THE NANKING ATROCITY, 1937–38

Asia-Pacific Studies

Series Editors:
J. S. Eades, *Professor of Asia Pacific Studies, Ritsumeikan Asian Pacific University*

David Askew, *Associate Professor (Legal Studies), Ritsumeikan Asian Pacific University*

Volume 1
Media and Nation Building: How the Iban Became Malaysian
John Postill

Volume 2
The Nanking Atrocity, 1937–38: Complicating the Picture
Edited by Bob Tadashi Wakabayashi

THE NANKING ATROCITY, 1937–38

Complicating the Picture

Edited by

Bob Tadashi Wakabayashi

Berghahn Books
New York • Oxford

First published in 2007 by
Berghahn Books
www.berghahnbooks.com
First paperback edition published in 2008
Paperback reprinted in 2009

Library of Congress Cataloging-in-Publication Data
The Nanking atrocity, 1937–38 : complicating the picture / edited by
Bob Tadashi Wakabayashi.
　　p. cm. — (Asia Pacific studies ; v. 2)
　　Includes bibliographical references.
　　ISBN 978-1-84545-180-6 (hardcover : alk. paper) — ISBN 978-1-84545-
200-5 (pbk. : alk. paper)
　　1. Nanking Massacre, Nanjing, Jiangsu Sheng, China, 1937.　2. Nanjing
(Jiangsu Sheng, China)—History—20th century.　3. Nanjing (Jiangsu
Sheng, China)—History—20th century—Historiography.　I. Wakabayashi,
Bob Tadashi, 1950–

DS797.56.N365N38 2007
951.04'2–dc22

　　　　　　　　　　　　　　　　　　　　　　　　　　　　2006100355

British Library Cataloguing in Publication Data
A catalogue record for this book is available from the British Library
Printed in the United States on acid-free paper

ISBN: 978-1-84545-180-6, hardback
ISBN: 978-1-84545-500-2, paperback

For two pioneers in critical
Nanking historical scholarship:

Hora Tomio (1906–2000)

and

Fujiwara Akira (1922–2003)

CONTENTS

Preface and Acknowledgments   ix

Wade-Giles to Pinyin Conversion Table   xii

Maps   xvi

Introduction

1. Bob Tadashi Wakabayashi, The Messiness of Historical Reality   3

2. Fujiwara Akira, The Nanking Atrocity: An Interpretive Overview   29

Section One: War Crimes and Doubts

3. Kasahara Tokushi, Massacres outside Nanking City   57

4. Ono Kenji, Massacres near Mufushan   70

5. David Askew, Part of the Numbers Issue: Demography and Civilian Victims   86

6. Bob Tadashi Wakabayashi, The Nanking 100-Man Killing Contest Debate, 1971–75   115

7. Timothy Brook, Radhabinod Pal on the Rape of Nanking: The Tokyo Judgment and the Guilt of History   149

Section Two: Agressors and Collaborators

8. Amano Saburô, Letters from a Reserve Officer Conscripted to Nanking   181

9. Timothy Brook, Chinese Collaboration in Nanking   196

10. David Askew, Westerners in Occupied Nanking: December 1937 to February 1938   227

11. Takashi Yoshida, Wartime Accounts of the Nanking Atrocity   248

Section Three: Another Denied Holocaust?

12. Joshua A. Fogel, The Nanking Atrocity and Chinese
    Historical Memory   267

13. Masahiro Yamamoto, A Tale of Two Atrocities: Critical Appraisal
    of American Historiography   285

14. Kasahara Tokushi, Higashinakano Osamichi: The Last Word
    in Denial   304

15. Kimura Takuji, Nanking: Denial and Atonement in
    Contemporary Japan   330

Postscript

16. Bob Tadashi Wakabayashi, Leftover Problems   357

Appendix   394

Bibliography   399

Notes on Contributors   418

Index   420

PREFACE

This volume presents a largely non-American perspective on the Nanking Atrocity; only two of its ten contributors are U.S. nationals, and both of them reside permanently in Canada. Several chapters originated as papers given at a conference in March 1999 funded by the Department of History, Faculty of Arts, and McLaughlin College at York University in Toronto. I did not purposely string this project along for eight years, scheming to make the book's publication coincide with the seventieth anniversary of the Atrocity, but as things turned out, I have come pretty close. Yang Daqing, a good friend and participant at the conference, urged me to publish the papers after it ended, but I wanted to solicit a wider range of essays and primary sources that would make our coverage more comprehensive. (The issue of sexual violence against women is our biggest remaining lacuna.) Since most of those materials were in Japanese, a good deal of time consuming translation work and follow-up correspondence ensued. The death of my mother, plus administrative duties at York, further delayed completion of the book. I apologize for the lateness and thank the authors for their saintly patience. Some are junior scholars who had hoped for an early publication date that would facilitate job hunting and tenure reviews, yet no one asked to withdraw his chapter for submission elsewhere despite my repeated delays.

I am responsible for all errors and shortcomings in this book, but I wish to express thanks to the many kind persons who helped my produce it. Forgive me if I leave anyone out. Kasahara Tokushi introduced me to leading Japanese scholars in the field, including the late Fujiwara Akira and Ono Kenji, whose findings on Nanking appear here for the first time in English. Professor Kasahara also presented me with books and articles that shaped my understanding of the Atrocity even when we disagree. I rely heavily on him on the issue of casualties found in Japanese military sources and that of the Atrocity's duration and spatial extent. Takashi Yoshida allowed me to read his superb work, *The Making of the "Rape of Nanking"* while it was in dissertation form. On an unusual note, I express gratitude to ideological adversaries in the Nanking controversy—Higashinakano Osamichi (Shûdô) of Asia University and Komori Yoshihisa of the *Sankei shinbun*. Both sent me copies of their publications knowing that I would publicize their flaws—although I have tried to point out their merits too. Gerald Jordan secured a conference venue and lodgings for participants at York's McLaughlin College in March 1999. Okamoto Kôichi, now a professor at Waseda University, served as a discussant at that conference and secured the participation of Kimura Takuji from Japan. Attefa Salihi cheerfully solved my computer crises, often on short notice. David and Rie Askew sent me materials from overseas, as did Matsuura Masataka, Janice Matsumura, Honda Itsuo, Iwafuchi Masashi, Megumi Wakabayashi, Takagi Tsutomu, Vicky T'ang, and Clark Taber. Joshua A. Fogel and Timothy Brook commented on drafts of chapters 1 and 16. Colin Green checked my romanization of Chinese terms. Yumiko, my long-suffering wife of 23 years, deserves a special mention. She has endured a life with books, papers, and newspaper clippings strewn about the house on the pretext that her (often irritable) husband is doing research. Yumiko's forbearance and other wonderful qualities have been priceless. Finally, few publishers today are willing to incur the costs and risks entailed by this large a collection of essays, so I am very grateful to Berghahn Books, and in particular, to Jeremy Eades, Marion Berghahn, Vivian Berghahn, Marilyn Silverman, and Melissa Spinelli.

A number of chapters originally appeared elsewhere in radically different versions. Igarashi Akio of Rikkyô University helped me obtain permission to edit, amend, translate into English, and republish work originally under Japanese copyright. But these chapters differ so much that they are, in effect, separate essays rewritten for a Western readership: Kasahara Tokushi, "Massacres outside Nanking City" appeared as "Nankin kinkô ni okeru zangyaku jiken" in Fujiwara Akira ed., *Nankin jiken o dô miru ka* (Tokyo: Aoki shoten, 1998), pp. 16–32; Ono Kenji, "Massacres near Mufushan," appeared as "Dai-13 shidan Yamada shitai no Nankin daigyakusatsu" in Fujiwara Akira ed., *Nankin jiken o dô miru ka* (Tokyo: Aoki shoten, 1998), pp. 43–70; Amano Saburô, "Letters from a Reserve Officer Conscripted to Nanking," appeared as "Amano Saburô gunji yûbin" in Ono Kenji, Fujiwara Akira, and Honda Katsuichi, eds., *Nankin daigyakusatsu o kiroku shita Kôgun heishi tachi* (Tokyo: Ôtsuki shoten, 1996), pp. 246–58; Masahiro Yamamoto, "A Tale of Two Atrocities: Critical Appraisal of American Historiography," appeared as "Amerika ni okeru 'Nankin' kenkyû no dôkô" in Higashinakano Osamichi (Shûdô), ed., *Nankin "Gyakusatsu" kenkyû no saizensen* (Tokyo: Tendensha, 2003) pp, 143–92; Kasahara Tokushi, "Higashinakano Osamichi: The Last Word in Denial," appeared as "Nankin gyakusatsu hiteiha no 'Shin kishu'" in *Nankin jiken to Nihonjin* (Tokyo: Kashiwa shobô, 2002), pp. 156–201. Two chapters are republished from English-language publications in revised form: Timothy Brook, "Radhabinod Pal on the Rape of Nanking: The Tokyo Judgment and the Guilt of History," appeared as "The Tokyo Judgment and the Rape of Nanking" in *Journal of Asian Studies* 60:3 (August 2001), pp. 673–700; and Bob Tadashi Wakabayashi, "The Nanking 100-Man Killing Contest Debate,

1971–75" appeared as "The Nanking 100-Man Killing Contest Debate: War Guilt Amid Fabricated Illusions, 1971–75," in *Journal of Japanese Studies* 26:2 (Summer 2000), pp. 307–340.

Surnames precede given names for Japanese nationals in this volume except for Masahiro Yamamoto and Takashi Yoshida, whose major works are published in English. I used the Hepburn system for romanizing Japanese terms and followed the convention of omitting diacritical marks over long vowels in familiar place names such as Tokyo. For the following reasons, I chose Wade-Giles over pinyin for romanizing Chinese terms. Wade-Giles appears in earlier historical scholarship, in standard reference works for nonspecialists, and in primary sources related to Nanking, many of which have been republished and are now in wide use. However, Westerners who left those sources were inconsistent in their romanization. They often transliterated names according to local dialects or the old Chinese post office system rather than according to standard Mandarin pronunciation. For example, the town romanized as Jurong in pinyin, which prominently figures in the 100-man killing contest, should be rendered as Chüjung in Wade-Giles. But it appeared as Kuyung in documents at the time, one of which has been reproduced in a popular textbook by Jonathan D. Spence. By contrast, the late Iris Chang rendered the name as Kajung in Wade-Giles and as Karong in pinyin. However, I have rendered better-known geographic terms in proper Wade-Giles. Thus, counties that Lewis Symthe listed as Kiangning and Kiangpu appear as Chiangning and Chiangp'u in this book. In sum, I have tried to be faithful to historical usage while avoiding confusion and inconsistency, and I have provided a conversion table for the two systems.

WADE-GILES TO PINYIN CONVERSION TABLE

ai – ai
ah – a
an – an
ang – ang
ao – ao

cha – zha
chai – zhai
chan – zhan
chang – zhang
chao – zhao
che – zhe
chen – zhen
cheng – zheng
chi – ji
chia – jia
chiang – jiang
chiao – jiao
chieh – jie
chien – jian
chih – zhi
chin – jin
ching – jing
chiu – jiu
chiung – jiong
cho – zhuo
chou – zhou
chu – zhu
chü – ju
chua – zhua

chuai – zhuai
chuan – zhuan

chüan – juan
chuang – zhuang
chüeh – jue
chui – zhui
chun – zhun

chün – jun
chung – zhong

ch'a – cha
ch'ai – chai
ch'an – chan
ch'ang – chang
ch'ao – chao
ch'e – che
ch'en – chen
ch'eng – cheng
ch'i – qi
ch'ia – qia
ch'iang – qiang
ch'iao – qiao
ch'ieh – qie
ch'ien – qian
ch'ih – chi
ch'in – qin
ch'ing – qing

ch'iu – qiu
ch'iung – qiong
ch'o – chuo
ch'ou – chou
ch'u – chu
ch'ü – qu
ch'uai – chuai
ch'uan – chuan
ch' üan – quan
ch'uang – chuang
ch'ün – qun
ch'ung – chong

eh – e
ei – ei
en – en
eng – eng
erh – er

fa – fa
fan – fan
gang – fang
fei – fei
feng –feng
fo – fo
fou – fou
fu – fu

ha – ha
hai – hai

han – han
hang – hang
hao – hao
hei – hei
hen – hen
heng – heng
ho – he
hsi – xi
hsia – xia
hsien – xian
hsiang – xiang
hsiao – xiao
hsieh – xie
hsin – xin
hsing – xing
hsiung – xiong
hsiu – xiu
hsü – xu
hsüan – xuan
hsüeh – xue
hsün – xun
hu – hu
hua – hua
huai – huai
huan – huan
huang – huang
hui – hui
hung – hong

i – yi

jan – ran
jang – rang
jao – rao
jeh – re
jen – ren
jeng – reng
jih – ri
jung – rong
jou – rou
ju – ru
juan – ruan
jui – rui

jun – run
jo – ruo

ka – ga
kai – gai
kan – gan
kang – gang
kao – gao
kei – gei
lem – gen
keng – geng
ko – ge
ku – gu
kua – gua
kuai – guai
kuan – guan
kuei – gui
kun – gun
kung – gong
kuo – guo

k'a –
k'ai – kai
k'an – kan
k'ang – kang
k'ao – kao
k'e – ke
k'en – ken
k'eng – keng
k'ung – kung
k'uo – kuo
k'u – ku
k'ua – kua
k'uai – kuai
k'uan – kuan
k'uang – kuang
k'uei – kuei
k'un – kun
k'uo – kuo

la – la
lai – lai
lan – lan

lang – lang
lao – lao
le (lo) – le
lei – lei
leng – leng
li – li
lia – lia
liang – liang
liao – liao
lieh – lie
lien – lian
lin – lin
ling – ling
liu – liu
lou – lou
lu – lu
lung – long
luan – luan
lun – lun
lo – luo

lü – lü
lüeh – lüe

ma – ma
mai – mai
man – man
mao – mao
mei – mei
men – men
meng – meng
mi – mi
miao – miao
mieh – mie
mien – mian
min – min
ming – ming
miu – miu
moh – mo
mou – mou
mu – mu

na – na

nai – nai
nan – nan
nang – nang
nao – nao
ne – ne
nei – nei
nen – nen
neng – neng
ni – ni
niang – niang
niao – niao
nieh – nie
nien – nian
nin – nin
ning – ning
niu – niu
no – nou
nu – nu
nuan – nuan
nuen – nun
nung – nong

nü – nü
nüeh – nüe

ou – ou

pa – ba
pai – bai
pan – ban
pang – bang
pao – bao
pei – bei
pen – ben
peng – beng
pi – bi
piao – biao
pieh – bie
pien – bian
pin – bin
po – bo
pu – bu

p'a – pa
p'ai – pai
p'an – pan
p'ang – pang
p'ao – pao
p'ei – pei
p'en – pen
p'eng – peng
p'i – pi
p'iao – piao
p'ieh – pie
p'ien – pian
p'in – pin
p'ing – ping
p'o – po
p'ou – pou
p'u – pu

sa – sa
sai – sai
san – san
sang – sang
sao – sao
seh – se
sen – sen
seng – seng
sha – sha
shai – shai
shan – shan
shang – shang
shao – shao
shei – shei
sheh – she
shen – shen
sheng – sheng
shih – shi
shou – shou
shu – shu
shua – shua
shuai – shuai
shuan – shuan
shuang – shuang
shui – shui

shun – shun
so – suo
sou – sou
ssu (szu) – si
su – su
suan – suan
sui – sui
sun – sun
sung – song

ta – da
tai – dai
tan – dan
tang – dang
tao – dao
teh – de
tei – dei
tuen – den
teng – deng
ti – di
tien – dian
tiao – diao
tieh – die
ting – ding
tiu – diu
to – duo
tou – dou
tsa – za
tsai – zai
tsan – zan
tsang – zang
tsao – zao
tse (tze) – ze
tsen – zen
tseng – zeng
tso – zou
tsuan – zuan
tsui – zui
tsun – zun
tsung – zong
tu – du
tuan – duan
tui – dui

tun – dun

tung – dung

t'i – ti

t'ien – tian

t'ieh – tieh

t'ing – ting

t'ong – tong

ts'u – cu

ts'uan – cuan

ts'ui – cui

ts'un – cuo

ts'ung – cong

ts'ou – cou

t'ung – tung

t'uan – tuan

t'ui – tui

t'un – tun

t'u – tu

tz'u – ci

wa – wa

wai – wai

wan – wan

wang – wang

wen – wen

weng – weng

wo – wo

wu – wu

ya – ya

yen – yen

yang – yang

yao – yao

yeh – ye

yi – yi (i)

yin – yin

ying – ying

yung – yung

yu – you

yuan (yüan) – yuan

yü – yu

yüeh – yue

yun (yün) – yun

MAPS

Map 1. Assault Routes to Nanking

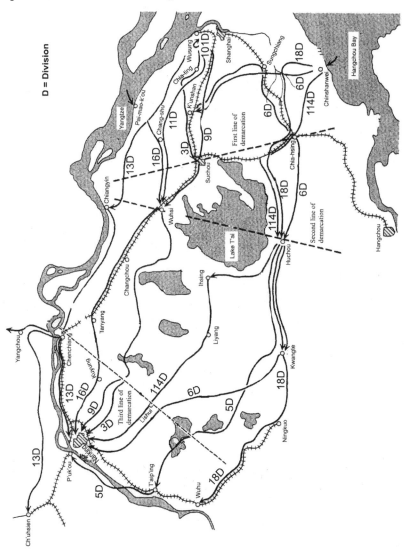

Map 2.   Nanking Special Administrative District (NSAD)

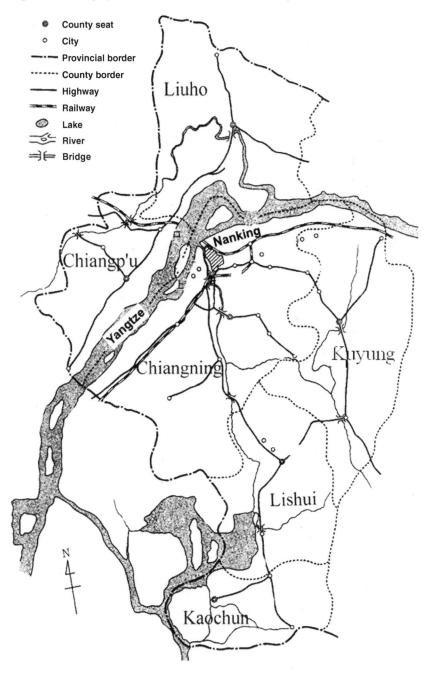

Map 3. NSAD and Yangtze Valley

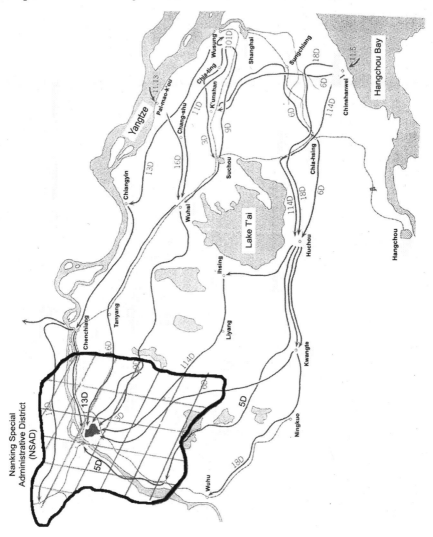

Map 4. Thirteenth Division and Yamada Detachment Assault Routes and Dates of Capture

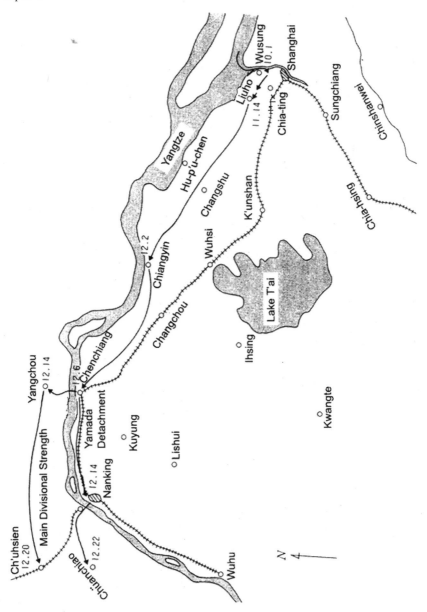

Map 5. Mufushan-Nanking Environs

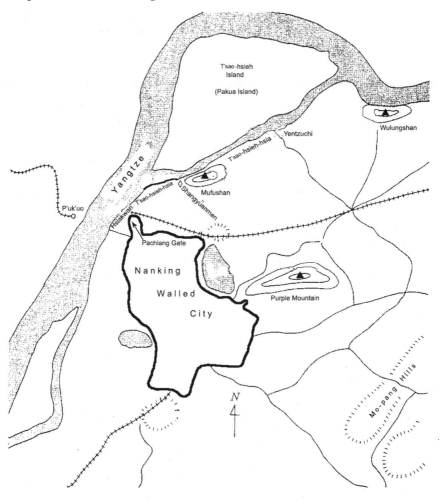

INTRODUCTION

1

THE MESSINESS OF
HISTORICAL REALITY

Bob Tadashi Wakabayashi

A Sordid Squabble

Seventy years, well over two generations, have past since the Nanking Atrocity of 1937–38, better known in English as the "Rape of Nanking" or "Nanking Massacre." Yet there is no fruitful or even civil dialogue about it between the Chinese and Japanese; indeed, venom now flows at peak levels. This was not always so. During the war, of course, the Chinese leader Chiang Kai-shek sought to win sympathy and aid from his U.S. ally by denouncing Japanese "barbarities" at his capital where, he claimed, "over 200,000 civilians were massacred within one week."[1] But this need to vilify a wartime enemy ended when Japan surrendered in August 1945. Thereafter, three factors minimized Sino-Japanese hostility until the 1980s.

First, Chiang and his Kuomintang (KMT) regime or Nationalist government did not revel in victors' justice. They were bent on getting even with Chinese collaborators, called *Han-chien,* or "traitors to the Han race," and on winning a civil war against Communist rivals, against whom they mobilized some Japanese units. In 1945–47, when over a million defeated Japanese were left in China at Chiang's mercy, his regime indicted 38,280 Chinese for treason as opposed to 883 Japanese for war crimes; it sentenced 15,391 Chinese, as opposed to 504 Japanese, to death or imprisonment on those charges; and, it refused to prosecute those Japanese responsible for massacres in northern areas of China that were sympathetic to the Communists.[2]

Second, some Japanese academics such as Inoue Kiyoshi in the 1950s and 1960s used the term *Massive Butchery* (*daigyakusatsu* or *ta-t'u-sha* in Chinese) when referring to Nanking.[3] Others wrote bestsellers that cited a death toll of 200,000 to 300,000, but qualified the figure as denoting civilian massacre victims and soldiers killed in action over five months along a battlefront that advanced 300 kilometers from Shanghai to Nanking. For the city of Nanking alone, they cited 42,000 Chinese deaths with no breakdown as to civilians and belligerents.[4]

Third, the Communist People's Republic of China (PRC), the regime that won the civil war in 1949, prioritized an anti-KMT, anti-U.S., antifeudal, antirevolutionary, agenda. It sought to discredit Chiang and the KMT, who had fled to Taiwan but threatened to retake the mainland with U.S. help during the Cold War. Thus the PRC denounced KMT incompetence and cowardice as an indirect cause of tragedies such as Nanking; that is, Chiang, who had appeased Japan from 1931, deserted his capital when its fall was imminent, as did his commander T'ang Sheng-chih, who vowed to die in its defense, only to flee at the last moment.[5] The PRC in the 1950s also insinuated complicity by U.S. residents in Nanking who reputedly "entertained themselves with wine, song, and dance, celebrated Christmas, and ate their fill of roast beef, roast duck, sweet potatoes and other fresh food" while the invaders ran amok. The PRC also accused U.S. residents of creating a refugee area, the Nanking Safety Zone (NSZ), so that Chinese could be more easily killed.[6] Today, a different PRC line depicts those same Americans, plus Nazi Party member and "good German" John Rabe, as heroic friends of China who rescued Nanking citizens from slaughter.[7]

The KMT in 1947, and PRC in 1960, cited "over 10 million" war deaths from 1937 to 1945. Both regimes presumed that Japanese militarism had been hateful, but voiced little overt criticism on the grounds that ordinary Japanese, like ordinary Chinese, had been its victims. Meanwhile, a few Japanese historians used the term "Massive Butchery," and several of them cited Nanking death tolls of 200,000 to 300,000. The Chinese accepted those figures and the inclusion therein of troops killed in action over five months from Shanghai to Nanking. Thus, the Chinese tacitly admitted the key distinction between "death tolls" that included belligerents killed in action and "massacre-victim tolls" of innocent noncombatants, and they admitted that these deaths took place in a wide area over several months. Finally, the PRC faced other problems: the Great Leap Forward, the Great Famine, and the Cultural Revolution. For classes branded "the black five antirevolutionaries"—capitalists, landlords, intellectuals, criminals, and KMT (right-wing) sympathizers—those other problems were certainly more recent than Japanese aggression and probably more painful too. Even females who had been raped or recruited in the war as "comfort women" suffered persecution for allegedly consorting with the enemy.[8] Thus, for more than thirty years after the war, Chinese on both sides of the Taiwan Strait, but especially in the PRC, directed most of their wrath at "traitors to the Han race" and class enemies—at other Chinese rather than at the Japanese. Terrible though it was, as massacres go in history, Nanking had been largely forgotten.

4

Things changed by the 1980s. PRC leaders consolidated their regime, which displaced Taiwan as the sole recognized government of China. To the extent that Taipei accepted this fact, regional Cold War tensions eased. Though with an eye to Japanese economic aid, the PRC dropped its anti-KMT, anti-U.S., "antiblack five" line and focused blame for Nanking on Japan, where it more rightly belonged.[9] Reflecting this changed PRC thinking, Americans and other Westerners formerly castigated as Japanese accomplices became courageous humanitarians. One writer has them "wrestling Chinese men away from execution sites, knocking Japanese soldiers off of women, even jumping in front of cannon and machine guns to prevent the Japanese from firing."[10] In Japan, nonacademics such as Suzuki Akira, Yamamoto Shichihei (a.k.a. Isaiah Ben-Dasan), and others said that the Massive Butchery was an illusion *(maboroshi)* because extant documents did not prove the allegation. Given their peculiarly Japanese use of "illusion," there was some truth to the claim, since reliable sources were still scarce. In 1982, sanitized textbooks in Japan dubbed wartime continental aggression an "advance," though it is unclear if this revision in terms took place on explicit government orders. Reacting to such Japanese "denials," the PRC in 1983 vehemently protested that the Massive Butchery at Nanking was no "illusion": "Over 300,000 innocent compatriots died; 190,000 corpses were cremated out of existence and 150,000 were buried by charitable societies. When the Japanese entered the city, they killed every man and raped every woman they set eyes on. After they finished raping, they killed the women."[11] The tacit distinction between "death tolls" and "massacre-victim tolls" disappeared, so that "over 300,000" now stood for nonbelligerents murdered in the city and *excluded* troops killed in action from Shanghai to Nanking in August to December. PRC insistence on this point provoked a fierce reaction in Japan. Nonacademics such as Tanaka Masaaki cited their own figures to argue that *less than* 300,000 civilians were in Nanking when it fell in December 1937, and that its population was *rising* by March 1938. For Tanaka, the Massive Butchery of over 300,000 victims—raised to 340,000 in 1983—was no innocent "illusion." It was a pernicious Chinese "myth" designed to slander and demonize the Japanese people.

Finally, a sea change in values and sensibility—a veritable revolution in individual-based victims' rights—began in the United States during the Civil Rights Movement and Vietnam War, and has spread around the globe to varying degrees. By the 1980s, Americans had come to feel that any abuse or deprivation of individual rights must end—especially toward nonmainstream racial, ethnic, religiocultural, gender, or disabled groups. In the past, members of minorities had accepted abuse and discrimination as facts of life to be left behind in their quest for assimilation. Now, such degradations became group-defining icons to be preserved and flaunted as a shared "memory" in multicultural society. Blacks, ethnics, females, native peoples, the disabled, homosexuals, and others had a "coming out" to reject conformity with dominant cultural norms. Demanding "redress now" by exalting past victimization, these groups forged activist identities to pursue empowerment through agency. North Americans of Japanese descent in 1988 won $20,000 in individual compensation for wartime internment deemed lawful at that time. Through affirmative action, persons in underrepresented target groups now obtain compensation for discrimination in hiring suffered generations ago. The Supreme Court of Canada ruled in September 2005 that tobacco companies can be sued for smoking-related deaths and illnesses going back to 1955. In sum, it is no longer good enough to express remorse for past wrongs and vow never to transgress again. Retroactive individual compensation is now demanded on humanitarian grounds, irrespective of legality at the time that those wrongs were committed. This revolution in individual-based victims' rights has decisively changed the ground rules on redress for wartime damages by impugning the adequacy and legitimacy of conventional state-to-state reparations agreed to in peace treaties that Taiwan, South Korea, the PRC, and other governments negotiated with Japan. Now, it is maintained, those postwar governments never had the moral authority to waive their citizens' rights to compensation for wartime injuries, losses, and injustice.

Historians identify U.S. Jews and their "memory" as pivotal to this sea change in values and sensibility.[12] Only in the 1970s did "holocaust"—which, with a small *h*, had generically denoted calamities involving fire—become "the Holocaust." Now, as a proper noun, with a capital *H* and definite article, it denotes the Nazis' "Final Solution to the Jewish problem."[13] To impugn the memory of death-camp survivors is deemed insensitive, if not disreputable; and, in Germany it is illegal. "The Holocaust" became a template for "the *Ta-t'u-sha*"—also upper cased with a definite article—standing for the Nanking Atrocity, and by extension, for Japanese war crimes in China that demand post hoc individual compensation.[14] Thus, in 1997 the late Iris Chang subtitled her bestseller "The Forgotten Holocaust of World War II." Earlier, in 1992, the editors of a scholarly book on the China war dedicated it to "the countless victims [of] an Asian Holocaust, probably on an even grander scale" than in Europe.[15]

Since the 1990s the PRC has implicitly likened Nanking to the Holocaust in an education system to foster patriotism, and deniers in Japan have pounced on this fact to validate their own ethnically biased view of the war. They cite the metaphor of "gray hair 3,000 *ch'ang* [6,750 meters] long"—derived from the T'ang poet Li Po (701–62)—as symbolizing a reputed Chinese penchant for exaggeration. Thus, deniers argue, the victim count of over 300,000 must be taken with a grain of salt.[16] But statistical imprecision holds true for literary expressions the world over; Japan's ninth-century *Man'yôshû* or "Collection of 10,000 Odes" has only 4,516. Do the Japanese also exaggerate? Other deniers point to similarities in Nanking massacre accounts and those found in the third-century *San-kuo chih* (History of the Three Kingdoms) or in the seventeenth-

6

century *Chia-ting t'u-ch'eng chi-lüeh* (Outline of the Butchery at Chia-ting). From these similarities, deniers in Japan argue that chroniclers in China embellished traditional narratives of dynastic decline with the stylized trope of a butchery or slaughter in besieged cities, especially when foreign invaders took part. This trope obtained at Chia-ting in 1645, where 20,000 Ming loyalists died at Manchu hands.[17] Deniers postulate that patriotic Chinese writers applied this literary convention to Japanese invaders at Nanking; and, as a result, it now passes for a "fact" in China. Ironically, this denial argument finds fortuitous limited support in Western scholarship on late-imperial China.[18]

Other deniers exhume the "blame Chiang Kai-shek and T'ang Sheng-chih" line to absolve Japan of culpability for Chinese military personnel killed in action at Nanking. (They repudiate civilian massacres.) To wit, Nanking in 1937 would have fared as well as Paris in 1940 if Chiang and T'ang had not fled for their lives. Few deaths and little damage would have resulted if they had declared an open city and supervised an orderly surrender as dictated by the laws of war and the codes of military professionalism. Likewise, deniers do admit the culpability of Japanese commanders for the orgy of rape and murder at Manila in 1945.[19] There is some validity on this point. The missionary Minnie Vautrin—rightly called "a goddess of mercy" at Nanking—reached this same conclusion on the scene in 1937.[20] And, the PRC itself adopted this view until the 1960s. That said, naked aggression is one thing; failure to surrender in good order is quite another. So Japanese moral culpability differs exponentially from that of the Chinese.

One historian sees hope for a "convergence" in Sino-Japanese views on Nanking.[21] To me, that seems impossible to a major extent anytime soon. The two peoples' historical experiences, basic values, and sociopolitical systems lie too far apart. But we can hope for a more modest goal—to begin a reasoned and courteous scholarly dialogue. For this to happen, both sides must admit that raw passions stand in the way, and that "memory"—although valuable for other purposes—cannot substitute for empirically verified facts in history as an academic discipline. As a start, both sides must abandon wartime ethnic slurs equivalent to "Jap" and "Chink" in English. (See the appendix to this volume.) Such terms have no place in our profession, except in direct quotations from primary sources when historicity must be preserved.[22] Finally, violence or threats of violence based on the rationale that "anything is permissible if motivated by patriotism" *(ai-kuo wu-tsui)* are even more detestable. A degree of civility is required before scholarly inquiry can take place.

"Forever Be Contrite"

What might be called the officially sanctioned PRC view of Nanking emerged early in the 1980s, long before Chang's 1997 book, which drew on and in turn bolstered it.[23] Almost all Chinese who express an opinion publicly today would aver that no room for debate exists on the Atrocity or on any Japanese war crimes. The PRC censors domestic and translated foreign works to allow few deviations from its official line.[24] Ultranationalists, often exploiting the anonymity of cyberspace, castigate and even physically attack persons who tolerate Japanese views or express an affinity for Japan, accusing them of being "traitors to the Han race," that wartime term of denigration.[25] While denouncing such extremists, most Chinese today deem that Japanese war guilt was settled at war crimes trials in Tokyo and Nanking—two of the East Asian sequels to Nuremberg—where a total of seven Japanese defendants were executed for the Nanking Atrocity.[26] As stated in Allied indictments and verdicts, Japan committed horrific war crimes at Nanking to cow KMT China into submission as part of a conspiracy to wage aggressive war, which constituted a "crime against peace." These war crimes included causing or failing to halt rapes of 20,000 to 80,000 women and massacres of 200,000 to 300,000 persons inside the city walls for 6 weeks starting on 13 December 1937. Historians at Nanking University recalculated the death toll at 400,000 in 1979, and the PRC recalculated it at 340,000 in 1983, but the key proviso is "noncombatants murdered within the city in six weeks." This "fact" is incontestable in China, and its corollary is that the victims at Nanking exceeded those in both nuclear attacks on Japan combined.[27] To execute a mere seven Japanese defendants was not sufficient punishment to fit this crime, so the Chinese feel they have a duty to sanctify their "Victims: 300,000"—a phrase carved in stone at a Nanking mausoleum built in 1985 to refute Japanese denial efforts. This mausoleum—plus similar memorials at Harbin for victims of Japan's chemical/biological warfare and at Marco Polo Bridge where Japan provoked full-scale war—are for the Chinese what Yad Vashem is for Israelis and Jews worldwide.

As this view goes, postwar Chinese have wanted to forgive and forget; that is why Nanking was a nonissue for decades. The KMT on Taiwan signed a peace treaty with Japan in 1952. The PRC signed a joint communiqué with Japan in 1972 and a peace treaty in 1978. Both regimes waived all rights to official state-to-state indemnities. They magnanimously declined desperately needed monies, to which they were entitled by any standard of justice, despite suffering 35 million deaths and $600 billion in losses from 1931 to 1945, as tabulated by the PRC in 1999.[28] (This compares with 10 million dead officially announced by the PRC in 1960.) The Chinese, who suffered imperialist aggression, remained mired in postwar destitution for decades while their imperialist victimizers used these savings to build Japan into an economic superpower. Further, as stipulated in Article XI of the San Francisco Peace Treaty signed with forty-eight states in 1951, Japan "accepts the judgments" at Allied war crimes trials, including ten held in China. Indeed, the Japanese text enjoins accepting the trials *(saiban)* themselves as valid and binding.[29]

After 1982, Japanese government-approved school textbooks admitted that the Nanking Atrocity was a historical fact—if belatedly and cursorily after diplomatic protests from livid Asian neighbors.

Above all, the Chinese would say, Nanking is but a small part of a far larger problem. Why do the Japanese refuse to express contrition for their wars of aggression that began in 1894, if not 1874? More and more Japanese people depict their history in positive, if not in glorified terms. One sticking point is repeated visits by government leaders to Yasukuni Shrine, where the souls of 2.5 million war dead rest, including war criminals. In 1979, it became publicly known that, a year earlier, Yasukuni priests enshrined fourteen A-class war crimes convicts, three of whom were implicated in the Atrocity.[30] (B-class criminals were enshrined beginning in 1959.) By visiting Yasukuni on 15 August, the anniversary of the war's end—or at any time of the year, for that matter[31]—high state officials honor men guilty of imperialist aggression against China. They include men who committed heinous crimes such as Matsui Iwane, commander of assault forces at Nanking, and two officer-swordsmen who staged a 100-man killing contest. Japanese leaders requite Chinese generosity with a cruel insult by eulogizing war criminals with the hackneyed line, "prosperity and peace are their sacred legacy to us." In 2001, the PRC halted high-level state visits to Tokyo, and "sternly ordered (or clearly told)" Prime Minister Koizumi Jun'ichirô not to visit Yasukuni. In November 2004, premier Wen Chia-pao (Jiabao) and president Hu Chin-T'ao (Jintao) refused to resume those visits unless Koizumi "takes proper action," and this situation still obtains in July 2006.[32]

Another sticking point lies in twisted portrayals of the "War of Resistance to Japanese Aggression" in which 35 million Chinese died, usually dated July 1937 to August 1945 in Taiwan, and September 1931 to August 1945 in the PRC. The Japanese, it is claimed, commit a "second rape" through revisionism that denies the truth about Nanking, or through textbooks that fail to relate its horror in graphic detail. This holds for works of art or fiction as well, such as movies like *Puraido: Unmei no toki* (Pride: Moment of Fate). This 1998 film portrayed the A-class war criminal Tôjô Hideki as a liberator of Asians during the war, and Indian Justice Radhabinod Pal as a jurist of integrity for his blanket "not guilty" opinion at the Tokyo trials. No Japanese person may renege on the San Francisco Peace Treaty by rejecting or ignoring the guilty judgments rendered at duly constituted Allied war crimes trials. The historical truth about Japan's militarist aggression and imperialism is undeniable. Friendship and trust are impossible until contrition takes place properly—as opposed to perfunctorily.

This official Chinese view presumes congruities with Jewish views of the Holocaust and of postwar German atonement for it. (1) Germany and Japan committed insuperably monstrous atrocities. (2) Guilty verdicts at Nuremberg and Tokyo are true, binding, and above reassessment. (3) Anyone who finds fault with these is a revisionist or denier beyond the pale of reputability. It is illegal to cast doubt on the Nuremberg verdicts or to deny the Holocaust publicly in Germany; Japan should follow suit but refuses. (4) Both states conducted systematic genocides; and, even though no centrally directed written orders have been found, this lack of documentation may not be cited as a lack of proof. (5) All Chinese who died in the war were innocent victims. Whether belligerents or civilians, all must enter the victim count: 340,000 at Nanking plus 35 million in the war as a whole. These figures, like that of 6 million Jews, are sacrosanct. (6) Eternal vigilance is needed to prevent relapses into genocide. Germans and Japanese must continue to admit guilt, apologize, compensate victims, and educate new generations. (7) To that end, Jews and Chinese may censure Germany and Japan to enforce compliance with demands for just contrition, even if this seems to interfere in those nations' internal affairs. (8) Germans have apologized and done penance fairly well; the Japanese are both morally and monetarily deficient by comparison.

"What More Do They Want, Blood?"

The Japanese narrative contains a more complex plurality of viewpoints. Ultranationalist thugs deny any moral wrongdoing on Japan's part and they issue threats of death or violent confrontation to silence anyone who says otherwise. Some authors in this volume have received such threats in the mail, over the phone, or in person at public lectures. But despite this abominable situation, serious and productive debates about Nanking and war guilt do take place. In brief, leftists try to approximate the official PRC view whereas conservatives—who may include but are not always identical with "revisionists" and "deniers"—try to disprove the Chinese view and thereby lessen Japanese war guilt in varying degrees. Rancor between leftists, conservatives, and deniers is so intense that they must exchange diatribes in print through partisan publishers rather than hold discussions under the same roof.[33] Yet they nevertheless share certain premises.

All parties concur that war crimes tribunals assumed unassailable legal force only by virtue of Allied fiat in the form of an unconditional surrender extracted under threats of renewed nuclear attack, but this fiat entailed no authority to establish historical truth for all time. Unlike government officials, scholars need not accept Article XI of the San Francisco Peace Treaty, so reexamination and revision of the war guilt issue are both permissible and desirable. "Conservative revisionists" reject guilty verdicts as punitive "victors' justice" never applied to Italians in Abyssinia, Russians in Finland, the Dutch in Indonesia, Britons in Malaysia, the French in Algeria, Chinese in Tibet, and Americans in Indochina. "Leftist revisionists" uphold the guilty judgments in general, but bemoan that war crimes tribunals did not go far enough; for instance, by not hanging the Shôwa emperor (r. 1926–89), by excusing colonial exploitation of Korea, by granting immunity to men guilty of chemical and biological warfare, or by failing to indict Japanese servicemen for violent crimes against Asian, as opposed to Caucasian, "sex slaves." Imperial Prince Asaka Yasuhiko, an uncle of the Shôwa emperor, commanded the Shanghai Expeditionary Army (SEA) or Shanghai Expeditionary Force (SEF) that assaulted Nanking, and he thus had the power to stop or punish Japanese troops who committed atrocities there. Unlike Matsui Iwane, however, Asaka was never subpoenaed to account for his war crimes of omission. He and the emperor enjoyed rounds of golf in the postwar era, blithely oblivious to their sordid wartime pasts.[34]

Japanese conservatives point out that the KMT regime was hardly a paragon of mercy. Its ten military tribunals executed or gave life sentences to 228 Japanese out of a total 500 found guilty of war crimes in China *other than* the Nanking Atrocity.[35] To execute only four men for this particular war crime suggests Chinese indifference to it or a lack of evidence to prove it. Conservatives in Japan ask: Why did it take until the 1980s for the Atrocity to become China's penultimate symbol of wartime victimization? Leftists retort by describing the PRC's humane treatment of Japanese war criminals; it repatriated all but forty-five of 1,109 detainees by 1956. Those forty-five faced trials at the Shenyang and Taiyuan military tribunals, but none received a sentence of more than twenty years' imprisonment and none served his term in full. PRC leader Chou (Zhou) En-lai intervened to extend leniency based on a belief that militarism, not the Japanese people, bore culpability for war crimes; thus, after the guilty men in prison confessed and atoned for their sins, they were forgiven and sent home.[36]

According to conservatives, postwar Japanese have not been stingy and mean; their naive generosity will lead to insolvency if continued. Since 1979, a year after normalizing relations, the Japanese government has voluntarily given the PRC financial aid worth 3 to 6 trillion yen in lieu of official state reparations or indemnities that the PRC declined when it signed its peace treaty with Japan.[37] Businesses have contributed trillions more in grants or loans at little or no interest. This aid helped finance PRC economic growth, industrial development, and arms buildups in nuclear weapons and missile systems; but PRC leaders hide the source of this aid, preferring to take all credit themselves. Taxes from Osaka citizens, for example, built the infrastructure that allowed Beijing to win out in bidding for the 2008 Olympics.[38] Japanese aid helped China launch a man into orbit in 2003—a feat replete with military applications. Thus the conservative journalist Komori Yoshihisa resents PRC leaders who feel entitled to demand this money on the grounds that their predecessors declined formal reparations in the 1970s.[39]

Conservatives note that PRC and Taiwanese citizens enjoy the right to sue the Japanese government and corporations for injuries suffered in the war, and sometimes win. Li Hsiu-ying, a survivor of the Nanking Atrocity, sued Matsumura Toshio for pointing out inconsistencies in her oral testimonies about it, and for suggesting that she was an impostor.[40] Matsumura fulminated: "If they can sue us for defamation just because we are skeptical [about reputed survivors], no one will be free to write anything about them."[41] Conservatives agree that Japan refuses to pay formal reparations or indemnities, but this refusal is sanctioned by international law in the form of mutually binding treaties between sovereign states. The Japanese government has, on occasion, provided informal humanitarian compensation, first in 1953–54, when Tokyo paid condolence monies to Taiwan and Italy for the wartime detention and/or murder of diplomats.[42] Chinese former "comfort women" were also permitted to apply for nonofficial compensation under the now-defunct Asian Women's Fund. Humanitarian compensation to PRC citizens took place most recently in 2003, when Tokyo gave 300 million yen to workers who were injured, and one who died, after handling poison gas canisters that the imperial army had abandoned in 1945.[43] The road to compensation is open to Chinese victims not only in Japan, but also in U.S. law courts since passage of the July 1999 Hayden Act in California, which allows wartime slave laborers to seek compensation from Japanese firms that exploited them.

Leftists contend that these arguments amount to shameless hypocrisy. Most "aid" took the form of capital grants and loans plus technical assistance needed for Japanese manufacturers and trading firms to forge inroads in Asian markets. Japan dispensed aid in ways that fueled its own economic growth and ensured corporate profits. Would-be plaintiffs could not travel to Japan for litigation until 1986, and its judicial system has granted no clear-cut victories to Chinese seeking compensation. Li Hsiu-ying first launched her lawsuit in 1999. The paltry sum of 1.5 million yen granted in May 2002, and upheld in April 2003, was highly anomalous. Matsumura Toshio appealed, and Li Hsiu-ying died in December 2004 after filing a similar suit in the PRC a month before.[44] Apart from the poison gas cases mentioned above, the Tokyo District Court ruled in September 2003 that roughly 190 million yen be paid to other Chinese victims killed or injured after handling abandoned Japanese poison gas shells. Leftists claim that such decisions are hopeful signs but are exceptions that prove the rule. Chinese victims can file lawsuits in Japan. Given their old age, plus the institutionalized snail's pace of Japan's judiciary, those acts are but symbolic protests, as Li's case shows. Lawsuits filed in U.S. courts have met with defeat as well.

Conservatives contend that, apart from being grossly inflated, PRC claims for wartime losses—35 million deaths and $600 billion in damages—omit the fact that not all of these losses resulted from Japanese actions. Massive internecine wars between warlords, Chiang's KMT, and Communist forces started before 1931 and continued past 1945. Even the leftist Kasahara Tokushi admits that T'ang Sheng-chih, the Chinese commander at Nanking, ordered some of his units to shoot and kill others that tried to flee.[45] Deniers also cite pro-

Chinese wartime Western journalists who reported that much of the death and carnage had resulted from Chinese earth-scorching and dyke-blasting tactics, or from KMT rapacity that caused mass starvation.[46] Less well-known is the fact that severe collateral damage resulted from U.S. air raids on Japanese targets in Chinese cities, the worst of which was in December 1944, when eighty-four B-29s indiscriminately attacked Hankow with incendiary bombs, causing fires that lasted three days.[47]

Conservatives argue that this decades-delayed indictment of Japan's wartime conduct—which assumed special intensity under Chiang Tse-min (Jiang Zemin)—is a propaganda tactic to vilify and isolate Japan.[48] Fighting and killing ended in 1945, but the Chinese today are renewing the war by non-military means to achieve furtive aims: (1) to extract ever more aid that will build Chinese economic hegemony in Asia; (2) to make PRC citizens forget horrors like the Great Leap Forward, the Great Famine, and the Cultural Revolution caused by their own leaders' abuse of power; (3) to defuse seething unrest spawned by official corruption, by suppressed civil rights and political freedoms, and by the huge gap between rich and poor created through distorted economic growth; and (4) finally, to divert foreign criticism from the PRC's own policies of imperialist aggression cum genocide against Tibetans, Uighurs, and other non-Han ethnic minorities.[49] Japan has waged no war to harm China or any other country since 1945, and even outlaws the exporting of arms and other war-making materials, but PRC government textbooks totally omit this postwar pacifism while exaggerating and distorting, if not fabricating, wartime atrocities such as "the Massive Butchery at Nanking."[50]

Conservatives answer Chinese criticism about Yasukuni Shrine by asserting that Japanese society has changed; virtually no one "worships" there any more. Visits to Yasukuni by state leaders may look the same as before 1945 on the surface, but these are now made from a desire to mourn the nation's war dead—a universal sentiment which, conservatives say, warrants no denunciation. They also note that denunciations are a recent phenomenon. From early in the postwar era, many prime ministers and the Shôwa emperor visited Yasukuni. Miki Takeo, Ôhira Masayoshi, and Nakasone Yasuhiro each made two to four yearly visits from the late-1970s to the mid-1980s despite the known fact that Yasukuni had enshrined A-class war criminals, yet no one incurred PRC wrath until Nakasone in 1985.[51] The upshot is that reasons other than hurt feelings or fears of resurgent Japanese militarism lie behind PRC protests. Conservatives also argue that the Chinese and Japanese view their dead differently. The Chinese spit on statues of "traitors to the Han race" such as the KMT collaborator Wang Ching-wei (Jingwei) and even the twelfth-century peacemaker Chin Kuei (Qin Gui)—plus those of their wives.[52] This stems from a belief that evil persons remain evil after death, so they and their kin deserve to be reviled forever.[53] Conservatives insist that even if war criminals such as Matsui Iwane were evil, folk beliefs in Japan hold that they are buddhas or shinto spirits after death and should be spared derisive abuse. Mourning *(tsuitô, aitô)* differs from the forms of worship *(sûhai)* or honor *(kenshô)* in pre-1945 militarism.[54] And, every people should have the right to mourn its war dead in its own way.

Most leftists have begun to tolerate such conservative views, and no longer call for an outright disestablishment of Yasukuni. They now argue that the shrine should respect the wishes of families who do not wish their kin to be enshrined there, or that to enshrine only those who died for the emperor violates the tradition of mourning friend and foe alike who fell in battle, or that foreign dignitaries refuse to visit as they would Arlington National Cemetery, or that neither the Shôwa emperor nor the present emperor visited Yasukuni after A-class war criminals were enshrined in 1978. Leftists conclude either that A-class war criminals must be disenshrined, or that a new national institution must be set up for foreign and Japanese war dead alike without giving offense.[55] Ironically, former Prime Minister Nakasone Yasuhiro—who paid an official visit to Yasukuni on 15 August 1985—began to argue in 2004 that a new public institution plus the disenshrinement of A-class war criminals are called for.[56] (But that will not solve the problem of 1,000 or so enshrined B-class war criminals.) An underlying assumption even among leftists is that, sixty years after the war's end, it is "natural" for the Japanese, and even prime ministers, to mourn their rank-and-file war dead—those drafted into service usually against their will.[57]

Conservatives retort that, owing to different folkways—exacerbated by anti-Japanese PRC patriotic education—the Chinese will continue to denounce any visits to Yasukuni. To paraphrase this argument: "They won't be happy until we reject all beliefs, customs, and values not to their liking." Popular opinion seems to be moving in this direction. A national poll done by the daily *Asahi shinbun* in April 2004 showed that 42 percent of all Japanese felt "it is good" for the current prime minister, Koizumi Jun'ichirô, to make more visits to Yasukuni, whereas 39 percent said "he should stop." But 55 percent of males in their twenties said "it is good" for him to continue.[58] In December 2004, a nationwide survey showed that Japanese who "feel friendly" toward China fell to 37.6 percent— the lowest level since formal resumption of relations in 1978—whereas those "do not feel friendly" rose to 58.2 percent, up from 48 percent in 1978.[59] These trends are continuing in mid-2006.

Finally, incessant charges that Japan has "never apologized" are factually wrong.[60] State leaders and private individuals have repeatedly done so and admitted culpability for war crimes. According to Ma Lieh-ch'eng, a PRC journalist formerly at the state-run *People's Daily*, Japan has apologized twenty-one times since 1972.[61] Japan has tried to make restitution for its past in many ways. Through measures such as the "consideration clause" of 1982, the government took pains to reform textbook screening in deference to the vic-

14

tims of Japanese aggression and colonialism. As a result, textbook depictions of Nanking became graphic, and victim tolls of 300,000 appeared, although these have since disappeared from some texts. This depiction of the Atrocity caused one Nanking denier, Tanaka Masaaki, to sue the government in 1984, citing emotional distress.[62] All rhetorical camps in Japan agree that textbook screening is done for accuracy, for internal consistency, and for some political concerns; but local public school boards are free to choose any of the seven or more textbooks that pass. As a result, to the great chagrin of conservatives, *Atarashii rekishi kyôkasho*—the nationalistic middle school history text criticized by the PRC and by other East Asian governments—gained only 1.2 percent of the total market share in 2001.[63] But the real issue is: "What is an adequate, proper apology?" Leftists uphold Chinese claims that whatever postwar Japan has done is belated, insincere, and deficient. Conservatives note that China keeps raising the bar, and lampoon conciliatory leaders as "self-flagellating monkeys" who conduct kowtow diplomacy.[64] Conservatives will admit that Japan waged a war of aggression, but hold that the issue was settled through peace treaties decades ago. Japan has not harmed China since 1945 and has paid trillions of yen in lieu of formal reparations. Some 1,100 to 1,600 Japanese servicemen suffered execution as war criminals, many of them unjustly in kangaroo courts. Conservative ire boils down to: "What more do they want, blood? How many more generations must we beg to be forgiven?"[65]

A Qualified Atrocity

On 12 July 2003, right-wing Diet member Etô Takami made two points about history: (1) Japan did not use illegal force to annex Korea in 1910; "the two states signed a treaty unconditionally approved by the U.N." (2) "The concocted Nanking Atroctiy of 300,000 people is a fat lie." On 15 July *Asahi shinbun,* the most liberal of Japan's five national dailies, reported protests from the PRC and South Korea. The PRC declared: "The Nanking Atrocity was a horrific crime for which there is incontrovertible proof; this is the definitive view accepted by international society. All chicanery to distort or deny this historical fact will fail." On 15 and 16 July, *Asahi shinbun* editorialists slammed Etô for his loutish tone and ignorance: Neither the UN nor its predecessor, the League of Nations, existed in 1910.[66] But the editorialists kept still about Nanking despite harsh diplomatic criticism and a long-standing *Asahi shinbun* policy of upbraiding public figures who deny the Nanking Atrocity, as Etô clearly had. This two-day silence could not have been mere happenstance. It signaled a queasy, qualified admission that the Atrocity is a "historical fact" for which "there is incontrovertible proof," but that 300,000-plus victims is not "the definitive view accepted by international society." This left-wing view went unstated to avoid blaspheming the less-than 300,000 yet still huge number of people who did die at Nanking, and to avoid enraging PRC leaders and scholars who brook no questioning of the official line.

The late Fujiwara Akira—a former imperial army officer who perpetrated aggression in China on the Ichigô Offensive, a fiercely left-wing historian, and a contributor to this volume—conceded in 1987 that Nanking victim counts of 300,000 to 400,000 and allegations about the 100-man killing contest are "mountains made out of molehills to an extent." In 1991 he wrote, "It's easy to point out inaccuracies and contradictions in testimonies by Chinese [victims]." Thus he granted the very points about which Nanking denier Matsumura Toshio was sued for making eight years later. The difference is that leftists such as Fujiwara deem it unconscionable for Japanese victimizers to harp on such points today, regardless of the facts.[67] Even Honda Katsuichi denies the existence of over 300,000 massacre victims within the time frame and geographic scope that the Chinese assert. But he avoids saying this publicly and deems that *all* Japanese, even those born decades after the war, qualify as victimizers who must defer to Chinese victims. Today, however, a generation with no sense of having harmed China dominates politics, journalism, and scholarship in Japan. The possibility of "convergence" in adversarial views on Nanking appears greatest there, not between the Japanese and Chinese. Less doctrinaire, younger Japanese on both the left and right are softening their views.[68]

As volume editor, I have asked authors to use the term *Nanking Atrocity* rather than the better-known *Nanking Massacre* or *Rape of Nanking.* (The sole exception is Timothy Brook, whose chapter seven deals with the Tokyo War Crimes Trials, which used the "Rape of Nanking.") "Rape" and "massacre" express but two dimensions of the event and mislead readers through an invidious form of reduction. Deniers argue that Westerners called this event a "rape" at the time, and that the Chinese adopt the label today alongside the "comfort women" issue to demonize Japanese males as sexual predators in a transhistorical fashion.[69] Thus I avoid this term. Some Japanese, even leftists such as Kasahara Tokushi and Yoshida Yutaka, use the term Nanking *Incident (jiken),* so readers should not automatically think of it as a cynical euphemism. Also, a separate problem of ambiguity may arise, since "incident" also connotes an armed disturbance of short duration *(jiken)* such as the Nanking Incident of 24 March 1927 between Chinese and Anglo-American forces, or an undeclared full-scale war *(jihen)* such as the China Incident of 1937–45. In this volume, therefore, "Nanking Atrocity" or "the Atrocity"—with a definite article and capital *A*—will serve as the overall designation for this event from late 1937 to early 1938, made up as it was of numerous "small-*a*" atrocities.[70] These comprised large-scale violent, inhumane acts including, but not limited to, rape, pillage, torture, arson, mass murders of prisoners of war (POWs) and civilians, and air raids on urban population centers.

16

Most of these "small-*a*" atrocities were also *war crimes,* but both terms connote slippery, politically contingent concepts that changed over time and still evolve today. Not all past atrocities were war crimes, and not all past war crimes seem atrocious any more. A submarine attack on a merchant ship without first securing the evacuation of its crew was an atrocity that became a war crime after World War I, but it stopped being one in World War II when the action became normal. The aerial bombardment of cities was deemed an atrocity after attacks on Chin-chou, Guernica, Shanghai, Nanking, Barcelona, and Canton shocked world opinion in the 1930s. But these were not formal war crimes unless military, industrial, or administrative centers of strategic importance were absent; and, every city has some targets that so qualify, or can be purported to qualify.[71] The bombing of cities with incendiary bombs became normal in World War II, yet their bombing with atomic weapons is still not a war crime today. Moreover, "total war" as it evolved in the 1940s led to a no-holds-barred effort to break the will to resist of entire enemy peoples. In total war, fought to "unconditional surrender" (another World War II concept), the side whose material and human resources was first to be exhausted lost. Civilians were bona fide military targets, and in some cases faced greater danger at home than did soldiers on active frontline duty. Thus, it seems, if enough people commit war crimes for a long enough time, these become legal and lose their power to shock.

The Nanking Atrocity belies popular perceptions and received wisdom in many ways. For example, when did it start? Orders to take the city did not come until 1 December, and troops did not breech its walls until 13 December, but atrocities began on 15 August when the imperial navy launched air raids from bases in Japan. Hawks and doves traded places at Nanking. Yamamoto Isoroku—a Harvard-educated admiral who opposed war with the United States—initiated aerial strikes on Chinese cities to justify naval budget increases vis-à-vis the army. Some 291 navy planes dropped 33.2 tons of bombs on Nanking by 25 September 1937. Yet by a cruel irony, or perhaps deliberate calculation, the first attack on 15 August took place three hours after the KMT regime provided a train with armed escorts and two diplomatic officials to evacuate Japanese civilians stranded in the city; this, to protect them from irate Nanking citizens.[72] Then there is the fallacy of anachronism. No one today suggests that Westerners abetted the Nanking Atrocity. But were they really humanitarians who rose above narrow national allegiances? Were they allies or enemies of Japan in December 1937? Germany and Japan signed an Anti-Comintern Pact in November 1936, but it was directed solely at Moscow and was not a formal military alliance. The United States, Britain, and Germany were in fact neutrals, but over seventy German military advisers flying the swastika fought Japanese troops in China until early-1938.[73] As John Rabe boasted in October 1937, these advisers "trained the [KMT] troops fighting so bravely near Shanghai" and supplied "flak batteries and antiaircraft artillery" to shoot down Japanese planes.[74] Legal experts in the imperial navy construed the laws of war as allowing them to arrest, try, and punish citizens of neutral states who aided nations at war with Japan.[75] This may be why Alexander von Falkenhausen—head of the German military mission directing KMT defenses—fled with Chiang Kai-shek and his wife five days before Nanking fell.[76]

Like defense counsels at the Tokyo trials, deniers today exploit this violated neutrality in order to justify Japan's attacks on the *Panay* and *Ladybird* which furtively escorted Chinese troops and war matériel to safety under U.S. and British colors. Deniers also reveal that the U.S. Defense Department in 1991 admitted a damning wartime allegation: 259 Flying Tigers, who fought in China while the United States remained neutral, were airmen on active duty, not civilian volunteers as claimed at the time.[77] Deniers castigate the "good German" John Rabe for aiding Chinese belligerents who discarded their uniforms and fled into the Nanking Safety Zone (NSZ), set up for genuine refugees. The Japanese suspected that Chinese weapons were hidden in the NSZ, which commander T'ang Sheng-chih had agreed to demilitarize. In fact, the Japanese found four tanks, thirty howitzers, forty-six heavy and light machine guns, 1,063 rifles and revolvers, and 55,000 hand grenades plus 25,300 summer uniforms and 2,300 sets of civilian clothes.[78] This leads deniers to charge that unlawful Chinese plainclothes troops posed as refugees and schemed to launch insurgencies from the NSZ. However, even the conservative Hata Ikuhiko allows that these arms may have been stored there much earlier, before anyone knew the NSZ would be made a refugee area.[79] And, I would add, nothing proves that the stored civilian clothes were meant for guerrilla use.

Still, it may be reasonable to suspect Westerners of exploiting the ruse of neutrality for partisan ends. As deniers argue, they saved Chinese lives, but did so by helping combatants evade interdiction—to live and fight another day.[80] John Rabe candidly wrote that he sheltered "Mr. Loh Fu Hsian, whose real name is Captain Huang Kuanghan," for over two months despite knowing that Huang was "an air force officer" who had "shot down several Japanese aircraft." Yet, Rabe wrote, "I will smuggle him aboard the *Bee* [a British ship] as my servant and that way he can finally escape from danger." Huang did escape to Hong Kong, and may have rejoined the war later.[81] But deniers push this anti-Japanese conspiracy thesis much too far. Rabe was destitute in postwar Germany after his company Siemens was implicated for using slave labor to build death-camp barracks and after his petition for denazification was rejected.[82] Yet he refused KMT offers of housing and a pension in return for testifying at the Tokyo War Crimes Trials. Before his death, Rabe explained why: "I didn't want to see any Japanese hang, although they deserved it.... There must be some atonement, some just punishment; but in my view the judgment should be spoken only by their own nation."[83]

Aims of This Volume

The ten authors in this volume try to deal sensitively yet honestly with the Nanking controversy by introducing new research findings. We contend that the Atrocity was a shameful violation of law and morality, but find ourselves in grudging and qualified agreement that certain intractable facts betray key points in the official Chinese narrative and in Western accounts that follow it. As editor, I wish to make explicit those criticisms that have gone unexpressed up to now. Kasahara Tokushi, who contributes chapters three and fourteen, for example, in another work calls the Nanking victim count of over 300,000 a "Chinese national and ethnic fantasy," but uses "fantasy" in the scholarly sense of now being unverifiable, yet subject to affirmation if better evidence comes to light.[84] This view, by a Japanese scholar sympathetic to China, differs decisively from right-wing denial. Masahiro Yamamoto in chapter thirteen is a conservative, but not a disreputable, "revisionist." The distinction turns on how one uses evidence. A survey of scholarship on the causes of World War II in Europe shows that revisionism has provided healthy correctives on emotional issues such as British appeasement. Historians now reject simple moralistic denunciations of leaders such as Neville Chamberlain, and admit that Hitler's territorial demands, at least up to Munich, were justified by the Wilsonian ideal of national self-determination.[85] To suggest that a broadly parallel role may exist for revisionism in studies of the China war is not to deny, excuse, or justify Japan's naked aggression.

The late Fujiwara Akira provides a narrative overview of the assault on Nanking and a trenchant analysis of the Atrocity's causes in chapter two. He also suggests that deniers purposely create political conditions at home to foster Japan's reemergence as a military power uninhibited from waging war. This chapter, finished in translation in 2002, seems prescient given the dispatch of armed Japanese troops to Iraq in January 2004 and the extension of their mission in December 2004. The government deployed them under none of the constraints to ensure nonengagement as imposed by the 1992 Peacekeeping Law.[86] Nor were there explicit rules stipulating conditions for withdrawal, although it took place in July 2006. Deployment, however, undeniably lessened opposition to a revision of Japan's pacifist constitution. A major article of postwar leftist faith is that Japan must never again be a "normal" nation that enjoys the right to wage war because Japanese armed forces at Nanking and elsewhere proved that they could not be trusted to behave in a lawful, humane, and responsible manner. Chapter two is Fujiwara's final testament to that article of faith.

Section One, "War Crimes and Doubts," opens with narrative accounts in chapters three and four by Kasahara Tokushi and Ono Kenji who describe Japanese war crimes *outside of* Nanking city. They present new and important

dimensions of the Atrocity that force us to rethink the PRC account and Western views that follow it on two key points: where the lion's share of killings
took place, and how many Chinese POWs were murdered at Mufushan, northeast of Nanking. Verdicts at the Nanking and Tokyo War Crimes Trials, which
anchor the official PRC view, held that 200,000 to 300,000 Chinese were
killed in six weeks inside the city. But Kasahara argues that most killings took
place in outlying rural areas, and Ono painstakingly found new documents
showing that 14,000 to 20,000 POWs died at Mufushan. Ono thus questions
the war crimes trial victim toll of 57,418 derived from one Chinese eyewitness, discredits Japanese deniers who totally ignore Mufushan, and criticizes
conservatives who admit that 1,000 to 3,000 POWs were killed there, but
only in response to lethal provocation.[87]

Other chapters in Section One, by David Askew, myself, and Timothy
Brook raise doubts about other key points in the official Chinese view. In chapter five, Askew revisits a point made in the 1980s by the denier Tanaka Masaaki
about Nanking's civilian population just before the attack, since that figure
placed one limit on the number of people who could be massacred. Askew
estimates an initial population of 200,000 to 250,000—which is less than the
putative total of 340,000 victims. He arrives at a civilian death toll of "up to
5,000" and admits—if not as forcefully as I would like—that Chinese troops
and POWs killed in violation of international law must be added to reach a
final victim toll. Many of our authors reject Askew's statistical findings. Kasahara, for example, elsewhere estimates an initial population of 400,000 to
500,000 based on the assumption that refugees fleeing into the city offset the
earlier loss of evacuees.[88] Nevertheless, Askew raises our awareness about the
vexing quantitative problems that we face. He rightly says that merely adding
up the number of corpses found in Chinese burial records will not yield an
accurate victim total; we must read those records critically to eliminate double counting, exclude fabrications, and discount exaggerations. His caveat may
seem banal except that so many writers ignore it. Askew also notes the need
to differentiate Chinese soldiers and plainclothes troops killed in action, who
were not Atrocity victims, from civilians murdered in cold blood, who were
victims. This omission of combatants from victims tolls is painful for the Chinese, who understandably beg to differ.

In chapter six, I argue that the 100-man killing contest—*pièce de résistance*
at the Nanking war crimes trial—was indeed "fabricated" in some respects,
but not for the reason or in the way that deniers insist. The killing contest was
based on Japanese newspaper articles at the time that depicted two Rambo-
type officer-swordsmen killing enemy belligerents in combat. But the two men
were convicted of B-class war crimes and executed by the KMT regime. I hold
that they did not commit this alleged crime. But unlike deniers, I argue that
the main significance of this incident is the public debate that it kicked off
in Japan early in the 1970s, which forced ordinary Japanese to confront issues

of culpability for their imperialist past. In chapter seven, Bro
far Justice Radhabinod Pal—glorified by Japanese deniers—ma
to submit a blanket not-guilty opinion at Tokyo. Brook ca
agreed that atrocities took place, and that prosecutors did no
Rape of Nanking," as they called it, but they did make it th
conspiracy thesis to justify indicting Japan for "crimes against peace." Thus,
Nanking was crucial for linking atrocities leading up to Pearl Harbor and the
"Bataan Death March." Brook ends by suggesting that a truth and conciliation commission may be one constructive way for the Chinese and Japanese
to reach common elements of historical understanding while respecting each
other's national sentiments.

Section Two, "Aggressors and Collaborators," addresses other sensitive issues.
The letters in chapter eight convey perspectives of the Chinese held by Amano
Saburô, a cultured reserve officer conversant in written Chinese, abruptly
wrenched from family life to pacify Ch'üan-chiao county across the Yangtze
from Nanking.[89] His letters passed army censorship and thus reveal the types
of frontline behavior that could be related to family members in Japan.
Equally important, they put a human, and not wholly abominable, face on
men uniformly cast as "Japanese devils." In chapter nine, Timothy Brook tack-
les the prickly issue of persons who collaborated with Amano's occupation
forces—an act vilified in Chinese "praise and blame" narratives. Brook asks if
Nanking residents may not have been better off because "traitors to the Han
race" such as Jimmy Wang assisted the invaders. Brook does not justify or
excuse wartime collaborators; rather, he states, they acted amid conditions that
perhaps made their choice seem inescapable or even sensible at the time. Thus,
he asks readers to venture beyond simple, ideologically fixed stereotypes of
good and evil.

In chapter ten, David Askew reexamines a topic somewhat familiar to
Western readers—the role played by foreigners in the Nanking Safety Zone
(NSZ), a refugee area. He holds that they, including the Nazi Party member
John Rabe, displayed a more mundane yet no-less heroic form of humanitarianism than that portrayed up to now. Their most significant work consisted
of attempts to broker a truce between Japanese and KMT armies, to maintain municipal administration and public works amid utter chaos, to police
the NSZ in order to prevent rape and looting by both sides, to treat wounded
Chinese troops abandoned by their own army, and to procure food for huge
numbers of refugees. This is how they saved Chinese lives. In chapter eleven,
Takashi Yoshida relates how journalists, propagandists, and other official
spokespersons in China, Japan, and the United States portrayed the Atrocity,
both as it was unfolding and later in the war. He thus provides the information needed to see past ideological uses to which polemicists have put the
Atrocity since the 1980s. Yoshida also exposes a deceitful non sequitur employed by deniers, who claim that nothing bad happened at Nanking because

21

KMT government officials did not protest against atrocities as these were taking place. He shows that protests did occur, and thus verifies that the Atrocity was not fabricated at war crimes trials, but also explains why the wartime Chinese responses were relatively restrained.

Section Three, "Another Denied Holocaust?", takes up what I call the "Nanking-Auschwitz congruity." In chapter twelve, Joshua A. Fogel cogently asserts that *comparisons with* the Final Solution help to contextualize and typologize past and present mass murders, but *comparisons to* it are morally and academically indefensible. Japan had no state-sponsored program to kill all Chinese persons or all members of any target group, be it race, class, or ethnicity. While affirming that the Atrocity did take place, Fogel explains that North Americans of Chinese descent and overseas Chinese exaggerate its scope in order to exploit it as a powerful symbol of shared suffering that creates an unassailable ethnic identity. As some suggest, we might define as a "target group" those Chinese who resisted Operation Burn All, Kill All, Plunder All *(jinmetsu sôtô sakusen)* in contested areas of northern China later in the war, and this might qualify as genocide.[90] But that tailored definition would still exclude pacified areas. Moreover, if the Chinese in that target group were to stop resisting and collaborate, they would not be murdered, except perhaps by other Han Chinese who deemed them traitors. Indeed, Japan armed well over a million Chinese collaborators in puppet armies—something inconceivable for Jews in Europe. In chapter thirteen Masahiro Yamamoto argues that the late Iris Chang's immense and continuing popularity stemmed from two factors in North American society: latent bias against ethnic Japanese and the inability of academic historians to correct public misperceptions created by her bestseller. To support his argument, he contrasts the rave reviews of her book with intense criticism directed at similarly flawed atrocity claims in James Bacque's *Other Losses*— that American and French armed forces deliberately starved 1.4 million German POWs to death at the end of World War II. Although some will find Yamamoto overly sensitive to anti-Japanese prejudice, his views and evidence warrant attention. Chang, after all, faced nothing like the studied, sustained criticism that Daniel Goldhagen endured for two books. As a result, he and his publisher corrected factual errors and a mislabeled photo in one of these, *A Moral Reckoning;* Chang and her publisher never did so for *The Rape of Nanking.*[91]

In chapter fourteen Kasahara exposes flaws in the work of Higashinakano Osamichi (Shûdô), the most persuasive Nanking denier in Japan, who reaches some conclusions similar to those of Fogel and Yamamoto; for instance, that Chang's bestseller lacks merit as a work of empirical history. Kasahara introduces Higashinakano as one of many right-wing scholars working to revise history textbooks along nationalistic lines, and argues that, rather than examine evidence and arrive at viable conclusions, Higashinakano begins from a "delusive fixation" that the Atrocity never took place, dismisses all contrary evidence, and twists the sources to form tautological arguments that confirm his original fixation. In chapter fifteen Kimura Takuji shows that, contrary to Chinese and Western perceptions, ordinary Japanese have done penance akin to their Germans counterparts since the 1980s, but he also explains why veterans and war-bereaved families find spiritual sustenance at Yasukuni Shrine. Without being apologetic or defensive, he shows why these segments of Japanese society support not only conservative revisionists who downplay the Atrocity, but also politicians who totally deny its basis in fact. Kimura suggests that Yasukuni Shrine is perhaps less a dangerous symbol of resurgent militarism than a source of solace for marginalized, alienated social groups.

In the Postscript, chapter sixteen, I try to convey subtle shades of nuance in terms used to describe the Nanking Atrocity, and explain why Japanese deniers insist that Chinese views of it are illusions or myths. I repudiate a presumed or implicit Nanking-Auschwitz congruity by showing that victim tolls of 340,000 or more cannot be empirically verified. I concede that deniers make some valid points that force us to question assumptions and conclusions embraced all too smugly until now, but many of their claims are inimical to academic honesty, so it is crucial to discern what they get right from what they get wrong. Finally, I suggest that a misplaced emphasis on Nanking makes us overlook Japanese atrocities later in the war that more justifiably demand condemnation and post hoc compensation.

Scholarly Integrity

Historians must try, at least, to rise above the personal, political, and ethnic biases that virtually all human beings harbor. But when studying this particular topic, that obligation must not lead us to commit a worse error in the opposite direction—the sophistry of choosing and arranging facts in ways that rid too much of the evil from Japanese actions. To understand why the Japanese acted as they did at Nanking is not to absolve them of guilt for having done so. The authors in this volume seek to clarify the nature and extent of that guilt more precisely, and to identify its causes and contexts more fairly. We affirm that naked Japanese aggression is the most crucial fact of all. To expand imperial privileges won since 1895, imperial Japan launched an unprovoked invasion and carried out a brutal occupation of China—not the other way around. True, the Japanese are not the only people to conquer and exploit foreign lands, but that does not lessen the pain they caused. True as well, the Chinese bear some responsible for atrocities at Nanking, but they committed far less, and did so in defense of their homes and families. Our task is to refine, not reject, the prevailing view of Japanese turpitude, Chinese victimization, and Western humanitarianism at Nanking. But we complicate that picture to make it better comport with historical facts, some of which were quite inconveniently established by Japanese deniers. Thus, we hope to give readers a more reliable, less emotionally distorted basis for reaching their own conclusions and moral judgments about what this tragic event was, and what it was not. Anyone who speaks or writes for the public, whether in or outside the classroom, is perforce a teacher. As teachers, we have a duty to provoke the critical examination of controversial, sensitive issues. But in doing so, we must not declare as true anything proved or even suspected to be false, and not depict as false anything reasonably shown to be true—no matter how much that deceit may gratify our ethnic or political loyalties.

Notes

1. Chiang, speech, 14 February 1942, "One Half of the World's People," p. 11.
2. Tokyo saiban handobukku henshû iinkai, ed., *Tokyo saiban handobukku*, p. 219; Liu [Ryû], *Kankan saiban*, p. 178. Hayashi cites different figures for "Chinese traitors," but makes the same general point and also points out that an estimated 1,000 Japanese were sentenced to death at kangaroo people's courts in China but stressed that an accurate figure is impossible to arrive at; see Hayashi, *BC-kyû senpan saiban*, p. 109. On the KMT using Japanese units against the Communists, see Ienaga, *Taiheiyô sensô: Dai-2 han*, p. 295; also, Hayashi, *BC-kyû senpan saiban*, pp. 104–6.
3. Inoue, Okonogi, and Suzuki, *Gendai Nihon no rekishi jô*, p. 167.
4. See Inoue, *Nihon no rekishi ge*, p. 193; Tôyama, Imai, and Fujiwara, *Shôwa shi*, p. 125; Tôyama, Imai, and Fujiwara, *Shôwa shi: Shinpan*, p. 152; Hashikawa, *Nihon no hyakunen 4: Ajia kaihô no yume*, p. 347; and Hayashi, *Nihon no rekishi 25: Taiheiyô sensô*, p. 64. They cited either the Tokyo War Crimes Tribunal or Snow's *Battle for Asia* as evidence for these figures.
5. Much of the above derives from Kasahara, *Nankin jiken to Nihonjin*, pp. 221–43.
6. Cited in Askew, "The Nanjing Incident," p. 2. The original source for this assertion is probably Fitch's diary entries for 25 December 1937; see Zhang, ed., *Eyewitnesses to Massacre*, p. 95; for alleged U.S. complicity in creating the NSZ as a butchering pen, see Yoshida, *Making of the "Rape of Nanking"*, p. 68.
7. The original version of Rabe's diary, edited by Wickert for German readers, is entitled *Der gute Deutsche von Nanking* (The Good German of Nanking), but its English translation reads The Good Man of Nanking. The different nuance speaks volumes for students of modern European history.
8. For the 10 million figure, see Kasahara, *Nankin jiken to sankô sakusen*, p. 76; on the persecution during the Cultural Revolution of antirevolutionary elements, Chinese former "comfort women" and Chinese women raped by the Japanese, see Kasahara, *Nankin jiken to Nihonjin*, pp. 231–34.
9. For this view of PRC "KMT-bashing" early in the Cold War and its let-up after Taiwan lost international recognition, see Hata in Sakamoto et al., "Rekishi to rekishi ninshiki," pp. 79–80. For an example of the toned-down criticism of T'ang prevalent today, see Sun, "Causes of the Nanking Massacre," pp. 43–45.
10. Chang, *Rape of Nanking*, pp. 138–39. I have found no basis in the sources for such a claim.
11. Nankin-shi bunshiryô kenkyûkai, ed., Kagami and Himeta, tran. *Shôgen: Nankin daigyakusatsu*, p. 14.
12. Novick, *Holocaust in American Life;* Finkelstein, *Holocaust Industry.*
13. Thus in 1976 Remak cited Hitler's resolve in 1933 to revise terms of the Versailles Treaty, and then commented with no hint of giving offense to Jews: "but he [Hitler] added that he had no desire for another holocaust. In fact, he was ready to offer certain proposals toward disarmament." See Remak, *Origins of the Second World War*, p. 11.

14. Indeed, one Chinese-Canadian urges her compatriots to use this term for their own "unique" experience, and to avoid "Holocaust," so that Jews would not feel "intruded upon." See the *GA Newsletter* 5:1 (March 1988), p. 35.
15. Hsiung and Levine, eds., *China's Bitter Victory.*
16. For but two of many examples of deniers who cite this metaphor, see Watanabe, *Nihonshi kara mita Nihonjin,* p. 434; and Takemoto and Ôhara, *Saishin: Nankin daigyakusatsu,* p. 40.
17. Brook mentions this incident as background to the Japanese massacre at Chia-ting in 1937. See Brook, "Pacification of Jiading [Chia-ding]," p. 52.
18. See, for example, Takigawa Masajirô cited in Tanaka, *Nankin jiken no sôkatsu,* pp. 240–53. Kobayashi and others have repeated the account. For a Western discussion of the massacre at Chia-ting based on the same late-Ming sources used by Takigawa and that cites the modern novelist Hu Shan-yuan in a way that corroborates the Japanese denial claims, see Dennerline, *Chia-ting Loyalists,* p. 6.
19. For the explicit hypothetical comparison of Nanking to Paris being spared as an open city and Japanese culpability for rapes and massacres at Manila, see Watanabe, *Nihonshi kara mita Nihonjin,* p. 438. Japanese writers who fix primary, as opposed to just secondary, responsibility on T'ang would include Watanabe Shôichi, Kobayashi Yoshinori, Fuji Nobuo, Tanaka Masaaki, Ôi Mitsuru, Matsumura Toshio, Fujioka Nobukatsu, and Nakamura Akira. See *Shokun!* ed. "Sanpa gôdô dai ankeeto," pp. 66–67, 170, 172, 176, 179, 181, 183, and 185.
20. Kasahara, ed., *Nankin jiken no hibi,* pp. 46–47.
21. Yang, "Convergence or Divergence?" pp. 842–65; also, Yang, "Toward a Common Historical Understanding," pp. 236–59.
22. Tobe makes such a case for *"Shina tsû,"* or "China experts" in the imperial army, but he uses the term within quotations marks. See Tobe, *Nihon rikugun to Chûgoku,* pp. 8–12. See the appendix for a critical discussion of these ethnic slurs.
23. See Eykholt, "Aggression, Victimization, and Chinese Historiography of the Nanjing Massacre," pp. 11–69; also Fogel's Chapter 12 in the present volume. An example of the Chinese official view in English is Zhang and Liu, *An Illustrated History of China's War of Resistance Against Japan,* pp. 35–42 and 51–56.
24. Many colleagues have had publications in the PRC canceled or expurgated without notice. For example, Kasahara once had his victim toll deleted because it was less than 300,000; see Kasahara, *Nankin jiken to Nihonjin,* p. 223. A case that received far wider publicity is Hillary Clinton's *Living History;* Chinese translators axed passages deemed offensive by the PRC regime. See the *New York Times* 24 September and 23 December 2003. One exception is Ma Lieh-ch'eng formerly of the *People's Daily.* In December 2002, Ma argued that it was in China's interests to stop bashing Japan over war guilt issues, but did not mention the Nanking Atrocity specifically. See Ma, "Waga Chûgoku yo, han-Nichi kôdô o tsutsushime," pp. 126–35.
25. One victim of such physical assault and threats was the actress Ch'ao Wei. After she modeled a dress patterned after the wartime Japanese naval flag in 2001, she was pummeled, splattered with excrement, and threatened with death. For such incidents by PRC ultranationalist thugs see Seki [Shih], *Chûgoku: "Aikoku jôi no byôri",* especially pp. 4–40; and Ma, "Waga Chûgoku yo, han-Nichi kôdô o tsutsushime" pp. 126–27. For a Western analysis of Chinese anti-Japanese ultranationalism from below, see Gries, *China's New Nationalism,* pp. 69–98.
26. These seven were executed specifically in connection with the Nanking Atrocity. The three at Tokyo were Matsui Iwane, Mutô Akira, and Hirota Kôki; the four at Nanking were Tani Hisao, Noda Tsuyoshi, Mukai Toshiaki, and Tanaka Gunkichi. Of course, more Japanese at the Tokyo, Nanking, and other tribunals received the death sentence for war crimes unrelated to Nanking. Also, Sasaki Tôichi, a notorious brigade commander at Nanking, died in PRC detention at the Fushun Detention Center in 1955 after his arrest for other war crimes. See Tobe, *Nihon rikugun to Chûgoku,* pp. 227–28.
27. See Chang, *Rape of Nanking,* p. 6; and also MacInnis, Foreword, p. ix–x.

28. Komori, *Nit-Chû yûkô no maboroshi,* p. 256.
29. On this controversy over wording, see Awaya, *Tokyo saiban ron,* pp. 182–91. For the English text, see Reischauer, *United States and Japan,* p. 368; for the Japanese translation, see Kadoya, *Shôwa jidai,* p. 311.
30. For a recent expression of official Chinese displeasure about Yasukuni, see the article, "Nihon no shidôsha no Yasukuni sanpai ni danko hantai" (Resolute opposition to Japanese leaders' worship at Yasukuni) by the PRC Foreign Affairs Ministry, translated from the *People'sDaily* in *Asahi shinbun* as web posted 12 February 2004. On the previous day, the mythical national foundation day of 11 February, Japanese media reported Prime Minister Koizumi Jun'ichirô as saying that he had no inhibitions about visiting Yasukuni even though A-class war criminals were enshrined there, and he had no intention of changing his mind owing to criticism from foreign nations; see *Asahi shinbun,* 11 February 2004. He has repeated this statement in 2005. The three A-class convicts implicated with the Nanking Atrocity are Matsui Iwane, Hirota Kôki, and Mutô Akira.
31. Koizumi has visited Yasukuni on five different dates during his tenure: 13 August 2001, 21 April 2002, 14 January 2003, 1 January 2004, and 15 August 2006.
32. *Asahi shinbun,* 16 March 2004, 1 December 2004, and 3 December 2004. Three year earlier, T'ang Chia-hsüan (Tang Jiaxuan) had reportedly told Koizumi in Japanese *genmei shita* which, depending on the ideographs intended, could meant either "sternly ordered" or "clearly told" him to stop visits to Yasukuni.
33. Leftists write for publishers and publications such as Iwanami shoten, Akashi shoten, Aoki shoten, Ôtsuki shoten, Kashiwa shobô, *Asahi shinbun, Mainichi shinbun, Ronza, Sekai,* and *Shûkan kin'yôbi;* conservatives, for Bungei shunjû, Chûôkôronsha, Kôdansha, Tendensha, Shôdensha, Shôgakkan, Sôshisha, PHP Kenkyûsho, *Sankei shinbun, Shokun!,* and *Seiron.* The number of conservative publishing venues has increased since the 1990s.
34. Irokawa, *Aru Shôwa shi,* pp. 64–6 and 69.
35. Tokyo saiban handobukku henshû iinkai, ed., *Tokyo saiban handobukku,* p. 219 and p. 224.
36. Wakabayashi, "Review: *Japanese Devils,*" p. 432.
37. For the 3 trillion figure, see editorials in the *Yomiuri shinbun* and *Sankei shinbun,* 17 October 2003; for 6 trillion, see Komori, *Nit-Chû yûkô no maboroshi,* p. 237 and p. 253.
38. Komori, *Nit-Chû saikô,* pp. 47–48.
39. Komori, *Nit-Chû yûkô no maboroshi,* pp. 236–37.
40. *Asahi shinbun,* 11 May 2002 and 11 April 2003. For Matsumura's original comments on Li as an impersonator, see Matsumura, *"Nankin gyakusatsu" e no daigimon,* pp. 158–63 and 363–65.
41. *Sankei shinbun,* 10 May 2002.
42. See *Asahi shinbun,* 24 December 2003.
43. The Japanese government first agreed to award 100 million yen, but raised the amount to 300 million in the face of official Chinese displeasure; see *Asahi shinbun,* 4 September 2003 and 17 October 2003. For an introductory treatment of poison gas warfare in history, Japanese poison gas operations in World War II, and current-day compensation, see Tsuneishi, *Kagaku heiki hanzai,* especially pp. 109–86 and 217–53.
44. *Asahi shinbun,* 24 November 2004 and 5 December 2004.
45. Kasahara, *Nankin jiken,* p. 132.
46. See White and Jacoby, *Thunder out of China,* pp. 166–78.
47. B-29s stationed at Chengtu made 9 raids on Japan proper, 9 on Manchuria (Northeast China), 1 on Taiwan, and 1 on Hankow. See Usui, *Shinpan: Nit-Chû sensô,* pp. 172–73.
48. For a recent comprehensive study of this issue, see Shimizu, *Chûgoku wa naze "han-Nichi" ni natta ka,* passim.
49. Komori, *Nit-Chû yûkô no maboroshi,* passim; Kobayashi, "Shin gômanizumu sengen 110," pp. 83–98.
50. Komori, *Nit-Chû saikô,* pp. 154–247.

51. Editorial, *Yomiuri shinbun,* 15 August 2003 and 4 April 2004.
52. A Japanese wartime account notes that the Chinese masses urinated on Chin Kuei's statue; see Sasaki, *Yasen yûbinki,* p. 240. For a photograph of the two statues, see Liu [Ryû] *Kankan saiban,* p. 245.
53. See Komori, *Nit-Chû yûkô no maboroshi,* pp. 262–70. See Shirokauer, *Brief History of Chinese and Japanese Civilizations,* p. 196 for this observation about Chin Kuei alone.
54. This conservative argument is valid at a high level of generalization. But, for example, imperial loyalists in the Bakumatsu era (1853–67) decapitated wooden statues of the Ashikaga shoguns—who revolted against the imperial line in the fourteenth century—and placed the heads on public display like those of common criminals.
55. Editorial, *Asahi shinbun,* 8 January 2004.
56. *Asahi shinbun,* 16 February 2004.
57. Editorial, *Asahi shinbun,* 8 April 2004.
58. *Asahi shinbun,* 20 April 2004.
59. *Asahi shinbun,* 19 December 2004.
60. The conservative *Sankei shinbun* claims that the *People's Daily,* a PRC government organ, admitted as much after a state visit by Chiang Tse-min (Jiang Zemin) in 1998; see the *Sankei* editorial, 17 October 2000.
61. Ma, "Nihon wa Chûgoku ni 21-kai shazai shità," p.183.
62. *Asahi shinbun,* 4 September 2001.
63. Komori et al. ed., *Rekishi kyôkasho,* p. 128.
64. The "self-flagellation" comes from *jigyakuteki,* or "masochistic," which is the curse word of choice among conservatives. "Monkey" comes from *hansei zaru,* or "monekys who 'reflect critically'" on sins committed not by themselves, but by other Japanese in the past. By doing that, conservatives claim, these leftists claim moral superiority to ordinary Japanese who do not. See Kamisaka, *Tsugunai wa sunde iru,* pp. 214–15. Among government leaders, Murayama Tomiichi (a Socialist), Miyazawa Kiichi, the late Hashimoto Ryûtarô, and Kôno Yôhei have come in for especially harsh criticism. Hashimoto was derided as "Prime Minister Ashimoto" for bowing on his hands and knees in apology at the feet *(ashimoto)* of Asians. See Kobayashi, *Sensô ron,* p. 144.
65. For the 1,100 figure, see Komori, *Nit-Chû yûkô no maboroshi,* p. 293. For the 1,600 figure (1,611 to be precise), see Kamisaka, *Tsugunai wa sunde iru,* p. 20. Based on Welfare Ministry records, Utusmi lists a figure of 984 B-class convicts sentenced to death and 920 actually executed; see Utsumi, *Chôsenjin B-, C-kyû senpan no kiroku,* p. 152. Recent example of the "how many more generations" line are Endô, and former consul to Hong Kong, Sassa Atsuyuki; see Sassa, "Tsumi kyûzoku ni oyobu..." p. 49.
66. *Asahi shinbun,* 13, 15, and 16 July 2003.
67. Fujiwara, *Shinpan: Nankin daigyakusatsu,* p. 60; Fujiwara, "Nankin daigyakusatsu to kyôkasho, kyôiku mondai," p. 20; Fujiwara, "Nankin kôryakusen no tenkai," pp. 90–91.
68. Note the critical self-reflection about an earlier book on Nanking recently made by left-wing historian, Yoshida Yutaka, Fujiwara's protégé at Hitotsubashi University. See Yoshida, *Nihon no guntai,* pp. 226–27.
69. See, for example, Fujioka and Higashinakano, *"Za reepu obu Nanking" no kenkyû,* pp. 146–70; and Nishio and Fujioka, *Kokumin no yudan,* pp. 220–60.
70. But as Fujiwara and Kasahara show (chapters 2 and 3), even within the left-wing Japanese camp, there are disagreements about precisely when the Nanking Atrocity began in 1937 and when it ended in 1938.
71. See Noam Chomsky's rebuttal to Telford Taylor as to the illegality of U.S. air strikes in Vietnam; Chomsky, *For Reasons of State,* pp. 212–22; Taylor, *Nuremberg and Vietnam,* pp. 36–38 and 89.
72. Kasahara, *Nankin jiken,* pp. 17–36.

73. For the figure "over 70" German military advisers, see Iriye, *Origins of the Second World War in Asia and the Pacific,* p. 43.

74. Rabe, *Good Man of Nanking,* p. 9.

75. Kita, *Nit-Chû kaisen,* pp. 24–29.

76. Kasahara, *Nankin jiken,* p. 116.

77. See Tanaka, *Paru hanji no Nihon muzai ron,* pp. 125–28; Ôi, *Shikumareta "Nankin daigyakusatsu,"* pp. 50–58; and Kobayashi, *Sensô ron,* p. 133.

78. Higashinakano, *"Nankin gyakusatsu" no tettei kenshô,* pp. 184–85.

79. Hata, Higashinakano, and Matsumoto, "Mondai wa 'horyo shodan' o dô miru ka," pp. 135–36.

80. Kobayashi, *Sensô ron,* pp. 137–38; Higashinakano, *"Nankin gyakusatsu" no tettei kenshô,* pp. 169–88; Watanabe and Komuro, *Fûin no Shôwa shi,* pp. 73–76.

81. Rabe, *Good Man of Nanking,* pp. 203 and 206.

82. Ibid., p. 251; on Siemens, see Rosenbaum, *Prosecuting Nazi War Criminals,* p. 80.

83. Rabe, *Good Man of Nanking,* p. 256.

84. See Kasahara, *Nankin jiken to Nihonjin,* pp. 204–23, especially pp. 213–14.

85. Compare Owen, *Guilty Men* in 1940 with works that came after A. J. P. Taylor, *Origins of the Second World War,* first edition in 1961. See also the brief survey of the literature in McDonough, *Hitler, Chamberlain and Appeasement,* pp. 77–86.

86. These restrictions to preclude participation in combat and to ensure neutrality included bans on arms exports, plus stipulations that operations could take place only under UN authorization and only after gaining express consent from the host nation.

87. In addition to Ono's chapter 4, see Ono, Fujiwara, and Honda, eds., *Nankin daigyakusatsu o kiroku shita kôgun heishi tachi.*

88. Kasahara, *Nankin jiken,* p. 220; Kasahara, "Sûji ijiri no fumô na ronsô wa jittai kaimei o tôzakeru," p. 85.

89. The original is in Ono, Fujiwara, and Honda, eds., *Nankin daigyakusatsu o kiroku shita kôgun heishi tachi,* pp. 245–58.

90. For this view, see McCormack, "Reflections on Modern Japanese History in the Context of the Concept of Genocide," pp. 270 and 274.

91. See the miscaptioned photograph in Goldhagen, *Moral Reckoning,* p. 117.

2

THE NANKING ATROCITY: AN INTERPRETIVE OVERVIEW*

Fujiwara Akira

Prelude

Modern Japan's aggression against China began with the Meiji-Ch'ing or First Sino-Japanese War of 1894–95, and continued with the Twenty-one Demands of 1915, the Shantung Expeditions of 1927–28, and the Manchurian Incident of 1931–33. But an all-out war of aggression began with the 7 July 1937 armed clash at Marco Polo Bridge outside Peking.[1] Culpability for turning that minor skirmish into an all-out war lay with Japan—primarily the imperial government and central army authorities. Although a local truce settled the affair on 11 July, Prime Minister Konoe Fumimaro's government expressed "grave resolve" in passing a cabinet resolution to send more troops on that same day. Konoe, an imperial prince, flaunted his regime's belligerence by inviting media representatives to his official residence and calling on them to foster national unity. Based on this cabinet resolution, commanders hastily sent two brigades from Manchuria and a division from Korea to northern China, the General Staff prepared to send three divisions from Japan, and the Army Ministry halted all discharges. At that time, two-year recruits received an early discharge in July—before their active duty actually ended—to go home for peak months of farm work when the labor of young men was sorely needed. By rescinding this provision, the government showed that Japan was gearing up for war in earnest.

Japan's hard line created a sense of crisis in China. Chiang Kai-shek of the Kuomintang (KMT) regime or Nationalist government met with Chou En-lai of the Chinese Communist Party (CCP) on 17 July to discuss stepped-up efforts for a united front and Chiang made a speech on the need for resolve in resisting Japan. The Chinese people's will to resist heightened as two more armed clashes broke out in the north China tinderbox. By 27 July, reinforcements from Korea and Manchuria had arrived, as did naval air force units; and the Shôwa emperor or Hirohito, as he is known in the West, issued Army Chief of Staff Order 64.[2] It read: "Along with its present duties, the China Garrison Army (CGA) shall chastise Chink forces in the Peking-Tientsin area and pacify [i.e., occupy] strategic points."[3] The emperor used the term *chastise* that Prime Minister Konoe later made famous. On 27 July, the government decided to send reinforcements from Japan proper. Chief of Staff Order 65, as issued by the emperor, called for sending three divisions and mobilizing another 209,000 men plus 54,000 horses.[4] Real fighting began on 28 July with a general offensive in the north that saw imperial troops occupy Peking and Tientsin.

This course of events was the converse of that which began the Manchurian Incident. In September 1931, the imperial government and central army authorities had wanted to settle that conflict quickly whereas field armies were intent on expanding it. Now, in July 1937, it was the government in Tokyo that escalated the war by sending massive reinforcements to northern China even though field armies had reached a settlement on 11 July. Ishiwara Kanji, Chief of the General Staff Operations Division, reversed his hawkish views of Manchurian Incident days, and was now an exception among central army authorities in opposing the extension of operations to China. More typical of that group was Army Minister Sugiyama Hajime, who sided with Prime Minister Konoe, Foreign Minister Hirota Kôki, and other civil government hawks. Even so, the initiative for future army decision making would ultimately lay with local commanders who zealously pushed for escalation despite their gravely flawed grasp of conditions in China. Blind to the patriotism forging national unity there, they persisted in disparaging the Chinese military and people in the belief that "one telling blow," or quick decisive victory, would make the enemy sue for peace.

In August 1937, naval marine units took the war to Shanghai on the pretext of protecting Japanese civilians against popular Chinese unrest. Army hawks dismissed opposition from more cautious elements such as Ishiwara Kanji, and boldly extended the scope of operations from northern to central China. The Shôwa emperor (Hirohito), as he himself would relate in 1946, sought to expand the war at this time by sending even more units from Manchuria. He berated Ishiwara for weakness and was instrumental in transferring units from Ch'ingtao in northern China to Shanghai.[5] Thus the central government started what became a full-scale war by dispatching huge army units, but offered no justification worthy of the name, saying only that imperial forces would "chastise the unruly Chinks"—a slogan that Konoe issued in lieu of formally declaring war. There were three main reasons for pursuing this conflict as an "incident" rather than as a war: (1) Even at this late date, army and government leaders felt convinced that "one telling blow" would end it; they did not dream that a major, long-term conflict would result. (2) Japan had no compelling reason for war. "Chastise the unruly Chinks" was hardly a war aim that would whip up popular support at home. (3) With the premiership of Hirota Kôki from March 1936 to February 1937, the army and navy had begun pursuing armament expansion programs that relied on imports of strategic matériel from the United States, a neutral power. Japan could not go on importing these key items easily under international law if it formally became a belligerent state by declaring war on China.

Central army leaders in Tokyo had no plan to attack China's capital of Nanking when they dispatched troops to Shanghai in August; in this, they differed from Matsui Iwane and Yanagawa Heisuke, who later led the assault on Nanking. Instead, leaders in Tokyo expected a quick local settlement like that which had ended the Shanghai Incident of January to May 1932.[6] This time, a Shanghai Expeditionary Army (SEA), or Shanghai Expeditionary Force (SEF), was assembled on 15 August 1937 under Matsui's command. It had strictly limited orders: "to protect imperial subjects by destroying enemy forces in and around Shanghai and occupying strategic points to the north."[7] Nanking, it bears noting, is roughly 300 kilometers west of Shanghai.[8] The SEA's initial strength was hastily set at two divisions, and a heavy artillery unit joined within two weeks. Three and a half more divisions joined in September, and one more in October. Thus the SEA came to comprise the Third, Ninth, Eleventh, Thirteenth, Sixteenth, One Hundred-first, and One Hundred-sixteenth divisions. The Tenth Army was formed under Yanagawa's command in October. It comprised three and a half divisions: the Sixth, Eighteenth, One Hundred-fourteenth, plus part of the Fifth. This Tenth Army was not supposed to attack Nanking either. Its mission, like that of the SEA, was to destroy Chinese armies and protect Japanese nationals in the Shanghai area—nothing more.[9]

The imperial army's foremost priority throughout the 1930s was to prepare for war with the Soviet Union. Army leaders had no wish to commit large forces in China for the long term, and most were convinced that this "incident" would end after they scored one major victory. But events at Shanghai shocked them. Shells ran perilously low. By 8 November, casualties had skyrocketed to 9,115 killed and 31,125 wounded. Reinforcements, which had never been anticipated, were sent repeatedly. The Third and Eleventh divisions, for example, had to be totally replenished.[10] Army leaders shifted the war's main theater from northern to central China in October and the Tenth Army landed behind Chinese lines at Hangchou Bay on 5 November. Only that daring move broke the bloody stalemate at Shanghai, but Chinese units beat a hasty full retreat to avoid encirclement and annihilation. Japan, then, did not deliver the "one telling blow" to wipe out enemy forces, and thus could not achieve victory in this "incident."

On 7 November, two days after the Tenth Army landed, it and the SEA combined to form a Central China Area Army (CCAA) under Matsui's overall command, with Imperial Prince Asaka Yasuhiko taking over the SEA. At its height, this newly-formed CCAA numbered an estimated 160,000 to 200,000 men.[11] The reorganization signified that Japanese forces were not just on an expedition to Shanghai, but would operate in a broader "central China area." Even so, the CCAA was still an impromptu amalgamation *(hengô)*, not a formal battle formation *(sentô joretsu)*, as reflected in its mission. Its orders read: "Destroy enemy forces in the Shanghai area, break their will to fight, and thereby bring an end to the conflict."[12] The Chief of the General Staff also stipulated a line of demarcation: "in general, east of the Süchou-Chia-hsing line" (see map 1). In other words, the CCAA was ordered to remain in the area east of Lake T'ai; that is why it received no support-and-supply units. Also, six of the CCAA's ten and a half divisions were "special divisions," weak in firepower, limited in maneuverability, and manned by second- or third-pool reservists hastily assembled. They were not officers and men on the active list, in the fighting prime of their early twenties. Their abrupt recall to active duty came in their mid- to late-thirties, or even their early-forties—long after they felt their military obligations were over and they had returned to civilian life as bread-winners. Hence, morale and amenability to military discipline were often poor. Amano Saburô, whose letters are translated in chapter 8, mentions these "old man troops" and hints at the anxieties felt by older reserve officers forced to command much younger troops years after their own twelve-month training period had ended.[13]

When the entire Chinese army began to retreat, the CCAA ignored orders and gave chase westward toward Nanking. Eguchi Keiichi cites SEA Chief of Staff Iinuma Mamoru's diary to show that, as early as 18 August, SEA commander Matsui Iwane already aspired to capture the enemy capital although central army leaders had no such plans, and even before the CCAA came into being. Matsui, disgruntled by the narrow scope of SEA operations, had to be chastised: "orders for military operations are no different from imperial rescripts; it is impudent to criticize these." But later that same day Matsui openly declared: "We must resolve to order troops into action as needed based on our traditional spirit of 'instant engagement, instant victory' by shifting our main forces from northern China to Nanking. We can debate the issue of where best to deliver the knock-out blow, but right now we absolutely must make Nanking our main target."[14]

After the Chinese flight began in November, frontline troops came to share the newly promoted CCAA commander Matsui's aspirations; they craved the glory of being first to enter Nanking. Their egregious forced marches, exacerbated by the absence of support-and-supply units, meant that the rank-and-file had to rely on plunder to survive en route. On 20 November, Imperial Headquarters (IH) was set up for the first time since the 1904–05 Russo-Japanese War—a decisive step both strategically and symbolically. Belittling the China war as a mere "incident," yet unable to win it, Japan had no choice. Given de facto wartime conditions of mass troop deployment and naval support, the coordinating of the two services' chains of command required an IH under the 1889 Imperial Constitution. Unlike the IH in wars before the Shôwa emperor's reign, however, this one was a purely military body in 1937. No civilian cabinet member, not even the prime minister, could join its deliberations. Instead, an ad hoc liaison council handled communications between the government and IH to ensure that cabinet acts of state conformed with the emperor's supreme command.[15] Thus began the most enormous, expensive, and deadly war in modern Japanese history—one waged without just cause or cogent reason.

The Atrocity Delimited

On 24 Novermber 1937, IH admitted reality and rescinded its first line of demarcation, that from Süchou to Chia-hsing east of Lake T'ai; only then did it begin to think seriously about attacking Nanking. IH now set up a second line of demarcation cutting across Lake T'ai from Wuhsi to Huchou, behind which forces would regroup before advancing further (see map 1). But frontline units ignored this line too, and pressed their attack.[16] On 1 December, the emperor's Army General Staff Order 7 converted the stopgap CCAA from an impromptu amalgamation *(hengô)* into a formal battle formation *(sentô joretsu)*. On the same day, the emperor's Army General Staff Order 8 read: "CCAA commanders shall assault the enemy capital of Nanking with support from the navy."[17] Thus, formal orders to attack Nanking came down only on 1 December. Based on Army General Staff Order 8, the CCAA commanded that: (1) the SEA launch operations on 5 December with its main force ready to move toward Tanyang and Kuyung while a subsidiary force attacked the enemy rear on the north shore of the Yangtze; and (2) the Tenth Army start operations on 3 December with its main force ready to move toward Lishui and a subsidiary force, toward Wuhu (see map 1). In fact, the SEA was already well past Chang-chou on 29 November. It occupied Tanyang on 2 December—something not scheduled to happen until the seventh. Likewise, the Tenth Army had already taken Kwangte on 30 November. Its commander, Lt. Gen. Yanagawa Heisuke, proclaimed at the head of his troops, "I will press the attack on Nanking as I deem fit." Thus, neither the SEA nor the Tenth Army bothered to wait for orders. The aim behind Army General Staff Order 8 was not to make an all-out rush for Nanking. Both CCAA armies were to advance along a broad front, regroup, encircle Chinese defense forces, and annihilate them. But glory-hungry, frontline units lusted to be first in the enemy capital and staged a mad dash for it. Thus the attack on Nanking, like that on Shanghai, was out of control from the start.

In determining the number of Chinese victims in the Nanking Atrocity, we must first define the event's time span and area. The SEA advancing from

Shanghai, and the Tenth Army after landing at Chinshanwei in Hangchou Bay, repeatedly indulged in rape, arson, plunder, and mass murder. In that sense, Yoshida Yutaka and Honda Katsuichi are correct when they argue that any study of the Atrocity must include these vicious acts en route to Nanking, not just those in and near the city.[18] Massacres took place all the way from Shanghai to Nanking, so in principle, all persons killed en route should enter into the total. But insofar as we call this the *Nanking* Atrocity—as opposed to those elsewhere—I delimit the event as lasting from 1 December 1937, when IH and the CCAA issued orders to attack Nanking, to 5 January 1938, when the imperial army felt that a measure of order had returned to the city. Area-wise, the Atrocity took place on both sides of the Yangtze, west of the Changchou-Kwangte line, where the two armies met on 1 December. Note that the temporal scope of the Atrocity as I define it is shorter than Kasahara Tokushi's in chapter 3, and the geographic area as I delimit it is wider than his definition. The SEA and Tenth Army main units advanced toward the capital parallel to the major roads and rail lines, while subsidiary units forded the Yangtze to march along its far bank under artillery support by the Eleventh Battle Fleet. Having let Chinese armies evade annihilation at Shanghai, the Japanese now sought to exploit geography to preclude a second escape by pushing them toward the Yangtze, which wrapped around and behind the city of Nanking. As Kasahara describes elsewhere, ill-advised Chinese plans to defend the capital at all costs despite these detrimental topographic conditions played into Japanese hands.[19] These flawed defense plans were a factor that contributed to the Atrocity, as did the fact that Nanking had a huge civilian population, which would be trapped alongside soldiers inside city walls.

Japanese Strategic Blunders

The Army General Staff had repeatedly worked out precise, detailed plans for war with the Soviet Union, but never seriously thought about fighting the Republic of China, led by Chiang Kai-shek's KMT regime after 1927, as a national entity. Thus, Japan had no long-range blueprint to conquer all of China. The General Staff revised its "Guidelines for Defense of the Empire," its tactical handbooks, and its troop strength levels in 1918, when it named "Russia, the U.S., and China" hypothetical enemies. A second revision took place in 1923, when the list read, "the United States, Russia, and China." However, just placing China on the list did not mean that the Army General Staff made careful plans to wage full-scale war against it as a unified nation. Strategic thinking remained tied to the notion that China was a collection of warlord satrapies; thus, Japan needed only to occupy key areas as tactical needs dictated. A third revision of "Guidelines for Defense of the Empire" appeared in June 1936. The text of its section on "Tactics toward China" has been lost.[20] But according to a later account by Shimanuki Takeharu, this simply called for the army to attack and destroy enemy forces in northern and central China so as to occupy key points there, and for the navy to support army operations by sinking the Chinese fleet on the Yangtze and along the seacoast.[21]

Based on these June 1936 "Guidelines," the General Staff in August 1936 drew up a plan titled, "Strategy for China: 1937." This stated that five hypothetical divisions in northern China might be bolstered by three more for use in the five provinces of Suiyuan, Jehol, Shantung, Hopei, and Shansi. Three hypothetical Ninth Army divisions in central China might occupy Shanghai, and a Tenth Army might be formed to land at Hangchou Bay. These Ninth and Tenth armies might march on Nanking and seize and occupy the strategic Shanghai-Hangchou-Nanking triangle, but in that case, no operations should take place elsewhere in China. In southern China, the plan would be for the deployment of one division, whose main force might occupy Foochou and whose subsidiary forces might occupy Amoy and Swatow. At this time, Japan's China Garrison Army, stationed in the Peking-T'ientsin area of northern China, had only recently risen in strength from 1771 to 5774 men.[22] This "Strategy for China: 1937" was the Army General Staff's first specific plan to occupy parts of northern China and to attack Nanking. But, it must be stressed, the "Strategy" was drawn up only in response to the Hirota government's "Second Guidelines for Settling the China Situation" of August 1936. This latter document envisioned a "Detachment of North China" that entailed the army's help to create an anti-Communist buffer zone of collaborator regimes. Likewise, the Army General Staff drew up plans for sending troops to Shanghai in central China, but only in response to stiffened Chinese defenses. Those plans, too, did not derive from Japanese initiative.

The "Strategy for China: 1937" drafted in August 1936, the creation of a SEA in August 1937, and actual assault on Nanking by the CCAA in December 1937, all stemmed from a grave misreading of affairs in China, which was fast moving toward national consolidation fed by anti-Japanese nationalism. The December 1936 Sian Incident, which saw the kidnapping of Chiang Kai-shek by his own generals, cleared the way for a second round of KMT-CCP cooperation culminating in a united front; it did not split China as the Japanese had hoped. These momentous events spawned a nationwide commitment to resist Japanese aggression after the July 1937 Marco Polo Bridge Incident, which led to full-scale hostilities. In sum, despite naming China a hypothetical enemy, Japanese military leaders neither deemed it a unified nation-state nor did serious strategic planning on that premise. This arrogance stemmed from the outdated notion that Japan need only occupy this or that key area in a strictly tactical fashion. Even in drawing up its "Strategy for China: 1937"—when the Army General Staff finally started thinking about sending troops to central China and Nanking—no one dreamed that this move would lead to a full-scale, long-term war. Japanese strategists could not understand broad political ramifications in attacking a national capital; that is why imperial army units sped lemming-like over the brink after they saw the Chinese army beat a retreat from Shanghai.

Such considerations shed light on three major underlying causes of the Nanking Atrocity. First, contempt for China as a modern nation led to a deficient concern for applying international law toward it. Just as serious fighting in northern China began, an undersecretary in the Army Ministry sent a notice dated 5 August 1937 to the China Garrison Army's Chief of Staff: "It is inappropriate to act strictly in accordance with various stipulations in 'Treaties and Practices Governing Land Warfare and Other Laws of War'."[23] Similar notices went out to other units as well. The message can only be construed as: "there is no need to obey international law." Second, this overweening attitude diluted concern for protecting Chinese civilians, as well as foreign diplomats and residents, from the horrors of war. The CCAA was formed haphazardly on 7 November 1937. Since it was not supposed to move far west of Shanghai, it had no supply-and-support units to provision troops, who could only rely on plunder to sustain themselves en route to Nanking. This increased their frequency of contacts with, and opportunities for violence toward, civilians. The SEA and the Tenth Army had no liaison staff or units trained in diplomacy; so those armies' relations with Japanese diplomatic officials in China were bad, to say the least. Troops viewed diplomats as a thorn in their side; diplomats who tried to stop army brutalities exposed themselves to danger. A third, related underlying cause of the Atrocity lay in the CCAA's disregard for upholding troop discipline and morality. It had no specialized military police (MP) units, and the few individual MPs who were on hand could not possibly maintain order. As one attached to the Tenth Army bewailed, "With less than 100 of us to control 200,000 men in several divisions, what could we do?"[24]

POWs and the Assault

The 1 December order to attack Nanking prescribed a third line of demarcation; troops were to regroup and consolidate a front from the Mo-pang Hills to Lishui (see map 1). From there, they would face off against Chinese defenders. This did nothing to deter the SEA's Ninth and Sixteenth divisions or the Tenth Army's Sixth and One Hundred-fourteenth divisions, which raced abreast of each other, intent on being the first to scale the walls of the enemy capital. The CCAA laid down a fourth line on 7 December, a "line of readiness," before the final push for the city; and, it issued instructions, "Essentials for Assaulting Nanking," listing orderly procedures for taking it. CCAA commander Matsui Iwane advised Chinese commander T'ang Sheng-chih to surrender the capital on 9 December, but received no reply by noon on 10 December. Matsui therefore ordered the attack to resume at 1:00 p.m. Frontline units ignored last-ditch efforts to contain the conflict, including those by the International Committee (IC), which established the Nanking Safety Zone (NSZ) described by David Askew in chapter 10. The SEA's Sixteenth division began to assault Purple Mountain just outside Nanking to the east on the tenth, and reached its summit by the twelfth. (See maps 1 and 5). The SEA's Ninth division rushed toward the city from the southeast. Some of its units reached Kuanghua Gate in the early hours on the ninth, but met fierce resistance for several days. The SEA pulled one regiment, the One Hundred-third Brigade, or Yamada Detachment, in the Thirteenth division, then on standby at Chen-chiang, and ordered this brigade to advance through Wulungshan and Mufushan on the right wing of a beefed-up Sixteenth division. On the eleventh, the SEA ordered a regiment in the Third division, then held in reserve, to augment the Ninth division's left wing as an advance raiding unit. The Tenth Army's Sixth and One Hundred-fourteenth divisions, advancing in parallel from the south, broke through Chinese front lines on 8 December and attacked the Fu-kuo encampment at Rain Flower Heights south of the city on the tenth. The Tenth Army then ordered the Hiroshima Fifth division's Kunisaki Detachment, on loan from its Ninth Brigade, to ford the Yangtze near Tz'u-hu-chen (T'aip'ing) and to advance on P'uk'ou. The Tenth Army also ordered its Eighteenth division, which had captured Wuhu on the tenth, to concentrate its forces on standby for an assault on Hangchou.

Thus the Ninth and Sixteenth divisions marched toward Nanking from the east; and the Sixth and One Hundred-fourteenth, from the south. On 13 December, the Thirteenth division's Yamada Detachment (or One Hundred-third Brigade) arrived from the north, and the Sixth division's Forty-fifth Regiment, from the south. Both had orders to plug Chinese escape routes between the city's western wall and the Yangtze. For good measure, the Eleventh Battle Fleet patrolled the Yangtze, and the Fifth division's Kunisaki Detachment advanced on its far bank to cut off Chinese troops trying to escape across the river. All told, CCAA forces assaulting Nanking numbered 57 infantry battalions or, as Kasahara estimates, between 160,000 and 200,000 men. They received artillery support from the seventeen-ship Eleventh Battle Fleet. Encirclement of the city would be complete by the early hours of 13 December. Across the lines, commander T'ang Sheng-chih did not order a retreat until 5:00 p.m. on the twelfth. T'ang was the very first to flee, crossing the Yangtze at 6 p.m. Tens of thousands of his troops—until then trapped in the city with orders to defend it at all costs—fled in chaos as their command structure totally broke down.

Japanese units learned of this retreat on the morning of the thirteenth. Skirmishes broke out in many areas as small groups of Chinese troops outside the city, now lacking a chain of command, desperately tried to slip past advancing Japanese forces. Then the surrendering began. Most of the Chinese troops still inside Nanking rushed to escape helter-skelter through Pa-chiang Gate, which led to the Hsiakwan wharf area. From Hsiakwan, they hoped to cross the Yangtze by boat, by raft, or by clinging desperately to scraps of lumber, or they madly ran up and down the riverbank, only to encounter Japanese forces sent to cut them off. Huge numbers of Chinese troops became prisoners of war (POWs) on the thirteenth and fourteenth at Hsiakwan, Mufushan, Chiang-tung Gate, and Hsiao-hua Gate. With no avenue of escape, Chinese soldiers lost all will to fight. Despite trying to surrender in droves, most were killed in the pell-mell of battle. Sixteenth division commander Nakajima Kesago's diary entries on 13 December describe the confusion:

> We see prisoners everywhere, so many that there is no way we can deal with them.... The general policy is: "Accept no prisoners!" So we ended up having to take care of them lot, stock, and barrel. But they came in hordes, in units of thousands or five-thousands; so we couldn't even disarm them.... Later I heard that the Sasaki Unit [the Thirtieth Brigade] alone disposed of about 1,500. A company commander guarding T'aip'ing Gate took care of another 1,300. Another 7,000 to 8,000 clustered at Hsienho Gate are still surrendering. We need a really huge ditch to handle those 7,000 to 8,000, but we can't find one, so someone suggested this plan: "Divide them up into groups of 100 to 200, and then lure them to some suitable spot for finishing off."[25]

Thirtieth Brigade commander Maj. Gen. Sasaki Tôichi wrote in his diary on 13 December:

> The number of abandoned enemy bodies in our area today was ten thousand plus thousands more. If we include those [Chinese] whose escape rafts or boats on the Yangtze were sunk by fire from our armored cars, plus POWs killed by our units, our detachment alone must have taken care of over 20,000. We finished the mop-up and secured our rear at about 2:00 p.m. While regrouping, we advanced to Ho-p'ing Gate. Later, the enemy surrendered in the thousands. Frenzied troops—rebuffing efforts by superiors to restrain them—finished off these POWs one after another. Even if they aren't soldiers [e.g., medics or priests], men would yell, "Kill the whole damn lot!" after recalling the past ten days of bloody fighting in which so many buddies had shed so much blood.[26]

Such diary entries by division and brigade commanders allow us to gauge the chaos of battle, and the extent of the slaughter of POWs. Official battle reports exist for some Japanese units that vividly describe how they handled POWs.[27] These sources are housed in the National Institute for Defense Studies, Military History Department Library in Tokyo. Most are included in the source collection, *Nankin senshi shiryô shû,* published by the Kaikôsha, a fraternal society of former imperial army officers and conservative revisionists. For instance, the Thirty-third Regiment's battle report for 10–14 December has a "Booty List" with an entry for POWs: "fourteen officers plus 3,082 NCOs and troops." Under the column "Remarks," it says, "disposed of POWs." As a rough number of "abandoned enemy corpses," it lists "220 on the tenth, 370 on the eleventh, 740 on the twelfth, and 5,500 on the thirteenth, for 6,830 all told." But, this battle report goes on, "the figure for 13 December includes defeated enemy troops whom we executed." The Thirty-third Regiment took 3,096 POWs on 13 December and "disposed of" them. The Sixty-sixth Regiment's First Battalion battle report says that it took "1,657" POWs outside Rain Flower Gate from the afternoon of the twelfth to the morning of the thirteenth. The appendix in the "Thirty-eighth Battalion Battle Report 12," says that its Tenth Company took "7,200" POWs on the morning of the fourteenth near Hsiao-hua Gate. Other battle reports listing numbers of POWs taken are those for the Kunisaki Detachment's Forty-first Regiment Twelfth Company, which took "2,350" at Chiang-hsin-chou from the night of the fourteenth to the morning of the fifteenth; the Thirty-third Regiment Second Battalion, which took "about 200" at Lion Hill on the 14th; and the Seventh Regiment, which took "6,670" in the Naking Safety Zone (NSZ), set up by Westerners as a refugee area, from the thirteenth to the twenty-fourth. Battlefield diaries left by Japanese units are another form of official source material. Only a few are extant and are housed in Defence Agency archives. Among these is that for the Twentieth Regiment's Fourth Company, which says that it took 328 POWs at the eastern side of the NSZ on the morning of the fourteenth, and shot all of them to death.

Thus battle reports and battlefield diaries—official, public, Japanese military sources—supplement and substantiate personal accounts by Westerners about mass executions of Chinese POWs. Japanese sources of this kind refute the Ministry of Education's claim, formerly used in textbook screening, that such killings were the acts of a few heartless soldiers in the heat of battle and did not take place in an organized way throughout the army as a whole. These sources also expose the falsity of arguments by Japanese conservative revisionists who, with studied ignorance of international law, insist that the killing of POWs was an extension of combat and thus does not constitute a massacre or an Atrocity. Imperial army records show that Japanese soldiers killed Chinese troops who, having lost all desire and ability to fight back, were begging to surrender so that their lives might be spared.

On the other hand, the fact that battle reports for other units are not extant does not mean that they did not take part in mass killings. One typical organized massacre of POWs occurred at Mufushan, northeast of Nanking. There, the Thirteenth division's Yamada Detachment or One Hundred-third Brigade, which included the Sixty-fifth Regiment (Morozumi Unit), took custody and "disposed of" 14,777 prisoners. Official, public army records do not mention this fact, but other contemporaneous sources do. These include newspapers such as the *Asahi shinbun* and volume 1 of the Army General Staff's own wartime official history, the *Shina jihen rikugun senshi*. And, as Ono Kenji reports in chapter 4, personal diaries and private notes by surviving Japanese soldiers in that detachment, brigade, and regiment—plus oral interviews with those men—show that more than 14,477 POWs were massacred.[28] Because of such damning sources, even the postwar Defense Agency's official war history, the *Senshi sôsho,* and the Kaikôsha's *Nankin senshi* cannot turn a blind eye to this massacre at Mufushan. The *Senshi sôsho* simply regurgitates an earlier account of the incident, now refuted. According to it, the Japanese units in question released half of their 14,777 men and incarcerated the other 8,000 or so, but half escaped. The units then tried to escort the remaining 4,000 POWs across the Yangtze in order to release them to safety, but the POWs attacked their Japanese guards, so the units had no choice but to open fire, kill 1,000 in self-defense, and let the rest escape.[29] This account is totally make-believe. The foot soldiers' personal diaries and other private sources that Ono unearthed—such as Amano Saburô's wartime letters, translated in chapter 8—conclusively prove that the Japanese units in question massacred all of the POWs held in custody in an organized manner.

Thus we can assume that many other Japanese units must have taken, and "taken care of," enormous numbers of POWs—even though this assumption cannot be verified irrefutably because so few battle reports, battlefield diaries, or other "official" records remain extant. The *Nankin senshi* adopts the position that killed Chinese POWs must enter the victim count when "official" records exist or when the testimonies of eyewitnesses abound, but in all other cases, there is no definitive evidence to substantiate the claim that POWs were taken and killed. This argument—which disparages nonofficial, private sources and oral testimonies—stems from a desire to lower the Chinese victim toll. Still another conservative revisionist argument is that numbers found in battle reports and in other official army records cannot be accepted at face value. As the *Nankin senshi* asserts, "units undoubtedly inflated figures used in reports to superiors so as to exaggerate their 'battlefield exploits'." Of course, statistics in these sources are not totally accurate, but we can only suspect ulterior motives when historians discount their validity solely to deflate Chinese victim counts. The key point here is that both official and nonofficial Japanese records—left by men who did the killing—aver that units "took care of," "dealt with, or "disposed of" POWs; and, in some cases, expressly say, "shot them dead." The men who left these documents used such expressions openly because they lacked any idea that the killing of POWs was a violation of international law and a grave crime against humanity. In response to conservative minimalists, we can just as easily conjecture that executions took place when the sources say only that units "took" prisoners, and omit explicit reference to "disposing of" them or "shooting them dead." Thus the claim that "there are no irrefutable records, ergo there were no massacres," and the counterclaim that "massacres occurred even though there is no express record thereof," offset each other—although neither is valid in and of itself.

Organized Nature of the Massacres

To repeat, on 13–14 December, Japanese forces encircled the Chinese army and captured Nanking. Chinese soldiers, lacking a command structure after being abandoned by their commander T'ang Sheng-chih, lost all will to resist and surrendered en masse only to suffer summary execution in an organized fashion. A key issue in the Nanking Atrocity, then, is to explain why these illegal and unjustifiable executions took place. One answer is that the imperial army—at least during the 1937–45 Sino-Japanese War—lacked any idea that enemy POWs should be treated in a humane fashion. The idea of universal human rights spread in modern Western states after the French Revolution. Laws governing land warfare were created one after another to ensure the humane treatment of prisoners. Those laws were consolidated in the form of internationally accepted conventions at the 1899 and 1907 Hague Peace Conferences. From 1868 to 1912—in the Meiji and Taishô eras before the Shôwa emperor's reign—Japan craved recognition as a civilized, modern state equal to the advanced Western powers; so, it strove to earn their respect by obeying international laws of war. That is why the Meiji and Taishô emperors included explicit clauses to that effect in rescripts declaring war on the Ch'ing Empire in 1894, on czarist Russia in 1904, and on imperial Germany in 1914. But the Shôwa emperor issued no rescript declaring war on the KMT Republic of China in 1937, although the scale of that conflict was unprecedented by far. As just noted, there were pragmatic reasons for calling this an "incident": the lack of a casus belli that the public would find acceptable, and the need to import strategic matériel from the United States. The government and military unwittingly escalated the up-to-then limited China conflict into a de facto war in August 1937, but even with hostilities spreading in northern China, central military officials in Tokyo told the China Garrison Army General Staff on 5 August 1937 that: "it is inappropriate to follow all specific clauses" in international laws of war, and "our empire is not in a full-scale war with China, so we must avoid using terms such as 'prisoner of war' or 'prize of war' that may imply the intent to start one."[30] The same message repeatedly went out to other units later. The Army Ministry's position was: the laws of war do not apply to an "incident," so do not use words that connote a formal state of war. This was a momentous change from the past, when imperial rescripts formally declared wars with the stern order for officers and men to obey international law.

Imperial army attitudes at this time exuded contempt for the Chinese army and people. A textbook for noncommissioned officers (NCOs) issued in January 1933 draws a telling distinction between Western states and China in a section titled, "Treatment of Prisoners": "There is no need to send them to the rear for confinement and wait to see how the war situation changes—as we would do with nationals of other [Western] powers. In the absence of special circumstances, it is alright to release them on the spot or to transport them elsewhere for release. The Chinks' domicile registration system is full of defects, and most Chink soldiers are the scum of society, so there is little way for anyone to check whether they are alive or where they are. Thus, even if you were to kill them or release them elsewhere, no one will broach the issue."[31]

In sum, central army officials instructed field armies not to apply international laws of war. Tokyo did not deem this nonapplication in China to be a war crime, so it is natural that local commanders issued orders to "take no POWs" or to "dispose of" them. Many veterans affirm that high ranking army- and division-level commanders gave such orders during the assault on Nanking. Thus Lt. Sawada Masahisa of the Independent Heavy Artillery's Second Battalion First Company states: "command headquarters ordered us to shoot to death on sight" 8,000 to 10,000 POWs taken at Hsien-ho Gate on 14 December. (Here, Sawada probably means SEA command headquarters; if so, its commander, Imperial Prince Asaka Yasuhiko, would be complicit.) Or, adjutant Kodama Yoshio of the Sixteenth Division's Thirty-eighth Regiment says that, when his unit got to a point one or two kilometers outside the Nanking city walls, the division's adjutant phoned in a command to "accept no Chink soldiers who try to surrender; dispose of them."[32] Official, public battlefield diaries and battle reports list formal commands to "take care of" POWs. One for the Thirty-eighth Regiment contains an order from the Thirtieth Brigade dated "14 December, 4:50 a.m." Clause 7 reads, "all units are forbidden to take POWs until directed by the [Sixteenth] Division." A Sixty-eighth Regiment, Third Battalion daily camp ledger dated 16 December reads: "Hereafter, make a cursory survey of troops taken prisoner; then units shall sternly dispose of them."[33] The Sixty-sixth Regiment's First Battalion took 1,657 Chinese POWs between 10 and 13 December comprising eighteen high-ranking officers plus 1,639 (NCOs) and troops. A battle report dated 13 December records in express detail how this unit killed them.

(8) Received the following order from our Regimental commander at 2:00 p.m.

A. Kill all POWs in accordance with [One Hundred Twenty-seventh] Brigade orders. As a method, we suggest tying them up in groups of less than twenty and shooting them one by one.

B. Collect their weapons and guard these until you receive instructions.

C. While the main force of our Regiment mops up inside the city, your duties are as outlined above.

(9) Based on the above Regimental command, we [in turn] ordered that the First, Third, and Fourth Companies collect, sort, and guard weapons. At 3:30 p.m., we assembled all companies and, after discussing how to deal with the POWs, decided on the following. We divided them up in 3 equal-sized units and assigned each of our 3 companies to oversee one of these. Each company would place POWs in a guard house to be led out in smaller groups of fifty. The First Company led its group to a valley

south of its camp; the Third Company, to a hilly area southwest of its camp; and the Fourth Company, to a valley southeast of its camp. Each company was then supposed to execute its POWs by bayonet, but take pains to guard them heavily, so that none would notice [anything suspicious] when they were being led out. All companies finished preparations and began the executions by 5:00 o'clock, so most were over by about 7:30 p.m. The First Company decided to change plans and instead tried to burn down its guard house. This failed. The POWs, resigned to their fate, stuck out their heads before our swords and stood tall before our bayonets with no sign of fear. Some of them, however, wailed and pleaded for mercy, especially when unit commanders came by to make the rounds.[34]

Only a few official battle reports and battlefield diaries are extant, but we have many personal diaries and reminiscences testifying that summary executions took place on command. There is no doubt that these reflected orders from above and took place systematically—not just haphazardly. The organized nature of the Atrocity was a focal point in Ienaga Saburô's third lawsuit against the government in January 1984. The Ministry of Education had tried to deny this fact by forcing him to retract an account of the Nanking Atrocity in his high school Japanese history textbook. He won the suit in October 1993, when the Tokyo District Higher Court ruled in his favor, and the Supreme Court upheld this decision in August 1997. In sum, Japanese law courts and the government now affirm that massacres took place in an organized way. Organized mass slaughters of POWs, such as that by the One Hundred Third Brigade and Sixty-fifth Regiment at Mufushan as substantiated by Ono Kenji in chapter 4, violated international law.

Defeated Stragglers and "Guerrillas"

The attack on Nanking was a classic example of encirclement. The SEA's Ninth and Sixteenth divisions plus the Thirteenth division's One Hundred Third Brigade advanced from the east. The Tenth Army's Sixth and One Hundred-fourteenth divisions advanced from the southeast. The Fifth division's Kunisaki Detachment advanced along the far bank of the Yangtze supported by the Eleventh Battle Fleet. Chinese commander T'ang Sheng-chih at first made no preparations to retreat, and indeed, ordered the city to be defended to the last man. But Chiang Kai-shek then ordered the army to escape for future fighting, and T'ang had a change of heart as well; so he ordered a retreat at 5:00 p.m. on the twelfth, before Japanese forces fully surrounded the city in the early hours of the thirteenth. In gross dereliction of his duty as defense commander, T'ang and his staff were the first to flee across the Yangtze River.

Abandoned without a chain of command, T'ang's troops lost all will to resist. Hordes of them east and south of the city were in chaos, while those trapped inside the city walls fled for Pa-chiang Gate, their sole escape hatch, only to find it shut. Masses of defeated Chinese troops and refugees had gathered at Hsiakwan wharf on the thirteenth, when the Eleventh Battle Fleet arrived at 5:00 p.m. According to Japanese naval sources, the fleet "fired fiercely on defeated stragglers who hoped to flee to the far shore and cut them to ribbons."[35] With their escape route by water cut off, masses of Chinese troops began madly rushing up and down the Yangtze river bank, desperately seeking safety. Victory was already decided; virtually all of the defeated Chinese soldiers lacked weapons and any will to resist. But the imperial army and navy fired on these helpless troops and also on civilians. It is clearly wrong to call this a combat operation; it was a slaughter, a massacre. An "annihilation of defeated enemy troops"—plus great numbers of civilians mixed in—was conducted by the Sixteenth Division at Hsiakwan, Pa-chiang Gate, and Machün; and by the Sixth Division at Hsiakwan, Hsin-ho-chen, and Chiang-tung Gate. In fact, each of these actions was simply a turkey shoot of defenseless people.

Defeated remnants of the Chinese army discarded weapons, stripped off their uniforms, and slipped into the city, where the imperial army began mop-up operations on 13 December with orders to round up anyone suspected of being a soldier. The Ninth division handled areas south of Chungshan Road; the Sixteenth division, those north of it. On the fourteenth, Japanese troops forayed into the Nanking Safety Zone (NSZ), claiming that defeated Chinese stragglers, disguised in civilian clothing; that is, guerrillas, had taken refuge therein. The reasons for this haste lay in the CCAA's decision to hold a triumphal entry procession into Nanking on the seventeenth—made despite SEA objections that this was too early to ensure safety. Newspapers at home had been playing up the capture of the enemy capital, so the CCAA could not lose face by seeming to dawdle. On top of that, Lt. Gen. Asaka Yasuhiko—an imperial prince and uncle of the Shôwa emperor—was to take a leading part in the ceremony as SEA commander. Thus the CCAA had to take every possible precaution to prevent harm from befalling his royal personage. The SEA's Ninth Division Seventh Regiment mopped up the Nanking Safety Zone from the thirteenth to the twenty-fourth, and its battle report records "6,670 [Chinese] killed by bullet and bayonet." This regiment's immediate superior officer, Brigade commander Maj. Gen. Akiyama Yoshimitsu, stipulated "Points to Note in Mop Up," dated 13 December. This document expressly said: "View all youths and adult males as defeated stragglers or soldiers disguised in civilian clothes; round up and detain all of them."[36] This implies that many civilians were likely among the 6,670 killed.

Seventh Regiment commander Col. Isa Kazuo, First Company Private First-Class Mizutani Sô, and Second Company Lance Cor. Inoie Mataichi left diaries. Isa made simple entries such as "Mopped up from the morning. The [Nanking] Safety Zone is in our area. It is said to hold about 10,000 refugees" on the fourteenth, or "we sternly disposed of about 6,500 over three days of mop up" on the sixteenth. By contrast, Inoie and Mizutani went into more specific detail. Inoie, for example, writes: "We set out in the afternoon as well and came back with 335 young captives. We ferreted out all males among the refugees who looked like defeated stragglers. Man! Some had family members there, and did they ever wail when we tried to take their men folk away! They'd latch on to our arms and bodies, pleading with us.... We took these 335 down near the Yangtze where other troops shot them dead."[37] Mizutani's entry for the sixteenth reads:

> In the afternoon we went to the [Nanking] Safety Zone for mop up. We placed sentries with bayonets at the intersections, blocked these off, and went about our work rounding up virtually all young men we came across. We roped them off, surrounded them with armed guards, tied them up in rows, and led them away so that they looked like kids playing choo-choo train. Our First Company clearly took less than other units, but we still got a hundred and several dozen. Lots of women, no doubt their mothers or wives, soon caught up with us to cry and beg for their release. Right away, we released those who clearly looked like civilians and shot thirty-six others to death. All of them wailed desperately to be spared, but there was nothing we could do. Even if some unfortunate innocent victims were mixed in (we couldn't tell for sure), it just couldn't be helped. Killing some innocent victims was unavoidable. [CCAA] Commander Matsui ordered us to clean out each and every anti-Japanese element and defeated straggler, so we did that in the harshest possible manner.[38]

The SEA Sixteenth Division's Twentieth Regiment also mopped up in the Safety Zone. Fourth Company Lance Corporal Masuda Rokusuke wrote: "14 December. Mop Up. Entered the [Nanking] Safety Zone. Cleaned out defeated stragglers mixed in with refugees. Our Fourth Company alone took care of no less than 500; we shot them dead next to Hsüan-wu Gate. I hear that all our units did the same thing."[39] In an account written on the order of his company commander after entering Nanking, Masuda noted:

> On the morning of the fourteenth we went to mop up the [Nanking] Safety Zone—run by some kind of international committee. We surrounded tens of thousands of defeated stragglers who had fiercely resisted us until yesterday. Not a single one would escape now. They all fled into that Safety Zone. But we were determined to go in, search every nook and cranny, flush them all out, and exact revenge for our fallen buddies. Each of our squads looked over all males in those big, complex Chink houses. In one of these, Lance Corporal Maebara and his troops found a few hundred defeated stragglers changing into civvies. Hearing of this, we went to have a look. What a sight! Next to them were tons of rifles, revolvers, swords, and other weapons. Some of those men were still in uniform. Some were hastily changing into ordinary Chink clothes. Others wore civvie shirts with army-uniform trousers. All of the clothes were either unsuited to winter or mismatched as to shirts and pants, so the men obviously had grabbed and donned these in a big rush. We led all of them off, stripped them down, checked them out, and tied them up with downed telephone wires.... With dusk

approaching, we marched close to 600 of these defeated stragglers over toward Hsüan-wu Gate and shot them dead.[40]

To execute soldiers lacking the will and means to resist on the pretext that they are "defeated stragglers" or "combatants disguised in civilian clothes" is unjustifiable, illegal, and inhumane. Worse still, it is a downright atrocity to slaughter huge numbers of civilians in the process without making an effort to ascertain if they in fact are military personnel. Even foreign nationals from states friendly to Japan concurred on this point. On 20 January 1938, the German Branch Consulate in Nanking sent this report to its Foreign Ministry:

Our few policemen could not stop vast numbers of Chinese soldiers from fleeing into the [Nanking] Safety Zone. (Some had thrown away their arms, but even when this was not the case, they lacked any means to resist.) On that pretext, the Japanese army began a massive search of houses and hauled away all Chinese suspected of being soldiers. The usual Japanese way of determining whom to seize was to check for abrasions or other tell-tale signs of having worn helmets on their heads, carried rifles on their shoulders, or lugged knapsacks on their backs. Foreign witnesses say that the Japanese tricked the Chinese by promising to give them work or to pardon them, but then led them away to be killed. The Japanese took no steps to declare martial law or anything of the sort. Why should we expect any such pretensions on their part? They flout the conventions of law in wartime as well as the rules of human decency?[41]

Conservative revisionists in Japan today deny the Nanking Atrocity or justify it by claiming that mop-up operations were conducted against Chinese soldiers disguised in civilian clothes. These guerrillas, or would-be guerrillas, it is claimed, pretended to be peace-loving civilians but actually bore concealed weapons waiting for a chance to snipe at Japanese troops. That form of combat violated international laws of war, so those Chinese combatants forfeited all legal rights that POWs enjoy. As this argument goes, it was a justifiable act of self-defense for Japanese units to kill them, and it was also permissible to capture and execute them for committing these acts, which were war crimes. Raids into the Nanking Safety Zone (NSZ), it is held, were legitimate combat operations to wipe out enemy soldiers disguised as civilians. In fact, however, Chinese soldiers who fled into the NSZ lacked the will to fight that was needed to become guerrillas. They had no place of refuge except the NSZ, and they changed into civilian clothes simply to avoid being killed by the invaders. It was indefensible for Japanese troops to kill them on the spot with no effort to ascertain their true status, or to execute them as war criminals without bringing them before military tribunals. Furthermore, it was even less justifiable to kill large numbers of innocent civilians based on arbitrary criteria such as having what seemed to be shoulder-strap or helmet abrasions, which purported "proved" that they were soldiers.

Atrocities against Civilians

As Takashi Yoshida relates in chapter 11, the "Rape of Nanking," as it was first called in 1937–38, became known the world over because of the huge number of rapes and mass murders committed against civilians. These atrocities took center stage at the Tokyo war crimes trials where Chinese victims and foreign witnesses testified, and the People's Republic of China (PRC) emphasizes this issue today by seeking out ever more victims and witnesses. Thus, crimes against the general civilian population remains *the* key point in the debate over Nanking. However, conservative revisionists in Japan remain mum on this point, ignoring all testimonies by Chinese victims, neutral foreign witnesses, and even Japanese victimizers as being uncorroborated in bona fide primary sources. These conservatives begrudge at most that: "The Japanese army did commit misdeeds against the civilian population. The International Committee for the Nanking Safety Zone protested against the killing of 47 civilians. Not all of these cases can be substantiated, but even if they could, that's a total of forty-seven—hardly a big number compared with other armies in history who captured and occupied foreign capitals in wartime."[42] Thus, conservative revisionists deny that Japanese troops perpetrated large-scale atrocities against Chinese civilians. But the imperial army itself admitted this fact at the time. On 4 January 1938, IH, in the name of Field Marshal Prince Kan'in Kotohito, an uncle of the Shôwa emperor, issued an unprecedented statement to CCAA commander Matsui Iwane: "If we look at actual conditions in the army, we must admit that much is less than blemish-free. Invidious incidents, especially as to troop discipline and morality, have occurred with increasing frequency of late. However much we may wish to disbelieve this fact, we cannot but have doubts." Though hardly blunt and direct, this imperial prince admonished against ongoing Japanese atrocities.

Other documents clearly show that troops were being disciplined for criminal acts at the time. For example, one source is a Tenth Army legal department daily ledger from 12 October 1937 to 23 February 1938; another is a CCAA battlefield courts martial daily ledger from 4 January to 6 February 1938. The absurdly small number of military police on hand could not control an invading army of well over 100,000; so we can be sure that only those men caught for the most egregious of crimes were court-martialed, and they were punished only as examples to deter others. Still, the following figures in the Tenth Army legal department daily ledger prove that rapes took place—although these represent the tip of an iceberg. Of the 102 men convicted as of 18 February 1938, twenty-two were for rape, twenty-seven, for murder; two for rape-and-murder; and two for causing bodily injury that resulted in death. Of the sixteen men awaiting trial on that date, two were charged with rape and one with murder. The occurrence of such heinous crimes is substantiated as well by a directive issued on 20 December 1937 that inveighs against the high incidence of rape in the Tenth Army: "We have told troops numerous times that looting, rape, and arson are forbidden, but judging from the shameful fact that over 100 incidents of rape came to light during the current assault on Nanking, we bring this matter to your attention yet again despite the repetition."[43]

Commander Matsui Iwane himself noted the reality of rape in the CCAA battlefield courts martial daily ledger. An entry for 20 December reads: "It seems that our troops committed acts of rape and looting (mainly items like furniture) at about 1:00 p.m.; the truth is that some such acts are unavoidable." Matsui's entry in the ledger for 26 December reads: "I again heard of looting and rape in and around Nanking and Hangchou."[44] In explaining these passages, the *Nankin senshi*'s (History of the Nanking Campaign) protective authors claim that Matsui "construed the so-called 'Nanking Incident' as comprising violations of foreign rights and privileges in China and incidents of violence and looting against the Chinese. He had no idea of an 'Atrocity' that would arise as a problem later on [at war crimes trials]."[45] If there was "a problem," however, it lay precisely in this lack of cognizance by the highest ranking Japanese commander during the Nanking campaign.

Indeed, then, the imperial army's upper echelons did know that troops were perpetrating rape and violence against Chinese civilians. Lt. Gen. Okamura Yasuji, who took over command of the Tenth Army before its assault on Wuhan in August 1938, later recalled: "I surmised the following based on what I heard from Staff Officer Miyazaki, CCAA Special Service Department Chief Harada, and Hangchou Special Service Department Chief Hagiwara a day or two after I arrived in Shanghai. First, it is true that tens of thousands of acts of violence, such as looting and rape, took place against civilians during the assault on Nanking. Second, front-line troops indulged in the evil practice of executing POWs on the pretext of [lacking] rations."[46]

Rapes were especially prevalent at Nanking, and were a focus of the third lawsuit that Tokyo University of Education professor Ienaga Saburô brought against the Japanese government. In its 1983 screening of high school history textbooks, the Ministry of Education ordered him to delete a footnote that read: "There were many officers and men in the Japanese army who violated Chinese women." The Ministry did admit that women were violated, but insisted that: "This occurred on all battlefields in all periods of human history. His [Ienaga's] selection of facts is problematic if he makes this point only in the case of the Japanese army." Rape is an immeasurably traumatic experience for the females involved; it leaves lifelong emotional scars. Given the shame-inducing nature of this crime, victims naturally wish to keep it secret; so written contemporaneous sources that document it are very rare. Nevertheless, rape by the imperial army was a major problem in the early stages of the 1937–45 Sino-Japanese War, especially at Nanking, even when compared with behavior in the Meiji-Ch'ing (or First Sino-Japanese) War and the Russo-Japanese War.

One source that sheds light on this matter is a directive issued in February 1939 by an Army Ministry undersecretary to units returning home from the China front. It sought to ensure that soldiers exercise discretion in talking about their experiences; in other words, they should keep still about what happened. An appendix to the source lists the following specific examples of verbal statements that the army wished to suppress:

(1) At XX, we took four people captive—parents and daughters. We played with the daughters as if they were whores and killed the parents because they kept on telling us to release the daughters. We had our kicks until the unit was ordered to leave; then we killed the daughters. (2) One company commander hinted that rape was OK, saying, "Make sure no problems arise later on; after you're finished, either pay them off or kill them outright." (3) Every soldier who fought in the war must be a murderer, armed robber, or rapist. (4) No one cared about rapes at the front; some guys even shot at MPs who caught them in the act. (5) The only skills I picked up after half a year in combat were how to rape and loot.[47]

These are documents left by the perpetrators. Needless to say, the victims left many as well. Foreigners also left testimonies and conducted surveys. Conservative revisionists say that these Western sources lack credibility because Britons and Americans were enemies who hated Japan at the time. But nationals of friendly states such as Germany, which signed the Anti-Comintern Pact with Japan in 1936, also left documents. I have already cited a message sent by the German Branch Consulate in Nanking. There are also reports to the German Foreign Ministry sent by Georg Rosen of the German Consulate staff and by John Rabe—a Nazi Party member, Siemens company employee, and head of the International Committee (IC) that administered the NSZ. Even these nationals friendly to Japan candidly exposed Japanese misdeeds. For example, on 24 December 1937, Rosen reported: "The most disgusting acts by Japanese soldiers against Chinese civilians have come to light; these clearly work against Germany's policy of thwarting the spread of Communism." On 15 January 1938, he reported: "Over a month has passed since the Japanese army occupied Nanking, but soldiers are still abducting and raping women and girls. In that sense, the Japanese army is erecting a monument to its own dishonor."[48] Rosen also noted that Japanese soldiers were breaking into the German Embassy and the ambassador's official residence demanding women.

John Rabe's diary describes horrible rapes by Japanese soldiers. For example, on 17 December he writes: "One of the Americans put it this way: 'The Safety Zone has turned into a public house for the Japanese soldiers.' That's very close to the truth. Last night up to 1,000 women and girls are said to have been raped, about 100 girls at Ginling Girls College alone. You hear of nothing but rape. If husbands or brothers intervene, they're shot. What you hear and see on all sides is the brutality and bestiality of the Japanese soldiery."[49] On 24 December Rabe noted: "Dr. Wilson used the opportunity to show me a few of his patients. The woman who was admitted because of a miscarriage and had the bayonet cuts all over her face is doing fairly well."[50] This woman is probably Li Hsiu-ying, one plaintiff in a lawsuit over wartime compensation launched by Chinese victims in the Tokyo District Court. Such objective contemporaneous reports by Westerners constitute undeniable evidence that huge numbers of rapes took place. And, I wish to stress, these reports were tendered by members of a nationality friendly to Japan, not by Chinese victims or by American, Australian, and British "enemies."

The imperial army responded to those criticisms by creating typically Japanese "comfort stations" staffed by so-called "comfort women." At an inquiry prior to the Tokyo War Crimes Trials, a former Kwantung Army staff officer, Tanaka Ryûkichi, gave this account of how the institution came into being: "[CCAA Staff Officer] Chô Isamu told me that officers and troops were raping too many women, so he set up brothels in Nanking to stop this."[51] Earlier, in the Siberian Intervention of 1918–22, Japanese troops had used "comfort women" to prevent rapes and the spread of venereal disease. Now, alarmed by the high incidence of rape at Nanking, the imperial army organized groups of such women to accompany troops during the later assault on Wuhan. Thereafter, the army officially recognized and set up comfort stations wherever it went. Because there were not enough Japanese women to meet the increased demand, Korean women were secured by fraud or force and sent to the front. Rapes occurred repeatedly all the way from Shanghai to Nanking and also in the capital after it fell. This was a major war crime perpetrated by the imperial army; indeed, the epithet "Rape of Nanking," as the event was called at the time, came to stand for the Atrocity as a whole. This war crime not only left deep scars on the Chinese, it also has had major implications for problems that plague Japan's relations with North and South Korea. Conservative revisionists in Japan deny that a Nanking Atrocity took place by asserting that *only* this or that many people were victimized, or that empirical evidence for their victimization is not ironclad. But we will never comprehend the true nature of Japanese atrocities at Nanking if we turn a blind eye to the tens of thousands of women reputedly raped there.

Historical Awareness

The Nanking Atrocity symbolized Japan's war of aggression against China. There were foreign embassies and news agencies in Nanking, then the capital of China, so reports of the Atrocity went out to the entire world. The Japanese people alone, with few exceptions, remained in the dark because of severe wartime censorship. Thus the great majority of Japanese learned about the Atrocity only during the Tokyo War Crimes Trials which, as Timothy Brook shows in chapter 7, first broached the issue of Japan's war guilt and culpability. Foreign physicians and missionaries who had lived in Nanking, plus Chinese persons victimized there, testified at Tokyo. Other types of evidence included sociologist Lewis Smythe's surveys of damages, burial records left by the Nanking branch of the Chinese Red Cross, the Red Swastika Society, and also those by other local organizations. As a result of this evidence, CCAA commander Matsui Iwane received the death sentence. The verdict read: "the total number of civilians and POWs murdered in Nanking and its vicinity during the first six weeks of the Japanese occupation was over 200,000." Article XI of the San Francisco Peace Treaty, signed in 1951, stipulates: "Japan accepts the verdicts of war crimes trials." In sum, the postwar Japanese government formally admits that imperial Japan waged a war of aggression and that it massacred over 200,000 people at Nanking.

But unlike its former ally Germany, Japan did not make an all-out effort to prosecute war crimes or criminals later in the postwar era after the Allied Occupation ended. Former wartime leaders, even some who had been convicted of A-class war crimes, returned to positions of power. Sentiments to affirm or even glorify the war became influential after the San Francisco Peace Treaty took effect and Japan regained sovereignty in April 1952. As seen in the Ienaga lawsuits beginning in 1967, the Ministry of Education censored school textbooks to ban words such as "aggression" or delete mention of the Nanking Atrocity. Moreover, conservative revisionists began to argue that the Atrocity was a fabrication or an illusion. From the 1970s onward, controversies threatening the very basis of historical fact have raged in Japan. In 1982, China and South Korea formally protested against Japan's government when they learned of conditions surrounding textbook screening. The Suzuki Zenkō regime, in power from July 1980 to November 1982, settled this diplomatic rift by having Miyazawa Kiichi, Director of the Cabinet Secretariat, proclaim that Japan "reaffirms the spirit of self-criticism espoused in the [1972] 'Sino-Japanese Joint Statement' and [1965] 'Joint Communiqué' between Japan and South Korea," and also that "the Japanese government will take responsibility for correcting textbook passages." As Kimura Takuji shows in chapter 15, hawks in the ruling Liberal Democratic Party as well as other right-wing elements lashed out at China and South Korea for allegedly intervening in Japanese internal affairs on this and other issues; and, as a result, debates over history flared up again, with deniers contending that the Nanking Atrocity was a fiction or a falsehood. In response, we formed the Society to Study the Nanking Incident (Nankin ken) in 1982, and it has continued publishing scholarly books and articles to this day. As more and more of these studies appeared, most aspects of the Atrocity have become clearly known.

The fatal scholarly blow to the conservative revisionist cause came between April 1984 and March 1985 when the Kaikōsha elicited testimonies from members who had served at Nanking for publication in its monthly, the *Kaikō*. Its editors hoped they would settle the controversy once and for all by publishing great numbers of eyewitness testimonies that denied major misdeeds. But contrary to those expectations, many Kaikôsha members sent in accounts affirming that massacres, rapes, and other acts of wanton violence took place. To their credit, the *Kaikô* editors published these materials unaltered, and Chief Editor Katogawa Kôtarô ended the series in March 1985 with an article titled, "Summing Up," in which he admitted the fact of illegal killings, and even of massacres. He cited estimated victim counts of 3,000 to 6,000 tendered by Unemoto Masami, and of 13,000, by Itakura Yoshiaki; and Katogawa concluded the series by saying:

We Deeply Apologize to the Chinese People

To repeat: 3,000 to 6,000 is a terrible figure; how much more so is 13,000. When we began compiling our history, we were prepared to accept that Japan was not innocent. Nevertheless, we can only reflect upon such huge numbers with deep sadness. No matter what the conditions of battle were, and no matter how that affected the hearts of men, such large-scale illegal killings cannot be justified. As someone affiliated with the former Japanese army, I can only apologize deeply to the Chinese people. I am truly sorry. We did horrible things to you.[52]

The Kaikôsha published a semi-official history, the *Nankin senshi,* plus a collection of primary sources, the *Nankin senshi shiryô shû.* These two works list 15,760 civilian casualties and 16,000 POWs summarily killed, but the editors took a reactionary step by insisting that not all of these were illegal or illegitimate killings, and that Chinese counterclaims of 200,000 or 300,000 victims are fabricated. Even so, by publishing primary sources that contain the facts and by admitting the Atrocity's historicity, the Kaikôsha conclusively repudiated false claims that the event never took place or was an illusion. Indeed, several contributors to the present volume, myself included, cite these Kaikôsha publications in our chapters. Thus, as a scholarly argument, denial was dead.

However, as further related by Kimura Takuji in chapter 15, the 1990s brought new developments. Konoe Fumimaro's grandson, Prime Minister Hosokawa Morihiro, in 1993 admitted that "aggressive acts"—though not aggression itself—took place in the last war. And, in 1995 Prime Minister Murayama Tomiichi from the Japan Socialist Party expressed self-criticism and sorrow for Japan's colonial rule and aggression in Asia. Those statements provoked more right-wing efforts to affirm and glorify the war and to deny historicity to the Nanking Atrocity—propositions that had suffered refutation in academic circles. Once more, battles over historical awareness erupted. Today, this is no longer a debate over facts or empirical proof, no longer a matter of scholarship. Conservative revisionists today who insist on denying the Nanking Atrocity—despite all evidence to the contrary—do so for political reasons. They wish to sanctify a road to future wars by glorifying the last one.

According to them, Japan is already an economic power; it now shoul~~d~~ the ranks of political and military powers too. This means winning a pe~~rma~~nent seat on the UN Security Council. To do that, they argue, Japan m~~u~~st make suitable international contributions by sending troops overseas to join in combat roles as part of UN armed forces. But before that can happen, the Japanese must amend or eliminate Article IX of their postwar Constitution so that their nation can once again use military force to settle international disputes. Such constitutional revision can not take place until the Japanese overcome their aversion to wars in general, based on misperceptions of the last one they fought, and until they stop their abject practice of "diplomacy by apology" due to unwarranted feelings of war guilt. In sum, as the conservative revisionist line goes, pacifism and servility are foolish because World War II was a just and glorious one for Japan. This is the nakedly political logic motivating those conservative revisionists who go on denying the Atrocity's factuality long after such claims have been exposed as scholarly bankrupt.

Notes

* Translated from Japanese by the editor.
1. When Chiang Kai-shek established Nanking as the capital of the Republic of China in 1928, he renamed Peking "Peip'ing." However, the city will be cited by its more familiar name, "Peking" in Wade-Giles rather than "Beijing," as the city is now known.
2. Translator's note. The emperor issued three types of orders: *rinsanmei,* conveyed by Chiefs of the Army or Navy General Staff, *tairikumei,* conveyed through the Army General Staff, and *daikairei,* conveyed by the Navy General Staff.
3. Usui et al., eds., *Gendai shi shiryô: 9 Nit-Chû sensô II,* pp. 19–20.
4. Ibid., pp. 20–24.
5. Terasaki and Terasaki Miller, eds., *Shôwa tennô dokuhaku roku,* pp. 36–37; Fujiwara, *Nankin no Nihongun,* pp. 11–12.
6. Fujiwara, *Nankin no Nihongun,* p. 18.
7. Bôeichô bôei kenshû sho senshi shitsu, ed., *Senshi sôsho: Shina jihen rikugun sakusen 1,* p. 26.
8. Kasahara, *Nankin jiken,* p. 72.
9. Bôeichô bôei kenshû sho senshi shitsu, ed., *Senshi sôsho: Shina jihen rikugun sakusen 1,* p. 386.
10. Fujiwara, *Nankin no Nihongun,* p. 18.
11. Kasahara, *Nankin jiken,* p. 79.
12. Bôeichô bôei kenshû sho senshi shitsu, ed., *Senshi sôsho: Shina jihen rikugun sakusen 1,* p. 397.
13. For more detail on these points, see Fujiwara, *Nankin no Nihongun,* pp. 83–94; and Fujiwara, "Kaisetsu," pp. ix–xxiv.
14. Quoted in Eguchi, "Shanhai sen to Nankin shingeki sen," pp. 17–21.
15. Fujiwara, *Nankin no Nihongun,* pp. 16–17.
16. Ibid.
17. Bôeichô bôei kenshû sho senshi shitsu, ed., *Senshi sôsho: Shina jihen rikugun sakusen 1,* p. 422.
18. Yoshida, *Tennô no guntai to Nankin jiken,* pp. 69–99; Honda, *Nanjing Massacre,* pp. 134–35.
19. Kasahara, "Nankin bôeisen to Chûgokugun," pp. 221–35.
20. Bôeichô bôei kenshû sho senshi shitsu, ed., *Senshi sôsho: Daihon'ei rikugunbu 1,* pp. 394–97.
21. Bôeichô bôei kenshû sho senshi shitsu, ed., *Shina jihen rikugun sakusen 1,* pp. 102–3.

22. Ibid., p. 103. The increase in the China Garrison Army came in April 1936; see Fujiwara, *Shôwa no rekishi 5: Nit-Chû zenmen sensô*, pp. 62–63.
23. Bôeichô bôei kenshû sho senshi shitsu, ed., *Senshi sôsho: Shina jihen rikusgun sakusen 2*, pp. 465–66.
24. Kamisago, *Kenpei sanjûichi nen*, p.175.
25. Nankin senshi henshû iiankai, ed., "Nakajima Kesago nikki," p. 326.
26. Sasaki, "Sasaki Tôichi shôshô shiki," pp. 377–78.
27. These were the Seventh, Thirty-third, and Thirty-eighth Regiments; and the Forty-first Regiment Twelfth Company, the Sixty-sixth Regiment First Battalion, and the Sixty-Eighth Regiment First and Third Battalions.
28. See Ono, Fujiwara, and Honda, eds., *Nankin daigyakusatsu o kiroku shita kôgun heishi tachi*.
29. Bôeichô bôei kenshû sho senshi shitsu, ed., *Senshi sôsho: Shina jihen rikugun sakusen 1*, p. 437.
30. Bôeichô bôei kenshû sho senshi shitsu, ed., *Senshi sôsho: Shina jihen rikusgun sakusen 2*, pp. 465–66.
31. N.p., *Tai-Shinagun sentôhô no kenkyû*, p. 74.
32. Unemoto, "Shôgen ni yoru *Nankin senshi* (5)," p. 7.
33. Nankin senshi henshû iinkai, ed., *Nankin senshi shiryô shû*, p. 545 and p. 648.
34. Ibid., pp. 673–74.
35. Kaigunshô kaigun gunji fukyûbu ed., "Shina jihen ni okeru teikoku kaigun no kôdô (Hottan yori Nankin kôryaku made)" document in National Defense Archives.
36. Nankin senshi henshû iinkai, ed., *Nankin senshi shiryô shû*, p. 630 and p. 551.
37. Ibid., p. 476.
38. Ibid., p. 502.
39. Iguchi et al., eds., *Nankin jiken Kyoto shidan kankei shiryô shû*, p. 7.
40. "Nankin jônai sôtô no maki," in ibid., pp. 322–23.
41. Document in former East German National Archives.
42. Fujioka, "'Nankin daigyakusatsu sanjûman' no uso," p. 565.
43. Yoshida, *Tennô no guntai to Nankin jiken*, p. 157.
44. Nankin senshi henshû iinkai, ed., *Nankin senshi shiryô shû*, pp. 22–24.
45. Ibid., p. 51.
46. Okamura, *Okamura Yasuji taishô shiryô jô*, p. 291.
47. Hora, ed., *Nit-Chû sensô shi shiryô 8: Nankin jiken I*, pp. 336–37.
48. Document in former East German National Archives.
49. Wickert, ed., *Good Man of Nanking*, p. 77.
50. Ibid., p. 92.
51. Awaya et al., eds., *Tokyo saiban shiryô: Tanaka Ryûkichi jinmon chôsho*, p. 257.
52. Katogawa, "Shôgen ni yoru Nankin senshi saishûkai: 'Sono sôkatsuteki kôsatsu'", p. 18.

Section One

WAR CRIMES AND DOUBTS

3

MASSACRES OUTSIDE NANKING CITY*

Kasahara Tokushi

Definitions and Dimensions

The Nanking Atrocity is a general term denoting barbarous acts that the imperial army and navy perpetrated in violation of humanitarian law and the international laws of war when those forces attacked and occupied Nanking, capital of the Republic of China, early in the Sino-Japanese War of 1937–45. I would delimit the Nanking Atrocity geographically and temporally as follows. Area-wise, it took place throughout the broad region known as the Nanking Special Administrative District (NSAD, see map 2). At that time, the NSAD comprised not only the walled city of Nanking itself, but also six adjacent counties *(hsien):* Liuho, Chiangp'u, Kaochun, Chiangning, Lishui, and Kuyung, although Kuyung is now part of Chen-chiang city. The NSAD corresponded with what the imperial army termed its Nanking theater of operations as well as with the zone of Japanese occupation after the capital city fell on 13 December 1937. Time-wise, the Atrocity began around 4 December 1937, after the Central China Area Army (CCAA) entered this theater of operations upon receiving formal orders from Imperial Headquarters (IH) dated 1 December 1937. Japanese field operations ceased on 14 February 1938, when IH rescinded its designation of the CCAA as a formal battle formation *(sentô joretsu),* but massacres and other hideous acts went on after mid-February. Therefore, it is more appropriate to date the end of the Atrocity on 28 March 1938 when the collaborationist "Reformed Government" under Liang Hung-chih came into being through CCAA machinations. Public order then returned to Nanking, and Japanese acts of rapine ceased. Those acts of rapine, which make up the Atrocity, fell under two broad headings: violations of life and limb, and violations of property rights.

Violations of Life and Limb

Ignoring international laws of war, the Japanese army killed Chinese soldiers and defeated stragglers who were wounded, in the act of surrendering, or even in custody. As part of their campaign to surround and exterminate the foe, Japanese troops arbitrarily killed adult males or civilians deemed to be enemy soldiers. Thus they stabbed or shot to death vast numbers of urban dwellers in the walled city of Nanking as well as rural residents in its adjacent counties on the pretext of "hunting down" or "mopping up" "defeated stragglers" on search and destroy missions. Instances of rape and gang rape were also prominent; and, although an exact count cannot be made, the International Committee (IC) for the Nanking Safety Zone (NSZ) estimated that these rapes ran into the tens of thousands. Acts of rape did not just injure women physically, these also produced trauma and cruel after-effects that might last for a lifetime. Some rape victims ended their own lives, some went insane, some became invalids owing to the venereal diseases that they contracted; and some, acting from a sense of shame, mutilated their bodies in attempts to abort unwanted pregnancies.

Violations of Property Rights

The imperial Japanese army instigated plunder and arson totally unrelated to the needs of combat. The IC conducted a survey showing that 74 percent of all Nanking city buildings were looted. Many areas in its central business district repeatedly suffered random acts of pillage by packs of soldiers as well as organized plunder that involved the use of army trucks—only to be torched afterward. Arson continued through early February 1938, and 24 percent of all Nanking city buildings were leveled by such fires. Japanese troops looted furniture, clothing, and cash from burned-out homes. They burned 40 percent of the farm houses in villages over wide areas of the NSAD. They pilfered wheat as fodder for army horses and stole produce from about half of the fields in Kuyung and Chiangning counties. The imperial army justified this large-scale plunder of food, crops, tools, stored grain, and barnyard animals through the battlefield imperative of "securing provisions" or "foraging" because it had neglected to provide adequate supply columns to feed its troops.

Estimates of Chinese Victimization

At this late date, seventy years after the event, it is virtually impossible to achieve an accurate Chinese victim count for the Atrocity, but we can estimate the loss of life to a certain extent based on sources discovered and research completed up to now. Although the distinction is admittedly blurry, Chinese victims fall into two categories: military personnel and civilians. On the military side of the ledger, my own preliminary research to this point in time shows that Gen. T'ang Sheng-chih, commander of Chinese defense forces in the Nanking theater of operations, stood at the head of 150,000 troops. Of that total, roughly 20,000 died in combat with Japanese forces, and thus must be left out of the victim count. Of the remaining 130,000 Chinese soldiers, about 50,000 survived. Roughly 40,000 of them retreated elsewhere to regroup, and about another 10,000 fled or went missing during their retreat. The remaining 80,000 Chinese soldiers in this theater of operations were massacred while trying to surrender, while in captivity, or on Japanese mop-up operations.

By contrast, the faulty nature of extant sources does not permit us to determine how many Chinese civilians died in the Atrocity. It is certain, however, that far more of them died in rural county towns and villages than inside the walled city of Nanking itself. The German national John Rabe, chair of the IC, estimated civilian Chinese deaths within the walled city at about 50,000 to 60,000. Based on surveys made in early 1938 by Dr. Lewis S. C. Smythe, an American sociology professor at Ginling College (now Nanking University), I calculate civilian deaths in the adjacent counties at over 30,000. Thus at this stage of my research, I contend that the total number of Chinese military and civilian victims in the Atrocity runs far above 100,000; indeed, the final figure approaches 200,000 and may actually be higher.[1] However, I will be able to refine these estimates in future research, after more Japanese primary sources are uncovered and made public and more Chinese damage surveys are conducted in surrounding county towns and villages.

In any case, two facts about the Nanking Atrocity are crystal-clear. First, it took place in the entire NSAD, first in the rural sections prior to the fall of Nanking city on 13 December. Second, Japanese troops massacred far more Chinese soldiers and civilians outside the walled city than in it. It is necessary to emphasize these points repeatedly, even at the risk of taxing the reader, because the more extreme conservative revisionists in Japan seek to deny or minimize the Atrocity by delimiting the event as narrowly as possible, both temporally and geographically. Through this clever sleight of hand, they reduce their victim counts to include only those Chinese killed inside the walled city immediately before and after 13 December when it fell to Japanese forces. I seek to place the Atrocity in its proper historical context by showing that it mainly took place outside the walled city beginning on or about 4 December 1937, and ending on 28 March 1938—roughly a four-month period. Thus, my chapter will serve to refute the distortions and false claims made by unscrupulous elements in the Japanese academic and journalistic camps. In thus defining the Atrocity, however, I differ from the late Prof. Fujiwara Akira in chapter 2, who dates it more narrowly from 1 December 1937 to 5 January 1938.

County Towns and Villages

As noted above, the NSAD comprised the walled city of Nanking plus Liuho, Chiangp'u, Lishui, Kaochun, Chiangning, and Kuyung counties. This broad area covers about 8,400 square kilometers or 3,240 square miles, which roughly equals the metropolitan Tokyo area combined with neighboring Saitama and Kanagawa prefectures. On a North American scale, this area would equal about 1.5 times the state of Delaware or the Canadian province of Prince Edward Island. The population of the six NSAD counties in 1997 (including Kuyung, though it is now under a different jurisdiction) was 3.17 million, a figure that outstripped the 2.62 million residents of Nanking city itself in that year, which covered an area of roughly forty square kilometers. These rural counties have historically had a high population density because they lie in the fertile Yangtze River rice-growing area.

The ratio of Nanking county-to-city residents in 1997 was quite similar to that in 1937 prior to the Japanese assault. Lewis Smythe's 1938 surveys omitted half of Liuho and all of Kaochun counties owing to obstruction by Chinese authorities. However, Smythe's surveys show that the remaining four and a half counties in early 1937 contained 1.20 to 1.35 million people compared with 1 million in the walled city.[2] Thus we would get a total rural population of well above 1.5 million in 1937 if we to include the one and a half counties that Smythe deleted from his survey; and, the entire NSAD population, including the walled city, would stand at over 2.5 million in early 1937, although huge numbers of people did flee in the summer and autumn of that year owing to Japanese air raids and in anticipation of an imminent Japanese assault.

The Nanking Atrocity first unfolded in these 6 outlying counties, not in the city itself. The Chinese army's outer line of defense ran through these counties, and its inner line of fortifications ran through the city. Thus the entire NSAD was a theater of operations, or war zone, where the Atrocity took place. When the imperial army's onslaught toward Nanking began at the beginning of December, over one million Chinese residents and refugees were estimated to remain in the 6 counties—with another 400,000 to 500,000 in the walled city and its immediate environs outside. (No more than 250,000 took refuge in the Nanking Safety Zone (NSZ) which covered roughly 3.8 square kilometers). Japan's 200,000-strong CCAA attacked from all directions in its campaign to exterminate the enemy. As a result, Chinese trapped inside the city found themselves surrounded and suffered huge losses.[3] Here, I wish to introduce a few specific examples of the barbarous acts that Japanese troops perpetrated in the six NSAD counties; for, to repeat, this is where the Atrocity began. It is important to note that these examples do not derive solely from Chinese oral and written sources, which Japanese deniers and conservative revisionists dismiss out of hand as fabricated or exaggerated. Instead, these examples are based on imperial Japanese army records that match corresponding Chinese accounts found in county gazetteers from the NSAD.

Lishui County

On 19 November the imperial navy received word that the Chinese army's general headquarters was in the country capital of Lishui, and assembled an air squadron of thirty-six bombers and fighters to attack that city at about noon. Lishui residents cooking lunch saw their city turn into hell on earth because of the bombings; fires broke out everywhere and great numbers of homes were destroyed. The panic-stricken masses fled, only to suffer more bombings and strafing. In the end, this hour-long air raid killed over 1,200 civilian residents and destroyed several thousand houses.[4]

Kuyung County

At 8:40 a.m. on 4 December, advance units of the Sixteenth division assaulting Tanyang entered the Nanking theater of operations when they attacked the village of Nit'ang, fifteen kilometers east of Kuyung city, the capital of Kuyung county, where an artillery school was located.[5] Thus it had immense strategic importance on the Chinese outer defense perimeter and was fortified by a maginot line of pillboxes to its east. Kuomintang (KMT) armies had destroyed a bridge leading westward from Nit'ang to Kuyung, so the Sixteenth division's Twentieth Regiment was forced to encamp at Nit'ang, where its members committed massacres. Adult males had already fled when Japanese troops arrived, but women, children, and the elderly remained. On hearing gunfire, women and children fled into the darkness or hid in nearby areas. Residents who could not escape Nit'ang, together with persons fleeing from other areas—about forty in all—fell captive to the Japanese troops. They forced these people into in the home of a villager named Ni An-jen, set it on fire, thus killing all forty. At 8:00 or 9:00 a.m. the next day, Japanese troops captured eighty refugees from another village including KMT army POWs. The Japanese led these eighty to a spot just off the Tanyang-Kuyung highway and machine-gunned them to death. Eight Japanese soldiers then gang raped a young woman on a reservoir bank, and she later died after having lost her mind. Before leaving the village of Nit'ang, Japanese troops set it on fire, so that all of its eighty structures were destroyed except for public buildings—a shrine, an oil factory, and a flour mill. Over 120 persons in total died in these massacres, but most were refugees who had fled to Nit'ang from other villages. Nit'ang natives were only seven in number, of whom two were female.[6]

At about 8:00 or 9:00 a.m. on 5 December, a Japanese army unit arrived at the village of Pen-hu north of Kuyung to mop up and secure provisions, but the villagers who viewed them from afar mistook them for KMT troops. Bearing spears and swords, about thirty men belonging to the Pen-hu village defense corps assembled in formation to welcome the arrivals, only to be captured. Together with ten other Chinese men captured nearby, these thirty were placed in the village's three-story, thatched-roof brewery that the Japanese soldiers then set on fire. They shot anyone who tried to escape, including a few men who managed to run out of the brewery and dive into a small nearby pond to squelch their burning clothes. Thus all forty of the captured men died except for Wan Jen-sheng, then a sixteen-year-old lad, who was able to dash from the burning structure and hide inside a hollowed-out wall.[7] Communications in out-lying areas were extremely poor, so people in many farming villages such as Pen-hu, far from highways or major roads, were caught unawares by Japanese attacks and suffered this sort of tragedy.

Kaochun County

After IH issued its 1 December general assault orders, the imperial navy air corps began to coordinate attacks on 4 December. It now deployed its main force in the Wuhu and Nanking areas. Already on 3 December, the navy air corps had built a base at Chang-chou, 140 kilometers east of Nanking, from which to step up its attacks in tandem with army units. On 4 December, the navy air corps set aloft a fleet of nineteen fighters, bombers, and reconnaissance aircraft. Kaochun county, at the southernmost part of the NSAD, was a key spot connected with Wuhu by water and with Nanking city by land. The navy bombed Kaochun city, the county seat, plus other towns in order to destroy bridges and canals and thereby block the KMT army's retreat toward Wuhu. Wuhu city—and especially its port of Tunghsiang linked with Shanghai by canal—suffered heavy damage from the air as well. Navy bombers concentrated their attacks on the main highway running through Tunghsiang. Corpses were strewn all over roads owing to bomb blasts, and fires gutted major streets. On this one day alone, eighty bombs fell, well over 100 Tunghsiang residents died, and over 200 homes turned into rubble.[8]

The Fifth Division's Kunisaki Detachment left Kwangte on 2 December and reached Langch'i on the third. After preparing for amphibious operations, this unit departed from Langch'i on the sixth. It then advanced by canal through Shuiyangchen and Kaochun, and captured Taip'ing on the ninth. On the 6th, however, the Kunisaki Detachment massacred thirty-six villagers en route from Shuiyangchen to Shuipich'iao village located on the county line; and on the seventh, this unit opened fire on townspeople when it captured Kaochun city. In Kaochun, it killed or wounded over 30 persons.[9]

Chiangp'u County

Chiangp'u and Liuho counties lie on the northern side of the Yangtze river, across from the Nanking walled city. The CCAA sought to encircle and annihilate the enemy on this Nanking campaign. Thus from the very start it sent units to cut off Chinese troops retreating through these two counties. Shanghai Expeditionary Army (SEA) Chief of Staff Iinuma Mamoru's diary entry for 11 December reads: "On hearing that the Kunisaki Detachment was fording the Yangtze, His Excellency [SEF commander] Prince Asaka [Yasuhiko] also was a bit anxious. He asked, 'Can't we get the Thirteenth Division across quickly to sever the Tientsin-P'ukou rail line?'" The Kunisaki Detachment crossed near Tz'u-hu-chen north of T'aip'ing, advanced toward Nanking parallel to the Yangtze, and attacked Chiangp'u city at 1:00 p.m. on the twelfth.

On the eleventh, over 2,000 men in the Kunisaki Detachment, who had captured already Wuchiangchen, then burst into the Nanking theater. They made their way to P'uk'ou in combat with the KMT army, killing civilians and burning houses en route. In this way, thirty farmers and refugees died before this unit took Chiangp'u, and forty-four farmers and fishermen died when it advanced from there to P'uk'ou. Also, the Hiroshima Fifth division was well-known for its marine combat capabilities, and the Kunisaki Detachment's 1,000-man amphibious unit used large and small assault craft to attack the small port of Hsichiangkou. There, men from this unit killed thirty farmers, merchants, and children; they also destroyed over 100 commercial vessels through shell fire. While boarding and searching privately owned Chinese boats, the troops discovered and raped over ten Chinese women.[10]

Wave Attacks

During the assault on Nanking, the 200,000-man imperial army sought to encircle and annihilate the enemy. Japanese divisions, brigades, regiments, and battalions advanced in waves toward the city from all sides. At the forefront were hell-bent-for-leather units vying for the honor of being first to set foot in the enemy capital. Behind them came second and third waves of support units, and finally, replenishment troops. These support and replenishment units were often of a stopgap nature, with ambiguous chains of command. Moreover, they were mostly taken from nonregular "special divisions," discussed by the late Fujiwara Akira in chapter 2. Hence they suffered from extremely loose discipline.

In early December, more than 1.5 million Chinese residents were still in the six NSAD counties—an area transformed into a war zone. Very few had the wherewithal to escape from the NSAD by car or train after the Japanese attackers arrived. In farm villages, younger people usually left the elderly behind to protect their homes. From there, the young fled from main roads into nearby hills, where they waited for the Japanese to leave. As a result, old folks left behind, farmers unable to escape, and people captured in the hills, all fell victim to the Japanese annihilation campaign. As a Sixteenth Division "Report on Conditions" dated 24 December states, "We make it a rule for men and horses to live off the land on this operation.... Fortunately, this is a lushly rich area, so we are generally well supplied."[11] In this way, plundering in both urban and rural areas proceeded apace, as an approximate total of 200,000 Japanese invaders "lived off the land." Hence, losses in barnyard animals, crops, and stored grain were vast. Victims employed the sardonic pun, *huang-chün*, to brand the "imperial army" an "army of locusts"—like that in the film *The Good Earth*. This human *huang-chün* devoured everything in its path, leaving nothing but desolation wherever it went.

Japanese troops, marching from all directions toward Nanking city, exhibited extremely lax military discipline. They torched village after village out of a desire to destroy, in order to vent pent-up frustrations, or simply from a perverted sense of pleasure. Countless Chinese villagers, their homes reduced to rubble and ashes, perforce became vagabonds in areas where their villages used to exist. As such, they were prime targets for Japanese search and destroy units eager to flush out and kill "plainclothes troops" deemed guerrillas. These helpless villagers had nowhere to escape and were, so to speak, fish caught in a net cast by the Japanese army. Japanese troops requisitioned Chinese males as porters and coolies, or arbitrarily called them "defeated stragglers" to be captured and killed en masse. Chinese women, on the other hand, suffered rape or gang rape, often coupled with murder in order to conceal the evidence. These unspeakable crimes were especially rampant in isolated rural villages. Chinese farmhouses—removed as these are from one another and rimmed by stone or earthen walls—provided just the privacy needed for this heinous crime. When Japanese soldiers found women hiding in hills or fields, the men had less inhibitions than if they were in towns or cities, subject to possible onlookers. For this reason too Japanese troops tended to murder rural women whom they raped all the more readily. Thus, Chinese village women suffered violation twice, losing their honor the first time and their lives, the second.

"Defeated Stragglers"

The NSAD contained the Chinese outer defense perimeter of fortifications. In that sense, it was enemy territory from which defeated remnants might launch counterattacks at any moment. In the eyes of Japanese troops, then, this was a war zone—the Nanking theater of battle—and they felt they had every right to destroy towns and villages on the way to the enemy capital if need be. They harbored few if any inhibitions against killing local residents whom they saw as indistinguishable and, indeed, inseparable from enemy forces. From the very start, the CCAA's Nanking campaign was intended to entrap and annihilate the Chinese army, and Japanese troops lacked the ability to tell civilians apart from military personnel. Chinese soldiers in the act of surrendering, defeated stragglers, and POWs all were fair game—as was any male whom the Japanese suspected as belonging to those categories. This was quite simply a kill-all. During search-and-destroy mop-up operations, defeated Chinese soldiers might flee and mix in with civilians; then, both ended up getting slaughtered.

The walled city of Nanking fell on 13 December, and the occupying CCAA conducted an all-out search and destroy mission in nearby county towns and villages. One Cantonese army defending Nanking had already broken loose from the Japanese encirclement and formed guerrilla units that harassed Japanese forces while retreating to the south. This experience set the CCAA on edge, and motivated it to wipe out all defeated enemy remnants in outlying towns and villages. Liuho, Chiangp'u, Kaochun, Lishui, and Kuyung county gazetteers describe massacres, rapes, and arson committed by Japanese troops on this pretext—atrocities no different from those perpetrated in the assault on Nanking city itself. Like countless stars in the night sky, villages lay spread out all over the NSAD, and Japanese atrocities occurred in all of them. Taken one by one, these atrocities may have been small in scope; taken together, however, they added up to an enormous number.

On 22 December CCAA commander Matsui Iwane left Nanking for Shanghai, and most Japanese units occupying the city were deployed on new missions elsewhere. However, the CCAA retained its Sixteenth division— whose lack of discipline was egregious—to maintain its military occupation of Nanking city and adjacent counties. As a result, the total number of atrocities fell; but instances of massacre, rape, pillage, arson, and other barbarities went on nonetheless. After the main CCAA units departed, Maj. Gen. Sasaki Tôichi, commander of the Sixteenth division's Thirtieth Brigade, was named security commander for the NSAD's western section, including the walled city. Sasaki launched a search-and-destroy mission to ferret out "defeated stragglers" from among the general populace. His diary reads: "5 January [1938]. Ended mop-up. As of today we flushed out about 2,000 defeated stragglers in the city.... We go on capturing those who persist in their insurgency, and we got rid of several thousand at Hsiakwan."[12]

This passage conclusively shows that defeated Chinese stragglers were hauled away to Hsiakwan, just outside the walled city on the banks of the Yangtze, where they were executed by the thousands (see Map 5). But much the same thing—plus rape, pillage, and arson—took place in villages and county capitals all over the NSAD on the pretext of "mopping up defeated stragglers." Here are a few examples as recorded in county gazetteers:

Chiangp'u County. 27 December. Forty Japanese soldiers searched villages, killed seventeen farmers and refugees, and raped six women.[13]

Chiangning County. Last third of December. Ten women at Shang-fang were raped and killed with iron rods thrust up their vaginas. Over 100 civilians who had fled the country capital were killed on mop-up missions at Lu-lang village on 8 September 1938; at that time eight women were raped and had their abdomens sliced open. The locality of Ch'a-lu is a convenient spot close to Nanking city, so Japanese troops often came "girl hunting." Over 250 women were raped and most of them killed. At Shih-ma village alone, over twenty were violated and killed. Japanese troops attacked Ts'ao village three times and killed fifty people.[14]

Lishui County. December. After the Japanese army occupied Che-t'ang-chen for use as a base of operations, farmers nearby were killed and women were raped. (During the [1937–45] Sino-Japanese War, twenty-nine villagers were killed and twenty-eight women were raped.)[15]

Kaochun County. January 1938. Raiding Japanese troops burned down two villages. Soldiers on mop-up and girl-hunting expeditions raped women in the county seat and in various villages, killing most of them. (During the [1937–45] Sino-Japanese War, several hundred women throughout this county were raped.)[16]

Smythe's Surveys: Flaws

Lewis S. C. Smythe, an American professor of sociology at Ginling College (now Nanking University) and a key member of the IC, was the author of the urban and rural sampling surveys in *War Damage in the Nanking Area: December, 1937 to March, 1938,* published in 1938.[17] Together with Chinese research assistants, he did the urban survey from 9 March to 2 April, and did supplementary work from 19 to 23 April. They conducted the rural survey from 8 March to 23 March, and made a separate "building investigation" from 15 March to 15 June. In his urban survey, Smythe arrived at a casualty figure of 7,450 for persons living inside the walled city. This number broke down to "3,250 killed by military action" plus another "4,200 taken away" and presumed dead. This figure of 7,450 victims reflects one huge limitation in his method, which was to survey surviving families who remained in the NSAD during the assault and after the city fell, or who returned to their homes shortly after. Symthe and his aides also made a careful study of Chinese burial records for Nanking city and for the immediate vicinity outside its walls, and he arrived at a total figure of about 12,000 killed.

On the other hand, Smythe's survey of four and a half counties in the NSAD (excluding county capitals) produced a figure of 26,870 rural persons killed. This comes to an average of 1 person per 7 farm families. Of that number, males constituted the great majority at 22,490. Eighty-five percent of them were young males up to the age of forty-five. This shows how harsh Japanese mop-up campaigns were in rural areas. The death of these young men had grave consequences for farm families who depended on male labor for survival. Among the 26,870 rural persons killed, Smythe found that women accounted for 4,380. Of that figure, 85 percent were aged forty-five or older, and of that 85 percent, half were elderly women over sixty years of age. Based on the age-old wisdom of life in rural Chinese villages, older married women believed they had nothing to fear from invading soldiers, so they remained at home after younger family members had fled, only to suffer many cases of rape and murder at Japanese hands.

As noted, Smythe and his associates limited their surveys to families who had remained in the NSAD all along, or who had returned to it by March and April of 1938. At that time, he made a sampling of one inhabited house in every fifty houses within the city, and one inhabited house in every ten houses in rural areas. Then he multiplied his findings by fifty and ten respectively, to arrive at his final estimates for urban and rural areas. Smythe's findings clearly were skewed on the low side because his method of sampling skipped over uninhabited houses and perforce omitted precisely those families who had been most victimized—those absent from the scene. These were families in which all of its members had died, and those who broke up and dispersed in the chaos of war. Perhaps most importantly, as Symthe himself expressly noted, "[t]here is reason to expect underreporting of deaths and violence at the hands of the Japanese soldiers, because of the fear of retaliation from the army of occupation." Despite all of these significant shortcomings, Symthe's urban and rural surveys are of immense value to historians of the Nanking Atrocity. These were, after all, the only academic, systematically conducted surveys made at the time of the event. Moreover, they support my contention that Chinese losses were far heavier in rural sections of the NSAD than in the walled city itself.

Furthermore, the results of Smythe's urban and rural surveys find corroboration in burial figures left by the Nanking branch of the Red Swastika Society (RSS), a Chinese charitable organization charged with burying corpses. Its figures stand at 1,793 for corpses buried in Nanking city, and at 41,330 for those buried in its immediate environs outside the walls. This gives a total of 43,123 deaths. Another Chinese charitable society, the Chungshant'ang (CST), separately lists burial figures of 7,549 for Nanking city and 104,718 for rural villages.[18] In Japan, conservative revisionists claim that the CST count for rural villages is unreliable because it came up this figure in the single month of April; so this must be an exaggeration. Of course we cannot take this one-month CST figure at face value. But we must remember that rural burials took place on barren land and in deserted fields; hence we can assume a much higher rate of corpse disposal there than in cities. Furthermore, the corpses of Chinese soldiers who died in combat—and thus, it might be claimed, are technically not victims of the Atrocity—are also included in these burial figures. But my key point is that, even discounting those factors, victim counts in rural sections of the NSAD were far higher than those within the walled city of Nanking itself.

Conclusion

The Chinese victim count is only one dimension of the Atrocity. As I have repeatedly stressed, rape, arson, pillage, torture, beatings, property loss, and other immoral, illegal forms of Japanese violence must also be factored in if we are to achieve a comprehensive understanding of what that event meant. Nevertheless, the victim count is one important element in gauging the overall scale of the Atrocity. At this point in my research, I would tentatively submit that the total number of Chinese victims; that is, those illegally and unjustifiably massacred, would break down as follows. In the entire NSAD, both in and outside Nanking city, some 80,000 military deaths took place in which Chinese troops were massacred while trying to surrender, while in captivity, or on Japanese mop-up operations. Inside the walled city, 50,000 to 60,000 civilian deaths took place. In rural sections of the NSAD, another 30,000 civilian deaths took place. This yields a total of well over 100,000 and approaching 200,000 Chinese soldiers and civilians. Moreover, with additional research, we may have to revise this figure upward still further.

There are at least two reasons why Chinese victimization was so much greater in outlying regions of the NSAD than in the walled city itself. First, at the time of the Japanese attack in early December, these outlying rural areas were heavily populated to begin with. Well over 1 million residents and refugees are estimated to have remained in rural sections of the Nanking theater after the Japanese onslaught had begun. This is far more than many conservative revisionists in Japan wish to admit, for they count only Nanking city residents in their estimates; and, they do so on a minimal basis by limiting their estimate to the 200,000 to 250,000 refugees who took refuge in the NSZ, on the assumption that few or no people remained in the city outside of it. Second, Western residents who comprised the IC vigorously protested to Japanese consular and military authorities against misconduct by imperial army troops within the walled city; and, also, American, German, and British diplomatic staffs began returning to Nanking from the middle of January 1938. This obtrusive Western presence helped curb Japanese atrocities within the walled city somewhat. By stark contrast, however, the law of the jungle governed surrounding rural areas. There, vicious Japanese acts of murder, rape, and pillage continued outside of foreign eyeshot well beyond March 1938.

If, as I have argued, we acknowledge the general fact that far more Chinese military and civilian personnel died in the rural areas of Nanking than in the walled city during the Atrocity, we still need greater detail, clarity, and precision to round out the picture. That detail, clarity, and precision can only be provided after Chinese local researchers conduct more surveys of rural damages, and after Japanese researchers unearth more imperial army records in the form of official battle reports plus personal battlefield diaries left by troops who participated in the Atrocity. In particular, the publication of more such primary sources on the Japanese side will effectively refute ongoing claims by conservative revisionists who assert that the Nanking Atrocity never took place, or that it was narrowly limited in scope, and hence was no different from similar events in all wars everywhere.

Notes

* Translated from Japanese by the editor.
1. Kasahara, *Nankin jiken*, especially pp. 214–28.
2. Smythe, ed., "Nankin chiku ni okeru sensô higai," pp. 211–77.
3. Kasahara, *Nankin jiken*, pp. 220–28.
4. Bôeichô bôei kenshûsho senshi shitsu, ed., *Senshi sôsho: Chûgoku hômen kaigun sakusen 1*, p. 509; Lishui hsien ti-fang-chih pien-kung-shih, ed., *Lishui hsien-chih*, pp. 650–51.
5. "Iinuma Mamoru nikki," in Nankin senshi henshû iinkai, ed., *Nankin senshi shiryô shû*, p. 206.
6. Kuyung hsien ti-fang-chih pien-tsuan-hui, ed., *Kuyung hsien-shih*, pp. 646–47.
7. Kuyung shih-shih pien-kung-shih, ed., "Jih-chün chun-Kuyung ch'i-chien pao-hang-lu," pp. 4–5.
8. *Senshi sôsho: Chûgoku hômen kaigun sakusen 1*, pp. 510–11; Kaochun hsien ti-fang-chih pien-tsuan-hui, ed., *Kaochun hsien-shih*, p. 581.
9. Bôeichô bôei kenshûsho senshi shitsu, ed., *Senshi sôsho: Shina jihen rikugun sakusen 1*, pp. 150–56; *Kaochun hsien-shih*, p. 581.
10. "Iinuma Mamoru nikki," p. 212; Chiangp'u hsien ti-fang-chih pien-tsuan-hui, ed., *Chiangp'u hsien-chih*, pp. 550–55; Chungkung Chiangp'u hsien tang-shih tzu-liao shou-tsi pien-kung-shih, ed., *Chiangp'u k'ang-Jih feng-huo*, pp. 16–17.
11. Nankin senshi henshû iinkai, ed., *Nankin senshi shiryô shû*, p. 577.
12. Sasaki, "Sasaki Tôichi shôshô shiki," pp. 381–82.
13. *Chiangp'u hsien-chih*, p. 550.
14. Chiangning hsien ti-fang-chih pien-tsuan-hui, ed., *Chiangning hsien-chih*, pp. 15–16 and 659–60.
15. Chiangsu wen-shih tzu-liao pien-chi-pu, ed., *Hsing-feng hsüeh-yü: Chin-hua Jih-chün Chiangsu pao-hang-lu*, p. 171.
16. *Kaochun hsien-chih*, pp. 582–83.
17. Smythe, "Nankin chiku ni okeru sensô higai," pp. 221–77
18. Ibid., pp. 270–76.

4

MASSACRES NEAR MUFUSHAN*

Ono Kenji

Introduction

This chapter focuses on the Thirteenth division's Yamada Detachment. It included the Sixty-fifth Regiment, also named the "Morozumi Unit" after its commander, Col. Morozumi Gyôsaku. For the sake of consistency, I will use the term Sixty-fifth Regiment. This regiment was part of Maj. Gen. Yamada Senji's One Hundred Third Brigade, subordinate to Lt. Gen. Ogisu Ryûhei's Thirteenth division, which in turn came under the aegis of the Shanghai Expeditionary Army (SEA), or Shanghai Expeditionary Force (SEF), commanded by Imperial Prince Asaka Yasuhiko. This Sixty-fifth Regiment was the main force in the Yamada Detachment, known for its role in the massive taking and massacre of Chinese prisoners in mid-December 1937 near Mufushan, north of Nanking. The massacres occurred at Yüleiying or Torpedo Encampment and at Tawantzu, both located on the banks of the Yangtze River in the T'sao-hsieh-hsia area, opposite T'sao-hsieh Island (a.k.a. Pakua Island) located in the middle of the river. (See maps 4 and 5). Note, though, that there is sharp disagreement among Japanese historians over the precise location of Yüleiying and Tawantzu in the T'sao-hsieh-hsia riverbank area along the Yangtze.[1]

The Sixty-fifth Regiment was formed at Aizu-Wakamatsu, Fukushima Prefecture. Almost all of the men in it were native to Fukushima, as is also true of myself, although I am of the postwar generation born in 1949. In 1988 I began conducting interviews with veterans from that regiment still living in Fukushima as well as with those who had moved to other localities such as Tokyo, Niigata, Miyazaki, and Ibaraki. From those elderly veterans, I collected about 200 oral testimonies, some recorded on tape or videotape, plus twenty-four war diaries and other primary sources dating from 1937 to 1938. Ôtsuki shoten published the written documents in 1996 under the title, *Nankin daigyakusatsu o kiroku shita kôgun heishi tachi* (Imperial Army Troops Who Recorded the Nanking Atrocity), and this is the source from which I draw most of the quotations cited in this chapter. Note, however, that most of the personal names that I employ when citing these documents—such as "Saitô Jirô," "Endô Takaaki," or "Kanno Yoshio"—are pseudonyms. (One exception is Amano Saburô, whose wartime correspondence is translated in chapter 8 by Bob Tadashi Wakabayashi.) This anonymity is needed to shield the authors and their families from threats, harassment, and possible violence from right-wing elements in Japan.

The Sixty-fifth Regiment was hastily assembled owing to the imperial army's acute need for increased manpower after the spread of fighting from northern to central China that followed the Marco Polo Bridge Incident of 7 July 1937. Like other "special units," discussed by the late Fujiwara Akira in chapter 2, this one comprised second- and third-pool reservists in their mid- to late-thirties and even early-forties—not current recruits in their early twenties who served in "regular" divisions, brigades, or regiments. The Sixty-fifth Regiment's mobilization as part of the Thirteenth division was complete by 18 September, and this 3,700-man regiment landed at a point near Shanghai on 1 October. It then took part in the bloody assault on Shanghai that claimed 1,720 casualties among men in the unit—620 killed in action and 1,100 incapacitated from wounds or illnesses. Only the repeated dispatch of replenishment troops allowed the regiment to attack the Chiangyin Batteries and march on toward Nanking.

On 6 December at Chen-chiang, the Sixty-fifth Regiment parted ways with the main force of the Eleventh division, which forded the Yangtze, marched along its northern bank to capture Yangchou on 14 December, and thereafter advanced toward Ch'uhsien. While that took place, the regiment joined four engineering and artillery units to form the Yamada Detachment. As the main component of this detachment, Morozumi's Sixty-fifth Regiment marched along the southern bank of the Yangtze with orders to cut off defeated Chinese stragglers who might be retreating toward T'sao-hsieh-hsia after fleeing from the elevated batteries on Wulungshan and Mufushan as well as from the city of Nanking.

By 14 December 1937, one day after Nanking fell, the Sixty-fifth Regiment reached a point south of Mufushan, which lies north of the walled city, between it and the southern bank of the Yangtze River. The following "Extra," put out by the *Tokyo Asahi shinbun* (now the *Asahi shinbun*) on 16 December, describes the situation that the regiment faced. This was the first report that Fukushima residents received about how their men at the front took massive numbers of Chinese prisoners:

Special Correspondent Yokota in Nanking
15 December
The Morozumi Unit [i.e., Sixty-fifth Regiment] advanced with vigor from Chen-chiang along the Yangtze River to capture elevated batteries on Wulungshan on the

thirteenth and those on Chaomushan [*recte:* Mufushan] on the fourteenth. There the men encountered a virtual avalanche of 14,777 retreating enemy troops belonging to the Chinese Army's Eighteenth and Eighty-eighth divisions as well as its Cadet Training Units. These enemy troops raised white flags and surrendered. What a splendid military achievement! The vastly outnumbered men in our Morozumi Unit captured intact well over 14,000 of the foe.

Nanking fell on 13 December, but Fukushima residents had been eagerly anticipating that historic event for several days. Partly in response to "guidance" from military authorities, they held lantern parades and other celebratory events all over the prefecture—including Aizu-Wakamatsu barracks—to mark the capture of the enemy capital. Just at that point, on the fifteenth, came news that the local Sixty-fifth Regiment had taken this huge number of the enemy as prisoners of war (POWs). As might be imagined, the Fukushima press played up this joyful event to the fullest. For the next two days, however, there was no news about what became of those prisoners. Then, on 17 December, the Fukushima edition of the *Tokyo Asahi shinbun* released an exclusive "Extra" bearing the headline, "The Morozumi Unit Captures 15,000. What a Tremendous Feat! What a Grand Battlefield Achievement!" The article in part read: "It was so wonderful to hear: 'They raised white flags and came forth to surrender.' [Our boys] really should have slaughtered them all. That's how we all feel—old and young, male and female, alike. An overwhelming sense of glee accompanies our celebrations to mark the capture of Nanking. Yet again we find ourselves delirious with glee."

Sadly, I am forced to conclude, the fate that befell these Chinese POWs was exactly what this *Tokyo Asahi shinbun* reporter hoped for, along with his gleeful Fukushima readers, no doubt. That is to say, having captured this huge number of prisoners, the Sixty-fifth Regiment went on to "slaughter them all." To the best of my knowledge, these massacres near Mufushan constitute the largest incident of mass murder in the entire Nanking Atrocity. The prisoners were detained in 22 Chinese army barracks located to the south of Mufushan where they awaited what turned out to be their execution. Like other imperial army units in China, the Sixty-fifth Regiment relied on "local procurements" for almost all of its needs on the march. In other words, it supplied itself by plundering from Chinese residents. Hence it had few if any rations to spare for feeding these prisoners. According to oral testimonies by veterans, each Chinese POW was supposed to receive one bowl of rice gruel, but in truth there was not enough to go around, so some were reduced to drinking urine and eating the weeds they found on barrack grounds. In any case, the Yamada Detachment would have its hands full coping with these POWs until most of the unit was ordered to leave Nanking for another mission on 20 December.

Previous Accounts

The sheer scale of the slaughter in the T'sao-hsieh-hsia riverbank area near Mufushan makes this particular incident stand out in the Nanking Atrocity as a whole. Thus it comes as no surprise that there are previous accounts, both in Chinese and Japanese. Chinese accounts date from the Tokyo War Crimes Trials and hold that 57,418 POWs were massacred. A controversy of sorts— though hardly scholarly—has been and continues to be waged about this incident in Japan.[2] The earliest Japanese account comes from a former wartime correspondent named Hata Kensuke, no relation to the present-day historian Hata Ikuhiko. Hata Kensuke accompanied the Sixty-fifth Regiment later on in the China war, and published "Horyo no chi ni mamireta Byakko butai" (The White Tiger Unit stained with POW blood) in 1957. The nickname "White Tiger" has evoked pride ever since the 1867–68 Restoration wars in Aizu-Wakamatsu, where a band of local young samurai by that name fought heroically against far superior Satsuma and Chôshû forces; hence the local regiment went by that unofficial appellation. Hata Kensuke was in a position to talk directly with men who earlier had participated in the Mufushan incident, and he also consulted four of their personal battlefield diaries before he wrote this piece. His article contains numerous errors of fact, but its overall conclusion is quite right: "What awaited this endless stream of prisoners was, most assuredly, death."[3] According to a second interpretation—expressly produced to refute Hata's—the Sixty-fifth Regiment admittedly fired on and killed a small number of Chinese prisoners near Mufushan. This account, however, goes on to exonerate the Fukushima regiment by claiming that it took these actions only in legitimate, unavoidable self-defense, after the Chinese had rioted. More extreme conservative revisionists in Japan today, who insist that the Nanking Atrocity is just a "fabrication" or an "illusion," eagerly embrace, embellish, and expand on this thesis of "unavoidable killing in self-defense." Finally, members of the left-wing Society to Study the Nanking Incident (Nankin ken), including the late Hora Tomio and Fujiwara Akira, Watada Susumu, Kasahara Tokushi, Honda Katsuichi, Yoshida Yutaka, and myself insist that this regiment did in fact perpetrate massacres on a vast scale in the T'sao-hsieh-hsia riverbank area near Mufushan. For the most part, we uphold Hata Kensuke's original 1957 conclusion, but correct factual inaccuracies in his narrative, and we contend that the real "fabricated illusion" lies in the conservative revisionists' thesis of "unavoidable killing in self-defense." The controversy thus turns on the validity of that thesis. When and under what specific circumstances did it first appear?

In December 1961, the editors of a prefectural newspaper, the *Fukushima shinbun*, began a long serial entitled "Kyôdo butai senki" (Accounts of our local units in the war). Such narratives describing the wartime exploits of local regiments were undertaken in all parts of Japan around that time. In this case, the Fukushima editors began their project in collaboration with the Fukushima War Bereaved Society plus prefectural branches of the Japan Disabled Veterans' Society and the Japan Local Veterans' Society—types of organizations discussed by Kimura Takuji in chapter 15. The portion of "Kyôdo butai senki" dealing with the Sixty-fifth Regiment ran to less than twenty pages in the original, but this serial as a whole was later expanded into a 3-volume work put out by the same publisher under the title, *Kyôdo butai senki: Moesakaru tairiku,* in 1965. An 8-volume variant from this same publisher was *Fukushima: Sensô to ningen* (Fukushima: War and people), which appeared in 1982.[4]

This Fukushima-rooted interpretation holds that the Yamada Detachment, which included the Sixty-fifth Regiment, captured roughly 15,000 Chinese near Mufushan. It released about half of them—the specific number varies— because they were noncombatants, and placed the rest in POW camps. However, a fire broke out at night that allowed half of these remaining detainees to escape. Finally, while escorting those remaining POWs—about a quarter of the original number—across the Yangtze to be set free, guards in the detachment drew enemy fire from the opposite shore. Quick to exploit this chance, the Chinese prisoners staged a riot, so Japanese guards had no choice but to shoot and kill 1,000 (3,000 in some versions) in self-defense. This account also cited the well-known "Shanghai Expeditionary Army Orders" for the detachment to "kill them all." But the spin put on this argument was that, by trying to release Chinese POWs to start with, the regiment had dared to violate orders issued by SEA commander, Lt. Gen. and Imperial Prince, Asaka Yasuhiko. In sum, this interpretation was designed to overturn that by Hata Kensuke which, Fukushima locals claimed, had blasphemed local sons in the Sixty-fifth Regiment and Yamada Detachment. Advocates of this "unavoidable killing in self-defense" thesis aver that these men acted in a humanitarian fashion as far as possible given battlefield exigencies and in the face of orders from above to massacre helpless prisoners.

Conservative circles throughout Japan welcomed this "unavoidable killing in self-defense" thesis. For example, the National Institute for Defense Studies, attached to the Defense Agency in Tokyo, maintains a Military History Department that produced a massive multivolume official history of Japanese operations in World War II. Not unsurprisingly, the Defense Agency cites this thesis in its relevant volume on the war against China published in 1975.[5] The same is true for conservative nonfiction writers such as Suzuki Akira in 1973 and Kojima Noboru in 1984, as well as for the local Fukushima writer Abe Teruo in 1989—if to differing degrees. The Kaikôsha, an organization of former imperial army officers and conservative revisionists, also adopted this interpretation in its 1989 narrative *Nankin senshi* (History of the Nanking Campaign).[6] In 1989, the Kaikôsha came out with its first volume of primary sources to accompany this historical narrative.

As related in chapters 2 and 15 by Fujiwara Akira and Kimura Takuji, the Kaikôsha began its project on Nanking with the self-assurance that it could collect irrefutable evidence, in the form of testimonies from members, to prove that no Atrocity ever took place. As the testimonies came in, however, Kaikôsha compilers had to abandon this article of faith and grudgingly admit that some massacres—if small in scope—did take place at Mufushan and elsewhere in Nanking. Citing the documents they had collected, plus testimonies from local Fukushima veterans, Kaikôsha editors issued the disclaimer that "oral testimonies are very vague and thus do not form a sure basis for establishing how many Chinese POWs the Yamada Detachment handled." But nevertheless, the editors went on to list:

Mufushan: The Yamada Detachment started out with 6,000
The Number ["taken care of"]: About 3,000
Escaped: 3,000

Later on, in 1993, the Kaikôsha published a second volume of primary sources related to Nanking. In the 4 years between 1989, when it produced *Nankin senshi* with its first volume of sources, and 1993, when it came out with this second document volume, I published full or partial texts of battlefield diaries obtained from Fukushima rank-and-file plus noncommissioned officers (NCOs) who took part in massacres near Mufushan, along with critical analyses of those sources.[7] Perhaps in response to my findings, the Kaikôsha editors wrote an explanatory essay in their 1993 document volume. A section in the essay was titled, "On Dispatching Prisoners near Mufushan: A Comprehensive Observation." In it, the editors declared that "low ranking officers, NCOs, and foot soldiers tended to record rumors and suppositions; hence, although their writings do constitute primary sources, the historical veracity of those documents is virtually impossible to substantiate today [in 1993], almost sixty years after the fact."[8]

In other words, the Kaikôsha compilers of the conservative *Nankin senshi* adopt a very queer criterion in primary-source criticism; that is, the only reliable wartime diaries are those written by high-ranking officers who, if still alive, would qualify to be fellow Kaikôsha members. By contrast, diaries obtained from the rank-and-file, NCOs, or lower ranking officers—those men who did the actual the killing—are unreliable. Stranger yet is the chameleon-like change in the attitude of Nanking researcher, the late Itakura Yoshiaki. Up to at least 1992, he had never missed a chance to snipe at Honda Katsuichi on this Mufushan issue. But by April 1994, Itakura came to admit that the Nanking Atrocity as a whole claimed "at most 10,000 to 20,000" victims. Even so, he insisted, "there is no decisive evidence in the primary sources" to support either left-wing contentions about huge massacres near Mufushan or the conservative Kaikôsha figure of 3,000 victims there.[9] Itakura's denial of our left-wing thesis is understandable enough; he simply refuses to believe the testimonies and battlefield diaries of men who admitted to "killing all" prisoners. But his statement vis-à-vis the Kaikôsha figure of 3,000 victims seems inexplicable, since he himself was a key member of the editorial team who compiled the volume that cites it as a historical fact.

Numbers and Methods

What, then, was the actual number of Chinese victims near Mufushan? When I began my research in 1988, I simply assumed that the 15 December 1937 *Tokyo Asahi shinbun* figure of 14,777 POWs represented their total number and that most men in the Sixty-fifth Regiment also accepted this figure as accurate. Many of those whom I interviewed, however, testified that the actual number of Chinese prisoners was 20,000. On the other hand, Saitô Jirô, who was assigned to regimental headquarters at that time, noted in the margin of his personal battlefield diary: "14,777 men captured; on the fourteenth, surveys by brigade headquarters."[10]

If 14,777 was the actual number of prisoners taken on 14 December, this had to have been the day when the Sixty-fifth Regiment first arrived in Nanking. Every imperial army unit routinely conducted mop-up operations as a safety measure before it occupied an area, so this 14,477 figure would represent the number of prisoners captured on that day during this mop-up. It is therefore a distinct possibility that the regiment took even more prisoners after 14 December. This supposition is borne out in the personal battlefield diary of Sublieutenant Endô Takaaki who belonged to the regiment's Eighth Company. Endô's entry for 15 December reads: "went [to mop up defeated stragglers] and took 306 prisoners."[11] Moreover, Private First Class (PFC) Kanno Yoshio, assigned to an artillery company in the regiment, left a battlefield notebook that relates: "14 [December]: Departed for [mop up] at 5:00 a.m. From about dawn, we took wave after wave of enemy troops prisoner.… We placed them in the [Chinese] army barracks and posted sentries in front. The prisoners numbered 15,000. 15 [December]: We continued taking more prisoners today; they come to about 20,000."[12]

Thus there is no doubt that the number of prisoners held by the Yamada Detachment and the Sixty-Fifth Regiment after 14 December amounted to more than the *Tokyo Asahi shinbun*'s reported figure of 14,777. Endô, for example, took his count down to the last man: "total number of prisoners—17,025."[13] I estimate the total to have been somewhere between 17,000 and 18,000, but the 20,000 figure cited by many of the men in their testimonies may well be accurate. We must note, then, that the 14,777 figure cited originally in the *Tokyo Asahi shinbun* and in the semiofficial Kaikôsha 1993 document volume, is for 14 December 1937 alone; it does not include Chinese POWs whom the Yamada Detachment captured after that date.

The Yamada Detachment and Sixty-fifth Regiment massacred this huge number of prisoners—whose total number approximated 20,000—over two days: 16 and 17 December. More correctly, we should say that the unit massacred all but the handful of prisoners lucky enough to escape. PFC Kanno Yoshio's battlefield notebook goes on to state: "16 [December]: There was a fire in the barracks around noon, and about half of the buildings burned down. Beginning that evening we took some of the prisoners to the banks of the Yangtze and shot them to death."[14] Kondô Eishirô, of the Mountain Artillery Nineteenth Regiment's Eighth Company, wrote in his personal battlefield diary:

> 16 [December]: ... The 20,000 prisoners committed arson. We filled in for troops from the company who went to guard them. Finally, it was decided today that we would shoot to death 7,000, or one-third of them, on the banks of the Yangtze. We went to provide an armed escort and finished taking care of them. Any who managed to survive, we stabbed or slashed to death with bayonet and sword. Bathed in the bright rays of the mid-December moon that hung over nearby hills, the prisoners' agonized cries of death were indescribably horrific. Only on the field of battle will one encounter such a sight. Having witnessed a scene never to be forgotten in our lives, we returned at about 9:30.[15]

We know from these veterans' personal battlefield diaries and from their oral testimonies that the Chinese POWs were massacred outside Yüleiying, or Torpedo Encampment, a KMT naval facility built on the banks of the Yangtze, opposite T'sao-hsieh-hsia (or Pakua) Island, which lies in the river. The Fukushima troops mounted heavy machine guns inside the encampment and bored holes in its thick concrete walls through which to aim and fire these weapons. Testimonies and war diaries tell us that some 2,000 to 3,000 Chinese prisoners docilely obeyed their Japanese captors while being brought here. The executions took place using light and heavy machine guns, but that did not kill all of the prisoners. Thus the order "charge" went out to troops guarding the periphery. They responded with bayonet and sword, making sure that no POW was overlooked. The personal battlefield diary of PFC Kurosu Tadanobu, assigned to the Mountain Artillery Third Battalion Quartermasters, describes the scene as follows:

> 16 December: Clear. At about 1 p.m., twenty men from our Quartermasters headed for Mafengshan [*recto:* Mufushan] on a search and destroy mission. Two or three days earlier we had taken about 5,000 of the Chink soldiers whom we held prisoner down to the Yangtze river bank and machine-gunned them to death. Afterwards, we cut and slashed them with bayonet and sword to our heart's content. I figured that I'd never get another chance like this, so I stabbed thirty of those damned Chinks. Climbing atop the mountain of corpses, I felt like a real devil-slayer, stabbing again and again, with all my might. "Ugh, ugh," the Chinks groaned. There were old folks as well as kids, but we killed them lot, stock, and barrel. I also borrowed a buddy's sword and tried to decapitate some. I've never experienced anything so unusual....[16]

After obtaining this particular document, I read and reread this passage transfixed. It is indeed self-explanatory. The reality of what this Fukushima artillery soldier starkly relates will not broach denial, no matter what kind of sophistry others may indulge in.

Furthermore, these primary sources that I uncovered give the lie to other important points in the conservative revisionists' "unavoidable killing in self-defense" thesis. For example, there was no release of noncombatants before the killing began, and the fire broke out in the daytime on the sixteenth, not at night time on the fourteenth or fifteenth, as claimed. PFC Kanno's battlefield notebook clearly states, "There was a fire in the barracks at around noon."[17] Sublieutenant Endô's personal battlefield diary also says that "A fire broke out in the barracks housing the prisoners at 12:30 p.m., so we were ordered to take action."[18] Hence it is clear that the fire occurred at about lunchtime on the sixteenth. But equally important, a perusal of other personal battlefield diaries that I discovered makes no reference to prisoners escaping. To the contrary, there are three photographs of POWs sitting on the ground in good order. It is quite likely that these are the ones who were burned out of their barracks. According to on-site surveys made by our research team, the Society to Study the Nanking Incident, shadows cast by Japanese guards indicate that these photos were taken sometime after the noon hour on a day in the middle of December. And, of course, there is a good possibility that the Chinese men in the photographs were some of the prisoners massacred on the sixteenth.

Under the conditions obtaining in mid-December 1937, an escape of POWs such as that purported by the conservative revisionists was totally impossible. To begin with, the barracks were under heavy guard and strict surveillance. According to the "unavoidable killing in self-defense" thesis, the Chinese prisoners fired arms after a fire broke out. But there is no record of Japanese guards being killed or wounded in my sources, nor is there any mention of escapees. The most that can be argued is that the POWs may have wished to fire on their captors in order to escape, but were unable to do so because of the strict surveillance. What, then, caused the fire? The most likely answer is this. A number of my interviewees spoke of staging a "trial execution" on 16 December. Hence, we may suppose that the Japanese captors set this fire as a pretext in order to lead prisoners away to their execution. The corpses were flushed down the Yangtze River on that very same day.

17 December

The Yamada Detachment considered this "trial execution" on the sixteenth a success. So it took the rest of the prisoners down to Tawantzu, on the banks of the Yangtze, to be massacred on the seventeenth. (However, some of the persons I interviewed noted the possibility that some Chinese POWs were taken to the same barracks at Yüleiying, or Torpedo Encampment, to be massacred.) In his personal battlefield diary, PFC Kanno explicitly wrote: "17 [December]: I took part in the unprecedented, grand spectacle marking our triumphant entry into Nanking. The ceremonies began at 1:30 [p.m.]. There was a review of troops by His Majesty, Lieutenant-General Prince Asaka [Yasuhiko], and by His Excellency, Supreme Commander Matsui [Iwane]. We shot to death the remaining 10,000 and some odd-thousand prisoners."[19]

The war diary of Sublieutenant Miyamoto Shôgo, of the Sixty-fifth Regiment's Fourth Company, reads: "17 [December]: Light snow.... We finally set out to dispose of the prisoners in the late-afternoon and early-evening after coming back [from the triumphal entry ceremonies]. Even allowing that they numbered over 20,000, we ended up making a fatal error that took a toll in casualties among our comrades."[20] Many men from the Sixty-fifth Regiment were assembled in a company that took part in the ceremonies. But almost all who did not, were assigned to massacre Chinese prisoners. In the morning they tied the prisoners' hands behind their backs with wire and also placed them in long chain-gang lines. The execution site was a broad bank of the Yangtze fenced off by barbed wire, with several heavy machine gun emplacements set up on the perimeter pointing inward. Oil was readied to burn the corpses, and phone lines were set up to link on-site troops with regiment and detachment headquarters. The chain-ganged POWs were led to this site in the afternoon, and all had arrived by the time dusk was setting in. The triggers were pulled just like the night before, but the number of prisoners shot differed.

In the following year while he was hospitalized, Lance Corporal Tanaka Saburô of the Sixty-fifth Regiment's Second Company drew a sketch of the massacre site (see the reproduction). His explanatory note to the sketch reads:

> [In the background] Yangtze River
> We said we would transport them temporarily to the island in the center [of the Yangtze], and assembled boats about halfway from shore. [But] after the boats pulled off, we fired on them from all sides at once to finish them off. In desperation, they climbed up on one another trying to evade our fire. They would pile on top of each other to a height of about three meters, fall down, pile on top of each other; and then repeat the process again.[21]

The prisoners were locked inside a semicircle of barbed-wire fencing with their backs to the Yangtze, and several heavy machine guns were mounted on the fence's perimeter pointing inward. Interviewees who fired the guns testified that they established an "allowable range of fire" beforehand in order to keep from shooting over or through the mass of prisoners and thereby killing comrades firing from the opposite side of the semicircle. Large bonfires were set up as markers at the two ends of the barbed-wire fence that ran into the river's edge. The gunners who manned each machine gun placed along the semicircle were ordered to limit their fire to points "in between the two bonfires" so

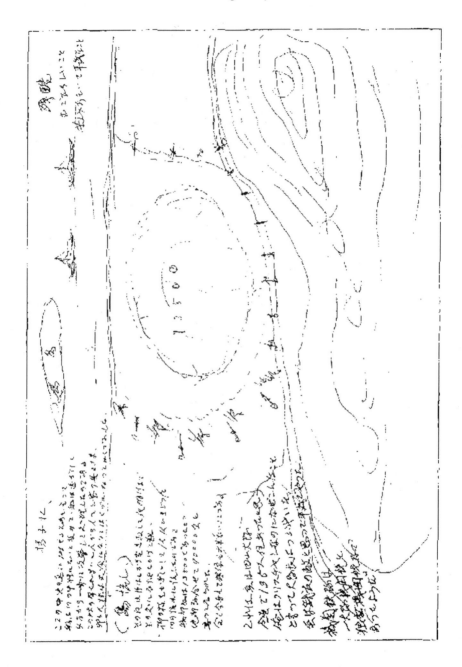

as to avoid hitting fellow-gunners on the other side by accident. This was their preestablished "allowable range of fire."

The "unavoidable firing in self-defense" thesis also holds that the Chinese prisoners were escorted for the purpose of being released. But as my primary sources clearly show, the POWs in truth were being escorted to be executed. In his war diary entry for 15 December, Maj. Gen. Yamada Senji, commander of the One Hundred Third Brigade, reiterated SEA orders and wrote: "That means 'kill them all'."[22] Endô's personal battlefield diary entry for the sixteenth reads: "Following orders, we took one-third of the prisoners down to the banks of the Yangtze River beginning in the evening. There, '[Roman numeral] I' shot them to death."[23] "[Roman numeral] I" refers to the Sixty-fifth Regiment's "First Battalion," comprising the First Machine Gun Company and the First to Fourth Infantry companies.[24]

Thus, just as our Society to Study the Nanking Incident suspected all along, these primary sources record orders coming from the SEA. And, they betray conservative revisionist claims that the Yamada Detachment and Sixty-fifth Regiment were escorting POWs to be set free in violation of orders issued by an imperial prince. Lance Corporal Tanaka Saburô's explanatory note to his sketch, which was just cited, explicitly states: "We said we would transport them temporarily to the island in the center [of the Yangtze]." Without doubt, this was a pretext to lead the prisoners away to their execution.

The machine gunners could not "finish off" all the prisoners, so the order to "charge" went out, just as on the night before. Tanaka's explanatory note continues:

(Flushing Them Away)

We killed them one after another from night time until dawn the next day. We splashed oil on the corpses and burned these. We used [forked] willow branches as hooks to drag the corpses over to the river one by one, where we flushed them downstream. Our own unit took care of 13,500 corpses, but other men were saying that the total would come to over 70,000 if all the units' killings were added up. It was a totally inconceivable, unimaginable sight.[25]

As a matter of course, the melee resulted amid great confusion. It is no wonder that POWs—faced with the abhorred prospect of dying—would resist to the bitter end. Even with hands tied behind their backs, they still numbered over 10,000; and, some may well have freed themselves during the machine gunning. Their battle with Japanese troops continued endlessly under cover of darkness. Yet, sadly, there was no way for the unarmed to prevail over the armed, so that all were stabbed or slashed to death. In order to make sure that all had died, the Yamada Detachment poured oil over the mass of corpses, set them on fire, and cut down any surviving POWs who dashed out of the burning heap, unable to bear the intense heat. These killings lasted until the morning of the eighteenth, with stand-by troops taking turns to help. PFC Kanno notes:

18 [December]: A light snow fell from the morning. We went to finish off those prisoners [not yet] taken care of by machine gunning. The smell was awful.

19 [December]: [Our unit] went to take care of the enemy soldiers again today, but I myself did not go.

20 [December]: We left at 10:00 a.m., boarded ships at Chungshan Wharf, and ended up camping out some 16 kilometers from P'uk'ou.[26]

There were so many corpses that it took virtually the whole Yamada Detachment three days—the eighteenth, nineteenth, and twentieth—to finish flushing all of these down the Yangtze past T'sao-hsieh Island in the middle of the river. And, even then the troops may have been unable to finish the job. The Detachment was originally ordered on a new mission on the nineteenth, but had to postponed its departure one day, until the twentieth, when its main force finally was able to leave Nanking.

18 December

Thus, it is clear that the Yamada Detachment and Sixty-fifth Regiment massacred the 17,000 to 18,000 Chinese prisoners captured near Mufushan, and that these massacres took place over two days and nights: the sixteenth and seventeenth of December. There are no later personal battlefield diary entries or testimonies about guarding the barracks where these POWs had been housed, so I assumed that all of the prisoners had been executed. But after I arrived at a clear estimate of the number of Chinese victims, another riddle surfaced. This took place when I obtained the personal battlefield diary left by Lance Corporal Meguro Fukuji, of the Quartermasters, Mountain Artillery Battalion III. Meguro's entries read:

16 December: Clear. Outside the walled city of Nanking....

At 4:00 p.m. we shot to death 7,000 prisoners taken by the Yamada Unit [Detachment]. The cliff on the Yangtze looked like a mountain of corpses for a time. That was truly an awful sight.

17 December: Clear. Outside the walled city of Nanking.

We left our encampment at 9:00 a.m. to take part in the grand historic ceremonies marking our commander's triumphant entry into the walled city of Nanking. At 5:00 p.m., we went to take up an assignment to execute about 13,000 enemy troops. Over 2 days, the Yamada Unit executed close to 20,000 of them. It seems that each of the units killed all the prisoners it held by gunfire.[27]

Thus, Meguro's entries for the sixteenth and seventeenth match those in other personal battlefield diaries. Moreover, his phrase "the cliff on the Yangtze" no doubt refers an area near Yüleiying, or Torpedo Encampment. His entry for the seventeenth—"Over two days, the Yamada Unit executed close to 20,000 of them"—leaves little doubt that the detachment finished killing all of its prisoners. However, momentous questions emerge from Meguro's next two entries.

> 18 December: Clear. Outside the walled city of Nanking.
>
> It was windy and rainy from about 3:00 a.m. Upon arising, we saw mountains capped in the whiteness of the season's first snow. We heard that the number of units concentrated in and around Nanking amount to roughly ten divisions. Break time. At about 5:00 p.m. we shot to death 13,000 defeated stragglers.
>
> 19 December: Clear. Outside the walled city of Nanking.
>
> We rose at 6:00 a.m. even though this was supposed to be a day off. Until 1:00 p.m., we flushed the corpses of enemy troops that we shot yesterday down the Yangtze—the number was 10,000 and several more thousand. We prepared to depart in the afternoon and performed guard duty at the command post.[28]

The dates of these entries cannot be wrong. Meguro correctly cites the triumphal entry ceremonies held on 17 December; and, furthermore, local weather records corroborate the fact that the first winter snow fell on 18 December.

So, what do we make of his entry for the eighteenth: "At about 5:00 p.m. we shot to death 13,000 defeated stragglers."? Should we take it at face value? Two possible explanations spring to mind: Meguro described the same massacre twice, or units other than the Yamada Detachment carried these out. But on the nineteenth, Meguro wrote: "Until 1 p.m., we flushed the corpses of enemy troops that we shot yesterday down the Yangtze—the number was 10,000 and several more thousand." Therefore, the massacre he mentions had to have occurred on the eighteenth. Be that as it may, Meguro's numbers are mind-boggling: "7000" on the sixteenth, "13,000" on the seventeenth, and "13,000" on the eighteenth, for a total of 33,000. On the seventeenth, he also noted vaguely: "It seems that each of the units killed all the prisoners it held by gunfire." These entries suggest that a plurality of massacres—apart from those at Yüleiying and Tawantzu—took place throughout the entire T'sao-hsieh-hsia area, for which Japanese historians have yet to account.

To date, Meguro's is the only personal battlefield diary I have found that mentions a massacre on 18 December. Trying to expand my search for sources beyond men in the Sixty-fifth Regiment, I looked for personal battlefield diaries left by former members of the Quartermasters, Mountain Artillery Nineteenth Regiment, Battalion III. I have been unable to locate any, however. On the other hand, I obtained a few testimonies from former members of the Sixty-fifth Regiment to the effect that massacres of prisoners took place on the banks of the Yangtze at sites other than Tawantzu. For example, one of the men said to me: "After our Sixty-fifth Regiment killed off our POWs, I saw another unit do exactly the same thing at some other desolate spot on the banks of the Yangtze, but I don't know which division or regiment it belonged to." Another man related to me: "At some other spot nearby on the banks of the Yangtze where buildings stood—but in a location different from ours—another unit killed POWs in the same way that we in the Sixty-fifth Regiment had done. It was some place where that unit had just passed through mountains. We in the Supply Corps also went over there to look at the corpses." I have ascertained that this "place where that unit had just passed through mountains" is Shangyüanmen Crossing. However, another of the men I interviewed said that "personnel in the heavy artillery from another regiment joined the massacre at Tawantzu." All of this raises the undeniable possibility that part of the Sixty-fifth Regiment was recruited to help other units massacre prisoners.

The other units stationed outside the walls of Nanking nearby the Sixty-fifth Regiment were the Sixteenth division's Thirty-third Regiment from Tsu in Mie Prefecture, along with that division's Thirty-eighth Regiment from Nara Prefecture, but we know little about what these two regiments did in the Nanking campaign. It is quite likely that they perpetrated other massacres in the T'sao-hsieh-hsia area cited in Chinese accounts dating from the Tokyo War Crimes Trials. These Chinese accounts are remarkably similar in nature to those in my sources, but place the number of victims in this area at 57,418. Only the unearthing and publication of official battle reports and personal battlefield diaries for those two units will settle this issue conclusively, however.

Conclusion

Personal battlefield diaries and oral testimonies obtained from veterans in the Fukushima Sixty-fifth Regiment—the main force in the Yamada Detachment—prove conclusively that the imperial army massacred an estimated 17,000 to 18,000 Chinese prisoners outside of Nanking city near Mufushan in the T'sao-hsieh-hsia area on 16 and 17 December 1937. The summary execution of POWs over whom armed forces had accepted custody is an inexcusable atrocity. It is also a clear violation of international treaties and laws of war that imperial Japan had pledged to honor. This was no impulsive or accidental act by a small number of troops suffering from battle fatigue or wartime hysteria. The two large-scale massacres at Tawantzu and Yüleiying described in my sources were premeditated and well-planned. And, above all, these mass murders were executed on orders from Lt. Gen. Prince Asaka Yasuhiko, who served as supreme commander of the SEA.

Previous Japanese accounts of this incident are demonstrably false in light of the primary sources introduced in this chapter. The Yamada Detachment and the Sixty-fifth Regiment never released half of their estimated 14,777 prisoners on the grounds of being noncombatants. These Fukushima units never intended to escort the remaining half to safety. They never killed the final one-quarter in a regrettable but unavoidable act of self-defense that claimed only 1,000 to 3,000 lives (varying from account to account). These units led 17,000 to 18,000—and perhaps 20,000—prisoners to the banks of the Yangtze River for the express purposes of killing them and disposing the corpses by burning or by flushing these downstream. Conservative revisionists in Japan who insist on clinging to their now-discredited, delusory versions of what happened at Mufushan do so from motives other than scholarly integrity and a search for historical truth.

Notes

*   Translated from Japanese by the editor.

1. See Hora and Watada, "Bakufusan no horyo shokei ni kansuru 'Shinsetsu' hihan."
2. For another analysis, see Watanabe, *Nankin gyakusatsu to Nihonjin.*
3. Hata, "Horyo no chi ni mamireta Byakko butai."
4. The relevant volumes are Fukushima minyû shinbun, ed., *Fukushima: Sensô to ningen,* vol 1, *Byakko hen;* and Fukushima minyû shinbun, ed., *Kyôbutai senki:* vol. 1, *Moesakru tairiku sensen.*
5. Bôeichô bôei kenshû sho senshishitsu, ed., *Shina jihen rikugun sakusen 1,* pp. 436–38.
6. Suzuki, *"Nankin daigyakusatsu" no maboroshi;* Kojima, *Nit-Chû sensô,* vol. 4, pp. 242–44; Abe, *Nankin no hisame,* passim; Nankin senshi henshû iinkai, ed., *Nankin senshi,* pp. 324–27.
7. Ono and Honda, "Bakufusan no horyo shûdan gyakusatsu"; Ono, "Nankin gyakusatsu no kôkei"; and Ono, "Mokugeki Nankin."
8. Kaikôsha, ed., "Bakusan fukin de no horyo shobun ni tsuite."
9. Itakura, "Nanking daigyakusatsu: gyakusatsu wa 'seizei' 10,000–20,000."
10. Ono, Fujiwara, and Honda eds., *Nankin daigyakusatsu o kiroku shita kôgun heishi tachi,* p. 37.
11. Ibid., p. 309.
12. Ibid., p. 309.
13. Ibid., p. 219.
14. Ibid., p. 309.
15. Ibid., p. 326.
16. Ibid., pp. 350–51.
17. Ibid., p 309.
18. Ibid., p. 219.
19. Ibid., p. 309.
20. Ibid., p. 134.
21. Ibid., pp. 376–77.
22. In Kaikôsha, ed., *Nankin senshi shiryô shû,* p. 331.
23. Ono, Fujiwara, and Honda, eds., *Nankin daigyakusatsu o kiroku shita kôgun heishi tachi,* p. 219.
24. However, we should note that the First Infantry Company was in fact deployed elsewhere at this time, so this statement is inaccurate in this respect.
25. Ono, Fujiwara, and Honda, eds., *Nankin daigyakusatsu o kiroku shita kôgun heishi tachi,* pp. 376–77.
26. Ibid., p . 309.
27. Ibid., pp. 373–74.
28. Ibid.

5

PART OF THE NUMBERS ISSUE: DEMOGRAPHY AND CIVILIAN VICTIMS

David Askew

Introduction

In this chapter, I hope to make a modest beginning for future quantitative studies of the tragic Nanking Atrocity, December 1937 to February 1938, by estimating how many Chinese civilians remained in the city before it fell on 13 December, and about how many died over the next several weeks at Japanese hands. Quantitative issues in the Atrocity are vexing in part because of the political and ideological baggage they carry. Writers choose vastly different time spans (short or long), geographic areas (narrow or wide), and definitions of "massacre" (whether or not those killed were combatants) to arrive at numbers that will "prove" how major or minor the Atrocity was. Through manipulations of this sort, the People's Republic of China (PRC) and its more zealous supporters insist there were no less than 300,000 victims, and perhaps over 400,000; in contrast, right-wing Japanese deniers claim there were zero to a few dozen.

Three groups witnessed the Atrocity: Japanese aggressors, Chinese victims, and Western residents. One irony is that many primary documents are in Western languages, mainly English, since the International Committee (IC), which established the Nanking Safety Zone (NSZ), was the only real municipal authority left after the city fell, and its members largely wrote in that language. In this chapter, I focus on official and private records left by those Westerners. Such a truncated focus and limited range of sources are two factors that serve to narrow my own definition of the Atrocity's time span and area, for many Westerners left Nanking a few weeks after it fell, and their purview was in any case limited to the city and its immediate environs. Indeed, they mainly witnessed events in or near the NSZ, a refugee area about one-eighth of the entire city. Thus their writings have huge limitations for historians seeking to reconstruct the Atrocity in its entirety. My limited focus has the advantage of closely following that adopted at the Tokyo and Nanking War Crimes Trials; that is, in and around the city for six weeks starting on 13 December. But it also has the drawback of being far narrower than that adopted by renowned historians such as the late Fujiwara Akira and Kasahara Tokushi in chapters 2 and 3. Due to the poor statistical data and the scarce official documentation just before the city's fall and during its occupation by the Japanese over these six weeks or so, I am forced place great weight on indirect pieces of evidence culled from nonofficial sources such as the Westerners' diaries, letters, and private papers.

However, my most grievous limitation is to exclude Chinese military personnel from this account even though huge numbers of them suffered a "massacre" in the sense of being killed in inhumane Japanese acts of violence that violated international laws of war. Thus it is crucial to stress that my estimated Chinese death toll would be far higher if I were to: (1) define the event in question more broadly as to time and area, (2) examine non-Western sources, such as written accounts and oral testimonies by the Japanese aggressors and Chinese victims, and (3) include Chinese military personnel in my calculations. In sum, I seek to quantify only Chinese civilian deaths, not all Chinese massacred in the Atrocity. I realize that critics may accuse me of defining "civilians" in an overly narrow way and of manipulating data to arrive at a minimal death toll. Thus, humility on my part is called for in the belief that other legitimate interpretations of the data are possible, which allow historians to reach higher victim totals. In these respects, I ask the reader to judge this chapter with a large dose of indulgence.

The Early and Later Population

Our starting point must be to estimate the population of Nanking in early-December, before the assault on city walls began. It had already plummeted due to repeated bombings, the approach of an invading army, and the flight by civil servants and wealthier classes. Those Chinese who stayed were, in John Rabe's words, "the poorest of the poor" who lacked the means to flee. He noted that 800,000 of the original population had left.[1] Some Western journalists estimated the number of people remaining at considerably less than 200,000. Lily Abegg, who herself left Nanking on 29 November, wrote in a 19 December *Frankfurter Zeitung* article that it was 150,000. The *New York Times* on 16 December said that the NSZ "shelters 150,000." Arthur Menken wrote on 17 December in the *Chicago Tribune* that "[m]ore than 100,000 Chinese sought refuge in the zone," and on 18 December, F. Tillman Durdin wrote of "upward of 100,000 noncombatants" in the NSZ with "residents, number-

ing upward of 50,000 who sought no sanctuary in the zone." These journalists believed that the entire population of Nanking city was about 150,000—
with 100,000 inside and 50,000 outside the NSZ. One hint that explains this
low early estimate may be George Fitch's statement in the *Los Angeles Times* of
18 March 1938 to the effect that the IC initially planned to feed and house only
100,000 refugees in the Zone, but a late rush increased the number to 250,000.

The most common Western estimate of 200,000 is found in two volumes
of sources: Harold J. Timperley, ed., *What War Means* (1938) and Hsü Shuhsi,
ed., *Documents of the Nanking Safety Zone* (1939). Timperley, an Australian
journalist and secret member of the Kuomintang [KMT] government's International Propaganda Department, edited the first detailed account of atrocities at Nanking.[2] Hsü was a "sometime Advisor to the [Chinese] Ministry of
Foreign Affairs." As I show below in tables 1 and 2, primary documents in

Table 5.1. Nanking Population, December 1937 to March 1938[3]

Official Documents of the IC	*Document No.*		*Date*	*Population*
	T6	H9	17 Dec. 1937	200,000
	T7	H10	18 Dec.	200,000
T = Timperley (1938)	T9	H20	21 Dec.	200,000
H = Hsü (1939)	T14	H26	27 Dec.	200,000
	T19	H41	14 Jan. 1938	250,000–300,000
	T22	H43	17 Jan.	250,000
		H46	18 Jan.	250,000
	T24	H47	19 Jan.	250,000
		H49	22 Jan.	250,000
	T26	H54	28 Jan.	250,000
		H68	10 Feb.	250,000
Survey	Smythe		12 Dec. 1937 to 13 March 1938	221,150
Registration	Japanese authorities		24 Dec. 1937 to 5 Jan. 1938	160,000
Registration	Japanese authorities		Late Feb.	172,502
Registration	Japanese authorities		Late Mar.	235,056
Reports	USA Embassy Report (Espy)		13 Jan.	200,000–250,000
	German Embassy Report (Rabe)		13 Jan.	200,000
Evidence (Tokyo Trials)	Bates		29 July 1946	221,000

Table 5.2.   Nanking Population as Recorded in Rabe's Diary

Source	Date	Population
Wolf Schenke	23 November	200,000
Telegram to Hitler	25 November	Over 200,000
Diary	25 November	Over 200,000
Telegram to Siemens Shanghai Office	25 November	Over 200,000
Chief of Police, Wang Kopang	28 November	200,000
Diary	10 December	200,000
Letter to Japanese Embassy	17 December	200,000
Letter to Japanese Embassy	18 December	200,000
Diary	25 December	200,000
Diary	26 December	200,000
Chancellor Scharffenberg	13 January	200,000
Letter to Siemens Management	14 January	200,000
Diary	17 January	250,000
Eduard Sperling	22 January (?)	200,000
Diary	12 February	250,000

these edited volumes reveal that: (1) the civilian population was an estimated 200,000 people, (2) it grew to about 250,000 by mid-January, and (3) the vast majority of these people were inside the NSZ, not in the rest of the city.

Geroge Fitch, Lewis Smythe, and other IC members agree that, as Smythe put it, "[a]t the time the city fell (December 12–13), its population was between 200,000 and 250,000" out of an estimated original "1,000,000" people. However, official documents dating after December 1937, such as Rabe's letter of 21 December (T9, H20) to the Japanese embassy, cite 200,000 civilians. The sole exception to that figure is in Rabe's letter to the Japanese embassy on 14 January: "We understand that you registered 160,000 people without including children under 10 years of age, and in some sections without including older women. Therefore there are probably 250,000 to 300,000 civilians in the city. To feed this population on normal rations of rice would require 2,000 tan [piculs] of rice per day (or 1,600 bags per day)."[4] Rabe probably derived this high figure of "250,000 to 300,000" from a published survey by Smythe: "On the basis of incomplete registrations carried out by the [Japanese] military authorities between the end of December and the end of January, members of the International Committee estimated the population of Nanking at that time to approach 250,000, a figure decidedly above their deliberately cautious guesses of earlier weeks. Semi-official Chinese conjectures ran closer to 300,000."[5] In this exceptional letter of 14 January, Rabe was pleading with the Japanese army for more food because many refugees inside the NSZ had none at all. Thus it was natural that, in this particular document, he sought to claim the existence of as many Chinese refugees as possible. On that very same day, he wrote to his company Siemens that the IC "has thus far succeeded in feeding the city's 200,000 residents packed into our [Nanking Safety] Zone," and also reported to the German embassy that the figure was 200,000.[6] As I show later on, the "semi-official Chinese conjectures" of "closer to 300,000" noted by Smythe are wrong if we accept his data on age-group distribution.

As seen from table 1, this initial population of 200,000 rose between 27 December and 14 January, probably due to the Japanese registration of civilians, announced on 22 December to begin on the twenty-fourth. On 17 January, Rabe wrote: "Estimates of the total population of the Zone are now around 250,000. The increase of about 50,000 comes from the ruined parts of the city."[7] At first glance, this seems to contradict his statements that people were not living outside the NSZ, but the contradiction disappears if he was referring to Chinese soldiers who had been hiding in those areas of the city. The Japanese finished registering the population by 14 January, when Western residents first noted an increase, and some Chinese ex-soldiers are known to have registered, so they probably account for part of that increase. Also, some residents who had fled to the surrounding countryside began returning from about 20 December, a week after Nanking fell. Thus, IC members consistently estimated the population at 250,000 under the Japanese occupation.

Location of the Population

On 28 November, Rabe noted, Chinese police chief Wang Kopang, "*repeatedly* declared that 200,000 Chinese are still living *in the city*" (italics added).[8] This shows that Chinese officials believed the population to be 200,000 in late November. Rabe's diary confirms where the people were. On 1 December, he says that the IC discussed whether to "order the remaining populace of Nanking into the neutral zone [i.e., the NSZ]," an order that was eventually issued. Moreover, the mayor of Nanking delegated "nearly all the functions of the City Government" to the IC. So it makes sense that the IC urged civilians to enter the NSZ—a move that foreshadowed orders by Chinese defense commander T'ang Sheng-chih later on. Rabe cites Chancellor P. Scharffenberg, writing to the German embassy that "the suburbs were burned down almost in their entirety by the Chinese, and the center of the city has largely been burned down by the Japanese. No one lives there now. The rest of the population—circa 200,000—is confined to the Safety Zone.... [T]he streets outside the Zone are deserted."[9] In an article published in October 1938, Smythe wrote that the population was 250,000 and that "[b]y the night of December 12th practically the entire population left in Nanking had moved into the Zone."[10]

Official documents in the Timperley and Hsü source volumes show that: (1) 200,000 people at first, and 250,000 people later on, were inside the NSZ; and (2) the rest of the city was virtually deserted. One memo dated 22 January 1938—after refugees had in fact started to return to their homes located outside the Zone—says that the IC "is now operating as a relief committee for the welfare of the 250,000 Chinese civilians living in the city. *Most of these people (at least 90 percent) are still living within the Zone.*"[11] Documents left by Miner S. Bates, Rabe, others in Timperley's volume, and Japanese soldiers also corroborate the view that "[p]ractically the whole population of Nanking moved within this area," and "[h]ardly anyone dares live outside the Zone," so "[l]ife hardly exists outside the walls, & little outside the Zone." The IC "estimated that about 250,000 people entered the Zone" but "[o]nly a relatively small number, probably not more than ten thousand in all, remained outside."[12] Verifying the existence of these 10,000 people—who are unmentioned in other documents—and their whereabouts is a topic for future research. Aside from this one possible exception, though, my point is that the IC believed that no significantly large groups of Chinese civilians, numbering in the tens or hundreds of thousands, were living in the city outside of the NSZ.

Other accounts at the time support this view. On 6 December, streets were "patrolled by small bands of troops wearing yellow armbands, signifying the enforcement of martial law." F. Tillman Durdin noted in the *New York Times* on 8 December that Chinese commander T'ang Sheng-chih "decreed that all noncombatants must concentrate in the internationally supervised safety zone" and "[m]ovement of noncombatants elsewhere in the city will be banned," so all civilians were to be moved off the streets as defense forces prepared to "fight to the last man." T'ang's decree and ban, preparations for street fighting elsewhere in the city, and widespread rumors that it was to be torched as part of China's scorched earth policy, all provided strong incentives to enter the NSZ. Thus it is wrong to assert—as do some writers such as even the conscientious historian, Hata Ikuhiko—that the 200,000 people mentioned in early documents, or the 250,000 in later ones, refer to only a part of Nanking's population.[13]

Many references say that, as Robert Wilson wrote on 10 January, the "entire" population of "some 150 or 200 thousand individuals," had "crowded into the zone." Miner Bates, Minnie Vautrin, John Magee, George Fitch, and James McCallum, all claimed virtually the same thing. Embassy reports by James Epsy to the U.S. ambassador in Hankow, as well as those by John Rabe to the German embassy, echo this view. Epsy wrote that "before the fall of Nanking, the Chinese armies and civilians had been steadily getting out of and away from Nanking. In the neighbourhood of four-fifths of the population had fled and the main body of Chinese troops had been withdrawn," and 200,000 to 250,000 out of the original population remained behind. Epsy's countryman, John Allison, reported on 10 January that 200,000 were concentrated in the NSZ.[14] On 14 January 1938, Rabe reported that Nanking's population of noncombatants was 200,000. Chancellor Paul Scharffenberg wrote several times about the population, as he did on 13 and 20 January, citing it as being 200,000 and 250,000. Kröger wrote that "all residents who remained in Nanking, about 200,000 to 250,000 individuals, fled to the [Safety Zone]."[15]

Of course, it is possible that civilians ignored T'ang Sheng-chih's order and the IC's promptings to move into the NSZ, preferring to stay in their homes elsewhere in the city, but it is not possible that tens of thousands of them existed. T'ang had been preparing to fight to the last man, and there were widespread rumors that he planned to torch the entire city. If large groups of people were hiding outside the NSZ, Japanese units would have found them, but only those units in the Seventh and Sixteenth divisions, those that searched the NSZ, filed reports about captured ex-soldiers. Finally, the Japanese never attacked the NSZ, and news of that fact probably induced both Chinese civilians and ex-soldiers outside of it to enter as time passed. Indeed, it is known that some Chinese ex-soldiers did hide in the NSZ. Many of the 16,000 troops conscripted just before the Japanese attack must have been local civilians, and those who survived it would have gone back to their homes in the city or suburbs.[16] The Japanese, at least sometimes, released men suspected of being ex-soldiers, so those last-minute conscripts who did survive the siege also help explain the population increase from 200,000 to 250,000 described earlier.

Smythe's "City Survey"

Another key primary source is Prof. Lewis S. S. Smythe's *Damage in the Nanking Area, December, 1937 to March, 1938,* which comprises agricultural and city surveys that he and his twenty or so Chinese assistants made under IC auspices during the Japanese occupation in 1938. Up to now, historians have given this document less attention than one might expect it deserves. The "Agricultural Survey," took place over 2,438 square miles in four and a half counties surrounding Nanking, but here I focus on the "City Survey" of every fiftieth inhabited house, defined by house number, in "the whole of the city inside the walls and the areas just outside some of the gates as well."[17] Smythe's survey took place from 9 March to 2 April 1938, with supplementary work from 19 to 23 April.

Historian Kitamura Minoru notes that Smythe received funding from the KMT regime's International Propaganda Division, and argues that he suitably inflated figures in his "Agricultural Survey."[18] Even if we were to grant that contention as being true, there is no reason to believe that Smythe—a University of Chicago Ph.D. in sociology with plentiful field experience in China—would have overlooked large populations or deliberately minimized data inside the city. As the only scholarly examination of the Atrocity published at the time, his "City Survey" deserves our respect and close attention.

Smythe studied 4,252 members of 906 families inside the city walls except for areas "not accessible to investigators." With the important proviso that this "number was probably 80 to 90 percent of the total residents," he estimated the city population at 212,600. This means that he thought the total for the city to be 236,000 to 266,000. As noted earlier, Smythe also stated that "[a]t the time the city fell (December 12–13), its population was between 200,000 and 250,000." Note that even as late as April 1938, a large proportion of the population was still in the NSZ (the "Refugee Camps" in table 3 were within it). This fact can perhaps be explained by Chinese scorched earth tactics before Nanking fell and widespread Japanese arson thereafter, plus the Japanese presence outside the NSZ. Smythe explicitly wrote that "areas outside the walls" were still dangerous, and Bates claimed that "there has latterly grown up in the rural areas a serious banditry which currently rivals and sometimes surpasses the robbery and violence by Japanese soldiers."[20]

Some historians accept Smythe's figure of 212,600 as the most accurate estimate of Nanking's population, but I contend that his data, combined with results of registration by the Japanese army, let us reach an even closer estimate. The Japanese army announced that civilians had to register from 24 December in order to receive identification papers—cited in Western sources as "passports," "registration cards," "good subject certificates," or "good citizen

Table 5.3. Families Studied and Estimated Population by City Sections[19]

Section	Number of Families Studied	Total Family Members if Families Studied	Average Size of Family	Estimated Total Number of Families	Estimated Total Family Members
A. Inside Wall	906	4,252	4.7	45,300	212,600
1. Safety Zone	298	1,358	4.6	14,900	67,900
2. Refugee Camps	114	550	4.8	5,700	27,500
3. Cheng Hsi	115	544	4.7	5,750	27,200
4. Cheng Tung	55	232	4.2	2,750	11,600
5. Cheng Pei	51	243	4.8	2,550	12,150
6. Men Hsi	126	631	5.0	6,300	31,500
7. Men Tung	103	451	4.4	5,150	22,600
8. Garden	44	243	5.5	2,200	12,150
B. Outside Wall	43	171	4.0	2,150	8,550
9. Hsiakwan	13	46	3.5	650	2,300
10. Chunghwamen	16	79	4.9	800	3,950
11. Shuihsimen	14	46	3.3	700	2,300
All Sections	**949**	**4,423**	**4.7**	**47,450**	**221,150**

certificates." The army also announced that "[t]hose without passports ... are not allowed to reside within the Nanking city wall[s]." Rabe's diary on 24 December and Robert Wilson's letter on 26 December also mention this Japanese decree. The army did not register all Chinese people; it excluded "children under ten" and "older women" in Nanking, at least in some cases. The number of these passports, then, is a means to help estimate the population, not an exact count of it. The army registered either 150,000 or 160,000 people (I accept 160,000 as on table 1). This was far less than the whole population, which the Japanese Special Service Agency (SSA) estimated to be 200,000 in a January report, and to be over 200,000 later on, noting that people had moved into the NSZ before the city had fallen.

As noted in table 4, Smythe provides population breakdowns by age and gender as of March 1938; 0–4 year-olds accounted for 8.4 percent, 5–9 year-olds for 12.5 percent, and 10–14 year-olds for 11.7 percent. Children 9-years-old or under would have accounted for 20.9 percent of the population. If 10-year-olds are included, the figure is roughly 23.3 percent. It is not as easy to calculate the number of "older females." Those in the 60-plus age group accounted for 11.7 percent of the total number of females—not of the whole population. Since the male-to-female ratio at the time was about 103:100, roughly 5.8 percent of the total population (one-half of 11.7 percent) were

Table 5.4.   Age and Gender Breakdown of the Population[21]

	Percent in Each Age Group			
Age Group	*Male*	*Female*	*Male and Female*	*Gender Ratio*
0–4	8.1	8.7	8.4	96.8
5–9	12.5	12.5	12.5	103.3
10–14	12.3	11.1	11.7	114.0
15–19	8.6	8.2	8.4	108.4
20–24	6.6	6.5	6.6	105.7
25–29	6.1	6.4	6.2	100.0
30–34	5.6	6.4	6.0	89.3
35–39	6.1	6.0	6.1	105.3
40–44	7.8	7.2	7.5	112.1
45–49	8.4	5.3	6.9	163.5
50–54	5.8	5.8	5.8	104.8
55–59	3.9	4.2	4.0	95.6
60 and over	8.2	11.7	9.9	75.2
Totals	100	100	100	103.4
0–14	33	32	32	105
15–49	49	46	48	111
50 and over	18	22	20	85
Totals	100	100	100	103

females above 60. If we round this off to 6 percent and assume that "older women" meant *all* women over 60, then "children and [all] older women" would amount to at most 29.3 percent of the population. If we take "older women" to mean 55 or above, this total increases slightly to less than 32 percent. Since the 160,000 people registered by the Japanese army were the remaining 70 percent of the population, its total would have been close to 226,000, which is about what other primary sources suggest. At 32 percent, the total would be roughly 235,000. Note that this assumes the Japanese did not register *any* "older women" in those age brackets. The estimate will fall to 217,000 if half of the women 60-plus were registered, to 223,500 if half of those 55-plus were registered, and to 232,000 if half of those 50-plus were registered. This can be double-checked. Using Smythe's data on the gender ratio and assuming a population of 221,500, we can calculate the number of males and females in each age group. If all males and females between 11 and 59, and all males 60-plus are added (there were 20,733 11–14 year-olds), we get a total of 157,508. We get 163,766 if half of those females 60-plus were registered, and 161,501 if half of those females 55-plus were registered.

Smythe missed those parts of the population in "dangerous areas," mainly outside the city gates, and he collected data some weeks after the Japanese registration ended. Nevertheless, we can accept his data for purposes of calculation, assuming that breakdowns in age and gender are consistent and that persons in "dangerous areas" were mainly males who, if anything, would have served to lower the estimates. Following his data, the total population figure would be larger if we included children under ten and "older women" not

Table 5.5. Population Distribution by Age and Gender

Age groups	%	Numbers	Gender ratio	Males	Females
Distribution of population, 1938 (assumed population: 221,150)					
0–4	8.4	18577	96.8	9137	9439
5–9	12.5	27644	103.3	14046	13598
10–14	11.7	25875	114.0	13784	12091
15–19	8.4	18577	108.4	9663	8914
20–24	6.6	14596	105.7	7500	7096
25–29	6.2	13711	100.0	6856	6856
30–34	6.0	13269	89.3	6259	7010
35–39	6.1	13490	105.3	6919	6571
40–44	7.5	16586	112.1	8766	7820
45–49	6.9	15259	163.5	9468	5791
50–54	5.8	12827	104.8	6564	6263
55–59	4.0	8846	95.6	4324	4522
60 and over	9.9	21894	75.2	9397	12496
Totals	**100**	**221,150**	**103.4**	**112,683**	**108,467**

registered, but it would still only be about 217,000 to 235,000. Figures from the Japanese registration of civilians, then, provide a basis for accepting the estimated range of 200,000 to 250,000 found in Western primary sources, and also for arguing that 224,500 is the closest possible estimate of the population. The Japanese army could not have overlooked 500,000 civilians, nor could the city outside the NSZ have contained 500,000 unregistered "children under ten" and "older women."

Thus based on Western sources combined with Japanese registration figures, I conclude: (1) even Chinese officials, such as the Nanking police chief Wang Kopang, accepted a population of 200,000 in late November; (2) Nanking's civilian population in early-December, before the Japanese began to assault the city, numbered 200,000 or perhaps even somewhat less—as foreign journalists believed at that time; (3) between mid-December and mid-January, this number seems to have risen to about 250,000; (4) the most accurate estimate is about 224,500—which I obtained by using Smythe's findings together with Japanese registration figures; and (5) virtually all of these 200,000 to 250,000 people were inside, not outside, the NSZ that occupied about one-eighth of the total city. If these conclusions are valid, it is impossible to agree with writers such as the late Iris Chang who, citing the PRC scholar Sun Chai-wei, argues for a population of some 600,000 to 700,000 people at the time Nanking fell.[22] This point is of crucial important because the initial size of Nanking's population places one major limit on the possible number of Chinese civilians the Japanese could have "massacred" during the Atrocity that would follow.

Civilian Casualties

It is difficult to estimate "civilian casualties" because IC members did not and, indeed, could not, make a distinction between three groups of Chinese: civilians, soldiers who changed into civilian clothes as the city fell ("ex-soldiers" or "former soldiers" as cited in Western sources), and plainclothes troops who were soldiers masquerading as civilians. Thus many persons and corpses identified by the Westerners as "civilians" in fact were, or had been, Chinese belligerents. There is no doubt, however, that the Japanese army did arrest and unjustly execute huge numbers of Chinese civilians assumed to be soldiers. In addition to that organized form of violence and murder, there is abundant evidence in the primary documentation attesting to random acts of rape and murder by countless numbers of Japanese troops, either as individuals or in small groups. As noted by Hata Ikuhiko, a leading historian of the Nanking Atrocity, huge numbers of Japanese soldiers were simply out of control.[23]

The IC documented and reported 405 cases of violent disorder to the Japanese embassy, some of which involved multiple victims. Many were not serious. For example, "on December 14th, Japanese soldiers entered the home of Miss Grace Bauer, an American missionary, and took a pair of fur-lined gloves, drank up all the milk on the table, and scooped up sugar with their hands."[24] Cases were often based on hearsay, and IC members hurriedly wrote down their accounts amid the pell-mell of fighting, so their English was often ambiguous. If our aim is to estimate the number of Chinese deaths at Japanese hands, the phrases "shot dead" and "shot but later recovered" are clear, but a simple "shot" is not. By my reckoning, those 405 cases reported by the IC included twenty-five in which fifty-five people were "murdered." However, the figures in table 6 will differ slightly according to how words and sentences are interpreted. Thus, Masahiro Yamamoto estimates forty-six murders; Itakura Yoshiaki, fifty-two.[25]

Most recorded incidents were secondhand accounts from Chinese persons. For example, IC members such as Rabe wrote in his diary and private letters that 1,000 women were raped on the night of 17 December, but the IC filed official reports to the Japanese embassy about twelve cases in which more that eighteen were raped (some were multiple rapes). The IC verified at least some cases of murder, rape, and other forms of violence; and it lodged official protests about these to the Japanese embassy. Hence Japanese deniers are wrong to dismiss out of hand all cases cited in Western documents as "mere hearsay." At the same time, cases noted in private sources such as letters and diaries must be treated with some caution.

Chinese death tolls cited in Timperley's edited volume range from a high of 40,000 to a low of 10,000. One major problem, however, is that these estimates do not distinguish between civilians and military personnel. Many Chinese soldiers were fighting in civilian clothes and young children were conscripted to support them, so it would have been impossible to determine if the corpse of an adult, let alone a ten- to twelve-year-old boy, was a bona fide civilian. A second problem is that Timperley was working as a paid propagandist in the KMT International Propaganda Division, and may have deliberately exaggerated his estimates in order to play up Japanese cruelty and Chinese victimization.[26]

Table 5.6. Reported Cases of Disorder by Japanese Soldiers[27]

Date	Murdered	Injured	Taken Away	Raped
12 Dec. – 18 Dec.	21	10	696	111 (3 cases of "many," 2 of "several")
19 Dec. – 10 Jan.	2	11	33 (1 case of several)	147 (2 cases of several)
11 Jan. – 7 Feb.	17	24	31 (1 case of "several")	84 (3 cases of "several")
Total	55	44	390	361

The high estimate of 40,000, Timperley said, came from a memo from a "foreign member of the University faculty" who, on close inspection, turns out to be Miner S. Bates. In his memo dated 25 January, Bates wrote that "burials indicate that close to 40,000 unarmed persons were killed within and near the walls of Nanking, of whom some 30% had never been soldiers."[28] This suggests that Bates believed that: (1) only the burial total by the Red Swastika Society (RSS)—a Chinese charitable organization charged with burying corpses—was accurate (its total reached 43,071); and (2) the 40,000 corpses included 28,000 soldiers (70 percent) and 12,000 civilians (30 percent). These figures included deaths in battle, so his phrase, "40,000 unarmed persons" is misleading. Moreover, to repeat for emphasis, it was impossible to differentiate the body of a civilian from that of a plainclothes soldier, or that of a civilian from a solider who had changed into civilian clothes. The "12,000 civilians" cited in Bates's 25 January memo, then, must have meant "12,000 bodies in civilian clothes" or "12,000 suspected soldiers executed."

If we accept Timperley's high estimate of 40,000 as breaking down to 28,000 deaths in battle and 12,000 suspected soldiers executed, then his low estimate of 10,000 is understandable. It came from "one of the most respected members of Nanking's foreign community who is noted for his fairmindedness." Again, this man is Bates, who had access to RSS records, as that society was working closely with IC members. Bates's memo of 10 January states: "[m]ore than 10,000 unarmed persons have been killed in cold blood.... These were Chinese soldiers who threw down their arms or surrendered after being trapped; and civilians recklessly shot and bayoneted."[29] Thus, Timperley's lower estimate clearly does not include Chinese deaths in battle. If this is true, the difference between his high figure of 40,000 and low figure of 10,000 narrows considerably. Either way, 10,000 to 12,000 soldiers, plain-clothed soldiers, and/or civilians were illegitimately executed. My own estimate based on other extant sources is about 16,000 illegitimate executions.

In *War Damage in the Nanking Area,* Smythe calculated Chinese deaths and injuries at Nanking, as well as the number of those "taken away" as laborers, and perhaps executed. As per table 7, his sampling survey showed that 850 Chinese "civilians" died in military action; 2,400 died owing to individual acts of violence by Japanese soldiers, and another 150 through unknown causes—for a total of 3,400. Another 3,350 were injured and 4,200 were "taken away." Smythe has limitations as a primary document. For example, especially in the "Agricultural Survey," how could he have determined how many deaths were at Japanese, as opposed to Chinese, hands? If, as Kitamura Minoru argues, the KMT government did indeed fund Smythe, he may have deliberately skewed his results to reinforce notions of Japanese brutality and Chinese victimization—again, in the "Agricultural Survey" especially. Yet on the other side of the ledger, the number of deaths that Smythe attributes to "unknown" causes

Table 5.7.   Number and Cause of Deaths and Injuries[30]

Date 1937–8	Deaths By			Injuries By			Taken Away	Total Killed and Injured	Percent Killed and Injured by Soldiers' Violence
	A	B	C	A	B	C			
Before 12 Dec.	600	—	—	50	—	—	—	650	—
12–13 Dec.	50	250	—	—	250	—	200	550	91
14 Dec.–13 Jan.	—	2000	150	—	2200	200	3700	4550	92
14 Jan.–15 Mar.	—	—	—	—	—	—	250	—	—
Date Unknown	200	150	—	—	600	50	50	1000	75
Total	850	2400	150	50	3050	250	4200	6750	81

A = Military Operations (bombing, shelling, or bullets fired in battle)
B = Soldiers' Violence
C = Unknown

seems far too low. I accept his results as they stand, however, and compare these with other information that he has provided.

First, the results dovetail fairly well with the 4,400 women who reported to him that their husbands had "been killed, injured or taken away"—of whom two-thirds, or 2,932, were killed or taken away. Second, Smythe's other data demonstrate that: (1) broken families of women and children rose to 6.6 percent of all families from the 3.4 percent in 1932, (2) women and children with relatives rose to 6.3 percent from 2.6 percent, and (3) women with relatives rose to 2.1 percent from 0.1 percent.[31] So, 8.9 percent of all families seem to have lost the male breadwinner. With a total of 47,450 families, this indicates that 4,223 men were missing. This figure almost exactly matches the 4,400 mentioned above and roughly corroborates the reported 3,400 killed plus the large number taken away. The Japanese took men to work as laborers, some for short periods of time, others for much longer.

Smythe mentions one more figure that indicates how many men were rounded up as forced labor.

Among the 13,530 applicant families investigated during March by the International Committee's Rehabilitation Commission, there were reported[ly] men taken away equivalent to almost 20 percent of all males of 16–50 years of age. That would mean for the whole city population [of] 10,860 men. There may well be an element of exaggeration in the statements of applicants for relief; but the majority of the difference between this figure and the 4,200 of the survey report is probably due to the inclusion of cases of detention or forced labor which the men are known to have survived.[32]

It may also be that families without a male breadwinner were seeking aid, so generalizations based on these families alone would exaggerate the number of males conscripted. Yet there is no doubt that the Japanese rounded up large numbers of men for work. Elsewhere, Smythe repeats Bates's estimate of 12,000 civilian deaths: "[a] careful estimate from the burials in the city and in areas adjacent to the wall indicates 12,000 civilians killed by violence." Smythe also claimed that "unarmed or disarmed soldiers are not considered in these lists," but he is almost surely wrong on this point. As with Bates, it was impossible to determine whether a corpse in civilian clothes was that of a soldier or a civilian.

Smythe's results can be compared with his data on Nanking's age and gender distribution. He says that the fall in the male-to-female gender ratio from 114:100 to 103:100 is "accounted for in part by the withdrawal of males not native to Nanking but formerly working here, and in part by the killing of males."[33] A drop of eleven points looks enormous, but we cannot know exactly what it means in the absence of hard population data for both years. Since the changes are in the *proportion* of men to women, it is theoretically possible that: (1) any drop could be explained by large numbers of women moving into the city, not by large numbers of men disappearing; (2) the total number of men went up, but the number of women increased even more; or (3) the number of women fell while the number of men fell even further. But we know that a disproportionate number of men did die, so Smythe's speculation seems plausible.

If the overall shift in the male-to-female gender ratio from 114 to 103 was attributable entirely to fewer males, if the female population remained static, and if the size of the original population on 13 December 1937 was 221,150—then the 1938 population would have been 209,782, consisting of 103,341 females and 106,441 males. Thus, the number of males "missing" would have been 11,368 or 9.36 percent. Similarly, if the female population remained more or less static, and the drop is explained by a loss through male migration or death; and if, say, half of the "missing" 11,368 men were migratory workers or individuals with no families, who thus could have left with relative ease, then there would be 5,684 individuals unaccounted for.

One fact noticeable from the tables is that the ratio of males dropped for virtually all age groups, with the inexplicable exception of the 45–49 and the 55–59 categories. The drop is fairly consistent across the range, although there are particularly steep declines in the 30–34, 25–29, and 50–54 age groups. The biggest decline—from 123.2 to 89.3 males for every 100 females—was in the 30–34 year-old group. If we cannot explain this enormous difference

Table 5.8. Age and Gender Distribution (Males per 100 Females): 1932 and 1938[34]

Age Group	1932	1938	Difference
0–4	101.3	96.8	− 4.5
5–9	109.3	103.3	− 6
10–14	119.2	114.0	− 5.2
15–19	123.4	108.4	− 15
20–24	124.5	105.7	− 18.8
25–29	128.1	100.0	− 28.1
30–34	123.2	89.3	− 33.9
35–39	123.4	105.3	− 18.1
40–44	124.5	112.1	− 12.4
45–49	121.0	163.5	+ 42.5
50–54	131.6	104.8	− 26.8
55–59	85.3	95.6	+ 10.3
60 and over	77.7	75.2	− 2.5
Totals	114.5	103.4	− 11.1
0–14	109	105	− 4
15–49	124	111	− 13
50 and over	94	85	− 9
Totals	114	103	− 11

by large numbers of men being conscripted by the KMT army and forced to leave the city before it fell, or by a large number of males being single or with families outside Nanking who left before the city fell, then it must be that this age group bore the brunt of Japanese conscription and/or executions. Smythe states explicitly that "areas outside the walls" were still dangerous, and that single men had started to return there. This may partly explain the discrepancies in certain age groups like men from 30–34. On the other hand, it is puzzling why there were so few women aged 45–49 compared with men. Perhaps women with young children had chosen to flee before 13 December, leaving men behind to protect their homes, or perhaps there was a large influx of single men aged 45–49.

It is interesting that table 8 shows how many males there were in almost every age group compared with females. Existing, albeit inflated, RSS burial records clearly indicate that the vast majority of all corpses buried were male.[35] So the large ratio of males cannot be explained by a large-scale massacre of females. We might think that there must have been a large influx of males into the city just before it fell, and a similar survey from 1932 shows that there were even more males for every age group except 45–49, 55–59, and 60-plus. For 10–14 year-olds, for instance, the large figure of 114.0 for 1938 was an even larger 119.2 in 1932, and the 112.1 figure for 40- to 44-year-olds was 124.5 in 1932. Thus we can conclude that Nanking was a city that attracted large numbers of single male migrants even before the war began.[36]

Table 5.9. Estimates Derived from Smythe

Source	Estimate	Notes
Sampling Survey	3,400 killed, 4,200 taken away	
Wives	2,932 killed or taken away	Married men only: underestimate?
Data on Broken Families	4,223 men missing	Male breadwinners: underestimate?
Applicant Families	10,860 men conscripted	Overestimate?
Gender Ratio	11,368 men missing	Highly speculative: some (half?) fled

Table 9 summarizes various estimates of men killed or conscripted, as directly provided by Smythe or derived from data apart from his overall estimate of 12,000 deaths. Following his sampling survey (where 44 percent of the total were killed), I recalculated the figures in table 10 to get an idea of how many civilians may have been killed. The average of the estimates is 3,266, or 3,232 excluding the sampling survey. His data thus indicate a possible civilian death toll of 3,200 to 3,400 (including any civilians killed in military action or by Chinese soldiers).

Rabe's estimates of the numbers killed varied. On 14 January, he reported to the German embassy that the Japanese had "slayed thousands of innocent civilians." Yet he appears to have revised this figure downward a fortnight later. In a letter dated 28 January to the British embassy in Nanking he stated, "there are many hundreds, if not thousands, of cases where the [family] wage-earner has either been taken away or killed."[37] From the context, it seems that he is talking only about men within the city walls after it fell, and that he is deliberately excluding those killed in fighting up to then, as well as those captured and executed outside the walls. His estimate of "many hundreds, if not thousands" of people conscripted as coolies or executed can be compared with Smythe's results, which show that 3,400 died through the violence of Japanese soldiers and that 4,200 were "taken away." Rabe does not estimate the

Table 5.10. Civilian Death Toll Derived from Smythe

1	Sampling Survey	3,400
2	Wives	1,290
3	Data on Broken Families	1,858
4	Applicant Families	4,778
5	Gender Ratio	5,002
Average		3,266

total number of deaths in his diary, but after returning to Germany in April 1938, he claimed that a total of 50,000 to 60,000 civilians and military personnel may have been killed inside and outside the walls of Nanking. This total included the bodies of 30,000 Chinese soldiers who died in fighting at Hsiakwan and were, as of 22 February, awaiting burial.[38] However, RSS records show that roughly 3,000 bodies were buried from Hsiakwan after this date. I therefore subtract 27,000 to revise Rabe's estimate to between 23,000 to 33,000 civilian and military deaths including deaths in action.

Estimates by other IC members varied (see table 13). On 19 December, John Magee wrote that 20,000 Chinese had been killed. On 5 January, he mentions the murder of "disarmed soldiers and thousands of civilians," and later noted thousands of civilians "done to death." On 11 January, he stated, "[i]t is impossible to say how many people have been murdered (including disarmed soldiers), but my guess is 20,000." In a letter on 29 December, James McCallum wrote that "thousands have been butchered in cold blood—how many it is hard to guess—some believe it would approach the 10,000 mark." Ernest Forster wrote on the same day that "[c]ountless people, civil and military, have been done to death," a figure he gave in another letter to a friend on 14 January as "[t]housands of men were ... executed." On 9 January, the journalist Tillman Durdin, almost certainly based on data provided by IC members, estimated that the total death toll was 33,000, of which executed soldiers accounted for 20,000. The vast majority of the remaining 13,000, it can be assumed, were soldiers who died in battle. In a report cited in Rabe's diary date 13 January, Christian Kröger wrote that the Japanese made a "rigorous search" to round up large numbers of suspected ex-soldiers and plain clothes soldiers, and "approximately 5,000 people were shot ... [t]hat number is probably too low an estimate." This appears to be an account of men led from the NSZ and executed—not of total deaths. Some civilians, at least 136 policemen among them, were so rounded up.[39]

On 21 March, Smythe reported "it is estimated that 10,000 persons were killed inside the walls of Nanking and about 30,000 outside the walls," adding that civilians comprised 30 percent of this total. He gives a lower figure in an October 1938 article: "It took the Red Swastika Society most of the spring to bury the bodies of the killed, and they reported burying 30,000 bodies, one third of which were civilians."[40] The first report is of great significance; it suggests that the IC may have counted those Chinese killed *outside* the walls as military personnel and those *inside* as civilians. The IC certainly argued that soldiers who threw down their weapons and changed into civilian clothes should be treated as civilians. The Japanese, on the other hand, viewed such men as guerrilla fighters who had violated international rules of warfare. Today, a main point of dispute in calculating the civilian death toll, as opposed to the total death toll, in the Nanking Atrocity derives from this difference of opinion.

The IC also collected data on husbands and sons reported missing. The missionary and teacher, Minnie Vautrin, mentions this data a number of times. She noted that 592 reports of missing men had been collected as of 13 January, 568 reports as of 21 January, 532 reports as of 24 January, 723 reports as of 7 February, and 738 reports as of 8 February. On 26 March, she again mentions that "more than 700" reports had been collected.[41] Why her data is lower than Smythe's—who reported 2,932 men killed or taken away—remains to be explained. Perhaps she collected data from only a subgroup of women. Or, perhaps women who knew their husbands or sons were dead appear in Smythe's data but not in Vautrin's.

On 21 March, Bates wrote that the civilian death toll was "about 12,000" in addition to "25,000 to 30,000 unarmed and passive remnants of the Chinese defense forces, killed within or near the walled city after the occupation."[42] These numbers suggest that the RSS was his source, which again means that Bates was misleading his readers, for much of the military death toll must have consisted of soldiers killed in action. Thus IC members seemingly believed that between 10,000 and 42,000 Chinese died in and immediately around Nanking, and that 10,000 to 20,000 may have been executed. Note that their larger figures, in the 30,000 to 42,000 range, are based on RSS estimates that included bodies of men who died in battle. Also note that these estimates do not always identify civilian casualties.

Although their initial estimates of the death toll were high, IC members such as Rabe seem to have revised these downward. On 18 February, the IC was renamed the Nanking International Relief Committee. Its "Report of Activities, November 22, 1937–April 15, 1938" lists "thousands" of Chinese murdered, imprisoned, or abducted. In a plea for contributions from abroad, the Relief Committee wrote: "When the great loss of thousands of families due to the murder, imprisonment, or abduction of the wage earner, is added to the tremendous economic loss which the people everywhere sustained, relief funds, even if multiplied a hundred fold, would still be inadequate."[43] Since the new committee made this estimate in the context of a plea for monetary donations, it could have chosen to exaggerate the scale of atrocities, so its downward revision of estimated civilian deaths is difficult to explain. This picture is complicated by a letter Wilson wrote on 7 March: "The Red Swastika Society had for the last month been feverishly burying bodies from all parts of the city outside the zone and from the surrounding countryside. A conservative estimate of the number of people slaughtered in cold blood is somewhere about 100,000 [10,000?], including of course thousand [thousands?] of soldiers that had thrown down their arms."[44]

Unfortunately, Wilson's original has been lost; this quotation is taken from a copy made during the war. As I suggest in brackets, he may have made mistakes in the original or these may have cropped into the copy. First, Wilson's own estimate of Nanking's population (150,000 to 200,000) seems inconsistent with 100,000 "people slaughtered in cold blood." All other casualty estimates at the time list executions as a very large percentage of deaths. Thus "thousands" of soldiers (with the *s*) executed in a total death toll of "10,000" (not 100,000) makes sense here. His source is obviously the RSS, either directly or through fellow IC members, which at first estimated a total of 40,000 bodies, although its original burial figure seems to have been about 32,000.

We also have a U.S. military attaché report from China dated June 1938, reports sent to the United States ambassador in Hankow by James Espy, and two reports sent to the German embassy, one by Rabe, the other an anonymous "Secret Report" (see table 13). The United States military attaché noted that "a reliable foreign investigator" calculated the death toll to be 41,000. Again the source must be the RSS, perhaps through Bates or Smythe. Espy's report, presumably based on data supplied by the IC, estimated that "well over" 20,000 Chinese had been executed. As noted above, in his report to the German embassy, Rabe estimated that, as of mid-January (by which time the large-scale executions were over), "thousands of innocent civilians" had been killed. The "Secret Report" by a German eyewitness sent to Berlin from Hankow said that, as of mid-January "the Japanese [had] shot dead at least 5,000 men."[45] I believe these men were executed soldiers who had been captured within the NSZ, and that this account does not include plainclothes soldiers captured and executed outside the city. As with the Kröger report, then, this figure provides an estimate only for those captured within the NSZ and subsequently executed, not for the total number of executions.

The records of various societies other than the RSS that claimed to have done burial work do not date from the time of the Atrocity. Instead, postwar Chinese government officials in the KMT produced these for the Nanking and Tokyo military tribunals as evidence of Japanese war crimes. Indeed, one such society in question, the Ch'ung-shan t'ang, may have totally fabricated its 112,266 burials. Hence, extreme care must be used in examining these postwar statistics, and in many cases these must be rejected as spurious. All primary sources dating from the time of the Atrocity mention a single organization involved in burials, the RSS, which after the war claimed to have buried 43,071 bodies. Thus an examination of RSS records, which historians accept as reasonably accurate, helps us draw an objective picture of burials in and around Nanking. In addition to other limitations noted in the next section, we must note that the RSS contracted work out, and statistics from those organizations appear in its records as well. Thus if we calculate figures for all such subcontractors, plus those for the RSS, as some writers do, multiple-counting will result. By checking original RSS documents against other contemporaneous sources, I found strong evidence that the RSS actually buried 17,500 bodies plus or minus 2,500; and, also that the original burial figures were to the tune of about 32,000.

Although not conclusive, this figure is a basis to estimate the minimum number of people killed at Nanking. However, I emphasize, the civilian death toll or number of Atrocity "victims" in the Atrocity is a separate matter because, in addition to persons executed by the Japanese, the 17,500 bodies plus or minus 2,500 that the RRS buried included many groups of Chinese "nonvictims." They included: (1) soldiers killed in action; (2) soldiers and civilians who died of wounds, infections, or disease; (3) retreating soldiers shot and killed by KMT "Supervising Units"; (4) civilians caught in cross-fires; (5) civilians killed by defeated Chinese troops as they desperately sought civilian clothes; and (6) at least some of the bodies of the thousands of people who attempted to swim across the Yangtze to escape from the Japanese.[46] In short, despite their undoubted value as historical materials, RSS burial records shed little light on the key issue of what percentage of the corpses it claimed to have buried were indeed civilian "massacre victims."

As Higashinakano Osamichi (Shûdô) stresses, the estimate of 40,000 deaths in Bates's 25 January memo—quoted in Timperley's *What War Means*—is a key issue that we must address. This large estimate was based on RSS figures and is one main basis for claims that 40,000 Chinese died in and around Nanking. In his original memo, Bates describes how groups of Chinese were led away to be executed and states: "Other incidents involved larger numbers of men than did this one. *Evidences from burials indicate that close to 40,000 unarmed persons were killed within and near the walls of Nanking, of whom some 30% had never been soldiers.* My special interest in these circumstances is twofold" (italics added).

To repeat, the RSS buried all Chinese dead, including soldiers who died in combat, so the suggestion here that all of the dead had been unarmed is misleading. But the main problem is that Bates printed this memo five times, noted in table 11 as Bates 1, Bates 2, Bates 3, Bates 4, and Bates 5. Bates 1 appeared in Timperley's *What War Means*. In *all other* four publications, the memo is reprinted except for the italicized sentence. Why was this italicized sentence—the only one in which Bates estimates this high a total death toll—omitted? Higashinakano holds that Bates "withdrew" his original accusation of 25 January that a massacre of 40,000 occurred at Nanking, as quoted in

Table 5.11. Bates on the Death Toll[47]

	Source	Date	Number
Bates 1	Timperley, *What War Means*	1938 (March)	40,000
Bates 2	Hsü ed., *The War Conduct of the Japanese*	1938 (April)	omitted
Bates 3	Hsü ed., *A Digest of Japanese War Conduct*	1939 (January)	omitted
Bates 4	*Chinese Yearbook 1938–39*	1939 (March)	omitted
Bates 5	Hsü ed., *Documents of the Nanking Safety Zone*	1939 (May)	omitted

What War Means. According to Higashinakano, Bates 2, Bates 3, and Bates 5 were published in works edited by Hsü Shuhsi. As an official of the KMT government, Hsü would not have published documents that contradicted its position on Nanking at that time. Higashinakano also argues that Bates 4 appeared in the *Chinese Yearbook,* another official KMT periodical, which would not print information that belied the official Chinese position.[48]

We may or may not accept Higashinakano's explanation for Bates's downward revision as representing the official Chinese statistical viewpoint at that time. But a downward revision does seem to have taken place, and its timing matched that of Smythe, Rabe, and the IC; all of them lowered figures by April 1938. Why the Westerners revised their estimates of the Chinese death toll downward is a mystery, but perhaps it is related to the completion of RSS burial efforts in early 1938, about which IC members had inside information.

Bates's figure of 40,000—as quoted by Timperley in *What War Means*—and perhaps his estimate of 37,000 to 42,000 deaths on 21 March are important for another reason. These figures appear to be the basis for Edgar Snow's claim in *The Battle for Asia* (1941) that the Japanese killed at least 42,000 people in and around Nanking. However, Snow inverts Bates's breakdown, claiming that "a large percentage" of those killed were "women and children." This manipulation by Snow was one of the first in a long history of factual distortions about Chinese casualties in the Nanking Atrocity. But it pales in comparison with that by Agnes Smedley in the *Battle Hymn of China* (1943). There, she argued that "Hundreds of severely wounded soldiers who could not be evacuated had been left in Nanking in the care of Chinese doctors and nurses ... when the Japanese Army occupied the city, they not only put to the sword some two hundred thousand civilians and unarmed soldiers, but fell upon the hospitals, slaughtering the wounded, the doctors, and the nurses."[49] Smedley lists no source for this information and at that time was with the Communist Eighth Route Army, far from Nanking.

Smedley's invective is important in that, far more than Timperley or Snow, she marks the start of a political campaign to propagandize the Atrocity, and of a concerted push to inflate the death toll. The only medical staff who remained in Nanking appear to have been two Americans, Wilson and Clifford Trimmer, two Chinese doctors, and several nurses who were not relieved until early June 1938.[50] All but one of the 500 wounded Chinese soldiers left in Nanking seem to have survived the occupation or to have died despite Japanese medical care. There is no documented account of any nurse being killed at Nanking, or of the Japanese slaughtering wounded patients there. Smedley's estimated death toll of 200,000 "civilians and unarmed soldiers" is totally unacceptable in that Nanking's entire civilian population at the time was 200,000 to 250,000 at most.

The location of bodies may provide a rough estimate of civilian deaths. Before Nanking fell, Chinese authorities moved civilians from surrounding

Table 5.12. Bodies Buried Inside Nanking by the RSS[51]

	Number of Bodies			
Date	*Men*	*Women*	*Children*	*Total*
22 Dec.	129			129
26 Jan.	124	1		125
2 Feb.	17	2		19
6 Feb.	49			49
7 Feb.	149		2	151
11 Feb.	16		4	20
14 Feb.	107	2		109
19 Feb.	650	2	20	672
20 Feb.	154			154
22 Feb.	29	1		30
27 Feb.	337			337
Total	1,759	8	26	1,793

areas into the city. They then torched suburbs outside the walls to deny the invaders cover and moved civilians into the NSZ. Thus, I would argue, most if not all bodies found outside the city walls were of Chinese soldiers, and even those found within the walls outside the NSZ were not civilians. The RSS claimed to have buried about 1,800 bodies inside the walls. Large numbers of Chinese men—at least 5,000 and perhaps even 9,000—were rounded up and executed by the Japanese Seventh and Sixteenth divisions clearing the NSZ from 13 December until 5 January. The total number of deaths within the city walls, or of people led from the NSZ for execution outside the city, is thus 5,700 at a minimum to 10,800 at a maximum. Theoretically, all or none of them could have been civilians, but I believe that some must have been civilians. If, for the sake of argument, we assume that 50 percent of those killed inside the walls were civilians, then the civilian death toll was 2,850 to 5,400. I believe that the number of bodies recovered from the city was 700 to 1,000 *at a minimum*, and that the number executed was at least 5,000. Again, assuming that half of them were civilians, this would indicate a minimum civilian death toll of 2,850 to 3,000. Although highly speculative, these figures seem to confirm much of what is recorded in other sources.

Quantitative Analysis

Among the various estimates of civilian deaths that appear in primary sources, Bates's is the most problematic because he appears to have withdrawn it, as Higashinakano suggests. Rabe 2 and the RSS figures must be treated with caution too. Internal evidence suggests that numbers were later added to the RSS figures, so these must be juxtaposed against other sources of the time unless an original RSS document turns up. A problem with some of these estimates is that all deaths—including those in battle as well as from drowning, friendly fire, legal and illegal executions, and civilians caught in crossfire—are lumped into a single figure. Even when Chinese "civilians" are explicitly listed as such in a certain body count, it would have been very difficult for the recorder to distinguish between the corpses of civilians, ex-soldiers in civilian clothes, and plainclothes soldiers.

The results of my analysis are presented in table 13, in chronological order of the documents. Raw data in the documents are in the third column. In the fourth column, I made "Revised Estimates" based on four admittedly contestable assumptions: (1) The vague figure "thousands" used by Westerners should be estimated at 5,000. (2) Of those deaths specified as "civilians" when based on a body count, half at most were in fact civilians and the other half were military personnel. (3) Following Bates, of all deaths unspecified as to civilians or military personnel, one-third at most were in fact civilians. (4) The Japanese army was fairly competent in identifying plainclothes soldiers in the NSZ, although there is very little data on this last point. My revised estimates will *not* lower the total number of estimated deaths, these only help us to conclude what percentage of those deaths may have been civilians; but these revised estimates also will produce an inflated number of civilian casualties and thereby reduce estimates of military deaths.

The IC's 55 civilian deaths were based on verified reports, so I accept these but revise the number to fifty-four because at least one of the executions was deemed "legitimate." Based on the assumptions listed above, I revise McCallum's "thousands to 10,000" to 1,666 to 3,333 civilians; in Magee 2, I revise his "thousands" to 5,000 civilians, and in Magee 1 and Magee 3, I revise the "20,000" executed to 6,666. The "Secret Report" to the German embassy lists "5,000 executed" as plainclothes soldiers, but they included some civilians, so I revise the estimate to 2,500 civilians. The source for Rabe 1, "thousands" of civilian casualties, was perhaps Smythe, who did try to distinguish between military personnel and civilians; so I accept it as it is. I am not sure of the source for Rabe 2, "hundreds, perhaps thousands." The "hundreds" may refer to genuine RSS figures for bodies collected in the city, or it may be based on data that Vautrin collected, but Rabe's source for "thousands" was again perhaps Smythe. Thus, I revised Rabe 2 to the minimum figure of about 700 bodies that the RSS collected and buried inside the city walls (a figure that roughly matches Vautrin), and the 6,750 casualties given by Smythe. Figures cited in Timperley 1 and Timperley 2 are from Bates, who had access to original RSS figures that are reasonably accurate. But Bates in Timperley 1 gives only a total number of bodies, so I assume that one-third were civilians. In Timperley 2, Bates almost certainly viewed the "40,000" bodies of plain-

Table 5.13. The Civilian Death Toll[52]

Source	Date	Estimated Number of Casualties	Revised Estimate
IC 1	15 Dec. 1937 – 7 Feb. 1938	55	54
Magee 1	19 December	20,000	6,666
McCallum	29 December 1937	thousands [5,000]–10,000	1,666 – 3,333
Magee 2	5 January 1938	thousands of civilians [5,000]	5,000
Bates (Timperley 1)	10 January	more than 10,000 (soldiers and civilians)	3,330
Magee 3	11 January 1938	20,000	6,666
Secret Report to German Embassy	13 January 1938	5,000 executed	2,500
Kröger's report	13 January 1938	5,000 executed	2,500
Rabe 1 (Embassy Report)	14 January 1938	thousands of civilians [5,000]	thousands [2,500]
Forster	14 January 1938	thousands of men [5,000]	1,666
Espy's Report	24 January 1938	20,000 executed	6,666
Bates (Timperley 2)	25 January 1938	40,000, of which 12,000 civilians	6,000
Rabe 2 (Letter)	28 January 1938	hundreds, perhaps thousands	700 – 6,750
Wilson (Letter)	7 March 1938	100,000 [10,000?]	[3,330?]
Smythe 1	21 March 1938	40,000 (30% civilians)	6,000
Bates 1	21 March 1938	37,000 – 42,000 (12,000 civilians)	6,000
Vautrin	26 March 1938	More than 700 men missing	738
IC 2	May 1938	thousands (murdered, imprisoned, abducted)	thousands [2,500]
US Military attaché report	June 1938	41,000	13,333
Rabe 3 (Report to Hitler)	June 1938	50,000 – 60,000 [23,000 – 33,000]	7,600 – 11,000
Smythe 2	August 1938	3,400 – 6,750	3,400 – 6,750
Smythe 3	August 1938	12,000 civilians	6,000
Smythe 4	October 1938	10,000 civilians	5,000
Bates 2	November 1938	12,000 civilians	6,000
Red Swastika Society	1946?	43,071 [17,500]	5,800

clothes soldiers as civilians, so I assume half of them were in fact ex-soldiers, and revise the figure to 6,000 civilians. The same holds for Smythe 1. The IC 2 estimate of "thousands murdered, imprisoned, or abducted" may be based on Smythe 2 and echoes Rabe 1, so I assume that up to 5,000 may have been murdered; of those, 2,500 or half, were civilians.

Rabe 3, his "Report to Hitler," is more problematic. As just noted, the original estimate of 50,000 to 60,000 includes 30,000 bodies that seem in fact to have been 3,000; so I subtract 27,000 to revise his original estimate to 23,000–33,000. This figure was for all bodies, including persons killed in battle, so I assume that *at most* one-third could be civilians and subtract 33.3 percent, but this leaves only 15,000 to 22,000 for military casualties, which is too low; so I revise the estimate of civilian casualties upward to one-half, to get 7,600 to 11,000 by subtracting 50 percent. I accept Smythe 2 verbatim based on his "City Survey" and assume that all of those "taken away" may have been executed. However, I assume that half of Smythe 3, based on a body count, were in fact Chinese soldiers in civilian clothes; so I reduce "12,000" by fifty percent to get an estimate of 6,000 civilians. Smythe 4, "10,000 civilians," is based on an examination and count of bodies, so I halve it to 5,000.

Finally, almost a decade after the Atrocity, the RSS claimed that it had disposed of 43,071 bodies. Close examination of various other sources shows that this number was almost certainly inflated; the figure 17,500 plus or minus 2500 is more accurate. Once more, I assume that *at most* one-third were civilians, but again this leaves only 10,000 to 10,700 military casualties, which is too low; so I revise the RSS figure for civilian casualties to 5,800. Another method to calculate the death toll is to add up the specific figures and divide by the number of figures to get an average. This gives an estimate of 4,779 to 5,003, or rounded off to 4,800 to 5,000.[53] If we want to compare this with the figure derived from Smythe's sampling survey, we should recalculate without Smythe 2, which gives 4,762. But the difference is too small to be significant.

Conclusion

I have examined primary sources left by Westerners within a narrowly limited geographic and temporal definition of "Nanking" inherent in those sources; that is, the walled city and its immediate environs from before the city fell in mid-December through the 6–7 week Japanese occupation ending in early-February. I found that the city's population was about 200,000 on the eve of its fall, and that it rose to about 250,000 in late-December to mid-January. Smythe's "City Survey" and Japanese registration figures, in particular, allowed me to estimate the population at roughly 224,500 from 24 December to 5

January. Western estimates of the civilian death toll at that time are all within a fairly narrow range. The one based on Smythe's sampling survey—3,400 killed and 4,200 conscripted for labor—and those derived from other data that he provides—1,300 to 5,000 killed—together provide a solid basis on which to compare other estimates of the death toll. I suggest that several Westerners—Rabe, Smythe, the IC, and most of all Bates—apparently revised their estimates downward early in 1938. Furthermore, I found that 4,800 to 5,000 seems to be reasonably accurate for the range of Chinese civilian deaths attested to by Westerners, and that range is confirmed by examining the location of corpses. In the last analysis, the best possible estimate range of civilians deaths, supported by all of the Western primary documents examined, is a low of 3400 to a high of 5000.

However, a fuller estimate and more meaningful conclusions must consider factors *other than* demography and the civilian victims; that is to say, in addition, how many military personnel, ex-soldiers, and surrendered soldiers were illegally killed and thus *massacred*—a term replete with politically laden definitions. At least up to 5,000 civilians were massacred in any case. I submit these findings as a starting point for further research that may well lead to higher figures and to a more accurate historical reconstruction of the Nanking Atrocity as a whole.

Notes

1. Smythe, *War Damage in the Nanking Area*, pp. 4 and 17; Rabe, *Good Man of Nanking*, p. 51.
2. See Suzuki, *Shin "Nankin daigyakusatsu" no maboroshi*, pp. 291–92.
3. Adapted from Itakura, *Hontô wa kô datta: Nankin jiken*, p. 56. In addition, statistics for "Registration" by "Japanese authorities" are from Inoue, ed., *Kachû senbu kôsaku shiryô*, pp. 148–69.
4. Rabe in Timperley, ed., *What War Means*, p. 254; Rabe, in Hsü, ed., *Documents of the Nanking Safety Zone*, p. 84.
5. Smythe, *War Damage in the Nanking Area*, footnote to Table 1.
6. Rabe, *Good Man of Nanking*, p. 130.
7. Ibid., p. 135.
8. Ibid., p. 39.
9. Ibid., p. 131.
10. Smythe, "What Happened in Nanking," p. 381.
11. Italics added; in Hsü, ed., *Documents on the Nanking Safety Zone*, pp. 95–96.
12. In Zhang, ed., *Eyewitnesses to Massacre*, p. 414; also see pp. 417 and 432.
13. Hata, "Nanking Atrocities," p. 51.
14. See reports by Epsy cited in Pritchard and Zaide, eds., *The Tokyo War Crimes Trials*, vol. 2, p. 4568 and Allison, "Nankin no jôkyô," p. 108.
15. Rabe, "Report from the German Foreign Office in China to the German Foreign Office in Berlin," in Pritchard and Zaide, eds., *Tokyo War Crimes Trials*, vol. 2, pp. 4593–94; for other relevant documents sent to the German embassy, see Ishida, ed., *Shiryô Doitsu gaikôkan no mita Nankin jiken*, pp. 52 and 111.
16. See Wilson, in Brook, ed., *Documents on the Rape of Nanking*, p. 210; and Askew, "Defending Nanking," pp. 148–73.

17. There were cases such as apartments where more than one family lived at a single address.
18. Kitamura, "GMD [KMT] International Propaganda Division."
19. Compiled from appendices in Smythe, *War Damage in the Nanking Area.*
20. Bates, Forward, to Smythe, *War Damage in the Nanking Area*, p. ii.
21. From Table 2 in appendexes of Smythe, *War Damage in the Nanking Area.*
22. Chang, *Rape of Nanking*, p. 100.
23. Hata, *Nankin jiken*, p. 179.
24. In Brook, ed., *Documents on the Rape of Nanking*, p. 11.
25. Yamamoto, *Nanking*, p. 128; Itakura, *Hontô wa kô datta*, p. 55.
26. See Suzuki, *Shin "Nankin daigyakusatsu" no kenkyû*, pp. 291–92; also, Kitamura, "GMD [KMT] International Propaganda Division."
27. Adapted from Itakura, *Hontô wa kô datta: Nankin jiken*, p. 55.
28. Timperely, ed., *What War Means*, p. 59.
29. Ibid., pp. 17, and 60–61.
30. From Table 4 in appendexes of Smythe, *War Damage in the Nanking Area.*
31. Smythe, *War Damage in the Nanking Area*, p. 6.
32. Ibid., p. 8, note 1.
33. Smythe, *War Damage in the Nanking Area*, p. 5.
34. Compiled from Smythe, "Composition of the Chinese Family," p. 382; and Table 2 in appendexes of Smythe, *War Damage in the Nanking Area.*
35. These RSS figures show 1,759 male, 8 female, and 26 child corpses inside the walls; and 41,183 male, 75 female, and 20 child corpses outside the walls.
36. See also, Bloch, "Chinese Population Problems," pp. 179–80.
37. Rabe, "Reports from the German Foreign Office in China to the German Foreign Office in Berlin," in Pritchard and Zaide, eds., *Tokyo War Crimes Trials*, p. 4594.
38. Rabe, "Hitoraa e no jôshinsho," p. 317; Rabe, *Good Man of Nanking*, p. 212.
39. Magee, in Zhang, ed., *Eyewitnesses to Massacre*, pp. 172 and 186; McCallum, in ibid., p. 231; Forster, in ibid., pp. 124 and 152; Durdin, in *New York Times*, 9 January 1938; Kröger, in Rabe, *Good Man of Nanking*, p. 144.
40. Smythe, in Zhang, ed., *Eyewitnesses to Massacre*, p. 315; Smythe, "What Happened in Nanking or the Situation in the Occupied Territory in China, p. 382.
41. Vautrin, in Zhang, ed., *Eyewitnesses to Massacre*, pp. 342 and 35.
42. Bates, "Notes on German Atrocities in Belgium," cited in Yamamoto, *Nanking*, p. 189, note 74; also, Bates, in Zhang, ed., *Eyewitnesses to Massacre*, p. 42.
43. In Smalley, ed., *American Missionary Eyewitnesses to the Nanking Massacre*, p. 12.
44. Wilson, in Brook, ed., *Documents of the Rape of Nanking*, pp. 253–54.
45. Reports cited in Yamamoto, *Nanking*, pp. 112 and 126, note 104; in Pritchard and Zaide, eds., *Tokyo War Crimes Trial*, pp. 4569, 4594, and 4601.
46. "Thousands, tens of thousands" of people died attempting to swin across the Yangtze; see Kasahara, *Nankin jiken*, p. 137.
47. From Higashinakano, *"Nankin gyakusatsu" no tettei kenshô*, p. 328.
48. Ibid., p. 339.
49. Snow, *Battle for Asia*, p. 57; Smedley, *Battle Hymn of China*, p. 151.
50. Smalley, ed., *American Missionary Eyewitnesses to the Nanking Massacre*, pp. 7 and 15.
51. Yamamoto, *Nanking*, p. 295, based on Shih-chieh Hung-wan-tsu-hui Nan-ching fen-hui chiu-chi-tui yen-mai-tsu yen-mai shih-t'i chu-shu t'ung-chi-piao.
52. The Secret Report to the German embassy was completed on 13 January, but not forwarded to Berlin until 16 February. Espy's report was prepared between 15 and 24 January, but not mailed until 2 February.
53. Magee 1 (6,666) + McCallum (2,500) + Magee 2 (5,000) + Bates (in Timperley 1) (3,330) + Secret Report (2,500) + Kröger Report (2,500) + Rabe 1 (2,500) + Forster (1,666) + Espy

(6,666) +Bates (in Timperley 2) (6,000) + Rabe 2 (3,725) + Smythe 1 (6000) + Vautrin (738) + IC 2 (2500) + Military Attaché Report (13,333) + Rabe 3 (9300) + Smythe 2 (5,075) + Smythe 4 (5,000) + RSS (5,800) ÷ 19 = 4,779. If Vautrin is left out, this figure becomes 5003. Cases where the same author has repeated exactly the same figure have been used once only. I have left out both IC 1 (54) and Wilson (100,000), as both would serve to skew the data.

6

THE NANKING 100-MAN KILLING CONTEST DEBATE, 1971–75[1]

Bob Tadashi Wakabayashi

In 1967, three decades after the event, Hora Tomio (1906–2000) published a 118-page essay on the "Nanking Incident," as he then called it. This was historiographically epoch-making. In previous survey histories there had been passing references to the Nanking Atrocity, but not until 1967 did a professional Japanese historian make an in-depth empirical study. Hora spent his teaching career at the private Waseda University, not an elite national school like the University of Tokyo. His publisher, Jinbutsu ôraisha, marketed popular titles for history buffs; it lacked the scholarly snob appeal of an Iwanami shoten. In short, Japanese historians placed scant value on Nanking as a research topic at that time. What roused them from this apathy was a 1971–75 debate about a 100-man killing contest that reputedly occurred during the Atrocity. The men who provoked this debate lacked high academic credentials or university affiliations. They were Honda Katsuichi (1932–), then a reporter for the liberal *Asahi shinbun*, a nationwide daily with a circulation of eight million at that time, and a convert to Islam; Yamamoto Shichihei (1921–91), a former imperial army officer posing as a Jew under the pseudonym Isaiah Ben-Dasan; and Imai Akio (1929–2003), a freelance writer using the nom de plume Suzuki Akira. Yamamoto and Suzuki wrote in the monthly *Shokun!*, which was affiliated with the conservative Bungei shunjû media group.

This debate began over the factuality of one incident, as disputed by left- and right-wing factions, and grew into a major ongoing controversy about the entire Nanking Atrocity. Both sides depict this historiographic rumble along partisan lines, and neither concedes defeat.[2] The left-wing faction holds and continues to hold that enormous war crimes took place at Nanking. The right-wing faction later divided into deniers, who insist that there was no Atrocity worthy of the name, and minimalists, who concede that minor or mid-scale crimes occurred at Nanking as in any war. Deniers and minimalists belong to a broad movement toward "conservative revisionism" led by academics, critics of social and political affairs *(hyôronka)*, journalists, and politicians. As my label implies, conservative revisionists seek to break what they see as a left-wing stranglehold on the historical consensus in Japan and thereby foster national pride by refuting shameful past events such as the Nanking Atrocity and other heinous war crimes.

The 1971–75 debate is significant for several reasons. It raised key prototypical issues still in dispute among historians of Nanking such as how, or whether, to distinguish the legitimate killing of combatants and guerrillas from the massacre of noncombatants and prisoners of war (POWs). Since the 1980s, when victim counts took on political import, variables of this sort have served to tilt the abacus as needed. The debate also presaged a flowering of scholarship on modern and contemporary Japan, as typified by Hora's own work. A pre-Meiji historian before 1967, he grew into one of Japan's leading expert on Nanking.[3] Replying to sustained attacks by critics, Hora wrote four books and many articles on the topic. In March 1984, he helped form a Society to Study the Nanking Incident (Nankin ken) whose members went on to produce scores of publications, as discussed by Kimura Takuji in chapter 15. They also edited major document collections to make Chinese and Western as well as Japanese sources accessible to interested readers in Japan. Similar publication efforts did not begin in the West until the late 1990s.

Finally, a decade *before* Chinese and Korean criticism about Japan's war guilt, the 1971–75 debate raised two key issues from the Japanese perspective. One is *sensô sekinin*: the culpability, responsibility, or accountability that ordinary Japanese bear for wartime sins. The other is *sengo sekinin:* the compounded culpability that stems from having evaded that culpability until today. For left-wing historians, *sensô sekinin* imputed meaning to the war, defined as a fifteen-year case of imperialist aggression mainly against Asians from 1931 to 1945. For human rights activists, *sengo sekinin* provided rationales to demand that their nation compensate both foreign and domestic victims of that aggression.[4] These ethical issues remain unresolved to this day. Leftists denounce their countrymen for moral sloth and callous greed compared with postwar Germans who, critics claim, have admitted past atrocities and paid foreign victims eighty times more in compensation money.[5] Conservative revisionists retort that young Japanese today live seventy years after Nanking, in a post-bubble age of prolonged recession, brutal restructuring, and burgeoning welfare costs; and, unlike their Chinese or Korean accusers, they have never waged a war of aggression since 1945. Why must they remain culpable for their grandparents' alleged misdeeds? As one minimalist reckons, claims for compensation will come to "at least an average of two million *yen* [about $20,000] per household—enough to keep one child from attending university.... And, if victimization claims are granted as demanded, the figure will be 10 to 100 times higher."[6]

We cannot know how Japanese in the twenty-first century will resolve these culpability issues, many of which first arose in this 1971–75 debate. But as I see it, Honda, Hora, and their leftist allies must admit that, at least as they first depicted it, the killing contest was an "illusion," and in one key sense it was "fabricated" as well. In that sense, they lost this early debate, but it sparked a far larger controversy over the Atrocity as a whole that, on the whole, vindicated their stand, and more importantly, heightened popular awareness of that event. This delayed victory forced postwar Japanese to confront their collective past as butchers, not just as victims, in a war of aggression that began a decade before Pearl Harbor. For such reasons, the debate warrants close examination.

The Contest First Portrayed

In his 1967 essay on Nanking, Hora examined Chinese, Japanese, and Western sources to sift rumor from fact about Japanese war crimes. He noted "two sublieutenants who began a 100-man killing contest at Kuyung,"[7] and quoted the following story from a Chinese Communist Party (CCP) official, as cited in a 1966 book by the journalist Ômori Minoru: "They competed to see who would be first to kill 100 men with military swords. Mukai scored 89 and Noda 78 by the time they reached the suburb of T'angshan, two kilometers from the city. There, they resumed the contest with permission from a superior officer. On reaching Chung-shan-ling [the Dr. Sun Yat-sen Tomb], Mukai had 107 and Noda 105. But neither could prove who killed 100 first, so they extended the contest by setting a new goal of 150."[8]

Hora said he "knew of this contest for a long time."[9] But, to my knowledge, Ômori in 1966 was the first postwar Japanese to write about it. Neither went beyond this thumbnail sketch. Neither related that the International Military Tribunal for the Far East (IMTFE), better known as the Tokyo War Crimes Trials, released Mukai and Noda from Sugamo Prison and extradited them to stand trial and suffer execution as B-class war criminals at the Nanking Military Tribunal (NMT), one of 10 that Chiang Kai-shek's Kuomintang (KMT) regime held. Chinese first learned of this "killing contest" from English-language articles in the *Japan Advertiser* on 7 and 14 December 1937. Harold J. Timperley, an Australian reporter for the *Manchester Guardian,* reprinted these as "Appendix F: The Nanking 'Murder Race'" in his 1938 document collection, *What War Means;* and, further-redacted accounts of the contest appeared in the 1 January 1938 issue of the *China Weekly Review* and other wartime Chinese publications, both Nationalist and Communist. These *Japan Advertiser* articles read:

[7 December 1937.] Sublieutenant Toshiaki Mukai and Sublieutenant Takeshi [*recte:* Tsuyoshi] Noda, both of the Katagiri unit at Kuyung, in a friendly contest to see which of them will first fell 100 Chinese in individual sword combat before the Japanese forces completely occupy Nanking, are well in the final phase of their race, running almost neck to neck. On Sunday when their unit was fighting outside Kuyung, the "score," according to the *Asahi* [*recte: Tokyo nichinichi shinbun*], was Mukai 89, Noda 78.

[14 December 1937.] The winner of the competition between Sublieutenants Toshi-aki Mukai and Iwao [*recte:* Tsuyoshi] Noda to see who would be the first to kill 100 Chinese with his Yamato sword has not been decided, the *Nichinichi* reports from the slopes of Purple Mountain, outside Nanking. Mukai has a score of 106 and his rival has dispatched 105 men, but the two have found it impossible to determine which passed the 100 mark first. Instead of settling it with a discussion, they are going to extend the goal by fifty. Mukai's blade was slightly damaged in the competition. He explained that this was the result of cutting a Chinese in half, helmet and all. The contest was "fun," he declared, and he thought it a good thing that both men had gone over the 100 mark without knowing that the other had done so. Early Saturday morning, when the *Nichinichi* man interviewed the sublieutenant at a point overlooking Dr. Sun Yat-sen's tomb, another Japanese unit set fire to the slopes of Purple Mountain in an attempt to drive out the Chinese troops. The action also smoked out Mukai and his unit, and the men stood idly by while bullets passed overhead. "Not a shot hits me while I am hold-ing this sword on my shoulder," he explained confidently.[10]

The *Japan Advertiser* articles—quoted by Timperley and circulated in China—held that a "murder race" took place between Kuyung and Purple Mountain (Tzuchinshan). These articles would be crucial as evidence in exe-cuting Noda Tsuyoshi (not Takeshi or Iwao) and Mukai Toshiaki for war crimes at the NMT. In works still in print as of July 2006, the late Iris Chang, Erwin Wickert, Jonathan D. Spence, and others cite these articles as historically fac-tual.[11] However, we should note, NMT records state that the defendants were executed for a recreational killing contest held entirely on Purple Mountain. Although both pleaded not guilty, NMT records continue, this "beastly and wicked killing" of innocent noncombatants and POWs was "unprecedented in the modern history of humanity." One defendant, Noda, protested that the contest never even took place. Instead, he said, reporters for the *Tokyo nichi-nichi shinbun*—which ran the original articles later translated and digested in the *Japan Advertiser*—fabricated the story after the other defendant, Mukai, had bragged about these imaginary feats. For his part, Mukai insisted that he never really killed anyone but boasted that he had, hoping the publicity would attract "a better wife" after he returned to Japan.[12]

Hora neither saw these NMT records, nor did he mention "Appendix F" despite citing a Japanese translation of Timperley's book, so he probably did not read the *Japan Advertiser* story before writing his 1967 essay. Actually, he omitted all of these details and devoted less than half a page to the "killing contest," probably because he felt it represented but one minor dimension of the Nanking "Incident"—as he then called the Atrocity. His 118-page essay was the first extended empirical study of Nanking based on Japanese, Chinese, and Western sources to appear anywhere. As with most pioneering works, it had errors; for example, that the alleged killing contest started at Kuyung. Still, left-wing historians such as Ienaga Saburô gave their immediate stamp of approval by citing it as evidence for the Nanking Atrocity in their own works.[13]

Backdrop to the Fray

Hora Tomio's landmark essay did not provoke a debate or inspire more research. Often, it is events in the political realm that spur pundits, and scholars, to take up their cudgels. It was the Vietnam War, after all, that sparked revisionist scholarship in the United States over who started the Cold War. Something like this happened in Japan. *Hyôronka,* or "critics of social and political affairs," kicked off a debate about Nanking in 1971–72, some years after Hora's essay, and it was their agitation that pulled in academic historians. Thus, a brief account of the sociopolitical milieu at the time is needed to place the killing contest debate and ensuing controversy over the Atrocity in historiographic context.[14]

After signing the 1951 San Francisco Peace Treaty, Japan regained sovereignty under the Shôwa emperor—known to Westerners and disrespectful Japanese as Hirohito. But a Mutual Defense Pact, signed at the same time, forced Japan to violate Article IX of its own Constitution and to snuggle into the U.S. orbit during the Cold War. This alignment entailed recognizing Taipei, not Peking. Japan also had to support American wars in Asia by stationing and servicing U.S. armed forces and by selling them weapons and strategic matériel. By 1970–71 the Vietnam War had reached its height, and leftists declared that Japan profited from it through special military-related procurements. The United States was starting to adjust its basic Asian policies to admit the reality of mainland China and its one billion inhabitants. In July 1971, Henry Kissinger secretly went to the People's Republic of China (PRC) and arranged for a visit by President Richard Nixon. Meanwhile, the United States expected and got full Japanese support in a futile attempt to block the PRC's entry into the United Nations in October 1971. Nixon paid his visit in February 1972—again without telling Japanese leaders—and announced that Taiwan was part of the PRC. His bolt from the blue repudiated the very China policy that America had forced Japan to follow since 1952. This was humiliating for the pro-Taipei Liberal Democratic Party (LDP) regime of Satô Eisaku who had stoutly resisted pressure from business and industrial circles to normalize relations with Peking. Unable to do this now-required about-face, Satô stepped down in June 1972 after claiming credit for regaining Okinawa—an event that he touted as ending the war for Japan. Tanaka Kakuei's regime began normalization with the PRC. He signed a joint communiqué in September that included an official apology for the war: "Japan keenly feels culpability and remorse for having caused grave injury to the Chinese people," and in the same month Hirohito began a 7-nation goodwill tour of Europe as Japan's titular head of state.

These achievements did seem to mark an end to the war for many Japanese, but other events at the time betrayed their sense of closure. In November 1970, Mishima Yukio launched an uprising at Japanese "army" headquarters; when it failed, he cut open his stomach. In February 1972, student radicals fought a pitched battle with police on Mt. Asama. The leaders went down fighting and murdered fourteen followers to keep them from surrendering. This bloody clash presaged over 300 more battles between rival student sects in the next two years. In May 1972, the Japanese Red Army Faction launched a suicide raid on Tel Aviv's Lod Airport. Perhaps most unsettling of all, three imperial army men were found to be still at war: Yokoi Shôîchi, Kozuka Kinshichi, and Onoda Hirô. Yokoi gave up in January 1972, but apologized to his commander in chief Hirohito for failing to perform his duty in full and proclaimed, "I am ashamed to have come back alive." Kozuka and Onoda exchanged gunfire with Philippine police in October 1972. Kozuka died in action; Onoda fled to the jungle and refused to give up until March 1974 when ordered by his former commanding officer. These events suggested that emperor-state militarism was alive and well. Almost as if in response, Chinese leaders chose to slow down normalization with a nation whose emperor had ordered massive invasions of their soil from 1931 to 1945. PRC officials said repeatedly that only Japanese militarists were culpable for the war; the Japanese people, like the Chinese people, were victims. But despite Tanaka's official apology in 1972 and further efforts at rapprochement, the PRC did not conclude a formal peace treaty with Japan for another six years.

In 1970–72, four issues dominated the media in this highly agitated situation. First, aside from disputing Hirohito's legal position as head of state, leftists censured his goodwill tour of Europe. Instead, they railed, he first should have shown goodwill to Asian peoples such as the Chinese and Koreans who suffered the most from his imperialist aggression and were shut out of postwar settlements. Second, leftists also criticized the LDP's use of him as a diplomatic tool to divert criticism of policies at home. Third, they reviled the lingering effects of Tôjô Hideki's 1941 *Senjinkun,* which enjoined death before the disgrace of surrender. Yokoi, Kozuka, and Onoda knew the war was over but kept on fighting it anyway. Even the young Mishima was enthralled with the samurai sword and *bushidô,* the warrior ethos on which *Senjinkun* was based. Fourth, all of this had implications for Sino-Japanese relations. What did the Chinese really mean by setting militarists apart from ordinary Japanese people? Did the PRC's refusal to sign a peace treaty signify genuine fears that Japan still embraced or was reviving militarism? Just what was needed to achieve friendly relations with the one billion Chinese living next door? Wartime Japanese soldiers may have committed atrocities, but how many apologies would it take to show that the postwar Japanese had repudiated their past? Or, were apologies really called for?

Round 1: Whose Culpability?

Political and diplomatic concerns of this type provoked the 100-man killing contest debate. It did not arise from idle curiosity or from a quest for historical veracity. The first salvo came from a reporter, Honda Katsuichi, of the *Asahi shinbun.* He toured the PRC for forty days in 1971 to interview victims of Japanese aggression, and published gut-wrenching reports accompanied by photographs in this newspaper from August to December. This was a tour de force in investigative reporting. It exposed in graphic detail fellow Japanese who perpetrated hideous atrocities. More than anyone else, Honda forced Japan to confront Nanking as an ethical issue for the first time since the IMTFE. In 1972 he republished these reports in *Chûgoku no Nihongun* (The Japanese army in China) and in *Chûgoku no tabi* (Travels in China). The latter became a best-seller and appeared in paperback. A Chinese translation came out in 1972, but Honda had a negligible impact elsewhere because his writings on Nanking were not translated into English until 1999.[15]

One of the 17 chapters in *Chûgoku no tabi* deals with Nanking. In it, Chiang Ken-fu, a CCP member and local official, described a 100-man killing contest that he had picked up from an eyewitness to the event, Wu Chang-te, who had testified at the IMTFE. Wu's account, as Chiang conveyed it, appeared in the *Asahi shinbun* on 5 November 1971:

> "This famous episode was also reported in Japan at the time [1937]." Chiang then described a 100-man killing contest by two Japanese soldiers. A superior officer egged on two sublieutenants, "A" and "B," into playing a game, saying, "I'll give a prize to the one who is first to kill 100 Chinese on the ten-kilometer route from Kuyung to T'angshan outside Nanking." The two began this game which ended with a score of eightynine for "A" and 78 for "B." On reaching T'angshan, the superior officer issued another order: "Try killing another 100 on the 15-kilometer route from T'angshan to Purple Mountain [Tzuchinshan]." It ended in a score of "A" 106, "B" 105. This time they did reach that goal, but the superior officer said, "You guys still can't tell me who did it first; so start over again. This time, kill 150 on the eight-kilometer route from Purple Mountain to Nanking." Chiang added that this last leg took them through a heavily populated area close to the city, so it was very likely that they reached their goal; but the result was unclear.[16]

Honda labeled this a "game" and did not state the type of weapon that the two officers used. He called them "A" and "B" in the *Asahi shinbun* article, and

"M" and "N" in *Chûgoku no tabi*. Honda's reporting carried a clear ideological slant, but he was not critical only of Japan; he declared that "the US army
in Vietnam commits far more frequent and hideous atrocities than did the
Japanese army [in China]."[17] Whether writing about Vietnamese peasants, U.S.
blacks, North American aboriginals, or Chinese at Nanking, he claimed to speak
up for "the side that got killed" because their story had been muffled by "the
side that did the killing."

Honda's point was that the truth about Japanese aggression in China was
suppressed for over forty years, first by the emperor state itself, and later by
Americans who forced a Cold War policy of hostility to the PRC on Japan.
This is why Japanese in 1971 did not know or had forgotten about what they
did in 1937. Self-styled "progressive men of culture" waxed eloquent about
pacifism in the media, but did so from a narrow sense of Japanese wartime
victimization. The U.S. volte-face on China now created a chance to right
those wrongs. Journalists must admit their past and present lies, but even the
most "progressive" went only halfway. They praised the U.S. media for exposing My Lai and other atrocities in Vietnam; now they had a duty to atone
for earlier sins by exposing the war crimes they refused to report four decades
before. Militarism and aggression were not abstract ideas for the Chinese;
these stood for the rape and murder of loved ones. Postwar Japanese had to feel
that pain, which had not abated with time. If not, they could never achieve
peace and friendship with the Chinese people or comprehend PRC charges
that emperor-state militarism was reviving.[18]

Honda censured the media for evading culpability toward China before
and after 1945. His aim in reporting events like the 100-man killing contest
was to show how Chinese victims perceived Japanese militarism. The precise
accuracy of their victim counts and of their historical memory did not overly
concern him. Thus, in rebutting objections by a skeptical Isaiah Ben-Dasan,
he snarled, "His reasoning makes me puke. If killing 100 was not mathe-
matically possible, maybe we should experiment to see if killing fifty was."[19]
Retelling Japanese victimization was not part of Honda's aim. That side of the
ledger was more than filled in by wartime and postwar accounts like those
that described the Chinese massacre of Japanese civilians at Tungchou in July
1937, before the outbreak of full-scale Sino-Japanese hostilities. Yet Honda's
attitude seemed cavalier to many Japanese—not all of them closet chauvin-
ists—who felt that journalists should get their facts and figures straight and
present both sides of the story.

Criticism over the killing contest emerged from a self-proclaimed Jew, Isaiah Ben-Dasan, with help from a Japanese translator, Yamamoto Shichihei.
Many guessed that they were the same person, especially after Ben-Dasan left
the debate in mid-1972 and Yamamoto took up the gauntlet in his stead. A
former sublieutenant himself, Yamamoto had caused the death of Philippine
civilians through inadvertent abuse, had cut off the limb of a dead comrade

with a sword, and had witnessed cannibalism among Japanese troops.[20] Thus he was an untried B-class war crimes suspect, who, unlike Mukai and Noda, chanced to escape trial.

Ben-Dasan drew on a rich store of Judeo-Christian knowledge and values to bash Honda and the *Asahi shinbun* for culture-bound hypocrisy. They preached that "all 100 million Japanese must repent" by saying *gomen nasai* or "forgive me" to the Chinese. As Ben-Dasan argued, the cabinet of Imperial Prince Higashikuni Naruhiko used this same rationale to shift responsibility for losing the war from the emperor state to the Japanese people back in September 1945. Through this bogus logic, individual Japanese absolved themselves of guilt by saying that everyone shared it. The *Asahi shinbun* too was compounding its wartime sins through this clever feint—exactly the opposite of what Honda claimed to be doing. According to Ben-Dasan, Japanese mothers scolded their children for not saying *gomen nasai* or *sumimasen* (I'm sorry) as the obligatory ritual condition to be pardoned, but that was not a true admission of guilt. By Judeo-Christian standards, Honda and the *Asahi shinbun* must do three things. First, they had to back up their words with deeds to ensure that Japan never again embraced militarism or pursued imperialism. Second, having accused "A" and "B" of war crimes, they had a responsibility to identify those men so that justice could be done. Third, the rank-and-file who committed such atrocities did not go to China willingly; they were drafted to fight, kill, and die there. Just as the Chinese said, these troops too were victims of Japanese militarism. So Honda and the *Asahi shinbun* must indict those at the top, those ultimately responsible. In this sly way, Ben-Dasan dared Honda and the *Asahi shinbun* to call Hirohito a war criminal in public.[21]

Honda deigned to retort that such views were banal. He had already presented them in *Enpitsu,* an *Asahi shinbun* company newsletter, and in *Gekkan Shakaitō,* an organ for what was then the Japan Socialist Party. He knew that apologizing was a weighty act overseas; it meant admitting guilt and accepting possible punishment. Personally, he refused to do that to the Chinese. He was a mere lad during the war, had committed no atrocities, and so had no reason to apologize. Moreover, formulaic apologies like Satô Eisaku's or Tanaka Kakuei's did not really atone for Japan's wartime culpability. The Chinese wanted measures to ensure that Japan had renounced wars of aggression, and they wanted those leaders responsible for the last one to face justice at Japanese hands.

Then Honda took Ben-Dasan's bait. He said that Japanese who kept still about Hirohito's war crimes had no business apologizing to China. These war crimes, like those of U.S. presidents in Vietnam, deserved the ultimate punishment. If Ben-Dasan were Chinese, he would clamor for Hirohito's execution as much as for Adolph Eichmann's. Honda lived by that conviction. Privately, he hated Japan's state-run broadcasting network, NHK, for lauding the emperor's 1971 visit to Europe. NHK used the most honorific language for Hirohito, and it signed on and off daily with *Kimigayo,* the extralegal national anthem and paean to Japan's *kimi* or sovereign ruler, which blatantly violated popular sovereignty as stipulated in the democratic postwar constitution. So Honda did not pay the monthly NHK subscription fee and wrote essays telling people how to skirt legal prosecution for this act of defiance.[22] Publicly, too, his journalism enlightened ordinary Japanese about Hirohito's primitive, barbaric nature as a shaman high priest, and about how absurd it was to keep on worshiping him: "Even the natives of New Guinea would scoff" at such backwardness. Honda also explained what the PRC meant by setting militarists apart from the Japanese people. Most Japanese were puzzled because they did not grasp the key Chinese idea of class. What the Chinese wanted, he said, was a class alliance from below that transcended state borders. It would bind "the side that got killed"—the common people in both states. And it would overthrow "the side that did the killing"—postwar regimes headed by war criminals, Hirohito and Chiang Kai-shek.[23]

Ben-Dasan retorted that Honda was evading culpability. Wartime Japanese had excused their sins by invoking the emperor's sanction; now Honda did that by saddling him with blame. Like a two-faced "old wife," he flirted with the next-door neighbor but did nothing to "get rid of" her old man after going back home. He wrote damning essays in obscure journals that few read; that was like cursing behind closed doors. Nor did nonpayment of NHK subscription fees indict Hirohito's war crimes. Honda should put his pen where his mouth was and publish an open letter specifying these as a step toward Hirohito's prosecution. If that were impossible, Honda should at least name names in the killing contest. Ben-Dasan protested the impossibility of such a "game." He reckoned that soldiers march about four kilometers an hour, so the officers' 10-kilometer trek from Kuyung to T'angshan, as Honda described it, would take 2.5 hours. To score eighty-nine kills along that route, 1 killing had to take place every minute and thirty-six seconds—clearly an absurd pace. Moreover, Ben-Dasan asked, just how did each officer tabulate and confirm not only his own, but also his opponent's, score? The term "100-man" was an exaggeration, a Chinese rhetorical flourish for "many"; it could just as well have been "1,000-man."[24] What the Chinese informant had orally conveyed was a legend. If Honda did not perceive its fictiveness, he was inept; if he did and reported it anyway, he was dishonest. It was one thing to report that the Chinese mistook a legend for historical fact, quite another to present it as such.[25]

Thus, Ben-Dasan made the crucial distinction, now often ignored or denied, between fact and memory. In any case, he said, Honda's refusal to name names proved the nonexistence of this event. Honda presumed himself to be the most advanced thinker in Japan. He exuded contempt for his backward countrymen; that is, everyone else, who clung to "absurd and barbaric customs" that "even the natives of New Guinea would scoff at." This slurred not only people in Japan and New Guinea. Jews practiced circumcision, a custom that predated shamanism and seemed even more "absurd and barbaric." Honda's lust to destroy everything he disliked reminded Ben-Dasan of Nazi motives behind the Holocaust.[26] Pedantically gracing his parting shot with citations from ancient Hebrew classics, Ben-Dasan delivered his most telling blow— one that Japanese leftists remain unable to counter to this day. Honda insisted that his cause lay with "the side that got killed," yet disavowed any personal culpability for the war because he was a boy and did not commit any atrocities himself. In response, Ben-Dasan argued that the Chinese feared this line of reasoning more than anything else. According to it, virtually all Japanese soon would belong to the postwar generation and be even less guilty than Honda. In a few years, *no* Japanese would need to bear *any* culpability for wartime deeds because they had not yet been born and were not personally involved. Postwar Japanese could then claim all the assets, yet repudiate all the liabilities, left by their forebears. Ben-Dasan disparaged Honda's attitude by contrasting it with that of West German premier Willy Brandt, who really did take "the side that got killed." Brandt had risked his life by opposing the Nazis in his youth; yet he apologized on his hands and knees to Jews in Warsaw for Nazi atrocities. He accepted responsibility for the guilt of fellow Germans, though wholly innocent himself. Thus Brandt, unlike Honda, earned the moral right to censure fellow nationals who had sinned.[27]

Honda retorted that Hirohito would never answer an open letter, inveighed against discriminatory editorial policies at *Shokun!* (which was true), and invoked a Jewish Studies friend to discredit Ben-Dasan's competence in ancient Hebrew.[28] Finally, Honda disclosed the following original wartime newspaper article—written by Asami Kazuo and Suzuki Jirô in Japanese—which he thought was the ace up his sleeve:

Sublieutenants Mukai Toshiaki and Noda Iwao [*recte:* Tsuyoshi]—those intrepid spirits in the Katagiri Unit—began a novel 100-man killing contest before entering Nanking. On the tenth, they reached a score of 106 to 105 while assaulting Purple Mountain [Tzuchinshan]. At about noon on the tenth, the two faced each other with swords in hand, although these were dented, as might be expected.

Noda: "I've *(ore)* got 105; how about you *(kisama)*?" Mukai: "I've *(ore)* got 106."

Both: "Ah, ha, ha. In the end, we didn't fuss about who reached 100 first. Instead, we agreed, 'Let's call this one a draw. Want to try another 150?' and began a new quest for 150 on the eleventh."

That's how Mukai described their "draw" while rounding up defeated Chinese on Purple Mountain directly overlooking Sun Yat-sen's tomb [Chungshanling] on the afternoon of the 11th. "It's great to find that we both got over 100 before we knew it. My *Seki no magoroku* got dented when I sliced a Chinese in half down the middle, steel helmet and all, like a hollow bamboo stalk *(kara take wari)*. That's when I vowed to donate this sword to your paper when the war ends. At 3 a.m. on the eleventh we used novel tactics to flush out the enemy on Purple Mountain. But I got flushed out myself and stood my ground amid a hail of bullets. With sword in hand, I cursed, 'Who gives a damn!' That nothing hits me is due to this baby," he said, pointing to the *Magoroku* that had just sipped the fresh blood of 106 men. All of this took place while we ignored the curtain of enemy gunfire streaming at us. Photo Caption: "Sublieutenants Noda Iwao [*recte*: Tsuyoshi], (right), and Mukai Toshiaki (left), who had a '100-man killing contest'." (Photo by Special Correspondent Satô [Shin]).[29]

This is the original Japanese-language article, dated 13 December 1937, on which the *Japan Advertiser* English-language digest of 14 December 1937 was based. Having thus named the culprits and cited the original source that damned them, Honda declared that his time was too precious to waste arguing with a juvenile smart aleck. Confident that he had clinched his point, he bade *Shokun!* readers a contemptuous "sayonara" and left the debate.

If Honda was openly abusive, Ben-Dasan satirically couched his derision in deferential language. Neither displayed much charm, but here we should reflect briefly on the importance of their run-in. Ben-Dasan deftly exploited the ruse of a foreign identity to "bash" Japan, and did so for right-wing rather than left-wing causes as is generally true today. In 1972, he chided postwar Japanese by contrasting them with Germans when it came to assuming culpability for the war. He hinted that Hirohito and other Japanese war criminals should be indicted by the Japanese people themselves, as the Germans had tried Nazis. Most telling of all, he accused Honda of siding with Japanese victimizers rather than with Chinese victims. Being a child or not yet being alive in 1937 did not absolve younger Japanese from culpability for war crimes and atrocities at Nanking. Ben-Dasan said, in effect, that children of a felon could not inherit his ill-gained fortune without also owning up to his crimes, at least on a moral plane.

Honda had reason to doubt Ben-Dasan's sincerity. A few years later, this same man—writing as Yamamoto Shichihei—chanted the mantra of right-wing excuses to absolve Hirohito from culpability for the war.[30] Yet in his assumed Jewish persona, Yamamoto ripped apart the cocoon of illusions wherein Japanese leftists took cozy refuge. Unable to refute his arguments, they went on to adopt these as their own—perhaps furtively at times, but unknowingly for the most part. In 1985, for example, Ienaga Saburô held that even generations born after the war bore responsibility for it because they inherited positive legacies left by forebears who committed atrocities.[31] In other words, young Japanese benefited from institutions built by the wartime-to-postwar generation, such as schools, hospitals, and the justice system. Having accepted these assets, they must bear the accompanying liabilities, such as compensating foreign and domestic victims of the war. Likewise, in a 1997 essay on Nanking, Honda reckoned that postwar Germans scored "50 out of 100" whereas Japanese rated "two or three out of 100" when it came to repenting and settling past accounts.[32] Yet another paradox lies in Honda's refusal to say *gomen nasai* (forgive me). That attitude lies at the heart of right-wing thinking about Japan's *non*culpability for the war.[33] Yet Honda's opponents in the later controversy over Nanking—Hata Ikuhiko and even the Kaikôsha army officers—have apologized to the Chinese people.[34]

Round 2: Indicting the Media

For academics, it is the Nuremberg and Tokyo tribunals that first spring to mind when the topic of war crimes trials arises. Those two tribunals were of revolutionary significance in establishing the principle that civilized nations would no longer tolerate A-class crimes against peace and humanity. Nuremberg and Tokyo set the ethical and legal precedent that state leaders who plan and pursue wars of aggression should be punished—even if international law must be applied retroactively to convict them. This precedent had dubious validity to start with, and it has been selectively ignored since then. No U.S. president, for example, ever stood trial for A-class war crimes in Indochina. Therein lies much of the interest for academics.

By contrast, the trials that jolted most ordinary postwar Japanese people were those for conventional B-class war crimes held at forty-nine sites in Asia and the Pacific. Many Japanese recall the drama, *Watashi wa kai ni naritai* (I want to be reborn as a shell-fish) that depicts an enlisted man unjustly charged and executed at the Yokohama tribunal for abusing Allied POWs. If international law had been consistently applied, Yamamoto Shichihei would have been a B-class war criminal. He never appeared in court. But some 5,700 other Japanese did; and well over 900 of them received the death sentence, often after what can only be called travesties of justice.[35] The execution of almost 1000 rank-and-file convicts had a greater impact on far more Japanese than did the hanging of 8 A-class convicts at the IMTFE. Conservative revisionists in Japan today denounce the Tokyo trial as "victors' justice," but few Japanese in 1948 shed tears over Tôjô Hideki and company. Indeed, Tôjô family members claim they were cruelly ostracized during, and for years after, the IMTFE.[36] Most Japanese worried about getting enough to eat everyday, and the general mood was that guilty verdicts were unavoidable since Japan lost the war. Yet many also felt that the A-class convicts got their comeuppance—though not for committing atrocities against foreigners at places such as Nanking. Instead, it was felt, those men should be made to answer for recklessly starting a hopeless war with the United States that caused Japan untold misery and death. This is the idea of *haisen sekinin*—"culpability for losing the war." The flip side, of course, is that no one would be culpable if Japan had picked on a weaker foe and won.[37]

In considering how ordinary postwar Japanese grasped this issue of culpability, we must examine the role played by the media in the wartime-to-postwar transition. German journalists and newspapers who praised Hitler and the Nazi war effort stopped publishing in the postwar era; Japanese journalists and newspapers that had played similar roles did not. They neither admitted nor atoned for whipping up hatred against China or for spreading lies about the war issued by Imperial Headquarters. Those wartime lies, for example, held that using the atomic bomb showed how desperate the United States had become, or that wearing thick clothing would protect people from radiation in further nuclear attacks.[38] As Senô Kappa's bestselling semifictional autobiography, *Shônen H,* relates: "More than the enemy who fire-bombed us, I hated those [Japanese] who kept deceiving us by lying or hiding the truth—the government, military, and newspapers."[39] It was to this sentiment—widespread among survivors of the war—that Yamamoto Shichihei and his timely ally Suzuki Akira appealed. They charged that the mass media avidly promoted imperialist aggression in the name of patriotism up to 1945, but these same journalists, often writing in the same papers, now fostered goodwill toward China by atoning for wartime sins. And, this newfound *taigi meibun,* or "unassailable just cause," meant retelling the 100-man killing contest with suitable embellishments to make Mukai and Noda scapegoats for a second time. Thus, round two in the killing contest debate centered on two points. First, Yamamoto and Suzuki sought to prove these defendants innocent, as if at a Nanking retrial. More importantly, though, these two critics exposed the sordid wartime behavior of postwar left-wing reporters such as Asami Kazuo. He was the *Tokyo nichinichi shinbun* (later *Mainichi shinbun*) reporter whom they accused of fabricating the killing contest in 1937 and refusing to admit that in 1947—when doing so would have saved Mukai and Noda from execution at the NMT.

Suzuki at first held that there were *illusions in* the Nanking massacre.[40] Although his position later changed, he did not originally claim that the whole Nanking Atrocity *was an illusion.* He admitted that imperial troops perpetrated random and inexcusable killings at Nanking starting on 13 December 1937, but insisted that these could not be accurately quantified owing to the dearth of reliable primary sources. In April 1972, his avowed aim was to show that some episodes—such as the 100-man killing contest—were "illusory." To that end, he quoted the following *Tokyo nichinichi shinbun* report of this contest dated 30 November 1937. It showed how badly mistaken the memories of Honda's Chinese informants had been:

Unit XX [identity disguised under wartime state censorship], whose demon-like assault from Ch'angshu to Wuhsi covered those 40 km in six days, now covered another forty from Wuhsi to Ch'angchou in three. Their attack was as swift as the gods and even more sweet. At the front, two young officers in the Katagiri Unit are staging a 100-man killing contest. We hear that one scored fifty-six and the other twenty-five soon after leaving Wuhsi. Sublieutenant Mukai Toshiaki, age twenty-six, of the Toyama [Takeo]

Unit, is from Kôjiro Village, Kuga County, Yamaguchi Prefecture. Noda Takeshi [*recte:* Tsuyoshi], age twenty-five, of the same Unit, from Tashiro Village, Kimotsuki County, Kagoshima Prefecture. Setting off from Wuhsi, Mukai advanced twenty-six or twenty-seven kilometers down a rail line, and Noda followed alongside until the two parted company. By the next morning, Noda reached Wuhsi Hamlet, about eight kilometers outside Wuhsi. Shouting out his name lest the enemy mistake it, Noda ferociously plunged toward a pillbox and cut down four men inside. On hearing Noda's war cry, Mukai plucked up his resolve, vowing not to be outdone. That night, Mukai and his men swooped down on enemy defenses at Henglinchen where fifty-five were felled. Later on, Noda cut down another nine at Henglinchen, six at Weikuanchen; and, on twenty-nine November, another six at Ch'angchou Station, for a total of twenty-five. Mukai later cut down four near the station. That's where we caught up with the two having a little encounter.

Mukai: "At this rate, I'll *(ore)* get 100 by the time we reach Tanyang; it won't take me until Nanking. Admit it, Noda; you lost. My blade sliced through fifty-six men with only one dent to show for it."

Noda: "We two *(bokura)* make it a rule not to cut down anyone who hightails it for dear life. I'm *(boku)* serving as an XX [XX o yatte iru], so it's not easy to up my numbers. But you'll see what a real record is by the time we reach Tanyang.[41]

When checked against this original Japanese-language *Tokyo nichinichi* story dated 30 November 1937, Suzuki Akira detected an "illusion" in all previous accounts that had depicted a game or a murder race against helpless noncombatants. As a written source contemporaneous to the event in question, Suzuki's document was more reliable than secondhand English-language *Japan Advertiser* accounts used by Harold J. Timperley, or the thirty-five-year-old memories orally conveyed by Honda Katsuichi's Chinese informants. This primary source shows that the contest took place in combat. Hence, it was not a war crime, for killing armed enemy soldiers in battle is what war is all about. Honda might retort that such killings would still constitute a war crime because the officers were part of an invading army that violated international law. But even if we grant him that point, imperial government leaders who ordered the invasion would be the ones to stand trial for A-class war crimes. No matter how many armed Chinese soldiers Mukai and Noda killed in combat, they could not legitimately be tried for B-class war crimes at the NMT.

Above all, however, Suzuki stressed how absurd it was for anyone to take this article seriously at all—whether in 1937 or in 1972. Asami Kazuo and the other writers made little attempt to imbue their stories with verisimilitude; and, we must concur, the tone does resemble that of *kôdanshi* or *katsuben*—traditional tale-tellers or narrators in silent movies. This is clear from the phrase, "slicing a man in half down the middle, steel helmet and all, like a hollow bamboo stalk" *(kara take wari)*." Also, Noda calling out his name before battle is a stock literary device dating from medieval war tales such as the *Heiki monogatari*. Suzuki reasoned that Asami wrote a propaganda-cum-entertainment piece in an era when journalists did that as part of the war effort. As common sense would dictate, no sword-wielding foot soldier could live to brag about charging headlong at enemy pillboxes equipped with machine guns.[42] As outside Western observers, we might liken these superhuman heroics to those depicted in the Japanese "three human bombs" saga fabricated during the 1932 Shanghai Incident, to wartime John Wayne movies, to the impossible exploits portrayed in the 1960s television series *Combat* or, more recently, to Rambo films.

Yet according to Suzuki, postwar leftists distorted this tale and exploited it as a symbol of Japanese bestiality that demanded continuing apologies in the name of friendship with China. And, not by chance, they lined their pockets doing so. Asami Kazuo was one such sinophile. He praised Mao Tse-tung and the Cultural Revolution in the 1970s. But Asami was in fact one of the *Tokyo nichinichi shinbun* reporters who contrived the 1937 killing contest story to inspire contempt for China and to raise fighting spirits at home. And, not by chance, he had curried favor with the army to advance his wartime career. In 1972 Asami wrote for the very same paper, although it had been renamed the *Mainichi shinbun* in January 1943. To Suzuki Akira, the integrity of Asami and other "progressive men of culture" seemed dubious. Contrary to Honda, Suzuki explored the issue of wartime culpability from "the side that did the killing." Partly this was to vindicate Mukai and Noda whom, Suzuki asserted, the KMT regime had unjustly executed as war criminals based on these news reports. After noting that there were few reliable primary sources in Japanese or Chinese, Suzuki critically examined third-party sources such as Edgar Snow's *Battle for Asia,* Agnes Smedley's *Battle Hymn of China,* and Harold J. Timperley's *What War Means.* Suzuki rejected these as products of virulent wartime anti-Japanese propaganda. He then contextualized Nanking by placing it amid the mass murder, rape, and pillage that he saw as characterizing modern Chinese history as a whole. Critics disparaged this tactic as minimizing, relativizing, or marginalizing Japanese atrocities through irrelevant comparisons. But in April 1972, Suzuki was consistent and even-handed in using it. He held that similar Japanese accounts of Chinese atrocities against Japanese residents at Tungchou in July 1937 were just as exaggerated and unreliable. In general, he said, victims of any nationality overstate their suffering in wartime; how much more so when they related 35-year-old memories of their suffering. Thus, for Suzuki, the truth about Nanking was destined to be shrouded forever by "illusions" like the alleged killing contest that could never be empirically verified. Nevertheless, he charged, Honda, Asami, and other leftists left-wing elevated these into potent symbols of Japanese bestiality for partisan reasons.[43]

Exploiting the techniques of oral history, Suzuki interviewed persons who had known Mukai Toshiaki and Noda Tsuyoshi; and his fieldwork turned up new sources to "prove" their innocence. From Mukai's widow Chieko, Suzuki learned the circumstances of his arrest and extradition to Taiwan in 1946.

Mukai had indeed found a new wife due to the fame derived from Asami's story. He remarried as an adopted son and took the surname Kitaoka. After the war, local police came to arraign "Mukai" Toshiaki on U.S. Occupation orders. But a Japanese constable helpfully hinted: "After all, this surname is different from yours, so if you're not the man that the [American] military police want, just say so."[44] American officials in the Allied Occupation relied on help from Japanese aides to carry out their measures. Thus, no follow-up efforts would have resulted if the suspect had chosen to take the hint and stay put. Yet he turned himself in. Chieko fearfully suggested connections to the "killing contest," but Toshiaki said that the news story had been based on "empty boasting," and "everyone from the government on down told similar lies during the war, so the Allies would have to try all of us Japanese." Then she replied, "Oh, so you lied to deceive me, did you?"

This dialogue shows that women like Chieko indeed aspired to marry men of Mukai's accomplishments, and it proves that she never doubted the veracity of Asami Kazuo's story until 1946, a year after the war ended. Chieko told Suzuki about memoirs by Kwantung Army staff officer Tsuji Masanobu as well. She said that, in effect, Tsuji had written, "Mukai was a damn fool for giving himself up."[45] Suzuki thus portrayed Mukai as an simple, honest man who turned himself in expecting exoneration from Allied courts of justice, and drew an oblique contrast between the naive gullibility of Mukai and the worldly guile of Tsuji—a far worse B-class war criminal who never owned up to his own culpability and deftly evaded prosecution by hiding out on the continent until it was safe to return home, after which he was elected to the Diet.[46] Suzuki discovered that the IMTFE in Tokyo chose not to prosecute Mukai and Noda, but the KMT insisted on their extradition for B-class war crimes. The NMT found them guilty because they submitted no "persuasive counter-evidence to refute the charges."[47] Suzuki cited NMT records left by Mukai and Noda. These instructed their kin to bear the Chinese people no ill will, and declared that they hoped their deaths would lay the bases for Sino-Japanese friendship. Chieko supplied a copy of a defense statement that Mukai Toshiaki filed at the NMT to protest his innocence. It said that: (1) the IMTFE subpoenaed him but took no legal action against him, (2) he belonged to an artillery platoon normally not engaged in frontline combat, (3) he saw action only in artillery shelling at Wuhsi and Tanyang on the road to Nanking, (4) he had met with and talked to Asami only at Wuhsi, (5) the *Tokyo nichinichi shinbun* reporters testified that none of them had seen any killings, and (6) Noda and he parted ways at Tanyang on 1 December and did not meet again until 16 December. Thus, Mukai's written statement contradicted all of the crucial events as reported by Asami.[48]

Suzuki also discovered that, just before Mukai Toshiaki's execution, his older brother, Mukai Takeshi, had tracked down other men who had served in Toshiaki's unit, plus Asami Kazuo himself. Mukai Toshiaki's former comrades gave oral statements and written testimonies in his support. Toyama Takeo, his former commanding officer, certified that Mukai was injured on 2 December 1937 at Tanyang and received medical treatment behind the lines from then until he rejoined his unit on 15 December at T'angshui (T'angshan). Thus, Mukai could not have killed anyone on the days stated in Asami's story.[49] Suzuki cited another statement, this one written by a Chinese defense counsel at the NMT, that Noda's mother had provided. It corroborated all of the points found in Mukai's statement.[50] Suzuki also cited a signed testimony by Asami dated 10 December 1946, obtained by Mukai Takeshi. Asami swore that: (1) he never actually saw any killings, (2) he based his articles on interviews with Mukai, (3) Mukai and Noda committed no atrocities against helpless POWs or other noncombatants, and (4) wartime government censorship would have suppressed any news report even remotely suggesting that Japanese troops committed such an atrocity.[51] But when Suzuki actually confronted Asami, the latter refused to admit having made up the story; instead, Asami said he had based it on verbal information that Mukai supplied. In Suzuki's eyes, this cost Mukai and Noda their lives.

Suzuki Akira also interviewed persons on Taiwan, including former chief justice at the NMT, Shih Mei-yu. Shih insisted, though erroneously, that the KMT regime had tried only 2,000 out of 1 million Japanese invaders and executed but a few dozen. (In fact, it tried 883 Japanese and sentenced 232 to death or life imprisonment.) The barbarity of this killing contest, Shih insisted, symbolized the entire Nanking Atrocity; yet only four men were found guilty and executed for it. Shih said that the NMT had Mukai's sword as evidence and that, when Shih pointed to a picture of Mukai in a Japanese book and asked "Is this you?," Mukai replied, "Yes." For such reasons, the newspaper stories alone had not caused his execution. As Shih stressed to Suzuki, "The Nanking Incident was enormous. By executing these men, we fully intended to make you understand what it meant to us." Also, Shih hinted, Chiang Kai-shek and his defense minister Ho Ying-chin had had a say in fixing the death sentence for these defendants.[52] Thus, Suzuki's account suggests that Chinese political considerations affected the outcome of the Nanking trials.

In the meantime, important new source materials had come out. Attracted by the debate, the mass weekly, *Shûkan shinchô,* published an issue on 29 July 1972 that carried short accounts by persons who had reported the wartime "contest." They included Suzuki Jirô (no relation to Akira), another reporter who covered the story, as well as Satô Shinju, the photographer who took the snapshot of Mukai and Noda at Ch'angchou that appeared in the *Tokyo nichinichi shinbun* on 13 December 1937.[53] These materials permitted new breakthroughs in the debate. Now writing under his own name, though referring to "Ben-Dasan" on occasion, Yamamoto Shichihei discussed the killing contest in the monthly periodical *Shokun!* from August 1972 to April 1974 as part of a rambling account of his experiences in the imperial army. This account appeared in hardcover in 1975, in paperback in 1983, and in a posthumous collection of his works in 1997. Thus, his Bungei shunjû publishers produced the very same account 4 times within 25 years—without editing or correcting obvious errors.[54] These multiple reissues show that many Japanese continue paying good money to "buy" Yamamoto's views.

Yamamoto's biggest contribution to the debate was an analysis of the wartime soldier's mental state based on firsthand experience in the imperial army. The obvious drawback to this approach is that its findings do not permit empirical testing by persons who lack that experience. Yet, Yamamoto exhibited shrewd intelligence and asked piercing questions. In essence, he defended Mukai's behavior by explaining the tortured wartime psychology that produced it, and he impugned Asami's integrity by exposing his four 1937 *Tokyo nichinichi shinbun* articles as specious. Yamamoto said that he was relating his wartime experiences to avoid a second sin; the first was his having fought in the war to start with. Postwar Japanese in the 1970s, he said, fell victim to the same duplicity exhibited under the old emperor system. Many readers in 1937 had perceived the fictive nature of Asami's story but said nothing for fear of being labeled traitors. Thus, its falsity went unexposed for so long that it took on enough plausibility to pass for the truth. Now, in the 1970s, those few Japanese who could see through those original lies kept still in deference to a new tenet of political correctness—friendship with China. Yamamoto admitted that imperial Japan had committed aggression in China and elsewhere, but asserted that this had not justified the execution of innocent B-class war crimes suspects. Worse still, by heaping blame on conveniently dead men, postwar left-wing journalists blocked efforts to uncover what really happened at Nanking and to expose those truly culpable.[55]

According to Yamamoto, Mukai did brag about fictive battlefield exploits to Asami, and did defend himself at the NMT by saying he had lied to attract "a better wife." But, Yamamoto insisted, readers should not caricature or excoriate Mukai. Instead, they should place his seemingly despicable conduct in proper context—the abnormal state of mind produced by brutalization in the imperial army. Treatment therein was such that, by modern Western standards, officers were guilty of war crimes against their own men. The Bataan Death March was no "atrocity"; it was normal practice. Owing to extreme physical and psychological abuse over time, all Japanese soldiers exhibited mental imbalance to varying degrees; and bragging was one way to preserve sanity. Only the infantry counted as "real men" in the army, Yamamoto stated. Those assigned to supply and transport or to duties in the rear became the butt of cruel taunts. Asami disguised Noda's duties, "serving as an XX," as required by wartime state censorship. In fact, Noda was an adjutant to a battalion chief and hence saw little or no action. Nor was Mukai an infantryman; he led an artillery platoon attached to the rear of an infantry unit. Thus, neither was a "real man" who fought tooth and nail at the front; both endured shame and inferiority for which they compensated by bragging. Moreover, the army phrases, "I want to find a nice wife" and "I want to perform filial piety," were code language for "I want a discharge to go home." Owing to imperial government censorship of defeatist sentiment, such cryptic expressions were the only way troops could publicly vent their true feelings.[56] Thus we might note, those phrases are like American slang expressions such as, "Tell it to the Marines" that cannot be taken literally.

Yamamoto then critically analyzed the texts of Asami's stories. First, he said, imperial army men would not use terms and idioms that Asami attributed to Mukai and Noda. No soldier would claim to be "serving as an XX" (XX *o yatte iru*). Anyone who blurted out *boku* or *ore* instead of *jibun* for "I," or who used *tetsukabuto* in place of *tetsubô* for "helmet," would suffer "discipline by the iron fist" before he could shut his mouth. In Yamamoto's eyes, Asami clearly fabricated the dialogue, so he likely fabricated the story as well. Second, no officer would offer a "prize" to kill the enemy in a "contest" because that desecrated a soldier's duty to the emperor. Third, if the officers truly did stage that contest, they would have been punished for appropriating the emperor's soldiers—the men under their command—for private purposes. Fourth, these officers served behind the lines, so any action at the front would entail abandoning their posts without authorization. Such dereliction of duty would subject them to courts martial. This is why Mukai said that he was "shocked and embarrassed" to read Asami's stories as these later appeared in print. Mukai bragged to attract "a better wife," but he never saw galley proofs and so could not know exactly how Asami would embellish that bragging. If Mukai had known he would be portrayed away without leave (AWOL), he would have been more reticent.[57]

Next, Yamamoto claimed that anyone who has actually used a Japanese sword in combat would know it could never cut up 100 men. Unlike Chinese swords made of one piece, Japanese swords were held together by a linchpin in the hilt and were prone to come undone. Also, blades were easily bent out of shape. In sum, they were too weak to withstand heavy use. In medieval Japan, when warfare actually took place, warriors favored bows and spears. In the following Edo period (1600–1867), a samurai carried swords for show—not usually to kill people. If one did kill someone, he needed a sword smith to fix the damage to his blade. And, unless he were a highly skilled swordsman, it was very hard to dispatch an adversary at one stroke. Invariably, several cuts were followed by a *coup de grâce* or *todome*—a thrust, not a cut, to some vital organ. Despite this reality, a pervasive myth grew up in the Edo period, which held that the samurai sword was the world's most awesome blade. The emperor state took over and sanctified this myth as part of the Japanese spirit after 1867. And, by the 1930s, anyone who publicly questioned that myth was attacked as a traitor, so most officers kept silent although they knew the swords they lugged into battle were useless. To prove this point, Yamamoto cited the expert wartime opinion of the sword smith Naruse Kanji, who had damned the Japanese sword through faint praise in order to skirt government censorship. But, as with the killing contest itself, this myth of the samurai sword went undebunked for so long that it now passed for the truth, especially among postwar Japanese who, unlike Yamamoto, had never used one to cut through flesh and bone.[58]

Finally, Yamamoto asserted that Asami typified many wartime civilians who, exuding militarist fervor, tried to appear more ferocious than real soldiers. Reporters were not allowed to mix with frontline troops in the heat of battle; that would have been perilous for both. If Asami did meet Noda and Mukai, it had to have been at some safe spot at the rear. More likely, he just used them as actors in a drama script to depict himself risking life and limb in vicious combat. That is why he contrived heroic lines such as: "We ignored the shower of enemy gunfire streaming at us." Asami's story was patently false, but he refused to admit that when Mukai Takeshi begged for a sworn testimony to save his brother's life at the NMT. Yamamoto therefore declared that, in order to atone for their wartime crimes, Asami and the *Mainichi shinbun* should retract earlier lies about the killing contest—which now enjoyed currency in the English- and Chinese-speaking worlds. In addition, they should issue a public apology to the victims' survivors and pay compensation for the mental anguish that their actions had caused. Mukai's daughter, in fact, filed a lawsuit against the *Mainichi shinbun* and the *Asahi shinbun,* and against Honda Katsuichi in April 2003. It was rejected by the court in August 2005.[59]

By 1974 Yamamoto came to conclude that 3,000 to 5,000 Chinese military personnel died at Nanking. He excluded all but a few casualties among civilians and other noncombatants from that figure.[60] Itô Takashi, an authority on modern Japan then teaching at the University of Tokyo, lauded this work as "splendid; a primer on critical source-analysis in contemporary history."[61] Not to be outdone, Suzuki Akira won the 1973 Ôya Sôichi prize for nonfiction, issued by the conservative Bungei shunju media group. He earned plaudits not only from right-wing circles and his own publisher. Even the ultra-radical critic Oda Makoto reluctantly found himself persuaded that the killing contest—though not the whole Nanking Atrocity—was an "illusion."[62]

Suzuki's thesis had a veiled subtle edge. He did not deny that a massacre of unknown magnitude X began on 13 December 1937 when Nanking fell. His illusion thesis *in this first stage* differed from that of later deniers, so we should view him as presaging the minimalists who concede that a small-scale massacre did occur. However, Suzuki refused to say how big or small that unknown magnitude X was. Instead, he stressed that verification and precise quantification were impossible; so he tried to show that at least this one incident in the Nanking Atrocity was "illusory." The implication was that, if others exposed more such illusions, magnitude X would shrink to the point where the whole Atrocity could be dismissed as inconsequential. To be fair, he did not say that to start with. Even in mid-1975, he expressed umbrage at being labeled a member of the denial school.[63] His early position was that Japanese leftists had elevated the killing contest into a "symbol" of the Nanking Atrocity for tainted reasons, so he would expose the falsity of this one event and let others draw their own conclusions. Later, however, he dropped these rhetorical complexities to claim that this one illusion denied substance to the whole phenomenon it reputedly symbolized.

Round 3: Prosecutor's Rally

Things looked bleak for the leftists toward the end of 1972. Hora Tomio found himself fighting an uphill battle, trying to show that the logic and evidence that Yamamoto Shichihei and Suzuki Akira employed were flawed and unscholarly. First, Hora reaffirmed that the killing contest was not just a Chinese "legend" as Isaiah Ben-Dasan claimed. Asami Kazuo's 1937 *Tokyo nichinichi shinbun* articles proved that Mukai and Noda did exist, and that they staged some sort of competition on the way to Nanking before it fell on 13 December 1937. Second, Hora deflated a seemingly cogent point made by Yamamoto—that it was impossible to kill 1 man every one minute and thirty-six seconds on the ten-kilometer, 2.5-hour route from Kuyung to T'angshan. Yamamoto had erred in accepting the Chinese oral account that Honda Katsuichi had cited. It mistakenly held that the killing contest took place from Kuyung to T'angshan.[64] But Honda failed to cite two additional *Tokyo nichinichi shinbun* articles, dated 4 and 6 December 1937.[65] These made a big difference. NMT records had claimed that the reputed killing contest occurred entirely on Purple Mountain outside Nanking whereas Timperley and the Chinese oral accounts cited by Hora, Ômori Minoru, and Honda had said that it first took place from Kuyung to T'angshan, and later was extended to Purple Mountain. But when read together, Hora's four Japanese sources showed that the contest began at Wuhsi on 26 November and ended at Purple Mountain on 10 December. Thus it occurred over a far longer distance than previously thought—from Wuhsi, not from Kuyung—until Purple Mountain. And, it began far earlier—on 25 November, not on 5 December—before ending on 13 December. Based on these more accurate written documents, Hora reckoned that Mukai and Noda needed to average about seven kills per day over this half-month span—hardly an impossible clip—to attain scores of 106 and 105, respectively.[66]

Hora had more trouble refuting Yamamoto's psychological interpretations based on army life—experiences that Hora lacked. And, as for the myth of the samurai sword, Hora used the same wartime publication by Naruse Kanji—plus another account cited by Uno Shintarô as cited by a certain Kumazawa Kyôjirô in *Tennô no guntai*—to redeem the honor of Japanese blades.[67] But this is really a moot point, a bit like suggesting that we redo Unit 731 vivisection experiments on humans to confirm their accuracy; and, the myth of the samurai sword becomes immaterial when viewed in the broader context of the Nanking Atrocity as a whole, apart from the guilt or innocence of Mukai and Noda as individuals. That is to say, neither side in this debate took the trouble to note that bayonets, not swords, were the blade of choice for killing Chinese.

Hora grudgingly praised Suzuki Akira for developing interview methods of oral history and for uncovering new document sources. Here, the professional historian relied on already-published materials whereas the amateur found and exploited new sources. Although reproaching himself for this role reversal, Hora pressed his attack to discredit these very sources that Suzuki Akira had discovered. First, Hora cited an article by Suzuki Jirô, Asami's fellow reporter:

> The articles came to the attention of [IMTFE] prosecutors who used these to support their charge of atrocities, and I got a summons to appear as a witness. Of course they viewed this [contest] as an atrocity. They grilled us about its truth or falsity, how we covered it, and what it meant. But no reporter actually saw the two men kill anyone with swords. They just said they had held the contest and related it as a tale of battlefield heroism, so we couldn't say it was an "atrocity." Based on the two men's word that they "make it a rule not to cut down anyone who high-tails it for dear life," Asami and I independently told the prosecutors: "This was not an atrocity because the two never killed anyone who ran away, only those enemy soldiers who came at them. They were true to the spirit of *bushidô* which says that common people should never be harmed." Our testimony certainly did not provide prosecutors with a strong case. When it finally came time for us to appear in court, Asami took the stand first. But ás soon as he recited the oath, they excused him on the grounds of "flawed documentation." So he returned to the waiting room with a dejected face. Soon, a clerk showed up to say," You guys don't have to come any more...." Later we heard that the two officers were turned over to the Chinese KMT regime and executed despite our affidavit to clear them.[68]

Here, Suzuki Jirô claims that Asami Kazuo had undergone questioning at the IMTFE but was dismissed from further interrogation on the grounds of "flawed documentation." Yamamoto and Suzuki Akira had used this document to assert either that the IMTFE had found the defendants innocent or released them for lack of evidence. But, Hora retorted, the IMTFE had not dismissed Mukai and Noda because it lacked the proof to convict them; instead, it did not indict them because they were not charged with the A-class war crimes that fell under its jurisdiction. So, the IMTFE quite properly sent them to face B-class war crimes trials at Nanking.[69] Thus, Hora argued that Yamamoto and Suzuki were guilty of a non sequitur.

Second, Hora asserted that the Mukai and Noda defense statements, plus sworn testimony given by Mukai's former commanding officer, Toyama Takeo, did not add up to a cogent alibi. Suzuki Akira used these documents to substantiate key contentions about Mukai's innocence: (1) Mukai belonged to a unit stationed far from the front and did not engage in close combat with the foe; (2) he saw action only at Wuhsi where he fired artillery shells from behind the lines; (3) he met Asami but once, at Wuhsi, not 3 times as depicted in the news stories; (4) he had no contact with Noda between 1 and 16 December; and (5) he was injured on 2 December at Tanyang, did not return to action until 15 December at T'angshui (T'angshan), and so could not have killed anyone during that interval. In disputing these claims of innocence, Hora pointed out that no official battle reports or other Japanese army documents dating from the time were extant. Thus, no bona fide primary sources corroborated the aforementioned contentions. Instead, Suzuki Akira had used post facto sources—the two defendants' defense statements and Toyama's testimony. These were produced after the NMT began in 1946, not in December 1937 when the 2 men allegedly committed their crimes. Hora believed that Mukai's brother Takeshi expressly urged Mukai, Noda, and Toyama to create latter-day documents designed to gain acquittals.[70]

In particular, Hora sought to destroy Mukai's alibi about being wounded and out of action between 2 and 15 December 1937. To that end, Hora cited testimony appearing in the 29 July 1972 issue of *Shûkan shinchô* written by the news journalist Satô Shinju, who photographed Mukai and Noda at Ch'angchou on 13 December 1937.[71] Satô said that he saw Asami talking with Mukai and taking notes at Ch'angchou one day before—which was after Mukai's unit left Wuhsi. So Satô's statement demolished Mukai's alibi about being hospitalized and also contradicted his claim of having met Asami but once, at Wuhsi. The skeptical Satô also asked Mukai and Noda about how they tabulated their scores—a point that Yamamoto Shichihei and Suzuki Akira claimed was impossible under battlefield conditions. According to Satô, the men replied that each assigned a subordinate to count the other's kills. To Hora, that degree of premeditation dispelled any doubt on this point. Hora also cited statements in *Shûkan shinchô* by Suzuki Jirô that Mukai and Noda bragged to Asami at the foot of Purple Mountain.[72] Furthermore, Suzuki Jirô disclosed that "flushing out" the enemy there took place through poison gas, not smoke, as Harold J. Timperley mistakenly adduced from the *Japan Advertiser*. (Yamamoto Shichihei too perceived from this account that Japanese forces used poison gas at Purple Mountain, and said so repeatedly in a matter-of-fact way that betrays total indifference about yet another war crime in China.[73]) The *Shûkan shinchô* editor concluded that Asami Kazuo did not make up reports of the contest on his own. Instead, Asami based these on the boasts made by Mukai and Noda, who did not really do what they claimed. Nevertheless, the editor concluded, they did make boastful self-incriminating assertions, so they had only themselves to blame for their tragic fate.[74]

Finally, Hora sought to exonerate Asami, whose honor Yamamoto and Suzuki Akira had besmirched. Asami in 1946, like Suzuki Jirô in 1972, insisted that none of the *Tokyo nichinichi shinbun* reporters actually saw Mukai or Noda kill anyone. In Hora's eyes, Asami was far from a villain. To the contrary, Asami had tried to help Mukai by testifying that wartime government censorship would have suppressed any news story that even hinted at atrocities being perpetrated against Chinese noncombatants. In truth, Hora concluded, Asami did falsify his 1937 story to deceive readers. Thus, Hora admitted that the killing contest was "fabricated" in one crucial sense. But this was not the same falsity, deception, and fabrication of which Yamamoto and Suzuki accused Asami. Nor was it the semifabrication that the *Shûkan shinchô* editor attributed to Asami. Instead, Hora proclaimed, Asami had falsified his 1937 story in order to circumvent imperial government censorship by portraying Mukai and Noda killing armed Chinese soldiers in combat when they had really decapitated helpless POWs.[75]

Hora backed up this claim with reference to two sources. One was *Tennô no guntai* by a certain Kumazawa Kyôjirô. It cites army veterans such as Uno Shintarô who testified that decapitations by sword were a frequent occurrence in China. But Hora's "clinching proof" came from a 1975 essay by Shijime Akira, a postwar labor leader who had been a primary school pupil during the war in Noda's home prefecture of Kagoshima. In 1944, Noda gave a talk about the killing contest that Shijime recalled in 1975 as follows:

> I learned of it when I was in primary school. This was my first experience with China. I'm sure it was in the spring of 1944, one year before I graduated... I recall that sub-lieutenant "N" stood very relaxed in front of us, not stiff and formal like most military men. He said serenely, "The newspapers call me a local hero and a valiant warrior who killed 100 men.... But in truth I only killed four or five men in actual hand-to-hand combat.... Whenever we took over a trench, we would shout *"Ni, lai, lai"* (Hey you, come, come). Chink soldiers are damn fools, so they would come out in hordes. We would line them up and cut down every last one.... I got a reputation for slicing up 100 men, but almost all of them were in this manner.... Two of us had a killing contest, but later on people would ask me, "Wasn't it really an easy matter?" And I would reply, "for me, it was nothing at all."[76]

Suzuki Akira and Yamamoto Shichihei never responded to this document, perhaps because they chose to wish it away. But Shijime's statement about Noda, though incriminating, is not quite the smoking gun that Hora Tomio held it to be and Honda Katsuichi still holds it to be. This is a hearsay account of the confession that Noda reputedly made to sixth-graders in 1944, recalled by Shijime 31 years later. The account would assume much more cogency if one or two of Shijime's classmates were to verify it, but is not incontrovertible evidence by itself. On the other hand, Kumazawa Kyôjirô's *Tennô no guntai*—which cites a similarly damning account by Uno Shintarô—is really a work by Honda Katsuichi and Naganuma Setsuo.[77] The disguised authorship may cast doubt on its reliability. Moreover, in the account cited above, Shijime says nothing about Mukai. Whether or not Mukai was hospitalized between 2 and 15 December, he was normally assigned to duties behind the lines, not in areas where front-line, hand-to-hand combat took place. No one ever saw Mukai actually kill anyone, and some persons whom Suzuki Akira interviewed insisted that Mukai had not. Above all, Mukai's wife Chieko stated that he turned himself in to the Americans to be questioned for war crimes even though he could have escaped when the Japanese constable assigned to arrest him offered to turn a blind eye. A guilty man is not likely to do that. Being a blabbermouth, and that alone, sealed his fate.

The Ramifications

Most incidents that make up the Nanking Atrocity yield more than one interpretation. The 100-man killing contest, it would seem, is exceptionally rich in this regard. There are six possibilities as these unfolded over time from 1937 to the present.

Factual/Guilty

This conventionally accepted view was espoused by Harold J. Timperley in 1937, the KMT government and NMT in 1946–7, Honda and Hora before 1972; and the late Iris Chang, Erwin Wickert, and Jonathan D. Spence today. They asserted (or continue to assert) that the 1937 *Japan Advertiser* English-language synopses plus postwar Chinese oral accounts based on memory accurately depict Mukai and Noda killing 211 helpless noncombatants in a "game" or a "murder race" at or near Purple Mountain outside the walled city of Nanking in December 1937. Thus, the two Japanese were guilty of B-class war crimes. At the time of this chapter's final editing in July 2006, the PRC cited this interpretation as a historically factual in school textbooks, and displays an exhibit graphically depicting the incident in its Nanking mausoleum.[78]

Factual/Innocent

From 1937 until 1946, Mukai's wife Chieko, along with many other Japanese readers including the historian Irokawa Daikichi,[79] believed that Asami Kazuo's original Japanese-language *Tokyo nichinichi shinbun* accounts were literally true; that is, the two officers killed 211 enemy soldiers in legitimate armed combat. This would make them wartime heroes, but they committed no war crime in the sense of murdering helpless nonbelligerents.

Semi-fabricated/Self-incriminated

In July 1972, the *Shûkan shinchô* editor concluded that Asami Kazuo made up his 1937 story based on vain boasting by Mukai and Noda at the time. No killings really took place, but this tongue-wagging sealed the two men's fate at the NMT, and responsibility for their executions lay with no one but themselves.

Fabricated/Innocent

Beginning in 1972, Suzuki Akira and Yamamoto Shichihei contended that the bragging issue is irrelevant. Asami Kazuo concocted his story knowing that no killings occurred on or off the battlefield, so he was responsible for the execution of two innocent war crimes suspects. In July 2006, these views remain in print in Japan and are endorsed by Mukai's daughter, Tadokoro Chieko.

Deviously Fabricated/Guilty

From 1975—and as a direct result of debating with Suzuki Akira and Yamamoto Shichihei after 1971—Honda Katsuichi and Hora Tomio had to revise their original claim of factual/guilty. Asami Kazuo, they now came to assert, made up this story for a sly purpose: to skirt wartime state censorship by portraying the murder of many—the precise number is immaterial—helpless Chinese POWs *as if* Mukai and Noda had killed belligerents in legitimate armed combat. This is the interpretation that appears, for example, in Honda's 1987 *Nankin e no michi* (The road to Nanking) and its 1999 English translation *The Nanjing Massacre: A Japanese Journalist Confronts Japan's National Shame*.

A Split Verdict

Based on Shijime Akira's 1971 oral account, we might construe that Mukai was innocent and Noda, guilty.

Historians often play judge and jury, but this almost never involves sentencing people to death. In penal proceedings, the criteria for judgment are far stricter, and the consequences of error are far graver, than in academic inquiries, so drawing analogies to a criminal trial distorts the nature of my historiographic analysis. Despite this caveat, I conclude that the evidence uncovered in this debate did not establish the two men's guilt beyond a reasonable doubt. The conventionally accepted factual/guilty view, as well as the factual/innocent view, are both untenable. Instead, the semi-fabricated/self-incriminated argument is probably closest to the truth, and the fabricated/innocent argument is next closest. In sum, I conclude that the two men were unjustly executed and that the incident was fictive, though not *wholly* fabricated, since Asami's account was based on boasting made by the two officers to him. This conclusion does not mean that the entire Nanking Atrocity was fabricated, or that the imperial army is absolved of war crimes. Hora and others since 1975 have found abundant proof that cruel and summary beheadings of noncombatants and POWs took place throughout China. It is quite possible that Mukai and Noda did the same thing at Nanking—even if their tally may have fallen short of 211. Guilt by association is impermissible in a court of law, but historians must draw conclusions under far less stringent constraints. Hence I remain fully open to the deviously fabricated/guilty argument as revised by Hora and Honda after this debate ended.

Yet, whatever we may conclude about the 1971–75 debate, it disclosed many points of great value. Disputants on both sides worked through a hypothesis, antithesis, and synthesis. This process diversified research methods, uncovered new documentary sources, honed interpretive analytic skills, increased our store of factual knowledge, and uncovered new avenues for research. For example, the debate disclosed an alleged war crime at Nanking—the use of poison gas—which still remains largely unheard of outside Japan. Yamamoto applied insights from psychohistory, if in a nonsystematic way, and Suzuki and Honda developed interviewing techniques needed for oral history. They did all of this at a time when narrowly document-based, mainstream academic historians in Japan derided those approaches as unscholarly or fit only for journalists and critics of sociopolitical affairs *(hyôronka)*. New methods are not an unqualified good; they have their own pitfalls. But in this case they made for a keener appreciation of complexities and nuances in the Atrocity.

At the end of the day, the debate unearthed new primary materials that exposed defects in earlier sources and the falsity of contentions based on those defects. Thus we can no longer assert that 1937 Japanese news stories, NMT prosecution charges, post hoc victimization testimonies based on memory, and current-day PRC assertions about the killing contest are true and reliable. What the Chinese victims interviewed by Honda in 1971 recalled from "memory" was a killing contest distorted by refraction through: (1) the early *Tokyo nichi nichi shinbun* articles (2) their redactions in English in the *Japan Advertiser*, (3) Appendix F in Timperley's *What War Means*, which quoted those redactions; (4) wartime colloquial Chinese news articles based on Appendix F; and (5) the prosecution's charges at postwar war crimes trials, the NMT. It is unlikely that any kind of killing contest took place at all, and certainly none took place in the way that KMT prosecutors charged at the NMT. In this key sense, the 100-man killing contest was *fictive,* though this term has different meanings for different people.

The debate kicked off further research and uncovered even more primary sources in Japan that removed all doubt about the factuality of the 1937–38 Nanking Atrocity as a whole. No one today can maintain academic credibility while saying that this event in its totality—as opposed to specific incidents within it—never occurred. The most that would-be deniers can do is minimize the number of victims, cite extenuating circumstances to explain it, or claim that all armies in all wars commit similar atrocities.[80] These are the main conservative revisionist positions today. Even Tokyo governor Ishihara Shintarô, who in 1990 vehemently denied the Atrocity in toto, has come to admit: "I'm not saying it's wholly untrue,… about 10,000 people got killed."[81] That is not a trivial concession.

Nevertheless, huge areas of uncertainly remain as to the fictive nature and the meaning of this contest. This early debate disclosed fundamentally different ways of assigning primacy to "truth" in history—whether this be allegorical or empirical. The Chinese resist charges that this contest is an "illusion" without grounding in fact, but its factuality really does not matter for them. Instead, the contest is emblematic of their acute wartime victimization at Japanese hands; its real value lies in commemorating victims and survivors, but most of all, in conveying allegorical truth. In the last analysis, the contest is parable rather than history for the Chinese. However, if Japanese critics of Suzuki Akira's stripe succeed in disproving the factuality not only of the killing contest, but of many more incidents in the Nanking Atrocity, the Chinese will be hard put to maintain credibility because modern-day historians will not accept narratives unless these are convincingly supported by empirical evidence.

The two Japanese camps in the killing contest debate displayed markedly different attitudes on this empirical front. Three tests of scholarly or journalistic integrity apply here. One is for authors and publishers to correct mistakes and to revise dubious or erroneous claims when confronted with superior evidence. Honda Katsuichi and Hora Tomio did this in later editions of their work. Yamamoto Shichihei did not. His absurd Chinese death toll of 3,000 to 5,000—limited to combatants—plus other blatant errors have been repeatedly reprinted down to the present. For two decades, Suzuki Akira argued that his *"Nankin daigyakusatsu" no maboroshi* should stand as a document of his views in 1972. But in 1999, Suzuki proclaimed affiliation with the denial school in a new book and refused to correct errors in it as pointed out by left-wing historians.[82] Thus for Yamamoto Shichihei and Suzuki Akira, the overall message to be gotten out was more important than its factual accuracy in details. A second test of scholarly integrity is to make one's sources publicly accessible and thus amenable to empirical verification or refutation. Beginning in 1973, Hora published volumes of primary documents, many translated from English and Chinese into Japanese. By contrast, Suzuki made public neither the taped interviews he made with NMT chief justice Shih Mei-yu, nor the sources provided by the Mukai and Noda families, cited as key evidence in his first book. This led Watada Susumu to conclude—after interviewing Shih himself on Taiwan in 1984—that Suzuki had never met this man and had "fabricated" his account of the interview.[83] Suzuki Akira died in 2003 without making his tapes public, so Watada's doubts seem justified. A third test of scholarly integrity is to apply both criticisms and excuses consistently; that is, toward one's adversaries and oneself alike. Yamamoto and Suzuki pilloried Asami Kazuo and the *Tokyo nichinichi shinbun* (now called the *Mainichi shinbun*) for failing to own up to wartime and postwar lies. Yet they never confronted their patrons at Bungei shunjû publishers with this charge. That task fell to a member of the enemy camp—Takazaki Ryûji.[84] Others in turn have eagerly exposed the now-left-wing *Asahi shinbun*'s sordid jingoistic role in wartime.[85] Muckraking is quite acceptable, but disputants should aspire to do it evenhandedly.

These tests of scholarly integrity—which, incidentally, equally obtain along the Chinese-Japanese ethnic divide—raise a troubling question: What if someone who fails them still makes a cogent point? Against the background of this moral ambiguity, the 1971–75 debate had salubrious effects in Japan. This is because it went beyond well-worn issues of *haisen sekinin*—or culpability for losing the war—that never went beyond blaming government leaders or faceless militarists for starting a war they could not hope to win, pursuing it through suicide tactics, or inviting nuclear holocaust by not surrendering early enough. By contrast, culpability as disputed in the killing contest debate was of a more profound and self-critical sort; this dispute pointed the finger at common, ordinary people *(minshû no sensô sekinin)*. In 1971–75, it bears repeating, the official PRC line was still that Japanese militarists alone bore responsibility for the war of aggression; "ordinary Japanese" were its victims along with "ordinary Chinese." Thus, through this debate, the Japanese side, not the Chinese side, first broached the painful issue of war guilt borne by Japanese men and women on the street, not just convicted A-class war criminals.

That and related issues have gained renewed focus in recent writings by Katô Norihiro.[86] He argues that there has been a series of vicious cycles involving Japan's public versus private memories of the war. Official apologies for the war have led to faux pas by politicians, protests by Asian governments, begrudged retractions plus dismissals from office, and more distrust because the apologies lack substance and sincerity. The repeated vicious cycle, Katô says, derives from a Jekyll-and-Hyde syndrome that makes many, perhaps most, Japanese say one thing publicly while believing otherwise at heart.[87] Ordinary Japanese in private life—like most ordinary people everywhere—yearn to cherish the memory of deceased loved ones. They find it unbearable when foreign critics or Japanese "progressive men of culture" carp on how those loved ones did nothing but commit atrocities in a dirty, shameful war. It is too painful to admit that family and friends acted like beasts. So they magnify those loved ones' suffering and sacrifices, which too are grounded in reality. Thus, no sooner does a public figure apologize for war crimes and say that the postwar generation must bear some responsibility, than someone else protests that Japan did not pursue imperialist aggression, that the alleged atrocities were "fabricated," or that left-wing accounts of these are skewed and overblown to depict Japan alone as guilty. Here we can grasp the widespread appeal of conservative revisionist arguments.

Katô's insights on a popular psychological level complement claims by the left-wing historian Yoshida Yutaka on the political level; that is, the postwar Japanese state has adopted a deceitful double standard of accountability for the war. In foreign affairs, the public sphere, it officially affirms the IMTFE verdicts and admits past guilt for aggression as stipulated in Article XI of the San Francisco Peace Treaty. Signing it, after all, was a precondition for ending the U.S. Occupation and regaining sovereignty. But in domestic politics and education, the private sphere, Japan denies responsibility for aggression, glorifies its role in the last war, and rewards the perpetrators of that war with pensions and decorations rather than prosecute them—while denying compensation to the Asian victims of that war.[88] From this standpoint, Japanese liberals contrast their countrymen very unfavorably with postwar Germans, though sometimes in superficial and unfair ways.

These points were central to the 100-man killing contest debate. Yamamoto and Suzuki—no less than Honda and Hora—tried to make large segments of Japanese society own up to their wartime sins and postwar denial of these. That was their main aim—at least at the start. Casting doubt on the contest's basis in historical fact was a means to achieve that end. But Yamamoto and Suzuki lost sight of ends and means in the heat of debate. And later, starting in the 1980s, they and their followers have denied not only the killing contest, but most, if not all, of the Nanking Atrocity. In extreme cases, that categorical imperative made later deniers such as Tanaka Masaaki stoop to alter disagreeable documents.[89] It also produced the self-fulfilling, facile logic displayed by Watanabe Shôichi: the Shôwa emperor, Hirohito, makes no mention of a Nanking Atrocity in his 1946 monologue, the *Dokuhaku roku;* this is clear proof that such an event never took place.[90]

However, when all is said and done, the real nub of this debate was, "Who victimized whom?" Yamamoto and Suzuki focused on Chinese who victimized Japanese by executing innocent war crimes suspects, or on Japanese journalists who spread lies to deceive and harm other Japanese. Honda and Hora, by contrast, exposed lies that covered up or glossed over Japanese victimization of the Chinese. Mukai's wife and daughter depict their family as tragic victims of bullying by Honda, the left-wing Japanese media, and foreign Japan-bashers such as the late Iris Chang.[91] Indeed, as first suggested by Yamamoto Shichihei three decades ago, Mukai's daughter has sued Honda, the *Asahi shinbun,* the *Mainichi shinbun,* and left-wing publisher Kashiwa shobô over this issue in 2003; and, after an unfavorable decision in 2005, she has launched an appeal.[92] Yet the Mukai family longed to believe a certain lie—that their beloved husband and father Toshiaki valiantly killed 106 Chinese soldiers in battle. It never dawned on them that he did so—if he really had—as an imperialist aggressor in an age when such conduct was becoming hard to justify before the world.

In this key sense, Honda's crusade on behalf of "the side that got killed" is all-important, despite Isaiah Ben-Dasan's rhetorical chicanery to obscure it. The postwar Japanese people could begin to confront their ignominious past only after feeling genuine remorse for victims of the war other than themselves—and even though, as conservative revisionists rightly insist, Caucasian imperialist aggressors still refuse to do so.

Notes

1. This chapter originally appeared as "The Nanking 100-Man Killing Contest Debate: War Guilt Amid Fabricated Illusions, 1977–75," in *Journal of Japanese Studies* 26:2 (Summer 2000), pp. 307–40.
2. See Kasahara, *Ajia no naka no Nihongun*, pp.15–39; Yang, "Convergence or Divergence?" pp. 842–65; and Yoshida, "A Battle Over History" pp. 70–132.
3. On Hora's career and publications, see *Shikan*, no. 95 (March 1977), pp. 90–117.
4. For example, Awaya et al., eds., *Sensô sekinin, sengo sekinin;* and Awaya, *Miketsu no sensô sekinin.*
5. Asahi shinbunsha ed., *Sengo hoshô to wa nani ka*, pp. 15–31 and 119–34.
6. Sakamoto, *Rekishi kyôiku o kangaeru*, p. 120 and p. 126.
7. Hora, *Kindai senshi no nazo*, p. 161.
8. Ibid., p. 162; also, Ômori, *Ten'anmon enjô*, pp. 186–87.
9. Hora, *Kindai senshi no nazo*, pp. 161–62.
10. Timperley, *What War Means*, pp. 284–85.
11. Chang, *Rape of Nanking*, pp. 55–56; Wickert, ed., *Good Man of Nanking*, pp. 283–84; Cheng, Lestz with Jonathan D. Spence, eds., *The Search for Modern China: A Documentary Collection.*
12. Portions of the NMT records are reproduced in *GA Newsletter* 5:1 (March 1998), pp. 87–88.
13. Ienaga, *Taiheiyô sensô*, pp. 214–15 and p. 315.
14. The paragraphs below derive from Fujiwara, *Taikei Nihon no rekishi 15: Sekai no naka no Nihon*, pp. 282–84 and pp. 293–94; and Miyamoto, *Shôwa no rekishi 10: Keizai taikoku zôhoban*, pp. 240–42.
15. In English we now have Honda, *Nanking Massacre.*
16. Honda, *Chûgoku no tabi*, p. 234.
17. Reprinted in Honda, *Korosu gawa no ronri*, p. 23.
18. Ibid., pp. 120–30.
19. Ibid., p. 195.
20. Yamamoto, *Watakushi no naka no Nihongun, ge*, pp. 163–90. I have used a two-volume paperback edition.
21. Reproduced in Honda, *Korosu gawa no ronri*, pp. 101–9.
22. Ibid., pp. 126–29. Also, *NKH jushinryô kyohi no ronri.*
23. Honda, *Korosu gawa no ronri*, pp. 116–35.
24. Yamamoto, *Watakushi no naka no Nihongun, jô*, pp. 262–68.
25. Honda, *Korosu gawa no ronri*, pp. 149–52.
26. Ibid., pp. 136–65.

27. Ibid., pp. 213–31.
28. Ibid., pp. 232–82.
29. Ibid., pp. 187–90.
30. Yamamoto, *Shôwa tennô no kenkyû*, pp. 235–58 and pp. 285–306.
31. Ienaga, *Sensô sekinin*, pp. 308–11.
32. In Nakamura, ed., *Rekishi to shinjitsu*, p. 160.
33. For an example of right-wing thinking, see Nishio, *Kotonaru higeki*.
34. Hata, *Nankin jiken*, p. 244; *Kaikô* (March 1985).
35. Iwakawa, *Kotô no tsuchi to narutomo*, p. 62.
36. Iwanami, *Sofu Tôjô Hideki"Issai kataru nakare,"* pp. 72–84. This book inspired the film "Pride: Unmei no toki" that cast Tôjô in a heroic light.
37. Gomikawa, *Gozen kaigi*, pp. 421–23; Ienaga, *Sensô sekinin*, p. 223.
38. *Asahi shinbun*, 8 August and 10 August 1945.
39. Senô, *Shônen H, ge*, p. 110.
40. Suzuki, *"Nankin daigyakusatu" no maboroshi*.
41. Ibid., pp. 14–15.
42. Ibid., pp. 16–17.
43. Ibid., pp. 11–56 and pp. 70–75.
44. Ibid., p. 71.
45. Ibid., p. 74.
46. On Tsuji, see Dower, *Embracing Defeat*, pp. 511–13.
47. Suzuki, *"Nankin daigyakusatsu" no maboroshi*, p. 97.
48. Ibid., pp. 63–67.
49. Ibid., pp. 96–97.
50. Ibid., pp. 87–90.
51. Ibid., p. 89 and pp. 95–96.
52. Ibid., p. 112.
53. *Shûkan shinchô* (29 July 1972), pp. 32–37.
54. For example, John G. Magee is cited as "Magoo"; *Watakushi no naka no Nihongun, ge*, p. 316.
55. Ibid., *jô* pp. 4–6; *ge*, p. 331.
56. Ibid., *jô*, p. 325, pp. 327–28.
57. Ibid., *jô*, pp. 215–19, pp. 227–28 and pp. 306–11; *ge*, p. 96.
58. Ibid., *ge*, pp. 71–123.
59. Ibid., *jô*, pp. 282–83; *Asahi shinbun*, web posted on 23 August 2005.
60. Ibid., *ge*, p. 298.
61. Quoted in Hora, *Nankin daigyakusatsu: "Maboroshi"ka kôsaku hihan*, p. 76.
62. Ibid., p. iv.
63. *Asahi geinô* (21 August 1975), p. 145.
64. Hora, *Nankin daigyakusatsu: "Maboroshi"ka kôsaku*, pp. 26–29.
65. Ibid., pp. 22–26.
66. Ibid., p. 26.
67. Ibid., pp. 91–104.
68. Ibid., pp. 42–43.
69. Ibid., pp. 110–16.
70. Ibid., pp. 38–47.
71. Ibid., pp. 34–45, and pp.126–31; *Shûkan shinchô* (29 July 1972), pp. 34–35.
72. Hora, *Nankin daigyakusatsu: "Maboroshi"ka kôsaku hihan*, pp. 35–36; *Shûkan shinchô* (29 July 1972), pp. 35–36.
73. Yamamoto, *Watakushi no naka no Nihongun, jô*, p. 241; *ge*, p. 281, pp. 286–87, p. 303, p. 317.
74. Hora, *Nankin daigyakusatsu: "Maboroshi"ka kôsaku hihan*, p. 36; *Shûkan shinchô* (29 July 1972), p. 36.

75. Hora, *Nankin daigyakusatsu: "Maboroshi"ka kôsaku hihan*, p. 73, pp. 104–110.
76. Ibid., pp. 49–50. Honda had also cited this source in his debate with Ben-Dasan.
77. Honda and Naganuma, *Tennô no guntai*, p. 413, where Honda admits having used this pen name in the original edition.
78. *Asahi shinbun*, 6 January 2000; Mukai, "'Mujitsu da!' Chichi no sakebi ga kikoeru" *Seiron* March 2000, p. 63–65.
79. Irokawa, *Aru Shôwa-shi*, p. 61.
80. Kasahara, *Nankin jiken to sankô sakusen*, pp. 43–71.
81. *Asahi shinbun*, 20 April 1999.
82. Suzuki, *"Nankin daigyakusatsu" no maboroshi*, pp. 295–96; Suzuki, *Shin "Nankin daigyakusatsu" no maboroshi*, pp. 307–505; *Seiron*, July 1999, pp. 226–36; *SAPIO*, 14 July 1999, pp. 16–19. For errors in Suzuki's book, see a review by Yoshida Yutaka in *Shûkan kinyôbi*, 27 August 1999, pp. 34–37.
83. *Asahi jaanaru*, 28 September 1984, pp. 6–9.
84. Ibid., pp. 16–19.
85. Yasuda and Ishibashi, *Asahi shinbun no sensô sekinin*.
86. Katô, *Haisengo ron*, pp. 46–62; *Asahi shinbun*, 15 September 1997.
87. This psychological analysis meets resistance from left-wing critics, including the clinical psychiatrist Noda Masaaki; see *Asahi shinbun*, 11 December 1998.
88. Yoshida, *Nihonjin no sensôkan*, pp. 78–104.
89. Tanaka Masaaki performed this document tampering on the *Matsui Iwane taishô no jinchû nisshi* in 1985.
90. Watanabe, paraphrased from *Shûkan bunshun*, December 1990, p. 43.
91. *Shûkan bunshun* 15 December 1988, pp. 166–70; *Shokun!* January 1989, pp. 40–55; *Seiron*, March 2000, pp. 60–67.
92. *Asahi shinbun*, 29 April 2003; *Asahi shinbun*, webposted on 23 August 2005.

7

RADHABINOD PAL ON THE RAPE OF NANKING: THE TOKYO JUDGMENT AND THE GUILT OF HISTORY

Timothy Brook

Nothing would be achieved by seeking any premature escape from the guilt of history.

—Radhabinod Pal

There were many wartime incidents in East Asia on which the International Military Tribunal for the Far East (IMTFE), better known as the Tokyo War Crimes Trial, was called to adjudicate during its sessions in Tokyo. Among the most notorious was Japan's assault on Nanking in December 1937. Two of the tribunal's constituents brought to the court particular concerns for what the prosecution and the bench regularly referred to as the "Rape of Nanking," or what other authors in this volume call the "Nanking Atrocity." China regarded the incident as the most atrocious event of the war and highlighted the brutalities at Nanking among the cases that it submitted to the United Nations War Crimes Commission (UNWCC) between 1944 and 1946.[1] The United States, as I shall observe later in this chapter, had a different concern, which was to use the incident as a linchpin for its argument that the leaders of Japan conspired to commit war crimes throughout the region and throughout the war. As a consequence of this double interest, two Japanese were convicted as A-class war criminals and executed for "crimes against peace."[2]

The majority on the Tokyo bench felt that, within the terms of the charter under which the Tokyo tribunal was convened and the charges that the prosecution laid before it, justice was done. Public opinion has been less confident. In an article published in the summer of 1947, the young Sung-period historian James T. C. Liu observed that the trial was then regarded as a "second-rate show," having lost whatever public interest it might have excited well before it was over.[3] Unlike Nuremberg, which judged German leaders expeditiously, Tokyo dragged on for two and a half years. More to the point, Tokyo fell under the shadow of the Cold War, trying to dispense justice after the political alignments that had enabled it to be convened, had dissolved.[4] The voluminous transcripts were deposited in public archives but not published, unlike Nuremberg, which alone became the representative judicial act ending the war. Tokyo was regarded as nothing more than a footnote to Nuremberg, and those who thought they were engaged in breaking new judicial ground there had fallen silent by 1953.[5] Japanese reluctance to acknowledge war responsibility, and Chinese war weariness, compounded by the political complications of the Communist seizure of power, conspired further to erode the authority of the Tokyo judgment. Scholarly assessments since the 1970s have wondered whether Tokyo achieved anything more than victors' justice. This sense of disrepute has led popular writers more recently to continue dismantling the Tokyo judgment, though by arguing in quite the other direction: not that the postwar victors' judgments on Japan were too harsh, but that they were too weak; that Japan has still to bear its "legal burden," particularly for what happened in Nanking.[6]

Did the Tokyo judgment impose too little on Japan, or did it impose too much? Should the Rape of Nanking be subjected anew to judicial scrutiny, or does this way of dealing with the memory that has passed to the next generation create undesirable effects? In this chapter I wish to reevaluate the judicial status of that atrocity by considering how the IMTFE invoked, examined, and interpreted what happened in Nanking. My methodology will be to work not just with the tribunal's judgment but against it as well, by giving particular attention to the contentious dissenting opinion of the Indian member of the bench, Radhabinod Pal (1886–1967). Of the four judges who dissented from the majority judgment, Pal was the most uncompromising in his rejection of everything the tribunal did or stood for. He expressed serious doubt as to the reliability of the evidence that the prosecution brought forward, questioned the judicial meanings that it attached to Nanking, and refused to condemn anyone for what happened there. Pal's interpretation stands in stark contrast to opinion then, which generally accepted at least one of the two convictions on the evidence from Nanking, and also to opinion now, which doubts that two convictions were enough. Pal did not deny that the incident occurred, though he did at times bend over backward to find doubt where his colleagues saw none. But he doubted that the victors had the right to judge, or that the losers had the obligation to assume guilt for, any atrocities Japanese committed during the war, Nanking included. In Pal's view, as we shall see, the guilt adhered not to the individuals who stood before the bench, but to history, specifically the history of Western imperialism in Asia. Until that legacy was resolved, Western nations had no authority to hold Japan responsible for evils committed during the war.

However controversial Pal's arguments were at the time (they were), and however partisan the purposes to which they have been put subsequently (they have been),[7] their high standard of jurisprudence obliges us to proceed cautiously with arguments that justice has not been done. It is essential to be aware of the precise legal grounds on which the Rape of Nanking was prosecuted, the procedural disagreements among the judges who sat on the bench, and the divergences in the finding of facts. Otherwise we cannot begin to assess whether the Tokyo judgment constituted a persuasive history of that Atrocity, an appropriate adjudication, or an adequate procedure for its redress. Pal's counterargument also provides a useful review of the difficulties of defining, assessing, and assigning war guilt more generally. Given that we have not stopped committing crimes against humanity, nor figured out how to bring these to satisfactory judgment, Pal's careful discriminations and high caution may prove to be a valuable point of reference in discussions beyond those concerned with revisiting Japanese responsibility for military misconduct in Nanking.

The IMTFE and the Rape of Nanking

The Tokyo indictment consists of fifty-five counts. The first thirty-six are grouped under "crimes against peace," the next sixteen under "murder," and the final three under "war crimes and crimes against humanity." The prosecution wrote the Japanese attack on Nanking into the indictment as a charge of "murder" in Count 45. This count charged that twelve of the Japanese defendants "on the 12th December 1937, and succeeding days, by unlawfully ordering, causing and permitting the armed forces of Japan to attack the City of Nanking in breach of the Treaty Articles mentioned in Count 2 hereof and to slaughter the inhabitants contrary to international law, unlawfully killed and murdered many thousands of civilians and disarmed soldiers of the Republic of China, whose names and number are at present unknown."[8]

That the prosecution gave this incident its own separate charge signals that it thought evidence of Japanese conduct in Nanking would secure convictions, and it devoted much time to bringing forward relevant evidence to implicate the twelve defendants named in Count 45. As the trial proceeded, though, the target narrowed to two people: Matsui Iwane, the overall commander of the Central China Area Army (CCAA) until February 1938, and Hirota Kôki, the foreign minister serving at the time until May 1938. Count 45 was not the only count toward which evidence was introduced at the trial. In fact, Count 45 soon disappeared from view, and the bench in the end chose not to rule on it.[9] Both the prosecution and the bench were more interested in applying evidence from Nanking to the general charge of "conspiracy to commit conventional war crimes and crimes against humanity," specifically Counts 54 and 55. Under Count 54, Matsui, Hirota, and others were charged with "having conspired to order, authorize or permit" their subordinates to "commit breaches of the laws and customs of war." Count 55 charged them with having "violated the laws of war" by having "deliberately and recklessly disregarded their legal duty to take adequate steps to secure the observance and prevent breaches thereof."[10] Although neither count named Nanking, the prosecution used evidence from this atrocity as its basis for arguing that Matsui and Hirota be found guilty under this section of the indictment. Convictions for the Rape of Nanking were thus argued on general rather than specific grounds.

The principal source on which the prosecution relied for evidence regarding the Rape of Nanking was *Documents of the Nanking Safety Zone*. The sixty-nine documents in this book were generated by the German and American members of the International Committee (IC) for the Nanking Safety Zone (NSZ). During the first two months of the Japanese occupation, the IC sought to secure the safety of the Chinese population in Nanking. The book was published in 1939 and distributed worldwide in the hope of stimulating international support for China's struggle against Japan. The effort would yield unexpected results after the war, for substantial portions of the book were read directly into the war crimes record.[11] The prosecution solicited additional evidence from some of the American members of the IC, who were asked to testify, either in person or by written affidavit, about what they knew and experienced.[12] The court's reliance on their testimony meant that the IC was pivotal in shaping the tribunal's perception of Japanese conduct during the capture of Nanking. The bench's reconstruction of the event in its final judgment closely follows that account.[13]

Matsui's Defense

Matsui Iwane's defense consisted of an affidavit regarding his command of the CCAA, which was read into the record on 24 November 1947, and his cross-examination on that day and the following.[14] In both, he denied the charge contained in Count 54 that he "ordered, authorized, or permitted" his troops to destroy the city of Nanking or butcher its population. This denial was generally accepted. It proved to be the easiest of the denials he would make, however, and would not be sufficient to relieve him, as the overall commander of the forces that took Nanking, of responsibility for war crimes. For there were lesser but equally damning charges that he had tacitly allowed his soldiers to run amok, or that he had done nothing to discipline their conduct.

Matsui had two defense strategies, and relied on both at different times. The first was to go on the offensive and deny that atrocities had been committed in Nanking, and therefore argue that he could not be held responsible for something that did not occur. At certain times he attempted to use this defense in a restricted capacity, as when he declared, "I do not know of any fact of Chinese women and children being killed within the walls of Nanking."[15] His second defense strategy was to admit that atrocities may have happened, but that he could not be held responsible for them. Two alternative strands of logic stemmed from this second line of defense. The stronger one was that atrocities occurred, but that he was unaware of these at the time. The other tack was to admit that he had some knowledge of troop misconduct, but that he lacked either the opportunity or the capacity to stop it. In either case, the point of vulnerability in his defense was knowledge, not action: the less he knew, the less he might be held responsible for what took place. This defense strategy put Matsui in the difficult position of deciding how much knowledge he should admit to, and remaining consistent in that admission. Slight knowledge might mitigate the degree of his responsibility, as he could not have acted effectively to stop something about which he knew little. Yet it would be difficult to know only a little about something this extensive, especially as Matsui was present in Nanking in mid-December when the atrocity was in full swing and would be expected to have had knowledge of the situation around him. The fuller his knowledge, however, the more persuasive the prosecution's reasoning that he should have intervened more forcefully than he apparently did.

Matsui's defense oscillated among these contradictory postures of no, little, or some knowledge, though as much as possible, he sought to privilege the limits of his knowledge over the extent of his action. Even his declaration that no women or children were killed within the walls of Nanking was couched as an assertion about his knowledge, not about whether such killings had actually occurred. Matsui's evasive representation of his knowledge of breaches of discipline attracted the close attention of the prosecution, which devoted almost half of its cross-examination to trying to sort out for the record what he did and did not know. Under the pressure of cross-examination, Matsui conceded that incidents may have occurred and that he acquired some knowledge of these after first entering Nanking on 17 December. This information does not appear in his affidavit, however. When asked to explain its absence, he responded that he put in it only such information as he had received in an official capacity. "As far as I remember," he stated, "no reports were made in my capacity as Commander-in-Chief [actually, overall commander] of the CCAA, official or unofficial."[16] Nor, he said, did the consular staff in Nanking inform him that foreigners on the IC were lodging complaints almost daily about the conduct of the Japanese army.[17] This became yet another line of defense: that he was obliged to admit to, and act on, only *official* knowledge. Rumors of misconduct, which was all that he admitted hearing, were not sufficient to require him to act.

The deaths that Matsui did acknowledge in his affidavit as having occurred during the taking of Nanking were as a result of military engagement with the enemy—and accordingly not to be construed as war crimes. He allowed in his prepared statement that "a great number of Chinese soldiers and civilians were killed or wounded by bombs, artillery shells and rifle bullets during the Nanking campaign," but defended himself against the charge of committing war crimes by denying that a massacre had been planned. "Nothing can be further from the truth than the slander that the staff of the Japanese Army ordered or tolerated the above deaths."[18] As for Chinese civilians, Matsui insisted that his knowledge was based entirely on what he learned from one conversation with refugees, which he noted vaguely, took place in a temple on the top of a mountain he could no longer identify.[19] A last-minute question from the bench tried to probe his knowledge of criminal behavior from a different direction by inquiring whether, after the event, he heard of Japanese soldiers being court-martialed for their misconduct in Nanking. "I did hear at the time that two or three cases were being tried in Shanghai," Matsui admitted. To weaken the implication that he had failed to act responsibly, he added that when he tried to find out more about these cases after being relieved of his command, he discovered that "as the documents in question had been burned and were missing, I was unable to carry it any further and I was unable to ascertain the actual figures." He thus interposed one more layer of ignorance insulating himself from the event.[20]

At this point in the proceedings, as the acting president of the tribunal was turning to other matters, Matsui spoke up on his own account to say that "the offenses for which these men were tried were rape, robbery, looting, outrages and murder."[21] It is not clear what he intended by making this unsolicited—and potentially damning—interjection. Was it to acknowledge that misconduct did occur but that it was dealt with according to the procedures of military law? Whatever his intention in volunteering this information, he was not asked to elaborate. Matsui thus managed to get through his testimony without ever making an unambiguous statement about the full extent of his knowledge of atrocious conduct, skating dexterously between the claims of knowing nothing of what was going on and knowing something—though not knowing about anything in sufficient detail, or in an official capacity, to make him duty-bound to investigate. He appeared to believe that he could adhere to any of these postures and still relieve himself of liability for having failed to act effectively to halt the atrocities.

In its later summation for the defense, Matsui's counsel argued that the attack on Nanking was a defensive response to an "offensive campaign" that China was preparing against legitimate Japanese interests in Kiangsu and Chekiang provinces. "Unless the Japanese occupied the Nanking base for the time being, it seemed difficult to maintain peace in Central China as a whole and secure our interests therein. Such being the case, the Japanese Government, in order to restore peace of the whole area south of the Yangtze, determined to attack Nanking." In other words, the attack was not aggressive, and not unjustified. Counsel also argued mitigating circumstances, observing that the CCAA had to mount the attack "in a hurry under many difficulties. But this Army, being originally organized to secure the region around Shanghai, was in its setup and maintenance defective." This supported Matsui's claim that he was unable to exercise full discipline. In addition, the withdrawal of Chiang Kai-shek's KMT army created an "uncontrollable situation" that could not be blamed on the Japanese forces. Counsel also reiterated at some length Matsui's insistence in his affidavit that he gave orders that Nanking be captured in an orderly fashion. When he entered Nanking for the first time, he heard of "a few offenders of breach of military discipline and morality and he was greatly hurt, so that he ordered strict compliance with his former orders." When "the rumor of the unlawful acts of the Japanese Army in Nanking" reached him in Shanghai, his counsel noted that he issued instructions calling for punishment of the perpetrators and compensation for the victims. According to his own lawyers, then, Matsui had extensive knowledge of the disaster in Nanking but availed himself of every possible means to right the situation. In preference to Matsui's claim of relative ignorance, therefore, his counsel rested its case on reasonable action. Apparently they did not regard this switch in defense strategy as compromising Matsui's own interpretation, for beyond both always stood the more assertive argument that "Matsui's operations in Shanghai and Nanking were within the category of war in self-defense."[22]

Near the end of the summation, Matsui's counsel made a surprising move toward a new line of defense by asking that the charges against Matsui be set in a broader context: "The losses and damages then inflicted on human lives and material things in Nanking, are almost insignificant when compared to those which the principal cities of Japan suffered in consequence of the war. More so, would it be, if compared to the indescribable horrors to which countless innocent Japanese women and children and other civilians in Hiroshima and Nagasaki were subjected by the atomic bomb."[23] The rhetorical device of setting Japanese civilian losses against Chinese civilian losses is here given direct statement in the transcripts of the IMTFE proceedings for the first time, to my knowledge. The defense had attempted on 3 March 1947 to introduce evidence about the atomic bomb as part of its general submissions, but was overruled.[24] Although the *tu quoque* defense of using an atrocity on one side to cancel out an atrocity on the other was not allowed in the context of the law governing the tribunal, it was a popular device, at least in Japan, for trying to offset the losses that Japan inflicted with those that it suffered. As if sensing that this approach might not win Matsui a reprieve, his counsel went on to offer two blanket defenses specific to the Rape of Nanking. One was that much evidence for atrocities, being based on fear, misjudgement, and rumor, was exaggerated and sensationalized. The second, in some measure of contradiction with the first, was that Chinese soldiers bore much of the responsibility for the violence and destruction that did occur. This would include Chinese women, who, counsel alleged, approached Japanese soldiers for sex and cried rape later.[25]

Judging the Rape of Nanking

Given the almost universal condemnation of Japan for this atrocity, Matsui's counsel faced grave difficulty in mounting a persuasive legal defense. Their client was too closely associated with the Rape, especially in Chinese eyes, to be excused for his part in this incident. Such expectations may have compromised the legal viability of the procedure that found Matsui guilty. Whatever the general had or had not done, or whatever his counsel did or did not argue, was unlikely to deflect the tribunal from holding someone among those arraigned as A-class war criminals for "crimes against peace" responsible for what happened in Nanking, and Matsui was the likeliest military candidate to cast in that role. Some of his counsel's arguments may have been responsible for persuading the bench to dismiss the first eight of the nine counts against Matsui, but it could not defeat Count 55. The bench did not hold that Matsui conspired to wage crimes against peace or even to commit atrocities at Nanking, but it did judge that he was guilty of failing to act in such a way as to prevent their occurrence. "The Tribunal is satisfied that Matsui knew what was happening," declared the judgment, showing that the defense of partial knowledge had not worked. But, the judgment went on, Matsui "did nothing, or nothing effective to abate these horrors. He did issue orders before the capture of the City enjoining propriety of conduct upon his troops and later he issued further orders to the same purport. These orders were of no effect as is now known, and as he must have known."[26] Matsui's knowledge, combined with his failure to act commensurately to that knowledge, amounted to criminal negligence.[27] On this count alone, Matsui was condemned.

Matsui was not alone in being found criminally liable for failing to take effective action. The IMTFE also condemned Hirota Kôki under the same Count 55, among others. Hirota was foreign minister at the time the CCAA occupied Nanking. The bench judged that, as he knew about the Rape of Nanking, he should have intervened more strenuously with the Army Ministry to correct the problem. His complicity in this matter was far less important to his overall conviction, however, than his earlier role in cabinet decisions. For it was Hirota who stepped in as the new premier in the wake of the abortive military coup of 26 February 1936, which effectively put the army in control of the government. (He lost his post when the army withdrew its support a year later.) Hirota's conviction on Count 55 was not unanimous among the members on the bench.[28] It also drew some opposition in diplomatic circles when it was announced. Robert Craigie, who knew Hirota while serving as British ambassador to Japan, wrote at once to the Foreign

Office urging that the British government intervene on Hirota's behalf. "It looks to me," he stated, "as if, through Russian and possibly Chinese misrepresentation, a serious miscarriage of justice may occur in this case unless immediate action is taken." Craigie suspected the Chinese government of having pressured the IMTFE to secure more than one conviction for the Rape of Nanking. The foreign secretary referred the appeal to a member of his staff for comment. After consulting with Comyns Carr, the British assistant prosecutor at Tokyo (who had managed to get Craigie's written testimony for the defense thrown out earlier that year), his staff person judged that Hirota had been intimately involved in working out the plan for Japanese aggression during his term as prime minister, as the other counts against Hirota alleged. The foreign secretary accordingly saw no point in raising Hirota's culpability under Count 55, as he felt justice was properly served on other grounds.[29]

The IMTFE judgments on Hirota and Matsui were among the innovations in international law that the postwar tribunals made. Individuals in positions of high authority could henceforth be held legally responsible for military atrocities committed by state personnel, even if these individuals did not directly plan or order them to be carried out. Nuremberg adopted the same principle of individual responsibility, but limited its applicability to actual participation, which had to be proved, rather than allow position alone to implicate a leader.[30] In terms of indictable offenses, Tokyo employed the categories used at Nuremberg, which in addition to conventional war crimes and "crimes against peace" (the latter covering atrocities against civilian populations) laid charges of "crimes against humanity" as introduced in the London Agreement.[31] Tokyo was disinclined, however, to define or pursue "crimes against humanity," preferring to lump these with "conventional war crimes" in the final section of the indictment (along with Counts 54 and 55) without defining or applying these "crimes against humanity" in legal argument.

With Count 55, however, Tokyo introduced an important innovation. It enlarged the concept of war crimes to include omission, or making failure to prevent war crimes, a war crime itself.[32] B. V. A. Röling, the Dutch justice and colleague most sympathetic to Radhabinod Pal, understood the criminalization of omission as crucial for gaining convictions at Tokyo. This was because, unlike at Nuremberg, "here it was less a question of orders to commit war crimes given on high authority, but rather of constant criminal practice both on land and sea."[33] The argument of conspiracy thus had to bear greater legal weight at Tokyo,[34] given that there was no Hitler, and no clique around a Hitler, to whom military aggression could unequivocally be traced. The emperor Hirohito, or Shōwa emperor, might have been cast as Hitler's functional equivalent in Japan, but the American Occupation authorities kept Hirohito out of the trial and ensured that none of the defendants incriminated him.[35] Even had he been indicted, it would have been difficult for the prosecution to present the emperor Hirohito as another Hitler, given the constitutional limitations on the emperor's powers and the ambiguity of the documentation regarding his role in decision making. The IMTFE judgment therefore argued that Japan's "far-reaching plans for waging wars of aggression and the prolonged and intricate preparation for and waging of these wars of aggression were not the work of one man," and thus had to be conceived as "the work of many leaders acting in pursuance of a common plan for the achievement of a common object."[36] With no final "high authority" at the top of the structure, the tribunal was hard-pressed to rely on conspiracy to convict the upper leaders. The criminalization of omission, under these awkward conditions, was therefore essential for securing convictions.[37]

Pal's Dissent

After the IMTFE had been set up, states organizing the tribunal decided to invite India and the Philippines—both victims of Japanese aggression and both in the process of decolonization—to appoint representatives to the bench and the prosecuting team. Pal was the Indian appointee (his home village today lies on the Bangladeshi side of the India-Bangladesh border that runs through Bengal). He reached Tokyo on 14 May and made his first appearance at the tribunal three days later, several weeks into the proceedings.[38] As a latecomer, Pal did not regard himself as bound by the agreement the original nine justices made before his arrival to deliver a unanimous judgment, as the bench at Nuremberg chose to do. For him to reject this agreement at the outset indicates that he must have gone to Tokyo with the foreknowledge that he would disagree with the majority. His decision undid the unanimity agreement and opened the way for four other separate opinions.[39] Pal missed substantial portions of the trial to return to Calcutta to care for his ailing wife, including the cross-examination of Matsui in November 1947, but he did not regard his absence as disqualifying him from delivering a judgment.[40] And that judgment was severe. In his dissenting opinion, which was numbered to 1,235 pages but exceeds that total, Pal laid out with care and in detail a host of objections to the majority judgment, and indeed to the entire judicial process. He objected to the constitution and jurisdiction of the tribunal, to the concepts of aggressive war and omission, and to the tribunal's loose rules of evidence and procedure. These objections led him to find none of the accused guilty.

At several points in his dissenting opinion, Pal addresses the charges arising from the Rape of Nanking, and it is on these passages that I will focus attention.[41] He did not deny that Japanese soldiers had acted evilly in Nanking, noting that "the evidence is still overwhelming that atrocities were perpetrated by the members of the Japanese armed forces against the civilian population." He accepted the fact that injury had been done. But he did not find that General Matsui failed to regulate the conduct of his troops, nor did he find foreign minister Hirota at fault for not intervening with the Army Ministry to stop brutalities in the field. More generally, Pal was disturbed by the retrospective moral uses to which the prosecution put the event, prompting him to decline to capitalize "rape" and to install the word in scare quotes when he used it. He preferred to speak in terms of "the Nanking Incident."

To understand his rejection of the charge of criminal responsibility for Nanking, it is necessary to review some of Pal's legal objections to the tribunal's composition, procedures, and legal reasoning.[42] We turn to each of these now.

1. The IMTFE was a military tribunal on which judges from the countries that had been victorious in war sat in judgment over the defeated. Only Japanese were indicted for their misconduct, and only their enemies could decide whether they had misconducted themselves. This arrangement might satisfy victors' justice, but it was not congruent with the judicial ideals that Pal believed should be in force at this momentous point in the development of international law. "As a judicial tribunal," Pal reminded his fellow judges in the conclusion to his opinion, "we cannot behave in any manner which may justify the feeling that the setting up of the tribunal was only for the attainment of an objective which was essentially political, though cloaked by a judicial appearance."[43] But that is precisely what the tribunal was: a device by which the chief victors over Japan, the Americans, sought to establish a narrative of war guilt for Japan that justified their new dominance in the Pacific. Pal was not alone in doubting the composition of the bench. Shortly after the trial, Röling expressed similar anxieties. The nations from which the judges were selected had "a strong interest in using a post-war trial to establish certain events, to whitewash themselves, to blame others." As he recalled later, "it was quite impossible to achieve the detachment one likes to observe in judges." Röling would have preferred sharing the bench with judges from neutral nations. "They would have been a constant element of objectivity, and often during our deliberations in chambers, I regretted their absence, which would have prevented things, which could, too easily now, go unchallenged."[44] At the outset of the trial, the Japanese counsel for former premier Tôjô Hideki attempted to challenge the impartiality of all the appointments to the bench on the allegation of prior interest.[45] He began with its Australian president, William Webb, who had headed Australia's national UNWCC office and as its war crimes commissioner had personally investigated war crimes in New Guinea in 1945, making him both prosecutor and judge.[46] Webb summarily dismissed the argument.

The quality of the bench was not enhanced by the qualifications of its members. Although they were versed in law, not all were acquainted with law relevant to this case, nor did any of them have a reputation as an international jurist.[47] Possibly the least qualified from a legal point of view was the second Chinese appointment to the Tokyo bench, Mei Ju-ao. Mei had received his legal education at the University of Chicago, but he had not practiced law extensively, nor had he any prior experience on the bench. He was appointed by the Chinese government not for his judicial capacity, but for his loyalty to the KMT political leadership. It is difficult to suppose that Mei would have supported a judgment that did not punish Japanese leaders for the Rape of Nanking.

2. From the faulty composition of the tribunal followed procedural flaws. Most serious was what Pal regarded as the tribunal's predisposition to find guilt. The IMTFE was mounted on the assumption that someone should be made responsible for the terrible disasters that the winning side had suffered. Reviewing the history of scapegoating since World War I, Pal noted that people of his generation had come to demand punishment when a despised military leader was defeated.[48] Even if the accused were guilty, Pal argued, that guilt had to be proved rather than adduced on the basis of prior moral reasoning or a misplaced idealism in the capacity of the international community to administer justice. As he expressed his caution in a later publication, "the burning of many a Joan [of Arc] may thus only need half an hour: but several centuries would always be needed to find out the truth." Single-minded pursuit of what appears to be the truth without due procedural caution can undercut the possibility of attaining it, for "every truth, however true in itself, yet taken apart from others becomes only a snare." The greater task is not assigning guilt, but "enlarging the human community so that the principles of order and justice should govern the international as well as national community."

Pal's concern that the tribunal was predisposed to accept culpability on assertion, rather than on proof, was tied to his sense that the bench failed to uphold the highest standards of evidence. He found the court too ready to admit second- and third-hand testimony that could not be corroborated. Article XIII of the Tokyo charter allowed that "the Tribunal shall not be bound by technical rules of evidence" and might "admit any evidence which it deems to have probative value."[49] Pal worried that this freedom with regard to evidence failed to filter out dubious testimony regarding atrocities, which could be expected to be animated by powerful emotions that always favored the prosecution's case. "Excited or prejudiced observers," as he put it, might well be tempted to relate more than they actually saw, or to present it in highly colored ways. He singled out for particular criticism the testimony of two Nanking witnesses brought before the court, Dr. Hsü Ch'uan-yin of the Red Swastika Society, a charitable organization in Nanking that buried many of the victims of the massacre, and John Magee of the IC that established the NSZ. "Both these witnesses have given us horrible accounts of the atrocities committed at Nanking," Pal acknowledged. "It is, however, difficult to read this evidence without feeling that there have been distortions and exaggerations." After reviewing what he considered inexact testimony about rapes and suicides by witnesses who could not have seen them happen, Pal comments: "I am not sure if we are not here getting accounts of events witnessed only by excited or prejudiced observers." He felt that the evidence of both witnesses, based on observations "of the most fleeting kind," was not sufficiently scrutinized for credibility. Under the circumstances, "All the irrelevancies of rumours and canny guesses became hidden under a predisposition to believe the worst, created perhaps by the emotions normal to the victims of injury."[50] While these emotions were to be expected, the bench should have been more cautious in accepting the testimonies they colored as evidence of what actually happened.

3. Rather than summarize Pal's objections to the tribunal's legal reasoning, I prefer to present his own succinct synopsis of those objections in a book on international law that he published 7 years after the trial:

1. The Charter did not define the crime in question.

2. (a) It was not within the competence of its author to define any crime.

   (b) Even if any crimes would have been defined by the Charter, that definition would have been *ultra vires* and would not have been binding on us.

3. It was within our competence to question the authority of the Charter in this respect.

4. The law applicable to the case must be international law as found by us.

5. The Pact of Paris did not affect the pre-existing legal position of war in international life. War in international life remains as before, outside the province of law, its conduct alone having been brought within the domain of law.

   (a) The Pact of Paris did not come within the category of law at all and consequently failed to introduce any change in the legal position of a belligerent state or in the jural incidence of belligerency.

6. No category of war became criminal or illegal in international life either by the Pact of Paris or as a result of the same or in any other way.

7. The individuals comprising the Governments and functioning as agents of that Government incur no criminal responsibility in international law for the acts alleged.

8. The international community has not as yet reached a stage which would make it expedient to include judicial process for condemning and punishing either states or individuals.[51]

Pal formulated these objections mainly in response to Article V (a) of the Tokyo charter, which defined "crimes against peace" as "the planning, preparation, initiation or waging of a declared or undeclared war of aggression, or a war in violation of international law, treaties, agreements or assurances, or participation in a common plan or conspiracy for the accomplishment of any of the foregoing."[52] This article, taken with minor revision from the Nuremberg charter, outlawed "aggressive war," declared a war that violated treaties illegal, and made conspiracy to wage such a war criminal. To justify the claims of the

Tokyo charter, the prosecution offered the Pact of Paris (or Kellogg-Briand Pact) of 1928, which renounced the use of war as national policy except in self-defense.[53] Pal was not persuaded that either this, or any other international agreement in effect as of 1937, specifically declared war illegal; nor did he find any definition of aggressive war either in prior jurisprudence or even in the Tokyo charter itself, hence his opening complaint that "the Charter did not define the crime in question." There were simply no adequate laws or precedents on which to make rulings about the illegality of war, and the Tokyo charter could not make war criminal after the fact. Similarly, Pal argued, international law had not yet determined that conspiracy to wage war was illegal. These legal difficulties were in any case beyond whatever extrapolations one might make from the Pact of Paris, inasmuch as Pal agreed with the defense counsels' claim that Japan had waged a war of self-defense. On the same grounds he had difficulties with the charter's assumptions that states could be found criminally liable for waging aggressive war, and that individuals serving those states could be punished for that service. As Pal argued in regard to the Rape of Nanking: "War is hell. Perhaps it has been truly said that if the members of the government can be tried and punished for happenings like this, it would make peace also a hell."[54] Pal doubted that the tribunal had adequate legal ground to find individuals responsible for activities that, at the time of their commission, had not been defined as crimes. Triumphant militaries might choose to execute those against whom they had fought, but a court could not put itself in the same relationship to an accused whom the victors might choose to bring before it.

Pal on the Rape of Nanking

Pal's fundamental rejection of the legal viability of the IMTFE left him no position from which even to pass judgment on conventional war crimes, defined in Article V (b) as "violations of the laws and customs of war," for which adequate law did exist. This rejection meant that he had to decline the authority that the Tokyo charter gave him to adjudicate on the conventional war crimes that occurred in Nanking, most starkly the execution of surrendered troops. The legal shortcomings of the process in which he was engaged trumped any claims of injury that might be made against the accused. To find Japanese leaders guilty of war crimes would be, for him, to succumb to the partiality of the entire proceedings, turn law into the device of the stronger against the weaker, and make a mockery of justice. If it also meant that no judgment could be passed on Nanking at this level of war crimes, it was a price Pal did not regard as too high to pay.

The starting point of Pal's difficulty with the prosecution's view of the Rape of Nanking was its contention that leaders can always exercise effective control over troops in the field. He noted from testimony that Matsui and other members of the government did attempt on several occasions to bring undisciplined soldiers to heel. Matsui's failure to be effective Pal attributed to a breakdown in the "machinery" of military organization, not to the general's inaction. The responsibility of other leaders was even more remote: "as members of the government, it was not their duty to control the troops in the field, nor was it within their power so to control them." A leader is "entitled to rely on the competency" of his field officers and should not be obliged to bear legal responsibility for every action of the soldiers under his command, so long— and this is the limiting condition—as he had fulfilled his "duty to take such appropriate measures as were in his power to control the troops under his command."[55] Pal thus sided with Matsui's counsel's argument that Matsui had known what was happening in Nanking, as well as with Matsui's own argument that he had acted in such a way as to show that atrocities against civilians were not policy. To hold Matsui or Hirota responsible by omission for the continuation of those atrocities was not justice but scapegoating.

Secondly, Pal objected to the representation that acts of misconduct had occurred in the context of aggressive war. He countered that Japan had not waged war aggressively as "national policy" but had acted in self-defense. Western powers had been pressuring Asia for decades prior to the outbreak of war with such force that Japan had to strike back to survive. Moreover, he deemed, Anglo-American interference in the conflict between China and Japan had been "in defiance of the theory of neutrality and of the fundamental obligations that the law of nations still imposes upon non-belligerent Powers."[56] However much Japan had breached the principle of sovereign inviolability in its conduct in China, that breach did not justify other states from becoming involved. Pal got around the Chinese claim that Japan had interfered with China's sovereignty by characterizing the conflict between them as an "internal" matter in which both sides had legitimate interests. In this view he was profoundly at odds with the rest of the bench, and possibly even with his own logic, which required the invocation of sovereignty as inviolable in order to challenge the presence of Western nations in Asia.

Pal's unwillingness to assign criminal liability for Nanking was rooted most deeply in his refusal to find conspiracy in the facts presented before the tribunal. The prosecution staked its overall case against Japan's leaders on this charge, that all of Japan's aggressive actions in East Asia between 1928 and 1945 were linked in a vast and comprehensive conspiracy, in which every act and decision confirmed what had preceded it and which led inexorably to the next. Pal was utterly contemptuous of this reading of Japan's actions in what he chose to call "Greater East Asia." "The alleged conspiracy which the prosecution has attempted to trace and describe is one of the most curious and unbelievable things ever sought to be drawn in a judicial proceeding," he declared. "A long series of isolated and disconnected events covering a period of at least fourteen years are marshalled together in a hodgepodge fashion; and out of this conglomeration the prosecution asks the Tribunal to find beyond all reasonable doubt that a 'common plan or conspiracy' existed to accomplish the objectives stated in the indictment."[57] In his estimation, the evidence of conspiracy was at best, and only, circumstantial. As he reminded his fellow judges, "for our present purpose, it is not for us to see whether or not the events and their spread could be *justified*. We are now only to see whether the happenings could be *explained* otherwise than by the existence of a conspiracy."[58] An alternative explanation was indeed available if one believed that Japan's survival was under threat. International politics may have forced Japan into a foreign policy that was consistent, but this did not mean that the Japanese government was conspiratorial in pursuing it. The victor nations sitting in judgment wanted conspiracy, and built it into the logic of the Tokyo charter as a net through which none of Japan's highest politicians, bureaucrats, or officers could escape; it also justified the desperate measures of the American total-war response, from firebombing to atomic detonation.

Moreover, the charge of conspiracy placed undue burden on Nanking. In the prosecution's narrative of war criminality, this was a key event; it marked the moment at which Japanese military domination of East Asia shifted from encroachment to atrocity. Every atrocity after Nanking could then be derived from this moment, forging a chain that demonstrated conspiracy. The prosecution was using Nanking not just to gain convictions for Matsui Iwane and Hirota Kôki, but also to construe "similar atrocities ... perpetrated subsequently in several other theaters of war" as conspiratorially tied to Japan's refusal to do anything about the "atrocious conduct of the Japanese Army" in Nanking.[59] The Rape of Nanking was thus installed as the moment of origin for a long series of "similar atrocities" stretching across Southeast Asia and into the Pacific. The continuity that the prosecution alleged between Nanking and subsequent Japanese war crimes proved that that misdeeds were consistent and so must have emanated conspiratorially from the central government. The underlying goal of the American-dominated prosecution in arguing for continuity, Pal believed, was to identify the mistreatment of American servicemen in the Pacific as being of the same category as the brutalization of Nanking residents. This connection is built into Count 44 (directly preceding Count 45 on Nanking), in which the prosecution charged the accused with the wholesale murder of both prisoners of war *and* civilians of the countries opposed to Japan, thereby unifying the two categories of victims, regardless of location or nationality or status as combatants, as a single object of judicial address. Condemnation of Japanese actions against Chinese civilians in Nanking thus entailed equal condemnation of actions against American combatants in the Pacific. Tying the two together was for Pal a fabrication of logic, not a link of substance. He categorically rejected that "such offenses were committed pursuant to any government policy. There is no evidence, testimonial or circumstantial, concomitant, prospectant, retrospectant, which would in any way lead to the inference that the government in any way permitted the commission of such offenses."[60] There was no conspiracy, and Nanking was not the place to anchor it. What happened in the Pacific had no necessary or legal connection with Nanking: each atrocity charge stood, and fell, on its own merits.

Culture as the Redundancy of the Political?

Pal's judgment did not come as a huge surprise to his fellow judges, but it did alarm their governments. As soon as the dissenting opinion was made available, the head of the British liaison mission in Tokyo hurried to figure out why Pal had broken ranks so completely with his colleagues on the bench. The Canadian justice, Stuart McDougall, told him that Pal had decided against joining in any condemnation of the accused from the time he first arrived in Tokyo.[61] There was discussion among the British as to whether the government of India had given Pal prior direction, but all that India's representative had recommended during diplomatic consultations with the British government prior to Pal's appointment was that no death sentences be handed down; no other instructions were given.[62] The head of the British liaison mission speculated that India may have wanted Pal to file a dissenting judgment "for political reasons," presumably to embarrass erstwhile colonial masters. This suggestion was dismissed in the foreign office on the grounds that even V. K. Krishna Menon, Congress' negotiator in Europe, was reported to have found the judgment disquieting.[63] Yet while British paranoia over the loss of India may have induced some exaggeration in their reading of Pal's dissent, the presence of a political understanding behind his opinion seems undeniable. The question we might ask is this: Did Pal's legal and political thinking coincide, or was one pressing the other into service?

To answer this question, we might first consider Pal's own scathing evaluation of the role of politics in the tribunal. As the head of the British mission himself put it when he telegraphed the news of Pal's dissenting opinion back to the foreign office, Pal regarded the IMTFE as "an attempt to achieve political ends with the appearance of legal justice."[64] At the root of Pal's dissatisfaction was the limitation on the IMTFE's jurisdiction to investigate only one side of the conflict and confer impunity on the other. Had both sides been arraigned, the tribunal would have been empowered to examine a much wider range of issues. In his own words, "It has been said that a victor can dispense to the vanquished everything from mercy to vindictiveness; but the one thing the victor cannot give to the vanquished is justice. At least, if a tribunal be rooted in politics as opposed to law, no matter what its form and pretenses, the apprehension thus expressed would be real, unless 'justice is really nothing else than the interest of the stronger'."[65]

Pal's complaint about the political ends that the tribunal served so offended the Filipino judge Delfin Jaranilla that he wrote his own concurring opinion to reaffirm the reasonableness of the legal logic underpinning the majority findings. If Pal refused to accept the law laid down in the Tokyo charter, specifically with respect to the illegality of aggressive war, Jaranilla reasoned, Pal never should have take the oath of office under the charter in the first place. And, Jaranilla bluntly dismissed Pal's view that individual leaders could not bear responsibility for Japan's wartime conduct as "absurd."[66] The stridency of Jaranilla's rebuke may have been fueled by the fact that the Philippines had been brutally occupied by Japan, whereas British India had not. There, anti-imperialist anger looked elsewhere than at Japan.

The most interesting attempt to decipher the logic of Pal's unique opposition to the IMTFE has come from the Indian psychoanalyst and social critic Ashis Nandy. In sympathy with his subject, Nandy has sought to probe Pal's intellectual and moral formation as a late-colonial Indian intellectual to make sense of the extraordinary position he took in Tokyo. To this inquiry Nandy brings his own desire to understand how colonial and postcolonial Indians have adapted to the oppression that their training in the ideals of Western civilization has placed on them, and to conceive of ways to bridge the polarities that colonialism has imposed.[67] Pal thus emerges easily into Nandy's view as a culture hero, whom he addresses as such via an implicit analogy with Krishna. Locating Pal on the historical cusp between colonial British India and postcolonial independent India (a cusp that in modified form Nandy himself occupies a generation later), Nandy argues that Pal judged as he did because his thinking as a modern jurist coexisted with a native Hindu "worldview that shuns binary oppositions." He perceives in Pal a unity between these worldviews where otherwise there appears only a stark bifurcation between the international jurist working at the International Law Commission in Geneva in the 1950s—where Pal continued to dispute prevailing wisdoms of international justice as he had done in Tokyo—and the Hindu legal philosopher distrustful of the moral simplicity of assigning all blame on one party in a dispute involving two. The latter impulse won out, according to Nandy, who himself desires to transcend the bifurcations imposed by living postcolonially in a global context. It was not "the culture of modern international law" that explains Pal's judgment at Tokyo, but "his long exposure to the traditional laws of India." Pal's manipulation of the language of international law camouflaged a very different conception of law as reconciliation to achieve an end to conflict. Nandy concludes that Pal was "both an Indian and a Victorian trying to transcend the moral dichotomy of the age," but for whom the Indian tradition trumped what otherwise appeared to be a commitment to the laws of the post-Enlightenment West.[68]

Nandy's analysis slightly condescends to what he regards as Pal's charming but misguided progressivism, which induced Pal "to provide a comparative picture and to explain India in Western terms."[69] By embedding Pal in his native culture, by bracketing the international with the local, Nandy restores the ground of Pal's personal identity, but it is a cultural move that makes Pal's anti-imperialist politics appear redundant to a worldview shaped by culture. This analysis neglects the particular world history that furnished Pal with the perspective from which he rendered his judgment at Tokyo, a world history intensely political in its content and usage. Pal's judgment does more than put the West equally at fault: it blames the West for the war. In Pal's view, the charge of "aggressive war" against Japan had to rebound on the West, for Western nations had waged aggressive war in Asia for centuries. Until the legacy of Western imperialism was brought to account, "even justice" for Japan was impossible.[70] His refusal to accept the tribunal's judgment thus rested less on a cultural objection, in my view, than on a political one. What mattered were not particular acts of the war and how to redress them, but the historical conditions that produced the war and blocked the establishment of world peace. To a Japanese defense lawyer serving at the IMTFE, Pal's refusal to join the Western powers in punishing Japan marked him as the only advocate of genuine world peace on the tribunal.[71] This observation may have involved its own "cultural" logic, but it too was essentially a political judgment.

Although Nandy acknowledges Pal's commitment to Asian solidarity, he treats Pal's anti-imperialist politics as a second-order expression of his consciousness, rather than credit it as a first-order sign of the commitments around which he organized his life. Nandy's downgrading of Pal's politics is analytically consistent with his own understanding that colonization forces a disjunction between politics and culture.[72] Yet by allowing that disjunction to dominate his analysis, and so leave out Pal's politics, Nandy neglects a significant element of Pal's particular historical experience. Against Nandy, I would argue that Pal's judgment at Tokyo was shaped by politics that do not resolve automatically into his Hindu consciousness, however much that consciousness shaped his appreciation of law's moral purpose.

Politics and the Redundancy of the Legal?

What was that politics? B. V. A. Röling, who continued his friendship with Pal even after the Tokyo trial, noted in a later reminiscence that Pal had accepted Japan's slogan of "Asia for the Asians" and regarded the war as just because it was waged "to liberate Asia from the Europeans." Röling also recalled Pal later saying that he had supported the Indian National Army (INA).[73] The INA was the force the Japanese recruited from Indian troops after the fall of Singapore in 1942 and sent against the British on the India-Burma border in 1943. As an educated Calcuttan who supported the INA, Pal shows himself to have been among the influential Bengali who followed the radical Indian nationalist, Subhas Chandra Bose. Bose, a prominent leader of the

Indian National Congress, was the figure around whom crystallized radical opposition to Mohandas Gandhi's moderate position within the Congress. He regarded Gandhi as hopelessly mired in capitulations and compromises with the British, which, he felt, would forever keep India back from crossing the threshold of independence.[74] After World War II was well underway, Bose broke with Gandhi completely. He turned in 1941 first to Germany, then to Japan, to seek support for an armed struggle for independence from Britain. He hoped to see the Japanese-organized INA become the revolutionary force that would drive the British out of India, though he died in an airplane crash off Taiwan before the war ended and that illusion was shattered. Had he lived, the British would have arraigned Bose on charges of treason, as they did many of the Indian officers and soldiers who joined the INA or the small Indian detachments that fought in Europe alongside Germans. Still, Indian opinion at the war's end regarded Bose as a martyr for the cause of independence; many revered him as Gandhi's equal.[75]

This background should alert the reader only to the obvious: Pal brought to the tribunal a particular orientation to issues of conflict, occupation, and war that was shaped by the colonial context in which he practiced law. His willingness to excuse all charges against Japanese leaders may have been legally argued, but it rested on his prior acceptance of Japan's claim that it had waged war to liberate Asia for Asians. As scandalous as this position may strike some observers today, it was far less controversial among educated Indians who desired to see the end of British rule in India, and who sympathized with Bose's desperate actions to bring that about. As an official in the British foreign office candidly recognized at the time, "there is no doubt that Mr. Pal's views are representative of a large section of Indian opinion. Many Indian papers have endorsed his judgment."[76] Indeed, within the coming year, legal opinion in India would go even further, dismissing the Tokyo tribunal purely as a war measure and doubting that it could have any valid constitution in law. As a caustic commentator phrased it, "to a mere lawyer, the trials appear as crude and ineffective attempts at clothing the sword with something like a wig, and he should let such attempts pass without further comments."[77] A dramatic affirmation of the political nature of his judgment, which cannot be confirmed, is the story that Pal visited the condemned men in prison after the trial ended. "You were the leaders of Japan," he is alleged to have told them. "Through that leadership Asia was liberated."[78] And this much was true: the effect of the war was to break Europe's colonial hold over Asia. That it did so at an extraordinary cost for Asians, particularly for Chinese, did not deflect Pal from his enthusiasm for Asian liberation.

There is a second element to Pal's politics that shaped his legal opinion—his view that the dropping of atomic bombs on civilian targets was the greatest atrocity of the war. Pal only occasionally mentions the atomic bomb in his judgment, as its evaluation was not part of the tribunal's mandate, but it casts a shadow across much of his text. Pal first treats it in the context of arguing against the contention that preparation for war was considered a crime before the Second World War. Dubious of the popular homily—popular in the West, that is—that the atomic blasts had forged a unity of all people and made war unthinkable, Pal argues that those who dropped the bombs did not share this understanding. They were simply using them to gain advantage over their enemy by means of a weapon that had not yet been declared illegal.

> I do not perceive much difference between what the German Emperor is alleged to have announced during the First World War in justification of the atrocious methods directed by him in the conduct of that war and what is being proclaimed after the Second World War in justification of these inhuman blasts. I am not sure if the atom bombs have really succeeded in blowing away all the pre-war humbug; we may be just dreaming. It is yet to be seen how far we have been alive to the fact that world's present problems are not merely the more complex reproductions of those which have plagued us since 1914; that the new problems are not merely old national problems with world implications, but are real world problems and problems of humanity.[79]

Much later in his text, Pal returns to this theme, and even to the same example of the German kaiser, to lead into an analysis of specific war crimes, the first of which is the Rape of Nanking. Like Matsui's counsel, he pits atrocities against each other and finds the "decision to use the atom bomb" the worse offense.[80] When he moves on to the question of the mistreatment of downed American bomber pilots, he again pits that misconduct against "the havoc which can be wrought by the indiscriminate launching of bombs and projectiles," both conventional and atomic, and judges the Americans as having inflicted the greater damage. He also slyly cites the opinion of the American jurist Ellery Stowell that the atomic bomb, rather than make war unthinkable, only changed its rules.[81] By excluding the atomic bomb from the jurisdiction of the IMTFE, the Americans in Tokyo ruled out the possibility of the tribunal undertaking a global evaluation of the war. If the tribunal had been prepared to face "the implications of atomic explosion," Pal observes in the concluding section of his judgment, the outcome of the tribunal would have been completely different.[82] Then it would have meant a judgment not just on Japan, but on all parties.

Pal made his observation in the context of deploring the politics in which the tribunal was fatally rooted. "Had we been openly called upon to decide such political issues," Pal observes, "the entire proceedings would have assumed a different appearance altogether, and the scope of our enquiry would have been much wider than what we allowed it to assume."[83] But it was not: this was a military tribunal convened within a particular political environment to dispense judgment on those who had committed aggression against those who had won the war. It also endorsed a particular view of history, one with which Pal disagreed. The IMTFE history narrated the injury done by Japanese to all of its Pacific neighbors since 1937, in the opening phase of which Matsui loomed large. It was a history that ended in August 1945 and in which the present—the emerging Cold War, atomic warfare, and American hegemony in the Pacific—never appeared. Pal's history, in contrast, went back several centuries and featured European colonialism as the defining feature of Asia in both the past and the present. In that history, Matsui's actions in China were of little consequence to larger patterns. To hold this general responsible for crimes that the West had committed many times over was to evade the real issue in Asia. It was in this context that Pal made the remark that appears at the head of this essay: "Nothing would be achieved by seeking any premature escape from the guilt of history."[84] The incompatibility of these histories was rooted in turn in the incommensurability between the two postcolonial futures that Radhabinod Pal and the other ten judges imagined for Asia: one out of, and the other still in, the shadow of Western imperialism.

If Pal's disagreement with the tribunal was political, are we justified in dismissing his legal reasoning as redundant, employed merely as second-order objections in the service of a different vision of how the world should be? Pal's exoneration of Matsui certainly raises this troubling question. His judgment suggests his own unease with combining legal and political reasoning. While declining to declare a leader legally responsible for crimes he did not order, Pal still found it necessary to note that Matsui acted to impose discipline after he learned of his troops' misconduct. Like Matsui, he played both sides of this issue—and conveniently could find Matsui guilty on neither. I suspect that he would have found a way to excuse Matsui even had he been unable to demonstrate that the general had taken appropriate action; for however well Pal argued the legal limits concerning an overall commander's responsibility over troops in the field, the exoneration rests ultimately on the political judgment that Japan was acting justly in Asia. Given this judgment, anything Matsui did was of only circumstantial relevance: Matsui disappeared from judicial scrutiny.

The redundancy that Pal's politics seems to impose on the legal logic of his decision is less disturbing if we step back from the substantive view of law that prevails in discussions of the Rape of Nanking and recognize that law never operates independently of politics and history. To insist that it does was an important illusion governing the IMTFE, an illusion that Pal strove to expose. Law mattered to Pal to the degree that it observed the highest standards of procedure, evidence, and definition; but law itself was only a tool for other things, to which we now briefly turn by way of conclusion.

Truth and Reconciliation

Pal's arguments, however persuasive separately, seem to tangle each other in contradictions when they are combined. While urging that Japanese leaders should not be held responsible for the conduct of their soldiers, he implies that leaders on the other side should have been indicted for the conduct of their soldiers. While declining to find Japan guilty of waging aggressive war, he suggests that the United States was guilty of committing aggression in Asia. While wanting to put Western imperialism on trial, he refuses to construe Japan's actions in Asia as another form of imperialism. The philosopher's distaste for assigning guilt to only one party goes against the jurist's duty to determine the guilt of the party before him; the jurist's conviction that insufficient evidence has been placed before him to assign guilt goes against the anti-imperialist's insistence that there is ample evidence to damn the Western powers; and the anti-imperialist's desire to blame the West for the war goes against the philosopher's distaste for blaming anyone. Pal's deft argumentation, which always seemed to get him wherever he wanted to go, becomes a logical Möbius strip from which there is no exit. Are we entitled therefore to dismiss Pal's prevarications as political opportunism and rule them out of the court of public opinion?

I would prefer to see his position as political idealism. This is a charge Pal would dispute, for he himself dismissed the innovations of the IMTFE as expressing at best a "commendable" but "unrealizable" moral idealism; yet his idealism/opportunism was of the same intensity and sprang from the same desire at the end of the war to eliminate war. Pal's idealism understood that the purpose of international justice was one of "enlarging the human community" so that people would move closer to "the essential spirit of communal life." He doubted that this was something a military tribunal was capable of doing. It could mete out punishments, but it could not bring about the reconciliation of all parties, which is the fundamental condition for world peace. Pal did not approve of Japan's military violence; his judgment stated unequivocally that "atrocities were perpetrated" in Nanking, and he regarded them as "wrongful and reprehensible."[85] But the task he felt that he faced as an international jurist in 1948, with the Cold War heating up around Asia, was not to assign retrospective blame for a conflict that was over. It was to figure out how best to address dangers that grew beyond the war. Without a reconstitution of the international political order that recognized the claims of the losers as well as the victors, punishment looked like nothing but vengeance.

We might better understand Pal's position by considering that what he aspired to was something that did not exist at the time and has only emerged in the practice of war crimes adjudication since the 1990s; that is, truth and reconciliation commissions. These bodies have been experimented with as supplements, and in some cases as alternatives, to judicial tribunals in nations seeking to heal deadly conflicts and work toward democratic rehabilitation. They have been criticized because, as extralegal entities, they cannot impose sanctions on those whom courts would otherwise find guilty. On the other hand, in conflicts that at least one side sustains out of fear of postconflict legal reprisals, truth and reconciliation commissions have been praised for providing exits through which both parties can back down to reestablish peace.[86] This is what I glimpse in the concluding recommendations of Pal's judgment. He wanted a widened scope of enquiry whose mandate would have been to examine "facts perhaps hitherto undisclosed" that could be used to address "the future threat of the 'public order and safety' of the world." To do anything less—which is exactly what he felt the IMTFE had done—was an "incipient failure of will and wisdom" that he could not condone and saw no reason to accept. "The name of Justice should not be allowed to be invoked only for the prolongation of the pursuit of vindictive retaliation. The world is really in need of generous magnanimity and understanding charity."[87] By preferring narrow vengeance to full disclosure, the Tokyo tribunal failed to provide either boon to the postwar world.

As already noted, Radhabinod Pal's political challenge to the majority judgment implied a different view of, and role for, history. The question with which I would like to conclude this chapter is what that presence of difference signifies for our understanding of Pal's project. In the process of determining who did what to whom and for what reasons, every judicial body writes a history of what has happened. For a military tribunal, that history need satisfy only the side that convened the tribunal. In the case of a truth and reconciliation commission, however, the history of the conflict has to bear the burden of constructing a plausible account that, rather than celebrate the victors' triumph over the losers, describes the honorable paths that both sides took to get to the exits. This operation is not an easy one because each side has already constructed a previous history that justifies its position and denies whatever history the other side offers. Blending two contradictory accounts into a single history requires each side to accept a portion of the other's account and as well to surrender elements of its own, thereby fashioning a common history that both sides can accept and recognize as their own. This revision of history must involve frank admission of guilt and full forgiveness of wrongs, concessions that both sides will resist so long as the advantages of sustaining the conflict (e.g., using it to legitimize a particular version of the state or to bolster an ethnic identity) appear greater than the benefits of reconciliation.

From this perspective, it becomes possible to suggest that those Japanese who, sixty years later, choose to deny war responsibility, and those Chinese who, at similar remove from the event, demand compensation, are engaged in the same operation: promoting a history that celebrates divergence and conflict so as to gain a windfall in nationalist or ethnic integrity. The concern on each side is not to "thin out" the particularities of identity that separate their two national groups, which is what contemporary human rights discourse strives to do in balancing the claims of one group against another.[88] Instead, such efforts "thicken" conceptions of who they are by packing the event with particularized cultural identities and exclusive collective memories through which they can honor themselves and disdain others. These are unilateral histories, not histories of reconciliation.

But is this what Pal too has done in composing his history of the war and setting it against the majority's? Certainly his intensely anti-imperialist posture does not read easily today. It falls under the sway of its own rhetoric, swinging far from what we would regard as a natural sympathy for the victims of atrocity. He argues that the West, having gained its advantages in Asia by "recourse to the sword," should give them up.[89] Yet he declines to suggest that Japan was bound to do the same in China. The history of Western imperialism in Asia may well be full of "scandalous stories."[90] But so too is the history of Japanese imperialism in China. Pal's version of truth will persuade few that the fundamental contradiction driving the war in East Asia was the fissure between Asia and the West, or that the legacy of colonial domination can displace the guilt for Nanking from real Japanese soldiers on to an abstract West.

If Pal declined to write a history that provides exits for all parties, he did so because the dominant party, the United States, never entered the arena. His sole alternative as a member of the Tokyo bench was to give an account of the war that contradicted the grand narrative leading ineluctably from the Rape of Nanjing to the American victory in the Pacific, and thence to the hanging of Hirota Kôki and Matsui Iwane. Pal's was a unilateral history in which the Americans could not recognize themselves, nor perceive the burden he felt they should bear. Nor could he see himself in theirs; and yet, by holding up a mirror in which motives and responsibilities were reversed, Pal tried to show that the majority history was also a unilateral account, one that did not provide a history in which all parties might recognize not only themselves but others as well.

The high judicial standard to which Pal worked should caution us nonetheless from rushing to the conclusion that he dissented for purely political reasons. In fact, his legal and constitutional objections to the IMTFE take us closer to the core problems of war crimes adjudication than does the blithe assertion of the majority that justice had been served; and his challenge to the prosecution's narrative of a just and appropriate victory helps us to read their judgment with a critical awareness of how the Rape of Nanking was used to win convictions, and would be unlikely to stand up in a war crimes tribunal today. The adequacy of the Tokyo findings on Nanking cannot be assessed in terms of the number of convictions it produced or the quota of retribution it conferred on those who suffered terrible losses in the war. Justice, as Pal suspected, is a much more difficult project. Its adequacy can be measured only in terms of the validity of the laws invoked and the success with which the rights of the defendants were protected. This is what a court does, and what the IMTFE, in retrospect, failed to do. Those who argue from the opposite point of view that the IMTFE did not go far enough in punishing those responsible for the Rape of Nanking see a different inadequacy in the judgment.

The debate may never end, for every future interpretation of the history of Japan's armed interventions in East Asia and the Pacific will suggest yet other grounds for revision. This, of course, is what history does: not sit in judgment, but ask what other ways we might consider in seeking a fuller account of the past. Whether the Tokyo judgment was adequate in law will continue to engage legal specialists. But by the same token, what actually happened in Nanking in December 1937 will remain beyond the capacity of any court to determine or resolve. If the resolution we seek is reconciliation, other means will be needed to construct it.

Notes

A different version of this chapter under the title, "The Tokyo Judgment and the Rape of Nanking" appeared in the *Journal of Asian Studies* 60:3 (August 2001), pp. 673–700.

1. UNWCC, *History of the United Nations War Crimes Commission*, pp. 121, 130, 151–53.
2. Involvement in the incident also resulted in Japanese convictions at other military tribunals throughout East Asia, including Nanking; see Piccigallo, *Japanese on Trial;* Iwakawa, *Kotô no tsuchi to naru tomo.*
3. Liu, "Tokyo Trial," p. 279.
4. As one of the prosecuting staff put it in 1950, the alliance that had made the trial possible was breaking apart as it ended. "New conflicts and new problems had arisen, and new alignments had been formed among the victors. It was therefore not surprising that in the darkening shadows of current events there were added to the voices of those who did not believe in the principles of the trial and who could see no illegality in war regardless of its aggressive character, the warnings of those who saw in the principles of Nuremberg and Tokyo a dangerous precedent which could be applied to our own leaders regardless of blame or guilt in the event we should lose a war"; Horowitz, "Tokyo Trial," p. 574. See also Brode, *Casual Slaughters and Accidental Judgments,* p. 176 and p. 199.
5. Several IMTFE participants published studies in the years during the tribunal and immediately afterward, for instance, Evans, "Trial of Major Japanese War Criminals"; Pal, "International Law"; Quentin-Baxter, "Task of the International Military Tribunal at Tokyo"; Horowitz, "Tokyo Trial"; and Röling, "Tokyo Trial and the Development of International Law." Only in the 1970s would the IMTFE come back into the ken of jurists. For a bibliography of the literature on the Tokyo trial, see Lewis, *Uncertain Judgment,* pp. 139–45.
6. Chang, *The Rape of Nanking,* p. 225. The quest for justice rides on considerable emotional disturbance. Chang, for instance, characterizes her anxiety that the "oral history" of the Atrocity she received from her parents might not survive their generation as "panic" (p. 10), and declares that the lack of a full published history of the incident causes her to feel "terrified" (p. 200). Such emotions hint at the degree to which the Atrocity has become implicated in the contemporary identity-formation of younger Chinese outside China. They may also betray an awareness that an ethnically channeled memory can be a weak base from which to build an identity that can be projected beyond ethnic lines into the larger representational field of moral landmarks such as Auschwitz and Kosovo.
7. As soon as the American occupation of Japan came to an end in 1952, Tanaka published Japanese translations of Pal's opinion, both partial *(Nihon muzairon: shinri no sabaki)* and full *(Zenyaku: Nihon muzairon),* in an attempt to overturn the authority of the majority judgment. Pal continues to be lionized by extreme Japanese nationalists as the lone voice of impartial justice for Japan. The 1998 movie *Puraido: unmei no toki* (Pride: The Fateful Moment), which

honors Tôjô for bowing to execution rather than betraying the emperor and the state, casts Pal in a ympathetic role.

8. IMTFE, "Indictment," p. 11.

9. IMTFE, "Judgment," p. 49,771. Count 45 was one of forty-five counts (including all the counts of "Murder") on which the bench declared itself unable to rule. The difficulty with Count 45 was technical: it phrased the charge of murder in terms of a conspiracy. The tribunal reasoned that the Tokyo Charter "does not confer any jurisdiction in respect of a conspiracy to commit any crimes other than a crime against peace. There is no specification of the crime of conspiracy to commit conventional war crimes" (p. 48,451). The specification of conspiracy with regard only to crimes against peace appears in Section II, Article 5(a) of the charter.

10. Ibid., p. 13.

11. IMTFE, "Proceedings," Exhibit No. 323, pp. 4,508–36, excerpting all or parts of Documents No. 2, 7, 8, 10, 14–18, 20, 24, 29, 31, and 58. The book has been reproduced in its entirety as the first part of Brook, *Documents on the Rape of Nanking.*

12. Wilson, Bates, and Magee appeared before the bench as witnesses; Smythe, Fitch, and McCallum filed affidavits; see IMTFE, "Proceedings," Exhibits No. 306, 307, and 309; pp. 1946–48, 4,456–63, and 4,467–79.

13. Ibid., pp. 49,238–39; 49,604–12; 49,814–16; 49,855–56. These passages from the IMTFE's judgment are reprinted in Brook, *Documents on the Rape of Nanking,* pp. 257–67.

14. IMTFE, "Proceedings," pp. 33,811–921.

15. Ibid., p. 33,866. For a lively description of Matsui on the stand, see Kuo, *Tung-fang ta-shen-p'an,* pp. 172–86.

16. Ibid., p. 33,879.

17. Ibid., p. 33,851. On the almost daily submission of documentation regarding atrocities by the International Committee to the Japanese consulate, see Brook, *Documents,* pp. 6–7.

18. IMTFE, "Proceedings," p. 33,824, quoting from Matsui's affidavit as it was read into the record on 24 November 1947.

19. Ibid., p. 33,861.

20. Ibid., p. 33,919. Matsui also insisted that his position in the chain of command over the two armies involved in the operation did not give him the power to investigate or intervene: "in the strict legal sense I did not conceive myself as having the power to give specific orders—orders in detail with regard to the maintenance of military discipline" (p. 33,883).

21. Ibid., pp. 33,919–20.

22. IMTFE, "Summation for Matsui, Iwane" (Defense Document No. 3096), pp. 37–38, 46, 56, 59. Matsui's counsel consisted of Floyd Mattice assisted by two Japanese lawyers, Itô Kiyoshi and Jôdai Takayoshi. The language and logic of the summation suggests that the Japanese were its principal authors, and that Mattice's role was mainly to deliver it at the tribunal. Röling understood that in general the American lawyer assigned to each defendant determined his defense strategy, and that the Japanese lawyers were unable to raise issues outside that defense; Röling, "Tokyo Trial and the Development of International Law," p. 6. This seems not to have been the case with Matsui's lawyers.

23. IMTFE, "Summation for Matsui, Iwane," p. 98.

24. IMTFE, "Proceedings," pp. 17,654–62.

25. IMFTE, "Summation for Matsui, Iwane," pp. 99 and pp. 101–8.

26. IMTFE, "Judgment of the IMTFE," in Brook, *Documents on the Rape of Nanking,* p. 266.

27. Cohen has charged that the Tokyo judgment failed to establish adequate tests to limit individual criminal responsibility in the case of criminal activities that a leader knew about but was personally derelict in preventing or redressing. This charge appears to apply to the judgment on Hirota, on which he makes his point, but not to the Matsui judgment, which was careful to take account of the extent of his knowledge and the inefficacy of his actions; see Cohen, "Beyond Nuremberg," pp. 78–85.

28. The Dutch justice, Röling, argued in his dissenting opinion both that Hirota was too far removed from the chain of command to bear responsibility for the Atrocity, and that although the army sought to block the flow of information coming out of Nanking, he did in fact intervene effectively, as evidence of which he cited the recall of Matsui along with some eighty staff officers in February 1938; Röling, "Opinion of Mr. Justice Röling," p. 209. For a concurring but differently argued interpretation, see Cohen, "Beyond Nuremberg," pp. 62–65.

29. Public Record Office (PRO), FO 371/69833, F16327/48/23: R. Craigie to O. Sargent, 18 November 1948; minute by Cheke, 19 November 1948. Regarding Carr's objection to the admissibility of Craigie's written answers to questions posed by the defense and introduced to challenge the charge of conspiracy, see IMTFE, "Proceedings," p. 37,013.

30. Cohen, "Beyond Nuremberg," pp. 60 and p. 67. As pointed out in note 27, however, the Tokyo tribunal was not indiscriminate in denying defense claims that leaders could be unable to intervene to prevent war crimes about which they had knowledge.

31. Beigbeder, *Judging War Criminals*, pp. 47–48.

32. The concept of criminal liability in situations where there is a legal duty to act has gained considerable ground since the Second World War and has been most prominently established in the provisions concerning victims of international conflicts in Protocol I Additional to the Geneva Conventions (1977). For a recent review of the concept of "omission" in civil and international law, see Boulesbaa, *U.N. Convention on Torture and the Prospects for Its Enforcement*, pp. 9–15.

33. Röling, Introduction, to Röling and Ruter, *Tokyo Judgment*, vol. 1, p. xv.

34. Cohen, "Beyond Nuremberg," p. 61.

35. Dower, *Embracing Defeat*, chap. 15. The extrajudicial decision not to charge the emperor with war crimes induced the tribunal's president, William Webb, to argue in his own dissenting opinion that none of the accused should be executed, on the grounds that British law exempts criminals from capital punishment when the leader of the crime has been granted immunity; Webb, "Separate Opinion of the President," p. 18.

36. IMTFE, "Judgment," p. 768.

37. MacArthur created the precedent for omission with the military commission he convened in Manila in October 1945 to try the Japanese commander in the Philippines, Yamashita Tomoyuki. Yamashita was convicted and executed not on the grounds that he had ordered offenses against American servicemen, or even known about them, but because he had been negligent in preventing the forces under his command from committing such offenses. As the American author of the standard study of this trial notes with some force, "Never has a military leader been prosecuted for an incident when he has neither ordered, condoned, nor even been aware of the atrocity in question" (Taylor, *Trial of Generals*, p. 221). If the Yamashita precedent shaped the Tokyo indictment, it may have worked initially in Matsui's favor by encouraging the Tokyo bench to demand unambiguous confirmation that Matsui did indeed know something of the atrocity for which he was being charged. Once knowledge was established, though, the Yamashita precedent of finding guilt by omission worked fatally against Matsui's defense.

38. PRO, FO 371/57424, U2331/5/73: "Inclusion of Indian Judge: Tokyo."

39. The other justices who filed separate opinions were Henri Bernard of France, Delfin Jaranilla of the Philippines, B.V.A. Röling of the Netherlands, and William Webb of Australia. Beigbeder, *Judging War Criminals*, p. 73, argues that Pal's decision to break ranks with the rest of the Tokyo bench "seriously weakened the value and impact of the tribunal's findings and sentences" on subsequent international law; on the other hand, it may have enriched case law.

40. Section I, article 4(c) of the Tokyo Charter provided for such absence without disqualification. The provision of full transcripts made it possible for a judge to review the sessions from which he was absent.

41. Pal, "Judgment of the Hon'ble Mr. Justice Pal," pp. 1–2; 1,050–51; 1,060–61; 1,063–65; 1,069; 1,091–99; 1,108–18; 1,225–26; and 1,232–35. These passages are reprinted in Brook, *Documents on the Rape of Nanking*, pp. 269–97.

42. For evaluations of Pal's dissenting opinion, see Minear, *Victor's Justice*, pp. 63–70, 130–33, 155–58; Hosoya, *Tokyo War Crimes Trial;* Röling, *Tokyo Trial and Beyond*, pp. 28–32; and Kopelman, "Ideology and International Law."
43. Brook, *Documents on the Rape of Nanking*, p. 294.
44. Röling, "Tokyo Trial and the Development of International Law," p. 5.
45. Evans, "Trial of Major Japanese War Criminals," pt. 4, p. 323.
46. UNWCC, *History of the United Nations War Crimes Commission*, pp. 121, 154, and 387.
47. Dower, *Embracing Defeat*, p. 465, suggests that Pal was the only judge appointed to the bench with significant experience in international law. I have found no evidence that Pal had such experience before the trial. He came widely read in historical and legal issues, but appears to have acquired his understanding of international law in the course of seeking to apply it at the Tokyo tribunal.
48. Brook, *Documents on the Rape of Nanking*, p. 273.
49. Section IV, Article 13(c), Subsection (1) permitted the admission of a state document "without proof of its issuance or signature"; Subsection (4), of "unsworn statements" in a private document. The wording on rules of evidence was taken verbatim from Article 13 of MacArthur's "Special Proclamation" governing the Military Commission in Manila that convicted Yamashita; see Taylor, *Trial of Generals*, p. 137. MacArthur's idea of justice, being military and retributive, was unconstrained by compunctions about cutting legal corners to expedite convictions.
50. Brook, *Documents on the Rape of Nanking*, pp. 277–78.
51. Pal, *Crimes in International Relations*, pp. 186–87.
52. Ginn, *Sugamo Prison*, p. 262.
53. The legal jurisdiction of the Kellogg-Briand Pact was a contentious issue in the early deliberations of the UNWCC. China argued with Czechoslovakia and Australia, and against Britain and the United States, that the pact signaled a general understanding in international law that aggressive war was a criminal act; see UNWCC, *History of the United Nations War Crimes Commission*, pp. 182–83.
54. Brook, *Documents on the Rape of Nanking*, p. 286.
55. Ibid., pp. 286, 288.
56. Pal, "Judgment of the Hon'ble Mr. Justice Pal," p. 978.
57. Ibid., p. 354.
58. Ibid., p. 980.
59. Brook, *Documents on the Rape of Nanking*, p. 283.
60. Ibid., pp. 285–86.
61. Although McDougall concurred with the majority judgment, in his internal communications to Ottawa, McDougall was fiercely critical of the IMTFE for its procedural mistakes, ignorance of precedents, and overall lack of principled jurisprudence. He asked to be taken off the bench, but was persuaded to remain so as not to embarrass Canada's allies, notably the United States; see Stanton, "Canada and War Crimes," pp. 392–94; also Brode, *Casual Slaughters and Accidental Judgments*, pp. 198–99. After the trial, McDougall wrote privately to MacArthur asking that the sentences on Tôgô Shigemitsu (the Japanese ambassador to Britain, 1938–41) be reduced; his appeal was rejected (PRO, FO 371/69834, F16646). He and Pal were among the five judges who met with MacArthur on 23 November to ask that the death sentences be commuted; see Dower, *Embracing Defeat*, p. 628, note 34.
62. It had been the GOI's representative to the UNWCC's Enforcement Committee who in August 1944, had proposed that supreme commanders be empowered to set up interim military tribunals to handle war criminals expeditiously, exactly as MacArthur had done in Tokyo; see UNWCC, *History of the United Nations War Crimes Commission*, p. 450.
63. PRO, FO 371/69834, F17460: "Judgment and sentences delivered by the members of the IMTFE on the major Japanese war criminals," 25 November 1948. Stein, *A History of India*,

p. 404 has characterized Menon as "Nehru's long-time friend, his delegate at the United Nations and perhaps his leftist conscience."

64. PRO, FO 371/69833, F15996: A. Gascoigne, "Major War Crimes Trials: Dissenting Judgments," 13 November 1948.
65. Ibid., p. 294.
66. Jaranilla, "Concurring Opinion of Mr. Justice Jaranilla," p. 31.
67. See Nandy, *Intimate Enemy.*
68. Nandy, "Other Within," pp. 53–54, 71, 80.
69. Ibid., p. 72.
70. Pal, *Crimes in International Relations,* p. vii, and p. ix.
71. Kondô Giichi's preface to Pal, *Nihon muzairon: shinri no sabaki.*
72. Nandy, *Intimate Self,* p. 2.
73. Röling, *Tokyo Trial and Beyond,* pp. 28–29.
74. The tension between Bose and Gandhi is interestingly portrayed, to Bose's advantage, in Sen, *Twin in the Twist.*
75. The Intelligence Bureau of the Government of India in the summer of 1945 reported several cases of Indian military personnel writing and chanting slogans honoring both Gandhi and Bose as the two great leaders of the Indian National Congress; British Library, Government of India, Home Department, R/3/1/330, pp. 31, 103. Nandy (p. 65) suggests the same sense of unity between Gandhians and Boseans by noting that Nehru served as defense counsel at the trial of three Indian officers who defected from the British forces to serve in the Indian National Army.
76. PRO, FO 371/69834, F17460: comment of W. B. Ledwidge, 17 December 1948, appended to Gascoigne, "Judgment and Sentences Delivered by the Members of the International Military Tribunal."
77. Basu, "Tokio Trials," p. 30.
78. Brackman, *Other Nuremberg,* p. 344. Praising the condemned men for liberating Asia continues to be popular at the extreme edge of Japanese public opinion; see Kuo, *Tung-fang ta shen-p'an,* p. 173.
79. Pal, "Judgment of the Hon'ble Mr. Justice Pal," p. 138.
80. Ibid., p. 1,090.
81. Ibid., p. 1,202–03. To give his opposition to the atomic bomb greater prominence when he published his judgment in India five years later, he appended a damning gallery of photographs from Hiroshima and Nagasaki. Jaranilla firmly rejected any appeal to the atomic bomb as a defense for the accused. In his view, what changed the nature of war in this conflict was not the atomic bomb, but the total mobilization of a population for war, thereby legitimizing the destruction of the home base. The bomb itself signified a difference only in the scale of destruction, not in its quality; Jaranilla, "Concurring Opinion by Mr Justice Delfin Jaranilla," pp. 24–25.
82. Brook, *Documents on the Rape of Nanking,* p. 296.
83. Ibid., p. 294.
84. Pal, *Crimes in International Relations,* p. viii.
85. Ibid., pp. vii–viii.
86. Beigbeder, *Judging War Criminals,* pp. 124–25; Hesse and Post, *Human Rights in Political Transitions,* pp. 13–21; Neier, "Rethinking Truth, Justice and Guilt after Bosnia and Rwanda."
87. Brook, *Documents on the Rape of Nanking,* pp. 294–95.
88. Hesse and Post, *Human Rights in Political Transitions,* pp. 30–31.
89. Pal, "Judgment of the Hon'ble Mr. Justice Pal," p. 279.
90. Pal, *Crimes in International Relations,* p. ix.

Section Two

AGGRESSORS AND COLLABORATORS

8

LETTERS FROM
A RESERVE OFFICER
CONSCRIPTED TO NANKING[*]

Amano Saburô[1]

Postmarked "Hiroșhima Station Plaza, 22 November 1937"[2]

[To Naoko, from Hiroshima],
   I arrived in Hiroshima in high spirits. I really appreciate your seeing me off so late at night. I got here at 10:00 a.m. on the twentieth; departure is tomorrow. I saw everyone in Tokyo, plus friends and company people in Nagoya. Hiroshima is a pretty city. There are thin clouds in the sky, and little or no breeze. If this is any indication, the Genkai Strait [off Kyushu] will be calm as well. I look forward to viewing the Seto Inland Sea tomorrow.

Postmarked "Hiroshima Station Plaza, 22 November 1937"

[To Tatsuo,]
   Just when I thought I had slept my last night on the soil of our homeland, we got orders to delay embarkment until tomorrow, so today I took advantage of this fine Indian summer to visit the [Rai] Sanyô Museum. Getting acquainted with his writings made me appreciate even more what a great man he was. I'll just take it easy for the day and not make the trek over to Miyajima.
                                                                    Saburô
                                                        Hiroshima, 22 November

Postmarked "Ujina [Hiroshima Port], 24 November 1937"

[To Tatsuo],

We're now starting to board ship and will be off to our destination. I'll come home safe and sound; don't worry about me. The weather is good, so the trip by sea should be calm.

Saburô

Ujina, Festival Day of Thanksgiving [23 November]

Postmarked "Moji, 24 November 1937"

[To Tatsuo,]

It's 11:15 a.m. on the twenty-fourth in Moji [Fukuoka Prefecture]. We set sail from Ujina at 5:45 p.m. on the twenty-third and are now anchored in Moji Harbor, but won't dock. It's pretty crowded onboard; this is a 6,000-ton hospital ship for transporting patients. It will be another forty to fifty hours before we leave ship. About three men sleep per *tatami* mat, and even here in the officers quarters, it's crammed. Wherever you look, there are troops and more troops; so I avoid going above deck if there are no duties to discharge. Instead, I read the [monthly] *Bungei shunjū* or just sleep in my spare time. From tomorrow onward, it will be "lights out."[3] Please circulate my letters in mimeograph or some other form starting with this one.

Saburô

Postmarked "Moji, 2 December 1937"

(24 November)

[To Tatsuo,]

We assembled at 11:30 a.m. at the Takeya Primary School grounds, Hiroshima city, and marched out at 11:50 with the Sixty-fifth Regiment bringing up the rear. At 1:46 we set out by steam barge. All we could hear were rousing cheers of "banzai, banzai." The little flags being waved on shore gradually receded into the background as we reached the 5,872.89-ton *Pacific Maru*, a hospital ship, anchored in port. Climbing the ladder rung by rung, we became seamen. In front of the ship's "Central Entrance," I turned around for a last look at the flags being waved at us on the Ujina quay. Wondering if this will be the last we ever see of our homeland, we were drawn into the ship's hold by some strange, powerful force. The excitement finally died down. I busied myself with the tasks of assigning day watch and seeing to mess preparations. I composed company orders too. The stickiest problem will be provisions. Chow seems to be over; it's 5:40 p.m. and the whistle sounds overhead. Time to set sail. Farewell, Hiroshima! What point is there in going above deck to take a final look?

I'll tell you a bit about the ship. The white-painted steel column in our officers' quarters has a sign pasted on it that says, "*Pacific Maru,* 5,872.89 tons, Tamanoi Commercial Shipping Co., 32 Akashi, Kobe Ward, Kobe city." The "officers' quarters" are in name only. Seventeen of us share this twelve-mat triangular area with one corner and a steel ceiling overhead. White curtains hitched to a couple of posts is all that separates us off from the One Hundred Sixteenth Regiment. This is a sturdy vessel, a freighter converted into a hospital ship. There is a blanket spread over our *tatami* mats and a desk set up in the center of the area. This is where we drink, smoke, and write assemblage reports. Some of these contain real knee-slappers. For instance, one of the "old-man" sublieutenants visited a brothel in Hiroshima. After returning to barracks, he realized that he had left his underpants behind, and it was time for his unit to board ship. Since he couldn't go to fetch them, only a desperate last-minute purchase in town saved the day. These are the kinds of assemblage reports that we submit.

This ship has made several hauls to the front and back since the [China] Incident began. It's a hospital ship; so, of course, there are lots of nurses. It's weird to see women, maybe sixty of them, on a ship for men only. More than anything else, transport officers are strict in the extreme about [protecting] these nurses, but that's only what one would expect. Somebody taped a cute little picture to a pillar; it shows two little girls viewing the moon over a rush-covered riverbank. There is also a photo of some foreign movie actress.

(25 November)

After wake-up and along with the roll call report this morning, I went above deck. The hills of Kyushu are visible. It's taking a long time to get my sea legs. The troops are docile today, no doubt because their store of booze has run out. We only brought a little with us at boarding. When we anchored in Moji, other ships pulled up alongside us, so we were able to exchange money for booze by passing back and forth baskets tied to ropes. That replenished our stock for a time, but it's now depleted, so the men are subdued. The Sixty-fifth is a quiet bunch. The One Hundred Sixteenth is full of rowdies.

(26th November)

The sea is calm today too. Not a single man is drunk. I haven't shaved since leaving Hiroshima, so the stubble on my face is growing and it's starting to bother me. We finally land tomorrow. I went above deck; there were lots of nurses. The "old-man" troops wear caps to camouflage their balding heads; if not, the nurses will ignore them, or at least that's how they see it.[4]

I hear that these nurses have made the Japan-Shanghai trip several times now. I also hear stories of some pitiable soldiers, but it would only make you worry if I wrote these down, and I don't want that, so I won't. I'll only say that we sometimes find bedding with vivid blood stains, and that the ship has a morgue for the bodies of men who die in transit. Among officers of the Sixty-fifth, I am the only bachelor onboard. Actually there is one more, though he's engaged. But that's fine; it means I've got no cares in the world. I saw the sun set into the sea tonight. Shanghai is just a short distance away; there, men are fighting tooth and nail. In contrast, how peaceful the sunset was! I am often struck by the solemnity of all this. Just then, two ships heading for Moji cruised past our port at a distance of one *ri* (four kilometers).[5] Dusk is nearing; beacons flash on and off along the Chink shoreline.[6] All of our thoughts remain unchanged. How many of us seventeen officers will return home safely?

(Finished writing at 9:30 p.m. on the 26th)
The order has come. All units must submit mess kits for filling before 10:00 p.m. and be ready to alight ship on paying anchor in Wusung Harbor at 2:00 a.m. This is it; preparations for battle. We pass out ammo and get ready to disembark. By 8:30 p.m., those preparations are done and the troops are asleep. In the officers' quarters, we draw up the last of those assemblage reports. I finished mine quickly and wrote this letter. It's now 9:30 p.m. The report is done, and so is this letter. Farewell to all. Please hold on to this original—written on a bamboo trunk in lieu of a desk—until the day of my triumphant return, if that should ever come. Sorry to trouble you, but for the time being, could you mimeograph copies and send these to [relatives in] Tokyo, Hokkaido, and Hosoda? I'll write again tomorrow if I can. We are supposed to alight either before the light of dawn, or else in the afternoon. The order reads, "after 2:00 a.m.," but who knows....

Postmarked "Ujina, 4 December 1937"

Saburô at Wusung, 27 November
Right now it's 2:45 and there's still no order to land. The food on board is about to run out. Maybe there is enough for one or two more meals, so we should get the order to land soon. There are about sixty vessels near Wusung.

(9:00 p.m. on the 28th)
The order just came for us to land tomorrow (in Shanghai) at around noon.

(29 November)
At 6:30 a.m., the ship set out for XX [disguised under wartime state censorship] wharf in Shanghai.

Postmarked "Ujina, 4 December 1937"

Saburō, on the *Pacific Maru* off the coast of Wusung at 7:00 p.m.;
28 November
To Tatsuo,

We were supposed to disembark on the twenty-sixth, but are unable to do so today, the twenty-seventh.[7] I hope we can do so tomorrow, the twenty-eighth. This morning a boat came to us from Wusung bringing a three-day stock of provisions. Viewed through binoculars, the Wusung fortresses look to be an abysmal wreck. This ship was anchored here during that artillery assault, and according to the crewmen, it was an awesome sight. Two or three warships with their names blackened out are anchored here too. Early in the morning a seaplane made a splendid takeoff from the surface of the water and flew off somewhere. Now and then heavy bombers, our own of course, fly by. We are now into our third day of being anchored here and have yet to see anything like an enemy plane—only a passenger ship flying the British flag. All other ships are Japanese. At about 2:30 p.m., the *Shanghai Maru*—which plies between Nagasaki and Shanghai—left Huang-fu-chiang on its way back to Japan. The waters of the Yangtze are really murky. We can see the horizon way down the river. Both its mouth and upper reaches now lie on the horizon; our ship is about two to 2.5 thousand ___ from the Wusung fortresses.[8] Today, two transports full of troops—I don't know what unit—entered the harbor. They too remain at anchor. We get no newspapers. There's only one radio; it's in the control room. I'm told that the Chinks jam it whenever Japanese newscasts come on, so there's no way to tell how far the assault on Nanking has advanced up to now. I'm pretty tired of the boredom on ship. But if we land tomorrow, it will be nothing but combat with the enemy, so I can't let my guard down. (Please send the application to Chiyoda Life Insurance or to its office in Miharu.)

That's it for today. Please copy this info and circulate it to everyone. Satô-kun from Mr. Ôgoshi's place seems well. Dawn comes to Shanghai at 7:00 a.m.; it gets dark at 6:00 p.m.

At Shanghai, Noon, 29 November
(This postcard will get to you ahead of the earlier others.) We completed landing at noon and looked about near the wharf. Total devastation! A result of bombs, artillery, and small arms fire. There is no trace of anyone, only Chink patrolmen, Indian traffic cops, and beyond that, the Japanese army and British automobiles. There are shops in some places, but no customers. The guys from Hama Street, who belong to marine transport units, got transferred here yesterday from XX, so I was able to meet a former upper classman from Sôma Middle School. Tomorrow we head for Chang-shu to catch up with the Morozumi Unit [Sixty-fifth Regiment], but tonight we camp out in Shanghai. The

trek will take about four days on foot. This means the assault on Nanking. I met my classmate Shibano-kun. Both Ôki-kun and Yokoyama [Shûichirô]-kun are well.

At Shanghai, Yang-chu-p'o [phonetic rendition], 10 a.m., 1 December,

We've been delayed for various reasons. Now we're supposed to leave Shanghai for Nan-hsiang on the afternoon of 1 December. That's seven *ri* [twenty-eight kilometers]. Given our current equipment and marching capacity, can we do it? Or will we leave tomorrow? In any case, it will take quite a few days to reach Chang-shu, so I guess it will be a tough go. Mr. Yabuuchi, a reporter for the *[Fukushima] Minyû-Hôchi [shinbun]* came for an interview yesterday, so I was able to find out something about conditions at the front. Enough for now.

4 p.m., 2 December

There has been a change in plans since my last letter. We are now supposed to travel up the Yangtze by boat and land on the coast northeast of Chang-shu on 2 December. We just now reached that spot and await landing craft.[9] We're pushing forward mightily to reach the capital in time for the assault. [Earlier] today on the wharf in Shanghai, I met Hashimoto-kun from Miharu, who was drafted at the same time as me. He is assigned to XX duties in Shanghai.

Shanghai Expeditionary Army, Ogisu [Thirteenth] Division, Morozumi [Sixty-fifth] Regiment, Taira [Third] Battalion, Kinoshita [Ninth] Company

Saburô, 12 December

I've completed a march right out of that poem I learned from Akiko on the way home from Higashiyama Hot Springs in Wakamatsu:

> We enter endless plains
> that lead to nowhere,
> advancing steel helmets,
> with the Rising Sun

We've broken past the forty *ri* mark [160 kilometers] since coming ashore, and entered Chen-chiang as dusk approached this evening.[10] The Eleventh division moved in the night before. Now, there is little more than occasional machine-gun fire—no real combat to speak of. We hear the distant peel of the Mishima heavy artillery division shelling towns north of the Yangtze from points south of it, plus the distant roar of our heavy bombers. The night stillness of an abandoned capital![11] On the sixth, I took command of the Third Platoon in the Ninth Company (led by Sublieutenant Kinoshita), under the Third Battalion (Taira Unit), of the Sixty-fifth Regiment (Morozumi Unit). We have marched four days since then, past Chiangyin city to reach Chenchiang on the tenth, today. Although I'm supposed to be a "platoon commander," this unit is down to twenty-seven men. That gives you an idea of just how awful the fighting has been. It's already eleven o'clock (Japan time). I'll write again tomorrow; that's it for today.

I didn't get a chance to mail the letter written the other day (the twelfth) at Chiangyin, so I've still got it. It's been one forward march after another ever since. On the fourteenth, the Sixty-fifth Regiment, led by Battalion commander [Maj. Gen. Yamada Senji], took over the Mufushan [elevated] batteries a little over one *ri* [four kilometers] northeast of Nanking. (The One Hundred Fourth is on the north shore of the Yangtze.) Right now, the Sixty-fifth is mopping up defeated enemy stragglers in the area. Part of it left for Nanking to take part in today's triumphal entry celebrations, but most of us are charged with dealing with POWs. The Sixty-fifth by itself has taken a number approaching 20,000 to date. We hold them in the Chink army compound beneath the elevated batteries. Provisions are inadequate, so lots of Chink troops have gone without food or water for a week already.[12] Yesterday morning, I was appointed as a guard officer and have yet to be relieved, so I can't leave the compound to go anywhere. Instead, I keep an eye on the Chinks who surrendered. Apart from the early morning, it's much warmer here than back home, so don't worry about me. It rained while we were aboard ship anchored off Wusung, but since then it's been clear everyday. I'll be relieved of this post tomorrow, so I'll be seeing the sights in Nanking. In two or three days, the Sixty-fifth will cross over to the northern bank of the Yangtze and join the main force of our division.

How's this for something absurd?[13] A defeated Chink straggler hiding behind my bunk, unknown to me for two nights, got caught and was shot immediately; in effect, we were sleeping together. I have no idea where we'll make our next thrust; you folks back home must have a better idea of how the war is shaping up. We left all of our supply units back in Shanghai, so we run out of stuff often and get by through requisitioning. Neither I, nor even men present from the start of the campaign, have ever gotten a "comfort bag" from home. I don't know when I'll get a chance to mail this, but I've written it; so I'll hang on to it and mail it when I can.

Saburô, 17 December 1937

A POW from the Chink army handed me this document in the hope that I could help them out. I attach it here for your reference.

Report

To the Commanding Officer of Great Japan:

After being cut off from our [retreating] army, we turned over our arms and surrendered to the military forces of Great Japan, imploring you to adopt appropriate measures on our behalf. Three days have passed since coming here, yet we still have no idea of how you will deal with us. Tens of thousands of pitiable men have gone hungry for over four days. We cannot survive on thin rice gruel alone; soon we will die of starvation. Oh, Great Japan! Tens of thousands [of us] lie on the verge of death, yet retain hope for life. We beg you to save our lives. If you should grant this entreaty, we will submit to you with all our hearts and repay your kind blessing by enduring fire and water to serve Great Japan henceforth. Please, please, I beseech you to bestow food on us so that we may live. We join in celebrating the Empire of Great Japan! Banzai!

Most respectfully submitted,

Fu Ho

Ad Hoc Representative for the Surrendered Army

Shanghai Expeditionary Army, Ogisu [Thirteenth] Division, Morozumi [Sixty-fifth] Regiment, Taira [Third] Battalion, Kinoshita [Ninth] Company

Amano Saburō

Dear Father,

While on patrol today (17 December), I met a reporter for the *Tokyo Nichinichi [shinbun]* and asked him to mail my letters. We've advanced unopposed ever since landing at Hu-p'u-chen. We took over the Mufushan [elevated] batteries about one *ri* [four kilometers] northeast of Nanking at dawn on the fourteenth. We took about 20,000 defeated stragglers prisoner nearby, placed them in a Chink army compound below the batteries, and keep close watch over them at present. Though unshaven and sunburned, officers and men alike are in high spirits. I plan to see the sights in Nanking tomorrow. Some of our men proudly took part in the triumphal entry into Nanking today, but I was on duty as a guard officer here, and so could not join them. As I said, tomorrow I'll be sightseeing.

In a few days, it's believed, we'll cross over to the northern riverbank. I've sent letters (through this reporter) to [the folks at] Miharu, so I think they will forward these or mimeograph copies for you. Please have a look. I met Abe and Niinuma from Nakamura town, as well as Hara from Tsukabe, Ōno village. They are medics in my company. I am very busy transporting prisoners, so my handwriting has gotten sloppy. We shoot those who run away. I heard gunfire just now, so we must have killed some men. We use revolvers stolen from the enemy; the orders [for weapons that] we placed with the regiment didn't arrive in time. In the daytime, it's warmer than back home, but the morning chill gets to us. We've had no rain since landing. It doesn't look like the war will end for sometime, but I'll gird my loins to stick it out, so don't worry about me. Our platoon has twenty-eight men including myself. I keep them on a tight rein, so there's no need to worry on this score either. They're hardened survivors of many battles, really a tough lot. Please send this to Uncle [Jirô] in Tokyo, to Kiku-chan in Miharu, and to the folks in Urawa, Hokkaido, and elsewhere because I don't have time to write each of them separately. That's it for now.

Saburô
17 December, 4:30 p.m.

Dear Uncle Jirô,

We're finally set to ford the Yangtze from a pier north of Nanking tomorrow, the twenty-first; our objective is Ch'uhsien. The regiment's main force is crossing today; our Third Battalion will follow early tomorrow morning. Yesterday, I was named officer in charge of loading the battalion on transports and am now busy seeing to that task. Each man is ordered to carry sandbags if possible, so we may be engaging a formidable foe.[14] As befitting the enemy capital, Nanking has massive walls; defense perimeters in its environs are particularly strong. I feel for the Chink army that had to abandon it without a fight. I hear that our planes bombed the capital many times, but it's strange to see how little damage they caused. Kuomintang government buildings remain unscratched, and the Sixteenth division is guarding these; so, unfortunately, I couldn't go inside. Wherever I went, there were stout-roofed shelters that people would enter during air raids. This shows just how much the enemy fears bombing attacks and how much of a national effort it makes to defend against these. I came away feeling that Japanese air raid drills were child's play in comparison.[15]

Actually, I have a favor to ask. While I was in the latrine yesterday morning some guy, probably from another unit, stole my sword sash. I only brought one with me because I didn't want to carry more gear than I had to. Right now I'm improvising, but it's a pain. Could you visit the Kaikōsha, buy one similar to the last time, and send it as soon as you can? It will take about a month to reach me. A "sword sash" is used to hold an officer's sword; Taka-chan should know what it is. I'm sorry to bother you so often. It's time to go on duty now, so I'll end here.

Saburô
20 December 1937, 9:45 a.m.

To: Mr. Watanabe Jirô
    1-339 Shimo-Ochiai
    Yodobashi-ku, Tokyo[16]

(1) Today we entered Nanking. It's cloudy with quite a strong, chilly wind; but I'm feeling great. Soon we will cross the Yangtze, so I steel myself for more ferocious fighting. The folks in Miharu and Hosoda have no doubt filled you in on my movements; I didn't have the time to write to you. There should be a field post office opening soon; I'll send this letter then.

(2) I forgot to mention this in my last letter, but I don't have enough gloves. I wonder if you could send me four or five pairs of sturdy cotton and woolen ones. Keep track of how much these cost. I'll write [home] to Sôma about this, so send all of the receipts to them for reimbursement. I'll be here on guard duty for a month here in Ch'üanchiao, an area across the Yangtze, to the west and north of Nanking. This is where we will greet the New Year. I'll write again.

23 December

Shanghai Expeditionary Army, Ogisu [Thirteenth] Division, Morozumi [Sixty-fifth] Regiment, Taira [Third] Battalion, Kinoshita [Ninth] Company

Amano Saburō
23 December

We embarked from Chung-shan Pier in Hsiakwan Port just outside Nanking to ford the Yangtze on the twenty-first, as scheduled. We arrived here in Ch'üanchiao county last night. I'll be here for a month or more assigned to guard duty, peace preservation, and propagation of the Imperial Way; so this is where I'll greet the New Year. The city [of Ch'üanchiao] had a population of 30,000 people, all of whom fled, to be replaced by many refugees from Nanking. It's a small walled city, just what you'd expect to find on the Chink landscape. Our emaciated officers and men will no doubt recover their strength eating [foraged] chicken and pork everyday, but they all say they'd love to get their hands on some freshly brewed Nada *sake*. I'll be OK for clothes after the transport unit ships my gear over from Shanghai; that should be soon. For the moment, I get by on locally requisitioned cigarettes. Sweets are hard to come by; at one point there were none at all. The other day, some guy swiped my sword sash, so I asked Uncle Jirô in Tokyo to send me one; but would you, elder brother, ask him too, either by getting a postcard off to him or just by circulating this letter?

All the residents here hate Chiang Kai-shek. This can't just be a ploy to get in good with the Japanese army. Some Chinks even say they look forward to having Japan govern them—the sooner the better. As befits a cultured nation, every house has its hanging scroll, painting, or sample of calligraphy on display. It's really impressive. Their bedding is far better than anything we have in Japan; I suppose it reflects a Chinese national trait of enjoying a hearty

190

night's sleep. Everyday I eat the local specialty, Nanking peanuts; but I absolutely hate another of these, Nanking rice. Just try leaving it in your mess kit overnight; the grains dry up and come unstuck the next day, so there's no way it can taste good. Today we finally got a meal of rice brought from Japan.

Hatred for Japan is especially strong south of the Yangtze, where reading charts hung in school classrooms are filled with nothing but anti-Japanese slogans. You hardly see anything like that up here, north of the river. Had we let this situation go on for another ten years, the results would have been terrifying. Japanese residents in Shanghai [last August] got angry when our navy stood by idly [despite Chinese rioting] for so long, so I shudder to think about how much future damage these pupils will cause to Japan-Chink relations. Twelve- and thirteen-year-old kids, who don't know any better, are told to shoot and kill Japanese; so they show up on the frontlines. It's the same with women, too. When I see both kids and women fighting at the battlefront, I think of how happy all of you are back in Japan. Many kids were mixed in with the enemy troops; they fought bravely on the front lines in battles near Nanking. When I saw them, hatred welled up inside me. Yet at the same time, I felt admiration even though they are the enemy.

I'm just rambling. A buddy will be going to Shanghai tomorrow, so I rushed to get these thoughts down on paper so that I can ask him to mail this letter. After I'm back on guard duty (for 5 days after 10 off), I'll be able to describe the situation for you. A field post office ought to be up and running pretty soon. When you address letters or packages to me, it's best to spell out in full my rank, surname, and given name. If you send packages, please include some newspapers or a copy of *Bungei shunjû* [magazine].

23 December, 8:30 p.m., Japan time

Correspondence Number 10—23 December, night

Dear Mother,

We crossed the Yangtze on 21 December, as scheduled. After a forced marched of over ten *ri* [forty kilometers] yesterday, we reached our present position, Ch'üanchiao County, just as the sun set. I'm here for a month on guard duty. At the same time, this is a mission to propagate the Imperial Way. So I'll greet the New Year here, and am now busy preparing for it. Every tenth day, I have five days on [guard] duty. I'll probably be busier when on duty, than when I'm in battle.

The [Thirteenth] division is at Ch'uhsien, about six *ri* [twenty-four kilometers] north of here. If you sent me something, I'll get it soon. The transport unit ought to be shipping my gear over from Shanghai, so I should be more or less OK for clothes; but I'd like to have a long-sleeve undershirt to wear under my woolen shirt. I'm making do with requisitioned cigarettes, so

I'd sure appreciate it if you sent me some "Bat" or canned "Hikari" brands from Japan. Send me some sweets too; hard-rock candy would be great, but no caramel or bonbons. With the arrival of a fourth batch of replenishment troops, this platoon now numbers thirty-six men, myself included. I'd like to give them a taste of Japan and peace in the New Year of 1938. So, I'm sorry to bother you, but could you send me some things?

There is no sound of shooting at all right now. North of the Yangtze here, there are lots of refugees from south of the river. They have taken over houses vacated by the locals who had fled earlier. They're a submissive lot who call Chiang Kai-shek a villain. Thanks to the Chink language that I took for awhile back in school, we can communicate pretty well by exchanging written notes. Late into the night by a campfire, our troops swap stories about their hometowns and talk incessantly about when they'll be able to make a triumphant return to Japan. Though I'm an officer who is younger than them, they obey me earnestly and perform their duties for me energetically [unlike in many units]. So don't worry about me. I haven't received a "comfort bag" yet. Warrant Officer Yokoyama Shûichrô, from Tamura Middle School in Miharu, is here in this company; and a student at [Hitotsubashi] Higher Commercial School one year junior to me has arrived with the fourth batch of replenishment troops. Abe Ichirô is in the Tenth company. I'm in the Ninth, so he's right nearby. It's now winter holidays for you, so you must be enjoying them. A powdery snow fell the other day. The daytime temperature is like early spring back home. It's cold in the mornings, but don't worry about me. Today, I went to a Chink-style public bath here in town—for free of course. I'll write again. Could you please give me the addresses of Kiku-chan and of Isamu-san in Hokkaido right away? Give my regards to everyone.

Saburô

P.S. Show this letter to elder sister Takeno. Please let [the folks in] Hokkaido and Kiku-chan know that I'm well and inform them of what unit I'm in also.

To Mr. Ôgoshi Kinji in Miharu town,

Back in Japan you must be busy getting ready for the New Year. I hope everyone in your household is well. Fortunately, I too have been fine ever since landing and performing my duties here starting on the twenty-second, so please don't worry about me. This division lacks a field post office, so I have to hang on to the letters I write, waiting for a chance to mail these. New Year's Day will see me on guard duty; I'll probably greet the year's first sunrise in a trench somewhere. Please give my regards to everyone. It's pretty warm here.

(From Ch'üanchiao County)

To Uncle and Taka-chan,

This map gives you an idea of the route I've taken since landing.[17] I will relate each move in detail when I write [home] to Sôma. They will forward that letter to [relatives in] Miharu, who in turn will send it to you. Just ask them for it. Tomorrow the regiment will conduct a memorial service to honor heroic comrades who died on campaigns since Shanghai. Rain turned to snow at around noon today and it's falling pretty heavily right now, so there should be quite a bit on the ground by tomorrow. I have absolutely no idea what action we will take hereafter. At 3:00 p.m. on the thirtieth, the day after tomorrow, I'll head for the front to take up guard duty with the [Third] battalion. So I'll celebrate the New Year's—and add one year to my age—in a trench together with dozens of troops under my command.[18] What greater happiness could accrue to a man in the Japanese empire! Early this morning I led the men in my platoon on a two-*li* (eight-kilometer) march outside of town to boost their physical stamina as well as to display the might of our imperial army. We returned to barracks at 2:00 p.m. amid rain. [Unlike many commanders,] I'm fortunate that these courageous men—who have cheated death in all of the fierce battles since Shanghai—obey my orders.

Did you get my letter written the other day [23 December] in which I asked you about the sword sash? Please buy one and send it to me. The field post office isn't up yet, but I should get a chance to mail this tomorrow, so I wrote it in a rush. The sentries on guard duty will have it cold tonight. We get [the continental cycle of] "three cold and four warm days," and the chill seems to be gaining strength. How is Saburô-san health-wise? I'm scribbling this beneath a dim lamp, so please try to decipher my scrawl. By the time it reaches you, your New Year holidays will probably be over. So much for now.

Saburō, 28 December, night

MILITARY POST

To: Mr. Amano Tatsujirô
      Hosoda, Nakamura town
      Sôma county, Fukushima prefecture
From: Amano Saburô
      Kinoshita [Ninth] Company, Morozumi [Sixth-fifth] Regiment,
      Ogisu [Thirteenth] Division, Shanghai Expeditionary Army
      29 December 1937

[Chronology]

Arrived in Shanghai—29 November
   Landed at 10:00 a.m.; camped out three nights in a Chink spinning factory here.

Arrived in Hu-p'u-chen—2 December, 6:00 p.m.

Change of route from land to sea. Boarded a Nisshin steamer. Advanced from 6:00 to 11:00 p.m. at night to reach Mei-li-chen. Several rounds of rifle fire heard. That morning [3 December], the Chink air force bombed Hu-p'u-chen.

Arrived in Changshu—3 December, 4:00 p.m.

En route, saw mounds of enemy corpses left strewn about, plus dead Japanese army horses

Arrived in Wuhsi—4 December, 8:00 p.m.

Same sight en route as yesterday. Changshu and Wuhsi both completely leveled by shells and bombs. Few tolerable private houses left standing [to camp out in], and no sign of inhabitants. Defeated stragglers appear and vanish out of thin air. Very dangerous, must dodge stray bullets now and then.

Chiangyin—

Forced march from Wuhsi on 5 December starting at 10:00 p.m. Covered tens of *ri* in one fell swoop to catch up with those men in our regiment on the very front lines. Accomplished our transport mission without losing a single man.

Chen-chiang—

After departing Chiang-yin on 7 December, several days' forced march required to reach the walled city of Chen-chiang, whose batteries overlook the Yangtze River, on 4 December.[19] Another unit conquered this city the day before. No defeated enemy remnants around. Saw electric lights on for the first time since landing [at Hu-p'u-chen], probably because our offensive left the Chinks with no time to destroy generating plants. An American flag flutters above the U.S. embassy on a low-lying hill; hatred welled up inside me.

From Chen-chiang to Nanking—

Departed Chen-chiang at 11:00 a.m. for the assault for Nanking. The ruins of some towns and villages en route clearly showed that retreating Chink armies ravaged all of these to their hearts' content. Finally established assault formations to attack the Mufushan [elevated] batteries at 11:30 a.m., on 14 December. Later heard that another unit captured the Wu-lung batteries earlier that morning. At 8:00 a.m., as the sun rose, we encountered the enemy about one *ri* (four kilometers) this side of the Mufushan batteries. Suffered slight losses; killed or wounded 15,000 of the enemy and captured mounds of weapons.

Ch'üanchiao County—

Crossed the Yangtze from Hsiakwan outside Nanking; got here after a two-day trek. Almost no sign of the enemy. Inhabitants seem fairly amicable toward the imperial army. Such extravagant provisions never seen before! Chickens and pigs more plentiful than vegetables, so we gorge on [plundered] meat everyday. Stone mortars are available [to pound *mochi*]. Also, we requisitioned sweet glutinous rice for making New Year's *mochi*. Will be here on guard duty for the time being.

This is a chronology of my movements since landing. Please send it to the folks in Miharu, and have them in turn forward it to relatives elsewhere. The last person should tuck it away for safekeeping.

Notes

* Translated from Japanese by the editor.
1. This is a translation of "Amano Saburô gunji yûbin," in Ono, Fujiwara, and Honda, eds., *Nankin daigyakusatsu o kiroku shita kôgun heishi tachi*, pp. 246–58.
2. Note that postmarked dates and dates of composition do not correspond for some of the letters.
3. Corrected from a misprint in the transcribed text.
4. Amano uses the English word "camouflage."
5. Amano, I assume, measures the unit as Japanese *ri*, or about 4 kilometers, rather than Chinese *li*, each of which would be 1.8 kilometers.
6. Throughout his correspondence, Amano employs the pejorative terms *Shina* and *Shinajin* commonly used in Japan at the time. I retain his historical usage by rendering these as "Chink." Also, see the appendix.
7. Amano wrote some letters over 2 or more days; hence the discrepancies between dates; for instance, "Wusung at 7:00 p.m.; 28 November" in the heading, and "today, the twenty-seventh" in the body.
8. The unit of measure is missing, either in the original or due to an omission in transcription.
9. As the Chronology indicates, this spot on the coast northeast of Changshu is Hu-p'u-chen.
10. As the Chronology indicates, Amano's company passed through Mei-li-chen, Changshu, Wuhsi, and Chiangyin on this forced march of over forty *li*, or 160 kilometers, from Hu-p'u-chen to Chin-chiang en route to Nanking. However, in this letter, he records his entrance into Chenchiang as taking place on either the tenth or twelth, whereas in his Chronology, he records it as being on "4 December." See note 19, below, however.
11. Amano may be referring to the fact that Chenchiang had been established as a prefectural capital in the Sung dynasty (960–1279).
12. If the POWs were taken on the fourteenth, this should be "3 days" rather than "a week already." By contrast, the Chinese "Report" cited below states "over 4 days."
13. Amano uses the English word "nonsense," which I render as "absurd."
14. The import of this sentence is unclear.
15. In August 1933, Kiryû Yûyû (1873–1941) said much the same thing in an article, "Derisive Laughter over the Great Kantô Air Raid Drill," in the *Shinano mainichi* shinbun. Kiryû was forced to resign for his offensive title and for describing the drill over Tokyo as a "puppet show." See Iide, *Teikô no shinbunjin*, pp. 156–75; especially, pp. 167–70. Also, Kiryû, *Chikushôdô no chikyû*, pp. 17–20.
16. Yodobashi-ku was established in 1932 as one of the then 35 *ku*, or "wards," in the city of Tokyo. In 1947 it was merged to form what is now Shinjuku-ku.
17. The map is not included in the published volume that contains this group of letters.
18. According to traditional East Asian custom, one calculated one's age by adding a year on each New Year's Day.
19. The date "4 December" is out of chronological order. Most likely, it should read "14 December." This may be a mistake in the original or in the transcription.

9

CHINESE COLLABORATION
IN NANKING

Timothy Brook

Introduction

On 22 January 1938, Lewis Smythe, a sociology professor at Nanking University, paused in his report on the complicated relief work of the International Committee (IC) for the Nanking Safety Zone (NSZ). He wrote a brief accolade for two men who were making extraordinary efforts to ease the plight of the 250,000 whom the Japanese army had turned into refugees in their own city: "A stirring story can be written some day about the strenuous efforts of Mr. Wang Cheng-tien (locally known as 'Jimmy'), the new Food Commissioner under the Self-Government Committee, and the head of his trucking committee, Mr. Charles Riggs ('Charlie'), who together are moving heaven and earth to get the Japanese to allow them to have more rice, flour and coal for the population and then to truck it in."[1]

Jimmy Wang and Charlie Riggs, made for a striking pair. Charlie Riggs was an American employed in the Agronomy Department at Nanking University who acted as the associate housing commissioner for the IC, which foreigners had organized in November 1937, in anticipation of the Japanese capture of the city. Assaulted on several occasions by Japanese officers when he intervened on behalf of the Chinese, Riggs was active organizing relief on university campuses inside the NSZ. This work brought him into close contact with Chinese relief workers, including members of the Red Swastika Society (RSS), a prominent charitable group that buried many of the victims of the Atrocity.[2]

Jimmy Wang was a local auctioneer of dubious reputation whom foreigners, Lewis Smythe among them, referred to as "the famous 'Jimmy'" with "many connections with the underworld in Nanking."[3] Wang emerged in the second week of the occupation as a man of extraordinary energy and resources, and was taken on as the IC's business manager while at the very same moment engineering for himself a position as adviser to the Nanking Self-Government Committee (*Nan-ching tzu-chih wei-yuan-hui,* or SGC), also called the Autonomous Government Committee. The SGC was a collaborationist organ that the Japanese cobbled together from RSS activists to create the illusion that this was a change in administration, not an occupation. When the old five-barred Republican flag was raised at the SGC's inauguration on 1 January 1938, it was Jimmy Wang who raised it. Wang not only got into both camps but made himself indispensable to both, and with an ease that inspired cynical but amused comments from the foreigners. When IC members learned five days later that he had been put in charge of SGC food supply operations, according to Smythe, "They all snorted and Searle [Bates] said, 'Well, rice must be going to be the most paying proposition.' But I remarked, 'Well he is the one man in the outfit that may get some rice moving before March first'." Two days after that, the secretary at the German legation, Georg Rosen, referred to Wang as "the most active member of the new system."[4] A smooth operator working from no obvious moral standards, Jimmy Wang became indispensable to all parties as a key facilitator for getting things done. Such a person would never have found a place in the historical record of Republican China were it not for the calamity that struck his city, his willingness to act rather than flee, and his dealings with foreigners who enjoyed writing about such a dubious but energetic character.

Jimmy Wang is a figure who challenges the categories of collaboration and resistance. In the heightened atmosphere of denial and moral outrage that surrounds the memory of the Nanking Atrocity, the Japanese are all bad guys, the Chinese all pitiable victims, the Westerners all saviors, and the collaborators all evil traitors. Jimmy Wang doesn't fit. He stands out in the first instance because he was not a victim. He looks like a collaborator, having joined the puppet administration that came into being while the Atrocity was still going on. And yet, as the German consul Paul Scharffenberg reported, he "has at least shown courage and told the Japanese: 'If you are against me, then you'd better shoot me here and now'!" Fixers such as Jimmy Wang can play pivotal roles in crisis situations, as the now well-known case of Oskar Schindler has made us aware. But Wang was not the sort of paragon that Chinese historiography on the Atrocity likes to celebrate.[5] Our sources are too meager to tell the "stunning story" that Lewis Smythe hoped one day would be told; Jimmy Wang has slipped too far into the past. Fragments of his doings can nonetheless be retrieved to sketch his role during that winter of 1937–38 and introduce a shade of ambiguity into events that otherwise seem unambiguous. My intention is not to overrule the moral condemnation that most persons choose to pass on the Nanking Atrocity, but to consider what else was going on, and to explore the places where that judgment may not extend.

Our knowledge of the Nanking Atrocity has been thoroughly organized within the concepts of invasion, war crimes, and national humiliation, with the last of these available to do double duty for either Chinese or Japanese, depending on whose historiography is in play. Collaboration is not a concept that receives much reflection. It is unattractive within Chinese historiography, which praises those who resisted as the sole figures of honor, and dismisses those who collaborated as morally unfit. It is also disturbing for Chinese national identity, which still relies on a heroic narrative of wartime resistance to Japan to sustain itself in the face of the many indignities China suffered throughout the twentieth century. The concept of collaboration is even more unexpected in narratives of the Nanking Atrocity. The Atrocity is regularly placed within a category of human experience too extreme to allow the shades of gray that collaboration casts between heroic defiance and abject subjection. Stories of betrayal are remembered as moments of terrible duress, the rare exceptions that prove the opposite: that Chinese did *not* collaborate with the Japanese invaders.

But "running dogs," to use the Chinese phrase, are not the only guise that collaborators can assume. Collaboration can also be about working within largely unalterable conditions to make life tolerable for others as well as for oneself. Until recently, the historiography of this Atrocity held that such room for maneuvering did not exist, and that it was anathema to Chinese culture to utilize it. For Chinese to suggest that other Chinese collaborated with the Japanese during the war goes against the theme of racial and national unity that runs through this historiography. By contrast, for Japanese to raise this possibility would be to court condemnation for trying to off-load moral responsibility for their war crimes and atrocities to Chinese agents. Yet in Nanking, as much as in any other location where the Japanese occupation appeared to have arrived as a fact of life, some Chinese did come forward to work out what accommodations they could with the new masters. Even as the Atrocity was underway, some Chinese were taking actions and making choices that fall into neither category of hero or victim. Jimmy Wang belongs within this unmarked realm, as does the political agency he chose to work for, the SGC. By reconstructing its brief history between December 1937 and April 1938, I hope to broaden the present historiography surrounding the Nanking Atrocity and, by so doing, complicate and improve on the problematically inert moral judgments that enclose it.

New Year's Day, 1938

At 2:00 p.m. on 1 January 1938, a thousand Chinese who had survived the Japanese army's takeover of Nanking stood assembled in the sunshine at the Drum Tower. They had been ordered there by the Nanking Special Service Agency (*Tokumu kikan,* or SSA), appointed to handle civil affairs on behalf of the occupying Japanese Central China Area Army (*Naka Shina hômengun,* or CCAA). On 30 December, SSA agents had informed leaders of the refugee camps around the city that every camp had to send an appropriate number of "representatives" to the unveiling of the new municipal government. This regime was to be inaugurated on New Year's Day, and it needed an audience. George Fitch, an American who headed the Nanking YMCA and served on the IC, called on the Japanese embassy that day just as preparations were being ordered:

> They were busy giving instructions to about sixty Chinese, most of them our camp managers, on how New Year was to be celebrated. The old five-barred flag is to replace the Nationalist flag, and they were told to make a thousand of these and also a thousand Japanese flags for that event. Camps of over a thousand must have twenty representatives present, smaller camps ten. At one o'clock New Year's Day the five-barred flag is to be raised above the Drum Tower, there will be "suitable" speeches and "music" (according to the program) and of course moving pictures will be taken of the happy people waving flags and welcoming the new regime.[6]

As the event called for at least the appearance of popular celebration, the SSA also distributed thousands of fireworks so that people could make appropriate noise to celebrate the formation of the SGC. Residents of the NSZ, however, used theirs to animate a New Year's ceremony prior to the inauguration to thank the German head of the IC, John Rabe, for his protection.

What was planned was precisely what happened. The Drum Tower was decorated with the old flag of the Chinese Republic, which hadn't been flown for a decade since it was replaced by the sun-and-sky iconography of Sun Yat-sen's Nationalist Party, the Kuomintang (KMT). Chinese and Japanese officials paraded in front of the assembly. Representing the Japanese army were CCAA Chief of Staff Iinuma Mamoru and Maj. Gen. Sasaki Tôichi, commandant of the Nanking Garrison. The navy was represented by its attaché, Nakahara Saburô, and the foreign ministry by Vice-Consul Tanaka Sueo and Second Secretary Fukui Kiyoshi. With them stood a small crowd of Chinese people, members of the fledgling SGC who were about to become the new municipal government. The senior figure dressed in a traditional gown was a white-whiskered lawyer named T'ao Hsi-san. Jimmy Wang was there, as the American surgeon Dr. Robert Wilson remarked in a letter that day: "One of the chief men has been working in a rather subordinate capacity under the International Committee and has a long record with many connections with the city underworld, and other undesirable characteristics. He is by business an auctioneer. The others hold various positions with the Red Swastika Society and most of them have been working for the Committee. It certainly is a second-hand crowd, but then there aren't any first classers in town."[7] Charlie Riggs, Wang's soon-to-be partner in food supply, punned, as did Wilson, on the man's auctioneering business by observing that Jimmy's role in the inauguration was "very fitting for a second-hand government."[8]

Standing at the head of his group, T'ao Hsi-san read out the SGC's five-point manifesto. Its first point committed the SGC to end the KMT's one-party rule. The second and third points declared the regime's goals to be cooperation with Japan to achieve peace in East Asia, the promotion of anti-Communism, and pro-Japanism. Fourth came the revival of the economy and the improvement of the people's welfare, and lastly the implementation of meritocracy at the center and self-government among the people. The committee was setting itself up as the agency that would finally bring Chiang Kai-shek's period of fledgling modernization, known as the Nanking Decade (1927–37), to an end. The air at the inauguration was thick with more than irony for, as John Rabe noted, "while the orators of the new Autonomous Government [the SGC] were speaking of cooperation, several buildings torched by the Japanese were burning to the right and left of Gulou [Drum Tower] Hospital where the ceremony took place."[9]

George Fitch noted that the Westerners were less concerned about a regime inauguration than about the two days' holiday that the Japanese army was granting in its honor, "for it means more drunken soldiers."[10] As predicted, many of them chose to celebrate the holiday by drinking and looking for women. According to some Japanese soldiers' diaries that survive, troops started the day with a morning ceremony in which they faced east and called out lòng life for the emperor. Then they had the rest of the day off to go drinking and "buy ass," to use their phrase for securing a prostitute's services. Others were willing to line up at the military brothel. One diarist mentions seeing Chinese on the streets waving Japanese flags as he headed over to join 500 other soldiers waiting to share the services of seventy prostitutes.[11] Many chose rape in their pursuit of similar pleasure. (IC records identify two of the victims as fourteen-year-olds, and two of the perpetrators as military police.[12]) One gang of New Year's revelers even had the temerity to show up at John Rabe's home that evening with a truck and ask him to fill it with girls, a request he declined.

The Nanking Special Service Agency (SSA)

The IC was not part of the Japanese plan for rehabilitating occupied China. This committee had three strikes against it: it had been spontaneously organized; it was already functioning as a local authority when the Japanese army arrived; and, most noxiously, it was composed of Westerners. The usual Japanese plan, which had been unfolding in county towns across the Yangtze delta in the wake of the army's westward advance, was to set up a temporary peace maintenance committee *(chih-an wei-ch'ih-hui)* of local Chinese. Once order was restored, the Special Service Department *(Tokumubu* or SSD) in Shanghai would send out a pacification team *(senbuhan)* to take charge of local civil affairs. That team would then regularize the peace maintenance committee into a self-government committee (*tzu-chih wei-yuan-hui* or SGC). From this latter committee, under the guidance of the pacification team, would emerge a new county administration.[13]

The process was altered for the national capital, however. The Japanese command saw Nanking as both a challenge and an opportunity. The opportunity was that its fall signaled the collapse of Chiang Kai-shek's military operations in central China and, it was hoped, of his government. The challenge was dealing with the huge refugee population under the watchful eyes of "third-country" observers, to use the Japanese phrase. CCAA commander Gen. Matsui Iwane was conscious of the foreign presence in Nanking and ordered the occupying force not to interfere with foreigners or their property when taking the city. But he did not anticipate the impact that foreign observation of his troops' conduct would have on world opinion at the time, nor could he have guessed the power of the IC's detailed record, published in 1939, to condemn him at his war crimes trial in 1946–48.[14] Matsui hoped that the orderly fall of the national capital would persuade the Chinese people of the folly of supporting Chiang's regime. In fact, the riotous conduct of Japanese soldiers cancelled out the possibility that Nanking's capture would lead to compassionate behavior toward the Chinese, conveying to the populace at large only that the occupation would be violent and uncompromising.

Regardless of the army's conduct, the task of pacification—reconstructing local order on a new civilian footing—had to go ahead. According to a review of pacification work in central China produced by the Shanghai office of the South Manchurian Railway Company (Mantetsu) on 16 March 1938, the original plan called for eight branch pacification departments across the Yangtze Delta. The one in Nanking would oversee four teams, one in the city and three others in the surrounding counties.[15] This plan was never carried out. Instead, the CCAA's SSD set up a direct branch operation in the capital. Its designation as a full Special Service Agency (*Tokumu kikan,* or SSA) signalled higher status than a regular pacification team. The first three members of the team were on site as soon as the city fell: Maj. Sakata Shigeki as agency head, assisted by two Mantetsu civilian employees, Matsuoka Isao and Mabuchi Seigô. Within two weeks of arriving, Sakata appealed to Shanghai for more men with strong China experience. The SSD selected four more for this task. The first to arrive, on 28 December, was Maruyama Susumu. In the second week of January Satô Tsukito, Kojima Tomô, and Kawano Masanao (transferred from Sung-kiang) came.[16] Two weeks later, Kawano disappeared, Sakata was transferred away, and Matsuoka took over the team. Sakata was a military officer who, it seems, was on loan to help set up the agency rather than to lead it in the long term.

At their first and only meeting with Maj. Sakata on 15 December, IC members clearly understood that he held military rank.[17] The mistaken sense that the SSA was primarily a military organ was still current in April, when Cabot Coville, a visiting American consular official, referred to the SSA as "the military mission" and noted that "its contact man was a pleasant officer, formerly attaché at Ottawa (named Hongô?)." Coville understood that Hongô was "quite without authority or influence, just a facade for pleasantness while the military could proceed with their own purposes."[18] At the brief meeting back in December, Sakata urged the IC to trust his army's "humanitarian attitude" with regard to "care for disarmed Chinese soldiers." Was this a pure fabrication on Sakata's part, or did he genuinely fail to anticipate that SSA soldiers would be employed to round up defeated Chinese troops, lead them to the Yangtze riverbank, and shoot them?[19] The SSA's principal responsibility, however, was to create a Chinese administration for the occupied area. On 21 December, it convened a meeting of Chinese sympathizers at the Japanese embassy to explore the possibility of forming a new municipal administration. In keeping with the seniority of the SSA, it bypassed the standard peace maintenance stage and proceeded directly to set up of a self-government committee.[20] The negotiations with these tag-ends of the old Nanking elite progressed smoothly. The SSA was able to call a second meeting two days later at which an SGC preparatory committee was struck. The "pacification" of Nanking was about to begin.

The Red Swastika Society

The network through which the Japanese would recruit personnel for the SGC was the Red Swastika Society (*Hung-wan-tzu hui* or RSS), a voluntary organization formed in imitation of the Red Cross, but reimagined in a non-Christian form. The Chinese Buddhist iconography of the swastika was a conservative assertion of the eastern pole of the East-West dichotomy with which so many tradition-oriented intellectuals felt burdened in the wake of May Fourth.[21] Nanking had two RSS branches, both founded in 1922, one inside the city and one in Hsiakwan, Nanking's river port on the Yangtze and home to some of the city's poorest residents. Before 1927, when the city lacked what could be called a municipal government, organizations such as this provided the destitute of Nanking with crucial aid in hard seasons. They also furnished traditional elites with a position and purpose in the new urban sphere. Even after the KMT regime made Nanking its national capital and set up a full municipal administration there, these benevolent societies, and the philanthropic elite that led them, continued their activities, dispensing food and clothing in winter and burying abandoned corpses. The RSS enjoyed close links with the new municipal government, sitting on the boards of government-organized relief projects and donating money to these. It also coordinated its work with missionary efforts in the city. It thus made complete sense

that the RSS would be the entity organizing relief during the winter of 1937–
38 as it had in previous winters, especially now that the municipal government had decamped.[22] Faced with disaster on a scale that dwarfed the worst
years of the 1930s, the RSS enlarged its membership to about 600 and set to
work.[23]

The relief work that the RSS did in the early months of the occupation,
supported by its tradition of cooperation with Chinese political regimes in
the city, brought its members in contact with the Japanese occupation force.
This contact became the conduit that led the Japanese to T'ao Hsi-san, the
RSS leader who became the head of the SGC. T'ao declined to serve initially,
though in any case he was not the first choice of the Japanese side. The
embassy, through Second Secretary Fukui Kiyoshi, tried first to woo Ch'en
Jung, a graduate of Hokkaido Imperial University and head of the Forestry
Department at Nanking University. Ch'en's fluency in Japanese and English,
as well as his good relations with the embassy, made him an attractive candidate, but he resisted and chose to work instead as an informal liaison between
the embassy and the IC. The embassy then approached Lou Hsiao-hsi. Lou
was a Nanking businessman who had studied in Japan and worked as an interpreter in Shanghai; more saliently, he had acted as an informal communication channel between the KMT regime and the Japanese embassy in Nanking.
Lou appears to have been willing, but the SSA blocked his candidacy on the
grounds that he would look too much like a puppet.

RSS leader T'ao Hsi-san, with his elegant white beard and good connections
into the old official networks of Nanking, was the third choice.[24] Allegedly,
T'ao demanded as his condition to serve that the Japanese army make a commitment not to kill any more people. The Japanese side agreed, but gave no
sign of intending to observe it. By not resigning in protest at that early
moment, T'ao found himself in a compromised position from which he could
neither extricate himself nor renegotiate terms. With T'ao locked in, the SSA
used the RSS network to recruit other men for the SGC. Vice-chair Sun Shu-
jung, Dr. Hsü Ch'uan-yin, and Jimmy Wang were known members, and it
appears from Robert Wilson's comment in his letter of 1 January, quoted earlier in this chapter, that most of the other committee members had RSS ties
as well. Not all RSS members were willing to cooperate with the Japanese,
however, and some fled the city to avoid entanglement.[25]

The Red Swastika's local prestige as a philanthropic organization made it
an attractive entity for the Japanese to work with. It also put them in touch
with the few people at the low end of the city's elite who had stayed behind.
These tended not to be the new KMT elite, but men whose deep ties into
Nanking society at all levels predated the KMT seizure of power and could
provide the Japanese access to local networks of patronage and brokerage. The
ubiquity of this old elite's hand in Nanking society flashes into view in John
Rabe's diary on 26 December. When Japanese military authorities entered

Ginling Women's College to recruit women for brothel service, the American missionary in charge, Minnie Vautrin, refused to cooperate. Rabe describes the scene: "She is not going to hand over even one of them willingly; but then something unexpected happens. A respectable member of the Red Swastika Society, someone we all know, but would never have suspected had any knowledge of the underworld, calls out a few friendly words into the hall—and lo and behold! A considerable number of young refugee girls step forward. Evidently former prostitutes, who are not at all sad to find work in a new bordello. Minnie is speechless!"[26] If Vautrin was taken aback by the connections that "a respectable member of the Red Swastika Society" had with the sex trade, Rabe was more amused than surprised. The SGC in fact set up three brothels at about this time and recruited women to work there. Collaborators accepted the provision of this sort of service as a concession they had to make to please the Japanese, especially if it got sex-starved soldiers away from other women.

The activism of the RSS proved to be a double-edged sword that cut both itself and the Japanese. The society was dishonored and disbanded after the war for being too visibly close to Japanese authorities during the occupation. On the other hand, the knowledge it thereby gained of Japanese actions and the records it kept would be used against Japan at the International Military Tribunal for the Far East (IMTFE), conducted in Tokyo after the war. For, besides its soup kitchens, the other signal service that the RSS performed was burying the dead. It kept a daily record of burials, which it submitted everyday to the SGC during the winter of 1937–38. The number of dead as of early March was 31,791, according to an SSA report in mid-March, but that number kept growing. An RSS petition to the SGC for financial support stated that, as of the beginning of April, its members had disposed of well over 30,000 corpses, mostly in the last three weeks of February, after the final wave of Japanese violence against city residents had subsided. A later report of the Nanking branch put the total number of burials between December 1937 and April 1938 at 43,121.[27] This is the figure that RSS member Dr. Hsü Ch'uan-yin would read into the record at the Tokyo war crimes trial in 1946.[28]

The Nanking Self-government Committee

The uncharitable assessment that Robert Wilson offered on inauguration day of the people whom the Japanese had drawn from RSS membership to make up the SGC was harsh but not unfair—"a second-hand crowd, but then there aren't any first classers in town." These men had little real public stature, and no experience in the management of urban affairs, as the SSA caustically pointed out in a confidential January 1938 report.[29] The official narrative of the founding of the occupation state, published in Japanese by the Propaganda Bureau of the Reformed Government's Executive Yuan in 1940, could not afford to be so uncomplimentary; it calls them instead "local capable men."[30] Not "first-classers," perhaps, but they were the sort of elites who occupied responsible leadership niches in conservative entities such as the RSS. To the extent that T'ao Hsi-san was "capable," it was not so much his native talents as his deep ties into Nanking society that enabled him to get things done. Elderly, respected, not in the pocket of the KMT, he was a "fine old man," in the words of Lewis Smythe. T'ao and his associates on the SGC were not the new intellectuals of the era, nor were they activists tied to the KMT cause. If anything qualified them for this job, it was the experience of having been driven out into the political cold by the KMT after it took power in 1927. (The same official narrative explains that the SGC had to be set up in order to control the "unexpected terrorist activities" of KMT soldiers and Communist agents hiding in the NSZ.)

Organizing an SGC was an SSA task, but the Japanese embassy had the local contacts needed to identify potential collaborators, and at the start it seemed to have the upper hand in forming the committee. George Fitch was even given to understand that the SGC was the creation of Japanese "Consul General" Tanaka Sueo.[31] The SGC's Muslim vice-chair, Sun Shu-jung, for instance, was an embassy employee—and for his close relations with Japanese in Nanking, he had been placed under early suspicion by the KMT as a spy before the city fell. The SSA did not care for some of the people the embassy put forward, however. Within a day or so, Rabe picked up a rumor that "the military command here does not want to recognize the Japanese-Chinese Committee that the Japanese legation has put together—one similar to our committee for the Safety Zone." SSA agent Maruyama Susumu characterizes the SGC in his memoir as "rather opposed to the Japanese army."[32] This is a sentiment that may reflect the feeling within the SSA that it did not want the sort of people the embassy put forward in local self-government organs. If they were thwarted in their expectations, though, they were no different from Japanese pacification agents elsewhere on the delta. How most Chinese could not be "rather opposed to the Japanese army," in Maruyama's felicitous phrase, is beyond my powers to imagine.

The six other members of the SGC were Chao Wei-shu, Chao Kung-chin, Ma Hsi-hou, Hu Ch'i-fa, Huang Yueh-hsuan, and Wang Ch'un-sheng.[33] Huang Yueh-hsuan was an RSS activist whose name appears among those who had sat on the winter aid committee the previous year.[34] Wang Ch'un-sheng had been a police officer before the KMT took over Nanking in 1927, after which he ran a hotel and mingled with the city's underworld. This network would serve him in good stead when he took charge of the SGC police force, which worked with both the SSA and the Japanese military police through January to root out Chinese soldiers who had taken refuge among the city's residents. Wang Ch'un-sheng had a prior connection to Japan, having received his police training there. So too did several other SGC members. T'ao Hsi-san was a graduate of Hôsei University in Tokyo.[35] Vice-chair Sun Shu-jung had spent two years in Japan and spoke good Japanese. Chao Kung-chin had been trained as a medical doctor in Nagasaki. Chao Wei-shu and the committee's secretary, Wang Chung-t'iao, had also been students in Japan. Among those who would run the day-to-day administration of Nanking, it turns out that a prior involvement with Japan was an important factor.

Five other men were appointed to the SGC as advisers: Chang Nan-wu, T'ao Chueh-san, Chan Jung-kuang, Hsü Ch'uan-yin, and Jimmy Wang. At least three had personal ties to T'ao Hsi-san: T'ao Chueh-san was a kinsman, Hsü Ch'uan-yin an RSS associate, and Chan Jung-kuang, who ran a patent medicine shop in the old commercial district around the Confucian Temple, was a personal friend. Chan was also fluent in Japanese, for Minnie Vautrin identifies him as "an interpreter" when she approached him on 1 January 1938 to see whether the Japanese registration of men on her campus could be stopped.[36] From the reference in her diary, Vautrin seem to have been unaware of what Chan had done the previous day. According to a Chinese history of the occupation, an eyewitness heard him address the men who had sought refuge in Ginling College on 31 December, advising soldiers to identify themselves to the Japanese and promising that they would receive lenient treatment for doing so. Chan could not have been ignorant that the consequence of turning oneself in was likelier execution than mercy, given what went on five days earlier in the refugee camp at Nanking University. According to history professor Searle Bates, "Chinese under the instructions of Japanese officers" encouraged Chinese soldiers to come forward voluntarily. Some Chinese soldiers complied. Those who did were taken off and either shot or bayoneted.[37] Chan Jung-kuang helped repeat that history at Ginling College.

Hsü Ch'uan-yin presents a very different figure. Educated in the United States, he had an engineering Ph.D. from the University of Illinois, and was wealthy enough to have both a Dodge and a piano stolen by Japanese soldiers. Hsü's command of English and his social connections with the foreign community made him the RSS's natural choice to serve as its liaison with the IC. He occupied nodes in many networks: vice-chair of the Nanking Red Swastika chapter, adviser to the SGC, housing commissioner for the NSZ, and IC liaison with the Japanese embassy. In the early weeks of the occupation, he was accordingly a pivotal figure in knitting together the many networks through which the occupation state was constructed, and in knowing how to cross from one to another in order to get something done. In mid-March, when Minnie Vautrin was trying to help women secure their husbands' release from Japanese incarceration, she sought advice from Hsü Ch'uan-yin about whom to approach in the regime. Deeply implicated in the work of shepherding in the new order, he would later reemerge as a star witness at the Tokyo trial in 1946 to testify against CCAA commander Gen. Matsui Iwane.

The SGC was not of the quality that some on the Japanese side hoped for. Whatever the objections, the SSA had resolved by 30 December that the inauguration could go ahead, though it kept the SGC on a close rein for the next four months. SSA control over the SGC was obvious to Westerners in Nanking, who regarded the SGC and the SSA as essentially the same authority: cosigning the same announcements, pursuing the same policies, and operating in a relationship of reciprocal obligation and support. As an American consular official scornfully noted in April, just prior to the SGC's dissolution, the final regulation of its published constitution read: "When these regulations are to be changed, permission must be obtained in advance from the Nanking Special Service Organ [i.e., the SSA]."[38] It was also obvious to the Westerners, especially after a meeting at the embassy on 19 December, that their only potential allies on the Japanese side, the consular staff, had zero influence with the army.[39] It was the army, in the guise of the SSA, not the foreign ministry, that would shape the process of pacification in Nanjing.

If the SGC was hopelessly tied to the Japanese SSA, the burden of connection went the other way as well. The SSA needed the SGC to undertake a range of activities beneficial to the Japanese in the city. Burying corpses and supplying prostitutes were only the beginning. The SSA needed the SGC to assume the important responsibilities of caring for the Chinese population. The SGC's ability to do so would be the measure of its success vis-à-vis the triple political burden it faced as a fledgling agency of collaboration: maintaining an effective relationship with the Japanese, working in cooperation with the IC, and asserting a plausible authority over Chinese residents of the city. Meeting these political challenges meant having to overcome even greater logistic difficulties: providing relief to tens of thousands of refugees over whom it claimed authority, procuring grain needed to supply relief stations, and reestablishing some measure of security and infrastructure so that ordinary people could survive in the truly appalling conditions that the Japanese had created after the Chinese army had withdrawn from Nanking.

The SGC could not accomplish these tasks without resources, but no government funds were left behind when the previous municipal administration departed. Furthermore, the SGC had no source of income initially, other than the financial and logistic support the Japanese army was willing to give. This reliance constituted the most basic condition of SGC collaboration. The financial underwriting of the SGC was a matter of anxiety for the collaborators, not because they were all squeamish about accepting Japanese money, but because the occupying CCAA was in no position to hand over a blank check. It would fund the SGC only in the short term. Fifty-eight percent of the committee's income for the month of January (17,895 of 31,085 yuan) came from the sale of confiscated grain and flour that the CCAA had provided as a way to kick-start its revenue flow. That amount roughly covered SGC salaries. Another third of the SGC's January income (10,000 yuan) was an outright gift from the CCAA. The SGC was able to generate only 3,190 yuan, or 10 percent, of its income on its own, through commercial levies and a rickshaw tax. After this first month, however, the revenue holiday was over. The SGC was forced to become self-supporting in February. Direct Japanese support—in the form of a gift from the embassy—was cut back to a miserable 1,000 yuan (two percent of its total income of 51,257 yuan). A few other gifts from Japan's military arm followed: 2,000 yuan from the Fujita unit, and 500 yuan from Maj. Gen. Harada Kumakichi, the head of the SSD in Shanghai. These amounts were not sufficient to fund a large city administration.[40] Once in, the SGC had to find its own means of support.

The SGC and the International Committee

The third item in the manifesto recited by T'ao Hsi-san on New Year's Day admitted that "the concept of reliance on Europe and America" was strong among the people of Nanking and that this had to be "corrected" in Japan's favor. The concept of "reliance on Europe and America" was a particular obsession of SSD propaganda, which sought to project to Chinese people the idea that Japan had released them from this humiliating condition. At the close of its section on political work, a central report on pacification in March 1938 avoids noting the role that Japanese atrocities played in generating that popular sense of reliance on the West by phrasing this dilemma as a preoccupation influence: "In places where foreign charitable organizations operate refugee zones, such as South City [in Shanghai], Nanking, and Wuhu, refugees have long been influenced by the compassion of foreign charitable organizations. This has deepened their reliance on Europe and America and has worked against the intentions guiding pacification under the Imperial Way. These organizations must be taken over and dissolved as speedily as possible and placed under the direction of the self-government committees."[41]

As the SSD report states, the solution proposed in Nanking as well as in other locations was to mobilize the SGC as an organizational counterweight to foreign influence. In its internal monthly report for January, the Nanking SSA complained that the IC was using its influence with the people to further foreign interests and to block the development of the SGC. In its internal monthly report for February, the SSA continued to complain of how difficult it was to win the hearts of the people of Nanking, and attributed their pro-Western attitude to the work of the IC, which was acting as Japan's main competitor as an organ for local order. A priority of Japan, and of the new collaborationist regime, had to be the elimination of this influence. This, the SSA would push by trying to set the SGC and IC against each other.[42]

The IC first got wind of this scheme on 31 December, when it learned that all money and food stocks under its control had been promised to the SGC by the embassy, so its members hoped to preempt confiscation by issuing a statement three days later, explaining that it was a private relief organization whose resources were held in trust and not transferable.[43] The SGC's response the following day was to position itself as the IC's legitimate alternative by announcing that it was assuming full care for the refugees in the NSZ. This was *not* an empty declaration. On the next day Japanese military authorities entered the NSZ to identify, remove, and execute soldiers and any other young males regarded as "anti-Japanese elements."[44] What is more, the Japanese claimed the right to do so because the NSZ was now under Chinese jurisdiction. Control of refugees at this point had nothing to do with regularizing administration and everything to do with exterminating Chinese males of military age. The SGC's declaration of responsibility for refugees on 4 January thus amounted to complicity in war crimes. This blossomed into proxy management as, over the following weeks, the SGC's Investigation Subcommittee and Wang Ch'un-sheng's police force helped the Japanese military police round up ex-soldiers for execution.

IC members understood that the SGC was created to replace it. Initially they adopted a cool attitude, suspecting the SGC of a resource grab. As John Rabe noted 2 days before the New Year's inauguration, "We have nothing against their taking over our work, but it looks to us as if they simply want to take over our money. I'll not voluntarily hand over anything." Within a day of the inauguration, Vice-chair Sun Shu-jung was telling Rabe that he wanted to open a discussion with the IC. Rabe was willing to hear overtures but was skeptical, and wrote that Sun "condescendingly informs me that he must speak to me very soon about an important matter. Please do, I've been waiting for this. I have a very good idea of what your intentions are!"[45] It quickly became apparent, though, that the SSA was the real force behind the SGC. When Attaché Fukuda Tokuyasu called on Rabe on 6 January, it was to inform him that "the military authorities"—by which he meant the SSA—had decided that the IC should dissolve itself and hand over its assets to the SGC.

The IC responded to this demand the next day by demanding in turn that the Japanese lay out a plan for restoring law and order. Rabe was careful to make clear that he was not opposed to handing over the administration of Nanking to the Chinese. As he wrote in his formal letter of reply of 7 January, the IC was eager for the SGC to "assume as speedily as possible all the usual functions of a local civic administration: policing, fire protection, sanitation, *et cetera*. The International Committee has, I am quite certain, no desire whatsoever to carry on any of these administration duties which are normally assumed by competent local authorities."[46] The issue was not administration in general, but relief, and concern that it be done responsibly and effectively. The problem was the virtual absence of "competent authorities." In his diary that day, Rabe wrote that the SGC "hasn't the vaguest idea how to tackle these problems, even though they are being advised by the Japanese. All that interests them are our assets."[47] One week into its existence, the SGC had not yet demonstrated much capacity to meet the challenge of housing 62,500 people (the average camp population in January[48]) and providing food aid to many more. But Rabe's real target in this struggle was the SSA, which he felt did not do anything for the people in the city. He phrases his expectations of the SSA as graciously as possible in a letter: "We hope also that the Japanese military authorities will cooperate, even more liberally than they are now doing, with the Self-Government Association [i.e., the SGC] in the provision of food and fuel for the refugees." The point for Rabe, who had no interest in securing for any of the players the political protection that so consumed Japanese attention, was not to fight over scarce goods, but to ensure that these did not go to waste, and to coordinate efforts to deliver them. "Even so the combined efforts of all agencies will scarcely overtake the need."

A recent mainland Chinese history of the occupation concludes from the evidence of tension between the two organizations that, in its particular jargon, "the bogus Self-Government Committee and the International Committee for the Nanking Safety Zone were in opposition from beginning to end."[49] That was certainly how things looked from a distance, especially during the first week of SGC operations. In fact, though, all sorts of factors encouraged quiet complicity: crossover appointments, friendships, common concerns, and a recognition that resources were limited. There was little that the SGC would or could "take over" without first having worked out the terms for doing so with the IC, though the SGC made some effort to please the Japanese by making that relationship appear conflictual. A smooth behind-the-scenes relationship was further guaranteed, since some members of the two committees knew each other prior to the Japanese arrival; some, such as Hsü Ch'uan-yin and Jimmy Wang, were active in both organizations. Two days after Rabe's objection to the SSA's plans for takeover, Jimmy makes his first appearance in Rabe's diary, and as well in the IC's published correspondence, where he is referred to as "the new Food Commissioner." He dropped by that morning to inform Rabe that the Japanese had decided not to close down the IC by force, as they had threatened. The new Japanese condition, more modest, was that the SGC take over the sale of rice to refugees. The IC agreed and suspended rice sales the following morning, though doing so before the SGC had organized its own distribution system. By that afternoon, however, Jimmy had opened an outlet inside the NSZ. The Japanese sought to make this arrangement final by cutting off the IC's supply of rice and coal as of noon the following day and by forbidding it from hauling these goods. Inasmuch as the IC had agreed to truck rice on behalf of the SGC, which lacked its own transport, one purpose thus defeated another. And given that that rice was coming to the SGC from the Japanese, the irony of the blockade was all the greater.[50] It was in this context of transporting grain for the SGC that Charlie Riggs and Jimmy Wang found themselves working side by side.

SGC Operations

From its office behind the Drum Tower, the SGC began to proliferate organizationally. On 10 January, a police bureau and the first of five ward offices were established. By 21 January SGC employees, including police, numbered 130, plus thirty firefighters. Ward-level police stations were also set up during January in a bid to reestablish neighborhood security and to convince people that they could leave the NSZ and return to their homes. One of the regime's first projects was to carry out a census and to impose neighborhood watch *(pao-chia)* registration, grouping every five families into a mutual surety unit *(wu-chia-lien)*. This task was given to Wang Ch'un-sheng's police force. According to the SSA's February report on the SGC, Chinese police operated under supervision by security personnel from the SSA and Japanese military police. The report specifies that its purpose was to expand the work of the military police's Amaya Squad in tracking down former soldiers and anti-Japanese activists.[51] The installation of SGC police under military police management was regarded as the third and final stage in the process of establishing security in occupied territory. The Japanese army carried out the first stage when it defeated the enemy; military police took over the second stage, which was to root out armed or organized opposition; and the SGC was given the final stage, which was the maintenance of Japanese-imposed order.

The Japanese army eyed the captive Nanking population as a deep pool of free or cheap labor. The SSA began dragooning people for coolie labor, though by its own records it had levied or hired only about 10,000 people between early-January and the end of February. To improve access to this pool, the SGC began cooperating in the provision of coolie labor to the Japanese army by setting up Coolie Reception centers in each of the five wards in early-February. The numbers of laborers engaged were not impressive: the reception centers furnished only about 500 men in February. The levies continued in March with greater efficiency, it seems, for the SSA and the reception centers together arranged for another 20,000 conscripts to work on a daily basis. This program kept the lumpen elements of Nanking under supervision, and took advantage of the unemployed by paying them, when paid at all, only in Japanese military scrip, which the army hoped would drive out KMT currency.[52]

The greater, and more immediate, operational task for the SGC was to provide relief. Distributing relief would prove to the refugees that the SGC had the right to claim authority over them; it would also displace the foreigners from the moral high ground they occupied by virtue of having done so much to keep the residents of Nanking alive during the first month of Japanese occupation. The SGC did not face an uncooperative IC when the issue of food distribution was involved, as already noted. Its bigger problem was finding the food to distribute. The SGC started out with no stocks of grain in its possession. Jimmy Wang in its first week of operation asked the Japanese army for 200,000 *tan,* suggesting half for free and half by sale (one *tan* of lower-middle grade rice weighed 62 kilograms). This extravagant proposal the army turned down flat, but it came back a few days later with a delivery of 1,250 sacks for free distribution, plus the promise of another 10,000 sacks to sell (one sack weighed 77.5 kilograms). The one condition was that the SGC distribute this rice outside the NSZ as an inducement for refugees to leave. As of the end of the month, 4,200 sacks of rice had been delivered—less than half of what had been promised, and barely three percent of Wang's original request. The army also promised 1,000 sacks of flour (one sack weighed 22.8 kilograms), again for distribution outside the NSZ, though no flour was delivered until February. Using the IC calculation that one sack of rice could feed 125 adults for a day, and then reducing that level to subsistence rations, the Japanese army had given the SGC in January enough grain to feed the city for barely three days.[53] Fortunately, many still had private stocks of rice to see them through the month.

After being frozen out of food distribution, the IC petitioned the Japanese embassy several times that it arrange with the army for permission to recover 10,933 sacks of rice and 10,000 sacks of flour that sat embargoed in a former government warehouse in Hsiakwan. On 28 January the IC also filed a letter with the SGC proposing that "if this rice is secured, we shall be glad to cooperate with you in making it available for free distribution to civilians both outside and inside the boundaries of the Safety Zone." When the Japanese embassy finally responded in the first week of February, it did so informally through John M. Allison, the ranking official at the American consulate, who spoke Japanese. Counselor Hidaka Shinrokurô asked Allison whether the IC was willing to cooperate with the SGC to distribute this food—even though this assurance had already been made and put into practice several times.[54] The Japanese, especially the SSA, were still anxious lest food confer political legitimacy on the Westerners. Hidaka wanted to make sure that if there was any symbolic capital accruing to the release of the precious grain stores, it would go to the SGC.

Starting in mid-January, the SGC began setting up rice shops around the city. Poor security meant that this process was not smooth, however. On the twenty-first, its newly opened rice shop on Shen-chou Road was held up by Japanese soldiers no fewer than three times in one day. These incidents induced the SGC to set up a somewhat complicated arrangement involving the issuing of rice tickets at one office, the payment of money at another, and the delivery of rice at a third. On the following day the SGC tried to open another rice shop on Pao-t'ai Street close by its headquarters, though it had difficulty maintaining security and organizing transport. The ability of SGC operations to evade Japanese predation remained precarious until at least the end of January. A week after the first rice shop opened, for example, soldiers showed up at the T'ien-min bathhouse on East Chung-shan Road, which had been reopened at the Japanese army's request. They robbed all the employees of their money and shot three, killing one.[55]

With the improvement in public order in February, the SGC was able to distribute food with less interference. T'ao Hsi-san moved to get rice shops in the abandoned residential areas reopened by bringing grain across the Yangtze into Nanking and making it available to them at below the market price. This strategy would have had the double effect of providing people with food and encouraging refugees to return home. His vice-chair, Sun Shu-jung, spoke out against what he regarded as T'ao's wasteful liberality. Sun felt that all grain should be distributed from the shops that the SGC had set up, both to protect SGC revenue and to demonstrate its importance to the Japanese. Sun even turned to the Japanese army to support his attempt to overturn T'ao's initiative, but the army was not interested in interfering.[56] It did interfere, however, with the IC's plan to bring beans into Nanking. This was formed when signs of nutritional diseases, including beriberi, appeared early in February. The IC arranged for 100 tons of beans to be shipped from Shanghai to the University Hospital, where it would be made into tofu and sold. It was able to negotiate shipment with the Japanese navy at both ends, but the army at the Nanking end refused—and had its radio station announce that the shipment had been blocked because the IC was showing a "lack of cooperation" with the SGC. Indeed, the IC did not want to lose control of the beans for fear that these would never reach the hospital, but the SSA did not wish to set a precedent that would permit a private institution to circumvent its supervision and control foodstuffs. The face-saving solution was for the SGC to provide a cover for the IC by receiving the beans, storing these, and then releasing these only on the IC's order, which the SGC was content to do.[57]

The SGC's best hope for taking control of supplying food was to monopolize distribution, and for that it had to rely on the Japanese army. Monopoly was made possible in the first instance by the CCAA's blockade of foodstuffs in the occupied areas, and in the second instance by links the SSA provided with Japanese trading companies in Shanghai. The SGC was able to lay the groundwork for its foodstuff operations in the latter part of January when it sent out representatives to neighboring commercial centers of Chenkiang, Wuhu, and Yangchow to survey commodity markets and to learn what goods were available at what prices. This information was preparatory to setting up the Central Wholesale Market on 15 February, through which the committee aimed to achieve a monopoly over commodity circulation in the city.[58] The SSA realized that the revival of the Nanking economy depended on more than hogging wholesale markets in foodstuffs and simple processed goods, however. Other initiatives, especially in production, were encouraged. To this end, on 7 February the SSA recruited five people to sit on yet another preparatory committee, this one to reestablish the Chamber of Commerce, whose formal inauguration did not take place for a full month, though the SSA in its report for March gives no reason for this delay. We might guess that chamber members were not yet content to be seen cooperating with the Japanese. As of early 1940, the chamber still had not been formally reconstituted.[59]

Part of the challenge of distributing food in the capital was finding the means to move it. This is where the association between Charlie Riggs and Jimmy Wang comes into the picture. Vehicles of every sort were in high demand, as most had been either commandeered or destroyed in the first weeks of the invasion. The cost of a car in good working order was running in late January as high as $1,900—the price for which someone tried to sell the Panchen Lama's car to the SGC. (The Panchen Lama maintained a residence in Nanking under the KMT regime.) The SGC knew that the man selling the car had given the Panchen Lama's servant only $200 for it, and was unwilling to pay him any more than $600.[60] We do not know if the sale went through, but we do know that the SGC was competing in the same profiteers' market with everyone else. Without fixers such as Jimmy Wang, the SGC would have been in an even worse situation, with recourse to their Japanese backers an ever dwindling option. (The Japanese army did come through on 8 February with a gift of 2,000 gallons of gas for the SGC's trucks to haul grain and coal.[61])

In the absence of fuller documentation, it is difficult to gauge the extent to which the SGC found its financial feet, if ever. The fact that it received a petition from the RSS on 4 April for 500 sacks of rice and a cash grant of 500 yuan to buy fuel for morgue trucks may indicate that the SGC's financial affairs were in better order.[62] On the other hand, these resources may simply have been reallocations from the Japanese army. The SGC's own revenue mechanisms involved little more than the imposition of exorbitant commercial taxes on farmers and peddlers whose Loyal Subject Certificates permitted them to bring foodstuffs into the city, and on the confiscation of KMT currency they found on anyone trying to leave.[63]

Return to Residences

The final proof that life in Nanking had returned to normal, and that the SGC was fulfilling its mandate to operate a normal urban administration, was the relocation of the huge masses of refugees back to their homes within and outside the city. The SSA was particularly eager to get them out from under the protection and influence of Westerners in the NSZ, which continued to gall the army. As Maj. Gen. Amaya Naojirô chose to interpret the situation to the assembled foreign diplomatic corps on 5 February, "Without foreign interference, the Sino-Japanese relationship in Nanking would have developed harmoniously!"[64] Closing the NSZ would end that embarrassing irritant. The SGC was supposed to be the agency through which the city would return to normal functioning, but it was the SSA and the CCAA that were issuing Loyal

Subject certificates that enabled people to pass through the city gates. More particularly, the SSA pressed the SGC to revive the ward-level administration necessary for allowing refugees to return to their homes, getting the SGC to designate ward boundaries on 10 January, and giving it until the end of the month to have every ward office up and running. Then, on 28 January, came orders that the refugee camps were to close within a week and that all refugees were to return to their homes. The SSA confidentially admitted that over half of the housing in the city had been destroyed in December and January.[65] But it made no provision to address the problem.

Eager for IC leaders to go along with this plan, the SSA called them to a meeting at SGC headquarters on the afternoon of 28 January. SSA leader Matsuoka Isao gave no indication of how the lack of housing would be resolved, other than to explain that the Japanese army would help to empty the camps by sending in soldiers to drive out refugees. The popular reaction was hysteria. The IC responded the following day by petitioning the SSA to extend the deadline and suggesting that the SGC make a first step toward gaining control of the camps by taking over refugee operations in government buildings. The SSA's response the day after was to repeat what Matsuoka had announced on 28 January: the refugee camps were to close, and that was final.[66] The SSA's leadership indicates that returning to residences was in effect not a transfer of authority from foreigners to Chinese, with which the IC would have been happy to oblige, but from foreigners to Japanese. The SGC dutifully put the SSA plan into operation by posting notices informing people of the 4 February deadline, and warning them that after that date the temporary structures in which they had been living would be torn down. Many were eager to return home and began to do so. What no one anticipated was the reaction of Japanese soldiers to this order, which was to prey on the returnees in a renewed surge of rape, abduction, theft, and murder. This mayhem peaked during the first three days after the notices went up, but continued for a week.[67] The soldiers' expectations were so aroused with the thought of easy pickings, in fact, that a truckload of armed soldiers pulled up to the SGC headquarters on the morning of 2 February "and demanded at least thirteen girls or as many more as they could find," reports John Magee in a letter written that day. "The Chinese tried to stall them off but they surrounded the place and were still there this afternoon. The Committee did succeed in finding two prostitutes but these were not enough."[68] Not even the SGC was safe from those it was supposed to serve. Only after a week of this riot was it feasible for refugees to live outside the camps without harassment. The procedure became more orderly toward the end of the second week of February. By the end of the month, by SSA count, 172,502 people had returned to their homes or to other makeshift dwellings outside the NSZ. The exception was the devastated Hsiakwan area, home to Nanking's poorest. Of all the refugees who returned home, only four percent went back to Hsiakwan.[69] When the American biologist Albert Steward passed through Hsiakwan the following December, most of it remained a flattened waste.[70]

Aftermaths

By the end of March, several indicators pointed to a modest restabilization of life in Nanking. One was that the number of refugees who had been resettled was up to 235,056. A second was the renewed flow of commercial rice into the city from the regional wholesale market upriver in Wuhu, which was easing supply difficulties and giving the SGC something to tax (it had to get SSA approval to levy sixty cents on each *tan*).[71] A third indicator, not as trivial as it may sound, was that the number of fire alarms fell to twenty-two from forty-eight the previous month.[72] Despite these modest steps forward, much of the city remained a shambles. On Sunday 24 April, Cabot Coville went with several others into the business section of the city, where he was struck by the extent of the damage but puzzled by its pattern: "There are few signs of bombardment; but individual shops and other buildings are gutted by pillage, looting, and fire. It is not that the entire area has been swept over by a conflagration. Places left here and there show such was not the case. One shop will be utterly barren of any contents; the next will be a charred wreck, set afire after the removal of most of its goods and equipment. Photographs taken now would be completely damning."[73] Coville was an American consular official based in Japan whose sympathies tended in that direction. His comment was meant to imply that the evidence of looting would be damning to the Chinese, and indeed many had resorted to looting. The burning, though, was largely the work of Japanese soldiers. People at the time wondered why the Japanese army would choose to engage in what Lewis Smythe in his report identified as "the deliberate burning of extensive commercial and industrial sections" of the city. Some speculated that it was to hide the extent of their looting; others, to punish the Chinese. It certainly did not make the task of restoring the capital to proper functioning any easier.

Coville's party then drove outside the city walls. There they were confronted with more shocking evidence of what Nanking had been through: "Leaving by one of the city gates we stop and walk into the official residence of the chairman of the executive yuan. It is a wreck. Huge shell holes pierce the brick walls, glass and brick is all over the place, one can walk in and out anywhere. In the center of the reception room is the carcass of a horse. There are trenches in the garden with exposed Chinese bodies. The Sun Yat Sen memorial seems unharmed. It is covered by bamboo scaffolding and straw mats. In the park below trenches run about without much plan. The Chinese bodies in them have not been covered."[74] The trenches had been part of Chinese preparations for withstanding the Japanese attack. The Japanese army had found these useful as mass graves.

The destruction Coville saw in April still marred the cityscape when American biologist Albert Steward visited in December 1938. In the southern part of the city, he found that "the destruction which has been wrought is beyond calculation. The people are still few, and in most places houses of business are still scattered." Referring to Lewis Smythe's survey of war damage, Steward proposed: "If both sides had cooperated in giving such protection to civilian life and property as would not have interfered with military operations, not over one or two percent of the actual loses need to have occurred."[75] This is precisely the sort of rationality that did not enter Japanese calculations a year earlier, when the logic at work was not profit and loss, but victory and humiliation. If Steward's hypothetical is a reasonable supposition as to what cooperation might have achieved, it is also retrospective testimony that the Nanking SGC and the SSA failed to achieve what they were put in place to produce. The people of the city paid the price for this failure well beyond the initial occupation. As of 1939, unemployment was seventy-three percent and average earnings were sixty percent below what they had been before the occupation. Minor S. Bates summarizes the situation in the final report on the work of the International Relief Committee, as the IC was retitled in February:

> The living standard of the whole Chinese population of Nanking is very close to that of the poorer groups selected in various Chinese cities for surveys by social workers before the war. The events of the last two years have reduced the native population to that level, which means of course that many are on the margin of survival.... The Committee's own experience and studies, as presented in this report, are crowded by a desperate poverty grossly abnormal for this region. No general economic improvement is in sight, while factors of a military and governmental nature continue to worsen the currency situation and potentially to endanger much else. It is not for us to assess the program of the Japanese authorities or the attentions of the Chinese; we are here merely observing the actual influences at work upon the people's livelihood.

For ordinary people living under the occupation state, the collaboration experiment was a failure. "Prosperity and security seem pitifully remote from the local people" was Bates' despondent conclusion.[76]

Sunday, 24 April 1938, the day that Cabot Coville was touring the ruined city, was by coincidence the date on which the SGC in Nanking disbanded. Its fate was tied to politics at a higher level, for a new "national" regime, the Reformed Government *(Wei-hsin cheng-fu)* of the Republic of China was to be installed in Nanking six days later. For its inauguration, the SSA mobilized the SGC and its police force to get out 30,000 spectators waving little flags of the new republic.[77] With a new regime in place, a reorganization of the capital administration followed. That Sunday, the twenty-fourth, the SGC was replaced by a new entity, the Nanking Municipal Commission, which went by the unwieldy Chinese title *Tu-pan Nan-ching shih-cheng kung-shu* (*Tu-pan* being the old designation of the provincial military governorship prior to 1927). This change took municipal leadership out of the local hands in which it had briefly rested for four months and brought Nanking back under the control of the center. The new city head, Jen Yuan-tao, was a powerful member of the new Reformed Government and its concurrent minister of pacification (the organ that handled military affairs, and to which the Nanking police reported). Nanking was once again subordinated to its national master, just as it had been under the KMT. Jen would give up the post in a further reorganization of the municipal government five months later and hand the mayoralty off to his vice-minister, Kao Kuan-wu.[78] Control of the city would be separated from the military ministry only when the Reformed Government dissolved in March 1940 to make way for Wang Ching-wei's regime. Gao at that time relinquished his ministry post and was appointed full-time head of the once-again renamed Nanking Special Municipality.

During his tenure with the Nanking SGC, T'ao Hsi-san achieved little. According to a Chinese account of the early occupation of Nanking, T'ao's first undertaking as chair was to issue the notice to Chinese soldiers who had been left behind in the city that they should surrender, and they would be taken care of, even given money to pay their expenses if they chose to return home. When over 300 came forward, the Japanese summarily executed all of them and gave T'ao's RSS the task of burying the bodies.[79] A Japanese diarist confirms that the SGC was actively involved in separating soldiers from civilians.[80] Some held at the time that T'ao was horrified but felt he was already in too deep with the Japanese to be able to pull out. Others condemned him as an out-and-out traitor. T'ao also faced—and was unable to control—debilitating factional conflicts within the SGC, notably with his vice-chair Sun Shu-jung, who soon overshadowed him. When the SGC was obliged to meet formally with Gen. Matsui Iwane at the Japanese embassy on 23 January, it presented a united and respectful front, but the next day T'ao submitted his resignation, citing advanced age and ill health. The Japanese refused to accept it. To T'ao's further dismay, five days later his new residence was cleaned out.[81] A postcard belonging to a Japanese soldier was found on the scene of the robbery and T'ao demanded that the SSA investigate, but it replied that it had no evidence on which to proceed. Nothing was ever done. T'ao never learned whether the robbery was a chance event—this was hardly the first break-in that occurred in occupied Nanking—or a threat directed at him personally. He complained at the time that he was now SGC chair in name only.

T'ao Hsi-san might have turned back but did not, neither then nor later when the SGC was dissolved. He was promoted to sinecures in the Reformed Government, first as vice-chair of its mass organization, the Great People's

Society *(Ta-min-hui)*, and then as a member of the Legislative Yuan, the latter on the recommendation of its president, Wen Tsung-yao. T'ao thus left the administration of Nanking behind, although in 1940 his kinsman T'ao Chueh-san was appointed as a councillor to the new Special Municipality. With the dissolution of the Reformed Government in March 1940, T'ao Hsi-san was given "advisory" positions under the collaborationist Wang Ching-wei regime. That December, he fell under investigation for corruption and his political career came to an end. A postwar tribunal under the KMT sentenced him to two years' imprisonment for collaboration. It was a modest punishment, suggesting that his case must have struck the tribunal judges, so many years after the SGC had briefly come and gone, as a minor bit of collaboration. T'ao died in Nanking in June 1948, two months after his release.

A few of the other original SGC members made the transition to the new regimes. One was Chao Kung-chin, who was promoted from head of the Transportation Department to director of the Industrial Bureau under both the Municipal Commission and the Special Municipality, surviving politically until at least 1941.[82] If many of the original SGC personnel did not appear in later municipal lineups it was because new political elites moved in to overtake them. But post-1938 documents show that their disappearance did not signal their having fallen out of the city's elite. They may have been pushed out of municipal posts, but they continued to have a public presence. This at least is the impression one gets from a list of the heads of public organizations in Nanking published in 1940. Several SGC activists appear there: former vice-chair Sun Shu-jung as the manager of the Nanking mosque, the hated Chan Jung-kuang as head of the Kiangsi Provincial Guild, Huang Yueh-hsuan running the Buddhist Charitable Orphanage and the Lodge for Sharing Goodness *(T'ung-shan t'ang)*, and policeman Wang Ch'un-sheng heading a charitable organization registered in August 1939 called the Lodge for Stimulating Goodness *(Hsing-shan t'ang)*. The list also names Mayor Kao Kuan-wu at the head of the Japan-China Buddhist League, and none other than T'ao Hsi-san running Kuang-feng Granary, a new institution registered in August 1939 (managing the granary may be where the corruption charge against him originated). These posts are just the positions where one would expect to find "local capable men," as the Japanese called them. The SGC elite was still socially in place. Yet it had lost its political traction. A small indicator of this loss is the decline of the RSS's political clout. It turns out that the leadership of the Nanking branch of the RSS was the only public position T'ao Hsi-san managed to hold on to past his corruption disgrace. This suggests that its leadership no longer translated into leadership elsewhere. Furthermore, as of September 1942, the other four members of the executive were political unknowns.[83] The RSS was no longer the temporary bridge of convenience by which the Japanese could make contact with local elites, discarded now that better contacts had been made.

Like the would-be politician T'ao, the would-be regime of Nanking, the SGC, was trapped in a narrow defile by conflicting pressures. Its goals were both modest and grand: modest in trying to get a ruined city back to some semblance of order, grand in hoping to build from that rubble the foundation of a healthy civic regime, albeit one they hoped to control. Its sources of assets were also internally contradictory: on the one hand, it had a foreign army of occupation to turn to for financial and political support in the short term; on the other, it had a well-organized body of Westerners both to compete and cooperate with, within certain limits. The Western presence, rather than disrupt the process of collaboration, complicated it by doubling layers of complicity. The SGC had to be complicitous with the Japanese who brought it into being; it had to be complicitous with the Westerners who were providing essential support for the residents of the city; and it was indebted to the willingness of the persons and organizations, such as the RSS, that furnished the original collaborators but later could be pushed aside. Finally, the SGC had to accede to its own dissolution in favor of a higher and more powerful collaborationist project. Given the continuing disruptive presence of the Japanese army in Nanking, it is difficult to determine how much the SGC actually achieved during its four months as the municipal administration. If Nanking did creep back to normalcy, it was in part because, as Mark Eykholt has pointed out, individuals emerged to scavenge, barter, and rebuild wherever they could without the interference or support of either Japanese or puppet authorities. The "popular order" that the SGC generated lasted only four months, but it helped provide a foundation for the return of a more responsible administration.[84] And yet there is ambiguity even in this autonomy, for this "popular order" depended on Japan's presence. One way to earn half a yen was to scavenge the ruined city for a hundred catties of scrap metal and sell it to the Japanese. The offer was attractive enough that Japanese buyers were able to acquire 700 tons of metal by the end of March.[85]

The Collaborator?

Most ambiguous of all is the slippery figure of Jimmy Wang. On the one hand, he was an activist for the collaborationist cause. One final glimpse of him in this context: An elderly Christian interviewed in the 1980s recalled a conversation he had with Jimmy when the two of them happened to have bedded down beside each other in an NSZ refugee camp. Jimmy tempted the man with a post as the head of an SGC ward office. When he declined, Jimmy responded, "Why should you miss such a good opportunity to make a fortune?" Jimmy then went on to talk about the advantages and drawbacks of the various wards he might want to run. He might not want Ward #1, which included the old pleasure quarter by the Confucian Temple, since that was "where the

Japanese will go for girls" and would be troublesome to control. But the man held firm. "You don't know how to appreciate favors," Jimmy grumbled as he rolled over to go to sleep.[86]

On the other hand, Jimmy Wang was also an activist for the IC: "a (secret) member of our organization" is how John Rabe refers to him in his diary.[87] One last glimpse of him in this other context: On 8 February, he accompanied Rabe and three other IC members to Lotus Lake to inspect the site of a group murder. Hsü Ch'uan-yin had gone to Rabe the previous afternoon to tell him that Japanese soldiers had shot an old man and three of his relatives the night before. The story Hsü got was that the man had been trying to retrieve a rickshaw that he had hidden near his house. Rabe and the American missionary Plumer Mills had gone out to the site that evening and decided to report the incident (case 425 in the IC's documentation of Japanese misconduct) the following morning to the SGC. The SGC in turn informed the SSA. Jimmy Wang chose to join Rabe and four other foreigners on a second inspection tour. Rabe describes their visit briefly in his diary:

> The four bodies had been wrapped in mats and lay ready to be buried on a little nearby hill. Jimmy hunted up a Chinese man from the neighborhood, who gave us the following account of the incident: "The old Chinese man, allegedly trying to rescue his ricksha, had in fact been trying to bring two chairs from a thatch hut to his house. It was on account of these two chairs, looted or bought cheaply somewhere, that the Japanese soldiers shot him. He lay gravely wounded in the field. When his wife (or sister?) came to his aid with two male relatives, hoping to take him away, they were all shot."[88]

Jimmy Wang's name does not appear in the official IC report on the Lotus Lake murders. The report names George Rosen, John Rabe, Eduard Sperling, and Lewis Smythe, and says that they talked to "the one man left in the area," but it does not say who found the man or translated what he said, but it carefully avoids naming any Chinese.[89] Jimmy Wang's work with the IC had to be kept quiet, lest any one of several interests cut him out of their confidence, even though his presence that day was essential for finding that "one man" who could testify to the shootings. IC members have been lauded for their work on behalf of the people of Nanking. What about their Chinese associates?

Then again, their Chinese associates were involved in matters that some at the time found distasteful. It turns out that Jimmy Wang was the key figure in getting Chinese brothels back in operation, as we learn from a confidential report to the German foreign ministry from legation secretary Georg Rosen:

> Among Jimmy's first official acts was the establishment of bordellos, for which he was able to recruit the necessary workers among those females still residing in the old amusement district around the Confucius Temple. It is said that he provided the requisite furniture free of charge from his own inventories, but is demanding payment for

furnishing similar institutions that are to be outfitted with Japanese ladies who have been brought in. At any rate Jimmy has done a great service to his fellow Chinese in providing a less perilous means by which to satisfy the amorous needs of the Japanese soldiery, which up until now has employed the Erl-King's method of abducting the honest women of Nanking.[90]

It was Jimmy Wang who winkled the girls at Ginling College out from under Minnie Vautrin's nose in order to make prostitutes available to Japanese soldiers. He had an eye for the fortune to be made in providing services to the Japanese, but he also thought that legal prostitution would reduce the incidence of rape. Collaboration brings gains and losses, and Jimmy was prepared to deal in both.

Jimmy Wang was everything but naive. As Lewis Smythe writes in a letter, "He told us about 'self-government': 'When the Japanese say "Yes," we do it'!"[91] If we choose to condemn him for his role as a fixer who served the Japanese, we neglect his role as a fixer who served the Chinese. We should be careful about exactly what it is that offends us about Jimmy Wang's tour of duty along the border between good and evil. Jimmy was simply one of the best—and perhaps also one of the worst—of those who came forward under the extraordinary conditions that gripped Nanking in December 1937 to play the role of collaborator. He fits no moral models, and offends many; he saw opportunities where others saw only horror and defeat, and made the most of these; he saved others, and in the process gained something for himself. To condemn him or the SGC for having facilitated the Japanese occupation of Nanking may depend too much on the comfort of hindsight, and not enough on a recognition of the moral and physical emergency in which the Nanking Atrocity placed ordinary people. This was the burden of collaboration, part of a wartime history that we can only now begin to imagine how to write.

Notes

1. Smythe, "Memorandum on Relief Situation," in Hsü, ed., *Documents of the Nanking Safety Zone*, p. 99. The Hsü volume has been included in its entirety in Brook, ed., *Documents on the Rape of Nanking*.
2. Hsü, *Documents of the Nanking Safety Zone*, p. 24 and p. 43; Rabe, *Good Man of Nanking*, pp. 93–94. Ginling University was the site of one of two soup kitchens operated by the Red Swastika, the other being Yung-ch'ing Monastery on Wu-t'ai Hill; China Number Two Historical Archives, Nanking (CNT), Record Group 257, File 224: printed account of branch activities 1937–42, item 4. Yongqing Monastery hosted one of the five winter soup kitchens in Nanking before the war, and was therefore a location to which refugees would have gone.
3. Smythe diary, entry for 24 December 1937, reprinted in Zhang [Chang], ed., *Eyewitnesses to Massacre*, p. 274; see also p. 275.
4. Rosen, "Report from the Nanking Office of the German Embassy to the Foreign Ministry" (20 January 1938), quoted in Rabe, *Good Man of Nanking*, p. 146.

5. Wang Ch'eng-tien's name appears without comment in a list of regime personnel in Wang Hsi-kuang, "Jih-wei han-chien cheng-fu" p. 5; he gets no mention in Hsia Ch'iang, "Wei-hu tso-chang ti tzu-chih wei-yuan-hui." Nor does he appear in Chang, *Rape of Nanking*, which focuses on the initial takeover, or in Eykholt, "Living the Limits of Occupation in Nanjing," chapter 2, which examines the emergence of collaboration in 1938.

6. Fitch, diary entry for 30 December 1937, reprinted anonymously in Timperley, ed., *What War Means,* p. 43; also reprinted in Zhang, ed., *Eyewitnesses to Massacre,* p. 98.

7. Wilson, letter of 1 January 1938, in Brook, *Documents on the Rape of Nanking,* p. 233.

8. Lewis Smythe, letter of 1 January 1938, in Zhang, ed., *Eyewitnesses to Massacre,* p. 284.

9. Rabe, *Good Man of Nanking,* p. 109. *Asahi shinbun* reported on the inauguration 2 days later, proclaiming that the SGC was able to "unite with all pro-Japanese organizations" in the city, without specifying what organizations those might be.

10. Fitch, diary entry for 30 December 1937, reprinted anonymously in Timperley, ed., *What War Means,* p. 43; also reprinted in Zhang, ed., *Eyewitnesses to Massacre,* p. 98.

11. Iguchi et al., eds., *Nankin jihen: Kyoto shidan kankei shiryô shū,* pp. 32, 75, and 310–11.

12. Hsü, *Documents of the Nanking Safety Zone,* pp. 62–63, and p. 66.

13. Mantetsu Shanhai jimusho, "Naka Shina senryô ni okeru senbu kôsaku gaiyô," in Inoue, ed., *Kachû senbu kôsaku shiryô,* p. 51. The stages of pacification are described in Brook, "Pacification of Jiading."

14. On Matsui's order that his troops avoid interfering with foreigners, see his testimony at the Tokyo War Crimes Trial as cited by Pal in Brook, *Documents on the Rape of Nanking,* p. 291–92. On the use of the International Committee's record of the Rape to condemn Matsui, see Brook, *Documents on the Rape of Nanking,* p. 16.

15. Mantetsu Shanhai jimusho, "Naka Shina senryō chiku ni okeru senbu kōsaku gaiyō," in Inoue, ed., *Kachū senbu kōsaku shiryō,* p. 50.

16. The personnel changes of the SSA have been reconstructed principally on the basis of Maruyama Susumu's memoir, "Watakushi no Shôwa shi—Nankin jiken no jissô," particularly the fifth instalment in *Mantetsu wakabakai kaihô,* no. 137 (8 September 2000), pp. 38–44. I am grateful to David Askew for giving me a copy. Occasional discrepancies with the SSA's own report raise doubts that Maruyama has accurately recollected everything.

17. "Memorandum of Interview with Chief of Special Service Corps" (15 December 1937), in Hsü, *Documents of the Nanking Safety Zone,* p. 6. At least Maruyama Susumu was a Mantetsu employee.

18. Coville diary: Hoover Institution Archives, Stanford University, (HIA): Stanley Hornbeck record group, Joseph C. Grew files, Box 185. Hong's name does not appear in internal Japanese pacification records that I have seen; he may simply have been a military officer seconded to the SSA because of his consular experience in an English-speaking country.

19. As reported on 22 December in the Kitayama diary, reprinted in Iguchi, *Nankin jihen: Kyoto shidan kankei shiryô shū,* p. 73.

20. At his postwar trial, Wen Tsung-yao stated that he was a member of an early collaborationist entity called the Nanking Peace Maintenance Committee; Nan-ching shih tang-an-kuan, ed., *Shen-hsun han-chien pi-lu,* p. 344. I have found no other reference to such a body. Wen may simply have been confused in his memory of the SGC's formal designation.

21. Duara provides a brief introduction to the Red Swastika Society (RSS) and Society of the Way in "Of Authencity and Woman."

22. SGC and RSS member Huang Yuexuan had served on the 1936 winter aid committee; personal communication from Zwia Lipkin.

23. A report of the activities of the Nanking branch of the RSS in this period is archived in CNT, Record Group 257, File 224: printed account of branch activities 1937–42, item 6.

24. Yin Chi-chün, *1937, Nan-ching ta-chiu-huan,* pp. 176–79. Yin provides no sources for his account of the Japanese attempts to recruit local leaders.

25. Cooperation between the RSS and the SGC is noted in an archived 1938 report of the Department of Public Health, reprinted in *Ch'in-hua jih-chün Nan-ching ta-t'u-sha tang-an,* ed. Chung-kuo ti-erh li-shih tang-an-kuan, p. 453. The report notes that the RSS did not clear all corpses, especially those in out-of-the-way areas. At least one prominent RSS member resisted involvement in the SGC; see Lin Na, "Hsüeh-lei hua chin-ling," p. 143.

26. Rabe, *Good Man of Nanking,* p. 99. Vautrin was in fact willing to provide limited cooperation in arranging for prostitutes' services, as noted in Hu, *American Goddess at the Rape of Nanking,* p. 101, though no reference is made in that biography to this incident.

27. Japanese figure: Nankin tokumu kikan report, p. 24, in Inoue, *Kachû senbu kôsaku shiryô,* p. 153. RSS figure: archived RSS document dated 4 April 1938, in Nan-ching t'u-shu-kuan, ed., *Ch'in-hua Jih-chün Nan-ching ta-t'u-sha tang-an,* p. 436. According to the RSS's running tally of burials, the total at the end of February was 28,589; ibid., p. 433. The internal RSS figure appears as item #6 in the printed account of branch activities for 1937–42 archived in CNT, Record Group 257, File 224.

28. IMTFE, "Proceedings," p. 2,574. Xu insisted that the figure of over 43,000 represented civilians only, and that "the number is really too small. The reason is [that] we [were] not allowed to give a true number of the people we buried." For the tribunal's invocation of the data in its judgment, see Brook, *Documents on the Rape of Nanking,* p. 261.

29. Nankin tokumu kikan January report, p. 6, in Inoue, *Kachû senbu kôsaku shiryô,* p. 149.

30. Hsing-cheng-yuan hsuan-ch'uan-chü, *Chûka minkoku ishin seifu gaishi,* p. 370. The names of less important Chinese are frequently misprinted in the book, errors that are consistent with how Japanese writers who knew the Chinese names by Japanese pronunciation might miswrite the characters (e.g., on p. 371, T'ao Hsi-san's given name is miswritten as Hsi-shan, and Hsü Ch'uan-yin's as Ch'uan-ying) and betray the book's Japanese authorship.

31. Fitch, diary entry for 24 December, in Zhang, ed., *Eyewitnesses to Massacre,* p. 95. Tanaka was in fact Vice-Consul.

32. Maruyama, "Watakushi no Shôwa shi," p. 39.

33. SGC personnel are surveyed in Wang, "Jih-wei han-chien cheng-fu," p. 5; Li, "Lun-ching wu-yueh chi," pp. 112–13; and Anon., "Shih-shou-hou ti Nan-ching," pp. 153–54.

34. I am grateful to Zwia Lipkin for bringing this fact to my attention.

35. T'ao may have had other connections to the Japanese. According to an anonymous source published in 1938, T'ao was a friend of Ch'i Hsieh-yuan during the years 1917–20, when Ch'i was the military commissioner of Chiang-ning, where T'ao practiced as a lawyer. Ch'i went on to be military governor of Kiangsu until 1924 with the support of Wu P'ei-fu. Fourteen years later, Ch'i was a prominent figure in the North China collaborationist regime; Anon., "Shih-shou-hou ti Nan-ching," p. 153.

36. Vautrin, diary entry of 1 January 1938, in Zhang, ed., *Eyewitnesses to Massacre,* p. 369.

37. Bates, "Memorandum on Aftermath of Registration of Refugees at Nanking University," in Hsü, *Documents of the Nanking Safety Zone,* p. 100.

38. Rabe, *Good Man of Nanking,* p. 183; "Memorandum of Chancellor Scharffenberg for the German Embassy in Hankow," in ibid., p. 204. American consular official: Cabot Coville, Diary, entry for 25 April 1938 (HIA, Stanley Hornbeck Record Group, Joseph C. Grew files, Box 185).

39. This perception of the 19 December meeting was shared by many, for example, Wilson, in Brook, *Documents on the Rape of Nanking,* p. 217; Fitch and Forster, in Zhang, *Eyewitnesses to Massacre,* p. 92 and p. 120.

40. Nankin tokumu kikan report, p. 17 and p. 58, in Inoue, *Kachû senbu kôsaku shiryô,* p. 152 and p. 162.

41. Mantetsu Shanhai jimusho, "Naka Shina senryô ni okeru senbu kôsaku gaiyô," p. 13, in Inoue, *Kachû senbu kôsaku shiryô,* p. 52.

42. Nankin tokumu kikan February report, p. 10 and p. 19, in Inoue, *Kachû senbu kôsaku shiryô,* p. 150 and p. 152.

43. Hsü, *Documents of the Nanking Safety Zone,* p. 74.

44. The SSA in one of its reports to Shanghai chose to represent the declaration as a fact, stating: "On New Year's Day, the Nanking Self-Government committee under the leadership of T'ao Hsi-san was founded, and at last on 5 January this committee took over the 200,000 refugees from the International Committee" (Nankin tokumu kikan January report, p. 4, in Inoue, *Kachû senbu ksaku shiryô,* p. 148). The report goes on to note that the following day the Japanese army began the process of weeding out soldiers and subversives from the refugees, and giving Loyal Subject Certificates to the rest, without saying how those selected out were subsequently treated. By the end of February, the SSA had distributed 100,000 certificates, and the Nakajima Corps of the CCAA had issued 150,000 (February report, p. 22, in ibid., p. 153).

45. Rabe, *Good Man of Nanking,* p. 105 and p. 109.

46. Hsü, *Documents of the Nanking Safety Zone,* pp. 66–67.

47. Rabe, *Good Man of Nanking,* p. 114.

48. The figure is that given by Bates in his "Report of the Nanking International Relief Committee," p. 422.

49. Sun, *Nan-ching ta-t'u-sha,* p. 476.

50. Ibid., pp.118–20 and p. 122; Hsü, *Documents of the Nanking Safety Zone,* p. 75.

51. Nankin tokumu kikan February report, pp. 15–16, in Inoue, *Kachû senbu kôsaku shiryô,* pp. 151.

52. Ibid., p. 27 and p. 70, in Inoue, *Kachû senbu kôsaku shiryô,* p. 154 and p. 165. After receiving their pay in military scrip, Chinese were sold food at a rate of 10 yen for 1 bag of rice and 2.5 yen for a sack of flour. These sales were made at Military Scrip Exchange Offices, which were operating in 4 of the 5 city wards (Hsiakwan being the exception) as of 15 January.

53. Information on food supply matters comes from Hsü, *Documents of the Nanking Safety Zone,* pp. 83, 91–93, 97, 110–11, 121, 137; Inoue #19, pp. 164; Timperley, *What War Means,* p. 205; and Smythe, diary entry for 9 January 1930, in Zhang, ed., *Eyewitnesses to Massacre,* p. 295. Equivalents for units of measure are taken from Bates' "Report of the Nanking International Relief Committee," in Zhang, ed., *Eyewitnesses to Massacre,* p. 422.

54. Letter to the SGC: Hsü, *Documents of the Nanking Safety Zone,* pp. 110–11; inquiry from Hidaka: Timperley, *What War Means,* p. 205.

55. Hsü, *Documents of the Nanking Safety Zone,* pp. 95, 120. T'ao was a bathhouse owner; it is unclear if he owned this enterprise.

56. Yin, *1937, Nan-ching ta-chiu-huan,* pp. 174–75 (Sun Shu-jung is misnamed as Sun Shu-yun).

57. Rabe, *Good Man of Nanking,* pp. 195–96; Bates, letter of 13 February 1938, in Zhang, ed., *Eyewitnesses to Massacre,* p. 29.

58. Nankin tokumu kikan February report, p. 17 pp. 29–30 and p. 58, in Inoue, *Kachû senbu kôsaku shiryô,* pp. 152, 155, 162.

59. *Nan-ching shih-cheng kai-k'uang 1939,* p. 86.

60. Rabe, *Good Man of Nanking,* p. 159.

61. Hsü, *Documents of the Nanking Safety Zone,* p. 163.

62. Archived RSS document dated 4 April 1938, in *Ch'in-hua Jih-chün Nan-ching ta-t'u-sha tangan,* p. 436.

63. Lin, "Hsüeh-lei hua Chin-ling," p. 145.

64. As reported in Rabe, *Good Man of Nanking,* p. 178.

65. Nankin tokumu kikan January report, p. 4, in Inoue, *Kachû senbu kôsaku shiryô,* p. 148.

66. Hsü, *Documents of the Nanking Safety Zone,* pp. 117–19.

67. On the surge of military misconduct at the end of January, see Brook, "Documenting the Rape of Nanking," pp. 8–9, also Hsü, *Documents of the Nanking Safety Zone,* pp. 122–33 and p. 141; the SGC notice is mentioned on p. 127.

68. Magee, letter of 2 February 1938, in Zhang, ed., *Eyewitnesses to Massacre,* p. 193.

69. Nankin tokumu kikan February report, pp. 20–21, in Inoue, *Kachû senbu kôsaku shiryô,* pp. 152–53.

70. Steward, diary entry of 10 December 1938, in Zhang, ed., *Eyewitnesses to Massacre*, p. 319.
71. On the reopening of the rice trade from Wuhu, see Smythe's notes of 21 March 1938, in Zhang, ed., *Eyewitnesses to Massacre*, p. 314.
72. Nankin tokumu kikan March report, pp. 62, 65, in Inoue, *Kachû senbu kôsaku shiryô*, pp. 163–64.
73. Coville diary, entry for 23 April 1938.
74. Ibid.
75. Steward, diary entry of 10 December 1938, in Zhang, ed., *Eyewitnesses to Massacre*, p. 333.
76. Bates, "Report of the Nanking International Relief Committee," p. 435 and p. 444.
77. This inauguration is reconstructed in Brook, "Creation of the Reformed Government in Central China, 1938." For the SSA's role, see the Nankin tokumu kikan March report, p. 71, in Inoue, *Kachû senbu kôsaku shiryô*, p. 165.
78. Hsing-cheng-yuan hsüan-ch'uan-chü, *Chûka minkoku ishin seifu gaishi*, pp. 370–72. Kao became mayor on 14 September. As part of this reorganization, the municipal office was moved to 216 Sun Yat-sen Road on 1 October 1938.
79. Li, "Lun-ching wu-yüeh chi," p. 112. These burials have not been included in the RSS records reprinted in *Ch'in-hua Jih-chün Nan-ching ta-t'u-sha tang-an*, pp. 431–35.
80. Uchida Yoshinao diary, in Nankin senshi henshū iinkai, ed., *Nankin senshi* p. 387; I am grateful to David Askew for this reference.
81. Eykholt's suggestion that T'ao was shot at appears to be based on a misreading of the account given by Wang Hsi-kuang. See Eykholt, "Living the Limits of Occupation in Nanking," pp. 68–69.
82. Hsing-cheng-yuan hsüan-ch'uan-chü, *Chûka minkoku ishin seifu gaishi*, p. 371 and p. 373; and Ts'ai and Sun, "Min-kuo ch'i-chien Nan-ching shih chih-kuan nien-piao," p. 48.
83. Wang, "Jih-wei han-chien cheng-fu," p. 5. On the 1942 executive of the RSS, see the Nanking branch report of 6 September 1942: CNT, Record Group 257, File 224. On Chao, see Hsing-cheng-yuan hsüan-ch'uan-chü, *Chûka minkoku ishin seifu gaishi*, p. 371 and p. 373; Ts'ai Hung-yuan and Sun Pi-yu, "Min-kuo ch'i-chien Nan-ching shih chih-kuan nien-piao," p. 48.
84. Eykholt, "Living the Limits of Occupation in Nanjing," p. 115.
85. Nankin tokumu kikan March report, p. 66, in Inoue, *Kachû senbu kôsaku shiryô*, p. 164.
86. Xu, *Lest We Forget*, pp. 117–18.
87. Ibid., p. 198.
88. Rabe, *Good Man of Nanking*, p. 184.
89. Hsü, *Documents of the Nanking Safety Zone*, pp. 161–62. On the Committee's reluctance to name Chinese assisting in its work to protect them from reprisals, see p. 134.
90. "Report from the Nanking Office of the German Embassy to the Foreign Ministry" (20 January 1938), in Rabe, *Good Man of Nanking*, p. 146.
91. Smythe, letter of 8 March 1938, in Zhang, ed., *Eyewitnesses to Massacre*, p. 307.

10

WESTERNERS IN OCCUPIED NANKING: DECEMBER 1937 TO FEBRUARY 1938

David Askew

Introduction

The International Committee (IC) for the Nanking Safety Zone (NSZ) comprised a curious mix of people: American missionaries and academics, Chinese Christian and Red Cross workers, a German Nazi businessman, members of the Red Swastika Society (RSS, a charitable body), and figures from the Nanking underworld. The IC had to deal not only with Japanese conquerors, but also with Chinese who suffered under, cooperated with, and actively resisted them. In September 1937 John Rabe wrote, "[a]ll the rich or better-off Chinese began some time ago to flee up the Yangtze to Hankow," and in November he noted the heavy traffic pouring out of the city.[1] Yet a small group of Westerners chose not to return home, but to remain and protect those Chinese too poor to flee. These Westerners would form the nucleus of the IC, which was inspired by a similar committee that Father Jacquinot de Besange had set up in Shanghai. Many credit W. Plumer Mills as the first to suggest creating a safety zone in Nanking. On 17 November, Mills, Miner S. Bates, and Lewis C. S. Smythe visited the home of Willys R. Peck, U.S. embassy counselor, to inform him of their plans to establish a refugee zone, and also asked for negotiations with Japanese and Chinese authorities for its formal recognition. Minnie Vautrin wrote to the embassy on the same day to propose a safety zone. On 19 November, Rabe noted, "An International Committee has been formed.... They want to try to create a refugee camp, or better, a neutral zone inside or outside the city, where noncombatants can take refuge in case the city comes under fire."[2] At this stage, the aim envisaged was to provide a place of refuge during the attack. Once the city fell, however, the

IC had to take on other duties: to feed, house, and protect the civilian population from Japanese invaders. As Mills noted in late January, "the chief usefulness of the Zone has been in the measure of protection it has afforded to the people since the occupation."[3]

An "International Committee for Establishing a Neutral Zone for Noncombatants in Nanking" met on 22 November. As a German national with whom, it was thought, the Japanese would be more willing to negotiate, Rabe was elected chair.[4] This committee sent a telegram to the Japanese ambassador in Shanghai that read in part, "An international committee composed of nationals of Denmark, Germany, Great Britain, and the United States, desires to suggest to the Chinese and Japanese authorities the establishment of a Safety Zone for Civilian Refugees in the unfortunate event of hostilities at or near Nanking." The IC sought guarantees from Chinese authorities that this neutral refugee zone, the NSZ, "be made and kept free" of "military establishments" and "armed men" (other than police). It also stated that "passage of soldiers or military officers in any capacity" through the NSZ would not be allowed.[5]

Though estimates of its size differ, the NSZ measured about one-eighth of the city in its northwestern part.[6] The site was chosen on "the advice of foreign military observers" such as Maj. [*recte*: Captain] Frank M. Roberts, assistant military attaché at the U.S. embassy, for having "the least military value."[7] Not all Chinese authorities welcomed this idea. John Rabe talked with one military officer who was "very close to the generalissimo," and may have reflected Chiang Kai-shek's position. This officer was absolutely opposed to the NSZ, saying, "Nanking must be defended to the last man … [without the Safety] Zone, people now flooding into the Zone could have helped our soldiers." But on 25 November, Chiang agreed to the scheme, and 4 days later, Nanking mayor Ma Ch'ao-chün formally announced the formation of the IC.[8] After Ma fled the city on 7 December, the IC was left in charge of the remaining civilian population of some 200,000 to 250,000.

On 27 November, Rabe telegrammed Hitler for help in gaining recognition for the NSZ, and the IC asked the Japanese for a quick response. On 1 December, Father Jacquinot relayed their reply in a less-than-perfect English translation: "Japanese authorities have duly noted request for safety zone but regret cannot grant it. In the event of Chinese forces misbehavior towards civilians and or property cannot assume responsibility, but they themselves will endeavor to respect the district as far as consistent with military necessity."[9] The Japanese doubted that the IC could keep the NSZ demilitarized, but the IC was pleased with this answer, finding it "generally favorable," and the last part, "very satisfactory." Defense commander, Gen. T'ang Sheng-chih, however, reportedly admitted to the foreign press on 27 November that "disorder" was inevitable as defeated Chinese soldiers were pushed back into the city. The Japanese cited this "extraordinary admission" as proof that "Chinese guarantees that the military would not penetrate the proposed Nanking safety zone are practically worthless." Even so, the IC decided to proceed, noting to Father Jacquinot on 3 December, that "[a]t the proper time and after inspection [we] will formally notify both Chinese and Japanese authorities that [the] Zone is in operation."[10]

On 1 December, "Mayor Ma virtually turned over to us the administrative responsibilities for the Safety Zone together with a police force of 450 men, 10,000 piculs (2,000 tons) of rice, 10,000 bags of flour, and some salt, also a promise of C$100,000 in cash—C$80,000 of which was subsequently received."[11] As noted in the next section, 30,000 piculs of rice were promised as well, but the IC secured only 10,000. In a later letter addressed to the Japanese embassy, the IC spelled out its administrative responsibilities in more detail, to include "police, supervision of essential utilities, fire department, housing regulation, food supply, and sanitation."[12] The IC set up a number of subgroups to deal with those areas: food, housing, and sanitation. A fourth subgroup that dealt with rehabilitation, was added later.[13]

On 4 December, the Japanese ambassador to China reiterated to his U.S. counterpart that, because of "Chinese military establishments in and around the said area," and because the IC could not prevent Chinese troops from using the NSZ for military purposes, Japan could not promise not to attack it, but at the same time would refrain from doing so if Chinese troops did not enter it for such purposes.[14] Mayor Ma had fled on 7 December, so the IC took over as Nanking's *de facto* government the next day. As Rabe noted, he was "like an acting mayor." The IC faced huge problems: moving Chinese refugees into the NSZ, arranging its finances, policing it to keep out military elements, and providing food, housing, transportation, utilities, and sanitation. Chiang Kai-shek promised the IC $100,000 on 29 November. According to Rabe, $20,000 was paid on 1 December, and another $20,000 on 7 December. Two colonels, Lung and Chow, deposited a further C$30,000 on 12 December.[15] David Magee received $23,000 for the Red Cross on 10 December as well.[16] All sources agree that, of the $100,000 promised, $80,000 was received, so an additional $10,000 must have been paid to the IC at some point in time. The IC proved adept at fund-raising. It enjoyed an income of $454,000 from 1 December 1937 to 31 May 1938, with a further $96,000 from 1 June 1938 to 30 April 1939.[17]

Diplomacy

One relatively unknown story is the role that the IC played in trying to arrange a truce before the city fell. This attempt ultimately failed, but deserves recognition as an example of grassroots diplomacy. It was clear that the foreign community had a good understanding of the situation as the Japanese advanced on Nanking. According to Li Tsung-jen, who attended the meeting where Chiang decided to defend the city, German military advisers had argued against making a stand because the city could not be defended, but Chiang overruled them. Word of this leaked out. On 28 November, the IC debated whether to urge the Chinese to surrender the city peacefully since, "from a military point of view any defense of Nanking is absurd."[18] The IC decided to wait before communicating this to the Chinese authorities, but its opinion remained unchanged. On 6 December, Rabe wrote that "Gen. von Falkenhausen and all the German advisers have pointed out that this [defense] is hopeless." The Chinese may have realized that they could not hold the city, but wanted to inflict damage on the Japanese and buy time for other military units to escape. W. Plumer Mills, at least, thought this might have been the case. "It was perfectly clear ... that the Chinese could not hold the city, though not so clear that they might not be able to make it somewhat costly for the Japanese." It is thus no surprise that the IC tried to organize the city's surrender. As just noted, Rabe asked Hitler to intercede with the Japanese to gain recognition of the NSZ, and the Americans used diplomatic channels to urge them to respect it.[19]

On 9 December, the Japanese scattered leaflets calling for a peaceful surrender. On the same day, the IC urged Gen. T'ang to abandon plans to defend the city. Rabe wrote: "To my great amazement, T'ang agrees to do so if we can get the permission of Generalissimo Chiang Kai-shek."[20] This volte-face by commander T'ang, who had advocated defending Nanking to the last man, was reported in the contemporary press, and it is possible that the IC deliberately leaked word of the plan to bring international pressure on the Chinese. On 10 December, the *London Times* reported, the IC appealed for a three-day truce "as many thousands of Chinese civilians are still in the city but not in the zone," and the *New York Times* mistook this as "to enable thousands of Chinese noncombatants concentrated within the zone to escape."[21] The IC's plan was actually more ambitious; it hoped to arrange a three-day truce, during which the Chinese military would leave Nanking and then hand over a neutral city to the Japanese. On the evening of 9 December, Rabe, Mills, and Miner S. Bates boarded the USS *Panay*, and sent two telegrams: one to Japanese military authorities in Shanghai, the other to Chiang Kai-shek. The Japanese may have been happy with the idea; it was very close to the proposal that commanding general Matsui Iwane had made the same day. But Chiang rejected this on 10 December.[22]

T'ang next approached the IC on 12 December, asking it again to arrange a 3-day truce. This time it was "transparently clear" to Rabe "that General Tang wanted to conclude an armistice without the generalissimo's consent." Eduard Sperling agreed to walk through the lines carrying a proposal, but it was now too late. As F. Tillman Durdin noted, "General Tang ... in the final days was almost frantic in his efforts to obtain a truce, but the Chinese collapse came too quickly to permit the formulation of arrangements from the Chinese side." George Fitch and Rabe also agreed that this second attempt was too late, saying that the Japanese were already at the gates.[23] While he frantically tried to arrange a truce, T'ang also made plans for his own escape. The city fell when he abandoned his troops and fled. Indeed, one major reason for Japanese atrocities in and around Nanking was the lack of a formal surrender and the fact that Chinese troops shed their uniforms to hide among civilians in the NSZ. The Japanese could not be sure who was an ex-solider and who was a civilian, and the IC refused to help them identify Chinese military personnel for obvious reasons. The potential threat of guerilla-type resistance—including sniper attacks (especially given the presence of Imperial Prince Asaka Yasuhiko), sabotage of key institutions, and attacks on Japanese troops—allowed the Japanese to justify their efforts to identify Chinese former soldiers. Since many of them so identified were executed—my estimate in chapter 5 is roughly 5,000—this effort inevitably caused civilian casualties.

Policing and Neutrality

Despite concerted attempts to remove Chinese soldiers from the NSZ, the IC was unable to do so even though it was given a police force of 450 men. Later, the IC proved to be helpless after the Japanese occupied the city. In fact, many of these police became victims of relentless Japanese searches for Chinese soldiers. On 16 December, fifty uniformed policemen and forty-six volunteers were marched off, and the next day another forty uniformed policemen were taken. The IC no doubt rightly assumed that the Japanese executed these men, but some survived, for Lewis Smythe stated that, as of 22 December "about half of the [ninety uniformed] police have returned," and on 9 January Smythe also noted that 160 police were cooperating with the Nanking Self-Government Committee (SGC), sometimes also cited as the Autonomous Government Committee, set up by the Japanese.[24] On 4 December, Rabe felt great frustration about Chinese combatants refusing to leave the NSZ, and reported that more were reported hiding there the next day. This inability to police the NSZ meant that, as the Japanese had feared, its neutrality could not be guaranteed. There were other issues too. On 11 December, Chinese police "nominally under our control" arrested a thief, and the IC had to decide what to do with him. He was sentenced to death, pardoned, and ordered into twenty-four hours' confinement, but released for lack of a jail.[25] The inability to keep Chinese troops out of the NSZ gave the Japanese an excuse to gather weapons, conduct mop-up operations, and arrest suspected soldiers therein. The Seventh Regiment, entrusted with this task, reported securing 6,670 ex-soldiers and, among other things, twelve water-cooled heavy machine guns, 133 light machine guns, 55,122 hand grenades, 960 pistols, and four tanks. The "ex-soldiers" were executed, for as Masahiro Yamamoto notes, 6,670 approximates the 7,000 rounds of ammunition used from 13 to 24 December by the regiment.[26]

After Nanking fell, Westerners helped to protect the Chinese population from a grossly underpoliced Japanese military—there were initially only seventeen military police for the 50,000 to 70,000 troops in Nanking. At the same time, collaboration and resistance emerged. Members of the SGC helped the Japanese identify Chinese ex-soldiers, and there is evidence that the police punished collaborators. On 22 December, Smythe tells of two Chinese "cronies" of the Japanese "put ... in safe keeping." Two days later, Fitch reported that the second of them, a spy for the Japanese, had been caught: "I just saved him from a bad beating, so [I] locked him up in our basement and later turned him over to the Chinese police. What will they do to him? Strangle him I suppose—but I have told them to be careful [i.e., kill him quietly]!"[27] Fitch and Smythe are silent about what happened to the other man, but he too must have been killed quietly. This is one aspect of the IC that historians have neglected to date.

IC members fought to guarantee the neutrality of the NSZ, but failed in the end because they could not police it. On 3 December, Rabe reported that three "new trenches and/or foundations for anti-aircraft batteries are being dug in the Zone." He threatened to resign if this work was not immediately stopped, and received written confirmation that his wishes would be respected. Yet on 4 December, he lamented, "[s]oldiers continue to build new trenches and install military telephones inside the Safety Zone." The next day, he visited commander T'ang, who said that the military could not be removed for another two weeks. "A nasty blow," Rabe wrote: "[i]t means that the Japanese condition that no Chinese soldiers are to be allowed in the Zone will not be fulfilled. For now at least we cannot even think of claiming to have a 'Safety Zone,' at most it's a 'refugee zone'." Rabe went on, "Dr. [Georg] Rosen curses the Chinese military roundly for, as he describes it, having slunk into our Zone, because it's safer next to all those vacant houses with German flags than it is outside the Zone. I can't swear that it's true. But the fact is that General T'ang himself received us today in a house inside the refugee zone." Chinese troops were reported hiding in the NSZ on 5 December. Three days later Rabe wrote, "we must deal with endless encroachments by the military, who still have not left our Zone and apparently are in no hurry to do so," and "[w]e are all close to despair. Chinese military headquarters is our worst problem." On 9 December, the IC discovered "a row of anti-aircraft batteries within the southwest border of our Zone."[28]

The next day, Rabe wrote that it was "a crying shame that the European war reporters who are still here can't tell the whole truth. Certain people should be exposed for not always keeping their promise to rid the Zone of the military."[29] On 11 December, Rabe stated, "there are still armed soldiers inside" the NSZ, so the IC "cannot tell the Japanese, as was our intention, that the

Zone is now free of all military." Later that day, he noted that trenches were being dug inside the NSZ outside the Kulou (Drum Flower) Hospital. The next day, "[a]ll over our Zone you still see Chinese troops with yellow armbands and armed to the teeth with rifles, pistols, and hand grenades." The police were armed with rifles "[c]ontrary to all agreements."[30] Thus the NSZ was not demilitarized despite IC assurances, yet it is clear that the Japanese nevertheless strove to spare it from artillery attacks. Dr. Robert Wilson admitted this, writing on 14 December that "[t]he Japanese seemed to respect the safety zone remarkably with their big gun fire."[31] Rabe also wrote that the NSZ had been spared except for a time between the evening of 12 December and 13 December, and that this attack was understandable given the "various circumstances," referring to the Wutaishan antiaircraft battery on the southern border of the Zone. Arthur Menken also noted that "[t]he Japanese refrained from bombing the safety zone." The IC's first letter to Japanese authorities stated, "[w]e come to thank you for the fine way your artillery spared the Safety Zone."[32] Note, however, the politics of the statement: the decision to pose as grateful supplicants may well have been a strategic one, and does not necessarily mean that the NSZ was in fact spared by the Japanese for humanitarian reasons.

Food

The Chinese victimization narrative on Nanking emphasizes that the IC defended the lives of residents from Japanese invaders over and above other duites, such as humanitarian work in obtaining and transporting provisions to the NSZ. IC members themselves, however, believed that the real threat of large-scale civilian deaths derived mainly from a lack of food. Rabe said as much to the Japanese embassy on 17 December: "It is hard to see how starvation may be prevented amongst many of the 200,000 Chinese civilians if order is not restored at once amongst the Japanese soldiers in the city."[33] Although this might be seen as an example of rhetoric, private letters and diaries reveal similar feelings. For Rabe, Japanese aggression was less dangerous for directly killing large numbers of civilians, but rather for disrupting the flow of food, and the IC as a whole shared his concern. On 30 November, Smythe informed Rabe by telephone that 60,000 sacks of rice were in Nanking, and another 34,000 were at Hsiakwan outside the city walls. The next day, the IC was promised 30,000 sacks of rice and 10,000 sacks of flour, but lacked the means to transport it into the NSZ. Rabe noted that "large quantities" of this promised supply had been pilfered by the Chinese military and that, a day later, "only 15,000 sacks of rice" were left. Rabe was more diplomatic toward Hitler, for he did not mention the Chinese military confiscating food, but said only that the IC lacked trucks to carry rice, so only about 9,000 sacks of rice and 2,000 sacks of flour were secured. Elsewhere, he notes that no flour was secured, although 1,000 bags were obtained from a separate source, the Ta Tung Flour Mill. On 7 December, Rabe wrote that the IC had managed "at best to get a quarter of the food promised us into the Zone."[34] This perhaps explains why George Fitch said the IC was promised only 10,000 piculs of rice.

The IC kept this information from the Japanese, later stating in a 27 December letter that it "succeeded in moving 10,000 *tan* [piculs] of rice and 1,000 bags of flour into the Zone. The remainder we hoped to get as soon as the fighting was over."[35] The strategy was as follows: pretend to believe that rice was waiting to be picked up and hope that the Japanese would make up for any shortfall. As Symthe said: "we should just assume we had a right to the remainder of the 30,000 *tan* of rice, and 10,000 bags of flour." The same letter also noted that the Chinese military had another 100,000 *tan* of rice "most of which fell into your hands," but a close reading of various texts shows that the 30,000 *tan* of rice promised to the IC was included in the 100,000 *tan* in and around Nanking.[36] It is also clear that the Chinese would have destroyed this supply rather than surrender it to the Japanese. This deception was extended to officials at the U.S., British, and German embassies. In a letter to them dated 26 January, Rabe wrote that, of 20,000 bags of rice and 10,000 sacks of flour, the IC had received only 10,000 bags of rice, stating that "Japanese authorities" had "confiscated" the rest (10,000 bags of rice at ninety-six kilograms each, and 10,000 sacks of flour at fifty pounds each), and asked for support from the embassies in getting the Japanese to make up the difference.[37] To Hitler, Rabe reported that a Chinese friend promised him two trucks and 1,000 sacks of flour but only one truck and 100 sacks of flour actually arrived. His diary gave a slightly different version: on 23 November he was offered "two trucks with 100 canisters of gasoline and 200 sacks of flour" by a Chinese friend of one of his workers. The benefactor, it later becomes clear, was a Mr. Sung, the proprietor of the I-Ho-Tung Brick Works, and what initially turned up was one empty truck, even though Rabe later obtained all the gasoline and twenty sacks of flour.[38]

The IC thus secured only part of what it wanted, and never had enough food after the city fell. On 21 December, Western nationals in Nanking wrote to the Japanese embassy, stating that the IC "has reserve food supplies to feed these 200,000 people [the Chinese population] one week only." On Christmas Eve, Fitch wrote to friends that the IC had "enough rice and flour for the 200,000 refugees for another three weeks and coal for ten days."[39] On 26 December, Rabe wrote that it was "getting more and more difficult to feed the 200,000 people," but he was "not that pessimistic" even though Smythe estimated rice reserves would only last a week. On 6 January, Rabe wrote that the Japanese had agreed to sell rice and flour to the IC, and that it had purchased rice and coal. By 10 January, when the Nanking population had risen by 50,000, "[s]ome 250,000 are here, almost all in the Safety Zone and fully 100,000 entirely dependent on the IC for food and shelter." On 13 January, Paul Scharffenberg of the German embassy said that food was "dangerously short," and people had started "to eat horse and dog meat." On 16 January, another member wrote that "food supplies are very short" and that the IC had "rice on hand for about three weeks." Smythe wrote, "we faced the daily fear [that]our rice would not hold out."[40]

The discrepancy between the claim to the Japanese that food would only last a week and the admission that 3 weeks' worth were secured is explained by a letter to the Japanese embassy wherein Rabe states, "[i]f we had to feed the whole population, our reserve would not last a week." As of 18 January, the IC was providing 50,000 individuals with free rice.[41] Since the IC claimed that it was only feeding about a third of the population, supplies sufficient to last three weeks would only last one week if all were fed. Smythe and Fitch made exactly the same point: if the entire population became dependent on the IC's supply, "it would only last [for] the 250,000 people one week." These references suggest a refugee population of 150,000, for if the one-third being fed referred to the 65,000 to 70,000 in the refugee camps, the entire population would be 195,000 to 210,000.[42] Quite understandably, the IC must have thought it best to emphasize the lack of food, and not explicitly tell the Japanese that supplies might last only three weeks.

On 13 January, Fitch noted in a letter to the acting Japanese consul-general Fukui Kiyoshi that the IC had purchased 9,000 bags of wheat and 3,000 of rice from the Shanghai Commercial and Savings Bank. These foodstuffs were located, he claimed, in and around Nanking, and he asked for permission to transport these to the NSZ. The Japanese army was unable to locate these supplies.[43] The Chinese had deliberately scorched suburban areas around Nanking to deny the Japanese cover and to destroy anything that might be helpful to them. Later, the Chinese and a very hungry Japanese army looted these areas. Furthermore, Hsiakwan, where the rice stores were located, was an area that saw some of the fiercest fighting when the city fell. But the IC was still trying to get these supplies almost a week later.[44] It also used Christian networks to bring foodstuffs from Shanghai. On 15 January Rabe told the Japanese embassy that "about 600 tons" of "supplementary food supplies" had been secured, and asked for permission to ship these into the city. Three days later, Fitch and the IC asked Shanghai for an extra 100 tons of Chinese green beans to avert widespread beriberi (the Japanese blocked attempts to have this shipment brought to the city). Despite huge difficulties, the IC obtained enough food to run soup kitchens that fed all needy Chinese in the early weeks of the occupation. Apart from a scare with beriberi, no diseases related to nutrition broke out.[45] The entire Nanking population of 200,000 to 250,000 was crowded into the NSZ, and roughly 65,000 to 70,000 of them lived in refugee camps therein. All of them were dependent on the IC for food, yet no one starved.

Medical Services

Accounts of the number of medical staff in Nanking differ slightly. A reporter, Arthur Menken, says that "the wounded were not cared for" except by three American missionaries.[46] Yet the IC was clearly keeping a close eye on the situation with regard to medical staff. On 24 November, Rabe noted that three Chinese doctors had bolted, and "[i]f the American missionary doctors don't hold out, I don't know what will become of all the many casualties." The next day, he expressed concern about "the doctor problem," and his report to Hitler stated that the only medical staff who remained in the city were Dr. Robert Wilson, Dr. C. S. Trimmer, and two nurses, Grace Bauer and Iva Hynds. Ernest Forster wrote on 12 December that "only three doctors are left, Wilson, Trimmer and a Chinese."[47] But Wilson noted that, in addition to himself and Trimmer, two Chinese doctors worked in a hospital within the NSZ. The International Red Cross Committee also cared for patients in three military hospitals at the KMT ministries of Foreign Affairs, Railways, and War after Chinese doctors and nurses had fled before the city was occupied.[48] According to F. Tillman Durdin, as early as November:

> Many times more than 2,000 wounded, after spending two to four days lying on straw in close-packed, jolting trucks or jarring freight cars en route to Nanking, were left lying on concrete platforms at Hsiakwan railway station here in the bitter cold for two or three days and nights without any dressings or sanitation whatever and often without even drinking water and food.…
>
> The luckiest of the wounded on the concrete floors had a single straw mat and a single cotton blanket while those on the un-walled station platforms—in some cases the roofs had been shattered—suffered untold misery. They were exposed to sweeping rains. Their clothes and bandages were soaking wet.… It is obvious that the few who can survive at all apparently are lacking sedatives and their moans and cries are audible for blocks.[49]

After the city fell, all 500 or so abandoned Chinese military patients were moved to the military hospital in the Ministry of Foreign Affairs, where Japanese doctors cared for them. The Japanese acted on an IC recommendation dated 14 December: "[i]f it is possible to put all the wounded in it, we suggest transferring all the Chinese wounded to the Ministry of Foreign Affairs building."[50] This hospital was soon declared off-limits to the foreign community and Chinese staff were not allowed in the building at first, but Rabe heard nothing bad about conditions there "except for one especially cold-blooded incident." A patient complained about his food, was slapped, and after voicing further complaints, was taken outside and bayoneted.[51] The informant was a Chinese nurse who either stayed behind or was recruited after the Japanese took the city. Since the IC, through the International Red Cross, had informants inside the hospital, we can assume that word would have gotten out if other atrocities had occurred. Rabe also wrote warmly of a Dr. Hirai, who spoke a little German and was in charge of Japanese military doctors there, and Rev. John Magee went so far as to call their treatment of wounded Chinese soldiers "exemplary," explaining this as having been "deliberately planned for propaganda purposes."[52]

Medical staff had very heavy workloads. Permission for two doctors and two nurses to come to Nanking was refused until mid-February, when a Dr. Brady returned to the city.[53] A clearer picture of workloads emerges from Dr. Robert Wilson's family letters. On 14 December, he wrote "I did eleven operations today, including the inevitable amputation. We have considerably over 100 patients now." Some of these operations were due to injuries sustained before the Japanese occupation of the city. The next day, "[t]here were about thirty admissions today and no discharges. We can't discharge any patients because they have no place to go [...] Today I had ten operations." Things improved by 19 December, when he had 6 operations and remarked with some relief, "[a]nother day has passed without an amputation." Writing to the Japanese embassy the same day, he noted that there were "over 150 patients" in the hospital. On 26 December, he stated, "[t]his afternoon I started off with another amputation and had a few cases." Yet the total number of patients in the hospital increased. On 28 December, Wilson wrote that there were about 175 patients in all, and on 3 January 1938, he had 150 patients (Dr. Trimmer would perhaps have had an extra twenty or so). On 3 January, Wilson also remarked that he had "had five operations this afternoon."[54] On 22 January, the "University Hospital has been kept full caring for seriously wounded civilians and now an increasing number of maternity cases." It can be assumed that heavily pregnant women would have been reluctant to flee from the advancing Japanese, and thus there would have been a larger number of such women than the size of the total population (200,000 to 250,000) would otherwise suggest. On 10 February, the total number of patients had dropped to 150.[55]

Wilson's letters allow us to draw a rough picture of the situation. During the first week of the occupation, there may have been thirty admissions a day, with a high of eleven operations at the start, dropping to six by the end of the week. These high numbers are explained at least in part by military action as the Japanese captured the city. The number of patients increased from over 100 at the start of the first week to 175 by the end of the second, and began to decline by February. Wilson makes it clear that he did not like to discharge patients, but he must have begun to do so, or else the number of new cases must have fallen dramatically. On 29 December Rev. James McCallum wrote that the "hospital is full and the lighter cases fill the University Dormitory building. Some we cannot dismiss for they have no place to go." This shows that some patients were discharged. He also noted that "fifteen or twenty babies [were born] within the last week," which shows that some of those in the hospital had come for reasons other than violence.[56]

The conclusions to be drawn from this limited data are perhaps surprising, and I must emphasize that this was the only hospital inside the NSZ. (The other hospital in Nanking was outside of the NSZ, at the KMT Ministry of Foreign Affairs, run by the Japanese for 500 or so Chinese military casualties.) First, a daily intake of thirty patients and five to ten operations a day, as cited by Wilson, seems unbelievably low. Is this much higher than one would expect for a population of 200,000 to 250,000 in peacetime? Second, although Wilson gives some truly horrific cases of Japanese brutality, the victims of which ended up on his operating table, the number of patients admitted does not square with our image of large-scale, indiscriminate violence. This is not to say that large-scale Japanese violence did not occur, just that Wilson's letters do not substantiate it on such a scale.

Housing

On 1 December, the IC discussed whether or not to order the populace of Nanking into the NSZ, and appears to have done so. The Chinese military authorities declared martial law and ordered civilians into the NSZ on 8 December. These orders made housing in the NSZ an urgent issue. John Rabe reported to Hitler that the IC's first step was to put posters on city walls advising the population to bring bedding and food and to move into the house of any friend who might be residing in the NSZ. The next step was to hand over empty houses therein to Nanking's poorer residents. The last step was to open facilities and buildings in schools and universities to lodge the poorest residents. On 18 December it was thought that those public buildings would hold only 35,000 people, but these eventually came to house almost double that number by 21 December and for another month. The poorest of the poor, Rabe estimated, numbered 65,000 and were fed 1,600 sacks of rice a day. Other estimates put the number at 69,000 and "approximately 70,000." On 22 January, when these camps still held 60,000, the IC was feeding 50,000 daily, either in the camps themselves or through soup kitchens run by the Red Cross and the RSS).[57]

The IC first believed that 200,000—the entire population of Nanking— might move into the NSZ in a worst-case scenario.[58] But the number peaked at 250,000. Chinese soldiers who survived the battle for Nanking must account for the bulk of this increase. Nevertheless, the IC managed. Its provision of medical services and housing, along with finance and food, count as "successes," whereas its policing and maintaining of neutrality were "failures." But indeed, it is incredible that the IC coped as well as it did given near-impossible circumstances: (1) the sudden collapse of government and local administration, whose members all fled before the city fell; (2) widespread looting in Nanking by Japanese, Chinese, or (to a far lesser extent) Westerners: (3) large numbers of heavily armed Japanese troops and at least some armed Chinese; and (4) the possible existence of an active Chinese resistance movement.[59] Given these conditions and the IC's limited resources, it did far better than anyone could have expected.

Western Cooperation and Resistance

Cooperation with the Japanese in occupied Nanking is a topic that falls outside the dominant narrative of Western humanitarianism today, but it is clear that some Westerners did cooperate, at least to an extent. Thus, as defense of the city collapsed, the IC disarmed Chinese soldiers (but then hid them, albeit in a few cases). Rabe worked to get the electricity works in Hsiakwan up and running, going to inspect these as early as 16 December. The IC acted as a dispatch service to provide labor to the Japanese and also helped their troops register the Chinese population. Rabe provided a Japanese embassy official with a car; and the NSZ mechanic, A. Zial, worked for the Japanese embassy fixing cars.[60] The politics behind the decision to cooperate are clear; there was no alternative. Yet, partly because of this limited cooperation, the Chinese government in the past was very critical of the IC. Scholars at Nanking University in the 1960s, for instance, unfairly condemned it for facilitating Japanese atrocities by turning a blind eye while feasting on Christmas dinner.[61] However, after the Cold War ended, Chinese fears of U.S. imperialism diminished and Japan became the target of official vitriol. Accordingly, Chinese views of the IC changed dramatically. In a work frequently based on vivid imagination rather than on reliable primary sources, the late Iris Chang claims that IC members jumped "in front of cannons and machine guns to prevent the Japanese from firing" on unarmed civilians.[62] This claim is pure fiction, but humanitarian work by the IC is highly lauded in all secondary sources on Nanking today and is one of the few areas about which all researchers agree.

IC members were realists who cooperated with the Japanese to a degree. As Rabe said, "we have to get along peacefully with the Japanese here somehow." Some members, the Austrian mechanic Rupert Hatz, for example, thought the Japanese acted in ways that could be justified. Others, such as the American George Fitch, who was highly critical of the Japanese, at times pretended to think in a similar manner. Fitch went on Shanghai radio on 3 February as "very much a friend of Japan."[63] The IC had no choice but to assume this pose. It saw itself as responsible for the welfare of 200,000 to 250,000 Chinese—who, it believed, were unable to look after themselves without a guiding, Western, patriarchal hand. Yet there were limits to that pose, and hints of resistance often underlay overt acts of cooperation. For instance, American members got the Japanese to send a telegram asking for a diplomatic representative to be dispatched to Nanking as soon as possible; and, according to Lewis C. S. Smythe, Rabe: "used very flowery German to tell Rosen [at the German embassy] that he was delighted to say that two German houses in the city positively had not been damaged, that Rosen's car, along with many other German cars, was rendering excellent service for the Japanese Military, and that he hoped he would be here for Christmas Eve because by then we hoped to have electricity and telephone going!"[64] As Smythe claimed, this was "a masterpiece" of superficial cooperation (reporting that two cars were not damaged) and underlying resistance (implying that all others were destroyed). The droll sense of humor also helps to explain why Rabe was popular in the Western community.

The IC resisted the Japanese in more substantial ways as well. Works edited by persons such as Harold J. Timperley and Hsü Shuhsi, both closely linked to the KMT regime, could not have been published without cooperation from IC members. Far more importantly, the IC as a whole hid at least one high-ranking Chinese air force officer, and Rabe hid at least two officers. All three lived in Rabe's house, so he took considerable risks, especially if they were engaged in anti-Japanese activities, as was likely. Apart from these three officers, twenty more people smuggled themselves into Rabe's garden during the Japanese registration of the population on 26 December. They were probably military personnel too. Rabe mentions a "high official of the former Chinese government" who stayed at his house at least once. (This man may, however, have been one of the three officers living there.) There is evidence that the IC hid other ex-soldiers from the Japanese from a very early stage. Rabe noted on 14 December that the IC found "lodging in some vacant buildings for a group of 125 Chinese refugees, before they fall into the hands of the Japanese military," and he was almost certainly referring to soldiers.[65] On 15 December, the IC told the Japanese embassy that it had kept the NSZ "entirely free of Chinese soldiers" until 13 December, when "several hundred soldiers" entered it. On 18 December, the IC reported that "we can safely assure you that there are no groups of disarmed Chinese soldiers in the Zone. Your searching squads have cleaned out all of them and many civilians along with them."[66] Both statements were deliberately and, of course, justifiably misleading. IC members knew full well that far more than "several hundred" Chinese soldiers were in the NSZ long before 13 December and that the Japanese had yet to identify all of these soldiers.

According to Chiang Kung-i, Eduard Sperling helped smuggle reports by Chinese military personnel out of the city to be forwarded to Chinese authorities.[67] One Chinese source claims that Rabe provided a Chinese individual with explosives and directed him to destroy installations that might prove useful to the Japanese. Fitch smuggled the negatives of a film that documented Japanese atrocities—known as "John Magee's Film"—out of the city sewn into the lining of his coat.[68] On returning to Berlin, Rabe wrote a long lecture on the fall of Nanking, which he gave on numerous occasions while showing Magee's film. When ordered to stop, he mailed a copy of his lecture to Hitler. The IC was thus far from neutral; some members, at least, actively helped in the Chinese resistance.

The End of the Committee

The IC was originally established to protect Chinese civilians from an invading army. Next, it shouldered the tasks of feeding and protecting them from an occupying army. Lastly, it provided relief to help return civilians to normal life. But the Japanese moved quickly to undermine the IC's moral authority and to replace it with a collaborationist Self-Government Committee (SGC). According to Fitch, this was formed on 22 December at the invitation of the Japanese embassy. On the same day, Rabe learned that the Japanese authorities wanted to establish "their own refugee committee." Its head, T'ao Hsi-san, also headed the RSS, and was the collaborationist figurehead in occupied Nanking. T'ao's house appears to have been burgled at least twice during the early weeks of the occupation, and a bathhouse that he may have operated was also robbed and its staff members killed. This might be seen as a form of reprisal from the Chinese military authorities still in the city.[69] As Timothy Brook relates in chapter 9, the aims of these two bodies, the SGC and the IC, may have been similar, and they even had some members in common, but they competed against each other for the hearts and minds of Nanking citizens. Thus, on 30 December, Rabe gloomily noted in his diary that the SGC "is to be our replacement." He added, "[w]e have nothing against their taking over our work, but it looks to us as if they simply want to take over our money," and also noted, "I'll not hand over anything. I'll yield only under greatest pressure, and then only under loud protest."[70]

On 1 January 1938, Rabe ironically noted that the SGC was "solemnly constituted." The next day, he gloomily noted that "Mr. Sun, who is the vice chairmen [*sic*]" of the new SGC and "member of the Red Swastika Society [who] speaks Japanese, condescendingly informs me that he must speak to me very soon about an important matter." This had to do with finances. On 6 January, "Mr. Fukuda paid me a visit to tell me that by decision of the military authorities our International Committee is to be dissolved and our supplies and monies are to be taken over by the Autonomous Government Committee [i.e., the SGC]." The IC resisted this move, seemingly because: (1) law and order needed to be first restored, and the SGC had not "the vaguest idea" about how to do this; and (2) it was thought that the SGC was not up to handling all the administrative tasks.[71] Members of the IC did not think much of their SGC Chinese successors: "most of the trained, intelligent and active people … all moved further west" before the city fell. Those Chinese who remained were, in Wilson's words, second-raters. Matsui Iwane, commander of Japanese forces, shared that opinion, noting on 7 February that the SGC lineup "cut a poor figure."[72] The IC tried to be conciliatory; Rabe wrote to Fukuda on 7 January, stating that it would be "glad" to have the SGC "assume as speedily as possible all the usual functions of a local civic administration." He also stated that the IC had "no desire whatsoever to carry on any of these administrative duties which are normally assumed by *competent* local administrations" (italics added).[73] But, Rabe continued, the IC was formed to care for civilians, and since funds and supplies provided to it were entrusted for that purpose, it should not give these up to another organization.[74] The IC was thus willing to have the SGC take responsibility for administration but unwilling to hand over its assets, and it took steps to gain support from the newly reopened embassies in this regard. In a letter on 10 January to John Allison, Smythe again made it clear that the IC was unwilling to surrender its resources, but happy to have the SGC take responsibility for administering the city.[75]

On 9 January, Jimmy Wang told Rabe that the IC was no longer allowed to sell rice to the Chinese. The IC stopped selling it the next day. Wang also told Rabe that the Japanese would now sell rice and flour only to the SGC, which "opened an outlet for rice" on 10 January. It seems that the SGC became the sole source of food thereafter. On 11 January, Rabe noted that "[t]he Japanese have cut off our rice supply today." Dispensing food to Nanking's poor obviously legitimized an agency, and the Japanese wanted this to be the SGC. In resisting these moves, the IC was fighting a losing battle. On 12 January, Rabe reported that it was also prohibited from handling coal. The Japanese wanted the Chinese population to leave the NSZ, so they made coal and food available outside of it in order to encourage people to return to their homes.[76] The low opinion that IC members had of the SGC was quickly substantiated. On 14 January, the SGC, unable to cope with the responsibilities thrust on it, asked the IC to truck supplies of rice. On 17 January, the IC noted with alarm that arrangements to distribute rice through the SGC had broken down, and that there had been no regular distribution for almost a week. Although the two committees were rivals, there is no doubt that the IC was, in Miner S. Bates's words, "in cahoots with" the SGC.[77] Again, Westerners had no choice if they wished to help the Chinese, but this entailed moral ambiguities in cooperating with a collaborationist organization.

Foreign embassies reopened at about the time that the Japanese completed registration of the Nanking population and the SGC replaced the IC. The U.S. embassy was the first, on 6 January 1938, when "Mr. [John] Allison, Mr. [James] Espey [*recte*: Espy], and Mr. [Archibald] McFadyen, arrived here today aboard the USS *Oahu* from Shanghai by way of Wuhu." The German and British embassies followed, on 9 January on the HMS *Cricket*.[78] The foreign community grew as embassy staffs returned and also changed as some original staff members left. Christian Kröger left for Shanghai on 23 January. George Fitch and H. I. Prideaux-Brunce left on the HMS *Bee* for Shanghai on 29 January, taking Rabe's diaries (Fitch did not return until 12 February).[79] In February, the Japanese started to close refugee camps and increased efforts to make Chinese return to homes outside the NSZ. When he left Nanking on 23 February, Rabe estimated that 100,000 people had moved out of it. A Mr. Bishopric was allowed to return to Nanking in late January—the first Westerner apart from diplomats. By 12 February, another Westerner, James Kearney, arrived (if only for three days).[80] On 18 February 1938, in recognizing these altered circumstances, especially the disappearance of the NSZ, the IC changed its name to the Nanking International Relief Committee.[81]

Conclusion

Almost all Chinese under IC care survived this key first stage of the Japanese occupation, when the NSZ began with a population of 200,000 and ended with 250,000. Apart from perhaps 5,000 individuals identified as Chinese military personnel and executed (as noted in my chapter 5), the IC protected those whom it sought to help. In the face of immense difficulties and despite harsh criticism from the Japanese, Westerners who chose to remain in Nanking rather than flee to safety achieved their humanitarian aims. They were by no means neutral in the hostilities, and they saved huge numbers of Chinese lives, acting heroically under very trying circumstances. Moreover, it is largely because of the primary source they wrote that we can reconstruct so much of the Nanking Atrocity's history. Their story is one of the few positive aspects in a grimly bleak chapter of Sino-Japanese relations.

Notes

1. Rabe, *Good Man of Nanking*, p. 4 and p. 22; Vautrin, "Review of the First Month," p. 332. On the depopulation of the city, see Askew, "Nanjing Incident" pp. 2–20.
2. Timperley ed., *What War Means*, p. 13; Mills, in Smalley, ed., *American Missionary Eyewitnesses*, p. 44, and Chang, ed., *Eyewitnesses to Massacre*, p. 245. Rabe, 21 February speech to the IC staff, in Nankin jiken chôsa kenkyûkai, ed., *Amerika kankei shiryô shû*, pp. 185–87. Chang, *Rape of Nanking*, p. 106 and pp. 254–55. Zhang [Chang], in *Eyewitnesses to Massacre*, pp. xix–xx, suggests that Hang Liwu was also behind the push to establish a zone. Memorandum 17 November, in *Amerika kankei shiryô shû*, pp. 122–23. Vautrin, in *Amerika kankei shiryô shû*, p. 124. Rabe, *Good Man*, p. 25.
3. Mills, in Smalley, ed., *American Missionary Eyewitnesses*, p. 45; Zhang, ed., *Eyewitnesses to Massacre*, p. 246.
4. Rabe, *Good Man of Nanking*, p. 27; Rabe, "Hitoraa e no jôshinsho," p. 298. Also, Kasahara, *Nankin nanminku no hyakunichi*, p. 69.

5. Rabe, *Good Man of Nanking*, p. 28. Also, *Amerika kankei shiryô shû*, pp. 125–26.
6. Woodhead ed., *The China Year Book, 1939*, says it was 2 x 1 miles, or 3.86 (*sic*) square kilometers. Citing Yin and Yung, Bartlett says it "measured about 2 x 3 km. (about 1 square mile)" which is clearly wrong since 2 x 3 kilometers is over 2 square miles. See Bartlett, Introduction, p. vii. Kasahara, *Nankin nanminku no hyakunichi*, p. 72, says it was 8.6 square kilometers.
7. Smythe, in Smalley, ed., *American Missionary Eyewitnesses to the Nanjing Massacre*, p. 300; *Amerika kankei shiryô shû*, p. 122.
8. Rabe, *Good Man of Nanking*, p. 57, 33, and 40.
9. Durdin, *New York Times*, 28 November 1937; Rabe, "Hitoraa e no jôshinsho," p. 301; *Good Man of Nanking;* p. 46; Menken, *London Times*, 4 December 1937.
10. Rabe, *Good Man of Nanking*, p. 46; *New York Times*, 29 November 1937; Durdin, *New York Times* 28 November 1937. Rabe, *Good Man of Nanking*, p. 47; *Amerika kankei shiryô shû*, p. 128.
11. Fitch, *My Eighty Years in China*, p. 100. Timperley ed., *What War Means*, p. 24, Hsü ed., *The War Conduct of the Japanese*, p. 155. Zhang, ed., *Eyewitnesses to Massacre* (p. 85) gives the 10,000 piculs of rice as "30,000." Timperley gives the sums of money as "£100,000 in cash, £80,000 of which was subsequently received." Also see "In Nanking To-day," where $100,000 in cash, 2,000 tons of rice, and 10,000 bags of flour are mentioned.
12. Timperley, ed., *What War Means*, p. 217; Hsü ed., *Documents of the Nanking Safety Zone*, p. 12.
13. "Report of the Nanking International Relief Committee," in Zhang, ed., *Eyewitnesses to Massacre*, p. 414. On another commission, Finance, see the Vautrin diary in Okada and Ihara trans., *Nankin jiken no hibi*, p. 29.
14. *Foreign Relations of the United States: Diplomatic Papers, 1937*, vol. 3, *The Far East*, pp. 757–58; also cited in Yamamoto, *Nanking*, pp. 62–63.
15. Rabe, *Good Man of Nanking*, pp. 42–54 and p. 64; Vautrin, *Nankin Jiken no Hibi*, p. 29.
16. Rabe, *Good Man of Nanking*, p. 58. Vautrin heard from Bates that this was $50,000; see Zhang, ed., *Eyewitnesses to Massacre*, p. 357. Durdin, *New York Times*, 27 November 1937, claimed that the Nanking Christian War Relief Committee headed by Magee received an extra C$30,000.
17. Zhang, ed., *Eyewitnesses to Massacre*, pp. 441–44, and pp. 446–49.
18. Tong and Li, *Memoirs of Li Tsung-jen*, pp. 326–28; Rabe, *Good Man of Nanking*, p. 38.
19. Rabe, *Good Man of Nanking*, p. 52; Mills, in Smalley, ed., *American Missionary Eyewitnesses*, p. 46; Zhang, ed., *Eyewitnesses to Massacre*, p. 247. Rabe's appeal to Hitler, "Hitoraa e no jôshinsho," p. 301, appeared in Durdin, *New York Times*, 28 November 1937. Also, Yamamoto, *Nanking*, p. 62.
20. For the text of the leaflets, see Higashinakano, *Nankin gyakusatsu no tettei kenshô*, p. 65, and Matsui's diary, 8–9 December, in *Nankin senshi shiryô shû*, vol. 2, p. 139. Rabe, *Good Man of Nanking*, p. 56.
21. *London Times*, 11 December 1937; *New York Times*, 11 December 1937.
22. Rabe, "Hitoraa e no jôshinsho," p. 307. Mills stated that he and Bates boarded the *Panay;* see Zhang, ed., *Eyewitnesses to Massacre*, p. 247. Rabe, *Good Man of Nanking*, p. 59. *Foreign Relations of the United States, 1937*, vol. 3, *The Far East*, pp. 781, 784. Also Yamamoto, *Nanking*, p. 64 and p. 79, note 115.
23. Rabe, *Good Man of Nanking*, p. 63; Smythe, in Zhang, ed., *Eyewitnesses to Massacre*, p. 253; Durdin, *New York Times*, 19 December 1937, p. 38; Rabe, *Good Man of Nanking*, p. 63, Fitch, in Zhang. ed., *Eyewitnesses to Massacre*, p. 86.
24. Hsü, ed., *Documents of the Nanking Safety Zone*, p. 14 and p. 22; Smythe, in Zhang, ed., *Eyewitnesses to Massacre*, p. 257; Zhang, ed., *Eyewitnesses to Massacre*, p. 296.
25. Rabe, *Good Man of Nanking*, p. 61.
26. Higashinakano, *"Nankin gyakusatsu" no tettei kenshô*, p. 185; Yamamoto, *Nanking*, p. 99.
27. Smythe, in Zhang, ed., *Eyewitnesses to Massacre*, p. 267–68; Fitch, *My Eighty Years in China*, p. 113; Hsü, ed., *War Conduct of the Japanese*, p. 171.
28. Rabe, *Good Man of Nanking*, pp. 48–56.

29. Ibid., p. 58.
30. Ibid., pp. 60–62.
31. See Wilson letters, in Brook ed., *Documents on the Rape of Nanking*, pp. 207–10.
32. Rabe, "Hitoraa e no Jôshinsho," p. 302; Rabe, *Good Man of Nanking*, p. 59; Menken, *Chicago Daily Tribune*, 17 December 1937, p. 4; Timperley ed., *What War Means*, p. 206, Hsü, ed., *Documents of the Nanking Safety Zone*, p. 1.
33. Timperley, *What War Means*, p. 223; Hsü, ed., *Documents of the Nanking Safety Zone*, pp. 12–18; Rabe, *Good Man of Nanking*, p. 271.
34. On the situation with rice, see Rabe, *Good Man of Nanking*, pp. 42–53. He also noted, "about 100,000 sacks" were in Nanking, "more than half" of which were stored outside the city walls. See "Hitoraa e no jôshinsho," pp. 302–3. Mayor Ma wrote two letters confirming the promise. Timperley, ed., *What War Means*, pp. 242–43; Hsü, ed., *Documents of the Nanking Safety Zone*, p. 56. Also see Smalley, ed., *American Missionary Eyewitnesses to the Nanking Massacre*, p. 11; Zhang, ed., *Eyewitnesses to Massacre*, p. 413, which says that "owing to difficulties in transportation, only 9,067 bags were finally brought."
35. Timperley, ed., *What War Means*, p. 242; Hsü, ed., *Documents of the Nanking Safety Zone*, p. 57.
36. Smythe, in Zhang, ed., *Eyewitnesses to Massacre*, p. 279; Timperley, ed., *What War Means*, p. 243; Hsü, ed., *Documents of the Nanking Safety Zone*, p. 57.
37. Timperley, ed., *What War Means*, pp. 264–65; Hsü, ed., *Documents of the Nanking Safety Zone*, pp. 107–8. Although promised 30,000 bags, it appears that the IC only had written proof of promises of 20,000, which explains why the figure of 20,000 was sometimes used in official documents.
38. Rabe, "Hitoraa e no jôshinsho," p. 303; Rabe, *Good Man of Nanking*, pp. 29, 32, 34, and 41.
39. Timperley, ed., *What War Means*, p. 236 and p. 22.
40. Rabe, *Good Man of Nanking*, pp. 98, 113, and 131; Timperley ed., *What War Means*, pp. 62 and 70; Smythe in Smalley ed., *American Missionary Eyewitnesses to the Nanking Massacre*, p. 111 [3]; Zhang, ed., *Eyewitnesses to Massacre*, p. 302.
41. Timperley, ed., *What War Means*, p. 243.
42. Smalley, ed., *American Missionary Eyewitnesses to the Nanking Massacre*, p. 111 [3]; Zhang, ed., *Eyewitnesses to Massacre*, p. 302; Fitch and Rabe, in Timperley ed., *What War Means*, pp. 259 and 270–71; Askew, "Nanjing Incident."
43. Timperley, ed., *What War Means*, pp. 251–52 and p. 260; Hsü, ed., *Documents of the Nanking Safety Zone*, pp. 81–82 and p. 91.
44. Hsü, ed., *Documents of the Nanking Safety Zone*, pp. 90–93.
45. Timperley ed., *What War Means*, pp. 251–52 and 255–59; Hsü, ed., *Documents of the Nanking Safety Zone*, pp. 81–82; Rabe, *Good Man of Nanking*, pp. 136, 194–95, and 198.
46. Menken, *Chicago Daily Tribune*, 17 December 1937.
47. Rabe, "Hitoraa e no jôshinsho," p. 305; Rabe, *Good Man of Nanking*, pp. 31, 32. Forster, in Zhang ed., *Eyewitnesses to Massacre*, pp. 148–50 and 116–18.
48. On 21 December, Wilson stated that he had a nursing staff of 20 or so, of whom only 4 had any training; see Brook, ed., *Documents on the Rape of Nanking*, pp. 207, 212, and 222. McCallum mentioned a hospital staff of 50, but this seems highly unlikely given the number of patients; Zhang, ed., *Eyewitnesses to Massacre*, p. 241. On 9 December, Rabe wrote: "there are no doctors, no nurses, no medics left [except at] Kulou Hospital with its couple of brave American doctors"; Rabe, *Good Man of Nanking*, p. 57; Rabe, "Hitoraa e no jôshinsho," p. 305. For an account by a Chinese doctor, see Nan-chng ta-tu-sha shih-liao pian-chi wei-yuan-hui and Nan-ching tu-shu-kuan eds., *Chin-Hua Jih-chün Nan-ching ta-tu-sha shih-liao*, pp. 60–100. According to this account, there were originally 8 military hospitals but, as the staff fled and as patients were shipped out, these were consolidated into two hospitals in the Ministry of Foreign Affairs and in the Ministry of War on 12 December.
49. Durdin, *New York Times*, 27 November 1937.

50. Timperley, ed., *What War Means*, p. 208; Hsü, ed., *Documents of the Nanking Safety Zone*, p. 3. Magee appears to have started to move patients from the morning of 13 December. See his diary, cited in Kasahara, *Nankin nanminku no hyakunichi*, p. 148.

51. Rabe, *Good Man of Nanking*, p. 68 and p. 143; Rabe, "Hitoraa e no jôshinsho," p. 305; Magee, in Zhang, ed., *Eyewitnesses to Massacre*, p. 170; Hsü, ed., *Documents of the Nanking Safety Zone*, pp. 94–95.

52. Rabe, *Good Man of Nanking*, p. 148; Rabe, "Hitoraa e no jôshinsho," p. 305. Magee, in Zhang, ed., *Eyewitnesses to Massacre*, p. 189.

53. Hsü, ed., *Documents of the Nanking Safety Zone*, p. 96; Kasahara, *Nankin nanminku no hyakunichi*, p. 308.

54. On Wilson's activities, see Brook ed., *Documents on the Rape on Nanking*, pp. 212–13, 218, 228–29, and 235–36. The amputation was "a leg I had been trying to save for several weeks." This seems to contradict Fitch, who wrote on Christmas Day that "Wilson reports that of the 240 cases [of injuries due to bayonets] in the hospital three-quarters are due to Japanese violence since the occupation." See Fitch, in Timperley, *What War Means*, pp. 43–44; and Hsü, ed., *War Conduct of the Japanese*, p. 172. There is no evidence that there were ever as many as 240 patients in the hospital at any one time, but there may have been 240 in total from 13 to 25 December. The 175 on 28 December included "about 20" of Dr. Trimmer's. Also, see Rabe, *Good Man of Nanking*, p. 69; Timperley, ed., *What War Means*, p. 234; and Hsü, ed., *Documents of the Nanking Safety Zone*, p. 26.

55. Hsü, ed., *Documents of the Nanking Safety Zone*, p. 96; Wilson, in Brook, ed., *Documents on the Rape of Nanking*, p. 250.

56. McCallum, in Smalley ed., *American Missionary Eyewitnesses to the Nanking Massacre*, p. 34; Zhang, ed., *Eyewitnesses to Massacre*, pp. 229–30. Rabe had 300 women in his garden where there were 2 births; Rabe, *Good Man of Nanking*, pp. 317–18.

57. On the order to evacuate and housing problem, see Rabe, *Good Man of Nanking*, p. 45; Rabe, "Hitoraa e no jôshinsho," p. 300; *Amerika kankei shiryô shû*, pp. 131–32; and Kasahara, *Nankin nanminku no hyakunichi*, pp. 76–77. Compare with Rabe's diary entry for 7 December, *Good Man of Nanking*, p. 53. For a list of all public buildings used to house refugees, see Timperley, ed., *What War Means*, pp. 229–30; and Hsü, ed., *Documents of the Nanking Safety Zone*, pp. 19, 25, 45, and 96–97. As early as 18 December, the IC noted that these "buildings were originally listed to accommodate 35,000 people; now … this has increased to 50,000." Letter to Japanese embassy, in Timperley, ed., *What War Means*, pp. 224–29. By 21 December, this had increased to 68,000, and a month later was still 60,000. See Timperley, ed., *What War Means*, p. 240 (which mistakenly gives 77,000 instead of 68,000). Smalley, ed., *American Missionary Eyewitnesses to the Nanking Massacre*, pp. 11 and 311 [3]; and Zhang ed., *Eyewitnesses to Massacre*, pp. 302 and 414.

58. Rabe, "Hitoraa e no jôshinsho," p. 300.

59. I briefly discussed the issue of looting by Westerners, the existence of armed Chinese, and the possibility of a resistance movement in Askew, "Nanking 1937–38."

60. Rabe, *Good Man of Nanking*, pp. 67, 75, 79, 83–87, 98, and 149; Smythe, in Zhang ed., *Eyewitnesses to Massacre*, pp. 268 and 273.

61. Gao Xingzu et al., "Riben giguozhuyi zai Nanjing datusha." This was smuggled out of China and translated by Robert Gray, www.cnd.org/njmassacre/njm-tran. Also Eykholt, "Aggression, Victimization, and Chinese Historiography of the Nanking Massacre," p. 25.

62. Chang, *Rape of Nanking*, p. 139.

63. Rabe, *Good Man of Nanking*, pp. 134, 166–67, and 174.

64. Zhang, ed., *Eyewitnesses to Massacre*, p. 265.

65. Rabe, *Good Man of Nanking*, pp. 97, 168–69 and 68–69.

66. Timperley, *What War Means*, p. 211 and p. 227; Hsü, ed., *Documents of the Nanking Safety Zone*, pp. 4–5 and 20.

67. Chiang, "Hsian-ching san-yueh-chi."
68. Zhang, ed., *Eyewitnesses to Massacre,* p. 101.
69. Fitch, in Timperley, ed., *What War Means,* pp. 42, 44; Hsü, ed., *War Conduct of the Japanese,* p. 171; Rabe, *Good Man of Nanking,* p. 86; Brook, chapter 9 in this volume; and Hsü, ed., *Documents of the Nanking Safety Zone,* case no. 70.
70. Rabe, *Good Man of Nanking,* p. 105. In a letter to Allison dated 10 January 1938, Smythe noted that, on 31 December and 1 January, "we were confidentially informed that the Japanese Consul had informed the group organising the Tze Chih Wei Yuan Hwei [the SGC] that they could have the supplies and money that the International Committee had." Hsü, ed., *Documents of the Nanking Safety Zone,* p. 74.
71. Rabe, *Good Man of Nanking,* pp. 108–14.
72. Matsui Diary, in *Nankin senshi shiryô shû,* vol. 2, p. 169.
73. Timperley, ed., *What War Means,* p. 246; Hsü, ed., *Documents of the Nanking Safety Zone,* p. 66.
74. Timperley, ed., *What War Means,* p. 247; Hsü, ed., *Documents of the Nanking Safety Zone,* pp. 66–67.
75. Hsü, ed., *Documents of the Nanking Safety Zone,* pp. 73–75.
76. Rabe, *Good Man of Nanking,* pp. 118–124; Rabe, "Hitoraa e no jôshinsho," p. 319.
77. Timperley, ed., *What War Means,* pp. 253 and 258; Hsü, ed., *Documents of the Nanking Safety Zone,* p. 83 and p. 86; Bates, in Zhang ed., *Eyewitnesses to Massacre,* pp. 28–29.
78. Rabe, *Good Man of Nanking,* p. 113; Wilson, in Brook, ed., *Documents on the Rape of Nanking,* pp. 236–37. Rabe noted on 9 January that Dr. Rosen, Hürter, and Scharffenberg had arrived, together with two members of the British embassy, Consul Prideaux-Brune and Colonel Lovat-Fraser; and, a Commander Walser was also present by 15 January. See Rabe, *Good Man of Nanking,* pp. 118 and 121. Fitch wrote that three representatives of the American embassy arrived on 6 January, followed by three from both the British and German embassies on 9 January; Timperley ed., *What War Means,* p. 49; Hsü, ed., *War Conduct of the Japanese,* p. 178. Finally, see Wilson, in Brook, ed., *Documents of the Rape of Nanking,* p. 241.
79. Forster, in Smalley ed., *American Missionary Eyewitnesses to the Nanjing Massacre,* pp. 46–49; Zhang, ed., *Eyewitnesses to Massacre,* p. 132; Rabe, *Good Man of Nanking,* pp. 192, 160, and 162.
80. Bates, in *Amerika kankei shiryô shû,* pp. 329–30; Zhang ed., *Eyewitnesses to Massacre,* pp. 382, 139, 143, 28, and 146.
81. Rabe, *Good Man of Nanking,* p. 200.

11

WARTIME ACCOUNTS OF THE NANKING ATROCITY*

Takashi Yoshida

Introduction

Present-day Japanese who deny the Nanking Atrocity of 1937–38 use a number of stratagems to claim that it is a postwar fabrication. One of these is to allege that the government of the Republic of China, the Kuomintang (KMT) regime, did not protest Japanese actions at Nanking to the League of Nations during the Asia-Pacific War of 1931–45. Furthermore, these present-day deniers claim, the Western media in 1937–38 rarely mentioned Japanese misdeeds at Nanking. Finally, the deniers contend that no one in Japan ever heard about these alleged atrocities until the postwar Tokyo War Crimes Trials, formally known as the International Military Tribunal for the Far East (IMTFE), where the victorious prosecutors had an ax to grind. In sum, the argument goes, there is no documented proof of a Nanking Atrocity that dates from the wartime era when it reputedly took place; therefore, the event never really occurred. This stratagem has been central to the claims of many deniers. Some of the more prominent include the late Tanaka Masaaki, a popular critic; Watanabe Shôichi, an emeritus professor at Sophia University; Fujioka Nobukatsu, an emeritus professor at the University of Tokyo; and Higashinakano Osamichi (Shûdô), a professor at Asia University.

Fujioka, for example, claims that Western observers on the scene listed only 47 Chinese deaths, a figure well within reason considering other wartime military occupations in modern world history; this wartime figure, he says, is nowhere near the "fabricated" Chinese claim of 300,000-plus victims or the

* For more detailed analysis of the history and memory of the atrocities in Nanking, see my *The Making of the "Rape of Nanking": History and Memory in Japan, China, and the United States* (New York: Oxford University Press, 2006).

"fabricated" IMTFE claim of 200,000 victims, both of which emerged after the war ended. Tanaka and Watanabe hold that Westerners in Nanking at the time reported only forty-nine civilian deaths at Japanese hands, some of which were legitimate executions. To give an example, they and Fujioka refuse to acknowledge as "victims" some 200 Chinese whom the Westerners, on one occasion, reported as have been taken away and gone "missing." Higashinakano asserts that the killing of Chinese stragglers and surrendered soldiers—which the Westerners indeed protested—did not violate international law because these men were combatants who had forfeited their right to treatment as bona fide nonbelligerents or as prisoners of war (POWs). Thus, present-day Japanese deniers argue, claims of a "Rape," a "Great Massacre," or an "Atrocity" at Nanking in 1937–38 actually date from *postwar* IMTFE proceedings—where post-facto evidence was concocted to obtain preordained guilty verdicts and to divert attention from Allied war crimes such as Hiroshima and Nagasaki. In other words, the deniers rhetorically question: If this alleged mega-massacre in the hundreds of thousands actually took place, why did Chinese, Westerners, and Japanese *at that time* fail to document it?[1]

Contrary to these denial claims, however, the KMT regime did in fact broach the issue of Japanese war crimes—including those at Nanking—at the League of Nations during the Asia-Pacific War. Also, the mass media in China, Britain, and the United States did report Japanese war crimes in the Nanking region at the time or shortly thereafter. Thus, as I will demonstrate, the Nanking Atrocity was a live issue long before the IMTFE. Most deniers make two fallacious assumptions in this regard: that the Atrocity produced the same consciousness and emotional response in everyone around the world, and that these responses remained the same over time. As a result, they fail to understand why Chinese protests against "atrocities" in 1937–38 placed less emphasis on Nanking than would otherwise have been the case; and, what is more, they dismiss wartime Western anti-Japanese propaganda as simply racist in nature, without considering its observed basis in war crimes at places such as Nanking. In this chapter, then, I examine wartime Chinese, American, and Japanese interpretations of Nanking in the political and temporal context of their day with a view to stressing their differences from each other and from current-day perspectives. Such a disclosure, I contend, will debunk some of the more popularly disseminated contemporary Japanese denial claims.

Chinese Accounts

In the late autumn of 1937, as the imperial Japanese army approached Nanking, regional Chinese newspapers such as the *Hankow Ta-kung-pao* reported the situation in detail. On 24 November, for example, this newspaper informed readers of the plan by resident Westerners to establish a neutral international safety zone in Nanking, the Nanking Safety Zone, or NSZ. On 7 December the Chinese press reported the imposed curfew in the city and food shortages in the NSZ. On 8 December, the press highlighted the facts that invading Japanese troops were approaching the city from three directions, that Chinese forces were thwarting the attack, and that they had killed dozens of Japanese soldiers. On 9 December, a Chinese correspondent revealed that some 30,000 civilians fled into the NSZ in a few hours on the previous morning, and that Japanese invaders had been attacking the city continuously for three days.[2]

The tone of these Chinese reports was little different from wartime patriotic news accounts in other nations. These reports uncritically supported China's military and political leaders, while cheering the deaths of Japanese troops and denouncing Japanese atrocities. On 17 December, the first reports of random Japanese killings and arson began to appear. Then, on the twenty-fifth, the press confirmed the previous report of Japanese atrocities in Nanking, including rape and looting; and, it estimated that 50,000 male refugees under forty years of age had been slaughtered after the city had fallen. This Chinese news writer stressed that Japanese atrocities in Nanking had produced outrage not only in China, but also abroad; and he also pointed out the hypocrisy of the Japanese government, which bore guilt for killing of tens of thousands of innocent Chinese civilians while claiming to fight to establish eternal peace in East Asia.[3]

Similarly, on 24 December the *China Press,* an English-language newspaper published at Shanghai, first reported Japanese outrages in Nanking. It had learned of these from articles in the *New York Times* and the *Shanghai Evening Post,* and stressed the collapse of discipline among Japanese troops, whose "looting, raping and other unprintable atrocities" surpassed in savagery those committed by Chinese bandits.[4] These depredations in Nanking reinforced in the mind of this *China Press* writer images of Japanese lawlessness and barbarism that stemmed from earlier news reports of Japanese planes having bombed the USS *Panay* and HMS *Ladybird* and of having conducted indiscriminate air attacks on open cities such as Canton. Contemporaneous Chinese reports of Japanese depredations at Nanking thus reaffirmed and exacerbated earlier impressions of Japanese rapacity.

As the historian Inoue Hisashi shows, both KMT and Chinese Communist Party (CCP) officials knew of atrocities in Nanking. On 10 March 1938, the KMT regime broadcast in Japanese a report entitled, "Barbaric Acts by the Imperial Army" that more or less repeated the *Hankow Ta-kung-pao* reports just cited. Chiang Kai-shek denounced Japanese atrocities in his diary in July 1938 and also in a "Declaration to the Japanese People" published in the same month. Although Chiang did not specifically mention the proper noun "Nanking" in that "Declaration," there is little doubt about the area to which was he referring, since no huge-scale atrocities of the type he mentions had yet been reported elsewhere in China. One of the earliest Chinese citations of the

Nanking Atrocity appeared in a CCP weekly published at Hankow, the *Ch'ün-chung*, dated 1 January 1938. It reported, though in a highly garbled fashion, the 100-man killing contest mentioned in the following section, and also discussed by Bob Tadashi Wakabayashi in chapter 6. On 14 December 1938—the first anniversary of Nanking's capitulation—the CCP organ, *Central China News*, declared that the imperial army had killed "200,000 compatriots."[5]

Furthermore, the KMT government denounced Japan's actions at Nanking before members of the League of Nations. On 2 February 1938, at the League Council's sixth meeting of its 100th session in Geneva—the first session after Nanking fell—Wellington Koo, or Koo Wei-jun, first delegate of the Republic of China, condemned Japan's "cruel and barbarous conduct" in Nanking and elsewhere. Koo decried Japan's indiscriminate bombings of open cities. His information about Nanking came from the *New York Times* by way of the *Times* of London, and he quoted from those reports to accuse the Japanese army of "wholesale looting, violation of women, murder of civilians, eviction of Chinese from their homes, mass executions of war prisoners, and the impressing of able-bodied men." Koo also referred to a separate article in the *Daily Telegraph and Morning Post* to estimate 20,000 Chinese civilian deaths and assaults on thousands of women. Denouncing Japanese lawlessness, he urged the council to take effective measures to halt Japanese aggression and to provide military and economic aid for China. In this speech, Koo stressed that Japan was a threat not only to China, but also to the West. He reminded delegates that Japan had sunk the *Panay*, damaged several other American and British ships, and assaulted the US Embassy in Nanking. He cited the 1929 "Tanaka Memorial" to disclose Japan's aim to conquer China, subjugate Asia, and finally dominate the world. Koo in 1938 thought the "Memorial" to be authentic because Japan's recent acts had roughly followed the aim mentioned therein.[6] Despite Koo's strong appeal, the council adopted a resolution that expressed only moral support and recommended that member states refrain from taking actions that might weaken China's resistance; it adopted no concrete, vigorous measures of the kind that Chinese delegates sought.

On 10 May 1938, at the one hundred-first session of the council, Koo delivered another speech requesting effective measures to deter Japanese aggression. He stressed that Chinese forces had recently prevailed at Taierchwang after desperate fighting and that the tide of the battle was now turning in China's favor. Yet he also emphasized that the Japanese invaders had become more cruel and barbarous in their desperation.

> The wanton slaughter of noncombatants by the indiscriminate bombing of undefended towns and nonmilitary centers has been continuing unabated. The unprecedented violence to women and ruthlessness to children and the deliberate massacre of hundreds of adult males amongst the civilian population, including those removed from refugee camps under false pretenses, form the subject of many reports by impartial foreign eyewitnesses. The cruel and barbarous conduct of Japanese troops towards

the Chinese people in the occupied areas not only shows the want of regard on the part of the Japanese army for the accepted rules of warfare but also betrays a disgraceful lack of discipline in its rank and file.[7]

Above all, Koo disclosed Japan's use of poison gas in Shantung, stressing Japan's contempt for international law. He demanded that the council carefully consider effective actions to deal with the Far Eastern situation.[8] But the council again adopted no measures except to express moral support for China.

On 16 September 1938, in the nineteenth session of the League's assembly, Koo once more appealed to it about the situation in China and urged it to take effective, concrete steps against Japan. He accused Japanese forces of murdering more than 1 million civilians over the past year, destroying priceless cultural and historical sites, and inflicting untold misery on ordinary people. He expressly referred to the Japanese "reign of terror" in Nanking and stressed that many other cities, towns, and villages faced similar violence and lawlessness. The KMT government called Japan's use of poison gas and air raids "the most inhuman" of all types of warfare waged against China. Yet in his address, Koo insisted that poison gas warfare was more reprehensible than indiscriminate aerial bombings because of its nature and effects. He accused Japan of violating the Hague conventions of 1899 and 1907, which prohibited the use of chemical weapons, and with transgressing the principles of humanity and civilization. Koo lamented the fact that the League had taken no effective measures against Japan such as embargoes on war matériel and financial credits. Above all, he reiterated that the principles of law and order, along with the peace and security of the international community, were at stake in the ongoing Sino-Japanese conflict.[9]

It was essential for Chinese government leaders not only to score moral points, but also to secure practical aid from a reluctant League. This is why they sent a cable prior to the assembly meeting that instructed Koo to take pains highlighting Japan's inhumane assault. But they did so in the context of that day. Thus, Chiang Kai-shek demanded that Koo tender a communiqué to the League Secretariat for circulation among member states in order to publicize as widely as possible Japan's use of poison gas. This telegram arrived on 3 September 1938 and conveys a feel for the KMT government's position:

> Nation wide meetings being organized support League demand [for] effective measures. Generalissimo desires [that] you strongly emphasize in speeches forthcoming Assembly and Council Japan's inhuman methods warfare particularly [the] frequent use [of] poison gas and demand effective measures.
>
> Same.
>
> Cabling you seperately [*sic*] authorative [*sic*] detailed account of Japanese gas attacks please communicate same immediately [to the] League Secretariat for circulation among member states [to] give [this] matter widest possible publicity. Compare para-

graph dealing with gas attacks cabled August 30th with this account and revise paragraph accordingly. When speaking before an assembly on [the] subject of gas, call members' attention to the detailed seperate [*sic*] account. As regarding [the] general statement of facts cabled 30th[,] it is intended as basic material for your speech. WCP[10]

The KMT regime not only instructed Koo to appeal to the League on this point; it also sent letters to the secretary-general that detailed Japan's use of poison gas and other atrocities. For example, Hoo Chi-tsai, director of the permanent office of the Chinese delegation to the League of Nations, sent a letter dated 5 August 1938 that included a report by H. Talbot, a British surgeon at Nanchang General Hospital. Talbot examined nineteen patients on 10 and 11 July 1938, and found that all had been poisoned by a type of mustard or chlorine gas. In another letter dated 5 September 1938, Hoo requested that the secretary-general circulate this detailed information on Japan's poison gas warfare against Chinese troops.[11]

On 19 September 1938, three days after his address to the Assembly, Koo appealed to the council at the one hundred-second session. He urged the League to recommend that member states commence embargoes of war-related materiel against Japan and that they send financial and material aid to China.[12] At this meeting, he forwarded "Some Recent Data Concerning Japan's Invasion of China and Her Conduct of Warfare" to the secretary-general. This document summarized speeches that he had delivered before the assembly on the sixteenth and on other occasions. Atrocities cited therein included the outrage at Nanking, Japan's aerial warfare, and Japanese gas attacks. As of September 1938, Chinese leaders described Nanking much as the Nanking International Relief Committee had. This humanitarian organization established by Americans and Europeans asserted that:

It was the deliberate act of violence by Japanese soldiers which was the direct cause of the killing of 74% out of 3,250, and the wounding of 98% out of 3,100 injured, under known circumstances. The total number of civilians killed, including those cases not yet verified, was estimated at 20,000; 4,200 Chinese were forcibly taken away under military arrest, most of whom are believed to have been killed. The number of the people thus affected by Japanese acts of massacre and violence represents one person in every twenty-three or one in every five families. In Nanking, 4,400 women had their husbands either killed, or wounded, or carried off, while 3,250 fathers shared a similar fate regarding their children. Thousands of women and girls aged between 14 and 50 were outraged. As regards material losses, 88% of the buildings in that city suffered damage or destruction at the hands of Japanese soldiers ... while only 2% suffered from military operations.[13]

Despite such efforts by the Chinese delegation, the League adopted no confrontational measures toward Japan which, in any case, was no longer a member, having bolted in March 1933 after being censured for its actions in "Manchuria" or, more properly, Northeast China. At this point, the League merely proposed inviting Japan to discuss the ongoing hostilities with China.[14] Only after Japan's attack on Pearl Harbor did the Republic of China receive significant assistance from Western states, apart from the Soviet Union. Meanwhile, the KMT government continued to appeal to the League about Japan's atrocities in China, but it stressed poison gas warfare rather than actions at Nanking.

However, this fact does not mean that Chinese leaders regarded Nanking as insignificant, nor does it mean that the Atrocity did not take place. Instead, China's KMT regime had compelling political and tactical reasons for placing greater emphasis on other types of Japanese atrocities. Western peoples were especially sensitive to poison gas perhaps because of their painful experiences in the Great War of 1914–18—only two decades before. Thus, Chinese leaders believed that the issue of Japanese chemical warfare, when exploited as a propaganda tool, would shock the conscience of leading member nations in the League. Moreover, the line between acts of war against combatants and unlawful acts of violence against civilians was not always clear, whereas the definition of illegal chemical warfare was spelled out in the Hague convention. Hence Japan's violations on this score were easier to establish and harder to excuse. Above all, the Nanking Atrocity was only one of many similar incidents across wartime China. Only later, under the postwar People's Republic, did Nanking achieve unique status *the* event that symbolized Japanese war crimes in China par excellence.

Accounts of Westerners in Nanking

KMT leaders were concerned with China overall rather than Nanking alone. In contrast are Western humanitarians such as members of the Nanking International Relief Committee—the successor to the International Committee (IC) for the Nanking Safety Zone (NSZ). These Westerners who remained in Nanking even after KMT government leaders fled, were most concerned with protecting the lives and restoring the livelihoods of the citizenry. Devastation in the Nanking area continued for weeks after the city fell on 13 December. The Relief Committee's primary goal was to appeal to the world about the crisis there in order to get financial aid. For this reason, its members wrote or backed the publication of several books and pamphlets for dissemination abroad. These included Lewis Smythe's *War Damage in the Nanking Area December, 1937 to March, 1938;* Miner S. Bates's *Crop Investigation in the Nanking Area and Sundry Economic Data,* and his *The Nanking Population: Employment, Earnings, and Expenditures.*

Smythe, an American professor of sociology at Nanking University, analyzed how the battles for Nanking city had affected people in the surrounding region. Bates, an American professor of history at the same university, wrote the foreword to Smythe's book, wherein he underscored the committee's political stance: "The Nanking International Relief Committee here makes known the results of its inquiries primarily for the information of those concerned with the practice and the support of relief work in this and other areas; secondarily, for the wider public which is or should be concerned with the ravages of warfare among civilians, in whatever country. Our own position is humanitarian, without regard to the nationality of war victims."[15]

Bates emphasized that losses to life and property from actual combat accounted for but 1 or two percent of the total devastation; if Chinese and Japanese troops had given proper consideration to the welfare of civilians, the rest of the damage could have been avoided. Chinese in the region first experienced serious harm at the hands of their own defenders, he wrote; KMT armies sacrificed the property of local citizens in the name of military necessity through scorched earth tactics and the like. Later on, however, destruction assumed an even greater scale under Japanese occupation.[16] After investigating both the walled city of Nanking and most of its five neighboring counties, Smythe estimated that Japanese troops had killed at least 12,000 civilians (excluding disarmed soldiers) in the city, and that 30,950 civilians had perished in outlying areas between December 1937 and March 1938.[17]

Bates emphasized different dimensions of the situation. His *Crop Investigation in the Nanking Area and Sundry Economic Data,* likewise published in 1938, describes in detail agricultural conditions in and around Nanking and provides information about the problems of food, fuel, and clothing. He did his field research in July 1938 and his findings told a grim story. War and floods had damaged crops severely, and the 1938 harvest was expected to be far below average. Despite great need, the cotton industry and trade were scant. Nearly half of the Nanking population lived in destitution, and employment was hard to find. Although Chinese farmers, workers, and merchants impressed Bates with their spirit and resourcefulness in dealing with difficulties, he concluded that "the life of the community [is] precariously maintained on a distressingly low level."[18]

In *The Nanking Population,* Bates analyzed working conditions in the walled city based on investigations conducted between November 1938 and January 1939. He found that the city had recovered and was able to achieve low levels of social and economic vitality, but that current economic policies along with military and political conditions precluded further improvement. Although the population was increasing, most of this increase derived from refugees fleeing to Nanking from the countryside. Males between the ages of fifteen and forty-nine comprised only twenty-two percent of the entire population. Of

255

those in that category before the war, less than a third remained. Although the employment rate had significantly improved since the early occupation, only twenty-seven percent of the total population had jobs, many in crude labor and meager peddling. Over half of the population in the city reported being partly or wholly unable to live on their current earnings.[19]

In addition to publishing these surveys, Westerners in the city were the prime force behind establishing the Nanking Safety Zone (NSZ) in November 1937. Between December 1937 and May 1938, they estimated that about 250,000 refugees entered this NSZ for shelter, food, and fuel.[20] Western humanitarians who remained in Nanking occasionally filed protests with the Japanese authorities in order to protect and improve the livelihoods of refugees in the NSZ.[21] These humanitarians also sent many diary-like letters to friends abroad and in other parts of China that highlighted Japanese outrages in Nanking. To give one example, the Chinese-born George Fitch, who served as a director of the NSZ, began a letter as follows:

X'mas Eve, 1937.

What I am about to relate is anything but a pleasant story; in fact, it is so very unpleasant that I cannot recommend anyone without a strong stomach to read it. For it is a story of such crime and horror as to be almost unbelievable, the story of the depredations of a horde of degraded criminals of incredible bestiality, who have been, and now are, working their will, unrestrained, on a peaceful, kindly, law-abiding people. Yet it is a story which I feel must be told, even if it is seen by only a few. I cannot rest until I have told it, and perhaps fortunately, I am one of a very few who are in a position to tell it. It is not complete,—only a small part of the whole; and God alone knows when it will be finished. I pray it may be soon—but I am afraid it is going to go on for many months to come, not just here but in other parts of China. I believe it has no parallel in modern history.[22]

Fitch's friends included Wellington Koo and Harold J. Timperley, an Australian correspondent for the *Manchester Guardian* in Shanghai. Timperley received the letter and included it in his exposé, *What War Means*, though he concealed Fitch's identity. This book was published in countries such as Britain, the United States, China, France, and even Japan—although imperial government censorship prevented ordinary Japanese from reading it.[23] Fitch and the other humanitarians witnessing Japanese atrocities at Nanking in 1937–38 could not prophesize about the levels of mass violence and murder that would be inflicted on civilian populations later on in the war—including the Holocaust of European Jewry and the nuclear attacks on Japanese cities. Therefore, they could not conceive of explicitly likening Nanking to such later atrocities. Nevertheless, these Western humanitarians asserted that Japanese violence in Nanking had "no parallel in modern history." To Western observers on the scene such as Dr. Robert Wilson, a surgeon at the University Hospital, Japanese brutality was "almost beyond belief."[24]

Accounts in the United States

The outrage in Nanking did not achieve symbolic status in either Japan or China during the war. In Japan, most people wholeheartedly supported the war effort and celebrated the capture of Nanking; and in China, Nanking was but one of many Japanese atrocities. By contrast, however, in the United States, and especially after Pearl Harbor, the Nanking Atrocity became a symbol of Japanese barbarism and ethnically encoded cruelty. Influential daily newspapers such as the *New York Times* and *Chicago Daily News* reported imperial army brutality in Nanking during and immediately after the event took place. On 18 December 1937, the *New York Times* printed an article by Tilman Durdin, who was in Nanking when it fell. He told of Japanese atrocities such as mass executions of Chinese men and citywide looting.[25] Durdin's second report in the *Times* appeared on 9 January 1938; it detailed day-by-day observations between 6 and 13 December. Durdin estimated that at least 33,000 Chinese died during this eight-day interlude and stressed that Japanese brutality was comparable only to "vandalism in [the] Dark Ages in Europe or the medieval Asiatic conquerors."[26]

As just noted, Timperley published *What War Means* in Britain in 1938, but this same book came out that year in the United States under the title *The Japanese Terror in China*. In its foreword, Timperley stressed that his goal was not "to stir up animosity against the Japanese," but instead "to give the world as accurately as possible the facts about the Japanese Army's treatment of the Chinese civilian population in the 1937–8 hostilities." Timperley included anonymous letters written by eyewitnesses to the Japanese atrocities, thus providing readers with vivid images of the horrors in Nanking and other areas. Moreover, he included an estimate by one foreign eyewitness that the war caused at least 300,000 military casualties plus another 300,000 civilian casualties in central China. In the book's conclusion, he urged American and British readers to give China arms or financial aid.[27]

In 1942, the year after Pearl Harbor, Timperley published *Japan: A World Problem* in the United States. Contrary to his earlier 1938 volume, which carefully avoided demonizing the entire Japanese people, this book explained Japanese aggression and atrocities through an alleged "national character." He stressed that deep-rooted psychological forces had driven the Japanese people as a whole to lust after world conquest: "History demonstrates that megalomaniacal ideas have been working in the blood of the Japanese, not merely for generations but for centuries, and that the minds of the Japanese people have been deliberately warped by their military masters. Obviously there can be no durable peace in the Far East, or for that matter in the world at large, until the power of the military oligarchy that now runs Japan has been finally broken."[28] Timperley did not acknowledge the conclusion that would seem to flow logically from these premises; namely, that there would be no peace in

Asia unless "the Japanese"—supposedly aggressive and brutal by their genetic nature—were totally liquidated.

Bradford Smith, an American who had taught at Tokyo Imperial University, presented similar views in his article, "Japan: Beauty and Beast." Smith too employed the notion of a "national character" to explain why family-loving, ordinary Japanese men could commit barbarous acts. To him, "the rape of Nanking, when 50,000 Japanese troops were let loose in the city and 42,000 innocent Chinese were murdered," was "one of the most barbarous mass-murders in history." Smith argued that Japanese soldiers acted as they did in Nanking owing to nine factors in their "racial background"; that is, their moral training limited to family and national loyalty, notions of divinity that set them apart from the rest of humanity, an inferiority psychosis, fear and hatred of individualism, disregard for the value of human life, unbridled sexuality, a background of head-hunting, a release from cramped social restrictions, and the lack of a religious literature based upon ethical and spiritual principles worthy of respect.[29]

James Young, an American journalist who also had lived in Japan, published *Our Enemy,* a twenty-five-cent paperback in 1942—long after Hitler's depredations against the Jews in Europe had become public knowledge. Young denounced Japan's "national character" as being inherently aggressive and barbarous. His book's cover shows an ominously slant-eyed, buck-toothed Japanese soldier wearing glasses and a Nazi-like uniform. In his right hand, a knife drips blood; in the other is a torn U.S. flag. Young claimed that: "In trickery, the breaking of promises, the violation of civilized principles, there is no limit. Japanese ways of thinking are not our ways of thinking, nor is Japanese honor our honor. Americans who have been in the Far East for any length of time have seen demonstrated, in Korea, Manchuria and China, the fact that the Japanese have studied and improved on all the brutalities which European conquerors of the past have employed. These Japanese know themselves qualified to duplicate all Nazi brutalities, exceed them, and add a whole satanic range of their own peculiar cruelties."[30] To Young, "the bloody, vicious record of Nanking" was "a crime so great, perhaps the greatest sack of a city in [the] world's history." His mistrust and hatred probably derived from a two-month period of imprisonment in Japan in 1940. To him, even U.S.-born Japanese-Americans were agents of imperial Japan preparing to aid Japanese troops when they landed on American shores.[31]

Works such as these published in the United States after Pearl Harbor stressed that the Japanese "national character" was unique and utterly different from that of Americans. In 1943, the editors of *Amerasia,* a left-liberal journal, expressed concern about the numerous books that popularized this monolithic negative image of the Japanese. In its April 1943 issue, for example, the editors carried a review article, "Is There Another Japan?" It examined Gustav Eckstein's *In Peace Japan Breeds War,* Jesse Steiner's *Behind the Japanese Mask,* and Alexander Pernikoff's *Bushido: The Anatomy of Terror.* Eckstein, a biographer of the humanitarian Japanese bacteriologist Noguchi Hideyo (1876–1928), held that the lack of ethnic minorities in Japan had produced a homogeneous culture wherein blind obedience and submission were instinctive and second nature to the Japanese. Steiner, a sociologist, also stressed a monolithic Japanese people who strongly hated the West and believed in their divine lineage from the Sun Goddess through the imperial line. Pernikoff, identified as a sensationalist by the journal editors, had written a "bloodcurdling story" about the Japanese treatment of White Russians in Manchuria. To the *Amerasia* editors, this stereotyping ignored the diversity of Japan. They urged readers to reject stereotypes that pronounced all Japanese as united by dreams of world conquest and pointed out that the imperial government had to employ police to silence democrats, socialists, and communists who opposed the war effort.[32]

In November 1943, *Amerasia* carried yet another review article that challenged this wave of anti-Japanese literature in the United States. This time, the editors reviewed three books, two of which attacked the Japanese character as being fixed genetically and psychologically. In one of these books, *Japan Fights for Asia* (1943), John Goette, a journalist and a former representative of the International News Service, emphasized that the "emperor, generals, junior officers, soldiers, civilian men, women, and children, and the Rising Sun flag are [a] unity." Similarly, Sydney Greenbie, lecturer and author, argued in his *Asia Unbound* (1943) that "It is not the generals, or even the military cliques, of Japan who are the true danger. It is the people. The people have been made literate—ninety-eight percent of them—but they have never used their heads. They simply do not know how to think. They are foggy. They are sentimental. They are hysterical and mystical." In contrast, Taro Yashima's *The New Sun* (1943) won the editors' applause by proving that racial and psychological theories were inaccurate. Yashima, a Japan-born leftist artist, wrote of his experiences in Japanese jails, where he met ethnic minorities as well as Japanese socialists and communists, all of whom the police imprisoned as being harmful to the empire. This review article urged readers not to ignore men like Yashima, whom the United States could use to build a new, peaceful Japan after the war ended.[33]

Amerasia was highly exceptional in being a high-brow, leftist publication. In general, the American media paid scant attention to Japanese like Yashima after Pearl Harbor. Instead, a monolithic image of the Japanese as bestial barbarians, who committed butchery in Nanking, became increasingly popular in the United States. That image justified not only America's war effort against imperial Japan and Japanese militarism, but also the mass murder of Japanese civilians by the fire bombing of major cities across the archipelago, ending with the atomic bombing of Hiroshima and Nagasaki. During the Pacific War (1941–45), the Nanking Atrocity was one objective piece of "evidence" that racially biased American authors used to "prove" their point.

Japanese Accounts

Japan's atrocities at Nanking and elsewhere did not appear in Japanese official histories or in the mass media during the Asia-Pacific War (1931–45). The imperial government justified its war effort in part by maintaining that the only atrocities in China were perpetrated by Chinese against Japanese nationals—often civilians, such as the one at Tungchou, noted below. Army and government censors banned all accounts that even hinted at the possibility that Japanese troops were conducting atrocities, including works of fiction such as Ishikawa Tatsuzô's *Ikite iru heitai* (Living soldiers).[34] Thus, unlike in the United States, where articles seemingly sympathetic to the Japanese enemy might appear in journals such as *Amerasia,* only government-approved accounts could legally be published or circulated in wartime Japanese society.

For example, as stressed in the state-prescribed sixth-grade history textbook of the time, Japan sent troops "to rectify mistaken Chinese ideas and to establish a permanent peace in the East."[35] Japanese newspapers and other government-authorized media played up Chinese brutalities, particularly after the Marco Polo Bridge Incident of 7 July 1937 and its aftermath, when imperial armed forces expanded hostilities to central China. On 4 August 1937, for example, the *Tokyo Asahi shinbun* detailed killing and looting by Chinese troops in Tungchou, near Peiping (as Peking was then called). It condemned Chinese "savagery" and expressed outrage at the murder of some 200 Japanese and Korean residents, including women, children, and infants.[36] Other major daily newspapers at home highlighted Chinese barbarism at Tungchou as part of concerted campaigns to stir up anti-Chinese sentiments among ordinary Japanese.[37]

As Japanese troops made their final advance on Nanking, newspapers enthusiastically predicted a dramatic conquest, whipping up nationalism to a fever pitch. The *Tokyo nichi nichi shinbun,* for example, reported a "killing contest" between two sublieutenants that reputedly took place on 30 November and on 4 and 6 December 1937. The correspondent proudly reported them competing to see who could first cut down 100 Chinese combatants.[38] On 8 December, the *Yomiuri shinbun* applauded the victorious imperial army and stressed that the capture of Nanking was imminent.[39] When Japanese troops surrounded the walled city, the press played up Japan's generosity and righteousness. To save the lives of Chinese soldiers as well as historical sites in Nanking, commander Matsui Iwane of the Central China Area Army (CCAA) urged his Chinese counterpart, T'ang Sheng-chih, to surrender, and waited a full day before launching his all-out attack. But, as the *Tokyo Asahi shinbun* put it, T'ang "rudely ignored Matsui's generous attitude of *bushidô* [the samurai ethos]" and forced the imperial army to attack the city, thereby causing needless death and destruction.[40]

In sum, official accounts and news reports cited no Japanese atrocities. The government censored all printed materials and radio programs in order to ban any accounts that might stir up antiwar sentiment among the Japanese people. Nevertheless, despite these highly restrictive circumstances, nonofficial, unauthorized accounts that disclosed Japanese atrocities—including those at Nanking—did circulate. One example is the essay, "Fassho kyôi no Nihon" (Japan under the Threat of Fascism) in *Kyokutô sensô nyûsu* (Far-Eastern War News), a Japanese newspaper printed in Seattle. This essay summarized a *New York Times* article about Nanking, thereby informing Japanese readers of the wholesale atrocities there.[41] Similarly, Japanese nationals such as Kaji Wataru, who left Japan for China and worked for the Chinese government, translated Timperley's *What War Means* into Japanese in order to describe the outrage that took place in Nanking.[42] Apparently, a surprising number of Japanese at home gained access to and read these smuggled documents, so the authorities aggressively suppressed these works whenever possible. Thus, the police confiscated three copies of "Fassho kyôi no Nihon" in February, ten copies in March, and three copies from April through June of 1938. As well, in February 1939 they confiscated eleven copies of the Japanese translation of *What War Means* from an American missionary living in Japan.[43]

However, as contemporary Nanking deniers claim, it is true that the Japanese public in general did not discover the vast pattern of atrocities that the imperial army perpetrated in Asia, including the one at Nanking, until the ITMFE convened after the war ended. Only then did the Japanese people as a whole realize that millions of lives had been destroyed both at home and abroad in the name of the emperor. But this wartime ignorance resulted from strict government censorship—not because the events did not take place or for a lack of documentary evidence.

Conclusion

During the Asia-Pacific War of 1931–45, ethnocentrism, nationalism, national interests, and demonization of the enemy heavily influenced American, Chinese, and Japanese views of atrocities in Nanking. In wartime China, the KMT government did not regard the outrage in Nanking as *the* symbol of Japanese wartime cruelty, as the postwar People's Republic has come to do. Instead, Chinese thought of Nanking as but one of innumerable Japanese atrocities in China at the time. Although Chinese delegates to the League of Nations did mention Nanking explicitly in protesting Japanese war crimes, they chose to emphasize Japan's use of chemical weapons and air raids on open cities because these types of atrocities, they reckoned, would more likely win world sympathy and aid. In wartime America, the "Rape of Nanking," as it was popularly called then, enjoyed wide circulation, first as a historically unprecedented atrocity prior to the Nazi Holocaust of European Jews, and later (after Pearl Harbor) as the negative icon of a monolithic "national character" exploited to demonize the Japanese people. In wartime Japan, government-authorized accounts of fighting at Nanking and in China as a whole never discussed mass murder, rape, and looting by imperial armed forces for fear that the truth would damage their image and call into question Japan's putative war aims of liberating Asians and creating a peaceful coprosperity sphere in the region. Nevertheless, some illicit documents pertaining to the Nanking Atrocity did slip through the network of state censorship and were available to a few Japanese readers. So, in sum, one of the main denial arguments fashionable among ethnocentric Japanese scholars today—that no documentary evidence of the Atrocity existed in China, the West, or Japan at the time or shortly thereafter—is patently false.

More disturbingly, however, the arguments put forth by contemporary Japanese deniers of the Nanking Atrocity are essentially the same as those expressed in wartime propaganda and government-authorized accounts. These deniers stress Japanese justice and Chinese injustice, and they value human lives differently based on ethnicity and nationality. The deniers also claim that they are "patriotic" whereas those Japanese who challenge them are traitorous leftists in league with Chinese leaders out to subvert Japan. Fujioka, Watanabe, and Higashinakano are former or current university professors. As teachers, they should remember that imperial Japan had many "patriots" like themselves, and that those patriots helped destroy millions of lives in Asia and the Pacific by supporting the imperial agenda. Is it not possible that the same national pride may lead to similar results again? It is to be hoped that educators such as Fujioka, Watanabe, and Higashinakano will never have to sing the elegiac song written in the early 1950s by another erstwhile academic patriot, a teacher named Takemoto Genji:

To My Students Who Died at War
Students who will never come back,
My hands are smeared with your blood.
I held one end of the rope that choked you to death.
Ah! And I was a teacher.
How can I excuse myself by claiming that "we were both deceived?"
How can I atone for my sin?
You will never be alive again.
I now wipe tears from my eyes, wash my blood-soaked hands, and promise you, "Never again!"[44]

Notes

1. Tanaka, *What Really Happened in Nanking,* pp. 76–78; Tanaka, *Nankin jiken no sôkatsu,* p. 174 and 114–21; Higashinakano, *"Nankin gyakusatsu" no tettei kenshô,* pp. 191–226, 340–42, and 362; Fujioka and Nishio, *Kokumin no yudan,* pp. 209–14 and 213; Watanabe, *Nihonshi kara mita Nihonjin: Shôwahen,* pp. 412–43.

2. In Nankin jiken chôsa kenkyûkai (Nankin ken), *Nankin jiken shiryôshû*, vol. 2, pp. 10–14.
3. Ibid., pp. 24–25.
4. "Collapse of Discipline of Japanese Forces in Nanking Is Revealed by N.Y. Times," *The China Press*, 24 December 1937, p. 1 and p. 8.
5. Inoue, "Sensô tôji Chûgoku de mo mondai ni sarete ita," pp. 60–71.
6. League of Nations, *Official Journal* 19:2 (February 1938), p. 122. Although some Japanese at the time may have dreamed of world conquest, the "Memorial" is now confirmed as a forged document. See, for instance, John Stephan, "Tanaka Memorial (1927), pp. 733–45.
7. League of Nations, *Official Journal,*19:5–6 (May–June 1938), p. 307.
8. Ibid.
9. League of Nations, *Official Journal,* Special Supplement, no. 183 (1938), pp. 52–55.
10. Wellington Koo Collection, Box 36, Rare Book and Manuscript Library, Columbia University.
11. League of Nations, *Official Journal,* 19:8–9 (August–September 1938), pp. 665–668.
12. Ibid., 19:11 (November 1938), p. 864.
13. Ibid., 19:12 (December 1938), p. 1133.
14. Ibid., 19:11 (November 1938), p. 865.
15. Smythe, *War Damage in the Nanking Area,* p. i.
16. *Ibid.,* pp. i–ii.
17. *Ibid.,* p. 8 note 1, 17, Table 25 (page number unknown).
18. Bates, *Crop Investigation in the Nanking Area and Sundry Economic Data,* p. 1.
19. Bates, *Nanking Population,* pp. 1 and 21–23. ·
20. The Nanking International Relief Committee, *Report of the Nanking International Relief Committee, November, 1937 to April 30, 1939,* pp. 413–15.
21. See, for example, Hsü, *Documents of the Nanking Safety Zone.*
22. Wellington Koo Collection, Box 25, Rare Book and Manuscript Library, Columbia University.
23. See *Japanese Terror in China*; *La Guerre Telle qu'elle Est: La Terreur Japonaise en Chine*; *Waiguoren muduzhongzhi Rijun baoxin*; and *Gaikokujin no mita Nihongun no bôkô.*
24. See Brook, *Documents on the Rape of Nanking,* p. 214.
25. Durdin, "U.S. Naval Display Reported Likely Unless Japan Guarantees Our Rights; Butchery Marked Capture of Nanking," *New York Times,* 18 December 1937, pp. 1 and 10.
26. Durdin, "Japanese Atrocities Marked Fall of Nanking After Chinese Command Fled," *New York Times,* 9 January 1938, p. 38.
27. Timperley, *Japanese Terror in China,* pp. 10, 15, and 139.
28. Timperley, *Japan: A World Problem,* pp. vii–viii.
29. Bradford Smith, "Japan: Beauty and the Beast," *Amerasia* 6:2 (April 1942), pp. 86–94.
30. Young, *Our Enemy,* p. 10.
31. Ibid., p. 10 and pp. 102–03.
32. Amerasia, ed., "Review Article: Is There another Japan?" pp. 35–42.
33. Amerasia, ed., "Review Article: The Nature of Our Enemy, Japan," pp. 389–92.
34. For a study in English, see Cook, "Reporting the 'Fall of Nanking' and the Suppression of a Japanese 'Memory' of the Nature of a War," pp. 121–53.
35. "Shôgaku kokushi jinjôka yô gekan," vol. 2, reprinted in *Nihon kyôkasho taikei kindai hen,* vol. 7, pp. 559–60.
36. *Tokyo Asahi shinbun,* 4 August 1937.
37. See, for example, Shinbun taimusu sha, *Shina jihen senshi,* vol. 1, pp. 264–88.
38. *Tokyo nichi nichi shinbun,* 30 November, 4 December, and 6 December 1937.
39. *Yomiuri shinbun,* 8 December 1937.
40. *Tokyo Asahi shinbun,* 11 December 1937.
41. "Fassho kyôi no Nihon," *Kyokutô sensô nyûsu,* no. 4 (10 January 1938); this was included in *Tokkô gaiji geppô,* (February 1938), pp. 12–13.
42. Hora, *Nit-Chû sensô: Nankin daigyakusatsu jiken shiryôshû,* vol. 2, pp. 4–5.

43. See *Tokkô gaiji geppô* (February 1938), 12; (March 1938), 10; and (June 1938), 14; also Hayashi, "Shina jihenka ni okeru fuon kôdô to sono taisaku ni tsuite," reprinted in *Shakai mondai sôsho*, 1:79, p. 185.
44. Included in *Runesansu*, a newsletter of the Japan Teachers' Union, Kôchi Prefecture, published on January 30, 1952. See Tokutake, *Kyôkasho no sengo shi*, pp. 73–74.

Section Three

ANOTHER DENIED
HOLOCAUST?

12

THE NANKING ATROCITY AND CHINESE HISTORICAL MEMORY

Joshua A. Fogel

Introduction

Serious scholars will continue to debate many aspects of the Nanking Atrocity perpetrated by the Japanese military from mid-December 1937 to early-February 1938. Why did it take place? How did Japanese military discipline break down? How many Chinese were massacred and raped? These and other questions remain open to scholarly debate. But no serious historian of any nationality doubts or denies that the Atrocity *did* take place. I stress this point at the outset because of, among other things, the grossly uninformed treatment this issue has received over the past decade in the American news media. The Atrocity has not achieved its full place in the catalog of world atrocities despite the great suffering that took place during those terrible weeks in Nanking, the Chinese capital city. Of course, the same can be said for other great acts of mass murder in the twentieth century, such as massacres of Armenians under the regime of the Young Turks during World War I, or the Porrajmos or Gypsy genocide by the Nazis during World War Two. But this hardly stanches the pain felt by survivors of Nanking and by their descendants. Over the past decade, there has been a dramatic surge of interest in Nanking and other atrocities committed by the Japanese in wartime China. This has taken place both in the People's Republic of China (PRC) and in Chinese diaspora communities, especially in North America. There is even a journal published in Chinese in the United States expressly devoted to the topic, the *Jih-pen ch'in-Hua yen-chiu* (Studies of Japanese Aggression against China), and there are now many websites focused on Nanking and similar Japanese wartime atrocities.[1] Organizations sponsoring the journal and websites have held many conferences and other commemorative events, such as a major symposium at Princeton University in November 1997, and a number of recent books by young Chinese nationalists have highlighted the Nanking Atrocity. In 2007, the seventieth anniversary of that event, it is important to examine the motives behind these highly politicized activities, which show little or no sign of abating.

Most significantly, in 1997 the late Iris Chang published her bestseller, *The Rape of Nanking: The Forgotten Holocaust of World War II.*[2] Not only has it sold several hundred thousand copies and been translated into a host of languages, Chang held numerous extremely successful book signings and appeared at many scholarly conferences before her death. In her book and lectures, she made the startling claim that, not only are the actions of the Japanese military in Nanking comparable to the Nazi Holocaust against the Jews of Europe; in fact, when properly calculated, the Nanking death count actually exceeds the "Shoah," as that event is known in Hebrew.[3] Although explicit references to the Holocaust in the PRC have been rare until very recently, young Chinese demonstrators did seize upon the swastika to vent their anger at the United States after the May 1999 NATO bombing of the Chinese embassy in Belgrade. Why are such comparisons being made both in the PRC and abroad? And why now? Why is it that young generations of Chinese both at home and in the diaspora overseas try to seize center stage from the established historical professions in the PRC, in Taiwan, and in Hong Kong? Why do they fervently seek to present the pain, suffering, and victimhood to the rest of the world on behalf of all Chinese?

The Nanking Atrocity and Postwar China(s)

From December 1937 to February 1938, at the actual time of the event in and around Nanking, few Chinese were in a position to comprehend the enormity of the mass murder going on around them; any who tried to gather data of this sort would have been in immediate mortal danger. Japanese soldiers who might have been able to report the scale of the killings obviously had no motivation to do so. Japanese journalists on the scene were subject to government censorship, or for the most part they suppressed the story voluntarily. The small Western community in Nanking was living in a compound, the Nanking Safety Zone (NSZ) set up in late-November. Although these men and women had some sense of what was going on and have left us with valuable records, they could not see or hear about what went on throughout the entire city and in areas outside of it until much later.[4]

After the war, the International Military Tribunal for the Far East (IMTFE), better known as the Tokyo War Crimes Trials, convened from 1946 to 1948; and a number of Japanese, Chinese, and foreigners in Nanking at the time were called as witnesses. The IMTFE came up with a figure of at least 200,000 Chinese murdered at Nanking. One Japanese convicted of war crimes at Nanking and sentenced to death was Gen. Matsui Iwane, the commander of Japanese forces, who had not even been in Nanking until 17 December. Matsui was aware of the brutal acts committed in the city and condemned his men for their savage excesses, having earlier demanded that Chinese prisoners of war (POWs) not be executed. But at his trial in Tokyo he denied that anything like a wholesale massacre had taken place. Nevertheless, the IMTFE found him guilty for not having prevented the crimes committed by men under his command, and he was hanged in 1948. By that time, however, the trials had become engulfed in more pressing concerns of the Cold War. There was considerable clamor among left-wing Japanese and among some elements of the general public to bring a much longer list of their own wartime leaders to the dock, but Gen. Douglass MacArthur, the commander of Allied Occupation forces, did not want to alienate conservative Japanese elites by prolonging the trials.

The Chinese Kuomintang (KMT) government under Chiang Kai-shek held much harsher postwar trials. These established the death toll at 300,000 and as a result, a number of implicated Japanese were executed. China at this time, however, was in the throes of a second civil war that the Chinese Communists under Mao Tse-tung would soon win. Shortly after its ouster from the mainland, the KMT dropped all claims to reparations for war damages. Chiang was concerned about diplomatic isolation and alienating the Japanese, and he needed East Asian allies in the Cold War as he established a new regime on Taiwan. When the Communists came to power on the mainland, they too refused war reparations as part of a policy of "self-reliance," and thus foreswore the PRC's ability to push that demand in the future. (Chinese individuals, however, can and do continue to sue the Japanese government and businesses for compensation.) Thus, in the immediate postwar period, the world did in effect recognize the Nanking Atrocity, but only a handful of Japanese were executed for their roles in it, and the Japanese government itself never tried any alleged war criminals. More importantly, though, nothing was implemented to keep the Atrocity in the public memory—such as a monument or annual commemoration. That situation obtained until the impressive stone memorial went up in Nanking on 15 August 1985.

The first postwar PRC generation produced little serious scholarship on the Atrocity, in part because they deemed it but one aspect of a horrific wartime experience interpreted in light of the subsequent Communist victory and the Cold War. As Mao Tse-tung putatively declared on the founding of the PRC, "China has stood up!" The Communists saw themselves, not the KMT, as victors in the war, and they had far bigger socioeconomic problems to contend with than seeking global recognition of Japanese war crimes. Most significantly, the PRC has always hampered serious scholarship on history in order to control the interpretation of it. The PRC government also strategically exploits history against international enemies, and deploys it to inspire shame in potential trading partners.[5] For example, it used the Atrocity as an ideological, albeit irrational, anti-US surrogate during the Korean War. In 1952 the PRC regime tried to implicate Americans in the Atrocity by claiming that the International Committee (IC)—an organization of Westerners who actually saved many thousands of Chinese civilians in the Nanking Safety Zone (NSZ)—was a gang of Western imperialists complicit with the Japanese invaders.[6] The PRC would again use the Atrocity during the 1960s to criticize the U.S. role in building up bases in Japan. Both of these deployments of the Atrocity helped escalate the Cold War. Yet at the same time, the PRC regime has been careful to control its criticism of the Atrocity owing to the importance of Sino-Japanese trade. Even before diplomatic normalization in 1972, the two countries had been engaged in trade that has grown to a massive volume today. PRC government leaders like to remind their Japanese counterparts of Japan's heinous wartime acts, usually at face-to-face meetings, and the Japanese government usually acquiesces in the interests of continuing this mammoth bilateral trade.

In order to maintain this strategic card, the PRC regime has tried to keep the Nanking issue from imploding among its populace, potentially injuring these lucrative Japanese contacts. Still far from a democracy, the Chinese government can exercise such prerogatives. It exploits the issue both to keep the Japanese in their place and to show its own people how it has gained the upper hand in Sino-Japanese relations, but it never mobilizes the masses to the point of seriously damaging trade. To be effective, then, the Peking regime has to walk a thin line. It must control public expressions of anti-Japanese sentiment by orchestrating demonstrations against Japan on other selected issues, such as the textbook controversy of the early 1980s, when the Japanese press leaked what proved to be inaccurate stories of the Ministry of Education's plans to soften the description of Japanese aggression in World War II.

Why Diaspora Chinese and Why Now?

Mainland Chinese have until very recently had their hands tied by their government. Overseas Chinese, however, have been much more active, not just in writing about Nanking and other wartime atrocities, but also in pushing for a wholesale condemnation of Japan and its alleged nonpayment of compensation. They believe that the Japanese, and other foreign peoples, have not accorded the 1937–38 Atrocity the importance that it warrants in modern world history, and that the Japanese government has not apologized sufficiently. At a number of international scholarly conferences I have attended, Chinese-American scholars have vociferously attacked Japanese academics and castigated fellow Chinese from the mainland for being "soft" on Japan. Overseas Chinese—and not just scholars—are justifiably angered by this or that right-wing Japanese group or individual who periodically denies the veracity of the Atrocity—although high-level Japanese government officials are forced to resign whenever they do this. But unlike Chinese living in the PRC, who cannot easily demonstrate their displeasure on such occasions, diaspora Chinese are free to express their opinions openly.

Recently, expressions of outrage among overseas Chinese about events in Nanking that occurred seventy years ago have become intricately tied to the complex issue of Chinese identity. Japan has inevitably played a crucial role in this identity formation given the close cultural and historical relationship between the two countries and the key role that Japan has played in China's own modernization since the late-nineteenth century. Despite the complexity and general amicability of this centuries-long history, the Atrocity has become *the* defining event in how many Chinese perceive Japan—to the extent of overshadowing over a millenium of previous relations. Even some gifted Chinese historians attribute not just World War II, but pre-twentieth century Japanese behavior, to an aggressive and expansionist Japanese "nature," usually connected with *bushidô* (the samurai ethos). As a symbol of Japan-as-aggressor, then, the Atrocity has become profoundly entwined with contemporary Chinese identity.

This issue has come to the fore among overseas Chinese only in the recent past. Other immigrant peoples have forged identities within a diaspora separated from their homelands over many centuries. Unlike them, however, the overseas Chinese experience did not really start until the mid-nineteenth century, and it has become seriously politicized only in the last 50 years or so. This politicization largely resulted from the post-1949 PRC-Taiwan rift, with growing numbers of ethnic Chinese living in Southeast Asia, Australia, the United States, and Canada. Whereas the overseas Chinese community was once strictly split between supporters of Taiwan and the PRC, it now reverberates with a multiplicity of voices. Moreover, increasing numbers of these ethnic Chinese were not born abroad. Especially since the 1970s, new modes of transportation—including jumbo jets and cheap air fares—have changed the very nature of immigration. People now move about between nations with considerably more ease, but perhaps ironically this has heightened their individual sense of ethnicity.[7]

New immigrants from Taiwan as well as highly educated PRC Chinese have brought new experiences and aspirations to the fore to create new fault lines within the overseas Chinese community. One of the more vocal groups of overseas Chinese not born abroad has been the scholarly community. Since the late-1980s, far more Chinese students and academics have been studying and teaching in Western institutions of higher learning than ever before. The West has afforded them more freedom, not only for academic pursuits, but for their gradually emerging political goals as well. This development has allowed many Chinese from the mainland to be less directly bound by their homeland than was true earlier. The worldwide web has also facilitated the expression of new voices by simplifying domestic and international communication to an unprecedented extent, and by providing a forum in which all views can be freely averred. The PRC government is desperately trying to control this phenomenon, but it is impossible to do so.[8] As various Chinese constituencies within the diaspora seek to assert themselves in the academic community and over the internet, they search for issues on which to ground their identities. The Nanking Atrocity has become the most prominent of these.

Thus, there are now more voices claiming to articulate Chinese identity than ever before, but paradoxically there is also a weaker basis on which to build that identity. One by-product of the modern era has been a kind of cultural deracination. Despite its obvious merits, the North American melting pot has had an unfortunate result: few of us are solidly grounded in the cultures, languages, and histories that are reputedly our own. As overseas Chinese—both those born in China and abroad—search for an identity in this the era of identity politics, they often find that they lack the tools needed to acquire one. Cultural deracination for the Chinese in China itself has been exacerbated by the trend toward iconoclasm in modern history with its self-conscious, often violent, rejection of China's long cultural heritage. This began in the New Culture Movement of the 1910s that blamed traditional culture for all of China's political, social, and economic ills; and it culminated in the Great Proletarian Cultural Revolution of the late-1960s and early-1970s. As a result, not only American- or Canadian-born ethnic Chinese, but even mainland Chinese who emigrate, are often ignorant of their culture and history. Entering the hot-house atmosphere of North American identity politics, they lack positive materials with which to forge their identity.[9] It is therefore tempting for them—like many other ethnic groups—to latch on to major negative instances in their history in order to forge that identity. For example, most North American Jews no longer know their own languages, religious texts, and cultural traditions in ways that their grandparents or great-grandparents did as a matter of course. So they have fastened on to the state of Israel and on to the sanctity of the Holocaust—the two are deeply interwoven—as basic to their Jewish identity. Many Chinese in the diaspora embrace the Atrocity, "the *Ta-t'u-sha*," in the same way.[10]

Why choose a negative instance—a horrific catastrophe in which so many of one's putative fellow ethnics died—as basic to one's identity? This is, I believe, because such an event represents something unassailable and irreproachable; it immediately links all members of an ethnic group in victimhood and bonds them in a way that cannot be questioned. This aspect of identity formation is elemental to the recent trends toward retribalization and toward the new sanctity of "difference," especially in the United States and Canada. Jews there have "remembered" and used the Holocaust in a similar way. For 2 decades after the end of the war, memory of the Shoah was faint as it went through a lag period, but took off dramatically from the 1960s and 1970s. By the late-1970s, Holocaust imagery was everywhere in North American Jewish culture—periodically punctuated with exclamation marks such as the famous eponymous TV melodrama, the Klaus Barbie trial in France, the trial of John Demjanjuk, and most recently the trials of Maurice Papon and Paul Touvier.[11] Overseas Chinese have experienced a similar lag, and manifested a similar response, toward the Nanking Atrocity.

The Fourth Generation on the Chinese Mainland

A new generation in the PRC has also begun to decry Japanese wartime behavior. Its members did not actually experience Japanese aggression in the 1930s and 1940s. Moreover, they are too young to have lived through the Communist victory over Chiang Kai-shek and the KMT in 1949, or to have suffered through the various Communist campaigns of suppression that culminated in the Cultural Revolution. In their mid- to late-thirties now, they grew up within the Communist regime and under its education system, so they acquired an accurate appreciation of their own historical culture with great difficulty, if at all. Unlike their immediate forebears, these young people no longer ascribe China's many pre-1949 defeats to the weaknesses or failings of pre-Communist regimes, such as the Ch'ing, the warlords, or the KMT. Nor are they content to focus on China's wartime resistance to Japan as a source of national identity and pride. Instead, they want to focus on China's victimization at the hands of foreigners.[12]

In one sense the views of this Fourth Generation *(ti-ssu-tai-jen)* match those of the Chinese Communist Party (CCP) regime, although these thirty-somethings are not all CCP hacks. They claim that China suffered exploitation in the past because it was weak, so its first national priority is to strengthen itself vis-à-vis Japan and the West. Among many publications, they have authored two best-selling books that exude nationalism and unvarnished antiforeignism—*Chung-kuo k'o-shuo pu* (China Can Say No) and its sequel, *Chung-kuo hai-shih neng shuo pu* (China Can Still Say No). Because these youths have suffered none of the hardships that their grandparents and parents did—and some have expressed a perverse envy of their elders in this regard—they also have no historical experience from which to form a meaningful identity. So, they vociferously strive to assert China's deserved but unrecognized international greatness. This entails an embittered assault on anyone who prevented China from assuming its due glory, and Japan is the preeminent culprit in their eyes.

In sum, members of this generation have championed China's status as a victim in order to compensate for the very insecurity produced by their lack of anything substantive on which to build an identity. As the China scholar

Peter Gries argues, its members' sense of victimization has but two aims: "quantifying the pain and presenting the Chinese case to the world."[13] Thus, their writings about the war do not focus on China's heroic resistance to and ultimate victory over Japan, but rather on the horrific losses incurred—with unusually inflated statistics. Thus they all cite a figure of *at least* 300,000 Chinese deaths in the Nanking Atrocity, the figure engraved in stone on the memorial in that city. This effort to gain the moral high ground is geared to silence anyone who disagrees, for the number of victims is simply not open to debate, except for upward revision. Anyone who disagrees is attacked or shouted down in public venues. Japanese professor Hata Ikuhiko, who has written extensively about the Atrocity for many years, concludes that 40,000-plus Chinese died in Nanking aside from prisoners of war (POWs). But he was shouted down by the largely Chinese and Chinese-American audience when he tried to present his views at an international conference at Princeton University in 1997. Similarly, the late Iris Chang, who was of the same generation, based her plea for international recognition of the Atrocity on what she presents as irrefutable numbers. She pointed out in an interview on American television—repeated in a *San Francisco Chronicle* interview—that the figure of 300,000 victims surpasses the combined death toll in the Hiroshima and Nagasaki atomic bombings.[14] Her implicit aim here is to establish a hierarchy of victimhood with China on top, especially because most Westerners cringe before the number of civilian lives lost in nuclear attacks on those Japanese cities. But why not compare the death toll at Nanking with those of Stalingrad or Leningrad, where even more civilians were killed? The same moral hierarchy simply does not hold for Chang.

The Fourth Generation rankles at yet another thought. The Japanese—who received their higher culture from China for centuries before victimizing China in the war—today enjoy great economic and political stature in the world, and many profit handsomely by investing in China's burgeoning economy. That has often led these Chinese thirty-somethings to criticize their own government. In their newfound nationalism, they find it galling that China depends on Japanese investment or aid, and they express their ire by constantly appealing to the memory of Chinese victimization. Their anger is, however, not directly solely at Japan, but at the entire world—and especially at the United States. As was true with Chang, members of China's younger generation do not work just to vilify Japan; they seek to marshal world opinion against it. That, first and foremost, means targeting the United States—Japan's number one trading partner and political ally in Asia. Young Chinese are trying to pressure Americans to make the Japan issue a complete *mea culpa*—a supreme apology for the war outdoing all previous ones, which they regard as insufficiently prostrate—and also to pay compensation for the war. That the American people and government apparently refuse to play this role angers them further.

Genocide? A Forgotten Holocaust?

The Fourth Generation in China focuses attention on numbers and victimization, but its members are still too removed from Western discourse to frame their critique in terms of the Holocaust. This is not true of Chang, Wu Tienwei (who founded the anti-Japanese journal, *Jih-pen ch'in-Hua yen-chiu,* and is an emeritus professor at Southern Illinois University), and other ethnic Chinese living in the West. The subtitle of Chang's book is *The Forgotten Holocaust of World War II,* and she insists that what transpired at Nanking was worse than the Holocaust of European Jewry. Wu has put forward the even more hyperbolic claim that what transpired in Nanking makes "the Auschwitz gas chambers appear humane."[15] It is surely safe to say that these lines are largely for shock value. Chang's claim remains grossly unproven in her book. Wu's is not only profoundly insensitive, and even vulgar; it is wholly unnecessary to his point. In any event, these two should not overly detain us.

At the discursive level, the term *the Holocaust* came to be used for the Judeicide some time in the early 1960s. Among many other things, it was a way of specially honoring those who perished in what many agreed was the worst mass murder in history. But, sadly, those on the left and right alike have frequently abused the term to advance their own agendas.[16] By the same token, many ethnic groups have seized on the term since the 1960s to honor their own people who fell victim in large numbers to some great man-made calamity. Each group's aim has been to bring its suffering to world attention, to garner the universal sympathy that this term elicits, to set its misfortune at a level beyond criticism, and thus to accord itself sacrosanct status. Hence there are Armenian, Roma and Sinti (Gypsy), African-American, Ukrainian, Cambodian, and Native-American holocausts. Finally, we now have a Chinese holocaust. The Jewish Holocaust shows that such victimhood can serve to shield one's group against all manner of criticism and strike shame and embarrassment in the hearts of governments. Of all modern genocides, only the Judeicide seems to have acquired this venerated, inviolable status. A few people still deny the existence of gas chambers at Auschwitz and other aspects of the Holocaust, but they are generally treated as pariahs. In stark contrast, it is possible to deny other genocides and not be so stigmatized. One can, for example, belittle or downplay the Turkish massacres, as the Turkish government itself regularly does, and go on with life more or less uninterrupted. The wartime and continuing suffering of the Roma and Sinti (the Gypsies) are regularly ignored or determinedly relegated to a secondary position. The right-wing critic Dinesh D'Souza recently went out of his way to tease positive side-effects out of the long history of African-American slavery. And, as the historian David Stannard has recently noted, scholars of the left, right, and center have all noted pointedly that eradicating the Native American way of life ultimately benefited surviving New World Indians.[17] Appreciation of the Nanking Atrocity lies somewhere amid these other "holocausts." Some in Japan deny it, including some academics and the occasional politician. But unlike Turkey, the Japanese government has acknowledged the Atrocity, and Japanese scholars are the world's most active and productive in researching it. Chinese and Chinese-Americans—like Armenians and other ethnic groups elsewhere—would like to see their particular tragedy elevated to sacrosanct status; then, only fringe elements could reject or disparage its veracity.

Nor is the idea of a "forgotten" holocaust original to Chang and others like her. Angus Frazer used it in his 1992 work, *The Gypsies,* referring of course to the Nazi genocide against them. He had borrowed the term from the French scholar Christian Bernadac, who authored a 1979 book entitled *L'Holocaust Oublié: Le Massacre des Tsiganes.* There is a 1986 book by R. C. Lukas entitled, *Forgotten Holocaust: The Poles under German Occupation, 1939–1944.* In an important 1981 study, *Genocide: Its Political Use in the Twentieth Century,* Leo Kuper called the Turkish mass murders of Armenians the "forgotten genocide of the twentieth century." R. J. Rummel, cataloged the great mass murders of the twentieth century in a 1994 article, "Democide in Totalitarian States: Mortacracies and Megamurderers." Referring to those killed by the Japanese in World War II, he wrote, "This is surely the forgotten democide"—"democide" being a neologism that he coined to mean the government-sponsored murder of persons of a specific group.[18] Finally, there is a 1999 article entitled, "The Circassians: A Forgotten Genocide." Thus, using the word "forgotten" as a modifier has a history of its own, and it usually constitutes efforts by the author to shock readers into altering long-held assumptions.

What needs to be asked, however, is this: does it help to assess the Nanking Atrocity by the standards of comparative genocide and Holocaust research? Can we better understand this event by placing it alongside other mind-boggling massacres? I previously resisted comparisons of this sort. But, on reflection, I have concluded that they need not establish a hierarchy of pain, nor need they detract from the uniqueness of a particular event. Every act of genocide and mass murder is unique, and none implies exclusivity; thus "distinctiveness" is a better word in this context. No group has monopolized suffering unto itself, and its rhetoric is offensive only when it flaunts its victimhood to denigrate the sufferings of other groups. Based on the intent of the murderers, the number or percentage of the target population killed, the circumstances of the killings, and other criteria, scholars have made compelling cases to deem mass murders of the Gypsies by the Nazis, of the Armenians by the Turks in 1915, and of the native inhabitants of North and South America by European immigrants, as being just as horrific as the Final Solution against the Jews.

Accepting comparison as a viable means of approaching genocide, let us take a look at criteria that scholars have devised to examine it. Raphael Lemkin coined the term *genocide* in 1933, and explained it eleven years later as "the destruction of a nation or an ethnic group. This new word, coined by the author to denote an old practice in its modern development, is made from the ancient Greek *genos* (race, tribe) and the Latin *cide* (killing), thus corresponding in its formation to such words as tyrannicide, homicide, infanticide, etc."[19] Fifteen years later, in 1948, the newly formed United Nations passed its famous Convention on Genocide that generally followed Lemkin's definition. He offers a succinct conceptual framework, but no guidelines on the size or scale that a mass murder must reach before it is "genocidal." In that vein, the social scientist Henry R. Huttenbach wrote: "How do we prevent ourselves from moving glibly from Auschwitz to Hiroshima and back, from the Death Camps to the Gulag, from genuine genocide to non-genocide, from lumping victims of *bona fide* extermination together with victims of massacres?"[20] Not all acts of mass murder are genocidal, and not all genocides may be placed on a plain with the Holocaust. Historian Michael R. Marrus has made perhaps the best argument for distinguishing the Holocaust from other larger-scale mass murders in the simple, terrible fact that the Nazis targeted for murder each and every Jew throughout the world.[21] Huttenbach offers his own succinct and useful definition: "[G]enocide is the destruction of a specific group within a national or even international population. The precise character of the group need not be spelled out." To see if an act deserves to be called genocidal, he suggests one key condition; we must ask, "Is this an act that puts the very existence of a group in jeopardy?"—and not just a case of extreme hardship or large-scale killings.[22]

There is no single process to genocide. Often it involves sadistic, crude methods of mass execution—despite a ready supply of ammunition—as a means of further terrorizing a subject population. In the 1975–76 Lebanese civil war, for example, sexual mutilation (often committed by well educated, otherwise rational men) was commonly performed by all levels of society, together with vicious acts of rape, desecration, torture, and murder. Whether this rose to a level commensurate with genocide remains to be proven, however. At other times, murders are committed more discretely, out of public view, and often in a way that separates the instigators of mass death from the actually killers. The Holocaust did not immediately become what we now know it as—the routinized mass murder by efficient means through industrialized, regularized, bureaucratically legitimated techniques. Before Kristallnacht in November 1938, the Nazis relied on the pogrom model. And, ultimately about one-third, or fully two million, of the Jews were slain by the *Einsatzgruppen*, mobile killing units set loose into Eastern Europe early in the war, aided by local collaborators such as the Romanian volunteers.[23] It was not until the Nazis established death camps, primarily in Poland in the early 1940s, that the Holocaust took on its most technologically advanced form—insulating the killers from the acts of killing, and making the victims invisible through ever more sophisticated weapons. This process was horrifically illustrated by the progression from the *Einsatzgruppen* to Zyklon B, the poison gas used to asphyxiate many thousands of victims. Zygmunt Bauman asks how it is that people who were not "moral degenerates" could commit mass murder on the scale of the Holocaust. And, he responds, the Holocaust shows that many never even faced moral choices: "moral aspects of actions are not immediately obvious or are deliberately prevented from discovery.... In other words, the moral character of action is either invisible or purposefully concealed."[24]

What form of violence did the Japanese military use at Nanking in 1937–38? In this instance, the murderers acted as if engaged in a continuous, bestial pogrom. There was some regularity to the killings, but there was no preconceived master plan of mass murder; and the perpetrators were castigated for their brutality and lack of discipline by their own commander, Matsui Iwane, when he arrived on the scene at Nanking. Most of the perpetrators were impoverished men who had led exceedingly hard lives up to conscription and the war. Moreover, their experiences in the military and on campaigns—particularly the battle of Shanghai before arriving in Nanking—were extremely harsh. They were not even supposed to have attacked Nanking, but were driven on by overzealous superior officers. They were not the refined, well-educated mass murderers who peopled the Gestapo or served as death-camp commandants, although some Japanese were not unlike many death- and concentration-camp guards or even some of the *Einsatzgruppen*. Whereas the Holocaust of European Jewry featured rational plans of murder en masse with bureaucratic regularity, the Nanking Atrocity can be more accurately described as a scene of mass murder run viciously amok.

Was there an ideology comparable to anti-Semitism or anti-Gypsy sentiment behind the Japanese war machine in China? Was there a pervasive ideology that so denigrated China or demonized the Chinese that it could legitimate or pave the way for mass murder—another trait found in genocide? There was certainly a widespread feeling that the Chinese were a weak and chaotic people incapable of running their own country and in need of urgent help. But there was nothing comparable to an ideology for sustaining mass murder, and there was most assuredly nothing comparable to the Nazi slogan that the Jews and Gypsies were "lives not worth living." In the Japanese treatment of China under occupation, there was not even anything comparable to the discriminatory Nuremberg Laws or the social isolation in ghettos that subsequently necessitated, in the diseased minds of Nazis, physical segregation of Jews and Gypsies into concentration- and death-camps. The Chinese were pitied or patronizingly looked down on, but they were never demeaned to a point justifying wholesale murder. Of course, in all wartime situations the enemy has to be deemed worthy of death—if only to motivate the troops—especially in cases of foreign aggression or total war. However, there was no Japanese plan to annihilate every Chinese man, woman, and child, as there was for the Jews following the Wannsee Conference of early 1942 in Nazi Germany. Nor was there the well-crafted plan of murder earlier in the twentieth century with respect to Armenians in Turkey. Even among the most retrograde, unattractive elements of the extreme Japanese right-wing and militarist cliques, one would be hard-pressed to locate such sentiments, let alone point to these as an overriding ideology in the 1930s and 1940s.

The only framework in Japan approaching an ideology behind the Nanking Atrocity was that of the emperor state which, from the 1930s, effectively deemed anyone who defied the imperial institution as unfit to live. This might be marshaled as a possible rallying call for Japanese troops in the field to attack Chinese who resisted, but it was by no means directed solely at China and the Chinese. Indeed, it applied with equal ferocity to Japanese Communists, which is one reason that so many of them underwent *tenkô* or a sudden reorientation of their views to abandon leftism and embrace the emperor system, usually while in jail or in anticipation of being arrested. Racism or ethnic hatred, understood in the broadest sense, was an essential component of the Holocaust and many acts of genocide—against New World Indians, Gypsies, Armenians, various peoples in Africa, and Ukrainian peasants. But it does not appear in any major way in Japanese constructions of China and the Chinese. In fact, one feature of late-nineteenth and twentieth century East Asian history has been a collapsing of the Chinese and Japanese into a "yellow race" to combat the white race. It is true that this notion may have been used to mask Japanese desires to "guide" the Chinese in a particular direction, or to "chastise" them for failing to go along, but it reflected a certain ideological solidarity vis-à-vis the West.

Moving from the level of an ideology constructed on the putative basis of a shared racial identity to visceral racism, did the latter play a significant part in Japanese formulations or views of the Chinese? Can we detect a visceral Japanese hatred of the Chinese as a people because of who they were? There was certainly much belittling of the Chinese in Japan at the time. But what enraged Japanese soldiers en route to and in Nanking in 1937–38 and what drove them to acts of mass murder had nothing to do with presumed Chinese weaknesses or endemic failings. Quite to the contrary, Japanese soldiers were stunned and out for revenge precisely because of the unexpected strength and perseverance of the Chinese they had confronted in the battle of Shanghai months earlier. This battle was of horrific proportions, second at the time only to the battle of Verdun in terms of overall numbers killed, in which many Japanese lost comrades. As one Japanese foot soldier later recalled in an interview with the famed journalist Honda Katsuichi: "[T]he assault on Nanjing took place as an extension of this fighting [in and around Shanghai]. It just wasn't the kind of atmosphere in which you'd immediately forgive and release your prisoners, merely because they had surrendered to you. The mood was one of avenging your dead comrades."[25]

Fourth Generation Chinese argue that racism—by which they mean the Japanese troops' dehumanization of the Chinese people—was indeed an essential part of the assault on China. The piece of evidence usually cited is the infamous 100-man killing contest, in which two Japanese soldiers allegedly vied to see who could first slay 100 Chinese en route to Nanking. Many have questioned the veracity of this story, and not only arch right-wingers in Japan. See Bob Tadashi Wakabayashi's chapter 6 in the present volume. But the Japanese press in November-December 1937 did give the story considerable play, the soldiers did receive death sentences at the postwar Nanking War Crimes Tribunal; so, as a result, anti-Japanese Chinese believe the story today. But despite the guilty verdict, to accept this story as true and accurate requires a leap of faith that no balanced historian can make.[26] If we interpret the story on another level, as symptomatic of the callous way in which Japanese troops acted on the way to Nanking, then we can conclude that dehumanization was elemental to their experience. But this is still not racism. And, when Fourth Generation members go even further, to that claim the slaughter in and around Nanking was not only deliberate but ordered by the emperor, they stray far from the historical record in an effort to find evidence for Japanese victimization of China. What is more, they often push this history of victimization back to the early Meiji era.

For obvious reasons, genocides usually occur where the targeted group is in a minority. This is not to say that the murderers necessarily are the majority, but the murdered are usually a minority, often in times of war or military occupation. Thus the Jews and Gypsies were usually in the minority, even if the Nazis were not the majority in Poland, Lithuania, and elsewhere in eastern and central Europe. Similarly, Armenians living on Turkish terrain were a minority. One exception to this generalization might be native peoples of the New World who were enslaved and murdered by smaller groups of white settlers. In 1937–38, by contrast, the Chinese were the overwhelmingly great majority at Nanking, although they had been abandoned by their army. If we follow Henry R. Huttenbach's definition of genocide as an act that "puts the very existence of a group in jeopardy," Japanese actions in China fall far short, if only because the Chinese population was so huge. Frequently the perpetrators of genocide use other ethnic groups to commit murder by proxy. Thus, the Nazis used apparently willing Ukrainians and other collaborators as guards in many of the death camps. In fact, the Nazis' ability to separate themselves from the killing went so far as to get Jewish complicity through the *Sonderkommandos* and through various Jewish ghetto councils *(Judenrätter)*.[27] Although there were Chinese collaborators, similar actions did not take place at Nanking; instead, Japanese military personnel did all the killing.

"Modern genocide is genocide with a purpose," notes Zygmunt Bauman. *"The end itself is a grand vision of a better and radically different society."* Because the victim group does not fit into this vision, it must by weeded out. Inasmuch as the modern bureaucracy has no moral component, but is solely directed at increased efficiency, it was the ideal instrument to orchestrate an efficient "gardening"—as much for Stalin and others as for Hitler.[28] Again, this was not

true for the Nanking Atrocity. An overarching purpose was missing. There was *nothing* political, military, ideological, or economic to be gained by committing this mass murder. And, there were no concentration- or death-camps, no elaborate system to distance the killers from the killing, and no bureaucratic organization for it except of the most primitive ad hoc sort. The Rwandan and Cambodian "genocides" of recent years also lacked the bureaucratic efficiency of the Holocaust. There was a vision of a "radically different society" in the case of Cambodia, but the torture and killing lacked the Nazi death machine's bureaucratic efficiency, even if the numbers of victims was ultimately quite high. Again, this in no way minimizes the suffering of Cambodians in the 1970s or other groups; it just distinguishes the organization of mass murder in different instances.

In sum, this rudimentary typology shows that the Nanking Atrocity was never an end in itself. Rather, it was an instance of impromptu, large-scale, mass murder perpetrated in the context of Japan's brutal war of aggression against the Chinese and other peoples in East and Southeast Asia. Thus the Atrocity in some respects resembles other events in Africa, Cambodia, and the New World that have acquired the label "genocidal." However, it fell far short both in numerical count and percentage of population slain, and it lacked the ideological impetus and bureaucratic efficiency that spurred on many of these other genocides. The Atrocity, then, was altogether different from the Shoah, the Porrajmos, or the Armenian experience in Turkey during World War I. I would ultimately have to agree with Justice Radhabinod Pal, the Indian judge at the Tokyo War Crimes Trials, who noted: "[T]he case of the present accused before us cannot in any way be likened to the case ... of Hitler."[29] Chief Justice William Webb effectively concurred: "[T]he crimes of the Germans accused were far more heinous, varied and extensive than those of the Japanese accused." This diminished assessment in no way slights the suffering of victims at Nanking; nor does it make the Atrocity less heinous. It merely is an attempt to understand these great human tragedies in a comparative perspective. Chinese victims have a serious case to make, but using the word "Holocaust" does not help us understand the Nanking Atrocity, nor does it shed light on genocides more generally. It has been more my task to examine the specific contexts in which claims of genocide have been made than to tally numbers or compare victimhood. Why did the issue seem less important to the Chinese in the 1940s and 1950s than it has become since the 1990s? This question involves the complex role of memory in identity formation. To be sure, the Nanking Atrocity deserves our solemn acknowledgment, not only so that the world will not forget, and not only because we need to affirm unequivocally that a great massacre was perpetrated against the Chinese people, which a handful of fringe elements in Japan continues to whitewash. Having said that, past injustices committed against a people do not license them and their descendants to denigrate others. Victimhood does not confer sainthood.

Context, Memory, and Identity

In this chapter, I have tried to demonstrate the importance of context in the ways that people perceive a historical event to form national or ethnic identities. Context is intricately tied to memory (constructed or otherwise), and shared memory is essential to identity. In this respect, China and Japan have been crucial to each other for many centuries. China was fundamental to the development of Japanese identity from at least the sixth century onward, and Japan has been crucial to China's since the end of the nineteenth century. In the First Sino-Japanese War, or Meiji-Ch'ing War, of 1894–95—a war fought when this turnabout began—the Japanese military committed horrific atrocities against Chinese civilians. The Chinese scholar-official Cheng Kuan-ying briefly catalogued these at the time, although he seems to have been recounting events listed in the foreign press rather than personally witnessed:

> When the Japanese occupied Lüshun, the entire town was massacred. Pregnant women in Hai-ch'eng were cut open…. When Niu-chuang was occupied,… our women were tied up and raped. Even innocent children could not escape. Japanese soldiers stabbed their bayonets into the children's anuses and then held up the body on their bayonets for fun…. When Japanese ships passed Teng-chou, they opened fire on villagers for no reason, and the homes of ordinary people were destroyed…. When they attacked Jung-ch'eng, they also opened fire everywhere, even at the houses of residents. People lost their homes and had to sleep outdoors in the fields. At that time, it was snowing heavily, and many died from cold and hunger…. It was so miserable and vicious that even the sky and sun would sigh. Oh, how brutal it was![30]

Why have these nineteenth-century atrocities been buried in historical oblivion whereas those of Nanking in 1937–38 continue to be cited routinely? The principal reason lies precisely in the issue of context. World War II is crucially important to those who make the case for a "Nanking Holocaust" because of guilt by association impugned to Japan which, after all, later became allied to Nazi Germany. For the historical record, a formal military alliance—as opposed to the Anti-Comintern Pact—was not formed until September 1940, well after the mass murders at Nanking took place. But this has not stopped the likes of Iris Chang, Wu Tien-wei, and others from claiming that imperial Japan and the Third Reich were full-fledged allies in 1937. Indeed, John Rabe's inveighing against what he witnessed—which, to her credit, Chang has brought to our attention—is transformed in a newspaper interview to: "So sickening was the spectacle that even the Nazis in the city were horrified."[31] This statement is a bit of a stretch. Chang and Wu link Japan with perhaps the worst murderous regime in our time, not just because of the subsequent alliance with Nazi Germany, but also because we have come to regard the European Holocaust as the most horrific act of genocide in recent human history.

The current outrage over events committed in Nanking seventy years ago is not directed at Japan alone, however. Sino-Japanese relations have taken on a new character since World War II. Globalization plus increased Chinese exposure and emigration to the West, especially over the past two or three decades, require that the entire world—which often means the West or, more specifically, the United States—verify China's victimhood. Chang, for example, was less interested in changing Japanese opinions—about which she knew next to nothing in any case—than in bringing the Atrocity to American attention. This is another reason for her to tally the death toll in Nanking higher than those for the two Japanese cities targeted by U.S. atomic bombs. Thus, like the younger generation in China, persons such as Chang are working—and successfully, it should be noted—to marshal the Western media against Japan. This has sadly become central to their identities.

The philosopher Avishai Margalit notes Sigmund Freud's description of a "neurotic person's disproportionate actions." Freud referred to a Londoner who, looking at a monument to the great fire of 1666, mourned aloud the destruction of three centuries earlier rather than feel joy or relief about the city's resilience.[32] A parallel neurosis of remembering plagues Chinese-American and Chinese groups discussed above. The journalist Ian Buruma recently recounted reading a piece by Iris Chang in which she told of an incident that followed a lecture she had given about the Nanking Atrocity. A Chinese-American woman came forward with tears in her eyes and said to Chang, "You make me proud to be Chinese." One would think that 5000 years of a resplendent world culture might suffice.

Notes

1. See, for example, the following websites: www.Nanking1937.org/; www.smn.co.jp/gallery/Nanking/; www.cnd.org/njmassacre/; www.skycitygallery.com/japan/japan.html; china.muzi.net/news/topics/massacre.html; www.cernet.edu.cn/history/www.arts.cuhk.hk/NankingAtrocity/NM.html
2. The website is: china.muzi.net/news/topics/massacre.shtml.
3. This argument is repeated at: www.skycitygallery.com/japan/japan.html.
4. See Rabe, *Good Man of Nanking;* Smalley ed., *American Missionary Eyewitnesses to the Nanking Massacre;* Brook, ed., *Documents on the Rape of Nanking;* and Zhang [Chang], ed., *Eyewitnesses to Massacre.*
5. This view has been noted by Japanese and Westerners alike. See, for example, Kojima, "Nit-Chû kankei no 'atarashii hatten dankai'." I would not go so far as to argue, as Newby does, that the Japanese play along out of a sense of guilt. See Newby, *Sino-Japanese Relations: China's Perspective,* p. 13. See also Gries, "Face Nationalism," chapter 4. Gries argues convincingly that this is not merely a phenomenon of the Communist Party dictating policy to the Chinese people, but that there is much popular support for anti-Japanese policies in China.
6. Yang, "Sino-Japanese Controversy," p. 16; also, Eykholt, "Aggression, Victimization, and Chinese Historiography of the Nanjing Massacre," pp. 24–25.
7. See Hirano, "Transnational Flows of People and International Exchanges," pp. 97–98.

8. Buruma, "China in Cyberspace," pp. 9–12.
9. I tried some years ago to describe the disbelief of one great Japanese sinologue, Naitô Konan (1866–1934), in the 1920s when he witnessed the assault by young Chinese on their own traditions. It make little or no sense to him and left him highly frustrated. See Fogel, *Politics and Sinology*, pp. 239–51.
10. Buruma has made a similar remark *en passant* in "Afterlife of Anne Frank," p. 7.
11. Novick, "Holocaust Memory in America," pp. 159–65, citation on p. 163. One line of analysis that Novick does not pursue is the role of the sharp decline in the popularity of Marxism and other leftist causes, together later with the collapse of the socialist states in Eastern Europe. Many Jews had invested their energies in socialist and other causes of social justice as a kind of secular religion, only to find either their non-Jewish fellows unsympathetic to the cause of Israel or their movement dissolve from within. Witness, for instance, the prominence of Jewish intellectuals among the "new-conservatives," virtually all of whom had been liberals or leftists prior to their "conversions" in the 1970s and 1980s.
12. See Gries, "Face Nationalism."
13. Ibid., p. 21.
14. *News Hour with Jim Lehrer,* 20 February 1998; Burress, "Wars of Memory."
15. Wu, Preface, p. iii.
16. See Marrus's excellent piece, "Is There a New Anti-Semitism," pp. 172–74 and p. 177.
17. Concerning the Armenian genocide and its denial, see Dadrian, "Comparative Aspects of the Armenian and Jewish Cases of Genocide," pp. 101–35; and Smith, Markusen, and Lifton, "Professional Ethics and the Denial of Armenian Genocide," pp. 1–22. On the Roma and Sinti, see Hancock, "Responses to the Porrajmos," pp. 39–64; and Lutz and Lutz, "Gypsies as Victims of the Holocaust," pp. 346–59. Concerning the "good" to be derived from black slavery, see D'Souza, *End of Racism: Principles for a Multiracial Society.* On Native Americans, see Stannard, "Uniqueness as Denial," pp. 163–208.
18. Kuper, *Genocide,* p. 105; Rummel, "Democide in Totalitarian States," p. 34.
19. Cited in Kuper, *Genocide,* p. 22.
20. Huttenbach, "Locating the Holocaust on the Genocide Spectrum," p. 291.
21. Marrus, *Holocaust in History,* p. 23 and p. 28.
22. Huttenbach, "Locating the Holocaust on the Genocide Spectrum," p. 259, p. 297 and p. 298.
23. Marrus, *Holocaust in History,* pp. 39, 79.
24. Bauman, *Modernity and the Holocaust* pp. 24–26, 74, and 89–90.
25. Honda, *Nanjing Massacre,* p. 240.
26. Also see Wakabayashi, "The Nanking 100-Man Killing Contest Debate," pp. 307–40.
27. Bauman, *Modernity and the Holocaust,* pp. 22–23, with obvious nods in the direction of Hannah Arendt.
28. Ibid., pp. 91–92, 102–6. Italics in the original.
29. Cited in Dower, *Embracing Defeat,* p. 459.
30. Cheng, "Chung-Jih chiao-chan hsi-wen-pao chi Jih-ping t'u-ch'eng ts'an-k'u t'u-shou hsü," pp. 486–87.
31. Burress, "Wars of Memory."
32. Margalit, *Ethics of Memory,* p. 4.

13

A TALE OF TWO ATROCITIES: CRITICAL APPRAISAL OF AMERICAN HISTORIOGRAPHY[1]

Masahiro Yamamoto

Introduction

The Nanking Atrocity has been intensely debated in the United States since the publication of Iris Chang's bestseller, *The Rape of Nanking: The Forgotten Holocaust of World War II,* in 1997. But the debate fails to focus on two crucial issues. First, commentators have neglected the factual history of the event and concentrated on its historiography. Second, those historiographic studies have dealt with Japanese and Chinese, but not American, writers. These failings are exemplified by *The Nanjing Massacre in History and Historiography* (2000), edited by Joshua A. Fogel. The volume examines how political contexts affected postwar scholarly and media treatments of the Atrocity in Japan and China, but the contributors devoted little space to the actual history of the Atrocity, and none of them addressed a crucially important issue: why Americans debated this incident so intensely in the wake of Chang's book. Given that the Atrocity has been known in the United States since 1937, thanks to media coverage by journalists such as F. Tillman Durdin and Archibald T. Steele, followed by extensive discussions in histories of modern China and Japan, the extreme sensation caused by Chang deserves close attention, especially because Americans were neither victims nor victimizers in the incident. Mark Eykholt, a contributor to Fogel's volume, suggests one reason: the Atrocity is an "international symbol" of suffering that unites all ethnic Chinese in the postwar era.[2] This, however, does not fully explain the "Chang boom" because those who extol her book are not limited to Chinese-Americans.

My analysis attributes the popularity of Chang's book in America to two intertwined factors: ethnic prejudice and the wide gap in interpretations of the Atrocity between professional historians and the general public. The professional historians' lack of fact-finding solidified the ordinary people's image of the Atrocity, already created by amateur historians, and reinforced popular ethnic prejudice. Regarding factual history, I presented my own interpretation in *Nanking: Anatomy of an Atrocity* (2000), a monograph that advances a "revisionist" thesis in contrast to the one presented by Chang and seemingly accepted by a majority of Americans. The label "revisionist" may raise suspicions that I am similar to Holocaust "deniers," but careful readers will find that my book emphasized the context of the Sino-Japanese War in which the Atrocity took place, and squarely blamed the Japanese army, although to a far less extent than usually recognized. The historian Yang Daqing, another of Fogel's contributors, states that: "Taken out of the context of Japan's aggression in China, the Nanking Massacre [Atrocity] would become a mere accident or an anecdote in the annals of military operation."[3] But I contend that, as far as the responsibility of Japanese commanders is concerned, the Atrocity was an accident, albeit a terrible one.

Critics may still find a parallel with Holocaust denial by arguing that my work downplays the "perpetrator-victim perspective."[4] But not every attempt to downplay an atrocity is equivalent to Holocaust denial. American and Western historians refuted charges of an atrocity allegedly committed by Americans on a scale that putatively equalized or surpassed that of the Nazis, but they were never damned as Holocaust deniers. Specifically, I refer to the debate over James Bacque's *Other Losses: An Investigation into the Mass Deaths of German Prisoners at the Hands of the French and Americans after World War II* (1989). First published in Canada, it became a bestseller in the United States and was translated into several languages. Bacque caught media attention into the early 1990s, but professional historians familiar with the topic soon arrived at a persuasive counterthesis. The Bacque phenomenon presents striking similarities to, and baffling contrasts with, the controversy over Chang's book. In this chapter, I examine the debates over these two bestsellers: both challenge professional historians to deal with narratives written by amateurs for mass audiences in a media age. The issue is how scholars and specialists can, or can not, influence or reshape popular attitudes about the past. More importantly, though, I argue that the contrasting academic and popular reactions to these two books underline latent ethnic prejudice against a particular nation in the United States.

Bacque and His Critics

The central thesis of *Other Losses* is that the Americans and French—acting under orders from Gen. Dwight D. Eisenhower, commander of Supreme Headquarters, Allied Expeditionary Force (SHAEF)—deliberately starved to death

800,000 to one million German prisoners of war (POWs) in custody. Bacque reached his radical new conclusion by reinterpreting primary sources and by interviewing eyewitnesses. He placed the blame on Eisenhower, whose personal "feelings against the Germans grew stronger the more desperately they fought, [and] the more he saw of the horrors of the concentration camps, until he felt ashamed that he bore a German name." Under his orders, the military command changed the status of German POWs to that of a "disarmed enemy force" (DEF) in order to kill them en masse by reducing their rations below levels stipulated by the Geneva convention even though food supplies were plentiful in postwar Europe. To support his claim, Bacque pointed to the item "other losses" in a document entitled "Weekly Prisoner of War and Disarmed Enemy Forces Report." "Other Losses," he said, was a euphemism similar to the Nazis' "final solution."[5] To underscore his claims, Bacque quoted eyewitnesses:

> Wolfgang Iff said that in his sub-section of perhaps 10,000 people at Rheinberg, 30 to 40 bodies were dragged out every day. A member of the burial commando, Iff was well placed to see what was going on.... Some of the corpses were dead of gangrene following frostbite suffered on the freezing nights of April. A dozen or more others, including a 14-year-old boy too weak to cling to the log flung across the ditch for a latrine, fell off and drowned.... Sometimes, as many as 200 died each day.[6]

Furthermore, Bacque cited then West German chancellor Conrad Adenauer's remarks in 1950 that 1,407,000 German soldiers were still unaccounted for, charged that most of them had died in Allied captivity, and argued that SHAEF censorship explained why such a horrible event went unnoticed after VE Day. Bacque found humanitarians who tried to save starving German POWs amid the horrible atrocity. These heroes included Jean-Pierre Pradervand, head of the delegations of the International Committee of the Red Cross in France; Jacques Fauvet, who contributed a story of German POWs to *Le Monde;* and Victor Gollanz, a British publisher famous for bringing out Harold J. Timperley's *What War Means* in 1938 and who later wrote a pamphlet criticizing Allied handling of German POWs. Finally, Bacque held that postwar Germans never raised this issue because they wanted their former enemies to forget about Nazi atrocities.[7]

Bacque hired 3 literary agents to "sell" his manuscript in the United States, but over thirty presses rejected it. In the process, the late Stephen Ambrose, a renowned U.S. historian of World War II, made some cautiously positive remarks on it. Even so, Ambrose dismissed its main thesis—that Eisenhower deliberately caused the death of so many German POWs—and surmised that it was this flawed thesis that had led publishers to reject the manuscript.[8] After the book appeared, a few reviewers accepted its claims, but with reservations. Roland Green said, "This book argued persuasively that many thousands of former German soldiers died unnecessarily while in Allied custody immediately after World War II," but added, "Bacque does not establish beyond a reasonable doubt that these deaths were caused deliberately."[9] *MacLean's* magazine in Canada said that "at least some American and French commanders were 'sinking toward the evil which we had all supposed we were fighting'," yet remained skeptical about the tabulated death toll.[10]

Academic historians reviewed the book in a very critical manner from the start. Arthur L. Smith Jr. of California State University, Los Angeles, said in a newspaper review, "The book needs to be put in perspective; it is the work of a novelist and should not be construed as history."[11] Then a group of historians launched a wholesale counterattack against Bacque in *Eisenhower and the German POWs: Facts against Falsehood*, a volume edited by Guenter Bischof and Steven E. Ambrose. Contributors to it argued that Bacque ignored the historical context that created conditions leading to the starvation of German POWs and civilians: "[T]here was, then, a volatile mix in Germany in May, 1945: angry GIs, frustrated recruits and revenge seeking Jewish officers, and former slave laborers and German soldiers packed into open camps. The result was unbearable conditions on a massive scale in a few of the large and grossly overpopulated holding camps on the Rhine River. There is simply no evidence that it was part of an organized, systematic Allied effort."[12]

Brian Loring Villa argued that Eisenhower had to report to higher authorities and thus was in no position to dictate policies on POWs.[13] James F. Tent refuted other assumptions, for example, that food was abundantly available, as well as the implicit logic that people die of malnutrition as soon as their food intake begins to fall below a minimum daily caloric requirement.[14] Albert E. Cowdrey presented his own estimate of slightly over 56,000 deaths at most, or about 1.1 percent of all German POWs in Allied hands.[15] Ruediger Overmans computed even smaller estimates of 5,000 to 10,000 at American, and over 21,000 at French, camps. He also quoted findings from the Bonn government's Maschke Commission, set up in 1957 to write a history of German POWs in World War II. Drawing on its report, Overmans concluded that what Bacque claimed to be the "missing million" mentioned by Adenauer was largely created on the Russian, not the Western, front. Based on the absence of corpses in locations where POW camps used to be, Overmans also discredited Bacque's allegation of mass deaths.[16] In order to disprove Bacque's interpretation of "other losses," critics cited this passage in a U.S. military document: "An additional group of 663,576 are listed as 'other losses', consisting largely of members of the *Volkssturm* [people's militia] released without formal discharge."[17] The critics conducted their own interview and obtained a recantation from 91-year-old former Col. Philip S. Lauben—whose confession about the meaning of "other losses" Bacque had sensationally presented in his book's introduction.[18] Finally, they questioned the originality of Bacque's monograph: Bacque neglected to refer to some crucial primary and secondary sources that touched on this issue.[19]

Despite such criticisms, these historians did admit that deplorable conditions existed at some Allied POW camps in Germany.[20] Nor did they dispute eyewitness accounts by German former POWs as quoted in *Other Losses:* "Bacque's six eyewitnesses fairly accurately reflect the appalling conditions in the Rhine meadow camps.... There can be little doubt that conditions in the worst of the camps were horrific—in the first weeks of May, even inhuman." Bischof, though, said that such stories do not corroborate the death rate and death toll that Bacque alleged: "to select out of five million German POWs in American hands six men who were held in three or four of the very worst camps is surely not the way to arrive at the most representative sample for making a persuasive case concerning the POW experience in American hands."[21] In like manner, Overmans criticized Bacque's faulty reasoning; that is, to assume that a condition existing in a few locations prevailed everywhere.[22]

The balance sheet favors those critics.[23] I too find them convincing. But they were not complacent about their achievement. Günther Bischof said that "professional historians ... will always find it difficult to refute convoluted conspiracy theories that are appealing to a lay audience."[24] His implication is that the general public is not usually attracted to carefully researched works of history, and that academic historians are sometimes losers in the realm of commercial publication. In sum, Bacque's *Other Losses* won over mass readers owing to its sensational charge of a monstrous atrocity committed by the Allies. As one critic lamented: "It [historical truth] can never be found by anyone who fails to set out carefully the context, which is to be found in a mass of documents. But that would take years of research and would hardly produce bestsellers."[25]

The Rape of Nanking Compared

The late Iris Chang detailed Japanese atrocities in Nanking, in part by drawing on her discovery of the diary of John Rabe, chair of the International Committee (IC) for the Nanking Safety Zone (NSZ). Her book immediately became a bestseller after appearing in late 1997 and has received largely positive reviews, especially from nonhistorians. As James Bacque's case shows, however, bestsellers are not necessarily carefully written scholarly monographs that stand up to academic scrutiny. Few critics doubt the authenticity of individual atrocity cases detailed in Rabe's diary as related by Chang, just as Bacque's critics did not deny the truthfulness of his individual eyewitness accounts. But there is ample room to question her on larger contextual issues: how and why did the Atrocity occur, and what was the actual extent of human losses?

Chang had a few early critics. In November 1997, *Kirkus Reviews* said, "this slight account will by no means be the last word" and concluded that she "rushes to simplify complex events and to universalize what happened at the expense of careful, comprehensive appreciation of a world violently destroyed."[26] The late Richard B. Finn of American University cast doubt on her high estimates of the death toll—200,000 to over 350,000—by calling attention to Rabe's own estimate of 50,000 to 60,000.[27] David M. Kennedy of Stanford University took critical note of the conspiracy theory implicit in Chang's book by pointing to her frequent references to David Bermamini's largely discredited book, *Japan's Imperial Conspiracy.*[28]

These criticisms suggest that Chang's work shares some elements that made Bacque's *Other Losses* popular among the ordinary public, and careful analysis indeed reveals some common traits. First, like Bacque, Chang's clamor for originality is conspicuous even though many of her sources have long been available to, and used by, scholars. For example, she claims to have "unearthed" a court exhibit from the International Military Tribunal for the Far East (IMTFE), better known as the Tokyo War Crimes Trials, for use in tabulating the Nanking victim count. Japanese historians, however, have not only mentioned the source countless times, but also reviewed its authenticity and credibility extensively.[29] Chang's discovery of Rabe's diary should be credited as a journalistic achievement, but even Carol Gluck of Columbia University, a bitter critics of Japanese deniers, says that it only corroborates information from existing sources.[30] Second, despite Chang's reserved statement about the emperor's role in Nanking, her eagerness to pin responsibility on the top echelon of Japanese leaders shows up in her conjectures that he knew about atrocities there.[31] Such an implicit resort to conspiracy theory finds a parallel with Bacque's *Other Losses,* and most likely has served to increase the popularity of Chang's work. Commenting on this shared trait, Thomas Baker, in a chapter in *Eisenhauer and the German POWs: Facts against Fiction,* cited "the general public's perennial receptivity to charges of conspiracy" as "the basic ingredient of a common recipe for writing bestsellers."[32] Third, Chang and Bacque emphasize the number of victims in order to illustrate the magnitude of the alleged atrocities. Openly or implicitly, both call these events equal to or worse than other mass killings in history including atomic warfare. Thus Bacque says that "by the end of May [1945], more people had died in the U.S. [POW] camps than died in the atomic blast at Hiroshima," and Chang says that her high-end estimate of 377,000 victims at Nanking "surpasses the death toll for the atomic blasts at Hiroshima and Nagasaki combined."[33] Fourth, Chang and Bacque both tell stories of heroes amid tragedy, effectively highlighting the victimizers' malicious character. Lastly, both authors assail collective indifference to their cases. Bacque says, "Not a word reached the press" after he referred to the number of A-bomb victims for comparison purposes. Chang too says, "The Rape of Nanking was front-page news across the world, and yet most of the world stood by and did nothing while an entire city was butchered."[34]

Dual Standards and Perceptions

Thus, sensationalism is striking in both books, but receptions differed. From the start, Bacque's critics questioned his estimated death toll and postulated motive behind the alleged mass killing. One review noted the "intrinsic impossibility that so vast an atrocity could so long have been utterly hidden."[35] The renowned military historian Michael Howard echoed: "the idea of getting a million prisoners starved to death, without anyone saying a word about it, for no reason except that Eisenhower disliked Germans, takes some swallowing."[36] In stark contrast, Iris Chang's reviewers, with few exceptions, swallowed her claims whole or opted for her higher estimates of casualties. Orville Schell of the University of California, Berkeley, said: "experts now believe the number to be over 350,000" and called it "an extraordinary figure."[37] Such reviewers ignored the commonsense approach adopted by Bacque's critics; that is, to doubt a figure precisely because it is extraordinary. Nor did they reason as did John H. Boyle in his college textbook on modern Japan: "One fact suggesting that the Chinese estimates are too high is that remarkably little notice of the incident was taken by either Chinese or the Western powers at the time."[38] Even the scholarly contributors to Josua A. Fogel's edited volume, *The Nanking Massacre in History and Historiography*—which could have played a role similar to Bischof and Ambrose, *Eisenhower and the German POWs: Facts against Falsehood*—chose not to examine factual details such as how many people actually did die.[39] Popular commentators accepted Chang's charge of collective, willful amnesia by the Japanese to this day. Thus George F. Will titled his review of her book, "Breaking a Sinister Silence."[40] Some reviews opposed these mainstay opinions, but these were a minority and appeared only later, largely in specialized periodicals that ordinary citizens do not read.[41] All of this contrasts with the Bacque debate: critical reviews of *Other Losses* appeared immediately in mass media sources, most notably the *New York Times*.[42]

One cannot overlook the oddity, if not a double standard, in the two books' receptions. *After* careful scrutiny, Bacque's reviewers rejected his thesis that a deliberate policy of starving Germans resulted in fatalities matching the number of atomic bomb victims, whereas *before* or *without* a similar probe or investigation, Chang's reviewers largely accepted her similar thesis as to the Japanese intent and Chinese death toll at Nanking. Regrettably, ethnic prejudice may be a factor explaining Chang's popularity. When I was a graduate student at the University of Alabama, Tuscaloosa, several years before Chang's book came out, I talked informally about Nanking with an American student and said that I doubted the often-quoted Chinese death figure of 300,000. Her response dumbfounded me: "Then, the Japanese troops killed *even more!*" Although a former 1-year exchange student in Japan who had favorable impressions of it, she still was not immune to this prejudicial wartime view.

Most critics neglect to dwell on this issue. Fogel's superb collection of essays is a case in point. His contributors speak of Japanese racism or chauvinism.[43] But they limit their analysis to deplorable Japanese and, to a lesser extent, Chinese attitudes while ignoring a similar American mindset. They may retort that the United States lies outside their purview, but given the heightened emotions surrounding Nanking there, and the worldwide impact that American opinions have, failure to address the issue of anti-Japanese sentiment is a serious omission or flaw. Thus, even those professional historians who do criticize Chang's book underestimate American anti-Japanese prejudice. They also unduly disregard the vast gap in scholarly and popular receptions of the books in question, whereas Bacque's critics were keenly aware of that gap. A review by Fogel of Iris Chang's book thus notes, "had a white person written this chapter [on Japanese martial mentality], I can imagine screams of racism ringing *through the halls of academe*" (italics added).[44] Unfortunately, a seemingly racially motivated statement by a white male *outside of academe* appeared and, as far as I know, has gone uncriticized. Russell Jenkins writes:

> consider that the United States, on all fronts, lost 323,000 in the four years of World War II. Or that at Auschwitz the Nazis killed on average 350,000 every two months. The Japanese killed roughly the same number in a few months without the benefit of the technology of mass murder available to the Nazis and without the advantage of concentration camps.... What's more, the Japanese troops weren't "specialized": nothing comparable to the *Einsatzgruppen* existed in their military. These were the boys next door.... *the Rape of Nanking reminds us how recently Japan emerged from its medieval age; a scant 140 years ago, less than 100 at the time of the Rape.*[45] (italics added)

Russell Jenkins was not alone. George F. Will, in the *Washington Post*, wrote, "Japanese soldiers murdered tens of thousands of surrendered Chinese soldiers, and almost certainly more than 300,000 noncombatants. (Civilian death at Hiroshima and Nagasaki totaled 210,000. Britain and France suffered a combined total of 169,000 civilian deaths from 1939 to 1945.)"[46] Donald MacInnis, in a foreward to Zhang Kaiyuan's *Eyewitnesses to Massacre: American Missionaries Bear Witness to Japanese Atrocities in Nanjing,* closely echoes Chang: "Estimates of soldiers and noncombatants killed range from 260,000 to 350,000—more than the combined death toll of both the atomic bombs dropped on Japan (140,000 and 70,000).[47] Will, MacInnis, and other nonspecialist commentators did not manifest racist overtones as explicitly as Jenkins. Yet one cannot but wonder if they uncritically accepted Chang's death toll of "over 350,000"—which defies conventional wisdom—because of the alleged perpetrators' nationality. This impression grows stronger when we contrast their comments with the skepticism of Bacque's critics toward his allegations about German victims.

Since most laypersons in North America do not read balanced academic opinions, their impression of Nanking will likely remain the one acquired from Chang's book—something visual and graphic rather than analytic and empirical. The perception gap between professional historians and general readers—an issue addressed by Bacque's critics—is far more acute regarding Nanking, perhaps owing to this ethnic factor, and is exacerbated by the neglect or failure by American and Western historians to investigate historical facts in the Nanking Atrocity. Fogel explicitly stated in his introduction to *The Nanjing Massacre in History and Historiography* that contributors would not delve into minute factual details of the Atrocity itself.[48] Except for my own monograph, later articles and books published in English on Nanking have mainly dealt with historiography, and very few with history.[49] A possible explanation for the scarcity of empirical research is that American and Western historians have already solidified an image of the Atrocity and are reluctant to reconsider it critically. Any challenge to the consensus is likely to be seen as "revisionism" worthy of the condemnation shown to Holocaust deniers. Fogel's introduction thus states, "We take for granted that those claims [of Nanking denial in Japan] have been made for an assortment of unsavory political reasons or misguided emotional or nationalistic ones."[50] Likewise, Carol Gluck identified Japanese scholars and journalists who in general agree with the official Chinese interpretation of "300,000 or more" victims as speaking "for honesty."[51] The implication is that anyone who opposes the left-wing Japanese view deserves condemnation for "dishonesty."

"Revisionists" Revisited

Yet is it fair to conclude outright that Nanking "revisionists" represent dishonesty? Bacque's critics fully affirm that comparative degrees of suffering and misery inflicted on victims cannot be measured, much less can one atrocity be used to cancel out another, but their main contention was that comparative degrees of evil in perpetrators *can* be measured. If this logic is valid, it is inconsistent to dismiss similar logic when applied to the Japanese at Nanking. This point bears repeating because so many insist that Nanking was an East Asian Holocaust, and Chang's death toll for it seems designed to highlight Japanese evil.[52] Thus, it is unfair to label all Japanese who question the prevailing American interpretation of Atrocity "Nanking deniers" analogous to those who refuse to admit the Holocaust's historicity. Those who advance their theses in an academic manner—as was true with Bacque's critics—should be treated as "revisionists" in the true sense.

Classifying these "revisionists" is tricky, however. Even left-wing historians fit the category if they seek to "revise" current interpretations of the IMTFE ruling. Timothy Brook in chapter 7 takes issue with virtually all scholars to date who overlook the awkward fact that both the bench and prosecution dropped charges of conspiracy at the IMTFE, and instead settled for Gen.

Matsui Iwane's guilty verdict in a crime of omission, not commission. In other words, the IMTFE found that Matsui failed to stop men under his command from committing war crimes, not that he planned or ordered these.[53] Left-wing historians also argue that the IMTFE and Nanking military tribunal were insufficient or flawed because the true culprits escaped legal retribution or died prematurely of natural causes.[54] But these attempts also seek to "revise" the prevailing interpretation of the IMTFE. Conversely, conservative "revisionists" strive to refute or lower the enormously high death figures claimed at the Tokyo and Nanking tribunals, as cited by Chang and by other commentators.

Whether revision is liberal or conservative, left-wing or right-wing, the basic guiding principle in historical study is, as Yang Daqing states, "vigorous [*recte:* rigorous] empirical research, critical evaluation of evidence, and responsible reappraisal."[55] Pitfalls lie in both directions. Takashi Yoshida, another of Fogel's contributors, criticizes conservative revisionists for "discrediting entire accounts by stressing partial inaccuracies."[56] This point has merit: some revisionists do reject whole documents or testimonies as worthless owing to pica-yune errors. But the obverse is equally fallacious; it is wrong to expand on the partial accuracy of one piece of evidence to extrapolate claims that it cannot support. One of James Bacque's critics says: "Where is the central mistake in Bacque's argument? Essentially, he assumes that the conditions that admittedly prevailed in sixteen of the 200 camps for a certain period (April to June or July, 1945, according to camp) in fact extended to all 200 American camps for the whole period 1945–1946, a basis of procedure that can be proved false."[57] Wittingly or not, Chang commits this fallacy when she cites the Sixty-sixth Regiment's order to execute Chinese POWs summarily as an example of Japanese army policy.[58] This implies that every Japanese unit issued the same order even though other sources, plus eyewitness accounts by a former Chinese soldier, suggests that army-wide treatment of POWs was inconsistent and in fact varied widely. The sources show that at least one unit released large numbers of POWs on the spot, whereas another interned POWs in holding camps inside the city.[59]

Another criticism against Japanese conservative "revisionists" is that they manipulate statistics to good advantage. Here again, the other side is guilty too. Chang declares, "Japanese treatment of their POWs surpassed in brutality even that of the Nazis. Only one in twenty-five American POWs died under Nazi captivity, in contrast to one in three under the Japanese."[60] These death rates may be accurate in and of themselves, but Chang totally ignores the Nazis' racist policy that accorded preferential treatment to Anglo-Saxon POWs, who numbered about 90,000, and wholly excludes from consideration the 3.7 million Russian POWs (out of a total 5.7 million captured) who died in German camps—to say nothing of six million Jews in the Holocaust.[61]

Thus Chang limits Nazi conduct on benign treatment of U.S. POWs but describes Japanese conduct in ways designed to impress readers with Japanese genocidal intent.

Left-wing scholars also allege that, in order to get a lower victim count, conservative "revisionists" purposely limit the spatial area of "Nanking" to the walled city and immediate vicinity and also shorten the Atrocity's time span to the six weeks immediately after the city fell.[62] A "proper" set of parameters, leftists say, requires adding several counties adjacent to the walled city and lengthening time span to three or four months. Fujiwara Akira and Kasahara Tokushi do that in chapters 2 and 3 of this volume, and this lets them reach much higher victim counts. But here, it is the left-wing, not the right-wing, camp that is being "revisionist." Ever since the IMTFE, the "traditionally" accepted parameters of this event have been the walled city and its environs within a time span of six weeks.

Some commentators can also be charged with ulterior motives in their "manipulation" of time and space; by severely limiting the area and time span involved, they play up the scale and intensity of Japanese barbarity. Tuan Yue-p'ing, a mainland Chinese historian, calculated the average number of victims in Nanking per day at an astounding 8,095 on the assumption that within six weeks "the Japanese military apparatus had slaughtered more than 340,000 Chinese POWs and civilians."[63] She then declares, "The fact that such a large number of people were slaughtered within such a short period of time is an extremely rare event in human history..., the daily death rate was one of the highest throughout World War II. For example, in Auschwitz, the infamous death camp in Poland, Nazi butchers exterminated 1.5 million people in 56 months (Jun. 1940–Jan. 1945), an average of 879 people per day."[64] Tuan's contention is based on fatally flawed data. As David Askew argues in chapter 5, there were *less than* 340,000 Chinese troops and civilians in the walled city and its immediate vicinity prior to the Japanese assault.[65] So, in this regard, those Japanese conservative "revisionists" who insist on the "traditional" limitations on space and time have a valid point.

A related problem of numerical evidence arises when leftist scholars claim that post hoc IMTFE evidence is more credible and has more probative value than that available eight to ten years earlier, at the time of the event in December 1937 or shortly after.[66] This is a crucial issue that divides the two camps in this debate. Apart from true deniers who turn a blind eye to any incriminating evidence, conservative "revisionists" deem contemporaneous evidence more reliable than that used to attest a larger-scale massacre later on at the IMTFE. Yet, despite endorsing the IMTFE's ruling, Mark Eykholt admits that at least one piece of IMTFE evidence was highly dubious—testimony by a Nanking citizen, Lu Su, about the massacre of 57,418 Chinese nonbelligerents at Mufushan.[67] Eykholt's position is intriguing because the bench's majority opinion in fact adopted Lu's figure in its ruling, along with several other dubious pieces of evidence, to create currently accepted victims counts of 200,000 to 350,000.[68] However, the point here is that, if disputing the probative value of IMTFE evidence is permissible to Eykholt, the same act should not be damned as a cunning "denial" tactic by Japanese conservative revisionists.

Finally, leftists such as Yang Daqing accuse Japanese conservative revisionists of "misguided empiricism" whereby they privilege those primary sources that lack references to the Nanking Atrocity in order to deny its basis in fact.[69] A notable specific case is that of the late Tanaka Masaaki, who argued that no Atrocity took place because Ho Ying-chin, Chinese defense minister at the time, said nothing about it in his 1938 military report.[70] Inoue Hisashi, another left-wing critic, dismissed this document, arguing that it is only natural that military reports did not discuss atrocities irrelevant to their main theme—the chronicling of military operations.[71] Ironically, Inoue's point would carry equal weight when used to dispute charges by Yang and Honda Katsuichi that the Japanese Defense Agency history of the war in China is a flawed source because it devotes only tiny space to the Nanking Atrocity. In other words, the Defense Agency's aim was to discuss military operations, not to describe atrocities, so its scant reference to the Atrocity does not constitute a cover-up.[72]

Since each historian has a field of special interest and cannot cover all aspects of an event, it is unfair to assign blame for ignoring a particular perspective. For example, Chang noted with amazement that Winston S. Churchill did not mention the Nanking Atrocity in his memoir on World War II. Apparently, she was unaware that in the same monograph, he only touched on prewar Nazi persecutions of Jews in Germany leading to the genuine Holocaust.[73] He did so, we can assume, because both atrocities lay outside his main focus of interest. Many Western military historians devote little space to the Nazi Holocaust in studies of World War Two. Basil H. Liddell-Hart's classic *History of the Second World War* hardly discusses death camps or the mobile killing units, the *Einsatzgruppen*. J. F. C. Fuller devoted but a few sentences to the Holocaust in a general section on atrocities.[74] Obviously, that does not make them Holocaust deniers. In the same manner, scant mention of the Nanking Atrocity does not necessarily mean that Japanese military historians deny or dismiss it as an illusion. Even some postwar Chinese works allocate little or no space to the Atrocity. *K'ang-chan chien-shih* and *Chung-Jih chan-chen-shih lueh,* published by the Taiwan Defense Ministry in Taipei, devote about eleven characters to the Atrocity. The same is true of Chiang Wei-kuo's *Kuo-min ke-ming chan-shih.*[75] F. F. Liu's standard *A Military History of Modern China: 1924–1949* made no mention of the Atrocity in his narrative of the Nanking campaign.[76] Obviously, none of these authors denied the Atrocity.

Propositions

Some scholars emphasize a need to establish common historical understanding that transcends national and ethnic boundaries.[77] This is certainly a desirable aim, and one can detect a positive sign conducive to this goal: there are some indications of convergence in the views of Japanese, Chinese, and Western professional historians.[78] As interest on Nanking grows, North Americans can play a pivotal role in achieving this goal since they are a third party to this historical event. But general trends in the United States do not seem to be moving in that direction. It is true that, swayed by chauvinism, some Japanese people make preposterous arguments that can hardly be academic. Yet reactions to Chang's *The Rape of Nanking* in the Unites States strongly imply the existence of similar twisted forms of nationalism there as well. In spite of scholarly analyses by Joshua A. Fogel and his colleagues, ordinary Americans seem beset with negative ethnic factors and sensationalism. Thus, the horizontal convergence emerging across national boundaries is not yet effective in narrowing the gap in perspectives between academics and the general public—a vertical gap in a sense.

Sadly, the less-informed sometimes exploit illegal means to advance their cause. Early in 2000, Tokyo metropolitan government computers were intruded by "Nanking Hackers," likely Chinese-Americans judging from their messages, who also tried to access Japanese central government sites without authorization. They left messages in English and Chinese giving their view of the Atrocity plus a note saying, "Japanese? As all people know, it's a folk that has no courage to face the truth of history. It's the disgrace of Asia!"[79] This incident, regrettably, substantiates Eykholt's view that Chinese and Chinese-American "knowledge of the Massacre [Nanking Atrocity] comes from family stories, school lessons, and newspaper accounts. Their information usually comes without much of the wartime context or the world situation at the time, and the feelings are patriotic and emotional, which in turn inspire hatred of Japan and tend to ignore the complicated situation surrounding the Massacre and its postwar metamorphosis."[80]

Japanese cruelty in World War Two forged empathy in the United States for ethnic Chinese.[81] Still, the United States was a third party to the Atrocity and there has been ample opportunity for ordinary Americans to initiate a meaningful and reasonable dialogue about it. Yet amid the current agitated environment, we are in need of some guiding principles in the debate over Nanking. I propose two, aimed mainly at professional historians, although not necessarily limited to them.

1. *Recognize a multiplicity of views and adhere to universally accepted scholarly standards.* Japanese conservative "revision," though postulating a smaller numerical range of victimization, differs from "denial." For example, I offer a range of 15,000 to 50,000 victims.[82] Historians probing into the Nanking

Atrocity are advised at least to recognize the scholarly legitimacy of such "revisionists" as long as they work within the rules of academe. Of course, this does not mean that historians must abandon higher estimates. All they have to do is "agree to disagree"—a common attitude not only in academic debates, but also in other realms of peaceful human activity. I advance this proposition because the Nanking debate has a polarized "all or nothing" nature; one almost has to accept the 300,000 figure or be damned as a "denier." Yang cites an example. Two Japanese scholars equivocated when an American historian declared: "The question about the Nanking Incident at this point is ... whether to recognize it. At the present, it is not necessary to admit whether there were 30,000 or 300,000 victims."[83] Although this is pure speculation, it may be that they felt trapped. If they said "no," they would be criticized for lacking moral compassion; but if they said "yes," their answer might be plucked out of context as affirming a massacre of 300,000. A better question to pose is: "Do you recognize a massacre of 300,000 or of 30,000, or deny both entirely?"

Left-wing scholars may dismiss my reasoning as a sophistic numbers game. Here again, the parallel to James Bacque is enlightening. His critic, Ruediger Overmans, tabulated deaths in the Allied POW camps and said, "it is certainly possible that some additional tens of thousands of deaths occurred, but a further 800,000 to 1,000,000 are not reconcilable with the facts"[84] My point is this: the gap between Bacque and his critics alters the debate's whole dimensions. If his critics were to accept his range, they would have no choice but to embrace his conclusion as well; that is, German POWs were starved to death *intentionally*. Their own numerical range, however, fits their conclusion that the deaths mainly stemmed from harsh circumstances in the wake of Nazi Germany's fall. It is noteworthy that neither side saw the numerical gap as just a margin of error; instead, they viewed it as a crucial indicator of radically different interpretations.

Although Fogel and his colleagues eschew numerical analysis, they too seem tied to an allowable numerical range under their interpretation. Fogel says, "whether 200,000 people were killed or 240,000 does not alter the dimensions of horror."[85] Why does he exclude Japanese "conservative"—whether in the sense of ideological or numerical—estimates of 40,000 or less? One can reason that it is because he and his contributors basically agree with the IMTFE ruling of 20,000 rapes and 200,000 killed in and around the city in 6 to 7 weeks. Several indications support this reasoning. The book's dust-jacket summary contains these numbers. Takashi Yoshida corrects Iris Chang's misquotation of the IMFTE's ruling, which implies his close attention to or endorsement of it. Mark Eykholt refers to much lower initial estimates of 50,000 to 60,000 made by Westerners in Nanking at the time such as John Rabe, but clearly states: "these initial estimates proved wholly inadequate as war crimes trials and burial records documented death totals that exceed 100,000 and possibly exceed 300,000."[86] Their underlying implication is that a figure as low as

40,000 will "alter the dimensions of horror" unacceptably. As in the Bacque debate, the numerical gap is too wide to be dismissed as just a margin error: it reflects two fundamentally opposed interpretations. Thus, scholars should pay more attention to the issue of numbers rather than dismiss it as a "game." That will allow for recognizing multiple positions on the Atrocity instead of a bipolar "moral high ground of 300,000" or "the damnable deniers' zero."

2. *Banish the terms* Holocaust *and* genocide *from this controversy.* One may argue that *holocaust* is not sensational: it is a generic term for any kind of atrocious or traumatic event. But at present, the same word starting with an uppercase letter means the Nazi genocide of Jewry. As Chang's subtitle, The Forgotten Holocaust of World War II, and passages in her book suggest, she equates Japanese with Nazi conduct: "Just as Hitler's Germany would do half a decade later, Japan used a highly developed military machine and a master-race mentality to set about establishing its right to rule its neighbors," or "another lesson to be gleaned from Nanking is the role of power in geno-cide."[87] Jacob Heilbrunn rightly criticized her: "This is unfortunate since the massacre was not—for all its murderous horror—an attempt to wipe out the Chinese as a race."[88] In chapter 12 of the present work, Fogel eloquently argues this point in detail.

The impact of "the Holocaust" is profound when transmitted verbally. Nonspecialists—who cannot tell if its first letter is in the upper or lower case—will visualize concentration camps, gas chambers, and mobile killing units *(Einsatzgruppen)* owing to the widely proliferating information on the gen-uine Holocaust. The result will be to place the Nanking Atrocity outside of its proper historical context. Again, Bacque's critics provide an apt warning. Brian Loring Villa writes: "sensation is the most easily achieved by simply wrenching a subject out of its context and discarding, ignoring, or distorting that context. Novel theses, striking revelations, and horrific criminality are easily achievable by such means.... Conspiracies have taken place in history, but they abound unnaturally in amateur historical writing because their authors are unwilling or incapable of examining the historical context."[89] A case in point was left on the Internet by an American from Massachusetts before Chang's book came out: "The Japanese killed millions of Chinese for racial purification.... The Japanese fought a war of aggression, based on the-ories of racial and ethnic purity."[90] It is not difficult to imagine that Chang's subtitle will misguide such uninformed persons even further.

The careless use of sensational vocabulary may produce, or has already pro-duced, highly undesirable effects on lay audiences. First, it may intensify prej-udice against Japanese and ethnic Japanese. Immediately after Chang's book appeared, the State Assembly in California—where anti-Japanese movements began in the last century—passed a resolution demanding that Tokyo com-pensate Nanking Atrocity victims. Second, because other atrocities in history also may improperly be likened to the Jewish Holocaust, its significance cannot but be slighted.[91] This is exactly what Holocaust deniers want. They are beginning to exploit Nanking as a rival "holocaust" to relativize the actual one, claiming that what the Nazis did was no different from other wartime tragedies.[92] Third, a conspiracy theory replete with sensationalist terms is spawning a counter-theory in kind. Some Japanese allege that the People's Republic of China and the Chinese Communist Party are backing Chang's followers in a scheme "to drive a wedge into the Japan-U.S. Alliance, which is an obstacle on the road to hegemony."[93] Such politicized accusations and counteraccusations are highly detrimental to a constructive dialogue toward historical truth.

Conclusion

As Yang Daqing argues, "historians alone cannot adequately cope with such an event or bring an end to the divergence of views or the emotional content of this subject."[94] Underlining this view, Honda Katsuichi has energetically striven to collect primary sources and to deepen our understanding of the Atrocity, although I am more or less critical of his conclusions.[95] Chang's discovery of John Rabe's diary should also be praised as a journalistic achievement. Yet including nonacademics in this debate allows the expression of extreme and sometimes egregiously mistaken opinions. The historian Edward Drea quotes intriguing remarks by a distinguished journalist, Marvin Kalb, about reports of an alleged U.S. army massacre of Korean civilians in the Korean War: "When journalists go back ten years and then forty and fifty years, they take on the tools of a historian. That requires a special kind of skill, which they don't have."[96] Professional historians should take note. In order to narrow the gap between our own admittedly varied perspectives on the Nanking Atrocity and those held by the general population, we must strive to correct unhealthy, irrational research and remarks by uninformed commentators.

Notes

1. I would like to thank Dr. Daniel Metraux of Mary Baldwin College, who encouraged me to write a preliminary essay, later published in the *Virginia Review of Asian Studies* (Fall 2000), pp. 39–73, on which this chapter was originally based. The Southern Japan Seminar invited me to give a paper condensed from that essay in Atlanta on 27 April 2001. The Japan "Nanking" Society invited me to speak on the same topic in Tokyo on 16 March 2002. A Japanese version of the present chapter appeared in *"Nankin" kenkyû no saizensen* (Tokyo: Tendensha, 2003), pp. 141–92.
2. Eykholt, "Aggression, Victimization, and Chinese Historiography of the Nanking Massacre," p. 57.
3. Yang, "Challenges of the Nanjing Massacre," p. 154.
4. Ibid., pp. 153–58; Chang, *Rape of Nanking*, p. 221.
5. Bacque, *Other Losses*, pp. 1–2, 24–26, 34, 51, 55–56, 64, 164, and 175–86.

6. Ibid., pp. 45–46.
7. Ibid, pp. 67, 70, 84–85, 93–97, 99–101, 103–5, and 158.
8. *Los Angeles Times,* 3 May 1990.
9. Green, review in *Booklist,* 15 June 1991.
10. *MacLean's,* 13 November 1989, p. 70.
11. *Los Angeles Times,* 13 May 1990.
12. Bischof and Ambrose, eds., *Eisenhower and the German POWs,* p. 18.
13. Villa, "Diplomatic and Political Context of the POW Camps Tragedy," pp. 53–61.
14. James F. Tent, "Food Shortages in Germany and Europe," pp. 95–112.
15. Albert E. Cowdrey, "Question of Numbers," p. 92. Cowdrey compared this rate to the overall death rate of 0.7 to 1 percent among Allied POWs in Axis hands. A possible problem is that he ignored the time factor; many of the German POWs died over several months whereas the less-than 1 per cent of Allied POW deaths occurred over the entire period of World War Two.
16. Overmans, "German Historiography, the War Losses, and the Prisoners of War," pp. 149, 151, and 16–68. As for corpses, he said, "Bacque's 726,000 dead would mean roughly 3,600 dead per kilometer, or 5,800 per mile—better than one corpse per foot. Yet despite the widespread construction work carried out after the war, not a single one of these legions of dead was found."
17. Bischof and Ambrose, eds., *Eisenhower and the German POWs,* p. 23.
18. Cowdrey, "Question of Numbers," p. 84.
19. Villa, "Diplomatic and Political Context," p. 53; Bischof, "Bacque and the Historical Evidence," p. 199.
20. Cowdey, "Question of Numbers," p. 92.
21. Bischof, "Bacque and Historical Evidence," p. 222.
22. Overmans, "German Historiography" p. 169.
23. Ibid.
24. Bischof, "Bacque and Historical Evidence," p. 222.
25. Villa, "Diplomatic and Political Context of the POW Camps Tragedy," p. 77.
26. *Kirkus Reviews,* 1 November 1997, p. 1,618.
27. Finn, letter to editor, *Washington Post,* 5 March 1998. Chang mentions Rabe's estimate but seemingly dismisses it as unreliable: "John Rabe ... never conducted a systematic count and left Nanking in February, before the slaughter ended." Chang, *Rape of Nanking,* p. 100. If we follow her logic, more people were massacred after Rabe departed in February 1938, but this contradicts her allegation that the "Rape of Nanking continued for months, although the worst of it was concentrated in the first six to eight weeks." Ibid., p. 159.
28. Kennedy, "Horror."
29. Chang, *Rape of Nanking,* pp. 101–02; for my own analysis, Yamamoto, *Nanking,* pp. 110–13.
30. Gluck, "Rape of Nanking."
31. Chang, *Rape of Nanking,* pp. 178–79.
32. Baker, "British Variety of Pseudohistory," p. 196.
33. Bacque, *Other Losses,* p. 68; Chang, *Rape of Nanking,* p. 101.
34. Bacque, *Other Losses,* p. 68; Chang, *Rape of Nanking,* p. 105.
35. *Economist,* 25 November 1989.
36. Howard, "A Million Lost Germans," *Times Literary Supplement,* 14–20 September 1990.
37. Schell, review in *New York Times Book Review,* 14 December 1997. Other reviews that uncritically accepted the higher estimate include *Publishers Weekly,* 27 October 1997, and *Booklist,* 1 December 1997. William J. Davis in *Marine Corps Gazette,* September 1998, says that he changed his earlier view of Nanking to accept Chang's claim of 300,000 "civilians" killed.
38. Boyle, *Modern Japan,* p. 189.
39. Fogel, Introduction, p. 5.
40. Will, *Washington Post,* 19 February 1998.

41. For example, see Finn's letter in *Washington Post*, 5 March 1998; Fogel's review in *Journal of Asian Studies*, August 1998; and Kennedy's in *Atlantic Monthly*, April 1998.
42. Ambrose, "Ike and Disappearing Atrocities," *New York Times Book Review*, 24 February 1991.
43. Eykholt, "Aggression, Victimization, and Chinese Historiography" p. 17; Yang, "Challenges of the Nanking Massacre," p. 159.
44. Fogel, review in *Journal of Asian Studies*, August 1998.
45. Jenkins, "The Japanese Holocaust." One can infer the absence of criticism from the fact that the same article is still posted on an internet web page (http://www.nationalreview.com/10nov97/jenkins111097. html) as of late November 2006.
46. *Washington Post*, 19 February 1998.
47. MacInnis, Foreword, p. ix.
48. Fogel, Introduction, p. 5.
49. Two possible exceptions are Honda, *The Nanjing Massacre*, and Hu, *American Goddess at the Rape of Nanking*. However, the former is a translation from Japanese, and the latter is focused on a personality rather than on the incident itself and it contains many factual errors.
50. Fogel, Introduction, p. 5.
51. Gluck, "Rape of Nanking."
52. Chang called the Nanking Atrocity the "Pacific Holocaust" at a meeting with Japanese guests in Flushing, New York on 28 June 1998; see Yoshida, "A Battle over History in Japan," pp. 131–32, note 191. Will, Schell, Green, Jenkins, and Davis all accept Chang high-end death count of 300,000 or even more.
53. For the details of the IMTFE deliberations, see Yamamoto, *Nanking*, chap. 6, and also, p. 217 for the change in the prosecution's strategy.
54. For example, see Eykholt, "Aggression, Victimization, and Chinese Historiography," pp. 18–24.
55. Yang, "Challenges of the Nanjing Massacre," p. 147.
56. Yoshida, "Battle over History in Japan," p. 107.
57. Overmans, "German Historiography," p. 169.
58. Chang, *Rape of Nanking*, p. 41.
59. On Japanese army treatment of Chinese POWs, see Yamamoto, *Nanking*, pp. 93–109.
60. Chang, *Rape of Nanking* p.173. Her note on pp. 273–74 cites Ken Ringle, "Still Waiting for an Apology," *Washington Post*, 16 March 1995; and Gavan Daws, *Prisoners of the Japanese*, pp. 360–61 and p. 437. She obviously accepts these analyses uncritically.
61. For the numerical data on Russian POWs in German hands, see Dallin, *German Rule in Russia 1941–1945*, p. 427.
62. Yoshida, "Battle over History in Japan," p. 104; Yang, "Challenges of the Nanjing Massacre," p. 149.
63. Cited in Li, "Unforgivable Atrocity."
64. Ibid., p. 17.
65. For estimates of Chinese troop strength and population, see Yamamoto, *Nanking*, pp. 46–48 and p. 65.
66. Eykholt, "Aggression, Victimization, and Chinese Historiography," p. 69, note 154.
67. Ibid., p. 52.
68. IMTFE, *Proceedings, 1946–1948*, p. 49 and p. 607; for other questionable Chinese evidence, see Yamamoto, *Nanking*, pp. 190–94 and 206.
69. Yang, "Challenges of the Nanking Massacre," pp. 146–47.
70. Tanaka, *Nankin gyakusatsu no kyokô*, pp. 55–58.
71. Inoue, "Nankin jiken to Chûgoku kyôsantô," pp. 168–69.
72. Yang, "Challenges of the Nanjing Massacre," p. 154; Honda, *Nanjing Massacre*, p. 139.
73. Chang, *Rape of Nanking*, p. 7; Churchill, *Second World War*, vol. 1, p. 139.
74. Liddell-Hart, *History of the Second World War;* its index includes neither "Holocaust" nor "Jews"; Fuller, *Second World War 1939–45;* pp. 407–8.

75. Kuo-fang-pu shih-cheng chu, ed., *K'ang-chan chien-shih* p. 52; Kuo-fang-pu shih-cheng chu, ed., *Chung-Jih chan-chen-shih lueh,* p. 198; Chiang, *Kuo-min ke-ming chan-shih Ti-3-pu K'ang-Jih yu-wu,* vol. 4, p. 75.
76. Liu, *Military History of Modern China,* pp. 198–99.
77. Yang, "Challenges of the Nanking Massacre," pp. 162–68.
78. Yang, "Convergence or Divergence?"
79. *Japan Times International,* 1–15 February 2000.
80. Eykholt, "Aggression, Victimization, and Chinese Historiography," p. 59.
81. Yamamoto, *Nanking,* pp. 178–81.
82. Ibid., p. 115.
83. Ibid.
84. Overmans, "German Historiography," p. 167.
85. Fogel, Introduction, p. 6.
86. Eykholt, "Aggression, Victimization, and Chinese Historiography," p. 69, note 154.
87. Chang, *Rape of Nanking,* pp. 2–4 and p. 220.
88. *Wall Street Journal,* 20 December 1997.
89. Villa, "Diplomatic and Political Context of the POW Camps Tragedy," p. 52.
90. See Joseph Edward Nemec, 8 September 1995, in *Tokyo Kaleidoscope,* "Decision of Dropping the A-Bomb in 1945 was right?" http:www.smn.cojp/square/bomb.htn-d.
91. Thus the historian John Hope Franklin called slavery "America's own Holocaust" in *Newsweek,* 8 December 1997.
92. For details, see Yamamoto, *Nanking,* p. 264.
93. Takemoto and Ōhara, *Alleged "Nanking Massacre,"* p. 140.
94. Yang, "Challenges of the Nanking Massacre," p. 172.
95. Yamamoto, *Nanking,* p. 249.
96. Drea, "Dispatches," p. 2.

14

HIGASHINAKANO OSAMICHI: THE LAST WORD IN DENIAL*

Kasahara Tokushi

Introduction

Asia University professor Higashinakano Osamichi (Shûdô) has not always been Japan's premier denier of the Nanking Atrocity. In fact, he was virtually unknown in his own field of Japanese social thought before 1995 when he began to find fault with left-wing historians of Nanking such as myself. Higashinakano owes his eminence as the denial faction's newest standard-bearer to his close collaboration with Fujioka Nobukatsu, then a University of Tokyo education professor, who spearheads "textbook reform" in a crusade against traitors within and enemies abroad. In the pivotal year of 1995, Japan commemorated the fiftieth anniversary of its defeat in the war, and the coalition government headed by socialist Prime Minister Murayama Tomiichi proposed a cabinet resolution to express critical self-reflection about Japan's war of imperialist aggression. Conservative nationalist elements in politics and society reacted with a sense of crisis. As shown by Kimura Takuji in chapter 15, their pressure tactics succeeded in greatly toning down the final document.[1] Taking heart in this "triumph," conservative nationalists sallied forth to attack history textbooks used in schools at that time. This set the stage for Fujioka and Higashinakano.

Traitors Within

Fujioka founded the Society for a Liberated View of History *(Jiyûshugi shikan kenkyûkai)* in 1995 in order to free schools from what he calls the "Comintern" and "Tokyo War Crimes Trial" views of Japanese history. These, he claims, inspire "masochistic" left-wing educators to write textbooks that depict Japan's past as one dark age after another, culminating in alleged war crimes like the Nanking Atrocity and sexual slavery in the imperial armed forces. The Comintern view, he holds, grew out of the biased interpretation of Japanese history dictated by Moscow and adopted in the 1932 Japan Communist Party platform. This view defined Meiji Japan as a system of emperor state absolutism to be overthrown by revolutionary struggle. On the other hand, the Tokyo War Crimes Trial view proclaims that all culpability for the last war lay with the criminal state of Japan. It was putatively foisted on the defeated nation by an all-mighty U.S. army of occupation through a brainwashing policy of shrewd indoctrination. And, it played up Japan's criminality in the Nanking Atrocity, an incident that Americans and Chinese "fabricated" at the punitive Tokyo tribunal. Fujioka insists that these two foreign-imposed views of the past now form the core of Japanese education in history whose adherents aid and abet foreign nations in denying any worth or decency to Japan. Presently used textbooks convey "masochistic views of the past that portray our nation as utterly treacherous and evil."[2]

In January 1997 Fujioka founded a new group, the Society to Create a New Japanese History Textbook, and became its vice-chair with Nishio Kanji as chair.[3] This society sought to create, and gain government certification for, textbooks that glorify Japan's war of imperialist aggression. Its "Statement of Purpose" declared: "Postwar education in history has not just ignored culture and tradition that must be passed on to the Japanese people; it has stripped them of all pride in being Japanese. The history of modern and contemporary Japan in particular is portrayed in ways that force children to view themselves as convicted felons bound by fate to apologize for past sins until they die. Even their children, grandchildren, and great-grandchildren too must continue to beg for forgiveness. Such masochistic trends in education intensified after the Cold War ended, so that textbooks now in use present wartime enemy propaganda as historical facts." This society's "Declaration of Foundation" reads: "We shall create and disseminate a textbook to halt the dissolution of high principles among our people that stems from having been deprived of a national history. This text will once again present an official history of our nation, one that will convey good sense and self-confidence to the next generation."[4] After founding this society, Fujioka was no longer bound to publish only in the relatively obscure journal that serves as the mouthpiece of his earlier Society for a Liberated View of History. He now gained access to conservative mass publishing houses such as Bungei shunjû, Shôgakkan, and the *Sankei shinbun*—a national daily newspaper. The *Sankei shinbun* connection is particularly significant because its subsidiary, the Fusôsha, in 2001 published the "new" textbook that his society sought "to create." Fujioka gave Higashinakano access to these mass-market publishers in order to publicize their views on Nanking.

Higashinakano responded by writing a critique of John Rabe's diary, which had been translated into Japanese and published in 1997. This appeared in the right-wing monthly *Seiron* put out by the Sankei publishing house.[5] Higashinakano also wrote a short piece on "The Nanking Incident" in the *Sankei shinbun* as part of its textbook campaign. In it, he declared: "Textbook authors ... draw conclusions based only on prosecution claims in the Tokyo War Crimes Trials. Until authors find reliable records and photographs definitely proving that an 'Atrocity' took place, they should not present it as a historical fact."[6] Later, he contributed a five-part article to the *Sankei shinbun* entitled "'Nankin' no shijitsu" (Historical facts on "Nanking") denying that anything like a "massive butchery" (*ta-t'u-sha* or *daigyakusatsu* as the Chinese and leftists in Japan call it) occurred. Since Fusôsha, a *Sankei* subsidiary, was to publish the new textbook, it was unethical and counter to established practices for the parent company to criticize textbooks put out by other publishers.

Enemies Abroad

In December 1997, the late Iris Chang, a Chinese-American journalist, published *The Rape of Nanking: The Forgotten Holocaust of World War II,* and it became a best seller with immediate sales of 600,000 copies. The admittedly "panic-stricken" Higashinakano and Fujioka countered in mid-1999 with *"Za reepu obu Nankin" no kenkyû: Chûgoku ni okeru "jôhôsen" no teguchi to senryaku* (Studies of *The Rape of Nanking:* Tricks and Stratagems in China's "Propaganda War"). In their preface, they redundantly carp: "Her book is quintessential Chinese propaganda—one demagogic lie after another. This is wartime Chinese propaganda recast sixty years later to wage a new propaganda war." If we ignore this book, "we will be at their mercy and suffer yet another 'postwar' era that denudes us of all pride.... If we turn the other cheek, her spurious piece of 'hate-Japan' propaganda will turn into a damning 'black book of myths'." So, they declared, "We rise up to counterattack Chang's propaganda.... This book records our struggle."[7]

According to Higashinakano and Fujioka, a foreign conspiracy is at work. Chang based her claim of 200,000 to 300,000 Nanking victims on testimonies and verdicts at the Tokyo War Crimes Trials. Those accounts were concocted in an Allied program of "mind control" to dupe postwar Japanese into believing that imperial Japan was irredeemably evil and thus had to embrace radical reforms imposed by alien conquerors posing as liberators. Higashinakano and Fujioka are not alone in citing Chang's best-seller status overseas as reflecting the reemergence of wartime and Occupation-era hatreds. For example, the right-wing Nihon seinen kyôgikai (Japan youth council) devoted a special edition of its periodical *Sokoku to seinen* (The fatherland and youth) entitled: "Thus Formed an International Anti-Japanese Ring of Encirclement."[8] Its editors wrote pieces such as "Iris Chang: Heroine for International Anti-Japanese Organizations" and "Chinese Machinations to Split Japan and America: What Lurks Behind the *Rape of Nanking* Campaign." Likewise, the once-liberal mass-publisher Shôgakkan's weekly *SAPIO* devoted an issue to "Why Are They Out to Get Us Now?: Machinations in the *Rape of Nanking* Campaign." It carried submissions by deniers, old and new, foreign and domestic: "The Chinese Government behind Support for Madame Chang" by Hamada Kazuyuki, "Then China Created the 'Rape of Nanking' Card to Contain Japan" by Suzuki Akira and Izawa Motohiko, and "China Schemes to Emasculate Japan through a War Game; Then It Will Rule Asia" by Ross H. Munro.[9] Chang-bashing must be viewed in the larger context of right-wing political maneuvers to rearm Japan. In November 1998 President Kiang Tse-min (Jiang Zemin) visited Japan and alleged that the Japanese government and people were not sufficiently repentant for their wartime aggression. His statement served as one more pretext for right-wing media appeals to the effect that, in the face of a threat from China, the Japanese people must take pride in their ancestors' achievements, reject masochistic textbooks, and alter or delete Article IX of their Constitution so that Japan can legally maintain armed forces and exercise their use as a sovereign right of the state. In sum, right-wing nationalists aim to make Japan into what they call a "normal nation"—one that can wage war. The timing of Kiang's (Jiang's) statement and of Chang's book, within months of each other, worked to their advantage.

To Win Hearts and Minds

There is another reason that Higashinakano and Fujioka welcomed Chang's *Rape of Nanking*. Left-wing Japanese historians share Chang's concerns, but even they note that it is fatally flawed as a work of empirical scholarship.[10] Besides committing countless gross errors of fact, she had scant regard for text critique in the use of primary sources. To support her claims, she marshaled any and all materials, including long-discredited photographs. She also played into the hands of Higashinakano and Fujioka in 1999 by blocking the publication of a Japanese translation of her book.[11] This allowed them to win glory at home by exposing her innumerable flaws. But more importantly, in hopes of staging a ninth-inning rally in the Nanking debate, they depict the work of bona fide Japanese historians who acknowledge the Atrocity as being on the same level as Chang. Among their ploys is the patently demagogic claim that a left-wing fifth column aids and abets foreigners in subverting Japan by lying about what took place in Nanking.

In June 1998, Fujioka, Higashinakano, Prof. Nakamura Akira of Dokkyô University, and Prof. Koyama Kazunobu of Kanagawa University held a news conference in Tokyo for thirty reporters at the Foreign Press Correspondents'

Club. In an English-language leaflet, they went beyond criticizing Chang's book for twisting historical facts and using flawed photos; they also argued, "the Nanking Incident is an illusion."[12] But Higashinakano really came into his own at the conference, *"Nanking gyakusatsu" no tettei kenshô* (A thoroughly critical examination of the "Nanking Massacre"), held by the Society for a Liberated View of History at the University of Tokyo in August 1998. There, he lambasted Chang for her anti-Japanese propaganda. But more importantly, old-time nonacademic deniers such as Tanaka Masaaki and Inukai Sôichirô attended this conference at the University of Tokyo, Japan's most prestigious citadel of learning, and pinned their hopes on Higashinakano to pull off a come-from-behind victory in the Nanking debate.

Thereafter, Higashinakano held conferences and symposia to "counterattack this spurious anti-Japanese tract." In September 1998, he and Inukai lectured on a "Total Refuting of *The Rape of Nanking*" at a conference held at Sanseidô Hall—owned by a major academic publisher—in Tokyo. Sponsored by the Society for a Liberated View of History, this conference described How *The Rape of Nanking* Falsifies History. The society held yet another conference, this one at the University of Tokyo's General Education campus at Komaba in December 1998. There, Higashinakano and Fujioka declared their determination to "join the information war; that is, propaganda war, by denying the Nanking Atrocity" and thus thwart this anti-Japanese plot by the People's Republic of China (PRC) and the U.S. State Department. On 31 July 1999 the two men feted the publication of *"Za reepu obu Nankin" no kenkyû* (Studies of [Chang's] *The Rape of Nanking*) by holding a conference at Kudan Hall near Yasukuni Shrine in Tokyo. Reportedly attended by about 1000 people, it was dedicated to "Debunking the Greatest Lie of the Twentieth Century: The 'Massive Butchery at Nanking'."[13]

Thus the Society for a Liberated View of History and Society to Create a New Japanese History Textbook—both led by Fujioka and Higashinakano—became activist and aggressive after the appearance of Chang's book, which they saw as part of a foreign plot to destroy Japan through propaganda warfare. For example, in February 1998 these two men started a Research Unit on Propaganda Photos within the Society for a Liberated View of History to "analyze the staged and faked photographs used in [books on] the Nanking Massacre." Its mission is "to study empirically photographs and illustrations concocted by those with anti-Japanese or masochistic biases, and force any authors and exhibitors who cite or display such materials to correct their mistakes." This unit works hand-in-glove with the Network of Prefectural Councillors to Rectify Biased War Museums—a political organization formed in February 1998 mainly by conservative Liberal Democratic Party members. These groups denounce public museums in Japan that display photos or pictures of imperial army atrocities and force the cancellation of these displays. Along with members of the right-wing Nippon kaigi (Japan Council), Fujioka and members of the Society for a Liberated View of History formed a Tokyo Citizens' Group to Contemplate Peace. With support from the *Sankei shinbun*, it staged protest rallies against the opening of a Tokyo Metropolitan Peace Museum, then being planned, on the grounds that it was overly critical of Japan's role in the war. Ever since 1999, when Nanking denier Ishihara Shintarô became governor of Tokyo, plans to open this museum have been stalled.

The Society for a Liberated View of History has set up a U.S.-Europe Unit within its Overseas Information Group to wage the information war. This unit's mission is to survey Western-language publications, periodicals, and media coverage on Nanking, Japanese wartime atrocities, and related subjects. In an all-out effort to "know your enemy," this unit publishes its findings in the society's organ and on its homepage under the heading "Overseas Media Watch." Both societies have organized their members in nationwide grassroots organizations to further their cause. Thus the Chiba Prefectural Association to Get at the Truth of the Nanking Incident pressured Kashiwa City to cancel a screening of *Nanking 1937*—a Chinese film produced in 1995 by Wu Tzu-niu—that a citizens' group had scheduled for October 1999. At a commercial theater in Yokohama, right-wing thugs launched loudspeaker trucks outside to intimidate would-be viewers and blocked the film's showing by slicing the screen to pieces. Since then, citizens' groups have encountered harassment and violence whenever they show this film at public venues in Japan. Similar dangers confront groups that invite left-wing scholars to lecture. I was a guest speaker at an October 1999 screening of *Nanking 1937* in Yamagata, but had to be ushered into and out of the building under protection by riot police. Seeking to get even, the Yamagata Prefectural Association to Get at the Truth of the Nanking Incident invited Higashinakano to lecture at the same venue in February 2000.

The Saitama Prefectural Association to Think about the Nanking Incident sponsored the conference, "Refuting the Now-Accepted Thesis: A Thoroughly Critical Examination of the 'Nanking Massacre'" at which Higashinakano and Fujioka were billed as "invincible scholars who will put an end to the debate." The leaflet advertising this event stated:

> Although the last war ended fifty-five years ago, elements who clamor about "Japan's war guilt" are now provoking the Chinese and Koreans, and even some U.S. State legislatures, to file law suits against us seeking indemnities. These elements always flaunt the so-called Nanking Incident as a symbol of our putative war guilt. They exploit this Incident to obstruct Japan's diplomatic and other state policies, thereby gravely harming our national interests. In order to break this deadlock, we comrades in Saitama must critically establish the facts and put an end to the debate once and for all.

Higashinakano provoked the ultimate confrontation on 23 January 2000 by holding the conference, "A Critique of the Greatest Lie in the Twentieth

Century: The Rape of Nanking." In content, it differed little from its predecessors; its significance lay in the venue. The organizers held it at the Osaka International Peace Center, commonly known as "Peace Osaka." This center was born amid left-wing fervor that prevailed in the 1970s and 1980s when large cites such as Tokyo, Osaka, and Kyoto had socialist governments. "Peace Osaka" had always held antiwar rallies and sponsored exhibits that exposed and harshly criticized Japanese war crimes such as Nanking. That Higashinakano should seek and gain approval to hold a denial conference in that venue signified a sea change in values to many Japanese, and even to some foreign observers, including reporters at the *New York Times*.[14]

The PRC government also took note. It expressed grave concern over the Peace Osaka conference, calling this "an anti-Chinese gathering to deny the Rape of Nanking and repudiate Japan's history of imperialist aggression." Based on concerns for overall Sino-Japanese relations, the Chinese Foreign Ministry, its embassy in Tokyo, and its consulate general in Osaka called on the Japanese government, and the Osaka municipal and prefectural governments to halt the opening of this conference. This call went unheeded, so the Chinese lodged vigorous protests, such as the one by PRC foreign minister T'ang Chia-hsüan, lodged with Japan's ambassador to China Tanino Sakutarô. In essence, T'ang held that the government of Japan had critically reflected on its aggression against China in the "Sino-Japanese Joint Statement" of November 1998 and in later official diplomatic documents. Moreover, recent Japanese prime ministers have critically reflected on, and officially apologized for, colonial rule and aggression in China based on the 15 August 1995 "Murayama Cabinet Resolution and Statement" marking the fiftieth anniversary of the end of the war. But all of that, T'ang charged, had been mere lip service:

> Once again, we strongly demand that the Japanese government demonstrate true sincerity by unmistakably assuming responsibility [for war crimes], by firmly halting reactionary right-wing elements from reviving militarism and repudiating their history of imperialist aggression, and by correctly instructing Japanese youth in that history—all in an effort to uphold the political bases of Sino-Japanese relations. Only in this way will the Japanese government win the trust of its Asian neighbors. Only in this way will it win the trust of peace-loving Japanese nationals as well as that of all peoples in nations throughout the world.

On 24 January 2000, some 500 Chinese from all walks of life braved the snow to hold a protest in front of the Mausoleum for Fellow Chinese Victims of the Nanking Atrocity. They declared: "Movements in Japan that deny the historicity of the Nanking Atrocity and of Japanese imperialist aggression against China gravely hurt Chinese popular sentiments and also basically destroy friendly Sino-Japanese relations."[15] *The People's Daily* and other Chinese media outlets, including television, reported the Peace Osaka conference as "a gathering to deny the Nanking Atrocity." The New China News Agency asked then foreign minister Kônô Yôhei for a statement, and he is reported to have replied, "It is an undeniable fact that looting and the killing of non-combatants occurred after Japan's army entered Nanking."[16]

On 28 October 2000 Higashinakano founded and became chair of the Japan Nanking Studies Association centered in Asia University. The association's leaflet states: "Our Society will facilitate an exchange of academic opinions that transcends differences of ideology." But a glance at its 24 advisers and directors is insightful for two reasons. First, thirteen of them are university professors and four are retired or visiting professors. This underscores a trend in Nanking studies over the past two or three decades. That is, earlier deniers were non-academics such as Yamamoto Shichihei, Suzuki Akira, Ara Ken'ichi, and Tanaka Masaaki; but today many are professional academics, although not necessarily historians. Second, most officers in this Japan Nanking Studies Association belong to the denial camp.

This political and ideological slant in part reflects the nature of Asia University itself. It was founded in 1955 by Ôta Kôzô—a well-known prewar ultranationalist and wartime minister of education, who was arrested as a war crimes suspect and purged under the Occupation. Asia University's current Board of Directors is chaired by former Imperial Headquarters staff officer Sejima Ryûzô, who supervised tactical planning for major operations in the Asia-Pacific War of 1931–45, and is currently an executive officer in the Itô Chû conglomerate.[17] Asia University's roots go back to 1941 when it was created as Kô-A Senmon Gakkô; its mission was to teach students how to "develop Asia" for Japanese purposes. Today this university provides financial assistance in support of Higashinakano's Japan Nanking Studies Association, for his own research, and for the dissemination of his findings. What is more, it takes the highly unusual step of allowing one of its department heads to serve as chair of the association's Steering Committee as well as on its Board of Directors. At the association's inauguration, the newly installed chair Higashinakano declared: "[Japanese defendants] received guilty verdicts with respect to the Nanking Incident at the Tokyo War Crimes Trials fifty-two years ago, but the more that I read in the sources, the more doubts I've come to embrace. To clarify the truth about the Incident, we must re-analyze mountains of existing documents, uncover new ones, and reconstruct the Incident as a whole in an accurate manner." About sixty members attended this inauguration, including Nihon University professor Hata Ikuhiko who is a minimalist in the Nanking controversy.[18] Higashinakano's association publishes its findings in its organ, the *Nihon "Nanking" gakkai nenpô* (Japan Nanking Studies Association Annual Report) as well as in other books and articles, both academic and popular.

Higashinakano's Background

Let us, then, examine Higashinakano and his scholarship. In the postscript to his *"Za reepu obu Nankin" no kenkyû,* he relates "one huge factor that drew me, a mere layman in the field, to begin research on Nanking." In August 1992, while on a trip to worship at Shôin jinja—a shinto shrine in the city of Hagi dedicated to Restoration martyr Yoshida Shôin—Higashinakano visited a elderly man named Moriô Migaku who lived nearby in Shimonoseki. Higashinakano describes Moriô as "a man of sterling character" who had served at Nanking as a captain in the Sixteenth Division and averred that he "neither saw nor heard of a 'Massacre' there." Above all, the normally soft-spoken Moriô fumed that he "could not stomach having the truth distorted."[19]

Up to then, Higashinakano's area of specialization had been in social thought or Japanese thought rather than in history per se. Biographical outlines contained in his published works tell us that he was born in 1947 and thus has no personal experience of the war. He earned a B.A. in Western history at Kagoshima University, and a Ph.D. at Osaka University. He taught Japanese intellectual history as a visiting professor at Western Washington University in 1985 and was a visiting fellow at the University of Hamburg in 1988. He is now a professor at Asia University, teaching the history of social thought. His books are *Shakai shisô no rekishi 18 kô* (A History of Social Thought: Eighteen Lectures) in 1988, *Higashi Doitsu shakaishugi taisei no kenkyû* (Studies on the East German Socialist Regime) in 1992, and *Kokka hasan: Higashi Doitsu shakaishugi no 45 nen* (Bankruptcy of the State: Forty-five Years of Socialism in East Germany) in 1992.[20] Judging from the last two titles, I initially assumed that Higashinakano specialized in East German socialism. So I consulted several historians of modern Germany, but no one had heard of him. A biographical sketch found in his first book shows that he has written essays and translations dealing with Yoshida Shôin and has published dictionary articles on *Hagakure,* a 1716 treatise by Yamamoto Tsunetomo that glorifies death for the samurai. This, plus Higashinakano's 1992 visit to Shôin jinja, led me to surmise that his expertise lay in right-wing Japanese thought, especially *bushidô* (the samurai ethos). Yet his main publications were dictionary articles; this probably explains why he was unknown to Japanese intellectual historians. Higashinakano's first book, *Shakai shisô no rekishi 18 kô,* is a course textbook that students use to supplement his undergraduate lectures. He wrote it along with *Kokka hasan: Higashi Doitsu shakaishugi no 45 nen* prior to his foray into Nanking studies, so an analysis of these two works should shed light on how his intellectual and scholarly background affected his later views on the Atrocity.

First we should note Higashinakano's old-style *kana* (syllabary) usage in his textbook on Japanese thought. This is extremely rare today even for persons born before 1945. Unlike them, he did not learn this old-style usage in school; instead, he went out of his way to acquire it. The Japanese language cannot be phonetically transcribed precisely under this old-style *kana* usage. Hence contemporary readers, and certainly young university students, would find it quaintly alien—much as American students today find Shakespeare. What is more, the few Japanese writers who insist on using this literary form today do so as a mode of protest. By clinging to it, they imply that the Japanese language as forcibly reformed by U.S. Occupation officials cannot fully convey the true beauty of traditional thought, culture, and values. This reactionary attitude betrays affinities with right-wing nativism.

Second, Higashinakano peppers his textbook and other writings with the pejorative terms *Shina* and *Shinajin*. These were formerly used to insult the Chinese government and people, and may be likened to the English term *Jap* for Japan or the Japanese. (See the appendix in the present volume.) Chinese government officials and private individuals from 1930 repeatedly protested against the use of this derogatory term, saying that *Chûka, Chûgoku,* and *Chûgokujin* were the proper forms of address. But the Japanese state and people arrogantly ignored those protests until forced to stop by the victorious Chinese after 1945. Today, apart from gross boors or elderly persons who grew up with those terms, Japanese shun the use of *Shina* and *Shinajin*. They display this deference toward Chinese feelings from a self-critical realization that the prejudice bound up in such discriminatory terms was a direct cause of imperialist aggression. But by flaunting these epithets, normally not used in polite company, Higashinakano displays an overweening wartime style of nationalism that sees nothing wrong about what Japanese armies did in China.

Third, in contrast to this contempt for the Chinese, Higashinakano pays undue adulation to figures in Japan's past. In writing about Prince Shôtoku (574–622), for example, the textbook employs highly honorific forms of language that the mass media reserve for imperial family members today. This is atypical in academic writing. It leads us to believe that Higashinakano reveres the imperial line and adheres to the government-sponsored pre-1945 view of Japan's past known as *kôkoku shikan*. This ultranationalistic view held that the main principle behind Japanese historical development was the unfolding of popular loyalty toward the imperial house descended from the Sun Goddess Amaterasu. This textbook devotes a full chapter to Saigô Takamori (1827–77), whom Higashinakano calls "the Meiji Restoration's most meritorious architect." He writes: "Saigô's words, 'European nations are barbaric, and not civilized states', remain alive even today—and we must never let these die." Higashinakano argues that left-wing Japanese historians—poisoned by the Tokyo War Crimes and Comintern views of history—"malign Saigô's idea of 'opening Korea to trade and diplomacy'" by calling it a plan to "conquer Korea" as the first step in Meiji imperialist aggression.[21] It is unusual to assign a whole chapter to Saigô's thought in a survey textbook. Higashinakano may have done this partly because he hails from Kagoshima Prefecture, Saigô's home. In any case, he ignores the postwar scholarly consensus about Saigô's triviality as a thinker. Higashinakano's idiosyncratic account stems from a subjective fixation with Saigô that brooks neither criticism nor compromise; it does not derive from a scrupulous study of the existing scholarship.

Fourth, this textbook on Japanese thought exudes a sense of ethnocentric superiority. In describing Prince Shôtoku's "ideal of harmony," for example, Higashinakano says that "Japanese history has never produced a dictator. Shôtoku's thought became Japanese political thought itself." "[Shôtoku's] ideal of harmony" in consensual decision-making "is now practiced by Japanese business firms abroad and is extolled as 'Japanese-style mangement'." Japanese-style management is now the butt of jokes, but this is lost on Higashinakano. In this same chapter, he lauds "Japanese wisdom" as shown in "the fact that there were no executions for 347 years, from 810 to until the [1156] Hôgen War." This "fact" supposedly proves that Japan is exceptional in world history for condemning violence, and that this condition obtains even today. Such Japanese "wisdom," Higashinakano exclaims, "was first evinced in Prince Shôtoku's ideas." This account is patently unhistorical. During Shôtoku's lifetime, there was no state called "Japan" and no people conscious of themselves as "Japanese." To imply that there were, suggests that Higashinakano subscribes to the old ultranationalistic *kôkoku shikan* view of history. This held that "the nation of Japan is governed by an unbroken imperial line coeval with Heaven and earth"; that is, eternal in nature. On a more basic level, this account lacks any sense of historical periods. Shôtoku tried to consolidate the ancient emperor state when he became regent in 592. His "ideal of harmony" properly belongs to that era. Higashinakano, however, cites it to "prove" Japanese excellence today. Furthermore, during the years 810 to 1156, there were several revolts among ruling elites, and the warrior and commoner classes also launched numerous uprisings. This period witnessed the ancient emperor state give way to courtier rule under the Fujiwara, and then to warrior rule under the Taira. It is a non sequitur to argue that a putative lack of executions predisposed "the nation to condemn violence," and that this constitutes "Japanese wisdom." Moreover, that premise itself is open to question because so many primary sources are lost to us. Higashinakano thus marshals one putative "fact"—that no executions took place for 347 years—to make a simplistic, sweeping, non-empirical, unhistorical assertion—that the Japanese people by nature have always abhorred violence. As we shall see, he often employs the converse of this polemic as well—that one discredited Chinese testimony denies historicity to the entire Nanking Atrocity.

Higashinakano's reportage, *Kokka hasan: Higashi Doitsu shakaishugi no 45 nen,* reveals other characteristics found in his later studies of Nanking. The book resulted from a 1-year stay in West Germany and a 2-month visit to East Germany just before the Berlin Wall collapsed. It presents an instructive ideological contrast to Honda Katsuichi's *Doitsu minshu kyôwakoku* (The German

Democratic Republic) written at about the same time and on roughly the topic.[22] (Honda has been a major participant in the Nanking controversy since early in the 1970s.) Honda seeks historical explanations for why the East German government system—born amid such good intentions—went on to fall. He did not write his book to praise West Germany; it is partly a lesson about the fate that capitalist, as well as socialist, societies may suffer. Moreover, Honda recognized a need to study the "failed" eastern part of Germany in later surveys after unification was complete. By contrast, Higashinakano unconditionally denounces Marxism as a religion "whose vacuous incantations got shoved down people's throats." He writes: "Marxist-Leninist dictators forced orthodox Marxism on the entire globe as a worldwide dictatorship." Yet, he continues, they branded internal dissidents heretical "enemies of the people." The secret police oppressed such enemies, put them in concentration camps, and even executed them. Thus the "12-year Nazi Reich and the 45-year [East German] Communist dictatorship were no different in being dictatorial." The Berlin Wall imprisoned the people just as Nazi concentration camps had. East German "field-tank Communism" crushed people who yearned for freedom and democracy. East Germany was "a state prison" boasting "the world's foremost secret police." "Communist Party aristocrats" lived in "red villages" whence they ruled over a "contemporary slave society." But in "the Peaceful Revolution of November 1989, 'the people'—who were cruelly victimized by lies and contradictions inherent in socialism—rose up to achieve the greatest revolution in European history—no, in all of world history." Thus, Higashinakano concludes, the fall of East Germany marked the final defeat of socialism and the total bankruptcy of Marxism.[23]

Honda's historically-based, multifaceted, empirical analysis admits many gray areas. By contrast, Higashinakano's account displays a simple black-and-white duality. The good guys triumphed; the bad guys got what they deserved. West Germany was a democracy destined to thrive; East Germany was a socialist dictatorship bound to fall. This either-or mode of thinking—unconditional good or unmitigated evil, absolute reality or pure fiction, an unequivocal "yes" or an indisputable "no"—predisposed Higashinakano to embrace certain fixations that spawned his denial thesis. Also, his ultranationalistic, emperor-worshiping view of history produced an intolerant hatred of Marxism, socialism, and communism—doctrines that opposed the imperial institution in Japan before 1945. His a priori, emotional hatred of communism resembles that of present-day right-wing circles. It precludes an open-minded, scholarly analysis of historical reasons to explain how socialist states in the twentieth century emerged, what positive role they played, and why they finally collapsed. Instead, Higashinakano embraces a phobia about socialist states; that is, they are evil nations out to "get" Japan by exploiting the so-called Nanking Atrocity in propaganda warfare.

315

A Delusive Fixation

Conservative revisionists rave over Higashinakano's latest book, *"Nanking gya-kusatsu" no tettei kenshô* (A Thoroughly Critical Examination of the "Nanking Massacre"), calling it the last word on this subject. The cartoonist Kobayashi Yoshinori—once a walking advertisement for the Society to Create a New Japanese History Textbook—remains one of Higashinakano's most enthusiastic mimics and vociferous supporters.[24] Kobayashi says, "This is the latest, most reliable historical study; if you can't refute it as a historian, you might as well close up shop." The *Sankei shinbun* columnist Ishikawa Mizuho states that "excellent scholars have emerged from the 'illusion faction' of late; Higashinakano is one of the best." But perhaps the ultimate platitude comes from University of Tokyo emeritus professor Fujioka Nobukatsu: "Higashinakano spent eight years completing this work.... Based on a wide-ranging study of the sources, he concludes with impeccable logic that 'there was no Atrocity.' The appearance of this book has raised the study of Nanking to new heights. It forms the scholarly beachhead from which to repudiate with finality Iris Chang's *The Rape of Nanking*." Indeed, Higashinakano's "thoroughly critical examination" raised Fujioka's own study of Nanking to new heights. Whereas he once followed Hata Ikuhiko's minimalist thesis, Fujioka is now a total denier.[25]

Actually, there is not much new in Higashinakano's thesis; it is largely a rehash of older arguments by the denial and illusion factions. Left-wing historians in the Society to Study the Nanking Incident (Nankin ken) have published *"Nankin daigyakusatsu hiteiron" 13 no uso* (Thirteen Lies to Deny the Nanking Atrocity), which exposes the logical inconsistencies in those arguments and the dearth of empirical documentation to support them. Here, I limit my critical analysis to Higashinakano's more egregiously mistaken methods and contentions. All stem from a common source: his delusive a priori fixation that precludes empirical analysis according to established rules of historical investigation. In the afterword to *"Za reepu obu Nankin" no kenkyû*, which he coauthored with Fujioka Nobukatsu, Higashinakano concisely relates his method:

> As to whether there "was" or "wasn't" a Nanking Atrocity, it's very hard to prove that there "wasn't." In fact it's virtually impossible to find direct evidence of this or any other negative proposition. Can anyone directly prove that there are no invisible men or aliens from outer space?... [But] there is one *indirect* way to prove that they do not exist. Let's say some man claims that these entities do exist. Then we must examine, down to the last minute detail, his every oral testimony and piece of written evidence in an effort to ascertain that these are absolutely reliable. If there is a speck of doubt as to the logic of an oral testimony or the reliability of a written piece of evidence, we must reject that man's claim. Logically speaking, this is the only proof—albeit indirect—that invisible men and aliens from outer space do not exist. This is the approach I take to the study of Nanking.[26]

316

In short, Higashinakano begins from the premise, or delusive fixation, that there was no Atrocity; then, he directs all of his efforts to corroborate it.

The scholarly rules of historical investigation operate differently. A historian first gathers primary documents and oral testimonies diligently; then, he or she studies these comprehensively, to arrive at "facts" that can be inductively substantiated. But Higashinakano's approach to Nanking is a perversion of this standard method. Admittedly, he cannot "find direct evidence" that the Atrocity never happened. So, instead, he "examine[s]—down to the last minute detail—every oral testimony and piece of written evidence" cited in left-wing secondary studies in order to pick out "a speck of doubt as to the logic ... and reliability" therein. When he finds a few, he claims that "this constitutes the sole proof—albeit indirect—" that the Atrocity never took place. This is a negative exercise at best. Bona fide historians have taken great pains and gone to great expense to gather oral testimonies and written documents in China and Japan upon which to reconstruct a comprehensive picture of what happened at Nanking. But Higashinakano, the self-styled "mere layman in this field," arbitrarily rakes through these primary sources with his fine-tooth comb, gleefully finds a few specks of vagueness or inconsistency, and proudly claims that these historians "disseminate propaganda with no basis in fact. [T]hey create their narratives by uncritically citing fourth- and fifth-rate sources."27

As with all topics of historical research, Nanking yields a wheat-and-chaff array of written documents and oral testimonies; some cannot but be inaccurate or erroneous. The same person may write partially inconsistent accounts in different documents, or may say slightly different things to different interviewers. A historian culls through this muddled heap of sources to sift the reliable from the less reliable or unreliable. Even accounts that seem unreliable at first may yield valuable insights when checked against other accounts to find common threads and remove inconsistencies. It is this comprehensive, critical weighing of innumerable sources of uneven quality that produces an inductive reconstruction of some past event. That is how a historian "proves" that the event took place. By contrast, Higashinakano wittingly or unwittingly rejects the logic behind this standard process of historical verification. He coats his Nanking studies with a meretricious veneer of scholarship that lends credence to his work—especially to people who lack the training or acumen needed to perceive his flaws, but who parrot his conclusions for political or ideological reasons. Higashinakano's flaw is to start from the delusive fixation— that no Atrocity took place. I say "delusive" or even "delusional" because the fixation is so deep-seated that he ignores massive documentation affirming the Atrocity's historicity. As of 2002, there are nine volumes of published sources available to him in Japanese, yet he turns a blind eye to any documents except those that yield "specks of vagueness and inconsistency." These, he marshals to support an outlandishly contrived thesis.

It is an established fact that the Atrocity took place; this is part of the scholarly consensus in Japan. The Nanking Atrocity is recounted not only in scholarly books on Chinese and Japanese history, but also in standard reference works such as historical dictionaries and encyclopedia, as well as in world and Japanese history textbooks. Any debate over Nanking should depart from this common reference point. What Higashinakano asserts is like saying, "the earth is flat." This can only stem from a delusive fixation. If shown photos of a spherical earth shot from outer space, he would no doubt reinforce his fixation by retorting: "This has to be a fabricated computer-graphic image, not a genuine photo. NASA must be conspiring to hide the truth from us."[28] Higashinakano seizes on any flawed Chinese photo, testimony, or document to claim that it was "fabricated" as part of a sinister anti-Japanese plot. These sources, he says, "prove" that the Chinese government and people are conspiring with traitorous Japanese historians and educators to disseminate a Comintern or Tokyo War Crimes view of history in order to crush Japan in a propaganda war.

Higashinakano's pre-Nanking writings show why he came to indulge in this delusive fixation. First, he embraces a sense of ethnic superiority and interprets Japanese history in line with the old *kôkoku shikan* that glorifies the reputedly divine imperial line. Thus, he cannot brook the possibility that Japan fought an unjust war or that the emperor's soldiers committed unspeakably evil deeds. Indeed, a "man of sterling character" like former captain Moriô Migaku avers that he "neither saw nor heard of an 'Atrocity' or a 'Massacre'" at Nanking, and indignantly declares he "could not stomach having the truth distorted." So, Higashinakano writes, Moriô "etched these words in my memory," and he vowed to vindicate Moriô's honor along with that of other soldiers likewise maligned. As noted above, this encounter with Moriô is what spurred Higashinakano to begin his research on Nanking.[29] Second, Higashinakano believes that Allied nations—especially Chinese and Americans—fabricated the Nanking Atrocity at the Tokyo War Crimes Trials as an extension of wartime propaganda that branded the imperial army as a criminal organization and Japan as a rogue state. He also believes that the PRC now uses this putatively fictive Atrocity as a potent weapon in its propaganda war to convince the world that the Japanese people and government have an enduring criminal nature.

Fallacious Contentions

Psychologists use the term *paranoid reaction* as follows: "[Such people] never question the rightness of the hypothetical fixation on which their paranoia rests. They not only explain present conditions based on it, they also reinterpret all past phenomena based on it, so as to assert its validity. In this way, it gradually becomes entrenched and systematized."[30] Higashinakano starts from the fixation that the Nanking Atrocity did not take place. Then, in order to validate it, he "reinterprets" all accounts of the Atrocity as being lies, fakes, errors, or plots. This produced the entrenched, systematized paranoia manifested in his "opus," *"Nanking gyakusatsu" no tettei kenshô*. "Reinterpreting" evidence is central to Higashinakano's method and to his emergence as the new standard-bearer in the denial cause. He appeared at a crucial time for that camp, after its arguments had lost credibility. Innumerable battlefield diaries and other sources left by Japanese military personnel who victimized the Chinese had already appeared in print. Also, because of limited democratization in the PRC, Chinese victims were becoming able to speak out about their experiences and even launch lawsuits in Japan. Japanese citizen groups actively aided them in addition to calling on their own government to apologize and pay compensation. Thus deniers lost the debate because it was impossible to go on claiming: "there are no primary sources," "there is no hard evidence," or "the Chinese themselves never complained about an 'Atrocity' in 1937–38."

Higashinakano emerged at that point, and deniers now count on him to clinch a wild-card play-off spot by advancing from the losers' division. Faced with reams of oral and written sources substantiating the scholarly consensus that an Atrocity did take place, they can no longer claim that sources do not exist.[31] Now, taking their cue from Higashinakano, they reinterpret new testimonies to be unreliable, and new documents to be "unauthenticated fourth- and fifth-rate" sources. When properly reinterpreted, they claim, these show that "accounts of massacres are in error," that "the Chinese really did these things but blamed us," or that "what the Chinese call 'massacres' are really combat deaths sanctioned by international law." Japanese deniers—who cling to their delusive fixation and refuse to admit defeat in scholarly debates—now turn to Higashinakano as their new hope. Below, I critically examine four of his main contentions.

A "Fake" Eye-witnesses

In November 2000, a 71-year-old lady who survived the Atrocity launched a lawsuit in Nanking against Higashinakano and his publisher, Tendensha. This lady, named Hsia Shu-chin, sought 21 million yen in compensation and a public apology for having defamed her as a "fake eyewitness" to the rape and murder of relatives and a neighboring family by Japanese troops. A China Fund to Advance Human Rights—led by the historian Jen Chi-yü—formed a support group for Hsia that included leaders of the All-China Lawyers' Association and the Society to Study the History of the War of Resistance against Japan. On 28 November 2000, they held a news conference to declare that Higashinakano's *"Nanking gyakusatsu" no tettei kenshô* and Matsumura Toshio's

"Nankin gyakusatsu" e no daigimon (both published by Tendensha), "denied the truth of the Atrocity, defamed surviving witnesses, and thus exerted a baneful influence on Japanese society."[32] Higashinakano bluntly replied, "If she really wants to disseminate the 'truth' about the 'Nanking Atrocity', her first job should be to dispel the doubts we raised—not sue us."[33] As some foreign critics claim, this crass denial today constitutes a cruel "second rape."

In December 1937, Hsia Shu-chin was eight *sui* by East Asian reckoning or seven-years-old by Western counting. She belonged to a nine-person family, seven of whom Japanese troops brutally raped and/or murdered. Shu-chin herself suffered a vicious bayonet wound. Although she recovered miraculously, the attack left her orphaned with only one relative, a four-year-old sister. The Hsias were living in a compound with another family at the entrance to Hsin-lu. Two weeks after the attack took place, Shu-chin was brought to the Nanking Safety Zone (NSZ) where she told John Magee about her ordeal. He immediately went to the site and captured on sixteen-millimeter film the victims' bodies wrapped in straw matting. Magee heard the story directly from Shu-chin, who had been in the house when the rapes and murders took place. He confirmed the story with an elderly lady who resided in the area and who had found Shu-chin hiding after the two-week interval. Magee also confirmed the story with Shu-chin's uncle, then taking refuge in the NSZ. Lewis Smythe cites Magee on the incident: "Mr. John Magee has an account of a family in South City of 13, of which eleven were killed, women raped and mutilated, on December 13–14 by Japanese soldiers. Two small children survived to tell the story." Hsü Shuhsi later quoted this account in his *Documents of the Nanking Safety Zone,* published in 1939.[34]

Magee went into more detail in his diary. He wrote that the eight-year-old girl's seventy-six-year-old grandfather, her seventy-four-year-old grandmother, her mother; and her 16-, 14-, and one-year old sisters had suffered rape and/or murder. Furthermore, Magee wrote, a one-year old child of their "landlord's family" also died in the attack; also, Hsia Shu-chin and "a four- or three-year old sister" fled into the next room where their mother had been raped and slain. There, they concealed themselves under bedding for two weeks in fear of Japanese troops who occasionally came back to search the compound. The girls survived on well water and *kuo-pa,* a kind of burned rice, until the elderly female neighbor—who had fled to the NSZ temporarily—returned to her residence at this site and rescued them.[35] Georg Rosen submitted an even more detailed report of this incident to the German embassy along with the Magee's film that included explanatory captions. Rosen dated the rapes and murders as occurring on 13 December, and he identified the landlord family's surname as "Ma." Rosen noted that the Ma couple's seven- or eight-year-old daughter had been killed as well.[36] In 1987, Honda Katsuichi published an oral account obtained from Hsia Shu-chin that repeats this story more fully. He also provided a sketch of the compound where she lived, clearly showing where each

corpse was located, and he included a photograph of Shu-chin with her stab wounds.[37] Finally, Robert Wilson and John Rabe cited brief accounts of the incident in their diaries at the time. Thus Hsia Shu-chin's plight has been documented in a plurality of accounts, and I have argued elsewhere that their number and similarity make for virtually an iron-clad case.[38]

However, Higashinakano insists that the woman who today claims to be Hsia is "an imposter" because "'the 8-year old girl' [in question]" was not a child of the Hsia or the Ma couple. He will not budge from this stance even though an accurate translation and a proper reading of Rosen's consular report—which he himself quotes in his book—would prove that the girl was Hsia Shu-chin.[39] As we have seen, Higashinakano presumes that "if there is a speck of doubt as to the logic or consistency" in relevant accounts, we should reject these as unreliable. Here he points out that, depending on which account we go by, either eleven or thirteen people were reported killed, and that Shu-chin's surviving sister was said to be either three or four years of age. Thus he inisists that "if Hsia Shu-chin were giving us the actual facts, there could be no inconsistencies of this type."[40]

This presumption violates the historian's method. Hsia Shu-chin did not write the sources that Higashinakano critically compares; Magee, Rosen, Rabe, and Wilson did. Likewise, Hsia's interviewer transcribed the oral testimony that she submitted in 1998. Therefore, it is only natural that the accounts do not match to a tee. Since the main points of her story are the same, slight discrepancies of this type should make no difference. All accounts confirm that: (1) more than ten persons in the two families were raped and/or killed; (2) the eight-year old Hsia Shu-chin survived a bayonet wound to the neck; and (3) she and her younger sister aged three or four were the only survivors. But Higashinakano insists that there can be no inconsistencies whatsoever; if there are, we should reject Hsia Shu-chin as an unreliable witness to the Atrocity.

The fallacy of his contention is clear to any historian who has done field interviews. In July 1998, for instance, I questioned seven survivors of the 12 July 1945 air raid on Utsunomiya city, northeast of Tokyo. Their replies differed greatly. Some said that the night of the attack was "cloudy." Some said it was "pouring rain." Some said it was a "misty rain." Some said they heard a warning siren. Others said they did not. Still others said that the siren came after the raid began. They disagreed about the sound made by falling bombs. Some said it was high-pitched; others, low-pitched. Some said the bombs made no sound at all. Above all, not one of those seven people said that he or she saw anyone die in the raid even though records list 521 victims.[41] But if we followed Higashinakano's methodology, this air raid never took place; it has to be an illusion, a myth, or a fabrication, because there are so many contradictory accounts. These oral accounts yield far more than "a speck" of vagueness or inconsistency, so the documents that cite 521 victims must be "fourth- or fifth-rate sources."

The Chinese Really Did It

Another ploy used by deniers such as Tanaka Masaaki and Higashinakano is to blame the Chinese for any misdeeds that did take place in this putatively non-existent Nanking Atrocity. All evil acts, Tanaka first wrote in 1987, were the work of Kuomintang (KMT) covert operations units lurking in the NSZ.[42] Higashinakano elaborated on this argument in 1998.[43] Those units, he said, reputedly numbered some 20,000 men disguised as Japanese troops.[44] They perpetrated acts of looting, rape, murder, and arson against helpless civilians or refugees in front of Westerners on the International Committee (IC) for the NSZ. In other words, those undercover KMT units duped foreign observers into reporting Chinese crimes to the outside world as the work of Japanese forces. Again, deniers commit a "second rape" by fobbing Japan's war crimes off on to China, thus reflecting the ethnic bias they harbor. Higashinakano gives free rein to his conspiratorial imagination. True, some KMT officers and men masqueraded as refugees in the NSZ, and some destitute Chinese civilians looted goods from abandoned houses to sell on the black market. But Higashinakano attributes to KMT covert operations units exactly what the Japanese Special Service Agency (SSA) were in fact doing. That is, the SSA was engaged in a calculated, covert propaganda campaign to pin responsibility on Chinese elements so that they, rather than the imperial army, would bear the brunt of international censure for war crimes at Nanking.

Western primary sources, fully available in Japanese translation, expose Higashinakano's fraud. For example, Secretary Georg Rosen in the Nanking Office of the German embassy sent a memo on "Japanese Propaganda Methods" to the foreign ministry in Berlin. It said that Japanese troops looting the French embassy threatened guards to make them "report this as the work of Chinese."[45] That is why Rosen felt a need to confirm and record cases of wanton Japanese pillage, arson, and destruction of German property before his embassy could demand compensation. Likewise, Prof. Miner S. Bates of Nanking University took great pains to document American losses resulting from Japanese pillage.[46] In other words, the Westerners who exposed imperial army atrocities and lodged formal protests with Japanese authorities did so knowing full well that the SSA was generating false reports designed to refute or deny such atrocities, or to accuse the Chinese of perpetrating these, so as to evade legal culpability. Western observers in Nanking were not as facile as Higashinakano portrays them.

Moreover, a bit of careful thinking reveals the contrived nature of Higashinakano's claim. Right after the fall and occupation of Nanking, some KMT troops did violate international law by fleeing into the NSZ. They discarded their uniforms to masquerade as refugees and hid their weapons and ammunition. But theirs was a very precarious existence. They were already being hunted down by Japanese mop-up patrols; hence they sought to remain as inconspic-

uous as possible. Furthermore, there were plenty of collaborators—called *Han chien* or "Chinese traitors" by the Chinese—who exposed the whereabouts of such KMT troops for a fee. Chinese refugees in the NSZ also tattled on these underground KMT troops for fear of indiscriminate retaliation if they should be discovered. Most of all, there were less than twenty Westerners left in Nanking, and the Japanese army had cut off virtually all means of communication with the outside world. Thus, KMT troops being hunted down in the NSZ had no reason to hope for widespread overseas media coverage. Why, then, would they risk revealing their whereabouts by engaging in these undercover acts? In sum, Higashinakano commits an anachronism unbecoming a historian. Writing in 1998, he knows for a fact that some Westerners journalists and residents in Nanking did report Japanese atrocities—as well as a few Chinese atrocities camouflaged as Japanese—to the outside world. He also presumes that underground KMT troops in the NSZ knew that fact as well. From these premises, he retroactively conjectures that these disguised KMT troops committed atrocities in front of Westerners so as to deceive them into reporting that Japanese forces were the real guilty party.[47]

"Lawful" POW Executions

As noted above, innumerable Japanese battlefield diaries and other primary documents have been unearthed and published over the past two decades to show unequivocally that the imperial army executed Chinese prisoners en masse. These sources—left by the very Japanese who committed massacres—are a key factor that exposed denial arguments to be bankrupt. To overcome this factor, Higashinakano idiosyncratically "reinterprets" the 1907 Hague Convention Concerning Laws and Customs of War—in effect repeating arguments made by Tanaka Masaaki in 1987—to claim that these killings were "legal."[48] According to Higashinakano, the Hague Convention—to which imperial Japan was bound as a signatory—stipulated that militia or volunteer corps had to meet certain conditions before they could enjoy the rights of combatants under international law, including the protection shown to prisoners of war (POWs). First, militia or volunteer groups had to be commanded by an officer responsible for overseeing their behavior. Second, they had to wear fixed, distinctive emblems setting them apart from noncombatants recognizable at a distance. Third, they had to carry weapons openly. Fourth, they had to conduct operations according to the laws and customs of war. So far, so good. But Higashinakano applies these stipulations—intended for militia and volunteer corps not in uniform—to regular Chinese troops so as to deny them protection as POWs under the laws of war. He argues that the Chinese at Nanking violated all four stipulations. Their commander, T'ang Sheng-chih, had fled and thus was derelict in his duty to oversee them and their surrender; this contravened the first condition. Those troops had cast off their uniforms and taken refuge in the NSZ where they hid their weapons and ammunition; this violated the second and third conditions. Finally, those actions ipso facto transgressed "the laws and customs of war." Thus, Higashinakano says, Chinese troops forfeited any right that they would otherwise have enjoyed as combatants. The Japanese side could then refuse to accept their surrender and instead kill them; and, this would constitute "legal" battlefield actions sanctioned by the Hague Convention.

Even if we were to grant him this point for the sake of argument, Higashinakano ignores other key articles in the convention. One of these stipulated that military tribunals be held before any killing of POWs might be deemed "legal." Another required signatory states to educate their armed forces about stipulations in the convention and the need to obey it as part of international law.[49] But the imperial army never held military tribunals for captured Chinese troops, and it instructed officers and men to ignore international law. Higashinakano parrots the argument that wartime Japanese field commanders had used to justify their massacres, thus underscoring their arrogance. His "reinterpretation" of the Hague Convention—plus his use of pejoratives such as *Shina* and *Shinajin*—present wartime Japanese prejudice in living color. In effect, he says that Japan did not need to obey international law when at war with the Chinese because they were despicable, inferior entities.

Nanking deniers such as Komuro Naoki and Watanabe Shôichi applaud Higashinakano's logic, but encounter trouble when they apply it to the Pacific theater. They concur that, in order for combatants to surrender under international laws of war, "their responsible commanding officer must formally request his counterpart on the other side to accept the surrender. If combatants try to surrender on their own, either singly or in groups, the opposing commander may refuse to take them because he has no way to ensure that they really will surrender [and not ambush unsuspecting would-be captors]. A formal surrender is like a contract; both sides must agree to it."[50] Thus, like Higashinakano, Komuro and Watanabe affirm that the Japanese army could "legally" slaughter T'ang Sheng-chih's men because he, as their responsible commanding officer, had fled the scene. As such, T'ang could neither request a formal surrender nor ensure that his men would comply with its terms. But these Nanking deniers also note:

> We usually hear that Japanese troops in the South Pacific died a glorious death, fighting to the last man. But in fact GIs killed almost all those who surrendered. Japanese captives who knew English were spared, to be exploited as a source of intelligence. But the rest got killed because GIs found them burdensome. The GIs slaughtered them and bulldozed the bodies into the ground. Those captives may not exactly qualify as "POWs," but the fact that they suffered this fate is duly recorded in U.S. documents.[51]

As Yoshida Yutaka points out, these nationalists would love to castigate American troops for their war crimes but cannot do so without repudiating Higashinakano's "reinterpretation" of international law.[52] Yet that perforce would deprive them of an argument needed to deny the Nanking Atrocity. Perhaps, then, it is they who have been brainwashed into espousing a "masochistic" "Tokyo War Crimes" view of Japan's past.

Faulty Text Critique

Higashinakano displays yet another quirk of logic to confirm his delusive hypothetical fixation. He contends that, if a later "official" document deletes any reference to the Nanking Atrocity or to a specific victim toll in it, this "proves" that earlier accounts had no basis in reality. For example, he cites a *North China Daily News* article dated 22 January 1938 that lists 10,000 victims, and compares this against the 1938 *China Yearbook,* put out by the same publisher, the North China News and Daily Herald, based in Shanghai. The *Yearbook,* he claims, is a "first-class source" since it is an "official document" issued by the Chinese government. Hence, it takes precedence over the "nonofficial" *North China Daily News*—clearly a fourth- or fifth-class source. The preface to this edition of the *Yearbook* is dated 2 February 1938. Chapter 19 on "Sino-Japanese Hostilities" says only that "the Japanese army occupied Nanking on 13 December 1937." From this, Higashinakano concludes that, since the authors were writing in late-January and early-February of 1938, they could not have failed to notice anything like a megamassacre; and, since they did not mention it, the KMT regime rejected the victim count found in the "nonofficial" *North China Daily News* article. This, he proudly deduces, is more proof that the Atrocity never occurred.

His claim rests on ignorance about what yearbooks are and how they are produced. Like all such works, the *China Yearbook* came out early in January. Writers had to finish manuscripts by late-November or early-December at the very latest in order for editing, printing, and binding to take place by the end of the year in time for publication. Since Japanese orders for the final assault on Nanking did not come until 1 December and the walled city did not fall until 13 December, we cannot reasonably expect a detailed narrative of the Atrocity in the *Yearbook.* Moreover, all stages of production were delayed owing to the Japanese invasion of central China that began at Shanghai in August 1937. The editor of the *Yearbook,* G. W. Woodhead, has a preface dated 2 February 1938, but it does not indicate the last stage of manuscript preparation. Rather, it means that the page proofs were ready for binding at that time. Thus the entry, "the Japanese army occupied Nanking on 13 December 1937" was the most detailed that can reasonably be expected in these circumstances. The *Yearbook* is also silent about how many Westerners died in the 12 December sinking of the USS *Panay*, an issue was of huge concern to English-language readers in China.

The *Yearbook* was a reference work, a compendium of general information about China. Its 593-page 1938 edition comprises twenty-nine chapters on geography, climate, history, culture, customs, economics, politics, recreation, health and welfare, and so on. In other words, it was not devoted just to military or political affairs. So the fact that it allots only thirty-one pages to "Sino-Japanese Hostilities" is not at all suspect. Such reference works are hardly the type of "first-class source" that Higashinakano claims, but if he wants to find corroboration of the Nanking Atrocity in such works, he should consult an entry entitled "The Battle for Nanking, December 4 to 13, 1937" found in the MacMillan *China Handbook: 1937–1945*. It relates that, after the Japanese invaders occupied Nanking, they cut off all means of transportation and communication with the outside world and began an organized, systematic looting of the city. Furthermore, it says, the invaders' huge massacres, rapes, and murders, plus their general atrocities and pillage were unparalleled in modern history.[53]

One more example of Higashinakano's flawed text critique of primary sources is revealing. He compares two edited versions of a letter originally written by Miner S. Bates. First, on the dust jacket of *"Nanking gyakusatsu" no tettei kenshô*, Higashinakano prominently quotes the following passage from Bates' letter as Harold Timperley reproduced it in his 1938 work, *What War Means*:

…ing Nanking. Other incidents involved larger numbers of men than did this one. <u>Evidences from burials indicate that close to forty thousand unarmed persons were killed within and near the walls of Nanking, of whom some 30 per cent had never been soldiers.</u> My special interest in these circumstances is twofold: first, because.…

Higashinakano added the underline to emphasize that this sentence is lacking in another yearbook, the *Chinese Yearbook: 1938–39*, which was "prepared from official sources by the Council of International Affairs under the directorship of Hsü Shuhsi."[54] Then, just below the first quotation on his book's dust jacket, Higashinakano quotes the same passage from Hsü's edited volume:

…occupying Nanking. Other incidents involved larger numbers of men than did this one. My special interest in the circumstances is twofold: first, because of the gross treachery of the…

From the deleted underlined sentence, Higashinakano argues that conscientious KMT editors such as Hsü rejected the "forty thousand" victim toll as groundless. Hsü showed scholarly integrity even toward his wartime Japanese enemy. Not only Hsü's *Chinese Yearbook: 1938–39*, but 3 other "official documents" edited under the Republic of China imprimatur, left out this damning sentence. By contrast, Higashinakano implies, Timperley's document collection, *What War Means,* is a "fourth- or fifth-class source" even though it appeared relatively soon after the event; hence we should dismiss it and the underlined victim count as products of wartime anti-Japanese propaganda.[55]

But common sense tells us that, unless Bates (who wrote the original letter) or Hsü (who edited the KMT source collections) explicitly stated that one of them deleted the victim count because it was false, we should assume that this deletion took place for other reasons, probably editorial in nature. For example, although this cannot be conclusively proved, it is more logical to surmise that the *Chinese Yearbook: 1938–39* had to shorten materials quoted therein, whereas Timperley faced no such constraints of space in *What War Means.* In any case, no sensible historian would hastily conclude that this passage disappeared in later edited works because the event in question never happened, or because the earlier reported death toll was unreal. If we took Higashinakano's claim to its logical conclusion, we would have to argue that each new edition of an annual periodical repudiates what was written the year before. Higashinakano jumps to this conclusion in all earnestness because he clings to a hypothetical fixation that the Atrocity never happened. This forces him to seize any shred of evidence, whether sound or not, to sustain and systematize that delusion.[56]

Conclusion

Higashinakano Osamichi (Shûdô) enjoys eminence as a new hope and standard-bearer among adherents of denial. He has earned this status mainly based on his opus, *"Nankin gyakusatsu" no tettei kenshô,* and *"Za reepu obu Nanking" no kenkyû*—the latter work he co-authored with Fujioka Nobukatsu. In fact, however, Higashinakano's credentials as a historian are suspect, and his contentions about Nanking are bankrupt—as demonstrated above. Two ominous points are noteworthy, though. One is the changed nature of the denial faction that acclaims Higashinakano. Two or three decades ago, denial was a somewhat sordid activity limited to nonacademics such as critics of sociopolitical affairs *(hyôronka)* or former military men. But denial today seems to have gained respectability, and the faction counts among its ranks many university professors who teach at some of Japan's finest universities, including the University of Tokyo. Second, the publication of Iris Chang's *The Rape of Nanking* as the exposé of a putatively "forgotten Holocaust" has given deniers the opportunity to stage a come-back that they have long sought. They exploit her flaws by demagogically portraying left-wing Japanese historians who affirm Nanking's historicity as being on the same unscholarly level as Chang and her supporters. Or, they even go so far as to call both parties enemies of the Japanese people in a propaganda war. Clearly, the situation calls for guarded pessimism.

Notes

*   Translated from Japanese by the editor.
1. See also, Kasahara, *Nankin jiken to sankô sakusen*, pp. 20–37.
2. Fujioka, *Kin-gendaishi kyôiku kaikaku*, pp. 1–2.
3. Fujioka suffered demotion to the Board of Directors in July 1999, but returned as Vice Chair in October 2001 after the resignation of Chair Nishio.
4. These quotations are from Atarashii kyôkasho o tsukurkai, ed., *Atarashii Nihon no rekishi ga hajimaru*, p. 314 and p. 320.
5. See "Aratamete *Rabe no nikki* o tettei kenshô suru."
6. See *Sankei shinbun*, 26 October 1999.
7. Fujioka and Higashinakano, *"Za reepu obu Nankin" no kenkyû*, pp. 1–3.
8. In *Sokoku to seinen*, September 1998.
9. *SAPIO,* 14 July 1999.
10. Tawara, et al., "Kokusai mondai no akujunkan o tatsu tame ni," pp. 10–15; Inoue, "Fuseikakusa yue ni hiteiha no hyôteki to naru, pp. 16–17.
11. The Kashiwa shobô publishers bought Japanese translation rights to Chang's book and had prepared a translation. However, Chang refused to allow a chapter of commentary and revisions to her numerous errors of fact, and blocked publication on these grounds at the last minute. The publisher did receive threats from right-wing elements, but this was not the main reason for canceling publication. See Haga, "'Za reepu obu Nankin' hôyaku chûshi no keii,"p. 17.
12. Later, in March 1999, they published a Japanese pamplet based on that leaflet, but Nakamura had parted company with the other three because he continued to hold a "minimalist" position about the Atrocity whereas Fujioka and the others had come to deny it totally.
13. For a more detailed account of their activities in the Atarashii kyôkasho o tsukuru kai, see Tawara, "Kyôkasho kôgeki-ha no saikin no dôkô."
14. *New York Times,* 20 January and 23 January 2000.
15. *Pei-ching chou-hao,* 1 February 2000, pp. 8–10.
16. *Mainichi shinbun,* 24 January 2000.
17. Sejima is also known as the model for Yamazaki Tomoko's protagonist in her novel, *Fumô chitai* (Zone of Barrenness).
18. *Sankei shinbun,* 29 October 2000.
19. Fujioka and Higashinakano, *"Za reepu obu Nankin" no kenkyû*, p. 272.
20. The publishers are, respectively: Ajia shobô shuppanbu, Nansôsha, and Tendensha.
21. Higashinakano, *Shakai shisô no rekishi 18 kô* , pp. 95, and 128–30.
22. In *Honda Katsuichi shû* vol. 29.
23. Higashinakano, *Kokka hasan*, p. 166, p. 183, p. 377, p. 389, p. 71, and p. 409.
24. Kobayashi left the society owing to differences of opinion and personality, but in October 2001, after Nishio resigned as chair, Kobayashi resumed his status as an "acting director," yet publicly announced his noninvolvement directly in the society's activities.
25. On his original position supporting Hata, see Fujioka, *Kin-gendaishi kyôiku kaikaku: Zendama-akudama shikan o koete*, pp. 23, 33, and 35; for his change after reading Higashinakano, see Fujioka, "Nakamura Akira shi no 'Nankin jiken 1-mannin gyakusatsu setsu' o hihan suru," passim.
26. Fujioka and Higashinakano,*"Za reepu obu Nankin" no kenkyû*, p. 273.
27. Ibid., p. 362.
28. See Nakayama, *Nihonjin wa naze tajûjinkaku na no ka*, p. 206.
29. Moriô in fact is an unreconstructed militarist who labels former fellow-officers such as historian Fujiwara Akira "minions of the Chinks" for affirming that the Nanking Atrocity took place after "being wined and dined for a week" in China. See Kasahara, *Nankin jiken to Nihonjin*, pp. 188–90.

30. Sotobayashi et al. eds., *Seishin: Shinrigaku jiten,* p. 432.
31. For example, see the battlefield diary of Sixteenth division commander Nakajima Kesago in Kaikôsha, ed., *Nankin senshi shiryô shû.* Also see battlefield diaries left by the rank and file in the Yamada Detachment, Thirteenth Division in Ono, Fujiwara, and Honda, eds., *Nankin daigyakusatsu o kiroku shita kôgun heishitachi.*
32. *Asahi shinbun,* 29 November 2000. Matsumura is being sued in the Tokyo District Court. I submitted a personal opinion to it attesting to the unscholarly nature of Matsumura's book.
33. In Hata, Higashinakano, and Matsumoto, "Mondai wa 'horyo shodan o dô miru ka," p. 144.
34. Reproduced in Brook, ed., *Documents on the Rape of Nanking,* p. 121.
35. Kasahara, *Nankin nanminku no hyakunichi,* pp. 254–55.
36. Ibid.
37. Honda, *Nanjing Massacre,* pp. 154–58.
38. Kasahara, *Nankin nanminku no hyakunichi,* pp. 249–56.
39. Higashinakano, *"Nanking gyakusatsu" no tettei kenshô,* pp. 241–42. Compare this with the accurate translation by Ishida, ed., *Shiryô: Doitsu gaikôkan no mita Nankin jiken,* p. 176.
40. Higashinakano, *Tettei kenshô,* pp. 246–48.
41. Interviews at "Utsunomiya kûshû no taiken o kataru kai," sponsored by the Utsunomiya heiwa kinen kaikan wo tsukuru kai, 31 July 1998.
42. Tanaka, *Nankin jiken no sôkatsu,* pp. 109–13.
43. Higashinakano, *Tettei kenshô,* pp. 274–78.
44. For the figure 20,000, see for example, Kobayashi, *Sensôron,* p. 45.
45. Ishida, ed., *Shiryô: Doitsu gaikôkan no mita Nankin jiken,* p. 180.
46. Nankin jiken chôsa kenkyû, ed., *Nankin jiken shiryô shû 1: Amerika kankei shiryô hen,"* p. 219.
47. For a more detailed discussion, see Kasahara, "Môsô ga umidashita 'Han-Nichi kakuran kôsaku tai' setsu," pp. 198–215.
48. On putative Chinese violations of the Hague Convention, see also Tanaka's earlier work, *Nankin jiken no sôkatsu,* pp. 114–16.
49. See Yoshida, "Kokusaihô no kaishaku de jiken o seitô dekiru ka," p. 162, and p. 175.
50. Komuro and Watanabe, *Fûin no Shôwashi,* p. 150.
51. Ibid., p. 72.
52. Yoshida, "Kokusaihô no kaishaku de jiken o seitô dekiru ka," p. 170.
53. *China Handbook: 1937–1945,* p. 303.
54. Higashinakano, *Tettei kenshô,* p. 357.
55. Ibid., pp. 355–62.
56. For a more detailed discussion, see Kasahara, "Riaru taimu de sekai kara hinan o abite ita Nankin jiken," pp. 52–56.

15

NANKING: DENIAL AND ATONEMENT IN CONTEMPORARY JAPAN*

Kimura Takuji

Introduction

There are three main objectives in this chapter. First, I briefly review the changing arguments by which conservative revisionists in Japan have tried to deny or minimize the Nanking Atrocity since the 1970s. Second, I describe their political activities and analyze their social bases of support. Third and most importantly, I examine how Japanese left-wing historical scholarship on World War II—and particularly the Atrocity—have spurred the emergence of numerous citizen-led movements from the 1980s into the 2000s aimed at educating the general public about imperial Japanese war crimes. Indeed, these civic groups go so far as to take legal action in attempts to force their own government to assume responsibility for war crimes by paying monetary compensation to Chinese and other foreign victims.

Postwar Japanese academic research on the Nanking Atrocity began in earnest with the appearance of two publications: Hora Tomio's chapter-length essay "Nankin jiken" in 1967, which was expanded and published in book form under the same title in 1972, and Honda Katsuichi's "Chûgoku no tabi," which was serialized in the *Asahi shinbun* in 1971 and appeared as a single volume in 1972. But Japanese scholarship on Nanking really took off from about 1984, one year after left-wing historians and journalists had founded a group known as Nankin ken, the Society to Study the Nanking Incident. Largely owing to its scholarly work, Japanese students of the Atrocity can now reconstruct its basic facts in a fairly comprehensive narrative structure. On the other hand, conservative revisionists in Japan have opposed these left-wing efforts by waging a thirty-five year propaganda campaign to trivialize the Atrocity.[1] Journalists, critics of social and political affairs, and some academics belong to this right-wing camp. They have twisted sources to fit their thesis, ignored evidence contrary to it, and engaged in other unscholarly practices that include document-tampering—all in an attempt to refute the historical facts of this event and other Japanese war crimes. Thus the left- and right-wing camps in Japan have engaged in a major battle that itself has become the object of numerous historiographical studies. One example of a non-Japanese scholar who analyzed the controversy surrounding the Nanking issue is Yang Daqing, a professor of Japanese history at George Washington University. Yang has argued that it is possible to arrive at a shared understanding of this highly traumatic event through collaborative efforts by Japanese, Chinese, and Western scholars. He holds that a common stock of historical facts and knowledge is forming on which we can begin a dialogue to overcome national or ethnic differences between the Japanese victimizers and Chinese victims.[2] However, Yang's tripartite analysis of the debate along mainly national lines—Japan, China, and the United States—does not fully account for differences of viewpoint between the various Japanese camps; nor does it adequately explain the conservative revisionists' tenacious staying power.

By contrast, the Japanese historian Hata Ikuhiko categorizes factions in the controversy over Nanking in Japan as: (1) a left-wing "great massacre faction," (2) an "illusion faction" (whom I call the "fabrication" faction), and (3) "moderates" or "middle-of-the-roaders" such as Hata himself (whom I call "minimizers,").[3] Hata's credentials as an academic historian are beyond doubt. Although adhering to a minimalist argument, he has produced an excellent study wherein he analyzes structural factors in the imperial army that precipitated the Atrocity.[4] But Hata's analysis of its historiography seems to place the three adversarial camps on an equal footing when in fact those whom he labels the illusion faction, and even some moderates, present several serious problems. They ignore inconvenient pieces of evidence, manipulate sources in arbitrary ways, and flaunt other unscholarly practices. Also, they repeat their hackneyed claims over and over, even though these have been effectively refuted in scholarly circles. Instead, it is more accurate to say that many in the minimizer and fabrication factions—backed by mass periodicals such as *Bungei shunjū, Shokun, Seiron, Sankei shinbun,* and other smaller right-wing publishers—are in league with conservative elements who seek to reinvent prewar institutions and to rebuild Japan into a great power by reinstilling nationalistic values dating from the imperial era among the Japanese people today.[5]

Japanese conservative revisionists adhere to a thesis that affirms the "Greater East Asia War." The basic points in this argument derive from wartime imperial government propaganda as reformulated in the 1950s and 1960s by those who wished to dismantle the Allied Occupation's reform policies. This nationalistic camp holds that imperial Japan could never have perpetrated anything like a Nanking Atrocity because it fought a just war to liberate Asia. If in fact anything resembling such an event did occur, this had to have been a "normal" atrocity, no different from those that take place in all wars in all ages. Hence, Japan alone should not have been demonized at the Tokyo War Crimes Trials and should not continue to be demonized on the international stage today, primarily at the instigation of Chinese and, to a lesser extent, Americans and Europeans.

This Greater East Asia War thesis refuses to see Japan as an aggressor. It is based on emotion, not evidence. Thus, no matter how scholarly bankrupt it is proven to be, its proponents will go on denying or minimizing the Nanking Atrocity and other shameful chapters of the recent Japanese past. However, it is undeniable that this thesis finds a degree of popular acceptance and political patronage today because certain limited segments of postwar Japanese society ardently support it. From this perspective, I examine political activities of the Society to Honor Our War Heroes *(Eirei ni kotaeru kai)* and its subgroups that comprise veterans and war-bereaved families. It is the existence of this society, plus its members' links with conservative politicians and bureaucrats, that helps to explain why seemingly large numbers of current-day Japanese refuse to acknowledge responsibility for war crimes such as at Nanking.

Above all, however, my purpose is to describe the sociopolitical impact that left-wing Japanese historians of the Nanking Atrocity have had since the 1980s. After the furor that broke out over textbook screening in 1982–83—when neighboring Asian governments protested against the Ministry of Education's (now the Ministry of Education and Science) whitewashing of issues such as Nanking and the so-called comfort women of World War II—many Japanese scholars and civic groups have vigorously exposed and publicized their nation's culpability for wartime aggression. The aforementioned Society to Study the Nanking Incident itself emerged in 1984; and, according to one of its most prominent younger members, it began its academic and sociopolitical undertakings with a sense of crisis in the historical profession.[6] In the wake of foreign diplomatic protests and conservative Japanese attempts to revive wartime propaganda about Nanking, the society not only convincingly proved that the event actually took place, it also helped launch citizen-led education and redress movements on behalf of Chinese victims.

As a result of this left-wing scholarship and sociopolitical activism, truly momentous changes took place in the Japanese government within fifteen years. For one thing, textbooks approved for use in schools by the Ministry of Education came to include mention of the Nanking Atrocity and other repugnant war crimes. Furthermore, in December 1998 the Ministry of Foreign Affairs, and in April 1999 Chief Cabinet Secretary Nonaka Hiromu, took the unprecedented step of officially conceding that the Atrocity took place. Chinese victims and their offspring are not likely to receive any significant monetary compensation for damages from the Japanese government, but its recognition of the event as a historical fact is a momentous reversal of position. And, it was primarily academic work by left-wing groups such as the Society to Study the Nanking Incident—plus spin-off effects in citizens' movements for education and redress—that forced the Japanese state to make this volte-face.

Deniers and Downplayers

There have been three stages in conservative revisionist efforts to deny the Nanking Atrocity. The illusion thesis appeared in the 1970s, the fabrication thesis in the early 1980s, and the minimalist thesis in the late 1980s.[7] Yamamoto Shichihei (Isaiah Ben-Dasan) and Suzuki Akira (both now deceased) were the main advocates of the illusion thesis. They did not explicitly deny the Atrocity but implied that it did not happen. Between 1971 and 1975, they engaged the left-wing Honda Katsuichi and the late Hora Tomio in a debate over the truth of a 100-man killing contest that allegedly took place as part of the Atrocity.[8] As described by Bob Tadashi Wakabayashi in chapter 6, Yamamoto and Suzuki held that the contest was fictive—a wartime propaganda story revived by the leftist postwar media in Japan to curry favor with the People's Republic of China (PRC). Yamamoto and Suzuki tried to cast doubt on the entire Atrocity by proving the "illusory" nature of this one incident that reputedly epitomized it. Suzuki also claimed that no reliable primary sources existed to substantiate the Atrocity; though, needless to say, he did not go far afield to find many new ones. Nor did he fully take into account extant sources. Moreover, Suzuki's artful arrangement and presentation of oral testimonies prompted left-wing critics such as Watada Susumu to accuse him of manipulating these in a dishonest way.[9]

The debate over Nanking died down in the late-1970s, but flared up again after the 1982–83 textbook furor just noted. In September 1983 Nanking denier Tanaka Masaaki published an article, later expanded into a book, that heralded the fabrication thesis.[10] Whereas Suzuki and Yamamoto in the 1970s only hinted that the Atrocity as a whole lacked reality, Tanaka averred outright that "the so-called 'Nanking Atrocity' is a total fabrication concocted for political reasons." In sum, he held, prosecutors at the Tokyo War Crimes Trials needed an issue comparable in barbarity to Auschwitz; so they made up the Nanking lie in order to establish "a theory of criminality running throughout Japanese history."[11] This assertion sparked new heights of acrimony. Tanaka used as his main source the battlefield diary of Gen. Matsui Iwane which he discovered. This was a key new source, since Matsui was commander of the Shanghai Expeditionary Army (SEA) and later of the Central China Area Army (CCAA) during the assault on Shanghai and Nanking from August to December 1937. Tanaka argued that, because Matsui tried to uphold military discipline after troops entered the city and because his diary lacked any mention of an Atrocity, this proved that none had occurred. Also, Tanaka stressed defects in Chinese military defenses such as commander T'ang Sheng-chih's last-minute flight and abandonment of his men—which were not untrue. But Tanaka stressed these Chinese defects so much that, in effect, he was claiming that the Chinese side was responsible for any mass killings that did take place, and that this absolved the Japanese side from culpability.

Both the illusion and fabrication factions were discredited in the late 1980s for 3 main reasons.[12] One was the discovery of irrefutable evidence left by Japanese troops who participated in the Atrocity. For example, the diary of Nakajima Kesago, commander of Kyoto's Sixteenth division, came out in 1984.[13] It records explicit orders to execute prisoners of war (POWs). As a result of this diary and other newly-found primary sources, the Kaikôsha, an organization of former high-ranking imperial army officers, reversed its avowed aim of proving the Atrocity to be false. Rather, the Kaikôsha conceded that the event took place and the chief editor of its organ, Katogawa Kôtarô, apologized to the Chinese people in March 1985.[14] Thus, a conservative and nationalistic organization of former imperial army officers grudgingly admitted that an Atrocity took place at Nanking. This action symbolized the bankruptcy of the illusion and fabrication factions. A second reason was that Tanaka in 1986 was found to have doctored Matsui's battlefield diary in roughly 900 places when he transcribed it for publication.[15] One of its main exposers was Itakura Yoshiaki, a seeming ally of Tanaka's. This infamous incident proved that the Atrocity's factuality could be denied only by fraudulent means. Third, and perhaps most importantly, the Society to Study the Nanking Incident began publishing scholarly findings to refute the deniers' assertions.

Thus by the late 1980s, persons wishing to deny the Atrocity's historical facts had no choice but to adopt the minimalist position first introduced by Itakura in 1984.[16] Itakura—who along with Hora had exposed Tanaka's document tampering in 1986—admits that massacres by the imperial army did take place at Nanking. However, in defining what an atrocity is, in delimiting its temporal and geographic extent, and in identifying types of persons who were and were not its victims—that is, the legal killings of combatants versus the illegal killings of noncombatants—Itakura and his followers strive mightily to downplay the scope of Japanese war crimes. These minimalists stress three points. The first deals with numbers. As Itakura put it:

> Any so-called Nanking "Atrocity" has to be defined as an event wherein huge massacres in the tens of thousands took place—as symbolically stated in the verdicts at the Tokyo War Crimes Trials and in the Nanking "Atrocity Mausoleum" that opened in August 1985. Thus someone like myself, who holds that illegal killings at Nanking numbered from about 10,000 to 20,000, can legitimately say that a Nanking "Incident" took place, but that it was not an "Atrocity."[17]

Itakura's aim is to trivialize the Atrocity or to portray it as an accidental battle-field occurrence and thus water down imperial Japan's culpability for wartime aggression. From political motives, he Itakura and his colleagues limit their discussion to the number of victims and thereby ignore qualitative issues that should be addressed in the debate such as rape, arson, looting, torture, and structural defects in the imperial army that gave birth to all of these shameful war crimes.

A second flaw is that the minimalist faction does not count as victims defeated Chinese soldiers who, lacking the will and means to resist (since they had discarded their weapons), fled into the Nanking Safety Zone (NSZ) where they were summarily executed by Japanese troops. Minimalists insist on viewing such Chinese as soldiers masquerading in civilian clothing, that is, as guerrillas who could legitimately be executed as part of combat operations. In fact, the imperial army killed huge numbers of actual civilians mistaken for Chinese guerrillas. But more to the point, such arguments mask the minimalists' desire to legitimize executions by exploiting the defective character of international law as it existed in 1937 and thus maximize the number of "legal" killings by the imperial army. As Yoshida Yutaka contends, international law in that era functioned as an ideological tool to strengthen and legitimize colonial control by American and European imperial powers; hence the laws of war afforded guerrillas minimal protection. Yet even within those strict discriminatory limits, international law in 1937 still required that military tribunals establish the guilt of POWs in order for them to be legally executed as guerrillas, and the imperial army invariably failed to comply with this requirement.[18]

Third, minimalists refuse to count murdered Chinese on the grounds that they died owing to spontaneously generated outbursts of hatred that "can't be helped" in battlefield situations.[19] Thus minimalists choose not to examine factors in Japanese society and in the imperial army that spawned such extreme hatred for Chinese in that period. Itakura writes, "through research on this tragic incident, we must uncover exactly what we Japanese did and where our defects lay [during the war], and we must use the findings as a basis for critical self-reflection."[20] At first glance, this seems to be a sincere and earnest attitude, but his actual methods veil political and ideological motives. Itakura and other minimalists in effect reduce the debate over Nanking to two issues— a deflated estimate of victims and the legality or illegality of POW executions. Their purpose is to deny that an Atrocity took place, or to assert that it was no different from those perpetrated by all armies in all wars.

Sources of Conservative Support

The illusion, denial, and minimalist factions presume that Japan fought World War II either in self-defense or to liberate fellow-Asians from Western colonial oppression. As noted above, this thesis to affirm the "Greater East Asia War" is a dogmatic rehash of wartime imperial government propaganda designed to conceal Japanese aggression under the cloak of pan-Asian struggle for emancipation. This reactionary view ignores historical realities and would gain no acceptance from an international readership, but a few segments of Japanese society embrace it on emotional grounds; and, what is more, it enjoys political influence through the activities of the Society to Honor Our War Heroes. This umbrella organization of veterans and war-bereaved families formed in 1976 to lobby the government to revive official standing for Yasukuni Shrine, a sanctuary of pre-1945 militarism. The existence of these veterans and war-bereaved families explains the ad nauseam efforts made by conservative revisionists to downplay or deny the Nanking Atrocity even though such claims lack scholarly credibility.

In 1869 the newly formed Meiji government created Yasukuni Shrine to honor the spirits of those who died on the loyalist side in the Restoration wars, and the shrine continued to instill a virulent form of militarism in the Japanese people until 1945.[21] Yasukuni stood atop a nationwide network of prefectural and local shrines that deified and honored the heroic souls *(eirei)* of persons who died faithfully for the emperor. By making all Japanese worship at Yasukuni, the imperial government fostered the idea that dying in Japan's wars was a cause for supreme pride and honor. After the defeat in 1945, Yasukuni changed from a state- to privately-run institution, but differs little otherwise. In that sense, it is a potentially dangerous religious entity that may serve as the rallying point to revive militarism. Movements to reestablish official standing and state support for Yasukuni failed from the 1950s to the 1970s. After that, various groups have tried to persuade cabinet ministers to worship there in their official capacities. Needless to say, if Yasukuni were again to come under state management or to sponsor official visits by cabinet ministers or prime ministers, that would violate the principle of separating government from religion as enshrined in Japan's postwar democratic constitution.

The Society to Honor Our War Heroes comprises several groups directly descended from the old imperial armed forces. These include army veterans, former army cadets (the Kaikôsha), former naval cadets, and families whose kin were military personnel killed in action (the Japan War-bereaved Families or *Nihon izokukai*).[22] These member groups insist that "Japan's peace and prosperity" today derive from the sacrifices of those who died in past wars, so all Japanese should offer thanks and respect, and the state should display utmost deference, to heroic souls enshrined at Yasukuni. These groups demand appreciation for loved ones whom the imperial government forced to die in action—not atonement for any evils they might have committed. Moreover, this demand is premised on the view that those loved ones died helping to liberate Asia as well as to defend Japan. This is why the Society to Honor Our War Heroes took out a full-page ad in the *Sankei shinbun,* a conservative nationwide daily, on 27 March 1997 proclaiming: "Japan was not an aggressor state! Nor did our heroic souls wage a war of aggression!"

The political activities of this society are noteworthy in two ways. First, ever since its inception in 1976, the organization has set up prefectural and other local branches with the goal of attaining 2.5 million members. This large a number, it correctly reckons, creates the impression that its appeals to prefectural assemblies enjoy broad grassroots support. Second, many of its component groups boast potent links with conservative Diet members.[23] For example, the Japan War-bereaved Families seeks help from politicians to raise its members' state pensions, to gain government support for Yasukuni, and to legalize worship there by government officials. In return for those benefits, the Society to Honor Our War Heroes mobilizes its member groups to campaign for and elect those politicians. In several well-known cases prior to the 2000s, right-wing Diet members or cabinet ministers have had to resign from their posts after voicing opinions such as, "we fought to liberate Asia," or "the 'Nanking Atrocity' was fabricated." Personal convictions aside, these reckless statements reflect a desire to curry favor with this society.[24]

Such conservative political links help explain certain key events in 1995. In that year, the National Committee to Mark the Fiftieth Anniversary of the War's End was formed, mainly by personnel from the Society to Honor Our War Heroes. At that time, a coalition government under the socialist Prime Minister Murayama Tomiichi pledged to enact a Cabinet Resolution of Apology and Critical Self-Reflection to mark the half-century since Japan's defeat in 1945. The conservative and nationalistic National Committee, however, promptly opposed Murayama's effort by drafting a Diet petition of protest signed by some 5.06 million people. Diet members from the Liberal Democratic Party and the New Progressive Party formed organizations (headed by Okuno Seisuke and Ozawa Tatsuo, respectively,) to battle Murayama's proposed Cabinet Resolution of Apology and Critical Self-Reflection.[25]

Thus, links between the Society to Honor Our War Heroes and conservative politicians grew stronger. All members of the New Progressive Party and many from the Liberal Democratic Party abstained from voting on 9 June 1995, when the lower house passed the cabinet resolution formally entitled, A Resolution to Reaffirm Our Vow to Promote Peace by Learning from History. Although the National Committee failed to scuttle the resolution totally, it did force the lower chamber to insert a key clause stating that not only Japan, but European nations and the United States as well, were guilty of aggression and colonial rule. That clause toned down Japan's culpability for the war to a degree unimagined by the resolution's original drafters. Not to be content, the National Committee then tried unsuccessfully to obstruct passage of the resolution in the upper house; and, in protest, went on to sponsor Resolutions to Offer Tribute and Gratitude to Our War Dead in prefectural assemblies, starting with Shiga. Only a month later, by the end of July 1995, 26 of Japan's 47 prefectural assemblies had passed such protest resolutions.[26]

Yet despite their all-out efforts, the National Committee and Society to Honor Our War Heroes could accomplish only so much, and these limitations are exemplified by the Resolution Concerning Tribute to Our War Dead and to Eternal Peace passed in the Tokushima prefectural assembly.

> On the occasion of this, the fiftieth year since the war's end, we in the Tokushima prefectural assembly resolve to offer tribute and gratitude to victims of that war—including 30,000 persons from Tokushima—who laid down their precious lives at home and abroad, praying for the peace and security of our ancestral land. What is more, in light of the innumerable acts of colonization and aggression that mark modern world history, we wish to express profound critical self-reflection about the enormous suffering endured by many peoples in Asia and all over the globe who were victimized by the horrors of war. We hereby solemnly pledge to heed the key role played by politics and to learn the lessons of history with humility, so that we will never again [perpetrate] the horrors of war, and thus contribute to an everlasting peace.
>
> So resolved on this fifteenth day of July in the seventh year of Heisei
> Tokushima Prefectural Assembly[27]

This resolution does indeed "offer tribute and gratitude" to Japanese "victims of the war," but it also manages to incorporate the left-wing view of the war as having been fought for aggressive aims. As this wording shows, despite intense lobbying by the National Committee, the Tokushima Assembly did not adopt the conservative revisionist thesis that unconditionally affirms Japan's role in World War II as having sacrificed itself to liberate Asians from Western colonial oppression. In other words, we can conclude, that reactionary view of the war does not find widespread acceptance in current-day Japanese society.

Yet the fact remains that the Society to Honor Our War Heroes and its constituent groups hold great attraction for many veterans and bereaved families. This allure stems from the acute mistrust and disgruntlement they bear toward Japanese society—this, despite the financially privileged treatment they enjoy compared with foreign victims of the war and even with Japanese civilian victims who, unlike former military personnel, receive no state pensions or benefits. There are deep-seated reasons for these groups' mistrust and disgruntlement. After losing homes in air raids and suffering destitution and hunger, most ordinary Japanese since 1945 have felt that *they*, and not foreign peoples, were the victims of the war. Thus, ordinary Japanese reacted with disgust and enmity toward soldiers or sailors who abused their privileged position to feather their own nests by pilfering military foodstuffs and supplies in the wake of Japan's defeat.[28] Also, the Tokyo War Crimes Trials laid bare the treacherous and barbaric wartime behavior of military leaders whom ordinary persons had been taught to hold in the highest esteem. On the one hand, by boosting postwar pacifism and foiling conservative attempts to revise Article IX of the new Constitution, this widespread disgust and enmity toward former soldiers has played a positive role in thwarting efforts to remilitarize postwar Japan. But on the other hand, that disgust and enmity have also led many Japanese to vilify and ostracize veterans and bereaved families, or at least to evade the problem of how those groups should be treated.

As a result, many veterans and bereaved families feel alienated from, and hostile toward, postwar Japanese society in general, and left-wing intellectuals in particular. These sentiments are understandable and, indeed, warranted to an extent. Indeed, many prominent postwar intellectuals embraced their left-wing creed only after acrobatically disowning the ultranationalism that they ardently spewed forth until 15 August 1945. As Bob Tadashi Wakabayashi shows in chapter 6, this mistrust of postwar liberals for their seeming duplicity and lack of moral integrity did much to fuel support for Yamamoto Shichihei and Suzuki Akira early in the Nanking controversy during the 1970s. For example, the well-known writer Agawa Hiroyuki, an award-winning biographer of the Meiji novelist Shiga Naoya (1883–1971), typifies this rancorous alienation. As a former naval cadet in training who survived the war, Agawa has this to say this about postwar left-wing apostates:

> Many "progressive" scholars and critics in the postwar era say the same thing; [that is, *kamikaze* pilots died for nothing]. It's one thing for the pilots themselves—as they took off on their one-way missions—to embrace doubts as to whether they were dying in vain. But it's quite another for this bunch of "progressive" scholars—from their safe havens now—to snort, "Those dumb saps died a worthless dog's death." Well, I for one, refuse to accept that those men died for nothing. This is the main reason I don't believe a word that those "progressives" say. In fact, I find them utterly despicable.[29]

Today, Yasukuni and its nationwide network of prefectural shrines, the *gokoku jinja,* are the only institutions that mitigate this deep-seated alienation. Yasukuni continues to proclaim that dying in Japan's wars was an honorable act—not a tragic, pitiable, or worthless one. Thus in the absence of other state-run institutions that show a concern for the war dead, Yasukuni emits strong appeal for veterans and bereaved families. Despite its militaristic trappings, Yasukuni enshrines and honors the souls of deceased loved ones or of comrades who fell in battle.[30]

Finally, and related to this last point, the postwar left-wing historical establishment must bear a share of the blame. The "progressive scholars," whom Agawa so thoroughly detests, have produced splendid empirical studies to lay bare the mechanics of modern Japanese aggression and its resulting war crimes. Left-wing scholars have shown in detail how the Fifteen-Year War (1931 to 1945) as we call it, was an imperialist folly from start to finish; and, they have documented how atrocities such as the one at Nanking stemmed from brutality built into the imperial armed forces. But no matter how impeccable their academic credentials, these left-wing "progressive scholars" ignore two key issues: how ordinary Japanese soldiers saw themselves during the war and how we should treat them today in their dual roles as brutal victimizers and brutalized recruits.[31] If a Japanese veteran or officer, such as a Kaikôsha member, subscribed to left-wing historical scholarship and admitted that the last war in Asia and the Pacific was nothing more than imperialist aggression, he would perforce deny any meaning to the ideals of his youth. Worse still, he would cruelly betray fallen comrades, those men whom he sent out on missions to die, and the families left behind by those men.[32] Yet, by evading such key academic and human issues, the postwar left-wing Japanese historical establishment has exposed itself to attacks from critics such as Agawa Hiroyuki and from conservative revisionists.

A "Liberated" View

Members of the Society for a Liberated View of History *(Jiyûshugi shikan kenkyûkai)*, formed in January 1995 by Fujioka Nobukatsu, then a professor at the University of Tokyo, have added yet another dimension to the debate over Nanking.[33] Their view of Japanese history is not "liberal" as a literal translation of the title would suggest. To the contrary, they boldly espouse a view of history "liberated" from what they deem to be the straightjacket of left-wing historical orthodoxy that pervades the media and school system. This baneful left-wing orthodoxy, the group insists, is offensive to veterans and bereaved families. It derives from the Tokyo War Crimes Trials, where Allied prosecutors sought to demonize the Japanese people as aggressors no different from the Nazis. Hence, it is argued, for the Japanese people to adopt that enemy view of history amounts to treason. However, this group laments, so many Japanese "masochistically" subscribe to this view because they were first deceived by propaganda units in the U.S. Occupation, were later deceived by the Marxist Japanese historical profession, and continue to be deceived by the allegedly Communist-inspired Japan Teachers' Association.[34]

Fujioka Nobukatsu, Nishio Kanji, Itô Takashi, the late Sakamoto Takao, Namikawa Eita, Okazaki Hisahiko, Kobayashi Yoshinori, and many others sympathetic to this group, condemn history textbooks approved for use by the Ministry of Education (now the Ministry of Education and Technology). It is noteworthy that Fujioka, Itô, and Sakamoto taught at prestigious national universities such as Tokyo and Gakushûin. They claim that, after coming under criticism from Asian governments in the 1982–83 Textbook Controversy, the Ministry caved in to adopt left-wing textbooks shot through with anti-Japanese bias. The movement spearheaded by this group took concrete shape in January 1996, when its members began serializing "The History Not Taught in Textbooks" in the *Sankei shinbun*. This same *Sankei* publishing group came out with paper and hardcover book editions of the serial in addition to publicizing it in the monthly *Seiron.*

In December 1996, these figures established a Society to Create New a Japanese History Textbook chaired by Nishio; and in August 1997 Fujioka penned an Urgent Appeal for the Ministry to "delete depictions of 'army comfort women' from middle school textbooks." Since that time, this society has been feverishly denouncing textbooks approved by the Ministry of Education because these allegedly encourage national masochism among students, and the society has been holding symposia throughout the nation in order to win public support.[35] Moreover, textbooks produced by the group for middle school courses in civics and Japanese history won government approval in 2002 and in 2005, and are being used in public schools—although in less than 1 percent of these institutions.

Fujioka, Nishio, Namikawa, and Kobayashi subscribe in varying degrees to the reactionary Greater East Asia War thesis that, as noted above, holds that Japan sacrificed itself to liberate Asians throughout modern history. Fujioka's group dogmatically propagates this "Japan *über alles*" view through school curricula designed to foster antiforeign nationalism in young people. This is why members condemn other textbooks that mention barbaric Japanese acts such as the sexual enslavement of Korean women and those of other nationalities during World War II. On the issue of Nanking, they simply regurgitate the denial, illusion, and minimalist positions discredited back in the 1970s and 1980s.[36] But they do so to good effect by holding large conferences such as that on 31 July 1999 in Tokyo. As reported in the *Sankei shinbun* on the following day, Fujioka lectured on "Deflating the Nanking Atrocity: The Biggest Lie of the Twentieth Century." On this occasion Fujioka also announced plans to form a Japan Society for Nanking Studies within a year that would "tell the real truth about the Nanking Incident." He carried out these plans in 2000, and this society has published numerous articles and books, including volumes of conference papers annually since 2002.

However, conservative revisionists have not enjoyed smooth sailing in all respects.[37] In July 1997, for example, Fujioka and Namikawa resigned as vice-chairs of the Society to Create a New Japanese History Textbook. This indicates that significant discord brews under the surface. The publication of chair Nishio's long-anticipated *Kokumin no rekishi,* a "pilot text" of the society's history textbook, met with several delays before it finally went on sale in November 1999. Members tout it as a record-breaking best-seller, but that is because sympathetic groups in and out of local governments buy the book in bulk and distribute free copies to school boards and individuals—including Japanese residing overseas. Slack sales of the society's mouthpiece, "Kingendaishi no jugyô kaikaku," indicate that members may be running out of fresh ideas. The group also may be at pains to maintain a coherent view of the Nanking Atrocity. Its most prominent specialist on this topic, Asia University professor

Higashinakano Osamichi, at first proclaimed a figure of forty-seven Chinese victims in June 1996.[38] But, as reported in the *Sankei shinbun* on 1 August 1999, he revised the figure to 15,000 in a lecture delivered at the society-sponsored conference on 31 July, organized to "deflate" the "lie" of the Atrocity. Higashinakano's lecture was slated to be published in the conservative monthly *Seiron* and was supposed to represent the consensus of the Japan Society for Nanking Studies, but due to opposition from other conference participants, it had to be scrapped. By contrast, Fujioka Nobukatsu may have abandoned his earlier support of Hata Ikuhiko's minimalist (or "moderate") position of "over 40,000 victims. In a 1999 book co-authored with Higashinakano, Fujioka seems to have approached outright denial. (See Kasahara Tokushi's chapter 14.)

Left-Wing Nanking Studies

The Society to Survey and Study the Nanking Incident comprises historians, journalists, and also interested citizens who share two aims. First, they seek to show objectively what happened at Nanking from a variety of scholarly perspectives in opposition to the illusion, fabrication, and minimalist factions who run roughshod over facts to suit their own agenda. Second, the members wish to apply the historical lessons of Nanking in fostering true friendship between Japan and China by prompting ordinary Japanese to develop a consciousness of their culpability for the last war.[39] Based on these shared aims, members meet monthly and several have undertaken trips to Nanking in search of data and materials with which to produce empirical studies.[40] Members also seek to uncover new primary sources within Japan, such as wartime diaries and testimonies by veterans who took part in the Nanking campaign. Moreover, members endeavor to obtain and translate records and testimonies on the Chinese side, along with documents left by Westerners in Nanking during the Japanese army's assault on and occupation of the city in 1937–38.[41]

Generally speaking, members of this society adopt three approaches. The first strives to gain an overall picture of the Atrocity by showing how imperial troops raped, pillaged, burned, massacred POWs, murdered civilians, and inflicted damage on other foreign nationals in addition to the Chinese that incurred international censure. Kasahara Tokushi exemplifies this approach in *Nankin jiken* and *Nit-Chû zenmen sensô to kaigun,* both published in 1997. *Nankin jiken* is the most comprehensive survey of the Atrocity by a Japanese historian, and is the standard by which future studies will be judged. It sheds light on events from a variety of perspectives, including one that left-wing Japanese historians had long avoided for political reasons; that is, how Chinese troops were ordered to fire on and kill other Chinese troops during their disorderly retreat. At his current preliminary stage of research, Kasahara says that the number of Chinese victims in the Nanking Special Administrative District (see map 2) "runs well over 100,000; indeed, the final figure approaches 200,000 and may even be higher."[42] A key characteristic of Kasahara's analysis is to stress that the Nanking Atrocity took place mainly outside the walled city, as typified in Chapter 3 of this volume. In *Nit-Chû zenmen sensô to kaigun,* Kasahara took up another issue ignored up to then; namely, the imperial navy's role in the Atrocity through air raids on civilian targets ordered by the supposedly pacifist admiral Yamamoto Isoroku. This is a pioneering study of the navy's culpability for escalating the China war in 1937 and suggests its links to the Pacific War that began in 1941.

The second approach adopted by society members is to analyze structural elements in the imperial army that transformed soldiers into a band of butchers on the march from Shanghai to Nanking. Here, the objectives are to identify those social and historical factors that predisposed Japanese forces to commit the Atrocity in a systematic and organized fashion. This approach is clearly at odds with the conservative revisionist view that Nanking was a fortuitous, spontaneous outburst of wartime emotion that "couldn't be helped." The late Fujiwara Akira exemplifies this approach in chapter 2 of the present volume and, in richer detail, in his 1997 *Nankin no Nihongun.* He traces the imperial army's actions on the march to Nanking and identifies five reasons for the Atrocity: (1) the extreme controls exercised over soldiers in the barracks plus insubordination by middle-grade staff officers based on an irrational faith in "fighting spirit," (2) an education and training system that produced staff officers oblivious to—indeed, contemptuous of—the laws of humanity and international laws governing war, (3) an overall deterioration in troop quality owing to unprecedented large-scale mobilizations, (4) a resulting decline in morale and discipline, and (5) the corruption of the rank-and-file who never knew what they were fighting for in China. Yoshida Yutaka, Fujiwara's doctoral student, followed this lead by analyzing the social and historical roots of Japanese war crimes during the Nanking Atrocity.[43] Henceforth left-wing historians can be expected to complete still more in-depth studies of the imperial Japanese society and mentality that produced and supported such armed forces.

The third approach—which contrasts somewhat with the second—deals with the Atrocity in relation to the imperial army's "Three 'Alls' Operations." This refers to army tactics adopted against Communists in northern China: to "kill all, burn all, and destroy all." Japanese research on the "Three 'Alls' Operations" has lagged far behind that on the Nanking Atrocity itself, which is deemed the epitome of contemptible Japanese aggression. However, with Eguchi Keiichi's 1988 "Chûgoku sensen no Nihongun," Kasahara Tokushi's 1999 *Nankin jiken to sankô sakusen,* and Kasahara's 2002 *Nankin jiken to Nihonjin,* the picture has begun to change. According to Eguchi and Kasahara, Japanese troops committed numerous outrages and massacres of Chinese POWs and civilians on the road from Shanghai to Nanking; and they would agree with Fujiwara that a few orders to that effect were issued at the divisional or army levels. However, all three scholars insist that the systematic extermination of virtually all Chinese—whether combatants or non-combatants—was *not* the imperial army's concerted aim in the central and south China theaters. In stark contrast, however, that policy *was* the army's express objective in Communist resistance areas throughout northern China, and this policy took concrete form in its "Three 'Alls' Operations."

This last point takes on great significance vis-a-vis the minimizers' efforts to downplay Japan's war of aggression in China by asserting that the Atrocity was "accidental," "spontaneous," and "unavoidable" in nature—as if Nanking had been an isolated occurrence, or as if similar atrocities take place in all wars. In sum, the paucity of left-wing research up to now on the "Three 'Alls' Operations"—and, to a lesser extent, on Japanese atrocities in China other than Nanking—has permitted minimizers to get away with their sophistry. Moreover, as Joshua A. Fogel and Masahiro Yamamoto deplore in chapters 12 and 13 of this volume, many Chinese and Western critics mistakenly, simplistically, or maliciously liken Nanking to the Holocaust. Nevertheless, as Kasahara argues, if we were to attempt to draw a parallel to the Nazis' systematic slaughter of European Jewry, it would have to be found in this "Three 'Alls' Operations"—not in the Nanking Atrocity.

Still, there are several problems and lacunae in left-wing Japanese research on the Nanking Atrocity apart from a lack of sympathy shown to veterans and to the war-bereaved, as noted above. First and foremost, left-wing scholars are at pains to explain why virtually no serious and sustained research took place from 1945 until the formation of the Society to Study the Nanking Incident in 1983. One reason for this belated start is that postwar Japanese historians presumed that they had to tackle "structural"—that is, theoretical Marxist— problems such as the nature of the emperor system or what stage of history the Meiji Restoration represented as a worldwide revolutionary event. To study the Nanking Atrocity was just not "proper scholarship" in their minds; it was something that social and political affairs critics *(hyôronka)* did.[44] Another explanation for this paucity of research was the lack of a freedom of information law in Japan before 1999. This was, and to a degree still remains, coupled with the Defense Agency's disinclination to declassify documents—which amounted to its virtual monopoly on sources. Until the 1980s, it was very hard to gain access to documents held in agency archives unless one were a former imperial army staff officer employed there, or unless one received a letter of introduction from an acceptable; that is, non-leftist, source. Needless to say, such highly restricted access to key primary sources made it very difficult for critical scholars to do research on the Nanking Atrocity and other sordid aspects of the war.[45]

Perhaps the most important task now before left-wing Japanese historians of Nanking is, as Yang Daqing points out, to arrive at universally applicable lessons through their research.[46] In sum, this means being able to explain

344

atrocities in general, not just Japanese atrocities such the one that occurred at Nanking. However, the rub comes in trying to do so without falling into the sophistry that the Atrocity was similar to—and hence, no worse than—other atrocities in history. Although Tanaka Toshiyuki (Yuki Tanaka) does not deal with Nanking per se, he provides some important leads in this respect. Tanaka employs a bipolar analytical framework of "particularity" to account for peculiarities in the Japanese imperial army as well as for the "universality" of war crimes elsewhere in the world down to the present.[47] He also insists on the need for examining these topics from a multiplicity of perspectives. By analyzing in detail war crimes committed by the Japanese in comparison to, and in contrast with, those by other nationalities, he suggests the need to arrive at conclusions that are universally valid. Ishida Yûji, a young Japanese historian working on the Third Reich, presented an important paper along those lines at a meeting of the Society to Study the Nanking Incident in September 1999.[48] According to Ishida, there are many points in common between atrocities by the imperial and Nazi armies. For example, he argues that Nanking and the northern China "Three 'Alls' Operations" can productively be compared to the Nazi army's mass murders of Serb civilians in violation of international law, or to its policy of creating no-man's-lands in occupied White Russian areas. As research in Japan by historians of modern Japan and Germany continue to develop, we can expect comparative studies on atrocities to emerge as an independent field.

Social Ramifications

Left-wing research on Nanking since the 1980s has had a number of highly positive results for Japanese society at large, two of which may be noted here. One area lies in the unearthing of new and crucially important primary sources. Here, the work of Ono Kenji is exemplary. An ordinary company employee and currently a member of the Society to Study the Nanking Incident, Ono painstakingly collected and published a key set of documents that led to a breakthrough in research. After returning from a citizens' tour of China in 1988 to survey the Atrocity, Ono quietly went about gathering battlefield diaries and oral testimonies from former low-ranking officers and men in the Thirteenth division's Sixty-fifth Regiment, which hailed from his home prefecture of Fukushima.[49] This regiment, also called the "Yamada Detachment," was long alleged to have murdered some 14,000 Chinese POWs at Mufushan just after the fall of Nanking. Ono's unpretentious yet tenacious efforts indisputably verified this long-held suspicion. He published those sources as *Nankin daigyakusatsu o kiroku shita kôgun heishitachi* (Imperial Army Men Who Recorded the Nanking Atrocity) in 1996. Some fruits of his labors can also be found in English in chapter 4 of the present volume.

A second area of positive social ramifications lies in the growth of events such as the Kyoto Exhibition on War for the Sake of Peace.[50] Held each summer, this elaborate exhibition attracted a total of 1.3 million people between 1981 and 1989. Until then, displays of this type tended to condemn war and teach the value of peace by underscoring the Japanese people's own suffering and victimization owing to air raids or nuclear attacks. The Kyoto Exhibition on War for the Sake of Peace—whose organizers included left-wing historians of Nanking such as Iguchi Kazuki, Kisaka Jun'ichirô, and Shimosato Masaki—went further. These citizens' groups created an event that explored the issue of why imperial Japan launched the Asia-Pacific War in China and depicted ordinary Japanese, including soldiers, as victimizers as well as victims. During their fourth annual exhibition in 1984, organizers mounted a display about the Kyoto Sixteenth division massacring over 20,000 Chinese POWs on its march to Nanking. While planning this exhibit, the organizers led by Iguchi, discovered several diaries left by former soldiers from Kyoto that vividly described their role in the Atrocity—precisely at a time that the fabrication faction was loudly denying its factuality. As with Ono's materials, these primary sources—written by men who actually took part in the Atrocity—confirm its historical factuality beyond any doubt. What is more, by publishing these diaries and other related source materials such as *Nankin jiken: Kyoto shidan kankei shiryôshû* in 1989, the exhibition's organizers facilitated future research on the Atrocity.

Left-wing historical research on Nanking should be viewed in relation to such citizen-led movements. Whether by gathering new evidence or by educating the public, these individuals and civic groups strive to condemn Japan for its culpability in the past war—a major theme since the 1980s.[51] These movements derive from a grave sense of crisis that emerged against the backdrop of government efforts to glorify imperial Japan. Those efforts took concrete form in the Ministry of Education's textbook screening that led to the 1982–83 Textbook Incident and in Premier Nakasone Yasuhiro's 1985 official visit to worship at Yasukuni Shrine—both of which drew loud protests from Asian governments. In a sense, these and other alarming political developments in the 1980s prompted ordinary Japanese such as Ono and organizers of the Kyoto exhibition to ponder anew the interrelated issues of wartime aggression in Asia and how postwar generations in Japan refused to make amends for it. For example, one group of citizens traveled to Nanking in May 1986 to plant 5000 trees in memory of the Atrocity victims and thus establish Sino-Japanese friendship. The citizens were motivated by "deep remorse and a keen sense of responsibility for the immense damage inflicted on the Chinese people."[52] This event symbolically shows that, when presented with the fruits of Nanking scholarship, many Japanese will take seriously the culpability that their parents or grandparents bear for war crimes. In a similar vein, an Association to Consider Postwar Culpability toward Asia was formed in

1983 in order to win compensation for Koreans abandoned on Sakhalin (Karafuto) after Japan's surrender; and, as noted below, this association launched legal proceedings for that very purpose in August 1990.

An Association to Consider War Victims in the Asia-Pacific and Inscribe Their Suffering on Our Hearts came into being in 1985. It attracted 900 members in Osaka and simultaneously held similar rallies in 10 cities all over Japan on 15 August 1986, the forty-first anniversary of the war's end. The "Association to Inscribe Suffering" set up a Postwar Redress Forum in the Asia-Pacific that prompted Asian war victims to sue the Japanese government and Japanese companies for compensation in 1991. The same association promoted an International Hearing on Japan's Postwar Compensation in 1992, and this led to the creation in 1993 of a Center for Research and Documentation on Japanese War Responsibility. This research center, staffed by left-wing scholars, serves as the central organ promoting research on Japanese war crimes. As well, the Asian Women's Fund was created to collect private donations in lieu of formal government compensation to former "comfort women," or sex slaves, of Korean and other nationalities.

Ôdate city in Akita Prefecture sponsored a memorial in 1985 for victims of the Hanaoka Incident of 1945 in which Chinese slave laborers forcibly brought to Japan launched an uprising to protest inhuman working conditions only to suffer torture and death in retaliation. This memorial sparked new interest in the issue of the forced wartime relocation of Chinese to Japan as slave labor. In 1987 an Association to Ponder Chinese Slave Labor and an Association to Prepare Commoners' Courts to Try Japan for Wartime Culpability toward Asia were formed. In December 2000, the latter organization hosted a mock trial by international women's groups in Tokyo modeled on a similar trial held by Bertrand Russell during the Vietnam War. Although this tribunal lacked the force of law, it pronounced the late Shôwa emperor (Hirohito) and other Japanese military leaders guilty of war crimes against Asian women for making them sex slaves. Also, from 1993 to the start of 1995, a Unit 731 Exhibition went on display in sixty-one Japanese cities, where 220,000 people visited it. The exhibition introduced the biological experiments that Unit 731 conducted on human guinea pigs euphemistically termed "logs" *(maruta),* which ended in the death and mutilation of some 3,000 people, most of them Chinese.

One of the most noteworthy social developments in the 1990s was real, not just symbolic, lawsuits brought against the Japanese government to win compensation for Asian victims of the war. These lawsuits became possible because Japanese citizen-led movements gained impetus due to the end of the Cold War, which produced liberalization and democratization in formerly authoritarian anti-Communist regimes such as South Korea, Taiwan, and the Philippines. Until then, governments there and in other Asian countries suppressed demands for compensation by their own peoples for fear of antagonizing Japan and thus losing a lucrative source of economic aid for development. Now, these Asian governments saw fit to stop this suppression and in some cases even encouraged their nationals to launch lawsuits as individuals in Japan, where they got help from sympathetic Japanese citizen groups.[53]

For example, groups of Koreans were relocated under imperial government orders to work on Sakhalin, which was Japanese territory during the war. But imperial armed forces abandoned them there in 1945 when the Soviet Union took over, and many remained stranded until the late 1990s. On 29 August 1990, some of the Koreans who had been able to return home sued the Japanese government for damages in the Tokyo District Court. Also, some wartime Koreans—as Japanese imperial subjects—served as soldiers, as guards in POW camps, and in other paramilitary capacities. Some of them were killed in action; or, after the war ended, some were executed or sentenced to penal servitude as Japanese war criminals for having mistreated Allied POWs. These men and their kin were unilaterally stripped of Japanese citizenship in 1952; and although they continued to live and pay taxes in Japan as resident aliens, they lost all rights to state pensions and social welfare benefits, such as medical treatment for wounds suffered in the war, because those rights were limited to Japanese citizens. On 12 November 1991, a group of such resident-alien Koreans sued the Japanese government for damages. In December 1991, we should note, the first group of Korean former "comfort women" launched a lawsuit against the Japanese government for their sexual enslavement by the imperial army during the war.[54]

Yet another lawsuit was launched to compensate wartime Hong Kong residents who had been paid wages in Japanese military scrip, and were forced to deposit these in Japanese financial institutions, only to find the scrip and their savings to be worthless after Japan surrendered in 1945. Later in the 1990s, still more lawsuits were launched against the Japanese government and Japanese companies on behalf of Chinese and Korean workers forcibly brought to Japan for slave labor during the war, and one of these lawsuits ended with an out-of-court settlement in November 2000 when Kashima Corporation agreed to award damages to former Chinese laborers and their offspring. As of 2003, there are some fifty lawsuits of this type being tried or appealed in Japanese courts of law. Asian victims will not likely win significant monetary compensation because Tokyo insists that peace treaties concluded with foreign governments stipulated that Japan pay only state-to-state reparations, and that any further claims for individual damages be waived. Japanese law courts almost invariably uphold this legal argument to disallow payment of compensation to foreign individuals on a state-to-person or a company-to-person basis. Nevertheless, the key point here is that victims have made serious attempts at redress, and none of these could have taken place without active cooperation from Japanese citizens who, owing to left-wing scholarship and public relations activities, feel a keen sense of accountability for war crimes committed 70-plus years ago. Such developments would have been barely conceivable prior to the sustained movements for education and redress that emerged from the 1980s and continue in the 2000s.

These movements have four important points in common.[55] First, and above all, they prove that ordinary Japanese are in fact owning up to the culpability that they, their parents, or their grandparents bear for the damages and suffering inflicted on Asians during the war. Second, by launching lawsuits against their own government to win compensation for victims of the war, these Japanese citizens are cultivating bonds of solidarity with those Asians. Third, younger Japanese have in general been the prime force behind these endeavors. Fourth, there has been a concomitant decline in influence enjoyed by conservative groups such as the Society to Honor Our War Heroes. This is epitomized by the fact that one group of dissident bereaved families bolted from the Japan War-Bereaved Families in 1996 in order to form their own Association of Pacifist War-Bereaved Families, which pursues goals informed by radically different principles.[56]

In sum, citizen-led movements have played a major role in educating ordinary Japanese people about the truth of the Nanking Atrocity and other hideous war crimes. What is more, these movements from below have forced various branches of the Japanese government and judiciary to acknowledge that truth—though with great reluctance. For example, in concluding the third Ienaga textbook lawsuit over the constitutionality of the government's system of textbook screening, the Tokyo Higher District Court ruled in October 1993 that, although the screening system itself was constitutional, the Ministry of Education illegally abused that system by forcing textbook authors to omit or tone down passages mentioning imperial army complicity in procuring comfort women.[57] It is noteworthy that all Japanese secondary school history textbooks issued during the 1980s and 1990s mentioned the Nanking Atrocity. Several relapsed into downplaying or omitting the Atrocity in their 2000 and 2001 editions, but that trend has been partly reversed since 2003.

It is no coincidence that, in response to a reporter's question regarding a lawsuit brought against Azuma Shirô, a reputed eyewitness to the Atrocity, a Ministry of Foreign Affairs official spokesperson on 25 December 1998 averred: "the Japanese government recognizes that there are numerous ways to interpret the 'Nanking Atrocity,' but it is an undeniable fact that mass killings or massacres of noncombatants did take place after the imperial army entered the walled city of Nanking."[58] In other words, even though two successive court decisions ruled against Azuma by concluding that he fabricated an account of one particularly cruel incident in the Atrocity, the government concedes that the Atrocity as a whole did take place. In April 1999, Chief Cabinet Secretary Nonaka Hiromu echoed this statement when he publicly repudiated a denial of the Atrocity made by Tokyo governor Ishihara Shintarô.[59] Ishihara himself later conceded that the event took place—though on a scale that accords with a minimalist definition. These developments prove that denying the historical fact of the Atrocity is becoming less and less acceptable in present-day Japanese society.

Key developments have taken place in judicial circles as well. For example, the Tokyo District Court on 22 September 1999 concluded a lawsuit launched over Unit 731, the Nanking Atrocity, and Indiscriminate Air Raids.[60] Its decision did not order the government to compensate Chinese victims, but it did affirm that, even by the standards of 1937–45, the Sino-Japanese War was an indefensible act of imperialist aggression and colonialism that inflicted immense suffering on enormous numbers of Chinese people. As to Nanking, the District Court explicitly conceded that "from several tens of thousands to as many as 300 thousand" Chinese were massacred; and as to Unit 731, it declared that this unit's existence and its biological experiments on human beings are facts beyond any doubt. Finally, the District Court's decision asserted that the Japanese government should apologize to the Chinese people in a sincere and heartfelt manner.[61] Again, although not ordering the government to pay monetary compensation, the Tokyo District and Tokyo Higher District courts in 2002 and 2003 upheld a 1999 defamation lawsuit launched by a Nanking survivor, Li Hsiu-ying, against the Nanking denier Matsumura Toshio and Tendensha, the publisher of his *Nankin gyakusatsu e no daigimon*.

Altered Views of the War

How have ordinary Japanese people's views of the war changed as a result of left-wing historical scholarship and citizen-led movements for education and redress? On 7 and 8 November 1993, the *Asahi shinbun* polled 3,000 eligible voters (citizens 20 years or older) nationwide about how Japan should deal with demands for postwar compensation made by foreign nationals. Of 2,319 persons who agreed to be interviewed, 51 percent answered that "we should respond" to those demands, whereas 37 percent said "we do not need to respond." This survey is noteworthy in that roughly 70 percent of the respondents in their twenties responded in the positive. As for whether Japan should pay compensation to former comfort women, fifty-one percent of all the respondents said "yes," whereas thirty-three percent said "no." Here too, over seventy percent of respondents in their twenties responded "yes." As these surveys show, however, the overall level of support for paying compensation remained at about fifty percent. An analysis of these polls indicate that there was still considerable support in 1993 for the view that violations of human rights are unavoidable in war to a degree. However, the idea that such violations are intolerable even during war was gaining ground, particularly among the young.[62] Contributing to the growth of such dissident views was the proliferation of citizen-led protest movements since the 1980s and the large number of lawsuits over postwar compensation that began in the 1990s. In that sense, social movements to force the Japanese state and people to face up to their culpability for wartime evils have indeed been efficacious.

In 1982, 1987, 1994, and 2000, Japan's national broadcasting corporation NHK conducted polls to gauge how the Japanese people made sense of their modern history. In October 1982, NHK conducted a nationwide survey of 3,600 persons aged 16 years and over, of whom 72.9 percent responded. In October 1987, 69.4 percent of 3,600 persons responded to a similar survey. In December 1994, NHK extended the nationwide survey to include 1,800 persons 20 years of age and over, of whom 64.2 percent responded. In May of 2000, NHK surveyed 2,000 persons 16 years or older. In October 1982, fifty-one percent of the respondents agreed that "the 50-year history of Japan from the [1894–95] Sino-Japanese War to the [1941–45] Pacific War was a history of aggression against neighboring Asian peoples." In October 1987, that figure dipped slightly to forty-eight percent, but in December 1994 it rebounded to fifty-two percent. And, in 2000 it remained at fifty-one percent. As for the avoidable or unavoidable nature of that aggression, in October 1982, forty-five percent of the respondents replied that "resource-poor Japan had no choice but to advance militarily into other countries if it were to survive" during this fifty-year period; so "[aggression] couldn't be helped." In October 1987, this figure fell to forty percent; and in December 1994, it fell even further, to thirty-two percent. Also, in October 1982, twenty-seven percent of the respondents replied that these fifty years represented a "history of aggression" that "was *not* something that 'couldn't be helped'." This figure remained at tewnty-six percent in October 1987, 27 percent in December 1994, and thirty percent in 2000.[63]

Overall, then, the NHK surveys indicate that most Japanese from 1982 to 2000 admitted that their forebears waged wars of aggression between 1894 and 1945, but that these wars were unavoidable; it was the only way for their resource-poor nation to survive in the world at that time. Looking at the figures in a positive light, we can say that very few Japanese accept the conservative revisionists' reactionary view that imperial Japan fought and sacrificed itself to liberate Asians during those fifty years. Yet it is just as important to note the opinion that wars from 1894 to 1945 "couldn't be helped." The persistence of this view discloses a troubling dimension; that is, the Japanese people still find it rather hard to face up to their wars of aggression, or they do not wish to learn from this history. As Yoshida Yutaka notes, if most Japanese believe that the wars "couldn't be helped" even as they admit that these were "wars of aggression," this means that they feel a need to apologize or to make amends only in a formalistic sense. In other words, they are not truly critical of modern Japan's policies toward Asia and lack a genuine sense of wrongdoing.[64] However, the 2000 NHK survey demonstrated that fifty percent of all respondents, and sixty percent of those born in 1959 or later, said that the post-war generation ought to "resolve the unsettled issues left over" from wartime; that is, discharge responsibility for the war. By contrast, thirty-two percent of all respondents, and twenty-seven percent of those born in 1959 or later, felt that the postwar generation did not need to discharge that responsibility or bore none at all. The remaining eighteen percent and thirteen percent of respondents "did not know" or entered other answers.[65]

Conclusion

Left-wing Japanese historians of the Nanking Atrocity have had an important sociopolitical impact in three key areas. First, their academic findings have done a great deal to clarify the overall nature and extent of the Atrocity. Second, they have directly or indirectly promoted broadly based citizens' movements that forced the Ministry of Education to permit mention of the Atrocity and other Japanese war crimes in school textbooks. Third, they currently assist Asian victims of the war who seek compensation for damages from the Japanese government and business firms. As a result of these endeavors, the government, as well as the majority of ordinary Japanese people, have come to accept that: (1) imperial Japan waged wars of aggression in Asia since 1894, (2) the Japanese people committed heinous war crimes between 1931 and 1945 of which the Atrocity was but one, and (3) the postwar generation ought to bear some responsibility for making atonement.

It is true that a minority of people in Japan continue to deny this history of aggression, are intent on claiming that the Nanking Atrocity was fabricated or grossly overblown, and repudiate any need for atonement. The continued existence of this minority is indeed lamentable. However, it is unlikely that those persons will exert a great deal of political influence in the future, as the wartime generation is totally replaced by persons born after the war. In that sense, both foreign critics such as the late Iris Chang and her followers, and Japanese such as Azuma Shirô (now exposed as having fabricated tales of atrocities at Nanking) grossly misrepresent contemporary Japanese society when making blanket condemnations of the Japanese people for willful ignorance about their history of aggression.[66] In fact, left-wing historians in Japan fully share those critics' goals of exposing the barbaric actions of imperial Japanese troops during the Atrocity in order to draw lessons from it, and also to win monetary compensation for foreign victims. But the reason that so many otherwise sympathetic Japanese scholars feel perturbed by the publications and journalistic activities of those "Japan bashers" lies precisely in the oversimplifications and distortions of present-day Japan that they insist on maintaining and propagating.[67]

Notes

*   Translated from Japanese by the editor.
1.   Kasahara, *Ajia no naka no Nihongun*, pp. 15–39.
2.   Yang, "Challenges of the Nanjing Massacre," pp. 133–79.
3.   Hata, "'Rabe kôka o sokutei suru," pp. 8–25.
4.   Hata, *Nankin jiken*, passim.
5.   Kasahara, *Ajia no nanka no Nihongun*, p. 19.
6.   Yoshida, "Kenkyûkai meguri," pp. 76–77.
7.   Kasahara, *Ajia no nanka no Nihongun*, p. 21.
8.   Suzuki, "'Nankin daigyakusatsu' no maboroshi," pp. 177–91.
9.   Watada, "Suzuki Akira shi no 'shuzai' o shuzai suru," p. 194.
10. Tanaka, *"Nankin daigyakusatsu" no kyokô*, passim.
11. Tanaka, "'Nankin daigyakusatsu': Matsui Iwane no jinchû nisshi," pp. 64–79.
12. Kasahara, *Ajia no naka no Nihongun*, p. 28.
13. Nakajima, "Nankin kôryakusen: *Nakajima dai-16 shidanchô nikki*," pp. 252–71.
14. Kimijima, "'Nankin jiken' no kôtei to 'Nankin daigyakusatsu' no hitei," pp. 105–20; *Kaikô*, (March 1984), p. 18.
15. Hora, "Matsui taishô jinchû nisshi kaizan atogaki," pp. 55–66; Itakura, "Matsui Iwane nikki no kaizan ni tsuite," pp. 187–94.
16. Itakura, "'30-man gyakusatsu' kyokô no shômei," pp. 50–54; Itakura, "'30-man gyakusatsu' kyokô no shômei, zoku: 'Nankin jiken no sûjiteki kenkyû," pp. 40–46; and Itakura, "Nankin jiken no sûjiteki kenkyû 3: Nankin de ittai nani ga atta no ka," pp. 36–43.
17. Itakura, "Matsui Iwane nikki no kaizan ni tsuite," p. 190.
18. Yoshida, "15-nen sensôshi kenkyû to sensô sekinin mondai," pp. 36–55.
19. Ibid., p. 47.
20. Itakura, "Matsui Iwane nikki no kaizan ni tsuite," p. 194.
21. On Yasukuni, see Murakami, *Irei to shôkon;* and Ôe, *Yasukuni jinja*.
22. Zenkoku senyû rengôkai, ed., *Senyûren jûnen no ayumi*.
23. Hata, "Izoku to seiji," p. 195, and p. 228.
24. Kasahara, *Nankin jiken to sankô sakusen*, p. 299; Sengo 50-nen shimin no fusen sengen iken kôkoku undô, ed., *"Sengo 50-nen" aratamete fusen de ikô*.
25. Shûsen gojûnen kokumin iinkai, ed., *Shûsen gojûsshûnen kokumin undo kiroku shû*.
26. Sengo 50-nen shimin no fusen sengen iken kôkoku undô, ed., *"Sengo 50-nen" aratamete fusen de ikô*, p. 195.
27. Ibid., p. 219.
28. Wada, *Sengo Nihon no heiwa ishiki*, passim.
29. Agawa, "'Aa, dôki no sakura' ni yoseru," pp. 112–24.
30. Yoshida, "Sensô no kioku," pp. 99–117.
31. Yoshida, "Nankin jiken no zenyô ga semaru rekishi ishiki," p. 65; Kasahara, *Nankin jiken to sankô sakusen*, p. 60.
32. Hosaka, "Chû-Kan no 'tai-Nichi hihan' ga okoru toki," p. 101.
33. Critical studies of the group include: Morita and Fujiwara, eds., *Kingendaishi no shinjitsu wa nani ka;* Kyôkasho kentei soshô o shien suru zenkoku renrakukai, ed., *Kyôkasho kara kesenai sensô no shinjitsu;* Yoshida, "Nihon kindaishi o dô toraeru ka," pp. 238–53; Ôgushi, "'Dai-3-ji kyôkasho kôgeki' no shinbu ni aru mono," pp. 15–26; Oguma, "'Hidari' o kii suru popyûrarizumu," pp. 94–105.
34. Typical of Fujioka's many publications are *"Jigyaku shikan" no byôri* and *Ojoku no kingendaishi*.
35. Tawara has monitored the groups' activities since 1997 in his home page, "Kodomo to kyôkasho zenkoku netto 21" found at: http//:www.asahi-net.co.jp/~prly-twr/

36. See, for example, Higashinakano, *"Nankin gyakusatsu" no tettei kenkyû*; also, Higashinakano and Fujioka, *"Za reepu obu Nankin" no kenkyû.*

37. Takashima, "Rekishikan X media = watching 3," pp. 37–45.

38. Higashinakano, "Rekishi no kenkyû ka, rekishi no waikyoku ka?," pp. 37–45.

39. Yoshida, "Kenkyûkai meguri," pp. 76–77.

40. Representative studies dating from the 1980s are Fujiwara, *Nankin daigyakusatsu;* Hora, *Nankin daigyakusatsu no shômei;* Honda, *Nankin e no michi;* Hora et al. eds., *Nankin daigyakusatsu no genba e;* Hora et al., *Nankin daigyakusatsu no kenkyû;* and others by Kasahara and Fujiwara discussed in the main text.

41. Their most recently published document collections include: Nankin jiken chôsa kenkyûkai, ed. and trans., *Nankin jiken shiryô shû 1: Amerika shiryô hen;* Nankin jiken chôsakenkyûkai, ed., and trans., *Nankin jiken shiryô shû 2: Chûgoku kankei shiryô hen;* and Ono, Fujiwara, and Honda, eds., *Nankin gyakusatsu o kiroku shita kôgun heishitachi.*

42. Kasahara, *Nankin jiken*, p. 228.

43. Yoshida, "Nankin jiken no zenyô ga semaru rekishi ninshiki," p. 59.

44. Yoshida, "15-sensô shi kenkyû to sensô sekinin mondai," p. 42.

45. Yoshida, *Nihonjin no sensôkan*, p. 90.

46. Yang, "Challenges of the Nanjing Massacre," passim.

47. See the English adaptation of his book (authored under his anglicized name) Yuki Tanaka, *Hidden Horrors,* passim.

48. Ishida, "Kenkyû dôkô shôkai: Doitsushi ni okeru gyakusatsu kenkyû."

49. Ono describes his labors in a postscript to his document collection, "Atogaki," pp. 375–82.

50. Yoshida and Iguchi, "Kyoto ni okeru sensôten undô to shiryô hakkutsu," pp. 442–65.

51. Uesugi, "Kowasenakatta 2-jû kijun no kabe," pp. 10–17.

52. Nankin daigyakusatsu higaisha tsuitô kenshoku hô-Chû dan, ed., *Midori no shokuzai,* vols. 1–4.

53. Ishida, "Sensô sekinin saikô," p. 32.

54. Tawara home page: www.asahi-net.co.jp/~prly-twr/

55. Uesugi, "Kowasenakatta 2-jû kijun no kabe," pp. 10–17.

56. Tanaka, "Senbotsusha o dô tsuitô suru ka," pp. 147–92.

57. Kasahara, *Nankin jiken to sankô sakusen,* p. 44.

58. *Mainichi shinbun,* 29 December 1998.

59. *Asahi shinbun,* 19 April 1999 (evening edition).

60. Chûgokujin sensô higaisha no yôkyû o sasaeru kai home page: www.threeweb.ad.jp/~suopei

61. *Asahi shinbun,* 23 September 1999; also, Oyama, "Mujun ni michita hanketsu no sekkyokumen to shôkyokumen," pp. 12–15.

62. Asahi shinbun, ed., *Sengo hoshô to wa nanika,* pp. 140–44.

63. For other surveys, see Kôno, et. al., ed., "Sekai no terebi wa sengo 50-nen o dô tsutaeta ka," pp. 1–109; Matsumoto, "Nihon no wakamono no 15-nen sensôkan to kyôkasho (ankeeto no matome)," pp. 199–231.

64. Yoshida, *Nihonjin no sensôkan,* p. 217.

65. NHK, ed., "Saki no sensô to sedai gyappu," web posted in September 2000.

66. Chang, *Rape of Nanking;* on Azuma's television appearances in China, *Sankei shinbun,* 2 June 1999.

67. Mizutani, "Watashi wa naze Azuma Shirô ni igi o tonaeru ka," pp. 219–25; Yoshida, "Kaisetsu," pp. 258–59. In Azuma's defense, see Nakakita et al., "'Azuma saiban' no shinjitsu o uttaeru," pp. 275–81.

POSTSCRIPT

16

LEFTOVER PROBLEMS

Bob Tadashi Wakabayashi

Massacres: Real and False

Massacres tend to provoke contention. U.S. but not British historians speak of a Boston Massacre in May 1770 that took five lives; the British commander was acquitted of all charges. In the more recent past, U.S. troops killed hundreds of Korean and Vietnamese civilians at No Gun Ri in July 1950 and at My Lai in March 1968. But most Americans deny that either event was a massacre entailing apologies, compensation, or execution of the men responsible. In January 2001 President Bill Clinton expressed "regret" but no official apology for No Gun Ri, and President Jimmy Carter earlier had refused reparations to Vietnam because "the destruction was mutual."[1] Palestinians insist that Israeli troops massacred 3,000 to 5,000 civilians at Jenin in April 2002, but Charles Krauthammer of the *Washington Post* disagrees: "The 'Jenin massacre' is more than a fiction. It is a hoax." He explains, "A massacre is the deliberate mass murder of the defenseless," and Jenin was a "phantom massacre," but earlier in 2002, sixty-two Israelis died in six "real massacres" one of which took the life of a single child.[2] Krauthammer's colleague at the *Post*, Richard Cohen, concurs: "The Jenin 'massacre' not only lives on in Palestinian mythology but also remains embedded in the files of many Western media outlets." Cohen grants that, "no doubt some bad things happened at Jenin," but still avers, "[g]iven the nature of the fighting, Israel can hardly be accused of a war crime."[3]

What makes for a *massacre* during an invasion or military occupation? First, a minimum numerical threshold must be cleared for the term to be meaningful. Of course, even 1 victim is too many from a humanitarian viewpoint, but if the number is five as at Boston in 1770, "the side that did the killing" will reject "massacre" as a hyperbole if not a slander. If we raised this minimum to 200 or 300, No Gun Ri and My Lai would qualify, but then the retort is that all states committed killings of that size sometime in the past, so it is unfair to indict only some for war crimes. Along with this key "numbers issue," I would posit four more attributes to define "massacre": the illegality of the killings, the lack of an overriding military necessity, the helplessness of the killed, and a cruelty that inflicts needless suffering. These five attributes entail hard judgment calls, which deniers may at times get right, as at Jenin, where evidence for a massacre of 3,000 to 5,000 seems questionable.

Those who, rightly or wrongly, deny that some massacre took place adopt some similar tactics. They place quotation marks around "X Massacre" to connote "the so-called" and imply, "this is a lie." They use terms like *phantom*, *hoax*, *fiction*, *myth*, and *illusion* to discredit accounts by the other side. Arithmetic and semantic precision suffer when "our side" gets killed. Thus, Tanaka Masaaki, Takemoto Tadao, Ôhara Yasuo, Higashinakano Osamichi (Shûdô), and other deniers cite the "massacre" of one Japanese officer; and Charles Krauthammer explicitly defines a "massacre" as "the deliberate mass murder of the defenseless," yet applies "mass" to one Israeli child. Members of "the Western media"—unnamed for Jenin but cited as Harold J. Timperley, Edgar Snow, and Agnes Smedley for Nanking—reputedly fabricated and perpetuated a "mythology." Deniers admit that "bad things" took place, like the inadvertent death of civilians, but insist that this was *not* a war crime because guerrillas in plainclothes, often including women and children, were not readily identifiable as enemy belligerents. "Given the nature of the fighting," Richard Cohen asks, "what, dear reader, would you have done?" This appeal won the day at official investigations of My Lai and No Gun Ri. President George W. Bush and Defense Secretary Donald Rumsfeld later used this logic to justify wars of dubious legality in Afghanistan and Iraq. For them, enemies disguised in civilian garb are "unlawful combatants" who abjured all rights reserved for bona fide prisoners of war (POWs), so humanitarian treatment and due process of law, including speedy trials before military tribunals, are not necessary; indefinite detainment or even summary execution is justifiable.

The Nanking Atrocity takes on new meaning in light of these recent events. Japanese deniers thus point to explicit images of sexual and sadistic abuse of Iraqi POWs by U.S. captors, liken these to similar photos used by the People's Republic of China (PRC) and by the late Iris Chang, and hold that the images were misused or doctored in order to demonize the enemy.[4] Higashinakano applies the category of unlawful combatants to plainclothes troops at Nanking. Kitamura Minoru tells how a distraught teenager—in fact the Kurdish ambassador's daughter—duped the U.S. Congress into authorizing the 1992 Gulf War, and likens her to agents for the Kuomintang (KMT) such as Snow and Timperley, who in 1938 posed as humanitarians while gaining Western support for China.[5] Educated persons after World War I tended to disbelieve atrocity claims because the British, hoping to draw the United States into that war as an ally, had falsely accused Germany of rapes and mass murders in Belgium.[6] Thus, Westerners in Nanking felt a need to preface their accounts in 1938 by warning that Japan and China laid "exclusive and exaggerated blame" on each other for atrocities.[7] Educated persons after World War II, by contrast, tend to believe atrocity claims because their verification has become so common. By sorting out some leftover problems about the Nanking Atrocity, we hope to avoid the twin evils of knee-jerk dismissal and gullible acceptance.

Ambiguity into Deception

Much misunderstanding, not all of it innocent, stems from terminology. The Chinese call what happened at Nanking "the *Ta-t'u-sha*"—"the massive butchery or slaughter." The ideographs *t'u-sha* (without *ta* or "massive") appear in the word "slaughter house," or the huge meatpacking plants where production-line workers kill and process livestock. "The *Ta-t'u-sha*" thus conjures up an image of defenseless creatures systematically butchered en masse in crudely violent ways. This accurately reflects the murder of 14,000 to 20,000 Chinese POWs detained at Mufushan that Ono Kenji describes in chapter 4. But the term is misleading in a key sense; it blurs a distinction that must be upheld even if Chinese who suffered a brutal invasion and occupation in an undeclared war rightfully beg to differ. That is, to qualify as a massacre, mass killings must be criminal in nature; belligerents killed in action differ from nonbelligerents murdered in cold blood. A lopsided kill ratio in battle may indicate a massive butchery, but the goal in war is to maximize enemy casualties and minimize one's own. War is a "killing contest" sanctioned by, yet constrained under, international law. The Marianas Turkey Shoot of June 1944 was a slaughter of Japanese pilots, helpless, given their inferior planes and training; but it did not entail moral censure, legal liability, and continuing apologies. In April 1945, U.S. forces killed a quarter of the civilian population on Okinawa, or 150,000 people, as opposed to killing 95,000 Japanese soldiers. But left-wing historians assert that the blame lies with the Shôwa emperor (Hirohito), whose "'august decision' [to surrender] came too late."[8] Deniers use this same logic to insist that some of the blame for Nanking lies with Chiang Kai-shek and T'ang Sheng-chih, who failed to surrender at all. This is one reason why they reject *ta-t'u-sha* (*daigyakusatsu* in Japanese) to describe what took place at Nanking. Adopting the arguments of Richard Cohen, Charles Krauthammer, George W. Bush, and Donald Rumsfeld, they argue that most Chinese civilian deaths at Nanking resulted from justifiable, legal battlefield actions against unlawful combatants who were armed or had access to arms in the Nanking Safety Zone (NSZ). Most of those Chinese killed, they hold, were guerrillas or persons mistaken for guerrillas; so no deliberate, large-scale massacre took place for which Japan must apologize and pay compensation. But deniers ignore the most basic fact of all; that is, although most

Japanese troops and noncommissioned officers at Nanking such as Amano Saburô were unwilling draftees, they illegally invaded and brutally occupied a foreign land. Thus, we must recognize, their Chinese adversaries felt justified in using illegal and unfair tactics to defend their homes and families.

The term *maboroshi* or "illusion" is problematic as well. It contains harmless elements of literary ambiguity, yet has a legitimate place in historical revision. In April 2004, the Associated Press announced, "Lost Bach Wedding Score Resurfaces after Eighty Years [in Japan]," but the original Japanese headline ran: "Bach '*maboroshi* no fu': Nihon ni" (underscore added).[9] Here, *maboroshi* denotes a long-lost musical arrangement. The late Fujiwara Akira once joked, "Iris Chang's translation is a *maboroshi* sitting in the publisher's warehouse."[10] Here, the word denotes books that are inaccessible to would-be readers because Chang forbade their sale and distribution in Japan.[11] In both cases the term stands for a nebulous entity, inferred from other sources to have existed in the past or present, whose exact nature cannot be ascertained because its cognitive traces lie beyond sight or hearing. Bach's composition stopped being a *maboroshi*, unknowable for being inaudible, when its score was found in 2004. Chang's Japanese translation too would lose its *maboroshi* status if the ban on its sale and distribution were to be lifted.

In this peculiar sense, Suzuki Akira was right when he called the Nanking Atrocity a *maboroshi* back in the early 1970s, when few reliable primary sources existed to verify oral testimonies that Chinese survivors conveyed to Honda Katsuichi. Suzuki's claim lost validity, however, after historians unearthed new sources that proved its factuality. Shrewd deniers then conflated *maboroshi* with "illusion" and "myth" as used by historical revisionists. L. L. Farrar lays bear *The Short-War Illusion* of July 1914 that made European leaders rush into a war they believed would end by Christmas. In *The "Hitler Myth,"* Ian Kershaw debunks common beliefs about the *Führer*, vastly at odds with reality, that Germans such as John Rabe embraced; for example, "if Hitler only knew" about an evil, he would end it.[12] Rana Mitter exposes *The Manchurian Myth* of mass resistance to Japan after 1931. Paul Cohen describes the Boxer Rebellion in China as "event, experience, and myth"—stressing that its memory differs from its historical reconstruction. Kasahara Tokushi is a revisionist who declares that victim counts of "over 300,000" at Nanking are "an ethnic Chinese fantasy." He differs from deniers, however, by affirming that the Atrocity did take place; only its scope is disputed. Suzuki made a valid point: the 100-man killing contest was an illusion. But he insinuated that the entire Atrocity was unreal.[13] This contest took pride of place at the Nanking War Crimes Tribunal where two Japanese officers were executed for it. The Chinese insist, however, that the contest is irrefutably true exactly as prosecutors charged, and that it symbolizes Japanese bestiality not only at Nanking, but all over China. Thus they play into the hands of deniers who exposed this one incident as false, and from it extrapolate malicious Japan bashing in all Chinese claims about war crimes. That in turn alienates persons in Japan who crave to accept Suzuki's views.[14] All states foster illusions and myths to bolster their prestige and authority. Japan has made 11 February a legal holiday to commemorate the founding of its imperial dynasty in 660 BC, and right-wing journalists seemingly depict the myth as factual.[15] The PRC too has its myths, and if deniers prove that many more incidents in the Nanking Atrocity are baseless in fact, we may have to rethink our overall understanding of it. There is nothing inherently pernicious in raising this possibility; our profession has no sacred cows.

Suitably Flexible Contours

The journalist Robert Marquand asserts: "What actually did happen [on] June 3–4 [1989] is still often confused with myth and misreporting" rooted in "fifteen years of unattributed rumor and discredited accounts of a 'massacre'." "[T]here was no massacre of students on the [T'ien-an-men] Square"; the true number of persons killed may have been "as low as a dozen."[16] At first glance, Marquand seems to deny that a massacre took place, but he actually affirms that one occurred; it is just that the vast majority of its victims were workers, and his figure of "a dozen" dead students obtains only for T'ien-an-men Square itself. Thus, he allows that thousands of Chinese, many of them students, may have died elsewhere in the city, but over four days rather than on one night.[17] This is an artful manipulation of spatial and temporal boundaries, but such artfulness exacts a price.

In analyzing any historical event, one must start by demarcating its contours. Disputants in the debate on Nanking harbor vastly different assumptions about how long the incident transpired and how broad an area it covered, but they usually fail to say so. Obviously, the longer a massacre is purported to have lasted and the wider its spatial scope, the higher its victim count will rise—and viceversa. A Japanese minimalist definition, which corresponds to the solid black area on map 3, restricts "Nanking" to forty square kilometers bounded by the walled city and its immediate environs, or even more narrowly, to the 3.8 square kilometer Nanking Safety Zone (NSZ). This minimalist definition, limits the massacre's temporal scope to five days: from 13 December when Japanese troops breeched the city's walls, to 17 December 1937 when Matsui Iwane held a triumphal entry, and it presumes that Nanking was just another assault-and-siege operation. Its extreme adherents limit their evidentiary base to one volume of official sources—*Documents of the International Safety Zone.* This lets them claim a total of under fifty victims; tens of thousands may have died, but did so in combat or its loosely defined extensions. At the other extreme, a maximal definition of Nanking, which corresponds to all of map 3, encompasses a 40,000-square-kilometer swath—the Yangtze delta region south from Shanghai past Lake T'ai through Hu-chou, Kwang-te, Ning-kuo, and Wuhu to Nanking, plus areas north from Yangchou to Ch'u-hsien in Ch'üan-chiao County.[18] This maximal definition extends the Atrocity's temporal scope to seven or eight months: from August 1937 when the Japanese attacked Shanghai, to February 1938 when a semblance of order returned to Nanking, or to March 1938 when the collaborationist Reformed Government arose. Proponents of maximal contours usually assume that all Chinese who died count as victims, irrespective of whether they were civilians or combatants. These maximal assumptions meld seamlessly with the even more extreme official Chinese view of over 300,000 victims—now pegged at 340,000—inside the forty-square-kilometer walled city within six weeks.

At the present stage of research, victimization estimates of under 40,000 and over 200,000 push the limits of reason, fairness, and evidence; but even within this range, much turns on one's prior normative assumptions; that is, Nanking was just a normal assault-and-siege operation with tragic collateral damage, or it was an East Asian equivalent of the Holocaust in which all Chinese were innocent victims, so that a distinction between belligerents and non-belligerents is immaterial. Even the leftist Honda Katsuichi, who adopts maximal contours, does not claim over 300,000 victims. The conservative Hata Ikuhiko, on the other hand, grants that 300,000—first cited in 1938 by Snow and Timperley and now dismissed as propaganda by deniers—is a fairly accurate total for Chinese belligerents and civilians killed in the five-month Shanghai-to-Nanking assault.[19] As noted in chapter 1, Japanese historians said just that in the 1950s to 1960s, and the Chinese voiced no disagreement.

The most sensible contours, corresponding to the criss-cross section of map 3, are those proposed by Kasahara Tokushi. He assumes that the Atrocity was both an assault-and-siege operation and a brutal military occupation, and thus dates the event from early December 1937 to March 1938, not the minimal contours of 13 to 17 December 1937, or the maximal contours of August 1937 to March 1938. He also assumes that most killings took place outside, not inside, the walled city, so he extends his spatial contours to the Nanking Special Administrative District (NSAD) on map 2; that is, the walled city and 6 adjacent counties, rather than limit his contours to the walled city alone. Thus, he does not extend these contours to the entire Yangtze valley from Shanghai to Nanking. This NSAD covers about 8400 square kilometers, or 1.5 times the size of Delaware. Within such middling contours, he estimates a victim toll approaching 200,000 or perhaps more, subject to revision after further research. A fellow leftist, the late Eguchi Keiichi, estimates a death toll of 100,000 plus a few thousand more, but this includes belligerents.[20] Hata's narrower contours produce a lower, yet still academically tenable, victim toll of over 40,000.[21] Thus, the admittedly vague range of "over 40,000 to under 200,000" has scholarly validity in the sense of being empirically supportable. Former staff officer Okumiya Masatake, who estimates about 40,000 victims, claims that Japanese forces encountered unlawful plainclothes combatants earlier in the China war, but not at Nanking.[22] Japanese sources cite guerrilla resistance after KMT armies were routed at Shanghai and beat a mad retreat, but few mention this after 13 December in Nanking itself, and Hata claims that military records show no Japanese casualties inside the NSZ, although deniers dispute his claim.[23] This is why Westerners inside the city—who had not seen Japanese troops killed by guerrillas en route to Nanking—denounced the rounding up and killing of Chinese "ex-soldiers" who shed uniforms and fled into the NSZ as refugees. However, it is duplicitous for deniers to adopt maximal contours in order to play up Japanese casualties from guerrilla actions outside the city while adopting minimal contours in order to play down the killing of Chinese ex-soldiers inside it.

A Nanking-Holocaust Congruity?

The historian William C. Kirby asserts that British poet W. H. Auden, who likened Nanking to Dachau in 1938, was one of the first to link Japan and Germany as "moral co-conspirators, violent aggressors, and perpetrators of what would ultimately be called 'crimes against humanity'."[24] Conservatives in Japan have always bristled at suggestions that their nation and Nazi Germany flocked together for reasons other than expedience. They retort that no defendant at the Tokyo War Crimes Trials was found guilty of crimes against humanity. By contrast, Japanese leftists point to the Axis partners' similarities—not single-party rule, a totalitarian state, or a *Führer* figure, all of which Japan lacked; but rather, the monstrous evils that both states committed. Critics abroad and leftists at home have incessantly derided Japan since the 1980s for insufficient penance compared with Germany, but this criticism presumes that Japan committed sins of a similar scale and severity; if not, an equal degree of penance is uncalled for. Of course, even small-scale atrocities are inexcusable, but deniers are right to insist that the numbers issue is crucial. If imperial Japan massacred 340,000 defenseless civilians at Nanking in six weeks and thirty-five million in China overall, a congruity with Nazi Germany becomes plausible. If not, the charge is unfair. So, should we stress what Japan and Germany had in common, or does the evidence show that Japan was not so bad after all?

Dissociation of Japan from Germany began at the dock in Tokyo. Takigawa Masajirô, a defense counsel there, wrote: "'crimes against humanity' was a special charge created to punish the Nazis for their inhumane massacres of Jews.... Japan committed no such massacres, but the Tokyo trial adopted this Nuremberg precedent, so we got hit with a cudgel meant for someone else."[25] Takigawa also criticized the Allies for violating *nullum crimen sine lege,* the principle that no act can be deemed a crime, subject to trial and punishment, without prior laws that make it illegal and that stipulate penalties for its commission. Senator Robert A. Taft said the same thing in 1946.[26] Where Takigawa differed was in holding that the Allies were right to ignore this principle in punishing the Germans, but that the "Nuremberg precedent" was inadmissible at the Tokyo trial because Japan did not commit a similar crime. The enormity of German guilt embossed "Japan's innocence"—the title of a 1963 book by Tanaka Masaaki. He argued that the Allies' failure to convict any Japanese defendant of crimes against humanity proved the incongruity between Japan and Germany. In 1963 Nanking was not yet a major issue, so Tanaka made no special effort to deny it in particular. Instead, he lionized the Indian Justice Radhabinod Pal, who denounced victorious Allied prosecutors for creating ex post facto laws to wreak vengeance. Tanaka thus criticized the Tokyo tribunal not for Nanking per se, but for its putative injustice overall. Nor was he yet anti-Chinese. He praised Chiang Kai-shek and deemed himself a pan-Asianist friend of the Republic of China like his former patron, Matsui Iwane. Tanaka became a denier in the 1980s owing to the PRC's hardline on victim counts that implied an equivalence to Nazi genocides. In 1984 he coined the catchphrase "Auschwitz in the west, Nanking in the east" to deride what he saw as unjust guilt by association.[27]

Ancillary issues surfaced in the 1980s: comfort women, biological/chemical warfare Unit 731, a "blame Japan" view of history that allegedly fosters uncritical pacifism, *sengo sekinin* or the culpability, never discharged by their grandparents, which postwar Japanese reputedly bear for war crimes, the government's formal apology for aggression and colonial rule issued on the fiftieth anniversary of defeat in 1995, and stepped-up demands by left-wing activists for Japanese to show true remorse by translating lip-service apologies into monetary compensation. "Bashing" from abroad weighed in heavily during the 1990s. The comfort women issue exploded, as foreign and domestic citizen groups held mock trials for long-dead war crimes suspects not indicted at Tokyo. The PRC assumed a strident anti-Japanese tone. *The People's Daily* in 1995 declared that Japan was culpable for over thirty-five million Chinese deaths in the war, and President Chiang Tse-min (Jiang Zemin) demanded a written apology in 1998. Richard von Weizsäcker, a former president of the German Federal Republic, made a speech in May 1985 that foreign and left-wing domestic critics would repeatedly cite as proving German moral superiority on the war guilt issue. In 1995, U.S. veterans forced the Smithsonian Institution to sanitize an exhibit on nuclear attacks against Japan, but in 1996, UNESCO named Hiroshima and Auschwitz as world heritage sites, and in 1997, Iris Chang retorted that more Chinese died at Nanking than did Japanese at Hiroshima and Nagasaki combined, but "Japan has doled out less than 1 percent of the amount that Germany has paid in war reparations."[28] She subtitled her best-seller of that year "The Forgotten Holocaust of World War II"—which soon became a worldwide clarion call.[29] Finally, in 1996 the U.S. Justice

Department put sixteen Japanese on a list of war criminals, until then limited to Nazis and their collaborators in Europe, banned from entering the United States; and in 1999, California passed the Hayden Act to permit lawsuits against German and Japanese firms that exploited wartime slave labor.

As if to mock Tanaka, Western polemicists took up "Auschwitz in the west, Nanking in the east" as an anti-Japanese leitmotif. Most early Nanking deniers in Japan had been nonacademics, but in the 1990s, elite University of Tokyo alumni such as Fujioka Nobukatsu, Nishio Kanji, and the late Sakamoto Takao took up the gauntlet, seeking to cut forever Japan's stigmatic link with the Nazis' Final Solution. Here I focus on Nishio, a specialist on German cultural and intellectual history, whose views on German war guilt and postwar restitution as related to Japan is the most detailed and comprehensive.[30]

How did Nishio repudiate charges of Japan's "forgotten Holocaust"? First, he argued that Richard von Weizsäcker never admitted guilt or apologized for the German past, and Germans never paid eighty times more in compensation for war crimes than Japan; so, he said, there is no factual basis for charging, as leftist and foreign critics incessantly do, that Japanese are despicably cheap and morally deficient in comparison. Postwar Germans apologized and paid compensation for *Nazi crimes,* but not for the *war crimes* they also committed. Second, this distinction lies at the core of Nishio's thesis. Germans abused comfort women in Europe more viciously than Japanese did in Asia; but for both, this was a normal, ordinary, conventional war crime since its aim was to gain victory by raising troop morale and effectiveness. Likewise, the United States waged atomic warfare, which should be a war crime, to defeat Japan; and, it granted amnesty to Unit 731 officers to gain data on chemical and biological warfare in order to win future wars. All nations commit such war crimes—categorized as B-class at Tokyo—to gain some strategic advantage. But they forgive and forget once the wars end. Thus, Nishio approvingly cites Nathaniel Thayer and John Dower who criticized the U.S. Justice Department's decision to lump Japanese former war criminals with Nazis for punitive treatment in 1996.[31] Third, Nishio rejected the idea that ordinary Germans, like other Europeans, were liberated from Nazism by the Allies, or that there were "good Germans" (like John Rabe) even among Nazis. Nishio stated that virtually all Germans supported Nazism before 1945, so they bore collective guilt *(Kollektivschuld)* for crimes against humanity, yet conveniently skirted it through the ruse of "individual guilt"—with the individuals being dead Nuremberg convicts. Fourth, Nishio said, Nazi crimes were committed under the cover of war, but apart from it, and even to the detriment of victory. Thus the *SS* and *Einsatzgruppen,* or special killing squads, could have been used in combat, funds for death camps could have gone to arms production, and trains hauling Jews for mass murder could have shipped rations to the front. Above all, Nazism was so evil that the Allies demanded an unconditional surrender; state-sponsored genocide precluded a compromise peace settlement, which was normal in war. Nishio held that all states commit murder some of the time, in war; but Germany legalized murder all of the time for some groups. Anne Frank, eulogized by Japanese pacifists, was not a victim of war. Germans would have murdered her even in peacetime because she was a Jew and could not change that biological fact. By contrast, killing in a war stops when one side surrenders and turns over its arms—which Chiang Kai-shek and T'ang Sheng-chih refused to do at Nanking. Thus, foreigners and leftists should not compare Japan *to* Nazi Germany in order to stress likenesses; they should compare Japan *with* Nazi Germany to highlight the crucial differences.

Nishio's fifth point is to refute arguments like that made by the Japan scholar, Donald Ritchie; that is, numbers are not the key issue at Nanking. Ritchie wrote, "four or forty is as atrocious as 140,000"—the high-end victim count he cited.[32] By contrast, Nishio held, "few if any of us deny that a massacre *(gyakusatsu)* occurred at Nanking; we only say that '300,000' as used in textbooks is far too high…. The number of murders *does* matter because it decisively alters the nature of a massacre."[33] He is thinking of numbers for the Boston Massacre, My Lai, No Gun Ri, or Jenin. Massacres of 5, 300, or 3,000 victims differ *qualitatively* from the cataclysmic 340,000 that allegedly occurred in six weeks over forty square kilometers—which insinuates a congruity with the Holocaust. In his view, no state, least of all the PRC, can claim innocence of "normal" war crimes wherein massacres of 5, 300, or 3,000 take place; hence Japan alone should not suffer vilification.

Nishio made valid points. He helped correct muddled leftist thinking by showing how murder differs from war, how conventional war crimes differ from the Nazi Final Solution, and how Japan's war guilt differs from Germany's. But he also had flaws. He claimed that only the *SS* and *Einsatzgruppen,* not regular Wehrmacht troops, committed genocide, and that Zyklon B (hydrogen cyanide) and high-tech death camps were essential in order to dispose of tens or hundreds of thousands of victims. These two points are crucial for him. The imperial army had no specialized, ideologically motivated exterminator units. Nishio reasons that Japanese troops could not kill 340,000 people inside Nanking city within six weeks because ordinary men require indoctrination akin to Nazification before they will commit so great a crime. Furthermore, the absence of highly toxic gases and death-camp furnaces made it impossible to burn 190,000 civilian corpses into oblivion, as the PRC has insisted since 1983. (It also claims burials of 150,000 more civilian victims.)

By the 1970s and 1980s, Michael Geyer, Manfred Messerschmidt, Christian Streit, Omer Bartov, Christopher R. Browning, and other revisionist historians debunked this myth of "the clean Wehrmacht"—fostered at Nuremberg and perpetuated by the Federal Republic. According to this myth, ordinary German officers and men were untainted by Nazism and uninvolved with racial extermination, but we now know that Wehrmacht troops did commit mass murders.[34] This finding destroyed the basis for Nishio's argument by analogy that "ordinary Japanese" troops also stood unblemished. Yet he, a German studies expert, ignored this scholarly consensus. Also, on four occasions, he distorted a key German account of three million Russian POWs purposely reduced to cannibalism and starvation.[35] Sebastian Haffner wrote: "Here, the borderline is blurred between the [ordinary] war crimes which are better forgotten and Hitler's mass murders." Nishio renders this as: "But abuse of POWs still falls under the category of [ordinary] war crimes."[36] Haffner did not include these murders in the Holocaust per se, but he drew a similarity to genocide that set them decisively apart from conventional war crimes. Nishio did the converse based on a legal technicality. He deemed this a normal war crime that might occur in any conflict simply because the bench at Nuremberg did not include these in the category "crimes against humanity."

This sleight of hand allows Nishio to skirt the issue of murdered Chinese POWs, and he opts to lower their number too. He rejects Ono Kenji's evidence in chapter 4, long available in Japan, that Japanese troops massacred 14,000 to 20,000 POWs at Mufushan. Instead, Nishio adopts the more congenial "unavoidable killing in self-defense thesis." It holds that, while escorting several thousand POWs for release, the Japanese had no choice but to kill 1,000 to 3,000 after they staged a riot in tandem with enemy fire from across the Yangtze. To be fair, as Ono notes, extenuating circumstances did exist at Mufushan. Chinese POWs far outnumbered their captors, posing the threat of revolt; and, those captors lacked enough provisions even for themselves, so they could not feed POWs. That said, criminality, cruelty, and the POWs' helplessness do not enter Nishio's calculus. No Japanese defendant was found guilty of "crimes against humanity," and only these constitute the Holocaust. Japanese committed *only* normal war crimes and have apologized and compensated victims for these, whereas Germans committed *both* war crimes and Nazi crimes, but have made amends *only* for the latter. Japan did nothing all that bad, so Chinese should drop this issue after sixty years of peace. In sum, Nishio refuses to see that, although the Holocaust was uniquely and insuperably monstrous, it might not be the only wartime atrocity of an extraordinarily evil nature that calls for enduring moral censure. Still, he is right to insist that, if Nanking was such an atrocity, deserving of such censure, then cogent evidence is needed to support this charge.

Memory and Written Evidence

Before postmodernism and the linguistic turn, historians demanded proof for assertions in written sources, ideally composed at or near the time of an event by people directly involved in it. Thus, John Vincent argues: "History is inescapably tied to the written word"; "no evidence, no history."[37] There is a reason for this privileging of written over oral accounts based on memory. Memory is vague to start with, and it changes over time without the subject noticing. The "written word" may be inaccurate or untrue, but it does *not* so change unless deliberately altered. Hugh Trevor-Roper derided "the worthlessness of mere human testimony" in debunking one by Karl Dönitz, widely accepted in 1946, that Hitler died at the head of his troops defending Berlin.[38] Another case in point is the memory of wartime Allied air raids on Dresden in February 1945, related by survivors to Frederick Taylor in the 1990s. Those survivors insisted that Dresden had been a purely cultural center without Nazis, Wehrmacht, or war industries; but Allied pilots used chemical weapons and machine guns to slaughter hundreds of thousands of helpless civilians. Taylor examined written sources to reach an empirically tenable estimate of 25,000 to 30,000 victims and to disprove other points in those oral testimonies. Yet the survivors remain convinced that their shard memory is true in all respects.[39] This is not to call the Dresden air raids an "illusion," or to deny that a terrible atrocity occurred—only to say that it did not take place in the way or to the extent that survivors remember today.

Similarly, in 1989 Timothy Brook sought to quantify the killings on T'ien-an-men Square a few months before. He wrote: "Where to begin? The experience [i.e., memory] of eyewitnesses is hardly the place. Many eyewitnesses saw people killed, but many did not. More to the point, none witnessed all the killing. People saw what was around them, at best a few dozen meters in any direction from where they happened to be standing when the guns went off. Their perceptions were muddled by fear and confusion and darkness. How can their individual experiences of the killing be summed into a total?"[40] Brook concluded that most student eyewitnesses recalled an impossibly high number of victims. In the opposite direction, Kôbe University professor Noguchi Takehiko noted that his own experience of the 1995 Great Hanshin Earthquake misled him to believe that the loss of life was far less than it really was. He had no idea that a catastrophe of over 6,300 fatalities took place—even though he survived being right in the middle of it: "No matter where anyone may be, one cannot see a disaster in its entirety. I learned of its massive scale from later TV reports. For anyone who directly experienced the disaster, it was either an awful tragedy or nothing all that bad, whichever the case had been. Even those who suffered losses could know only what occurred around their persons. They could not even begin to imagine that a massive natural calamity took place."[41]

Historians privilege written over oral accounts in order to prevent mistakes of this type, based on memory; this is what distinguishes history from behavioral sciences that study pre-, non-, or slightly-literate societies. Given a lack or dearth of written records, members of such societies can "know" a past event only by remembering and retelling it; for them, recalled experience or memory is the only form of historical truth or reality possible. Behavioral scientists who study them have no way to tell how closely this memory replicates a past event, or to discover when and how the memory of it changed over time through retellings. This is why historians tend to dismiss oral accounts based on memory as "worthless" unless substantiated by written records. To reject this dictum is to repudiate history as an academic discipline. As postmodernists rightly point out, however, that dictum stacks the deck against illiterate, inarticulate, and oppressed members of a society who cannot write accounts to reveal their side of the story and repudiate their oppressors'. But by contrast, the rich, powerful, literate members of society leave self-serving documents that latter-day historians use to construct its dominant narrative.

A full discussion of this and other cogent postmodernist concerns lies beyond this study.[42] But we must note three relevant points: (1) Wartime Nanking residents could not produce official, public sources that portrayed their Japanese masters unfavorably, nor could they produce many nonofficial, private sources of that nature because well-to-do, literate strata in society had fled. This discredits a popular denial myth; that is, if a "massive butchery of 340,000" people had occurred, Chinese at the time would have recorded it, but the lack of such records proves that none occurred. (2) Japanese troops held the Chinese in contempt as an ethnic group, but *at least early in the war,* this did not translate into the view that it was virtuous to kill helpless civilians en masse. The Japanese would still need to violate their own moral precepts in order to reach that point which, I hold, took place later in the war. This *incongruity* with Wehrmacht troops is important. As Claudia Koonz, Hannes Heer, and others argue, many Germans followed a "Nazi conscience" that placed certain groups beyond the pale of legal and ethical concern, and they acquiesced in the "moralization of crime." This sanctioned massacres and the compilation of murder lists.[43] But, by contrast, official, public Japanese sources recorded only the murder of Chinese belligerents, *at least early in the China war;* and, the murder of belligerents in war is permitted under international law. (3) If we seek to verify and quantify the mass murder of civilians at Nanking, we must rely mainly on nonofficial, nonpublic oral sources; that is, post hoc testimonies by Chinese victims and Japanese victimizers based on memory. Deniers, however, invariably criticize not only Chinese, but also Japanese, oral sources of this type on the same grounds that Hugh Trevor-Roper dismissed Karl Dönitz's.[44]

The Documentary Record

Japanese Military Sources

We first turn to documents left by the Japanese armed forces in 1937—official battle reports and private field diaries. Under critical scrutiny, these unwittingly expose incriminating evidence. Table 1 is taken from Kasahara Tokushi, as amended by myself.[45] Figures are in units of 1,000. I calculate "several 1s" as 5,000 but left "over 10" as "10,000."

We must cull these Japanese sources for information that the compilers never intended to convey, so problems of interpretation arise. First, the figures are for Chinese military personnel, as defined by Japanese troops, who held that soldiers donning civilian garb and fleeing into the NSZ remained belligerents. Rightly or wrongly, they felt justified in killing such men. By this Japanese definition, only Chinese who had never been soldiers counted as civilians; those killed after discarding their uniforms were *not* massacre victims. The "side that got killed" does not accept this distinction between belligerents and nonbelligerents; all Chinese who died resisting an illegal, immoral invasion qualify as victims. But my point is that Japanese troops would not record masses of murdered civilians (by their definition) in non-secret sources. Illegal, unjustifiable murders of civilians did occur, but documents analyzed here do not tell how many, so we cannot add them to a victim count. Japanese military sources thus have a built-in bias favoring "the side that did the killing"—a point that we cannot stress too much.

How many "surmised but not expressly recorded kills"—registered as "??" figures—may we include in the tally? I arbitrarily assumed that fifty percent actually occurred, and so subtracted 26,425 from 135,900 to get 109,475. These figures were rough guesses made in the pell-mell of battle, so their accuracy is suspect to begin with. On top of that, units inflated kill counts to

Table 16.1. Mass Killings of Chinese Military Personnel (Unit = Thousands)

Based on Estimates Expressly Recorded in Japanese Military Sources
Symbols: IR = infantry regiment, IB = infantry brigade, C = company, HAB = heavy artillery battalion, ?? = "surmised kills" based on other sources not recorded by the unit in question

	Date	Unit	Number	Description
		By the Sixteenth Division (Kyoto, Regular)		
(1)	13 Dec.	38IR	5–6	while fleeing across the Yangtze
(2)		33IR	about 2	while fleeing across the Yangtze
(3)		30IB	over 10	defeated stragglers
(4)		30IB	several 1s	while trying to surrender
(5)		1C	1.3	while trying to surrender
(6)		2HAB	7–8	while trying to surrender
(7)	14 Dec.	30IB	about 20??	taken as captives
(8)		20IR	0.8??	after disarming
(9)		20IR	0.31	rifled after disarming
(10)		20IR	about 1.8??	captives led off
(11)		20IR	0.15–0.16	captives incinerated
(12)		20IR	0.6	defeated stragglers led off, executed
(13)	24 Dec.-5 Jan.	30IB	several 1s	execution during mop-up operations

By the Thirteenth Division (Sendai, Special)

	Date	Unit	Number	Description
(14)	14 Dec.	103IB	about 1	mop-up of defeated stragglers
(15)	16–17 Dec.	103IB	about 20	captives in custody

By the Ninth Division (Kanazawa, Regular)

	Date	Unit	Number	Description
(16)	13–24 Dec.	7IR	6.670	suspected soldiers in ISZ

By the One Hundred-fourteenth Division (Utsunomiya, Special)

	Date	Unit	Number	Description
(17)	13 Dec.	66IR	over 1.5	captives executed after promises of mercy

By the Sixth Division (Kumamoto, Regular)

	Date	Unit	Number	Description
(18)	10–13 Dec.	unclear	5.5??	while trying to surrender
(19)	10–13 Dec.	unclear	12.7??	bodies in Hsiakwan area

By the Fifth Division (Hiroshima, Regular)

	Date	Unit	Number	Description
(20)	13 Dec.	9IB	about 5??	left disposal of captives to Tenth Army
(21)	14 Dec	41IR	2.35??	captives left for later disposal

By Unknown Unit(s) (so may be a duplication of Case 19)

	Date	Unit	Number	Description
(22)	16–17 Dec.	unclear	about 4??	execution of defeated stragglers at Hsiakwan

By the Eleventh Battle Fleet

	Date	Unit	Number	Description
(22)	13 Dec		about 10	while fleeing across the Yangtze
(23)	14 Dec		about 0.7??	while disarming defeated stragglers
(24)	15 Dec		about 1.2	defeated stragglers
(25)	about 16 Dec		several 1s	defeated stragglers on island in the Yangtze

Findings

A. Killings

Total Killings Listed: 135,900 (?? Surmised Killings: 52,850; 50 percent of 52,850 = 26,425)
Estimated Death Count: 109,475 (135,900 minus 26,425)

B. "Massacre Victims"

Clearly Illegal, Unjustifiable Killings: 29,240 (Underlined without ??)
?? Surmised Illegal Killings: 33,950 (Underlined with ??); 50 percent of 33,950 = 16,975
Estimated Illegal, Unjustifiable Killings = "Massacre Victims": 46,215 (29,240 plus 16,975)

C. Arguably Illegal, Unjustifiable Killings: 63,260 (109,475 minus 46,215)

impress superiors. Staff officer Anami Korechika stated that units regularly padded kill counts by threefold; others cite a twofold to fivefold padding rate.[46] Thus we might lower kill counts to that extent, but sources of this type exist only for about one-third of the units at Nanking.[47] So I let these factors cancel each other out and kept the figure 109,475. This is how many Chinese persons—not massacre victims—died in or near the walled city in December 1937.

Broad latitude thus exists for statistical interpretation or, less charitably, for manipulation. Conservatives can cite table 1 to limit victim tolls at "over 40,000." Deniers can cite it to prove that all 109,475 were belligerents killed in action and thus were *not* victims. Leftists can argue that all 109,475 were massacre victims, to whom we must add tens of thousands more killed in rural areas outside the city. I hold that some of these 109,475 were belligerents legally killed in battle and were not victims. How many? That hinges on how much empathy one has for "the side that did the killing"; the "arguably illegal" count will decrease to this degree. Judgment calls are hard to make. For example, it was illegal at the time to execute POWs until military tribunals judged that they were spies or guerrillas.[48] But deniers justify summary executions on the grounds that Chinese captives had already violated the laws of war by not surrendering under a responsible commanding officer, by changing into plainclothes, and by fleeing into the NSZ where they had access to hidden arms caches that included tanks, howitzers, machine guns, revolvers, rifles, and hand grenades.[49] As this logic goes, Chinese soldiers chose to be unlawful combatants within reach of weapons, so the Japanese could dispense with due process and humanitarian treatment reserved for bona fide POWs.[50] Despite reservations, I reject this claim and assert that all "captives" taken into custody and killed (the underlined figures) were massacre victims, whether unlawful combatants or bona fide POWs. This produces a bare minimum of 29,240 unjustifiable killings or "massacre victims," and more likely, 46,215 when we add estimated illegal killings. Cases 16 and 17 are irrefutably inexcusable; Japanese troops killed these men after telling the Westerners who had turned them in: "Trust [the] humanitarian attitude of [the] Japanese army to care for the disarmed Chinese soldiers."[51]

Likewise, I would include as "massacre victims" Chinese troops in uniform or persons in plainclothes killed while trying to surrender. To be fair, though, in private diaries and papers, the Japanese record cases of Chinese troops and civilians feigning surrender to kill would-be captors with concealed guns, or of waving the Rising Sun to ambush Japanese troops, which led to bans on displaying the national flag.[52] We cannot know how common these ruses were or how many Japanese troops harbored such fears inside Nanking city; and, it may be too much to expect mercy from fearful, hungry, exhausted troops brutalized by their own officers and shot at by guerrillas en route to Nanking. This too is a hard judgment call, and deniers, who empathize with "the side that did the killing," might be excused a bit for wanting to lower Chinese victim counts in these cases.

Japanese troops in 1937 were largely kept ignorant of international laws about POWs, but they appealed to ideas of military necessity similar to those found in the U.S. Lieber Rules of 1863. These hold that troops may give no quarter when their own security or the success of their mission is at risk. Thus, a commander can order enemy troops killed if so many of them try to surrender that his men cannot safely guard or escort them to the rear.[53] (This does not apply after taking them into custody, however.) Few Japanese troops knew of the Lieber Rules per se, but all nurtured similar notions that permit killing enemy soldiers when it was impossible to secure their incarceration. Also, the Japanese were so ill-supplied that the rank-and-file normally foraged for their own provisions en masse, and so could not feed POWs in huge numbers. This was their main pretext for killing Chinese troops who tried to surrender or, less justifiably, POWs already in custody.[54]

Contrary to humanitarian sentiments today, I hold that those Chinese in uniform shot while in flight; for instance, "across the Yangtze," were not massacre victims. International law at the time deemed interdiction operations legal.[55] Japanese troops had cause to err on the side of caution, since the act of fleeing might conceal an intent to rejoin battle later on.[56] In chapter 3, Kasahara Tokushi estimates that 50,000 of a total 150,000 Chinese troops fled from the Nanking theater; many must have seen future action against Japanese forces. Westerners thought of Chinese troops who changed into civilian garb and fled into the NSZ as "ex-soldiers" or "former soldiers," no different from refugees.[57] But the Japanese deemed them defeated stragglers *(haizan hei)* or enemy remnants *(zanteki)*—as legitimate targets on mop-up operations *(zanteki sôtô)*.[58] This judgment call too is not easily made today: Did enemy remnants who fled into the NSZ really pose a threat later on? Might the Chinese ex-soldiers shed their "ex-" status and return to kill Japanese troops? If so, it was justifiable to nip guerrilla insurgencies in the bud. Apart from taking the KMT capital, the aim of this Shanghai-to-Nanking campaign was to "exterminate" KMT armies. The Japanese did find large Chinese arms caches in the NSZ; and, one may argue that, even when their nation wages a vicious war of aggression, draftees retain the right to shoot if threatened by guerrillas. On the other hand, if one's sympathy lies with "the side that got killed," one will argue that these helpless "ex-soldiers" shed uniforms, donned civilian garb, and joined other refugees in the NSZ simply to stay alive. This uncertainty was reinforced by the Chinese custom of defeated troops shedding their uniforms to merge into civilian populations. That caused no problem in Chinese civil wars, when Hague conventions were not a factor, but Japanese troops came from a different military tradition that disallowed masquerading as civilians to seek cover in their midst.[59]

Despite these and other problems of interpretation, we can conclude that Japanese military sources culled by Kasahara Tokushi, and emended by myself, verify the killing of about 109,475 Chinese in or near Nanking in December 1937; of these, a minimum of 29,240—and more likely 46,215—were illegally killed massacre victims. To this figure, we must add an appropriate number from the 63,260 arguably illegal killings to get a subtotal. To reach a final total, we must add figures for the Nanking Special Administrative District (NSAD)—the walled city plus six adjacent counties—from 1 December 1937 to 31 March 1938. (See map 3.) Thus, no single victim count is definitive. Instead, we get an academically valid range of from "over 40,000 to under 200,000" that will vary according to factors noted above. Either way, these figures are strictly for Chinese belligerents—as defined by Japanese troops who left these sources. They would not record large numbers of murdered Chinese civilians in non-secret public documents. But many such murders certainly took place, and to get an idea of how many, we must look at wartime Western, plus postwar Chinese, documents.

Wartime Western Sources

Private sources left by Westerners such as letters, diaries, and personal papers tend to be imprecise and impressionistic. They mention thousands of rapes, but do so largely in a second- or third-hand manner. Yet, as deniers stress, one official Western source, *Documents of the Nanking Safety Zone,* lists under fifty murders. If we read Western documents against the strict rules of source criticism required by our profession, quantification is skewed both upward and downward. Deniers savor the high number of rape reports for being hearsay, and the official death tolls for being so low.

One of the best Western sources is *War Damage in the Nanking Area: December, 1937 to March, 1938* by Lewis S. C. Smythe, a Nanking University professor of sociology. The historian Kitamura Minoru argues that he was a paid KMT adviser.[60] That is no surprise. Like the Meiji government, which hired foreign advisers, the modernizing KMT regime wanted to exploit Western expertise. The rub comes when Kitamura suggests that Symthe being a KMT adviser compromised the reliability of this study. This is untrue. Symthe employed some twenty Chinese teaching assistants to conduct on-the-spot city and rural surveys in early 1938—just after the Atrocity ended. Thus, *War Damage in the Nanking Area* is a primary source of huge importance, too often ignored by researchers. Smythe mentions interference from Chinese troops while conducting his surveys.[61] Yet he says nothing about the Japanese interfering, even though they did suppress fictional works on Nanking in 1938 such as Ishikawa Tatsuzô's *Ikite iru heitai,* modeled on the Sixteenth Division's Thirty-third Regiment. (By contrast, Sasaki Motokatsu's nonfictional *Yasen yûbinki,* which described atrocities in China, was not suppressed in 1941.) Japan, then, did not halt the publication and circulation in China of Smythe's *War Dam-*

age in the Nanking Area. Critics may argue that it escaped suppression due to its low death tolls, but this is unconvincing. Unlike other Westerners at Nanking, Smythe refused to take the stand in Tokyo against Japanese defendants; he declared that he stood by statements in *War Damage in the Nanking Area* and also in *Documents of the Nanking Safety Zone.*[62]

Smythe's figures for deaths and injuries appear in table 2, taken from Smythe's own "Table 4." These are indeed low. Even assuming that all of those "injured" and "taken away" later died, his total for mid-December to mid-March is 10,950. If we subtract the 850 killed "by military actions" or combat—and Smythe thought the distinction worth making—we get 10,100 deaths. Leftist scholars find this total hard to deal with. In chapter 3, Kasahara Tokushi describes flaws in Smythe's sampling method that skew it toward underreporting, and elsewhere concludes that, if properly interpreted, "Smythe's surveys yield over 38,870 civilian massacre victims."[63] Indeed, Smythe also notes that "31,000 or 29 per 1,000 residents" were killed outside the walled city, and "eighty-seven percent of the deaths were caused by violence, most of them the intentional acts of soldiers."[64] Thus, we must assume that figures in table 2 are for the walled city alone, but he did not state this explicitly, and some Japanese deniers misrepresent this figure of 10,100 as his estimate for *all* deaths and injuries at Nanking.

Smythe himself admitted a flaw in his study: "There is reason to expect under-reporting of deaths and violence at the hands of the Japanese soldiers, because of the fear of retaliation from the army of occupation."[65] Tucked away in a footnote, though, we find traces of bias in this era that made him omit *all* casualties in another category: "The seriousness of 'taking away' is underlined by the fact that all so listed were males. Actually many women were taken for shorter or longer service as waitresses, for laundry work, and as prostitutes. But none of them is listed."[66] Females "taken away" were not a matter of "seriousness" for Smythe, so he left them out of his statistics. Not until the comfort women controversy in the 1990s, precipitated by feminist activism, would historians grasp the importance of such references to wartime sexual slavery and violence toward women.[67] Thus, Smythe's 4,200 "taken away" in reality were far higher and, assuming that most of them wound up dead, his aggregate massacre toll would rise greatly as well.

Table 16.2.   Smythe, *War Damage in the Nanking Area* [completed June 1938]

Dates	Deaths (A)	Injured (B)	Taken Away (C)	Total A + C	Total A+B+C
Pre-12 Dec. to 15 Mar.	3,400	3,350	4,200	7,600	10,950

(Adapted from Smythe's "Table 4: Number and Cause of Deaths and Injuries, by Date")

"Deaths (A)" includes 850 Chinese killed by "military actions" meaning "bombing, shelling, or bullets fired in battle."

Another statistical problem is John Rabe's often-cited estimate to Hitler in 1938 of "50,000 to 60,000" civilian deaths.[68] This too was based on hearsay, as is true for Western estimates about Nanking's population being 200,000 to 250,000 before the city fell, which David Askew discusses in chapter 5. Western observers lived and interacted in a tight enclave, the NSZ and its environs, where they exhibited an insular mentality, repeating and reinforcing one another's estimates. These were mutually reinforced guesses giving the illusion of agreement, not independently reached estimates. This figure of 200,000 to 250,000 is at odds with some other Western estimates. Rabe himself reckoned that Nanking's original population of 1,350,000 decreased in the fall of 1937, as "800,000 propertied citizens" fled before the attackers.[69] If so, 550,000 people remained in the city and might die at Japanese hands. Likewise, in a note to Table 1 in *War Damage in the Nanking Area,* Smythe lists a figure of "500,000 in early November."[70] As Kasahara stresses, refugees fled *into* the city from the east, and their number may have approached that of those who left earlier.[71] Thus, Western estimates of the city's population being 200,000 to 250,000 in mid-December carry no absolute guarantee of accuracy. Still, a victim toll of 340,000 is not tenable. Even with an influx of new refugees, the Japanese still would have to kill one-third to one-half of Nanking residents in order to reach that figure. The population was rising in March 1938 when the collaborationist Reformed Government was formed. No such regime could hope for popular support or a pretense of legitimacy if its Japanese patrons had massacred so many civilians 4 months before.

Early Postwar Chinese Sources

Smythe noted that Nanking residents could not publicly express suffering or record death tolls owing to "fear of retaliation from the army of occupation." This is one reason that official, public Chinese records dating from 1937 mention no "massive butchery." Rabe estimated that "800,000 propertied citizens" fled from Nanking before the Japanese assault. They were well-to-do, literate classes who normally kept diaries and wrote letters that might articulate grief and tally victims. Incalculable numbers of such private sources thus did not get written until after the war.[72] But early postwar Chinese sources pose major problems. Many date from 1946, eight years after the event, and were created at the behest of prosecutors at war crimes trials. Also, the Chinese did not employ rigor in compiling their materials, so deniers have reason to reject some of these as worthless when judged by strict criteria of source criticism. Some biases are inherent in the sources, since they were generated expressly to gain convictions in court, but more egregious biases stem from misuse for political purposes. The irony is that Japanese denial arguments gain in credence as a result.

In 1946, the Nanking District Court Prosecutor's Office had difficulty finding evidence of Japanese war crimes. Its "Report on Enemy War Crimes" states: "Like winter cicadas, people [fearfully] refused to speak," yet "they denied the truth [of a massacre]" as well.[73] Leftists stress the first explanation, that people kept still out of fear; deniers, the second, a refusal to make up stories. Table 3 summarizes the report sent by the Prosecutor's Office to military tribunals at Nanking and at Tokyo. Its numbers do not add up. The stated total of 279,586 is 51,995 *more than* the true total of 227,591. The figures derive from: (1) testimonies by eyewitnesses who recalled events eight years before, of whom the most prominent was Lu Su, who recounted seeing 57,418 victims killed; and (2) burial records by two charities, the Hung-wan-tzu-hui (Red Swastika Society or RSS) and Ch'ung-shan-t'ang (CST), which together listed 155,300 victims.

The Nanking tribunal proclaimed that Japanese troops massacred "over 300,000." The Tokyo sentence to Matsui read "upwards of 100,000" and its overall judgment, "over 200,000."[74] Justices at Tokyo took the burial records at face value: "That these estimates [of 200,000] are not exaggerated is borne out by the fact that burial societies and other organizations counted more than 155,000 bodies which they buried."[75] To get a total of 200,000 deaths, the bench at Tokyo also had to have uncritically accepted oral accounts by witnesses, most of all Lu Su's figure of 57,418. Lu's testimony raises suspicions of contrived verisimilitude. He is precise to the final digit, unlike other witnesses—apart from Sheng Cheng and Ch'ang Kai-sing—who rounded off to the thousands, which would seem more natural given the chaos at the time. Lu Su testified that he saw 57,418 people bound in the city after dark; they then were marched to the Yangtze, machine-gunned to death, and had their corpses burned and/or flushed downstream.[76] As Nishio Kanji argues, it was impossible to burn so many corpses in one night given the lack of death-camp

Table 16.3. Nanking District Court Prosecutor's Office

Report on Enemy War Crimes (1946)		
Area	*Testimonies By*	*Number of Victims*
(1) Hsin-ho	Sheng Cheng, Ch'ang Kai-sing	2,873
(2) Arsenal and Shen-miao	Jui Fang-yang, Yang Tu-T'sai	7,000
(3) Tsao-hsieh-hsia	Lu Su	57,418
(4) Han-chung Gate	Wu Ch'ang-te, Ch'en Yung-tsing	2,000
(5) Ling-ku Temple	Kao Kuan-wu, Temple Tombstone	3,000
(6) Burial Records	RSS + CST	155,300#
TOTAL		279,586 [sic]*

Breakdown: RSS—43,123; CST—112,266 = 155,389

* A mistake in addition; the total should read **227,591**. There is an overcount of 51,995

incinerators. And, as Hata Ikuhiko suggests, if tens of thousands of corpses had been flushed down the river at one time, sailors on Japanese, Chinese, and Western vessels plying it should have noticed, and someone would have written an account; yet none exists.[77] Ono Kenji partly corroborates Lu Su's account, however. Ono found that 14,000 to 20,000 POWs were killed at Mufushan and disposed of by burning and flushing downstream, but in smaller groups and to an imperfect extent. Thus, we cannot take Lu's oral account at face value. The true number killed is closer to 14,000 to 20,000—which is still horrific. Figures in items (2), (4), and (5) in table 3 may be true but would be more credible if corroborated by other sources. Figures by Sheng and Ch'ang in item (1) may be true, but would be misused in 1983, as noted in a following section.

What of the burial records, then? Deniers and many conservatives look askance at these because Japan's Special Service Agency (SSA) in Nanking paid charities like the RSS to bury corpses, so there was reason to overreport.[78] The best study of this issue is by former Defense Agency historian, Hara Takeshi. Tables 5 to 9 and much of my analysis here derive from Hara.[79] Item (6) on tables 3 and 9 contains burial records for the RSS and CST. Table 3 also gives a breakdown in burial figures: 43,123 for the RSS, and 112,266 for the CST.

Table 4 shows that the RSS buried almost all corpses outside city walls, with only 1,793 of 43,123 buried inside. Table 5 gives a monthly breakdown.

Table 16.4. Red Swastika Society (RSS)

	Inside the Walls	Outside the Walls	Total
	1,793	41,330	43,123

Table 16.5. RSS Burials by Month

Month	Inside the Walls	Outside the Walls	Total
Dec. '37	129	7,118	7,247
Jan. '38	125	1,427	1,552
Feb.	1,539	20,042	21,581
Mar.	nil	8,398	8,398
Apr.	nil	3,132	3,132
May	nil	1,024	1,024
Jun.	nil	26	26
Jul.	nil	35	35
Aug.	nil	18	18
Sep.	nil	48	48
Oct.	nil	62	62
Total	1,793	41,330	43,123

The RSS was a charitable body cited at the time, but with statistical discrepancies. Japanese sources say that it began burials in early January, not December, and ended on 15 March 1938; and list 1,793 burials inside and 29,998 outside the city walls for a total of 31,791. The RSS total of 1,793 for inside the city walls thus tallies with Japanese sources. Its total of 43,123 for outside the walls contrasts with the Japanese figure of 29,998. But Japanese sources may be wrong, for the difference lessens if we subtract the RSS figure of 7,247 for December; and John Rabe noted that RSS burials began on 13 December. In 1938, Minnie Vautrin repeated the RSS figures of 1,793 burials inside and 39,589 outside the walls, and the Nanking International Relief Committee credited the RSS with a rounded-off figure of 40,000 burials.

Sporadic references in primary sources reveal the RRS's capacity for burial work. Japanese documents say that it had 600 men in February and 200 to 300 in March, with five or six trucks. Chinese sources say that the RSS had 200 men at first and 600 later on. In his report to Hitler, Rabe said that 200 corpses a day was the most it could bury. The German diplomat Georg Rosen reported in March that it was doing 500 to 600 burials a day. Thus, 200 to 600 burials a day, varying by month, seems reasonable. The 20,042 burials outside the city walls in February may be problematic. Even if 600 men did the work, it means that they had to bury 715 corpses a day for twenty-eight days. This is quite high. Daily-entry logs show the RSS burying 6,468 corpses on 28 December, 4,685 on 9 February, and 5,705 on 21 February. Those figures also seem high, but might be explained by the recorder having combined several days' or weeks' burials in one entry. In sum, 40,000 to 43,000 burials seem to be a reasonably credible total for the RSS. In the 1960s to 1970s, Japanese historians listed 42,000 deaths for Nanking city, and the Chinese did not object.

But today the numbers issue looms all-important. As David Askew notes in chapter 5, Higashinakano Osamichi (Shûdô) has shown that Harold J. Timperley added 43,000 deaths to a letter by Miner Searle Bates that Timperley placed in a 1938 sourcebook, *What War Means*. Two passages, not in Bates's original, appear in Timperley's edited version: (a) "Burial gangs report 3,000 bodies at the point" and (b) "Evidences from burials indicate that close to 40,000 unarmed persons were killed within or near the walls of Nanking, of whom 30% had never been soldiers."[80] Thus, Timperley altered Bates's letter, and Higashinakano has made a laudable scholarly find, but he extrapolates invalid or overblown claims from it. First, he casts aspersions by saying that Timperley added these 43,000 deaths because he was on the KMT payroll— an aspersion supported with some nonconclusive evidence. Higashinakano then implies that Timperley fabricated the 43,000 deaths, argues that we must reduce the victim tally by this amount, concludes that *What War Means* is a worthless historical source, and insists that even the wartime enemy regime that employed Timperley shared this conclusion because it deleted the figure of 43,000 from four official document collections in 1938. Finally, Higashin-akano asserts, Timperley added to Bates's letter a declaration that 40,000 of these 43,000 corpses were "unarmed persons, of whom 30% had never been soldiers"—without any way to verify this assertion.[81]

My view on these points is as follows: (1) 43,000 deaths correspond to the RSS burial total, which Timperley subsequently added to Bates's letter after the figure became known. (2) The KMT likely used Bates's original letter in compiling its source collections, not Timperley's later edited version. (3) Tim-perley's conjecture that "30% had never been soldiers" ironically supports denial arguments. He made this claim in order to pre-empt or counteract Japanese protests that *all* corpses were those of future insurgents masquerad-ing as refugees, but it shows he believed that, conversely seventy percent of those 40,000—or 28,000—*probably had been* ex-soldiers who shed uniforms and fled into the city and NSZ, where huge stocks of arms were later unearthed. But, having discredited Timperley for being a KMT agent and per-nicious anti-Japanese propagandist, Higashinakano cannot very well use him to support this denial claim. (4) The weight of evidence seems to support, if anything, a reversal of Timperley's percentages; that is, thirty percent at most had been ex-soldiers, and seventy percent at least "had never been soldiers."

The RRS burial records are authentic, being corroborated by other primary sources, and their total of about 43,000 burials is generally reliable, but they do not disclose the combatant or noncombatant status of persons buried or the legality or illegality of how the Japanese killed them, assuming that most died at Japanese hands. Thus, not all of these 43,000 burials are of "massacre victims" as the Chinese insist, but neither are they all "illegal combatants" jus-tifiably killed in action as Japanese deniers argue.

Table 6 shows a breakdown for CST statistics inside and outside the city walls, and table 7 shows a chronological breakdown, though not monthly, for those figures by work crews one to four. Hara Takeshi notes four suspicious points about the CST.[82] First, it purportedly buried three times more corpses than the RRS, but its name appears on no extant sources dating from 1937–38. We first find its name in sources used by the Nanking District Pros-ecutor's Office to compile its 1946 "Report on Enemy War Crimes," prepared as evidence to convict Japanese war criminals. Thus, it may be that sources citing the CST, reputedly dating from 1937–38, were forged in 1946. Two sources used in the 1946 report say that the CST had four work crews, but disagree as to the number of laborers. One source says that there were four groups of twelve men each plus a foreman, for forty-nine men in all; the other,

Table 16.6. Ch'ung-shan-t'ang (CST)

Inside the Walls	Outside the Walls	Total
7,549	104,718	112,267

Table 16.7. CST Burials, Chronological

Dates	Inside the Walls	Outside the Walls	Totals
26 Dec.–28 Jan.	1,011	nil	1,011
30 Jan.–4 Feb.	1,556	nil	1,556
5 Feb.–6 Mar.	2,507	nil	2,507
7 Mar.–8 Apr.	2,475	nil	2,475
9 Apr.–1 May	nil	104,718	104,718
Totals	7,549	104,718	112,267

that these four groups had ten men each, for a total of forty. Neither source tells of a later increase, so we will assume that at most fifty workers did all of the CST burials.

Second, between 26 December and 8 April, CST crews buried 7,549 corpses, or seventy-four a day for 102 days, inside the city walls and none outside; but from 9 April to 1 May, they buried 104,718 corpses, or 4,553 per day over twenty-three days, outside the city walls and none inside. If we assume that the number of workers was forty-five, each buried an average of about 101 corpses a day over those twenty-three days from 9 April to 1 May. But by contrast, even at the height of RSS operations in February, and perhaps aided by five to six trucks, 600 RSS workers buried 20,042 corpses over twenty-eight days, for an average of 33.4 corpses per day, or 1.2 corpses per worker per day. This gross discrepancy in corpse-disposal capacity, about a hundredfold, must be explained. RSS workers may have been inordinately slow by comparison, but Western and Japanese sources attest to their speed, so we must rule out that possibility. This means that 104,718 CST burials is far too high to be credible.

Third, CST work crews three and four in table 8 reputedly buried a total of 59,318 corpses, but this could not have taken place where listed. We know that KMT troops practiced scorched earth tactics in those areas, so few civilians were living there when the city fell. Japanese records show that under 20,000 Chinese troops were in those areas and that 13,000 of them died in

Table 16.8. CST Burials Outside the Walls

Crew	Dates	Place	Totals
1	9–18 Apr.	Outside Chung-hua Gate and Arsenal at Yuhuantai to Hua-shen-miao	26,612
2	9–23 Apr.	Shui-Hsi Gate to Shang-Hsin-he	18,788
3	9 Apr.–1 May	Chung-shan Gate to Ma-chung	33,828
4	7–20 Apr.	T'ung-chi Gate to Fang-shan	25,490
TOTAL			104,718

battle, although this kill count was no doubt padded; so 59,318 is also untenably high. Fourth, according to postwar sources, the CST did burials in the eastern part of the city and the RRS, in the western part; but table 8 lists CST crews one and two doing burials where the RSS claimed credit. This suggests specious entries or double-counting. Furthermore, the twenty to twenty-two men in those two CST crews buried a total of 45,400 corpses in fifteen days between 9 and 23 April. Inoue Hisashi argues that the CST had at least one truck.[83] But still, this figure is far out of line with the RSS, which reputedly buried less than half that number, or 22,000 corpses, in the same areas despite employing hundreds more workers and at least one or two trucks.

For such reasons, Japanese deniers insist that early postwar documents mentioning the CST are latter-day forgeries made to pad Chinese death tolls for war crimes trials, and that the CST never existed. A more generous view is that it did exist, but took on burials as a subcontractor to the RRS. This view gained support owing to testimony by Maruyama Susumu, a former Nanking SSA member, interviewed by Higashinakano.[84] Either way, we must conclude that 112,267 burials by the CST—especially those outside the city—are highly exaggerated if not fictive. Responding to such skepticism, Kasahara Tokushi insists in chapter 3 that it was easier to bury bodies quickly in rural areas; and Inoue elsewhere argues that most were temporary burials in shallow graves, so work took place far faster outside the city.[85] These rebuttals, however, ring hollow.

Following Hara Takeshi, I conclude that the RSS total of 43,123 burials is admissible, but that the CST total of 112,267 burials is inadmissible, as evidence of massacres. Both the Nanking and Tokyo War Crimes Tribunals were wrong in accepting CST statistics as proof of illegal mass murders. Thus, we must lower their death tolls by about 112,000. In line with Ono Kenji's findings in chapter 4 of 14,000 to 20,000 massacres at Mufushan, we must discount Lu Su's testimony at the Tokyo trial by about another 40,000. These 152,000 or so victims never existed. Finally, an unknowable number of the 42,123 RRS corpses were those of Chinese belligerents who do not count as victims. Article XI of the San Francisco Peace Treaty enjoins Japan's government to "accept the judgments" of all Allied war crimes trials, plus their victim counts, but that treaty is irrelevant for historians.

Later Postwar Chinese Sources

Damage surveys made during or just after catastrophic events are sometimes flawed and result in erroneous findings that later studies must rectify. Initial fatality estimates for Chernobyl in 1986, for the 9/11 World Trade Center attack in 2001, and for Hurricane Katrina in 2005 are cases in point—although later revisions were all downward. Yet the opposite also happens. Early reports of the 1995 Great Hanshin Earthquake listed 500 to 600 deaths, but later surveys proved over 6,300 fatalities, for more than a tenfold increase. The same may obtain for the Nanking Atrocity. Initial estimates may have been too low and require upward revision based on better evidence found later on.

Table 9 sums up PRC findings by the Nanking Municipal Group to Study Documentary Historical Sources in 1983, translated into Japanese in 1984. Items (1) to (6) in table 9 are identical to those in table 3 for the 1946 "Report on Enemy War Crimes" except for the "Number of Victims" in item (1). Items (7) to (10) in table 9 were added in 1983 to produce a revised grand total of 340,000 deaths, which break down as "190,000 burned to nonexistence; 150,000 buried by charitable societies." As deniers argue, there are problems. First, "150,000 buried by charitable societies" repeats the figure reached at the Nanking and Tokyo War Crimes Trials and ignores criticisms noted above that the CST total of 112,267 is largely specious and the that RSS total of 43,123 includes belligerents killed in battle. A second problem lies in items (8) and (9). Findings by Ono Kenji indicate the possibility that these duplicate item (3), based on Lu Su's testimony in 1946—which was dubious to start with.[86] A third problem lies in item (1) in table 9, the figure 28,730. It was apparently reached through a multiplication by 10 of 2,873, the figure listed in

Table 16.9. Report of Survivors' Testimonies [1983]

Area	Witnesses	Number of Victims
(1) Hsin-ho	Sheng Cheng, Ch'ang Kai-sing	28,73**0** [sic]*
(2) Arsenal and Shen-miao	Jui Fang-yang, Yang Tu-T'sai	7,000
(3) Tsao-hsieh-hsia	Lu Su	57,418
(4) Han-chung Gate	Wu Ch'ang-te, Ch'en Yung-tsing	2,000
(5) Ling-ku Temple	Kao Kuan-wu; Temple Tombstone	3,000
SUBTOTAL		[**98,148**]#
(6) Burial Records	RSS + CST	155,300
TOTAL		[**253,448**]#
(7) Safety Zone to Hsiakwan	Hsü Chia-lu and son	Tens of thousands
(8) Torpedo Encampment (Yüleiying)	Tuan Yu-you	9,000
(9) Yen-tzu-chi	Ch'en Wan-lu	50,000
(10) Others		10,100
Grand Total: 190,000 burned to nonexistence; 150,000 buried by charitable societies		

* The original entry of 2,873 in table 3, Item (1) has been multiplied by ten.

Accordingly, the actual totals are **72,291** and **227,591**, respectively.

item (1) in Table 3, so that 2,873 victims in 1946 became 28,730 in 1983. This 1983 PRC study thus reinforces the stereotype of the Chinese sporting "gray hair 3,000 *ch'ang* [6,750 meters] long," or being prone to exaggeration, and it weakens the hand of Japanese leftists sympathetic to the Chinese cause.

This later study does not corroborate claims that Japanese troops murdered "over 300,000" or "340,000" innocent civilians inside the walled city of Nanking within 6 weeks from December 1937 to January 1938. But Lee En-han, the late Iris Chang, Shi Young, James Yin, and others insist that the "official figure of more than 300,000 victims has been reconfirmed by Hirota Kôbi [recte: Kôki]" in a telegram on 17 January 1938. Hirota was foreign minister and later hanged for A-class war crimes in relation to Nanking.[87] But this telegram is not the smoking gun it is claimed to be. Masahiro Yamamoto and others cite contextual evidence that Hirota quoted a hearsay account by Harold J. Timperley, and Lu Suping identifies Father de Besange Jacquinot as Timperley's source of information.[88] Father Jacquinot was in Shanghai, some 300 kilometers away and in no position to provide accurate information. Thus, Hirota's telegram cited "more than 300,000 victims" as an unfounded Western rumor, not as a fact, in January 1938. However, as conservatives admit, the figure 300,000 does represent a credible total for Chinese belligerents and civilians killed in the entire Yangtze delta area from Shanghai to Nanking over the period August to December 1937.

Summing Up

Japanese military sources dating from 1937, such as official battle reports and private field diaries, are the most reliable and revealing of all the sources examined here. Left by "the side that did the killing," these documents are self-incriminating in ways that their compilers did not intend. When read critically, they attest that Japanese troops illegally and unjustifiably massacred *at least* 29,240 Chinese—and I would say 46,215—just before and after Nanking fell. Beyond that, there is room for honest debate. Conservatives adhere to this academically reputable low-end estimate of over 40,000. By contrast, I hold that we must add several tens of thousands more Chinese illegally and unjustifiably killed from early December 1937 to the end of March 1938 in the NSAD—the walled city and 6 adjacent counties (see map 3). This is a longer time span and a wider area than conservatives and deniers will allow. Largely following Kasahara Tokushi, then, I conclude that a final victim total will far exceed 100,000 but fall short of 200,000 in the absence of new evidence. But, to repeat for emphasis, an empirically verifiable, scholarly valid victimization range is from over 40,000 to under 200,000. The broad latitude derives from how one defines the event, which in turn largely depends on whether one sympathizes with "the side that did the killing," or that which "got killed."

Memory, History, Invective

Hugh Trevor-Roper once rudely derided "the worthlessness" of oral testimonies, but owing to the revolution in victims' rights noted in chapter 1, few of us today would adopt so callous an attitude toward survivors of the Holocaust and Nanking Atrocity. Yet, in 1986, the director of the Yad Vashem Archives, Shmuel Krakowski, declared that most of the 20,000 survivor testimonies preserved there are not reliable as historical sources: "[M]any were never in the places where they claim to have witnessed atrocities, while others relied on second-hand information given them by friends or passing strangers."[89] Likewise, the Jewish-American historian, Peter Novick, quotes the Holocaust survivor Primo Levi lamenting: "The greater part of the witnesses ... have ever more blurred and stylized memories, often, unbeknownst to them, influenced by information gained from later readings or the stories of others.... A memory evoked too often and expressed in the form of a story tends to become fixed in a stereotype ... crystallized, perfected, adorned, installing itself in the place of the raw memory and growing at its expense."[90] Primo Levi's lament obtains for many testimonies by Chinese and Japanese eyewitnesses to the Nanking Atrocity as well. Few post hoc oral accounts are corroborated as cogently as that by the late Li Hsiu-ying, introduced by Kasahara Tokushi in chapter 14. Likewise, confessions by Japanese victimizers such as Sone Kazuo, Azuma Shirô, Ôta Hisao, and Sumi Yoshiharu stand discredited in part, though by no means wholly.[91]

Historians today judiciously use oral accounts based on memory to help reconstruct past events, for subjects may unwittingly convey shades of meaning and reveal types of evidence not found in documentary sources. But when using oral sources, we must be wary of their pitfalls. The late Iris Chang fell short here. In her 1997 bestseller, she wrote: "That the Nanking massacre of my childhood memories was not merely folk myth, but accurate oral history hit me in December 1994."[92] Chang was born in the United States in 1968, so those "childhood memories" were not her own, but perforce derived from recalled experiences verbally conveyed by survivors decades *after* the event. A second- and third-hand "memory" of this type defines "the *Ta- t'u-sha*" as a Massive Butchery equal to "the Holocaust" for Jews. This Nanking-to-Auschwitz congruity hinges on cataclysmically high, yet unverifiable, victim tolls. Nanking was far more horrific than No Gun Ri, My Lai, or Jenin; and, far more Chinese than Japanese died from 1931 to 1945. What I oppose in the Chang-PRC view of history is its intolerance. Adherents of that view will not brook any different empirically tenable views, each of which has its own degree of validity; for, the verity of their message obviates a need to prove it. Thus, they ignore contrary evidence, refuse to retract or recaption fraudulent or misused photos, leave dozens of factual errors in print, and incessantly repeat unsubstantiated or, indeed, demonstrably false claims.[93] This fundamentalism is that of Japanese deniers in reverse; but, unlike theirs, it finds all-too-ready acceptance in an age of sensitivity for victims. Four resulting areas of harm outweigh all of the benefits from an enhanced appreciation for Nanking's tragedy which, to their credit, Chang, the PRC, and their followers have prompted in all of us.

The first area of harm lies in twisted views of Nanking, the war, and Japanese attitudes that derive from gross errors by Chang and the PRC, as for instance, when *New York Times* editorialists on 13 February 2006 indicted Japan for its amnesia about "the sadistic slaughter of hundreds of thousands of Chinese civilians in the city of Nanking." This harm extends beyond the mass media, to academic historians. Michael Shermer and Alex Grobman as well swallow Chang's "forgotten Holocaust" hook, line, and sinker. They praise her book as "an exemplar of first-rate historical detective work," and conclude that "Nanking denial is part and parcel with Holocaust denial in methodologies, arguments, and motivations."[94] Niall Ferguson tells how Chinese "prisoners were hung by their tongues from meat hooks and fed to ravenous dogs," and John A. Lynn argues that Nanking "may not have been a holocaust for an entire national group, but it was [a] holocaust for one city."[95]

The Nanking Atrocity evokes no pride in being Japanese, but one thing is certain: Deaths and damage were light compared with alternative plans for the city. On 30 November 1937, the Tenth Army command drew up "Nankin kôryaku ni kansuru iken" (Views on attacking Nanking). It listed two plans, A and B, devised 1 day before commander Yanagawa Heisuke received orders for the assault. Plan A, in fact adopted, was to build on battlefield momentum in a headlong rush for the city. But if this were to fail, Plan B would take effect. It read:

> [S]urround Nanking completely and bomb it from the air thoroughly for about a week—with special attention to incendiary bombs and mustard-gas canisters—to reduce the city to rubble. Should the enemy resist and defend the walled fortress to the bitter end, the [Tenth] Army will use the smallest force possible to maintain the siege; 2.5 divisions should do. It will keep up air attacks to destroy the enemy while refusing to storm the city by force.... Poison gas is imperative in this assault. It is totally unacceptable to sustain the same losses we did at Shanghai owing to qualms about poison gas here.[96]

Had Plan B kicked in, there would have been a "holocaust for one city" in more than hyperbole. Even at this early, relatively mild stage of aggression in China, Yanagawa would have ignored the laws of war and humanity. But chief of staff Imperial Prince Kan'in Kotohito squashed Plan B by instructing Yanagawa's immediate superior, Matsui Iwane, that "the use of gas and tear gas shall await further directives."[97]

A second area of harm lies in the diversion of attention from Japanese war crimes worse than those at Nanking. The Shanghai Expeditionary Army (SEA) used chemical weapons in its attack on Ta-ch'ang-chen near Shanghai on 16 October 1937, before it marched on Nanking. But Japan's use of chemical weapons early in the war was generally marked by restraint. Tenth Army staff officer Tanabe Masatake issued a directive on 25 October 1937 that read: "Green canister [tear] gas is not toxic. Each unit should use it as required, but only when absolutely needed, since we lack sufficient replenishments." Tanabe meant that tear gas was not an illegal toxic gas owing to its nonlethal nature, so using it to incapacitate enemy troops from afar, before killing them in close quarters by bullet or bayonet, did not violate any treaties.[98] Later in the war, commanders dropped these scruples and used lethal toxic gases, not just tear gas, some 2,091 times to produce an estimated 90,000 casualties, of which about 10,000 were deaths. In April 1939, the imperial army formed a sister-unit to Unit 731 in Nanking that developed biological weapons for use in the area, and bombed Ningpo from the air with pathogens on 27 October 1940.[99]

U.S. prosecutors at the Tokyo War Crimes Trials had evidence to substantiate charges of chemical and biological warfare, but they turned a blind eye in order to gain Japanese data for potential use against Communist enemies. For different reasons, KMT prosecutors failed to see justice served at 10 war crimes trials in China. Out of 1,556 counts brought against 883 Japanese suspects, KMT prosecutors entered one count of chemical weapons use and none for biological warfare.[100] This is a "forgotten atrocity," if not a "forgotten Holocaust," with more reason to be remembered. Why do 2,091 poison gas attacks, such as at the Hopei village of P'ei-t'an in May 1942 that took about 1,000 lives, get lost in the uproar over Nanking? Some 400,000 poison gas canisters and shells left in China produce casualties even today, and in September 2005, evidence surfaced that their abandonment took place on imperial army orders.[101]

A third area of harm lies in the view that Nanking was emblematic of Japanese bestiality not just in one city over six weeks, but in all of China from 1931 to 1945. Some Japanese leftists go even further, to claim that the Atrocity symbolized everything evil in their entire modern history.[102] Sweeping vistas like these demand far more of Nanking than it can bear, and preclude a proper historical understanding of the China war overall. There were large regional variations in Japanese occupation policy during that war. Even Kasahara Tokushi admits that, unlike in contested areas, troops did not commonly rape and murder in pacified areas, where their prime concern was to uphold order. Early stages of combat, including the Shanghai-to-Nanking assault from August to December 1937, mainly comprised positional warfare against regular KMT forces. Although resistance by partisans did occur, Japan waged a conventional if undeclared war for limited aggressive aims, as mediated by the German ambassador to China, Oskar Trautmann. History would have been different if Tokyo had accepted his terms, agreed to by Chiang Kai-shek's KMT regime, rather than succumb to the hubris of battlefield victory.[103]

After the fall of Hankou, Wuhan, and Canton in autumn 1938—which marked the end of sustained KMT resistance through positional warfare—Japanese troop conduct degenerated grievously, especially in contested areas. Escalation occurred in chemical weapons use, from reputedly nonlethal tear gas to indisputably toxic gases. After the Hundred Regiments' Offensive by Chinese Communist units in summer 1940, Japan launched Operation Burn All, Kill All, Plunder All *(jinmetsu sôtô sakusen)*. Troops in Nanking city had earlier come under limited observation by neutral Westerners with some leverage to curb depredations. But after Pearl Harbor in December 1941, Westerners in China were either enemy nationals unable to halt Japanese atrocities or allied nationals unwilling to do so. Although the "China Incident" began in July 1937 as a conventional war for limited aggressive objectives, bit by bit it turned into an anti-insurgency war entailing a barbarization of Japanese troops that made their earlier atrocities at Nanking look tame by comparison.

In sum, the China war was not a Nanking Atrocity writ large. It degenerated into a vicious, dirty, anti-Communist crusade fought mainly against guerrillas and their village-based supporters. It became a war with no rules, no strategic advantages to be gained, and no peace to be hoped for. When targeted by irregular plainclothes combatants of all ages and both genders, ordinary men turned into packs of Japanese devils *(Jih-pen kuei-tzu)* without moral inhibitions. Things then got exponentially worse for the Chinese, especially in rural contested areas; military necessity, less and less restrained by pangs of conscience, excused any and all Japanese atrocities. The distinction between war and mass murder, fuzzy to start with, disappeared. But it is anachronistic to read this later condition back to the 1937 Shanghai-to-Nanking campaign. We as historians should try to explain how and why the hostilities changed over time, plus what those changes meant for both sides. A monolithic, good-for-all-time demonization of the Japanese does nothing to help.

Fourth, the Chang-PRC invective thwarts any aim of furthering Japanese penance. To the contrary, rowdy cat-callers at supposedly academic conferences produce grist for right-wing denial mills in Japan. More tragically, such tirades make enemies out of many Japanese who once expressed contrition about their war of aggression and remorse for its Chinese victims. The historian Hata Ikuhiko is a case in point. In a 1986 paperback study of the Nanking Atrocity, he poignantly confessed:

> It is a brutal fact that Japan perpetrated aggression against China for over 10 years after the Manchurian Incident [1931–33]. We inflicted immense pain on the Chinese, and caused them massive losses at Nanking and elsewhere. However, they not only refused to take revenge against more than a million defeated Japanese soldiers and civilians stranded there after the war, they allowed those Japanese to return home safely. And, contrary to our fears, China did not demand reparations when diplomatic relations were restored in 1972. All Japanese old enough to remember these events are twice indebted to the Chinese, or at least should be. But some have forgotten. Heartless per-

sons [Tanaka Masaaki] alter primary sources to argue, "there was no 'massive butchery' at Nanking," or they take issue with the symbolic figure of 300,000 to 400,000 victims claimed by the PRC. What if anti-Japanese groups in the U.S. latched on to victim counts for the atomic bombings in our textbooks, which we cannot be absolutely certain about either, and then declared, "That's too high," or "That's an illusion"? Then how would Japanese victims feel? There is no agreement on numbers, but it is an indisputable fact that the Japanese army committed huge massacres plus many other evils at Nanking. As a Japanese, I too wish to apologize to the Chinese people from the bottom of my heart.[104]

In 1986, there was no reason to doubt Hata's sincerity. In 1989, even his bitter rhetorical adversary, Honda Katsuichi, expressed admiration.[105] Hata changed his tune after encounters with Chinese and Chinese-Americans who repeatedly booed and shouted him down at Princeton, Keiô, and other universities.[106] Speaking at the inaugural meeting of a Nanking denial society in October 2001, Hata quipped that, in order to get a total of thirty-five million victims, "they would have to throw in deaths from the Great Leap Forward and Cultural Revolution." Today, Hata bluntly calls on the Chinese to "grow up a little," and he derides "the Nanking industry," replete with lawsuits and tear-jerking survivor tales that he likens to "the Holocaust industry" denounced by Norman Finkelstein.[107] It is time to stop fighting the China war and start understanding it as history without hatred. A nuanced, textured depiction of Nanking as part of that war—sensitive to the memories of both peoples yet faithful to empirical evidence—can be written and must be read.

Notes

1. Hanley, Choe, and Mendoza, *Bridge at No Gun Ri,* p. 287; Young, "Incident at No Gun Ri," p. 257; Young, *Vietnam Wars,* pp. 301–2.
2. *Washington Post,* 3 May 2002.
3. *Washington Post,* 6 August 2002
4. "Sankei shô" column in *Sankei shinbun,* 17 May 2004. The most recent in this genre of exposés of fake photos, which began in 1973 with Suzuki, *"Nankin daigyakusatsu" no maboroshi,* is Matsuo, *Puropaganda sen "Nankin jiken."*
5. Higashinakano, *"1937: Nankin Kôryaku no shinjitsu,* pp. 152–58; Kitamura, "Nankin de daigyakusatsu wa atta no ka," pp. 273–74; Higashinakano, "Nankin 'gyakusatsu,'" pp. 288–95.
6. See Lipstadt, *Beyond Belief,* pp. 8–9, 17, and 137; for actual examples of such propaganda, see Shevin-Coetzee and Coetzee, eds., *World War I and European Society,* pp. 323–29.
7. Smythe, *War Damage in the Nanking Area,* p. i. Timperley makes a similar statement in *What War Means,* pp. 8–9.
8. Yamada and Kôketsu, *Ososugita seidan,* passim. Likewise, Kitaoka blames Japanese commanders for the massive death and destruction at Okinawa; see Kitaoka, "Iwarenaki Nihon hihan o haisu," p. 61. For the death tolls, see Yamada, "Okinawa de no gekisen," p. 111.
9. Italics added. *Toronto Star,* 5 April 2004; *Asahi shinbun,* 4 April 2004.
10. Quoted in Ishikawa, "Tettei kenshô "Nankin ronten seirigaku," p. 159.

11. For background on the reasons, see a statement by the publisher in Haga, "'Za reepu obu Nankin' hôyaku chûshi no keii," p. 17. For a view from the denial side, see Higashinakano and Fujioka, *"Za reepu obu Nankin" no kenkyû,* pp. 222–69.

12. For examples of the belief, see Bartov, *Hitler's Army,* pp. 118–19; for Rabe's faith in the belief, see Rabe, *Good Man of Nanking,* pp. 34, 38, 40, 46, and 56; for Rabe's report to Hitler pleading for him to save the people of Nanking, see Rabe, *Nankin no shinjitsu,* pp. 288–321.

13. He also said that the massacre of Chinese POWs at Mufushan was a myth, but Ono refutes this.

14. This is probably why he recycled his old title, *"Nankin daigyakusatsu" no maboroshi,* for a totally different book in 1999; he simply prefixed the word New *(shin)* to it.

15. See the *Sankei shinbun* editorial on 11 Febraury 2004.

16. *Christian Science Monitor,* 3 June 2004.

17. For T'ien-an-men, see Brook, *Quelling the People,* pp. 151–69.

18. The distance is calculated from the legend on the map in Hata, *Nankin jiken,* p. 87.

19. Hata, Higashinakano and Matsumoto, "Mondai ha 'horyo shodan' o dô miru ka," p. 142.

20. Eguchi, in *Shokun!* (February 2002), p. 194.

21. This is "38,000 to 42,000" in Hata, *Nankin jiken,* p. 214; he rounds this off to "40,000" in Hata, "Nankin jiken: Ronten to kenkyû kadai," p. 18. He stated it was "over 40,000" during a conference at Keiô University in December 1997.

22. Okumiya, *Watakushi no mita Nankin jiken,* pp. 60–61

23. Hata, in Sakamoto et al., "Rekishi to rekishi ninshiki," pp. 87–88; cf, Higashinakano, "Nankin 'gyakusatsu'," pp. 283–86.

24. See Kirby's Foreword, p. xi.

25. Paraphrased in Tanaka, *Paru hanji no Nihon muzai ron,* pp. 35–36. Tanaka's first edition, titled *Paru hakase no Nihon muzai ron,* was published in 1963. For Takigawa's original arguments, see Takigawa, *Shinpan Tokyo saiban o sabaku* (jô), pp. 121–23.

26. See the celebrated account of Taft in Kennedy, *Profiles in Courage,* pp. 179–91.

27. Tanaka, *Nankin jiken no kyokô,* pp. 287–99; Tanaka, *Nankin jiken no sôkatsu,* pp. 20–31. He had part of the second book published in an English translation in 2000 in order to counteract Iris Chang. For a review, see Wakabayashi, "Nanking Massacre."

28. Chang, *The Rape of Nanking,* pp. 6 and 12.

29. For an example, see the Chinese-Canadian Peter Li's "Asian- Pacific War," pp. 109–37.

30. Nishio, *Rekishi o sabaku orokasa,* pp. 122–260; Nishio, *Kotonaru higeki,* pp. 11–119 and 310–16; Nishio and Fujioka, *Kokumin no yudan,* pp. 209–15 and 251–60; Sakamoto, "Kaisetsu," pp. 342–46; Sakamoto, "Sengo 50-nen towareru Nihonjin no rekishi kankaku," pp. 58–71; and Nishio, *Kokumin no rekishi,* pp. 728–44.

31. Nishio, *Rekishi o sabaku orokasa,* pp. 175–76 and 207–08.

32. Ritchie, in *Japan Times* 5 December 2000.

33. Nishio, *Rekishi o sabaku orokasa,* pp. 157–58.

34. Whitney Harris, a staff member for the U.S. Counsel at Nuremberg, writes that German armed forces "in the main, lived up to standards of humane warfare." See Harris, *Tyranny on Trial,* p. 175, also, p. 315 and p. 371. For ordinary German troops and genocide, see Bartov, *Hitler's Army,* pp. 59–105 Bartov, *The Eastern Front,* pp. 106–56; and Browning, *Ordinary Men,* especially pp. 159–89 and 191–223. For a brief discussion of the literature in German on the "clean Wehrmacht," see Berghahn, Preface pp. xv–xviii; Naumann, "'Unblemished' Wehrmacht" pp. 417–27; Streit, "Soviet Prisoners of War in the Hand of the Wehrmacht," pp. 80–91; Shepherd, *War in the Wild East* (passim); and Bessel, *Nazism and War,* pp. 201–03.

35. This is a pseudonym assumed from Johann <u>Sebastian</u> Bach and Mozart's <u>Haffner</u> Symphony. His true name is Raymund Pretzel. See Haffner, *Defying Hitler,* pp. 298–304. The first distortion by Nishio came in a 1993 article and was republished in *Kotonaru higeki* in 1994 and 1997. Nishio also repeated the distortion in *Kokumin no rekishi* in 1999.

36. Haffner, *Meaning of Hitler*, p. 136; Nishio, *Kotonaru higeki*, p. 96.
37. Vincent, *Intelligent Person's Guide to History*, pp. 9 and 29.
38. Trevor-Roper, *Last Days of Hitler*, p. xxi.
39. Taylor, *Dresden*, pp. 347–456.
40. Brook, *Quelling the People*, p. 152.
41. Noguchi, *Asahi shinbun*, 21 February 1995; cited in Kasahara, *Nankin nanminku no hyakunichi*, p. 330.
42. An excellent discussion is Evans, *In Defence of History*, especially pp. 75–128 and 191–253.
43. See Koonz, *Nazi Conscience*, pp. 1–16; and Heer, "How Amorality Became Normality," pp. 338–41.
44. See Ara, "'Nankin sen moto heishi 102-nin no shôgen' no detarame," pp. 96–102; also, Higashinakano, "'Nankin sen' moto heishi giwaku no 'shôgen'," pp. 162–73.
45. Kasahara, *Nankin jiken*, pp. 224–25.
46. Cited in Itakura, *Hontô wa kô datta Nankin jiken*, p. 375. Anami's son, Koreshige, was ambassador to the PRC from January 2001 to December 2005. Saitô, *Rikugun hohei yomoyama monogatari*, pp. 244–46.
47. Fujiwara quoted in Kasahara, *Nankin jiken*, pp. 218–19.
48. For example, Yoshida, "Kokusaihô no kaishaku de jiken o seitôka dekiru ka," pp. 167–68.
49. Higashinakano, *"Nankin gyakusatsu" no tettei kenshô*," pp. 184–85; for another example of such a find, see Rabe, *Good Man of Nanking*, p. 173.
50. Higashinakano, "Nankin 'gyakusatsu'," pp. 288–95; Komuro and Watanabe, *Fûin no Shôwa shi*, pp. 66–76, 83–86, 136–50.
51. Rabe, *Good Man of Nanking*, p. 71.
52. Sasaki, *Yasen yûbinki*, p. 58 and 71; Ono, Fujiwara, and Honda, ed., *Nankin daigryaksusatsu o kiroku shita kôgun heishi tachi*, p. 361. See also chap. 8 in the present volume.
53. See Taylor, *Nuremberg and Vietnam*, p. 36.
54. For an exceptionally articulate example, see the battlefield diary of Murata Kazushirô; Murata, *Nit-Chû sensô nikki*, vol.1, pp. 165–67.
55. Taylor, *Dresden*, p. 89.
56. On this point, see, for example, Itakura, *Hontô wa kô datta Nankin jiken*, p. 199.
57. Rabe also called them "deserters." See Rabe, *The Good Man of Nanking*, p. 57.
58. Okumiya uses this term to describe all U.S. military actions in the Pacific after Japan's decisive loss in the Marianas in June 1944. See Okumiya, *Watakushi no mita Nankin jiken*, p. 210.
59. Japanese troops, however, would do much the same thing on Okinawa, which in turn spawned American arguments to use atomic weapons out of military necessity.
60. Kitamura, *"Nankin jiken" no tankyû*, pp. 25–27 and 164–74.
61. Smythe, *War Damage in the Nanking Area*, p. 28.
62. Tanaka, *Nankin jiken no sôkatsu*, pp. 201–3; for Smythe's statement itself, see Lu, *They Were in Nanjing*, pp. 333–34.
63. Kasahara, *Nankin nanminku no hyakunichi*, pp. 353–54.
64. Smythe, *War Damage in the Nanking Area*, p. 22.
65. Ibid., p. 7.
66. Ibid.
67. For a critical survey of the scholarship, see Wakabayashi, "Comfort Women," pp. 223–58.
68. Rabe, *Good Man of Nanking*, p. 212; for the entire document, see Hirano, trans, *Nankin no shinjitsu*, pp. 289–321. For this citation, see p. 317.
69. For the 800,000 figure, see Rabe, *Good Man of Nanking*, p. 52; for the 1,350,000 figure in July 1937, see Hirano, trans., *Nankin no shinjitsu*, p. 196.
70. Smythe, *War Damage in the Nanking Area*, note 1 to Table 1, n.p.
71. Kasahara, "Sûji ijiri no fumô na ronsô wa gyakusatsu no jittai o tôzakeru," pp. 85–86; Kasahara, *Nankin jiken* pp. 219–21.

72. Some Chinese sources reputedly from wartime Nanking fail to withstand critical scrutiny. See Kitamura, *"Nankin jiken" no tankyû*, pp. 126–40.
73. Ibid., pp. 141–44; Takemoto and Ôhara, *Saishin "Nankin daigyakusatsu,"* pp. 143–44.
74. See Hara, "Iwayuru 'Nankin daigyakusatsu jiken' no maisô kiroku no saikentô," pp. 45–6; and Brook, *Documents on the Rape of Nanking*, pp. 261 and 266.
75. Brook, *Documents on the Rape of Nanking*, p. 261.
76. See Wakabayashi, "Nanking Massacre," p. 524.
77. Hata, Higashinakano, and Matsumoto, "Mondai was 'horyo shodan' o dô miru ka," p. 142.
78. Both the leftist Inoue and the denier Higashinakano agree on this point, based on the 16 April 1938 article in the *Osaka Asahi shinbun*, but they disagree on the motive involved; Inoue, "Itai maisô kiroku wa gizô shiryô de wa nai," p. 130; Higashinakano, *"Nankin gyakusatsu" no tettei kenshô*, p. 303. Maruyama Susumu, a member of the SSA at Nanking corroborates its payment for burials in Higashinakano, "Nankin tokumu kikan (Mantetsu shain) Maruyama Susumu no kaisô," pp. 221–22.
79. Hara, "Iwayuru 'Nankin daigyakusatsu jiken' no maisô kiroku no saikentô," pp. 43–59.
80. Timperley, *What War Means*, pp. 57 and 59. I thank Timothy Brook for helping me obtain Bates's original letter from the Yale Divinity School Library.
81. See Higashinakano, *"Nankin gyakusatsu" no tettei kenkyû*, pp. 323–30.
82. Hara, "Iwayuru 'Nankin daigyakusatsu jiken' no maisô kiroku no saikentô," pp. 43–59.
83. Inoue, "Itai maisô kiroku wa gizô shiryô de wa nai," p. 133.
84. See Higashinakano, "Nankin tokumu kikan (Mantetsu shain) Maruyama Susumu no kaisô," pp. 223–24 and pp. 247–49, note 3.
85. Inoue, "Itai maisô kiroku wa gizô shiryô de wa nai," pp. 136–37.
86. On this controversy, see Honda and Ono, "Bakufu-san no horyo shûdan gyakusatsu," pp. 128–149; also, Hora and Watada, "Baku-san no horyo shodan ni kansuru 'Shinsetsu' hihan," pp. 150–96.
87. Lee, "Nanking Massacre Reassessed," p. 56; Chang, *Rape of Nanking*, pp. 103–04; Young and Yin, *Rape of Nanking*, pp. 262 and 276–78.
88. Yamamoto, *Nanking*, p. 285; Lu, *They Were in Nanjing*, p. 352, note 57.
89. Quoted in Novick, *Holocaust in American Life*, p. 275 and note 21.
90. Ibid., p. 275.
91. See Fujioka, *"Jigyaku shikan" no byôri*, pp. 162–74; and Itakura, *Hontô wa kô datta Nankin jiken*, pp. 234–94.
92. Chang, *Rape of Nanking*, p. 9.
93. For a catalog of criticisms about factual errors and misused photographs made by Japanese deniers that have gone unanswered, see Hata, "'Nankin gyakusatsu' 'shôko shashin' o kantei suru," pp. 82–93; Higashinakano and Fujioka, *"Za reepu obu Nankin" no kenkyû*, pp. 52–220; and Matsuo, *Propaganda sen "Nankin jiken"*, pp. 54–115. In 2004, Chang wrote that KMT armies lost "250,000 troops in the battle for Shanghai," after which the Japanese "raped and slaughtered hundreds of thousands of civilians, presaging a war that would last eight years and claim as many as 35 million Chinese lives." See Chang, *Chinese in America*, p. 216.
94. Sherman and Grobman, *Denying History*, pp. 231–256, especially, pp. 231–37.
95. Ferguson, *Empire*, p. 332; Lynn, *Battle*, p. 227.
96. Yoshimi and Matsuno, eds., *Jûgo nen sensô gokuhi shiryô shû hokan 2: Doku gasu sen kankei shiryô II*, pp. 277–79.
97. Yoshimi, *Dokugasu sen to Nihon gun*, p. 53.
98. Ibid., pp. 50–51.
99. Tsuneishi, *Nana-san-ichi butai*, pp. 11–12 and 142–46.
100. Ibid., pp. 83–145 and 195–230; also, Awaya, *Chûgoku Sansei-shô ni okeru Nihon gun no dokugasu sen*, pp. 3–164; Obara, Arai, Yamabe, and Okada, *Nihon gun no dokugasu sen*, 18–65; and Chi, *Nihon gun no kagaku sen*, p. 325. On immunity at the Tokyo trials for poi-

son gas use, see Awaya and Yoshimi, "Kaisetsu," pp. 21–29. On the KMT failure to prosecute poison gas warfare, see Hayashi, *BC-kyû senpan saiban,* p. 64 and p. 105.

101. See Ishikiriyama, *Nihon gun doku gasu sen no mura,* which combines interviews with survivors and research in Japanese primary sources; on the ordering of poison gas shells to be abandoned in August 1945 by throwing these down a well outside of Harbin, see *Asahi shinbun,* 15 September 2005.

102. Fujiwara, *Shinpan Nankin daigyakusatsu,* p. 61; Yoshida, *Tennô no guntai to Nankin jiken,* p. 4.

103. See Ôsugi, *Nit-Chû jûgonen sensô,* pp. 298–312.

104. Hata, *Nankin jiken,* p. 244.

105. Honda, *Nankin e no michi,* p. 387. This is in the Afterword to the paperback *(bunko)* edition.

106. Hata, Kasahara, and Gries attest to the intense booing and shouting down of Hata at Princeton; I personally witness the same at Keiô. See Hata, Higashinakano, and Matsumoto, "Mondai wa 'horyo shodan' o dô miru ka," p. 144; Hata, "Nankin jiken, ronten to kenkyû kadai," p. 19; Kasahara, *Nankin jiken to sankô sakusen,* pp. 225–26; and Gries, *China's New Nationalism,* p. 81.

107. Hata, "Nankin jiken, ronten to kenkyû kadai," pp. 16–17; Hata, Higashinakano, and Matsumoto, "Mondai wa 'horyo shodan' o dô miru ka," pp. 131–32 and 144; Finkelstein, *The Holocaust Industry,* passim.

APPENDIX

Present-day Chinese pejoratives for Japan and the Japanese people—roughly equivalent to the English "Jap"—include Hsiao-Jih-pen (puny Japanese), Wo-nu (runty Japanese lackies), Wo-chu (runty Japanese pigs), Jih-pen kuei-tzu (beastly Japanese devils), and Jih-k'ou (Japanese bandits). Hsiao-Jih-pen was the term favored by violent hooligans at the Asian World Cup in Chungking, Tsinan, and Peking in July-August 2004 and in China-wide anti-Japanese rioting in the spring of 2005. These outbreaks of violence developed into major diplomatic incidents that remain unresolved as of July 2006.[1] According to Komori Yoshihisa, a journalist for the ultraconservative *Sankei shinbun,* Jih-k'ou, is actually translated into English as "Japs" on a public monument to Chinese war dead at Marco Polo Bridge.[2] Peter Hays Gries cites the terms Kuei-tzu and Wo-k'ou, and translates these as "Japs" in order to convey the sense of a slur.[3] For historians, Jih-k'ou calls to mind the premodern term, Wo-k'ou, better known in its Japanese form, Wakô. During the twelfth to fifteenth centuries, it connoted "Japanese pirates" who raided the coasts of China and Korea, but most of them in fact were non-Japanese and, in any case, ethnic consciousness was still weak among both peoples in that premodern era.[4] As opposed to Jih-k'ou, Wo-k'ou is now a purely historical term devoid of negative nuances.

Komori goes on to assert that, although Western nationals have stopped using the wartime pejoratives Jap and Nip in everyday life as well as in formal writing or at scholarly conferences, by contrast, educated Chinese commonly insist on using analogous ethnic slurs even today.[5] He argues that, in the twenty-first century, the vast majority of Japanese think of the war with China beginning in either 1931 or 1937 and ending in 1945 as being in the past, not in the present. In his avowedly conservative view, an insensitive lack of critical self-reflection by the Chinese—as manifested in their regular use of Wo-nu, Wo-chu, Hsiao-Jih-pen and other pejorative terms—cannot be justified by wartime atrocities and imperialist aggression perpetrated seventy years ago. The implication of Komori's arguments is that the Chinese should stop using such words today if the Japanese find these hurtful and offensive.

On the Japanese side, the derogatory terms Shina, Shinajin, Shinago refer to China, Chinese persons, and the Chinese language in all of its dialects. Generally speaking, as discussed below, postwar Japanese have stopped using these terms, but exceptions and qualifications complicate this generalization.[6] Even in the era of Japanese imperialism and colonialism up to 1945, Shina was far less pejorative when written in the native *katakana* syllabary. In other words, it is the *kanji* or Chinese ideographs for Shina that seems to offend the Chinese. This is the rationale by which Watanabe Shôichi, a Sophia University emeritus professor and Nanking denier, employs the *katakana* notation for Shina.[7] Moreover, at least two present-day uses of Shina, if expressed verbally or in *katakana*, seem permissible: (1) Shina *soba*, or Chinese noodles, the prewar expression for *raamen* (taken from the Chinese *lo mein*), rings nostalgic in the ears of older Japanese; it is increasingly seen in print and heard in speech; and (2) Higashi Shina kai, or the East China Sea, appears on Japanese maps with Shina in *katakana*. "Higashi Shina kai" is seen and heard daily on television and radio weather reports. Neither the People's Republic of China (PRC) nor Taiwan has expressed displeasure or opposition to the Japanese government over the use of this geographic term, at least on maps used outside of China proper. Chinese diplomatic acceptance of the term stands in marked contrast to the attitude shown by Seoul and by Pyongyang. Both adamantly reject the use of Nihon kai, or "Sea of Japan" on maps. Indeed, South Korea has lodged formal protests with the United Nations, insisting that the "Sea of Japan" is a vestige of odious Japanese colonial domination, and that "the East Sea" must be used to designate this body of saltwater.[8]

In the second half of the Edo period (1600–1867), under the influence of Western and Native Learning, Shina, had come into common use, but after the Meiji Restoration of 1867, the Japanese government generally called China "Ch'ing," after the ruling dynasty's name. After the 1911 Revolution, which created a Republic of China (ROC), the Japanese government used Shina. Various Chinese regimes, including the later Kuomintang (KMT) or Nationalist government; lodged formal protests over this use of Shina in diplomatic documents. According to the University of Tokyo history professor Katô Yôko, the imperial government issued a cabinet decision in 1930 to abandon Shina for Chûgoku (Chung-kuo in Chinese) as the official diplomatic designation for the ROC.[9] In actual practice, however, as Kasahara Tokushi notes in chapter 14, the Japanese government and armed services regularly ignored such Chinese protests until Japan surrendered to the Allied powers, the ROC included, in 1945. Nevertheless, use of Shina continued in the early postwar period at public venues such as the Tokyo War Crimes Trials, where that term was recorded in *kanji* in official tribunal transcripts. The Shôwa emperor called China Shina in *kanji* in his *Dokuhaku roku*, dictated to trusted aides in the early part of 1946. At that time, he feared the possibility of being called to the dock at those trials, either as a witness or as a defendant. Thus, he had this document transcribed beforehand to "prove" his innocence of any possible war crimes charges. As such, the *Dokuhaku roku* was meant to be tendered in the public domain, and it demonstrates the contemptuous view of China and the Chinese people that the Shôwa emperor and his government held even after their defeat, partly at Chinese hands.

Present-day left-wing historians such as Kasahara Tokushi and the late Fujiwara Akira argue that the use of Shina by the Japanese before 1945 not only reeked of contempt, it also reflects an attitude that led to fatal mistakes in foreign policy. Thus, they contend, those postwar Japanese with any measure of sense and good taste have abandoned the term. As Fujiwara Akira states in chapter 2, imperial Japanese military planners never formulated realistic strategies toward China as a nation-state because they despised the Chinese people as Shinajin who lacked a sense of patriotism, an ability to form a nation-state, and the will to fight in its defense. Thus, according to Japanese leftists, the overwhelming majority of postwar Japanese have stopped using Shina, Shinajin, and Shinago (the Chinese language and its dialects) as a result of critical self-reflection on their recent history of imperialist aggression, which in no small part was rooted in mistaken concepts of ethnic superiority to Chinese, Koreans, and other Asians. In the eyes of left-wing Japanese, this is the proper attitude that the Japanese today ought to take, both in deference to the feelings of their neighbors, and also to prevent similar lapses into foreign policy hubris. With respect to this sort of critical self-reflection, we might liken the situation in postwar Japan with that in the United States, where the overwhelming majority of Americans have abandoned the racist epithet *nigger* after the Civil Rights Movement, even though it had been in common use toward blacks previously. Generally speaking, both Japanese and Americans shun designations deemed offensive to the ethnic groups in question—at least when speaking in educated, polite company or in writing.

However, two classes of postwar Japanese have continued to use derogatory terms like Shina. Poorly educated and/or elderly persons who grew up with the terms go on using these from force of habit. An example would be Yamakawa Saki (b. 1871), a *karayuki-san* who related her life story as an oral history to Yamazaki Tomoko in 1968. Yamazaki transcribed Yamakawa's words "Shinajin" and "Shinago" in *kanji;* and, this book, first published in 1972, remains in print without revision or explanation.[10] The second group comprises educated and cultured persons who seek to make an a pointed right-wing statement, such as Nanking denial or minimalization, without much consideration for Chinese sentiments. Some prominent examples include Watanabe Shôichi, Komuro Naoki, the late Sakamoto Takao, Nishio Kanji, Kobayashi Yoshinori, Higashinakano Osamichi (Shûdô), Tanizawa Eiichi, Ôi Mitsuru, Endô Kôichi, and others.[11] Sakamoto (1950–2002), who writes the *kanji* for Shina, asserts that the number of victims at Hiroshima and Nagasaki outnumbered those at Nanking "several tens of times over"—although he gives no figures.[12]

This second group tends to justify their continued use of Shina through historical and etymological arguments. Nishio, one of the authors of the 2001 nationalistic textbook derided by Asian governments, appeals to history. He, Watanabe, and others argue that Chinese dynasties forced neighboring barbarian peoples refer to China throughout history by the honorific term Chûka or Chûgoku (Chung-hua and Chung-kuo in Chinese)—literally the "Central Realm," "Central Efflorescence," or "Middle Kingdom." These right-wing writers contend that the involuntary use of this term in premodern times was a form of tribute-bearing by East Asian peoples that affirmed China's putative position as the fountainhead of world civilization. In other words, foreign peoples kowtowed to China by calling it "Chung-hua" and "Chung-kuo, but in the Edo period (1600–1867), Japanese scholars of Western and Native Learning began to use "Shina" as a neutral term that was neither pejorative from the Chinese, nor demeaning from the Japanese, standpoint. Given this history, the right-wing argument goes, continued use of Shina requires no apology today; indeed, when the PRC assumes pretensions of sinocentric hegemony in East Asia, the practice is perfectly justifiable. To draw a strained analogy, we might observe, this would be like Irish nationalists arguing that it is demeaning for themselves, and hegemonic for the English, to insist on use of the term "Great Britain" instead of a simple "Britain" to denote England, Scotland, Wales, and North Ireland.

Right-wing Japanese also appeal to etymology in trying to ascribe respectability to the continued use of Shina. Higashinanakano, Kobayashi, Katō (although not a rightist), as well as others, point out that Shina derives from the Ch'in (Qin) dynasty of 221–206 BC, which established the first unified Chinese empire. Thus if anything, Japanese right-wingers contend, Shina ought to evoke ethnic pride for Han Chinese. Higashinakano points out that an officially approved PRC web site uses the variant form sina in its http domain address sina.com. Kobayashi adopts an even more radical argument. He says that, in order to be fair and consistent, ultranationalistic Chinese who condemn Japanese people for using "Shina" perforce must condemn Westerners for using "China" as well, since both terms are of identical etymology. However, Kobayashi goes on, the Chinese criticize only the Japanese on this score; this amounts to sycophancy toward the West and contempt for Japan.[13]

Such right-wing arguments based on historical usage and etymology ring hollow; indeed, one senses that these are but rationalizations for being meanspirited. The term Jap also has nonpejorative etymological origins, since it derives from Zippangu in Marco Polo's *Travels*. But Higashinakano and Kobayashi would no doubt be incensed—as Komori indeed is incensed—when foreigners refer to them by that three-letter derisive epithet. If the Chinese today say they are hurt by the terms Shina or Shinajin, then common courtesy enjoins the Japanese to stop using these terms, whatever the etymology or historical usage might be. Japanese right-wing writers can use the English term "China" in the Japanized *katakana* form of *"Chaina"* if they find Chûka and Chûgoku too demeaning. Indeed, Tanizawa Eiichi attaches these *katakana* to the side of the *kanji* "Shina."[14]

In sum, both conservatives such as Komori and leftists such as Kasahara make valid points. Courtesy is, after all, a two-way street. If Chinese historians who write about Nanking and other Japanese war crimes cling to their use of ethnic slurs—however legitimate this may seem in their own eyes owing to past victimization—the result will be to alienate increasing numbers of younger Japanese who otherwise would be sympathetic to the Chinese cause. Likewise, conservatives and the right-wing in Japan need to exercise maturity by abandoning prejudice and the sophistry they use to justify it. I propose that the Chinese use Jih-pen and Jih-pen-jen, and that the Japanese use Chûgoku and Chûgokujin, in reference to one another.

Notes

1. The news media in Japan covered and commented on these incidents heavily. See, for example, the "Tôron seidan" column in *Mainichi shinbun*, 15 August 2004.
2. See Komori, *Nit-Chû yûkô no maboroshi*, pp. 2–4; also Komori, *Nit-Chû saikô*, pp. 18–19, 36, 170–71, 198, and 220.
3. Gries, *China's New Nationalism*, p. 51 and p. 57.
4. By the early nineteenth century, protonationalists in Japan were construing this offensive term in a positive way—as a Chinese tribute to the ferocity and navigational skill of Japanese fighting men. See Wakabayashi, *Anti-Foreignism and Western Learning in Early-Modern Japan*, p. 210.
5. Komori, *Nit-Chû yûkô no maboroshi*, pp. 4–6.
6. For a recent discussion of whether "Shina" in either written form should be used, see *Asahi shinbun*, 3 June 2003.
7. For example, see Watanabe, *Nihonshi kara mita Nihonjin: Shôwa hen*, p. 458, passim.
8. *Yomiuri shinbun*, web posted on 22 April 2004.
9. Katô, *Sensô no Nihon kin-gendai shi*, pp. 50–51.
10. See Yamazaki, *Sandakan hachiban shôkan*, pp. 87, 92, 97, 98, 99, 118, 120, 121,128, and 136.
11. For example, Watanabe and Komuro, *Fûin no Shôwa shi*, p. 10; and, most recently, Endô, Chûgoku ni shippo o furu *Asahi* to pochi seijika no taizai," pp. 24, 26, and 27. Note that Endô, although born in the postwar era, employs the old-style *kana* usage common to right-wing thinkers discussed by Kasahara in chapter 14.
12. Sakamoto in "Rekishi to rekishi ninshiki," pp. 82 and 90; Sakamoto, *Rekishi kyôiku o kangaeru*, p. 120.
13. See Higashinakano, ed., *1937: Nanking kôryakusen no shinjitsu*, pp. 42–43; see Kobayashi, *"Ko to kô" ron*, pp. 205–206.
14. Tanizawa, *Konna Nihon ni dare ga shita*, pp. 186–87, *passim;* also, Tanizawa *Akuma no shisô*, *passim.*

BIBLIOGRAPHY

Abe, Teruo. *Nankin no hisame: Gyakusatsu no kôzô o otte* (Tokyo: Kyôiku shoseki, 1989).

Agawa, Hiroyuki. "'Aa, dôki no sakura' ni yoseru," in Agawa, *Agawa Hiroyuki no hon* (Tokyo: KK besuto seraazu, 1970).

Amerasia, ed. "Review Article: Is There another Japan?" in *Amerasia* 7:2 (April 1943), pp. 35–42.

————. "Review Article: The Nature of Our Enemy, Japan," in *Amerasia* 7:12 (November 1943), pp. 389–92.

Anonymous. "Shih-shou-hou ti Nan-ching" (1938), reprinted in Nan-ching t'u-shu kuan, ed., *Chin-hua Jih-chün Nan-ching ta-t'u-sha shih-liao* (Nan-ching: Chiangsu ku-chi ch'u-pan-she, 1985), pp. 148–55.

Ara, Ken'ichi. "'Nankin sen moto heishi 102 nin no shôgen' no detarame," in *Seiron* (November 2002), pp. 96–102.

Asahi shinbunsha, ed., *Sengo hoshō to wa nani ka* (Tokyo: Asahi shinbunsha, 1994).

Asami [Kazuo], Mitsumoto, and Yasuda. "Hyakuningiri kyôso! Ryôshôi mo hachijûnin," in *Tokyo nichinichi shinbun*, 30 November 1937.

Asami [Kazuo] and Suzuki, Jirô. "Hyakuningiri 'Chôkiroku'—Mukai 106—Noda 105—Ryôshi sara ni enchô," in *Tokyo nichinichi shinbun*, 13 December 1937.

Askew, David. "The International Committee for the Nanking Safety Zone: An Introduction," in *Sino-Japanese Studies* vol. 14 (April 2002), 3–23.

————. "The Nanjing Incident: An Examination of the Civilian Population," in *Sino-Japanese Studies* 13:2 (March 2001), pp. 2–20.

————. "The Nanjing Incident: Recent Research and Trends" (unpublished manuscript).

Atarashii kyôkasho o tsukuru kai, ed. *Atarashii Nihon no rekishi ga hajimaru* (Tokyo: Gentôsha, 1997).

Awaya, Kentarō. *Chûgoku Sansei-shô ni okeru Nihon gun no dokugasu sen* (Tokyo: Ôtsuki shoten, 2002).

————. *Miketsu no sensô sekinin* (Tokyo: Kashiwa shobô, 1994).

————. et al., eds., *Sensô sekinin, sengo sekinin* (Tokyo: Asahi shinbunsha, 1994).

————. *Tokyo saiban ron* (Tokyo: Ôtsuki shoten, 1989).

————. et al., eds., *Tokyo saiban shiryô: Tanaka Ryūkichi jinmon chôsho* (Tokyo: Ôtsuki shoten, 1994).

Awaya Kentarô, and Yoshimi Yoshiaki, "Kaisetsu," in Awaya, and Yoshimi, eds., *Jûgonen sensô gokuhi shiryô shû 18: Doku gasu sen kankei shiryô*, pp. 3–32.

Awaya, Kentarô and Yoshimi Yoshiaki., ed., *Jûgonen sensô gokuhi shiryô shû 18: Doku gasu sen kankei shiryô* (Tokyo: Fuji shuppan, 1989).

Bacque, James. *Other Losses: An Investigation into the Mass Deaths of German Prisoners at the Hands of the French and Americans after World War II* (Toronto: Stoddard, 1989).

Baker, Thomas S. "A Variety of British Pseudohistory," in Bischof and Ambrose, eds., *Eisenhauer and the German POWs*, pp. 183–98.

Bartlett, Beatrice. Introduction, in Smalley, ed., *American Missionary Eyewitnesses to the Nanking Massacre, 1937–1938*, pp. v–xvi.

Bartov, Omer. *The Eastern Front, 1941–45: German Troops and the Barbarisation of Warfare* (New York: St. Martin's, 1986).

———. *Hitler's Army: Soldiers, Nazis, and War in the Third Reich* (New York: Oxford University Press, 1991).

Bartov, Omer, Grossmann, Atina, and Nolan, Mary, eds., *Crimes of War: Guilt and Denial in the Twentieth Century* (New York: New Press, 2002).

Basu, K. K. "Tokio Trials," in *Indian Law Review* 3:1 (1949), pp. 25–30.

Bates, M. S. *Crop Investigation in the Nanking Area and Sundry Economic Data* (Shanghai: Mercury Press, 1938).

———. *The Nanking Population: Employment, Earnings and Expenditures* (Shanghai: Mercury Press, 1938).

———. "Report of the Nanking International Relief Committee, November, 1937 to April, 1939" in Chang, ed., *Eyewitnesses to Massacre*, pp. 413–45.

Bauman, Zygmunt. *Modernity and the Holocaust* (Cambridge: Polity Press, 1989).

Beigbeder, Yves. *Judging War Criminals: The Politics of International Justice* (London: Macmillan, 1999).

Berghahn, Volker. R. Preface in Heer, Hannes and Maumann, Klaus, eds., *War of Extermination*, pp. xii–xix.

Bernadac, Christian. *L'Holocauste Oublié: Le Massacre des Tsiganes* (Paris: France-Empire, 1979).

Bessel, Richard. *Nazism and War* (New York: Modern Library, 2004).

Bischof, Guenter. "Bacque and Historical Evidence," in Bischof and Ambrose, eds., *Eisenhauer and the German POWs*, pp. 199–234.

Bischof, Guenter, and Ambrose, Stephen E. Eds., *Eisenhauer and the German POWs: Facts against Fiction* (Baton Rougue: Louisiana State University Press, 1992).

Bôeichô bôei kenshû sho senshishitsu, ed., *Senshi sôsho: Chûgoku hômen kaigun sakusen 1* (Tokyo: Asagumo shinbunsha, 1974).

———. *Senshi sôsho: Daihon'ei rikugunbu 1* (Tokyo: Asagumo shinbunsha, 1974)

———. *Senshi sôsho: Shina jihen rikugun sakusen 1* (Tokyo: Asagumo shinbunsha, 1972).

———. *Senshi sôsho: Shina jihen rikugun sakusen 2* (Tokyo: Asagumo shinbunsha, 1967).

Boulesbaa, Ahcene. *The U.N. Convention on Torture and the Prospects for Enforcement* (The Hague: Martinus Nijhoff, 1999).

Boyle, John Hunter. *Modern Japan: The American Nexus* (Fort Worth: Harcourt, 1993).

Barchman, Arnold C. *The Other Nuremberg: The Untold Story of the Tokyo War Crimes Trials* (New York: Morrow, 1987).

Brook, Timothy. "Collaborationist Nationalism in Occupied Wartime China," in Brook, and Schmid, eds., *Nation Work: Asian Elites and National Identities* (Ann Arbor: University of Michigan Press, 1999), pp. 159–90.

————. ed., *Documents on the Nanking Safety Zone* (Ann Arbor: University of Michigan Press, 1999).

————. "The Creation of the Reformed Government in Central China, 1938," in Barret and Shyu, eds., *Chinese Collaboration with Japan: The Limits of Accommodation* (Stanford: Stanford University Press, 2001), pp. 79–101.

————. "The Pacification of Jiading," in Lary and MacKinnon, eds., *The Scars of War* (Vancouver: University of British Columbia Press, 2001), pp. 50–74.

————. "Documenting the Rape of Nanking." in Brook, ed., *Documents on the Rape of Nanking,* pp. 1–29.

————. ed. *Documents on the Rape of Nanking.* (Ann Arbor: University of Michigan Press, 1999).

————. *Quelling the People: The Military Suppression of the Beijing Democracy Movement* (Toronto: Lester Publishing, 1992).

Browning, Christopher R. *Ordinary Men: Reserve Police Battalion 101 and the Final Solution in Poland* (New York: Harper, 1998).

Burress. Charles. "Wars of Memory," in *San Francisco Chronicle* (26 July 1998).

Buruma, Ian. "The Afterlife of Anne Frank," in *New York Review of Books* 46:3 (19 February 1999).

————. "China in Cyberspace," in *New York Review of Books* 46:12 (4 November 1999), pp. 9–12.

Chang, Iris. *The Chinese in America* (New York: Penguin, 2004).

————. *The Rape of Nanking: The Forgotten Holocaust of World War II* (New York: Basic, 1997).

Chang [Zhang] K'ai-yuan, ed. *Eyewitnesses to Massacre: American Missionaries Bear Witness to Japanese Atrocities in Nanjing* (Armonk, NY: M. E. Sharpe, 2001).

Cheng, Kuan-ying. "Chung-Jih chiao-chan hsi-wen-pao chi Jih-ping t'u-ch'eng ts'ai-k'ut'u-shuo hsü," in Hsia, ed., *Cheng Kuan-ying chi (hsia)* (Shanghai: Shanghai jen-min ch'u-pan-she, 1988).

Chen, Pei-kai, Lestz, Michael, and Spence, Jonathan, eds., *The Search for Modern China: A Documentary Collection* (New York: Norton, 1999).

Chi, Hsüeh-jen. Murata Tadayoshi, trans., *Nihongun no kagakusen* (Tokyo: Ôtsuki shoten, 1996).

Chiang Kung-yi, "Hsian-ching san-yüeh-chi." (Manuscript, n.p.)

Chiangning hsien ti-fang-chih pien-tsuan-hui, ed., *Chiangning hsien-chih* (Nan-ching: T'ang-an ch'u-pan-she, 1989).

Chiang-p'u hsien ti-fang-chih pien-tsuan-hui, ed., *Chiangp'u hsien-chih* (Nan-ching: Ho-hai ta-hsüeh ch'u-pan-she).

Chiang-p'u k'ang-Jih feng-huo. (Manuscript, n.p.)

Chiangsu-wen-shih tzu-liao pien-chi-pu, ed., *Hsing-feng hsüeh-yü: Chin-hua Jih-chün Chiangsu pao-hang-lu* (Nan-ching: Chiangsu-sheng cheng-hsieh wen-shih tzu-liao wei-yüan-hui, 1995).

Chiang, Kai-shek. 'One Half of the World's People," in Chiang, *All We Are and All We Have* (New York: John Day Company, 1942).

Chiang, Wei-kuo. *Kuo-min ke-ming chan-shih ti-3-pu K'ang-Jih yu-wu* (Taipei: Li-ming Culture Enterprise, 1978), vol. 4.

China Number Two Historical Archives (CNT), ed., *Ch'in-hua Jih-chün Nan-ching ta-t'u-sha tang-an* (Nan-ching: Chiangsu k'u-chi ch'u-pan-she, 1987).

Chomsky, Noam. *For Reasons of State* (New York: Vintage, 1973).

Chungkung Chiangp'u hsien taing-shih tzu-liao shou-tsi pien-kung-shih, ed., *Chiangp'u k'ang-Jih feng-huo.*

Cohen, David. "Beyond Nuremberg: Individual Responsibility for War Crimes," in Hesse and Post, eds., *Human Rights in Political Transition*, pp. 53–92.

Cook, Haruko Taya. "Reporting the 'Fall of Nanking' and the Suppression of a Japanese 'Memory' of the Nature of a War," in Li, Sabella, and Liu, eds., *Nanking 1937*, pp. 121–53.

Cowdrey, Albert E. "Question of Numbers," in Bischof and Ambrose, ed., *Eisenhauer and the German POWs*, pp. 78–92.

Dallin, Alexander. German Rule in Russia: 1941–1945 (London: MacMillan, 1957).

Dadrian, Vahakn. "The Comparative Aspects of the Armenian and Jewish Cases of Genocide: A Sociohisotircal Perspective," in Rosenbaum, Alan S., ed., *Is The Holocaust Unique?: Perpsectives on Compariative Genocide* (Boulder: Westview Press, 1998), pp. 101–35.

Daws, Gavan. *Prisoners of the Japanese* (New York: Morrow, 1994).

Dennerling, Jerry. *The Chia-ting Loyalists: Confucian Leadership and Social Change in Seventeenth-Century China* (New Haven: Yale University Press, 1981).

Department of State. *Foreign Relations of the United States: Diplomatic Papers, 1937,* vol. 3, The Far East (Washington, DC: Government Printing Office, 1954).

Dower, John. *Embracing Defeat: Japan in the Wake of World War II* (New York: Norton, 1999).

D'Souza, Dinesh. *The End of Racism: Principles for a Multiracial Society* (New York: Free Press, 1995).

Drea, Edward. "Dispatches: Military History in the News," in *Quarterly Journal of Military History* (Autumn 2000).

Duara, Prasenjit. "Of Authencitiy and Woman: Personal Narratives of Middle-Class Women in Modern China" in Wen-hsin Yeh, ed., *Becoming Chinese: Passages to Modernity and Beyond* (Berkeley: University of California Press, 2000) pp. 342–64.

Eguchi, Keiichi. "Shanhai sen to Nankin shingeki sen," in Hora, et. al. eds., *Nankin daigyakusatsu no kenkyû,* pp. 12–51.

Endô, Kôichi. "Chûgoku ni shippo o furu *Asahi* to pochi seijika no taizai," in *Shokun* (August 2005), pp. 22–35.

Evans, Harold. "The Trial of Major Japanese War Criminals" 4 pts. *New Zealand Law Journal,* vol. 23, pp. 8–10, 21–23, 37–38, and 322–24 (21 January, 4 February, 18 February, 2 December 1947).

Evans, Richard. *In Defence of History* (London: Granta Books, 1997).

Eykholt, Mark. "Agression, Victimization, and Chinese Historiography of the Nanjing Massacre," in Fogel, ed., *Nanjing Massacre in History and Historiography,* pp. 11–69.

———. "Living the Limits of Occupation in Nanjing, China, 1937–1945." Ph.D. diss., University of California at San Diego, 1998.

Ferguson, Niall. *Empire: How Britain Made the Modern World* (London: Allen Lane, 2003).

Finkelstein, Norman. *The Holocaust Industry* (London: Verso, 2000).

Fitch, George A. *My Eighty Years in China* (Taipei: Mei Ya Publications, rev. ed., 1974).

Fogel, Joshua A., ed., *The Nanking Massacre in History and Historiography* (Berkeley: University of California Press, 2000).

————. *Politics and Sinology: The Case of Naitô Konan (1866–1934)* (Cambridge: Harvard University Press, 1984).

Frazer, Angus. *The Gypsies* (London: Blackwell Publishers, 1992).

Fu, Posek. *Passivity, Resistance, and Collaboration: Intellectual Choices in Occupied Shanghai, 1937–1945* (Stanford: Stanford University Press, 1993).

Fujioka, Nobukatsu. "Aratamete Raabe no nikki o tettei kenshô suru," in *Seiron* (April 1998).

————. *"Jigyaku shikan" no byôri* (Tokyo: Bungei shunjûsha, 1997).

————. *Kin-gendaishi kyôiku no kaikaku: Akutama-zendama shikan o koete* (Tokyo: Meiji tosho, 1996).

————. "Nakamura Akira shi no 'Nankin jiken 1-mannin gyakusatsu setsu' o hihan suru," in *Seiron* (March 1999).

————. "Nankin daigyakusatsu sanjûman no uso," in Fujioka and Nishio, eds., *Kokumin no yudan,* pp. 251–58.

————. *Ojoku no kingendaishi* (Tokyo: Tokuma shoten, 1996).

Fujioka, Nobukatsu, and Nishio, Kanji. *Kokumin no yudan: Rekishi kyôkasho ga abunai* (Tokyo: PHP kenkyûsho, 1996).

Fujiwara, Akira. "Kaisetsu," in Ono, et. al. eds., *Nankin daigyakusatsu o kiroku shita kôgun heishi tachi,* pp. ix–xxiv.

————. *Nankin daigyakusatsu* (Tokyo: Iwanami shoten, 1985).

————. "Nankin daigyakusatsu to kyôkasho, kyôiku mondai," in Hora, et al., eds., *Nankin jiken o kangaeru,* pp. 12–34.

————. "Nankin kôryakusen no tenkai," in Hora, Fujiwara, and Honda, eds., *Nankin daigyakusatsu no kenkyû,* pp. 52–94.

————. *Nankin no Nihongun* (Tokyo: Ôtsuki shoten, 1997).

————. *Shinpan: Nankin daigyakusatsu* (Tokyo: Iwanami shoten, 1991).

————. et. al. ed., *Shôwa 20-nen: 1945-nen* (Tokyo: Shôgakkan, 1995).

————. *Shôwa no rekishi 5: Nit-Chû zenmen sensô* (Tokyo: Shôgakkan, 1989).

————. *Taikei Nihon no rekishi 15: Sekai no naka no Nihon* (Tokyo: Shôgakkan, 1993).

Fukushima minyû shinbun, ed., *Fukushima: Sensô to ningen, Byakko hen,* vol. 1 (Fukushima: Fukushima minyû shinbun, 1982).

————. *Kyôdo butai senki, Moesakaru tairiku,* vol. 1 (Fukushima: Fukushima minyû shinbun shinbun, 1965).

GA Newsletter 5:1 (March 1998), pp. 87–88.

Ginn, John L. *Sugamo Prison: An Account of the Trial and Sentencing of Japanese War Criminals in 1948* (Jefferson, NC: McFarland & Co., 1992).

Gluck, Carol. "The Rape of Nanking: How 'the Nazi Buddha' Resisted the Japanese," in *Times Literary Supplement* (27 June 1997).

Gomikawa, Shunpei. *Gozen kaigi* (Tokyo: Bungei shunjûsha, 1984).

Gries, Peter Hays. *China's New Nationalism: Pride, Politics, and Diplomacy* (Berkeley: University of California Press, 2004.

————. "Face Nationalism: Power and Passion in Chinese Anti-Foreignism" (University of California, Berkeley, Ph.D. dissertation 1999).

Haga, Hiraku. "'Za reepu obu Nankin' hôyaku chûshi no keii," in *Shûkan kinyôbi* (5 November 1999), p. 17.

Haffner, Sebastian. *Defying Hitler: A Memoir* (New York: Farrar, 2000).

————. *The Meaning of Hitler* (London: Phoenix Press, 1979).

Hancock, Ian. "Responses to the Porrajmos: The Romani Holocaust," in Rosenbaum, Alan S. ed., *Is The Holocaust Unique?: Perspectives on Comparative Genocide* (Boulder: Westview Press, 1998), pp. 39–64.

Hanley, Charles J., Choe, Sang-hun, and Mendoza, Martha. *The Bridge at No Gun Ri* (New York: Henry Holt, 2001).

Hara, Takeshi. "Iwayuru 'Nankin daigyakusatsu jiken' no maisô kiroku no saikentô" in Higashinakano, ed., *Nankin "gyakusatsu" kenkyû no saizensen, 2002.*

Harris, Whitney. *Tyranny on Trial* (Dallas: Southern Methodist University Press, 1999 revised ed.) orig. ed., 1954.

Hashikawa, Bunzô, et al., eds., *Nihon no hyakunen 4: Ajia kaihô no yume* (Tokyo: Chikuma shobô, 1967).

Hata, Ikuhiko. *Nankin jiken: "Gyakusatsu" no kôzô* (Tokyo: Chûôkôron sha, 1986).

———. "Nankin jiken, ronten to kenkyû kadai" in Higashinakano, ed., *Nankin "gyakusatsu" kenkyû no saizensen, 2002,* pp. 11–39.

———. "Raabe kôka o sokutei suru" in Hata, *Gendaishi no sôten* (Tokyo: Bungei shunjû, 1998).

Hata, Ikuhiko, Higashinakano, Osamichi, and Matsumoto, Ken'ichi. "Mondai ha 'horyo shodan' o dô miru ka," in *Shokun* (February 2001), pp. 128–44.

Hata, Kensuke. "Horyo no chi ni mamireta Byakko butai" in *Nihon shûhô* (25 February 1957), pp. 13–15.

Hata, Nagami. "Izoku to seiji," in Tanaka, et. al. ed., *Izoku to seiji.*

Hayashi, Hirofumi. *BC-kyû senpan saiban* (Tokyo: Iwanami shoten, 2005).

Hayashi, Shigeru. *Nihon no rekishi 25: Taiheiyô sensô* (Tokyo: Chûôkôronsha, 1967).

Hayashi, Zensuke. "Shina jihenka ni okeru fuon kôdô to sono taisaku ni tsuite," in *Shakai mondai sôsho* 1:79 (Kyoto: Tôyô bunka sha, 1978).

Heer, Hannes. "How Amorality Became Normality," in Heer and Naumann, eds., *War of Extermination,* pp. 329–44.

Herr, Hannes, and Naumann, Klaus, ed., *War of Extermination: The German Military in World War II, 1941–1944* (New York: Berghahn Books, 2004).

Hesse, Carla, and Post, Robert, eds., *Human Rights in Political Transitions: Gettysburg to Bosnia* (New York: Zone Books, 1999).

Hidaka, Rokurô, ed., *Kyôkasho ni kakarenakatta sensô: part 19, Nihon to Chûgoku no wakamono tchi no rekishi ninshiki* (Tokyo: Nashinoki sha, 1995).

Higashinakano, Osamichi (Shûdô). *1937: Nankin kôryakusen no shinjitsu* (Tokyo: Shôgakkan, 2003).

———. *Kokka hasan: Higashi Doitsu shakaishugi no 45 nen* (Tokyo: Tendensha, 1992).

———. "Nankin 'gyakusatsu': Dai-ni kokkyô gassakuka no sensô puropaganda," in Higashinakano, ed., *Nankin "gyakusatsu" kenkyû no saizensen: 2003* (Tokyo: Tendensha, 2003) pp. 257–319.

———. *"Nankin Gyakusatsu" no tettei kenshô* (Tokyo: Tendensha, 1998).

———. "'Nankin sen' moto heishi, giwaku no shôgen," in *Shokun!* (November 2002), pp. 162–73.

———. "Nankin tokumu kikan (Mantetsu shain) Maruyama Susumu no kaisô" in Higashinakano, ed., *Nankin "gyakusatsu" kenkyû no saizensen, 2002.*

———. "Rekishi no kenkyû ka, rekishi no waikyoku ka," in *"Kingendai shi" no jugyô kaikaku* no. 424 (June 1996).

———. *Shakai shisô no rekishi 18 kô* (Tokyo: Ajia shobô shuppanbu, 1998).

Higashinakano, Osamichi (Shûdô), and Fujioka Nobukatsu. *"Za reepu obu Nankin" no kenkyû: Chûgoku ni okeru "jôhôsen" no teguchi to senryaku* (Tokyo: Shôdensha,1999).

Hirano, Ken'ichirô. "Transnational Flows of People and International Exchanges: Phenomena and Activities," in Yamamoto, Yoshinobu ed., *Globalism, Regionalism and Nationalism: Asia in Search of its Roles in the Twenty-first Century* (London: Blackwell Publishers, 1999), pp. 93–104.

Honda, Katsuichi. *Chûgoku no tabi* (Tokyo: Asahi shinbunsha, 1991).

———. *Doitsu minshu kyôwakoku* vol. 29 in *Honda Katsuichi shû* (Tokyo: Asahi shinbunsha, 1992).

———. *Korosu gawa no ronri* (Tokyo: Asahi shinbunsha, 1992).

———. *Nankin e no michi* (Tokyo: Asahi shinbunsha, 1987).

———. *The Nanjing Massacre: A Japanese Journalist Confronts Japan's National Shame* (Armonk, NY: M. E. Sharpe, 1998).

———. *NHK jushinryô kyohi no ronri* (Tokyo: Asahi shinbunsha, 1991).

Honda, Katsuichi, and Naganuma, Setsuo. *Tennô no guntai* (Tokyo: Asahi shinbunsha, 1991).

Honda, Katsuichi, and Ono, Kenji. "Bakufusan no horyo shûdan gyakusatsu" in Hora, Fujiwara, and Honda, eds., *Nankin daigyakusatsu no kenkyû*, pp. 128–49.

Hoover Institution Archives, Stanley Hornbeck Record Group, Joseph C. Grew Files.

Hora, Tomio. *Kindai senshi no nazo* (Tokyo: Jinbutsu ôraisha, 1967).

———. "Matsui taishô jinchû nisshi kaizan atogaki," in Hora, et al. eds., *Nankin jiken o kangaeru*, pp. 55–66.

Hora, Tomio et al. eds., *Nankin daigyakusatsu no genba e* (Tokyo: Asahi shinbunsha, 1988).

Hora, Tomio, Fujiwara, Akira, and Honda, Katsuichi, eds., *Nankin daigyakusatsu no kenkyû* (Tokyo: Banseisha, 1992).

———. *Nankin daigyakusatsu no shômei* (Tokyo: Asahi shinbunsha, 1987).

———. *Nankin daigyakusatsu: "Maboroshi" ka kôsaku hihan* (Tokyo: Gendaishi shuppankai, 1975).

Hora, Tomio, et al. eds., *Nankin jiken o kangaeru* (Tokyo: Ôtsuki shoten, 1987).

Hora, Tomio, et al. eds., *Nankin daigyakusatsu no kenkyû* (Tokyo: Banseisha, 1992).

Hora, Tomio, ed., *Nit-Chû sensô Nankin daizangyaku jiken shiryô shû 2: Eibun shiryô hen* (Tokyo: Aoki shoten, 1985).

Hora, Tomio, and Watada, Susumu. "Bakufusan no horyo shokei ni kansuru 'Shinsetsu' hihan" in Hora, et al. eds., *Nankin daigyakusatsu no kenkyû*, pp. 150–195.

Horwitz, Solis. "The Tokyo Trial," in *International Conciliation,* no. 45 (November 1950), pp. 473–584.

Hsia, Ch'iang. "Wei-hu tso-chang ti tzu-chih wei-yuan-hui," in *Nan-ching shih-chih,* 1989, no. 5.

Hsing-cheng-yuan hsüan-ch'uan-chü, ed. *Chûka minkoku ishin seifu gaishi.* (Nan-ching: Wei-hsin cheng-fu, 1940).

Hsiung, James C., and Levine, Steven I., eds., *China's Bitter Victory: The War with Japan 1937–1945* (Armonk: M. E. Sharpe, 1992).

Hsü, Shuhsi., ed., *Documents of the Nanking Safety Zone* (Shanghai: Kelley and Walsh, 1939), protoreproduced in Brook, ed., *Documents on the Rape of Nanking,* pp. 1–167.

Hu, Hua-ling. *American Goddess at the Rape of Nanking: The Courage of Minnie Vautrin.* (Carbondale: Southern Illinois University Press, 2000).

Huttenbach, Henry R. "Locating the Holocaust on the Genocide Spectrum: Towards a Methodology of Definition and Categorization," in *Holocaust and Genocide Studies* 3:3 (1988), pp. 289–303.

Ienaga, Saburô. *Sensô sekinin* (Tokyo: Iwanami shoten, 1985).

———. *Taiheiyô sensô* (Tokyo: Iwanami shoten, 1968).

———. *Taiheiyô sensô: Dai-2 han* (Tokyo: Iwanami shoten, 1986).

Iguchi, Kazuki, et al, eds., *Nankin jihen: Kyoto shidan kankei shiryôshû.* (Tokyo: Aoki shoten, 1989).

Iide, Magoroku. *Teikô no shinbunjin: Kiryû Yûyû* (Tokyo: Iwanami shoten, 1980).

Iinuma, Mamoru. "Iinuma Mamoru nikki," in Nankin senshi henshû iinkai, ed., *Nankin senshi shiryôshû.*

International Military Tribunal for the Far East (IMTFE). "Summation for Matsui, Iwane" (Def. Doc. No. 3096), Hoover Institution Archives, p. 62.

———. "Indictment." 1946, photo-reproduced in Pritchard, and Zaide, eds., *The Tokyo War Crimes Trial* vol. 1.

———. "Judgment." 1948, photo-reproduced in Pritchard Zaide, Sonia, eds., *The Tokyo War Crimes Trial* vol. 20, reprinted in Rölling, B., and Rüter, C., ed., *The Tokyo Judgment* vol. 1, pp. 17–468.

———. "Proceedings." 1946–48, photo-reproduced in Pritchard and Zaide, eds., *The Tokyo War Crimes Trial* vols. 1–19.

Inoue, Hisashi. "Fuseikakusa yue ni hiteiha no hyôteki to naru," in *Shûkan kinyôbi* (5 November 1999), pp. 16–17.

———. "Itai maisô kiroku wa gizô shiryô de wa nai" in Nankin ken, ed., *Nankin daigyakusatsu itei ron 13 no uso* (Tokyo: Kashiwa shobô, 1999).

Inoue, Hisashi. ed., *Kachû senbu kôsaku shirô* (Tokyo: Fuji shuppan, 1989).

———. "Nankin jiken to Chûgoku kyôsantô," in Hora, et. al. ed., *Nankin jiken o kangaeru* (Tokyo: Ôtuski shoten, 1987), pp. 166–82.

Inoue, Kiyoshi. *Nihon no rekishi ge* (Tokyo: Iwanami shoten, 1966).

Inoue, Kiyoshi, Okonogi, Shinzaburô, and Suzuki, Seishi. *Gendai Nihon no rekishi jô* (Tokyo: Aoki shoten, 1952).

Iriye, Akira. *The Origins of the Second World War in Aisa and the Pacific* (London: Longman, 1987).

Irokawa, Daikichi. *Aru Shôwa shi: Jibun shi no kokoromi* (Tokyo: Chûôkôronsha, 1975).

Ishida, Takeshi. "Sensô sekinin saikô," in *Nenpô: Nihon gendaishi,* no. 2 (1996).

Ishida, Yûji. "Kenkyû dôkô shôkai: Doitsushi ni okeru gyakustsu kenkyû," (unpublished paper).

Ishida, Yûji ed., *Shiryô: Doitsu gaikôkan no mita Nankin jiken* (Tokyo: Ôtsuki shoten, 2001).

Ishikawa, Mizuho. "Tettei kenshô 'Nankin ronten seirigaku'," in *Shokun!* (February 2001), pp. 146–63.

Ishikawa, Tatsuzô. *Ikite iru heitai* in *Gendai bungaku taikei 48: Ishikawa Tatsuzô shû* (Tokyo: Chikuma shobô, 1964), pp. 140–218.

Ishikiriyama, Hideaki. *Nihon gun doku gasu sen no mura: Chûgoku Kahoku shô, Heitan mura de okotta koto* (Tokyo: Kôbunken, 2003).

Ishin seifu, ed., *Chûka minkoku ishin seifu gaishi* (N.P., 1940).

Itakura, Yoshiaki. "'30-man gyakusatsu' kyokô no shômei," in *Zenbô* (March 1984), pp. 50–54.

———. "'30-man gyakusatsu' kyokô no shômei: Zoku, Nankin jiken no sûjiteki kenkyû" in *Zenbô* (October 1984), pp. 40–46.

———. *Hontô wa kô datta Nankin jiken* (Tokyo: Nihon tosho kankôkai, 1999).

———. "Matsui Iwane nikki no kaizan ni tsuite," in *Bungei shunjû* (January 1986), pp. 187–94.

———. "'Nankin daigyakusatsu nijûman' setsu e no hanshô," in *"Kingendai shi" no jugyô kaikaku* no. 412 (September 1995), pp. 71–79.

———. "Nankin jiken no sûjiteki kenkyû 3: Nankin de ittai nani ga atta no ka," in *Zenbô* (April 1985), pp. 36–43.

———. "'Nankin daigyakusatsu: gyakusatsu wa 'seizei' 10,000–20,000," in *Bizunesuinterigensu* (August 1994), pp. 16–19.

Iwakawa, Takashi. *Kotô no tsuchi ni naru tomo: B-C kyû senpan saiban* (Tokyo: Kôdansha, 1995).

Iwanami, Yûko. *Sofu Tôjô Hideki "Issai kataru nakare"* (Tokyo: Bungei shunjûsha, 1995).

Jaranilla, Delfin. "Concurring Opinion of Mr. Justice Jaranilla, Member from the Republic of the Philippines." IMFTE, 1948, photoreproduced in Pritchard and Zaide, eds., *The Tokyo War Crimes Trial,* vol. 21, reprinted in Rölling, and Rüter, eds., *The Tokyo Judgment,* vol. 1, pp. 497–515.

Jenkins, Russell. "The Japanese Holocaust," in *National Review* (10 November 1997).

Kadoya, Fumio. *Shôwa jidai: 15-nen sensô shiryô shû* (Tokyo: Gakuyô shoten, 1973).

Kaikôsha, ed., "Bakufusan fukin de no horyo shobun ni tsuite: Sono sôgôteki kôsatsu," in Kaikôsha, *Nankin senshi shiryô shû.*

Kaikôsha, ed., *Nankin senshi* (Tokyo: Kaikôsha, 1989).

Kaikôsha, ed., *Nankin senshi shiryô shû* (Tokyo: Kaikôsha, 1989).

Kamisago, Katsushichi. *Kenpei sanjûichi nen* (Tokyo: Tokyo raifu sha, 1955).

Kamisaka, Fuyuko. *Tsugunai wa sunde iru* (Tokyo: Kôdansha, 2000).

Kao, Hsing-tsu. "Jih-pen ch'i-kuo chu-i tsai Nan-ching ta-t'u-sha," trans., Robert Gray http://www.cnd.org/njmassacre/njm-tran.

Kaochun hsien ti-fang-chih pien-tsuan-hui, ed., *Kaochun hsien-chih* (Nan-ching: Chiangsu ku-tsi ch'u-pan-she, 1988).

Kasahara, Tokushi. *Ajia no naka no Nihongun: Sensô sekinin to rekishigaku, rekishi kyôiku* (Tokyo: Aoki shoten, 1994).

———. "Môsô ga umidashita 'Han-Nichi kakuran kôsakutai' setsu," in Nankin ken, ed., *Nankin daigyakusatsu hiteiron 13 no uso,* pp. 198–217 .

———. *Nankin jiken* (Tokyo: Iwanami shoten, 1997).

———. *Nankin jiken to Nihonjin* (Tokyo: Kashiwa shobô, 2002).

———. *Nankin jiken to sankô sakusen* (Tokyo: Aoki shoten, 1999).

———. *Nankin nanminku no hyakunichi: Gyakusatsu o mita gaikokujin* (Tokyo: Iwanami shoten, 1995).

———. "Riaru taimu de sekai kara hinan o abite ita Nankin jiken," in Nankin ken, ed., *Nankin daigyakusatsu hiteiron 13 no uso,* pp. 40–57.

———. "Sûji ijiri no fumô na ronsô wa gyakusatsu no jittai kaimei o tôzakeru," in Nankin ken, ed., *Nankin digaykusatsu hiteiron 13 no uso,* pp. 74–96.

Katô, Norihiro. *Haisengo ron* (Tokyo: Kôdansha, 1997).

Katô, Yôko. *Sensô no kin-gendai shi* (Tokyo: Kôdansha, 2002).

Katogawa, Kôtarô. "Shôgen ni yoru Nankin senshi saishôkai: 'Sono sôkatsuteki kôsatsu'," in *Kaikô* (March 1985).

Kennedy, David M. "The Horror," in *Atlantic Monthly* (April 1998).

Kennedy, John F. *Profiles in Courage* (New York: Pocket Books, 1957).

Kimijima, Kazuhiko. "'Nankin jiken' no kôtei to 'Nankin daigyakusatsu' no hitei," in Hora, et al. eds., *Nankin jiken o kangaeru*, pp. 105–20.

Kirby, William C. Foreword, in Chang, *Rape of Nanking*, pp. ix–xi.

Kiryû Yûyû. *Chikushôdô no chikyû* (Tokyo: Chûôkôronsha, 1989).

Kita, Hiroaki. *Nit-Chû kaisen: Gun hômukyoku bunsho kara mita kyokoku itchi taisei e no michi* (Tokyo: Chûôkôronsha, 1994).

Kitamura, Minoru. "The GMD [KMT] International Propaganda Division" (forthcoming).

———. "Nankin de daigyakusatsu wa atta no ka," in *Bungei shunjû* (October 2003), pp. 272–74.

———. *"Nankin jiken" no tankyû: Sono jitsuzô o motomete* (Tokyo: Bungei shunjûsha, 2001.

Kitaoka, Shin'ichi. "Iwarenaki Nihon hihan o haisu," in *Chûôkôron* (June 2005), pp. 54–63.

Kobayashi, Yoshinori. *"Ko" to "kô" ron* (Tokyo: Gentôsha, 2000).

———. *Sensôron* (Tokyo: Gentôsha, 1998).

———. "Shin gômanizumu sengen 110," in *SAPIO* (9 February 2000), pp. 83–98.

Kojima, Tomoyuki. "Nit-Chû kankei no 'atarashii hatten dankai': kyôsôteki kyôzon no tame ni," in Kojima, Tomoyuki ed., *Ajia jidai no Nit-Chû kankei: kako to mirai* (Tokyo: Simul Press, 1995), pp. 1–34.

Kojima, Noboru. *Nit-Chû sensô* (Tokyo: Bungei shunjûsha, paperback edition, 1988), 5 vols.

Komori, Yôichi et at., eds., *Rekishi kyôkasho: Nani ga mondai ka* (Tokyo: Iwanami shoten, 2001).

Komori, Yoshihisa. *Nit-Chû saikô* (Tokyo: Sankei shinbunsha, 2001).

———. *Nit-Chû yûkô no maboroshi* (Tokyo: Shôgakkan, 2002).

Komuro, Naoki, and Watanbe Shôichi. *Fûin no Shôwa shi: "Sengo 50 nen" jigyaku no shûen* (Tokyo: Tokuma shoten,1995)

Kôno, Kensuke, et al. eds. "Sekai no terebi wa sengo 50-nen o dô tsutaeta ka," in *NHK hôsôbunka chôsa kenkyû nenpô*, no. 41 (1996), pp. 1–109.

Koonz, Claudia. *The Nazi Conscience* (Cambridge: Harvard University Press, 2003).

Kopelman. Elizabeth S. "Ideology and International Law: The Dissent of the Indian Justice at the Tokyo War Crimes Trial," in *New York University of International Law and Politics* 23:2 (1991), pp. 373–444.

Kuo-fang-pu shih-cheng chu. ed. *K'ang-chan chien-shih* (Taipei: Defense Department History Section, 1952).

———. *Chung-Jih chan-chen-shih lueh* (Taipei: Defense Department History Section, 1962).

Kuo, Hsiao-hua. *Tung-fang ta-shen-p'an: shen-p'an ch'in Hua Jih-chün chan-fan chi-shih* (Peking: Chieh-fang-chün wen-I ch'u-pan-she, 1995).

Kuper, Leo. *Genocide: Its Political Use in the Twentieth Century* (New Haven: Yale University Press, 1981).

Kuyung hsien ti-fang-chih pien-tsuan-hui. ed. *Kuyung hsien-chih* (Nan-ching: Chiangsu jen-min ch'u-pan-she, 1990).

Kuyung shih-shih pien-kung-shih, ed. "Jih-chün chun-Kuyung ch'i-chien pao-hang-lu." (Manuscript, n.p.)

Kyôkasho kentei soshô o shien suru zenkoku renrakukai, ed., *Kyôkasho kara kesenai sensô no shinjitsu: Rekishi o yugameru Fujioka Nobukatsu shira e no hihan* (Tokyo: Aoki shoten, 1996).

League of Nations. *Official Journal.*

Lee, En-han. "The Nanking Massacre Reassesed: A Study of the Sino-Japanese Controversy over the Factual Number of Massacred Victims," in Li, Sabella, and Liu, eds., *Nanking 1937: Memory and Healing* (Armonk: M. E. Sharpe, 2002), pp. 47–74.

Lewis, John R. *Uncertain Judgment: A Bibliography of War Crimes Trials* (Santa Barbara: ABC-Clio, 1979).

Li, Fei Fei, Sabella, Robert, and Liu, David, ed., *Nanking 1937: Memory and Healing* (Armonk, NY: M. E. Sharpe, 2002).

Li, Haibo. "Unforgivable Atrocity," in *Beijing Review* (14–20 August 1995).

Li, K'o-lang. "Lun-ching wu-yüeh chi," in Nan-ching t'u-shu kuan, ed., *Chin-hua Jih-chün Nan-ching ta-t'u-sha shih-liao*, pp. 101–18.

Li, Peter. "The Asian-Pacific War, 1931–1945: Japanese Atrocities and the Quest for Post-War Reconcilliation," in *East Asia: An International Quarterly* (Spring 1999), pp. 109–37.

Liddell-Hart, Basil H. *History of the Second World War* (New York: Paragon Books, 1979).

Lin, Na. "Hsüeh-lei hua Chin-ling," in Nan-ching t'u-shu kuan, ed., *Chin-hua Jih-chün Nan-ching ta-t'u-sha shih-liao*, pp. 141–47.

Lishui hsien ti-fang-chih pien-tsuan-hui, ed., *Lishui hsien-chih.*

Lipstadt, Deborah E. *Beyond Belief: The American Press and the Coming of the Holocaust, 1933–1945* (New York: Free Press, 1986).

Liu Chieh [Ryû Ketsu]. *Kankan saiban* (Tokyo: Chûôkôronsha, 2000).

Liu, Frederick F. *A Military History of China: 1924–1949* (Princeton: Princeton University Press, 1956).

Liu, James T. C. "The Tokyo Trial," 2 pts. *China Monthly* 8:7 (July 1947) pp. 242–47; 8:8 (August 1947) pp. 279–80.

Lu, Suping. *They Were in Nanjing: The Nanjing Massacre Witnessed by American and British Nationals* (Hong Kong: Hong Kong University Press, 2004).

Lukas, R. C. *Forgotten Holocaust: The Poles under German Occupation, 1939–1944* (Lexington: University of Kentucky Press, 1986).

Lutz, Brenda Davis, and Lutz, James M. "Gypsies as Victims of the Holocaust," in *Holocaust and Genocide Studies* 9:3 (Winter 1995), pp. 346–59.

Lynn, John A. *Battle: A History of Combat and Culture* (Boulder: Westview Press, 2003).

Ma, Lieh-ch'eng. "Nihon wa Chûgoku ni 21 kai shazai shita," in *Bungei shunjû* (October 2003), pp. 178–84.

———. "Waga Chûgoku yo, han-Nichi kôdô o tsutsushime," in *Bungei shunjû* (March 2003), pp. 126–35.

MacInnis, Donald. Foreword in Zhang, ed., *Eyewitnesses to Massacre*, pp. ix–xi.

Mantetsu Shanhai jimusho. "Naka Shina senryô ni okeru senbu kôsaku gaiyô," in Inoue, ed., *Kachû senbu kôsaku shiryô*, pp. 48–53.

Margalit, Avishai. *The Ethics of Memory* (Cambridge: Harvard University Press, 2002).

Marrus, Michael R. *The Holocaust in History* (Hanover: University Press of New England, 1987).

———. "Is There a New Anti-Semitism," in Curtis, Michael., ed., *Anti-Semitism in the Contemporary World* (Boulder: Westview Press, 1986), pp.

Maruyama, Susumu. "Watakushi no Shôwa shi: Nankin jiken no jissô, 6 pts., in *Mantetsu wakabakai kaihô*, nos. 133–38 (5 August–1 October 2000).

Matsumura, Toshio. *"Nankin gyakusatsu" e no daigimon* (Tokyo: Tendensha, 1998).

Matsumoto, Yasushi. "Nihon no wakamono no 15-nen sensôkan to kyôkasho (ankeeto no matome)," in Hidaka, ed., *Kyôkasho in kakarenakatta sensô: Part 19, Nihon to Chûgoku no wakamono tchi no rekishi ninshiki*, pp. 199–231.

Matsuo, Ichirô. *Puropaganda sen "Nankin jiken"* (Tokyo: Kôjinsha, 2004).

Matsuoka, Tamaki. *Nankin sen: Tozasareta kiroku o tazunete* (Tokyo: Shakai hyôronsha, 2002).

McCormack, Gavan. "Reflections on Modern Japanese History in the Context and the Concept of Genocide," in Gellately, Robert, and Kiernan, Ben, E., ed., *The Specter of Genocide: Mass Murder in Historical Perpspective* (Cambridge: Cambridge University Press, 2003), pp. 265–86.

McDonough, Frank. *Hitler, Chamberlain, and Appeasement* (New York: Cambridge University Press, 2002).

Minear, Richard. *Victor's Justice: The Tokyo War Crimes Trial* (Princeton: Princeton University Press, 1971).

Miyamoto, Ken'ichi. *Shôwa no rekishi 10: Keizai taikoku zôhoban* (Tokyo: Shôgakkan, 1989).

Mizutani, Naoko. "Watashi wa naze Azuma Shirô ni igi o tonaeru ka," in *Sekai*, no. 664 (August 1999), pp. 219–25.

Morita, Toshio, and Fujiwara, Akira, eds., *Kingendaishi no shinjitsu wa nani ka: Fujioka Nobukatsu shi no "rekishi kyôiku, shakai kyôiku" ron hihan* (Tokyo: Ôtsuki shoten, 1996).

Mukai, Chieko. "'Mujitsu da!' Chichi no sakebi ga kikoeru," in *Seiron* (March 2000), pp. 60–67.

Murakami, Shigeyoshi. *Irei no shôkon: Yasukuni no shisô* (Tokyo: Iwanami shoten, 1974).

Murata, Kazushirô. *Nit-Chû sensô nikki (I)* (Tokyo: Hôwa shuppan, 1984).

Nakajima, Kesago. "Nankin kôryakusen: Nakajima dai-16 shidanchô nikki," in *Zôkan: Rekishi to jinbutsu* (December 1984), pp. 252–71.

Nakakita, Ryûtarô, et al. "'Azuma saiban' no shinjitsu o uttaeru: 8-gatsu gô Miztuani Naoko shi ronbun hihan," in *Sekai*, no. 666 (October 1999), pp. 275–81.

Nakamura, Masanori. ed., *Rekishi to shinjitsu* (Tokyo: Chikuma shobô, 1997).

Nakano, Yoshio. "Hito to bungaku," in *Gendai bungaku taikei 48: Ishikawa Tatsuzô shû* (Tokyo: Chikuma shobô, 1964), pp. 464–88.

Nakayama, Osamu. *Nihonhin wa naze tajû jinkaku na no ka* (Tokyo: Yôsensha, 1999).

Nan-ching shih tang-an-kuan, ed. *Shen-hsün Wang-wei han-chien pi-lu*, 2 vols. (Nanching: Chiangsu ku-chi ch'u-pan-she, 1992).

Nan-ching ta-tu-sha shih-liao pian-chi wei-yuan-hui and Nan-ching tu-shu-kuan, eds., *Chin-Hua Jih-chün Nan-ching ta-tu-sha shih-liao* (Nan-ching: Chiangsu ku-chi ch'u-pan-she, 1992).

Nan-ching tu-shu-kuan, ed. *Ch'in-hua Jih-chün Nan-ching ta-t'u-sha tang-an* (Nanching: Chiangsu ku-chi ch'u-pan-she, 1987).

———. *Shen-shün Wangwei hanchien pi-lu* (Nan-ching: Chiangsu ku-chi ch'u-pan-she, 1985) 2 vol.

Nandy, Ashis. *The Intimate Enemy: Loss and Recovery of Self under Colonialism* (Delhi: Oxford University Press, 1983).

———. "The Other Within: The Strange Case of Radhabinod Pal's Judgment of Culpability" in Nandy, *The Savage Freud and Other Essays or Possible and Retrievale Selves*, pp. 53–80.

———. *The Savage Freud and other Essays on Possible and Retrievable Selves* (Princeton: Princeton University Press, 1996).

Nankin daigyakusatsu higaisha tsuitô hô-Chû-dan, ed., *Midori no shokuzai: Nankin, tsuitô kenshoku hô-Chû-dan no kiroku*, 4 vols. (Tokyo: Nankin daigyakusatsu higasha tsuitô hô-Chû-dan, 1987–90).

Nankin tokumu kikan. Untitled reports for January, February, and March 1938, in Inoue, ed., *Kachû senbu kôsaku shiryô*, pp. 148–69.

Nankin ken (Nankin jiken chôsa kenkyû kai), ed., *Nankin daigyakusatsu hiteiron 13 no uso* (Tokyo: Kashiwa shobô, 1999).

———. *Nankin jiken shiryô shû 1: Amerika kankei shiryô shû* (Tokyo: Aoki shoten 1985).

———. *Nankin jiken shiryô shû 2: Chûgoku kankei shiryô shû* (Tokyo: Aoki shoten 1985).

Nankin senshi henshû iinkai, ed., "Bakufusan fukin de no horyo shobun ni tsuite: Sono sôgôteki kôsatsu in Nankin senshi, pp. 13–14.

———. *Nankin senshi* (Tokyo: Kaikôsha, 1989).

———. *Nankin senshi shiryô shû* (Tokyo: Kaikôsha, 1989).

———. *Nankin senshi shiryô shû* 2nd ed., (Tokyo: Kaikôsha, 1993).

Nankin shi bunshiryô kenkyûkai ed., *Shôgen: Nankin daigyakusatsu* (Tokyo: Aoki shoten, 1984).

Nanking International Relief Committe. "Report of the Nanking International Relief Committe," in Zhang, ed., *Eyewitnesses to Massacre*, pp. 413–45.

Naumann, Klaus. "The 'Unblemished' Wehrmacht" in Heer and Naumann, eds., *War of Extermination*, pp. 417–29.

Newby, Laura. *Sino-Japanese Relations: China's Perspective* (New York: Routledge, 1988).

"News Hour with Jim Lehrer," (20 February 1998).

NHK, ed., "Saki no sensô to sedai gyappu," web posted, September 2000.

Nihon Kyôkasho taikei: Kindai hen (Tokyo: Kôdansha, 1965).

Nishio, Kanji. *Kokumin no rekishi* (Tokyo: Sankei shinbunsha, 1999).

———. *Kotonaru higeki: Nihon to Doitsu* (Tokyo: Bungei shunjûsha, 1994).

———. *Rekishi o sabaku orokashisa* (Tokyo: PHP bunko, 2000).

Nishio, Kanji, and Fujioka, Nobukatsu. *Kokumin no yudan* (Tokyo: PHP bunko, 2000).

Novick, Peter. *The Holocaust in American Life* (Boston: Houghton Mifflin, 2000).

———. "Holocaust Memory in America," in Young, James E., ed., *The Art of Memory: Holocaust Memorials in History* (New York: Prestel-Lerlag, 1994), pp. 159–65.

Obara, Hiroto, Arai, Toshiaki, Yamabe, Yukiko, and Okada, Hisao. *Nihon gun no dokugasu sen: Semarareru ikidan shori* (Tokyo: Nit-Chû shuppan, 1997).

Ôe, Shinobu. *Yasukuni jinja* (Tokyo: Iwanami shoten, 1984).

Oguma, Eiji. "'Hidari' o kii suru popyûrarizumu," in *Sekai* no. 656 (December 1998), pp. 94–105.

Ôgushi, Junji. "Dai-3-ji kyôkasho kôgeki no shinbu ni aru mono," in *Rekishi hyôron* no. 579 (July 1998), pp. 238–53.

Okamura, Yasuji. *Okamura Yasuji taishô shiryô jô* (Tokyo: Hara shobô, 1970).

Okumiya, Masatake. *Watakushi no mita Nankin jiken* (Tokyo: PHP kenkyûsho, 1997).

Ômori, Minoru. *Ten'anmon enjô* (Tokyo: Ushio shuppansha, 1966).

Ono, Kenji. "Atogaki," in Ono, et al. eds., *Nankin daigyakusatsu o kiroku shita kôgun heishitachi,* pp. 375–82.

———. "Mokugeki Nankin daigyakusatsu: Hohei dai-65 rentai to Chûgokujin horyo," in *Shûkan kinyôbi* (4 February 1994), pp. 26–31.

———. "'Nankin gyakusatsu no kôkei': Hohei dai-52 rentai heishi no jinchû nikki o otte," in *Shûkan kinyôbi* (10 December 1993), pp. 8–13.

Ono, Kenji, Fujiwara, Akira, and Honda, Katsuichi, eds. *Nankin daigyakusatsu o kiroku shita kôgun heishitachi* (Tokyo: Ôtsuki shoten, 1996).

Ono, Kenji, and Honda, Katsuichi. "Bakufusan no horyo shûdan gyakusatsu" in Hora, Fujiwara, and Honda, eds., *Nankin daigyakusatsu no kenkyû,* pp. 128–49.

Ôsugi, Kazuo. *Nit-Chû jûgonen sensô* (Tokyo: Chûôkôronsha,1996).

Overmans, Ruediger. "German Historiography, the War Losses, and the Prisoners of War," in Bischof and Amrose, eds., *Eisenhauer and the German POWs,* pp. 127–69.

Owen, Frank. *Guilty Men* (London: Gollancz, 1940).

Pal, Radhabinod. *Crimes in International Relations* (Calcutta: University of Calcutta Press, 1955).

———. *International Military Tribunal for the Far East: Dissentient Judgment* (Calcutta: Sanyal, 1953).

———. "International Law," *Indian Law Review* 3:1 (1949), pp. 31–60.

———. "Judgement of the Hon'ble Mr. Justice Pal, Member from India," IMTFE, 1948. photoreproduced in Pritchard and Zaide, eds., *The Tokyo War Crimes Trial,* vol. 21, reprinted in Röling and Rüter, eds., *Tokyo Judgment,* vol. 2. pp. 517–1039.

———. *Nihon muzairon: shinri no sabaki,* Tanaka Masaaki, ed. (Tokyo: Taiheiyô shuppansha, 1952).

———. *Zen'yaku: Nihon muzairon,* Tanaka Masaaki, ed., (Tokyo: Nihon shobô, 1952).

Piccigallo, Philip. *The Japanese on Trial: Allied War Crimes Operations in the East, 1945–1951* (Austin: University of Texas Press, 1979).

Pritchard, John, and Zaide, Sonia., ed. *The Tokyo War Crimes Trial* 22 vol. (New York: Garland Publishing 1981).

Quentin-Baxter, R. Q. "The Task of the international Military Tribunal at Tokyo," in *New Zealand Law Journal,* vol. 25 (7 June 1949), pp. 133–38.

Rabe, John. *The Good Man of Nanking: The Diaries of John Rabe,* ed., Erwin Wickert, trans. John E. Woods (New York: Knopf, 1998).

———. "Hittoraa e no jôshinsho," in Rabe, *Nankin no shinjitsu,* Hirano Keiko, trans. (Tokyo: Kôdansha, 1997), pp. 275–321.

Reishauer, Edwin O. *The United States and Japan* (New York: Viking, 1965).

Remak, Joachim. *The Origins of the Second World War* (Englewood Cliffs: Prentice-Hall 1976).

Röling, B. V. A. "Opinion of Mr. Justice Röling, Member for the Netherlands," in IMTFE, 1948, photoreproduced in Pritchard and Zaide, ed., *Tokyo War Crimes Trial,* vol. reprinted in Röling and Rüter, ed., *Tokyo Judgement,* vol. 2, pp. 1041–1148.

———. *The Tokyo Trial and Beyond: Reflections of a Peacemonger,* Cassese, Antony, ed., (Cambridge: Polity Press, 1993).

———. "The Tokyo Trial and the Development of International Law," in *Indian Law Review* 7:1 (1953), pp. 4–14

Röling, B. V. A. and Rüter, C. F. *The Tokyo Judgement: The International Military Tribunal for the Far East, 29 April 1946–12 November 1948,* 3 vols. (Amsterdam: AAPA University Press, 1997).

Rosenbaum, Alan S. *Prosecuting Nazi War Criminals* (Boulder: Westview Press, 1993).

Rummel, R. J. *China's Bloody Century: Genocide and Mass Murder since 1900* (New Brunswick: Transactions Publishers, 1991).

———. "Democide in Totalitarian States: Mortacracies and Megamurderers," in Charny, Israel ed., *The Widening Circle of Genocide* (New Brunswick: Transactions Publishers, 1994), pp. 3–39.

Saitô, Kunio. *Rikugun hohei yomoyama monogatari* (Tokyo: Kôjinsha, 1997).

Sakamoto, Takao. *Rekishi kyôiku o kangaeru* (Tokyo: PHP Kenkyûsho, 1998).

Sakamoto, Takao et. al. "Rekishi to rekishi ninshiki," in *Shokun* (February 2002), pp. 48–122.

Sakamoto, Takao. "Sengo 50-nen towareru Nihonjin no rekishi kankaku," in *Chûôkôron* (September 1995), pp. 58–71.

Sasaki, Motokatsu. *Yasen yûbinki* (Tokyo: Gendaishi shuppankai, 1973)

Sasaki, Tôichi. "Sasaki Tôichi shôshô shiki," in Nankin senshi henshû iinkai, ed., *Nankin senshi shiryô shû.*

Sassa, Atsuyuki. "Tsumi kyûzoku ni oyobu…" in *Shokun!* (August 2005), pp. 46–56.

Schirokauer, Conrad. *A Brief History of Chinese and Japanese Civilizations* (New York: Harcourt, 1989).

Sen, Ranjit. *The Twin in the Twist: Bose and Gandhi* (Delhi: Asia Pacific Research Information, 1997).

Sengo 50-nen shimin no fusen sengen iken kôkoku umdô, ed. *"Sengo 50-nen": Aratamete fusen de ikô* (Tokyo: Shakai hyôronsha, 1995).

Seno, Kappa. *Shônen H,* 2 vols. (Tokyo: Kôdansha, 1997).

Shenfield, Stephen D. "The Circassians: A Forgotten Genocide?" in Levene, Mark and Roberts, Penny, eds., *The Massacre in History* (New York: Berghahn Books, 1999), pp. 149–63.

Shepherd, Ben. *War in the Wild East: The German Army and Soviet Partisans* (Cambridge: Harvard University Press, 2004).

Sherman, Michael, and Grobman, Alex. *Denying History: Who Says the Holocaust Never Happened and Why Do They Say It?* (Berkeley: University of California Press, 2002).

Shevin-Coetzee, and Coetzee, Frans. eds. *World War I & European Society: A Sourcebook* (Lexington, MA: D.C. Heath, 1995).

Seki, Hei [Shih, P'ing]. *Chûgoku: "Aikoku jôi" no byôri* (Tokyo: Shôgakkan, 2002).

Shijime, Akira. "Nit-Chû sensô no tsuioku: Hyakuningiri kyôsô," in *Chûgoku,* December 1971.

Shimizu, Yoshikazu. *Chûgoku wa naze han-Nichi ni natta ka* (Tokyo: Chûôkôronsha, 2004).

Shinbun taimuzu sha, ed. *Shina jihen senshi,* vol. 1 (Tokyo: Kôtoku hôsankai shuppan, 1937).

Shokun!, ed., "Sanpa gôdô dai ankeeto" in *Shokun!* (February 2001), pp. 164–203.

Shûsen gojûnen kokumin iinkai, ed. *Shûsen gojûsshûnen kokumin undo kiroku shû: Shûsen gojûsshûnen, daitô-A sensô no shinjitsu o tsutaete* (n.p., 1996).

Smalley, Martha Lund ed. *American Missionary Eyewitnesses to the Nanking Massacre, 1937–1938* (New Haven: Yale Divinity School Library, 1977).

Smith, Bradford. "Japan: Beauty and the Beast," in *Amerasia* 6:2 (April 1942), pp. 86–94.

Smith, Roger W., Markusen, Eric, and Lifton, Robert Jay. "Professional Ethics and the Denial of Armenian Genocide," in *Holocaust and Genocide Studies* 9:1 (Spring 1995), pp. 1–22.

Smythe, Lewis. "Nankin chiku ni okeru sensô higai," in Hora, Tomio, ed. *Nit-Chû sensô Nankin daigyakusatsu jiken shiryô shû 2: Eibun shiryô hen* (Tokyo: Aoki shoten, 1985), pp. 211–77.

————. *War Damage in the Nanking Area, December, 1937 to March, 1938* (Shanghai: Mercury Press, 1938).

Sotobayashi, Daisaku. et al. ed. *Seishin: Shinrigaku jiten* (Tokyo: Seishin shobô 1981).

Stannard, David. "Uniqueness as Denial: The Politics of Genocide Scholarship," in Rosenbaum, Alan S., ed., *Is The Holocaust Unique?: Perpsectives on Compariative Genocide* (Boulder: Westview Press, 1998), pp. 163–208.

Stanton, John. "Canada and War Crimes: Judgment at Tokyo," in *International Journal* 55:3 (Summer 2000), pp. 376–400.

Stein, Burton. *A History of India* (Oxford: Blackwell, 1998).

Stephan, John. "The Tanaka Memorial (1927): Authentic or Suprious?" in *Modern Asian Studies* 7:4 (1973), pp. 733–45.

Streit, Christian. "Soviet Prisoners in the Hands of the Wehrmacht," in Heer and Naumann, eds., *War of Extermination*, pp. 80–91.

Sun, Chai-wei, ed. *Nan-ching ta-t'u-sha* (Peking: Bei-ching ch'u-pan-she, 1997).

Sun, Zhaiwei (Chai-wei). "Causes of the Nanking Massacre," in Li, Sabella, and Liu, eds., *Nanking: 1937*, pp. 35–46.

Suzuki, Akira. "Nankin daigyakusatsu' no maboroshi," in *Shokun* (April 1972), pp. 177–91.

————. *"Nankin daigyakusatsu" no maboroshi* (Tokyo: Bungei shunjûsha, 1983).

————. *Shin "Nankin daigyakusatsu" no maboroshi* (Tokyo: Asuka shinsha, 1999).

Suzuki, Jirô. "Watakushi wa ano 'Nankin no higeki' o mokugeki shita," in *Maru*, November 1971.

Takashima, Nobuyoshi. "Rekishikan X media = watching 3: Rotei shita Yomiuri shinbun no 'Sankeika,'" in *Kikan: Sensô sekinin kenkyû*, no. 25 (Fall 1999), pp. 80–86.

Takemoto, Tadao and Ôhara, Yasuo. *"The Alleged "Nanking Massacre": Japan's Rebuttal to China's Forged Claims* (Tokyo: Meiseisha, 2000).

Takigawa, Masajirô. *Shinpan Tokyo saiban o sabaku (ge)* (Tokyo: Sôtakusha, 1978) orig. ed., 1953.

Tanaka, Masaaki. "'Nankin daigyakusatsu': Matsui Iwane no jinchû nisshi," in *Shokun* (September 1983), pp. 64–79.

————. *"Nankin gyakusatsu" no kyokô: Matsui taishô no nikki o megutte* (Tokyo: Nihon kyôbunkan, 1984).

————. *Nankin jiken no sôkatsu* (Tokyo: Kenkôsha, 1987).

————. *Paru hanji no Nihon muzai ron* (Tokyo: Shôgakkan, 2001), orig. pub. 1963.

————. *What Really Happened in Nanking: The Refutation of a Common Myth* (Tokyo: Sekai shuppan, 2000).

Tanaka, Nobumasa et al., eds., *Izoku to Seiji* (Tokyo: Iwanami shoten, 1995).

Tanaka, Yuki. *Hidden Horrors: Japanese War Crimes in World War II* (Boulder: Westview Press, 1998).

Tanizawa, Eiichi. *Akuma no shisô* (Tokyo: Kuresutosha, 1996).

————. *Konna Nihon ni dare ga shita* (Tokyo: Kuresutosha, 1995).

Tawara, Yoshifumi. "Kyôkasho kôgeki-ha no saikin no dôkô: Kôenkai, shinpojiumu nado no dôkô" (Unpublished paper).

Tawara, Yoshifumi et al., "Kokusai mondai no akujunkan o tatsu tame ni," in *Shûkan kinyôbi* (5 November 1999), pp. 10–15.

Taylor, A. J. P. *The Origins of the Second World War.* (New York: Atheneum, 1983).

Taylor, Frederick. *Dresden: Tuesday, Feburary 13, 1945* (New York: Harper, 2004).

Taylor, Laurence. *A Trial of Generals; Homma, Yamashita, MacArther* (South Bend: Icarus, 1981).

Taylor, Telford. *Nuremberg and Vietnam: An American Tragedy* (New York: Bantam, 1971).

Timperley, Harold J. ed., *Gaikokujin no mita Nihongun no bôkô* (Tokyo: Ryûkeisho sha, 1972).

————. *La Guerre Telle qu'elle Est: La Terreur Japnaise en Chine* (Paris: Editions A. Pedone, 1939).

————. *The Japanese Terror in China* (New York: Modern Age Books, 1938).

————. *Waiuoren muduzhongshi Rijun baoxin* (Hankou: Guomin chubanshe, 1938).

————. *What War Means: The Japanese Terror in China* (London: Victor Gollancz, 1938).

Tobe, Ryôichi. *Nihon rikugun to Chûgoku* (Tokyo: Kôdansha, 1999).

Tokutake, Toshio. *Kyôkasho no sengo shi* (Tokyo: Shin Nihon shuppansha, 1995).

Tokyo saiban handobukku henshû iinkai, ed., *Tokyo saiban handobukku* (Tokyo: Aoki shoten, 1989).

Tong, Te-kong, and Li, Tsung-jen. *The Memoirs of Li Tsung-jen* (Boulder: Westview Press, 1979).

Tôyama, Shigeki, Imai, Seiichi, and Fujiwara, Akira. *Shôwa shi* (Tokyo: Iwanami shoten, 1955).

Tôyama, Shigeki. Imai, Seiichi, and Fujiwara Akira. *Shôwa shi: Shinpan* (Tokyo: Iwanami shoten, 1959).

Trent, James F. "Food Shortages in Germany and Europe," in Bischof and Ambrose, ed., *Eisenhauer and the German POWs,* pp. 95–112.

Trevor-Roper, Hugh. *The Last Days of Hitler* (London: PAN Books, 1995) orig. ed., 1947.

Ts'ai, Hung-yüan, and Sun, Pi-yu. "Min-kuo ch'i-chien Nan-ching-shih chih-kuan nien-piao," in *Nan-ching shih-chih,* vol. 1 (1983), pp. 47–48.

Tsuneishi, Keiichi. *Nana-san-ichi butai* (Tokyo: Kôdansha, 1995).

Uesugi, Satoshi. "Kowasenakatta 2-jû kijun no kabe: Ajia e no hoshô o motomeru shimin undô kara," in *Sensô sekinin kenkyû,* no. 11 (Spring 1996), pp. 10–17.

Unemoto, Masami. "Shôgen ni yoru Nankin senshi (5)," in *Kaikô* (August 1984).

United Nations War Crimes Commission. *History of the United Nations War Crimes Commission and the Development of the Laws of War* (London: His Majesty's Stationery Office, 1948).

Usui, Katsumi et al., eds., *Gendai shi shiryô 9: Nit-Chû sensô II* (Tokyo: Misuzu shobô, 1964).

Usui, Katsumi. *Shinpan: Nit-Chû sensô* (Tokyo: Chûôkôronsha, 2000).

Utsumi, Aiko. *Chôsenjin B- C-kyû senpan no kiroku* (Tokyo: Keisô shobô, 1982).

Vautrin, Minnie. "A Review of the First Month," in Zhang, ed., *Eyewitnesses to Massacre,* pp. 330–44.

————. *Nankin jiken no hibi: Minii Bôtorin no nikki,* Okada Ryônosuke et al., trans. (Tokyo: Ôtsuki shoten, 1999).

Vidal-Naquet, Pierre. *Assassins of Memory: Essays on the Denial of the Holocaust,* trans. Jeffrey Mehlman (New York: Columbia University Press, 1992).

Villa, Brian Loring. "The Diplomatic and Poltical Context of the POW Camps Tragedy," in Bischof and Ambrose, eds., *Eisenhauer and the German POWs,* pp. 53–61.

Vincent, John. *An Intelligent Person's Guide to History* (London: Duckworth, 1996).

Wang, Hsi-kuang, "Jih-wei han chien cheng-fu: Nan-ching tzu-chih wei-yüan-hui," in *Nan-ching shih-chih* 4 (1987), pp. 4–6.

Wada, Susumu. *Sengo Nihon no heiwa ishiki* (Tokyo: Aoki shoten, 1995).

Wakabayashi, Bob Tadashi. *Anti-Foreignism and Western Learning in Early-Modern Japan* (Cambridge: Harvard University Press, 1986).

————. "Comfort Women: Beyond Litigious Feminism" in *Monumenta Nipponica* (Summer 2003), pp. 223–58.

————. "The Nanking Massacre: Now You See It,…" in *Monumenta Nipponica* (Winter 2001), pp. 521–44.

————. "Review: *Japanese Devils*" in *Journal of Japanese Studies* 28:2 (Winter 2002), pp. 430–435.

Watada, Susumu. "Suzuki Akira shi no 'shuzai' o shuzai suru," in Hora et al., eds., *Nankin jiken o kangaeru* (Tokyo: Ôtsuki shoten, 1987), pp. 192–200.

Watanabe Hiroshi. *Nankin gyakusatsu to Nihonjin* (Tokyo: Akashi shoten, 1997).

Watanabe, Shôichi. *Nihonshi kara mita Nihonjin: Shôwa hen* (Tokyo: Shôdensha, 2000).

Watanabe, Shôichi, and Komuro Naoki. *Fûin no Shôwa shi: "Sengo 50-nen" jigyaku no shûen* (Tokyo: Tokuma shoten, 1995).

Webb, William. "Separate Opinion of the President," IMTFE, 1948. Photoreproduced in Pritchard and Zadia, eds., *Tokyo War Crimes Trial,* vol. 21.

White, Theodore, and Jacoby, Annalee. *Thunder Out of China* (New York: DaCapo, 1980).

Wichert. Erwin, ed. *The Good Man of Nanking: The Diaries of John Rabe* (New York: Knopf, 1998).

Woodhead, H. G. W., ed. *The China Yearbook, 1939* (Shanghai: North China News Daily and Herald, 1940).

Wu, Tien-wei. Preface in Smalley, ed., *American Missionary Eyewitnesses to the Nanking Massacre, 1937–1938,* pp. iii–iv.

Xu, Zhigeng (Hsü Chih-keng). *Lest We Forget: Nanjing Massacre, 1937.* Chang T'ing-ch'üan and Lin, Wu-sun, trans. (Peking: Panda Books, 1995).

Yamada, Akira. "Okinawa de no gekisen," in Fujiwara et al., eds., *Shôwa 20-nen: 1945-nen* (Tokyo: Shôgakkan, 1995), pp. 108–111.

Yamada, Akira, and Kôketsu, Atsushi. *Ososugita seidan: Shôwa tennô no sensô shidô to sensô sekinin* (Tokyo: Shôwa shuppan, 1991).

Yamamoto, Masahiro. *Nanking: Anatomy of an Atrocity* (Westport, CN: Praegar, 2000).

Yamamoto, Shichihei. *Shôwa tennô no kenkyû* (Tokyo: Shôdensha, 1989).

————. *Watakushi no naka no Nihongun,* 2 vols. (Tokyo: Bungei shunjûsha, 1997).

Yamazaki, Tomoko. *Sandakan hachiban shôkan* (Tokyo: Bungei shunjûsha, 1975).

Yang, Daqing. "The Challenges of the Nanjin Massacre," in Fogel, ed., *The Nanjing Massacre in History and Historiography,* pp. 133–79.

————. "'Convergence or Divergence': Recent Historical Writings on the Rape of Nanjing," in *American Historical Review* 104:3 (June 1999), pp. 842–65.

————. "Rekishi e no chôsen: 'Nankin atoroshitei' kenkyû o megutte," in *Shisô* no. 890 (August 1998), pp. 83–109.

————. "A Sino-Japanese Controversy: The Nanking Atrocity as History," in *Sino-Japanese Studies* 3:1 (November 1990), pp. 14–35.

Yasuda, Shôzô, and Ishibashi, Kôtarô. *Asahi shinbun no sensô sekinin* (Tokyo: Ôta shuppan 1995).

Yin, Chi-Chün. *1937, Nan-ching ta-chiu-huan: Hsi-fang jen-shih ho kuo-chi an-ch'üan-ch'u* (Shanghai:Wen-hui ch'u-pan-she, 1997).

Yoshida, Takashi. "A Battle over History: The Nanjing Massacre in Japan" in Fogel ed., *The Nanjing Massacre in History and Historiography*, pp. 70–132.

————. *The Making of the "Rape of Nanking": History and Memory in Japan, China, and the United States* (New York: Oxford University Press, 2006).

Yoshida, Tamotsu, and Iguchi, Kazuki. "Kyoto ni okeru sensô ten undô to shiryô hakkutsu," in Iguchi et al., eds., *Nankin jiken: Kyoto shidan kankei shiryô*, pp. 442–65.

Yoshida, Yutaka. "15-nen sensô shi kenkyû to sensô sekinin mondai," in *Hitosubashi ronsô* 97:2 (February 1987), pp. 36–55.

————. *Gendai rekishigaku to sensô sekinin* (Tokyo: Aoki shoten, 1997).

————. "Kaisetsu," in *Sekai*, no. 667 (November 1999), pp. 258–59.

————. "Kenkyûkai meguri: Nankin jiken chôsa kenkyûkai," in *Chikaki ni arite*, no. 8 (November 1985), pp. 76–77.

Yoshida, Yutaka. "Kokusaihô no kaishaku de jiken o seitôka dekiru ka," in Nankin ken, ed., *Nankin daigyakusatsu hiteiron 13 no uso*, pp. 160–76.

————. "Nankin jiken no zenyô ga semaru rekishi ninshiki," in *Zen'ei*, no. 695 (January 1998), pp. 58–67.

————. *Nihon no guntai* (Tokyo: Iwanami shoten, 2002).

————. "Nihon kindaishi o dô toraeru ka: Jiyûshugi shikan kenkyûkai no rekishikan, sensôkan," in Yoshida, *Gendai rekishigaku to sensô sekinin*, pp. 238–53.

————. *Nihonjin no sensôkan* (Tokyo: Iwanami shoten, 1990).

————. "Sensô no kioku," in Iwanami shoten, ed., *Iwanami kôza sekaishi 25: Sensô to heiwa* (Tokyo: Iwanami shoten, 1997), pp. 99–117.

————. *Tennô no guntai to Nankin jiken* (Tokyo: Aoki shoten, 1986).

Yoshimi, Yoshiaki. *Dokugasu sen to Nihon gun* (Tokyo: Iwanami shoten, 2004).

Yoshimi, Yoshiaki, and Matsuno, Seiya, eds., *Jûgo nen sensô gokuhi shiryô shû hokan 2: Doku gasu sen kankei shiryô II* (Tokyo: Fuji shuppan, 1997).

Young, James. *Our Enemy* (Philadelphia: David McKay Co., 1942).

Young, Marilyn. "An Incident at No Gun Ri," in Bartov Grossmann, and Nolan, eds., *Crimes of War*, pp. 242–58.

————. *The Vietnam Wars, 1945–1990* (New York: Harper Colins, 1991).

Zenkoku senyû rengôkai, ed. *Senyûren jûnen no ayumi* (Tokyo: Zenkoku senyû rengôkai, 1979).

Zhang, Chengjun, and Liu, Jianye. *An Illustrated History of China's War of Resistance Against Japan* (Beijing: Foreign Languages Press, 1995).

Zhang [Chang], Kaiyuan, ed. *Eyewitnesses to Massacre: American Missionaries Bear Witness to Japanese Atrocities in Nanjing* (Armonk NY: M. E. Sharpe, 2001).

NOTES ON CONTRIBUTORS

David Askew is an associate professor at Ritsumeikan Asia Pacific University in Beppu, Japan. Recent publications include (with Paul Close) *Asia Pacific and Human Rights* (Ashgate Publishing, 2004) and (with Morimura Susumu, et., al.,) *Ribatarianizumu tokuhon* (Keisô shobô, 2005).

Timothy Brook, a specialist in late-imperial and twentieth-century China, is Shaw Chair of Chinese Studies at Oxford University. Recent publications include *Collaboration* (Harvard University Press, 2005) and *The Chinese State in Ming Society* (Routledge Curzon, 2005).

Joshua A. Fogel, is Canada Research Chair in Modern China at York University in Canada. He is interested in Sino-Japanese relations and his many publications include *The Literature of Travel in the Japanese Rediscovery of Japan* (Stanford University Press 1996) and *Manchuria under Japanese Dominion* (University of Pennsylvania Press, 2006), a translation of Yamamura Shin'ichi, *Kimera: Manshûkoku no shôzô*.

Fujiwara Akira was a professor at Hitotsubashi University in Tokyo before his death in 2003. A specialist in modern and contemporary Japanese history, his last major works were *Uejini shita eirei tachi* (Aoki shoten, 2001), *Chûgoku sensen jûgun ki* (Ôtsuki shoten, 2002), and the posthumously published *Tennô no guntai to Nit-Chû sensô* (Ôtsuki shoten, 2006).

Kasahara Tokushi is a professor of comparative cultural studies at Tsuru University in Yamanashi, Japan. His research interests lie in the Japanese army's "Three-All Policy" during the Chinese national movement in World War II. His many publications include *Nankin nanminku no hyakunichi* (Iwanami shoten, 1995) and *Nankin jiken* (Iwanami shoten, 1997).

Kimura Takuji, a specialist in contemporary Japanese history, is a doctoral candidate at Hitotsubashi University in Tokyo. His research interests center on veterans and military pensions in postwar Japan. Recent publications include

"Fukuin," in Yoshida Yutaka, ed., *Nihon no jidai shi 26* (Yoshikawa kôkun-kan, 2004) and "Gunjin tachi no sengo" in *Iwanami kôza Ajia-Taiheiyô sensô 5* (Iwanami shoten, 2006).

Ono Kenji, whose research interests lie in the Nanking Atrocity, is a private scholar from Fukushima, Japan. His publications include the collection of primary sources, *Nankin daigyakusatsu o kiroku shita kôgun heishi tachi* (Ôtsuki shoten, 1996).

Masahiro Yamamoto is an assistant professor at the University of Wyoming in the United States. His research interests lie in military and naval history and in modern Japanese history. Recent publications include *Nanking: Anatomy of an Atrocity* (Praeger, 2000) and articles in Japanese.

Takashi Yoshida is an assistant professor of history at Western Michigan University in the United States. His research has focused on the Asia-Pacific War (1931–45) and on memory in East Asia and the United States. Recent publications include *The Making of the "Rape of Nanking": History and Memory in Japan, China, and the United States* (Oxford University Press, 2006).

INDEX

A

Abegg, Lily, 87
Adenauer, Conrad, 287
Agawa Hiroyuki, 339
Akiyama Yoshimitsu, 44
Amano Saburô
    on activities in Ch'üanchiao county,
        191–93, 194
    journey from Hiroshima to Shanghai,
        182–85
    march from Shanghai to Ch'üanchiao
        county, 186–91, 194
    on older reserve officers, 32
    on plundering of Chinese provisions, 194–95
    on POWs, 40, 187, 188–89
    as an unwilling draftee, 12, 360
Ambrose, Stephen E., 287, 288, 291
Amerasia, 258–59
Anti-Comintern Pact, 17, 49, 282
Armenians, 267, 275, 276, 279
Asahi shinbun, 15–16
Asaka Yasuhiko, 11, 32, 44, 63, 70, 84
Asami Kazuo
    accusations of fabricating a killing contest,
        128, 129–30, 132, 134–35, 137, 141
    article about a killing contest, 125–26, 132,
        138–39, 142
Asian Women's Fund, 12, 347
Asia Unbound (Greenbie), 259
Asia University, 311
Askew, David, 20, 21, 295, 376, 379
atomic warfare, 168–69, 259
Auden, W. H., 363
Azuma Shirô, 349, 352, 385

B

Bacque, James, 22, 286–91, 292, 294, 298,
    299
Baker, Thomas, 290
Bates, Miner S.
    attempts to arrange a truce, 230
    on banditry in rural areas, 93
    documentation of American losses, 322
    estimate of the Nanking death toll, 98,
        100, 104, 106–7, 108, 112, 326
    on the IC's collaboration with the SGC,
        242
    on living standards in Nanking, 217
    publications by, 255–56
Bauman, Zygmunt, 278, 280
Behind the Japanese Mask (Steiner), 258, 259
Ben-Dasan, Isaiah. See Yamamoto Shichihei
Bischof, Guenter, 288, 289, 291
Bose, Subhas Chandra, 168–69
Boston Massacre, 357, 366
Boyle, John H., 291
Brandt, Willy, 125
Brook, Timothy, x, 21, 50, 241, 293–94, 368
Buruma, Ian, 283
Bush, George W., 358, 359
Bushido (Pernikoff), 258, 259

C

Cambodia, 281
Carter, Jimmy, 357
Center for Research and Documentation on
    Japanese War Responsibility, 347
Central China Area Army (CCAA)
    assault on Nanking, 34, 36, 37, 45, 57
    assault on outlying counties, 60–63, 65
    formation of, 31–32, 36
    funding of the SGC, 207–8
    issuing of Loyal Subject certificates, 214–15
    lack of control over troops, 33, 36, 47, 65
    See also Shanghai Expeditionary Army
        (SEA); Tenth Army

Chang, Iris
  estimate of Nanking's population, 96
  exaggeration of IC member's efforts, 239
  hierarchy of victimhood established by, 274, 283, 364
  intolerance of different opinions about the Nanking Atrocity, 385–89
  misquotation of the IMTFE's ruling, 298
  misrepresentation of contemporary Japanese society, 352
  on the Nanking death toll, 384
  The Rape of Nanking. See Rape of Nanking, The (Chang)
  view of Japan and the Third Reich as allies, 282
  view of a 100-man killing contest, 140
Ch'ang Kai-sing, 377, 378
Chan Jung-kuang, 206, 219
Chao Kung-chin, 205, 206, 219
Chao Wei-shu, 205, 206
chemical weapons, 138, 252–53, 254, 261, 386–87, 388
Cheng Kuan-ying, 282
Ch'en Jung, 203
Chiang Kai-shek
  denouncement of Japanese atrocities, 3, 250
  desertion of Nanking, 4, 7, 76
  establishment of a new regime in Taiwan, 269
  funding of the IC, 229
  kidnapping of, 35
  ordering of the Chinese army to retreat, 43
  refusal to surrender, 29, 230, 359, 366, 387
  role in Mukai's and Noda's death sentences, 132
Chiang Ken-fu, 121
Chiangning county, 66
Chiangp'u county, 63, 65, 66
Chiang Tse-min, 13, 364
China. *See* People's Republic of China (PRC); Republic of China
China Yearbook, 325–26
Chinese diaspora communities, 174n6, 267, 270–73
Chou En-lai, 11, 29
Ch'üanchiao county, 190–93, 194
Chungshant'ang (CST), 67, 105, 377, 379, 380–82, 383
Churchill, Winston S., 296
citizen-led movements, 345–52

civilian casualties, 47–50, 96–107, 109–11, 112, 255
Clinton, Bill, 357
Cohen, Paul, 360
Cohen, Richard, 357, 358
collaboration, 3, 4, 197, 198, 232, 323
comfort women
  compensation for, 12, 348, 350
  Japanese troops' use of, 50, 332, 341, 364, 375
  postwar persecution of, 4
compensation
  for comfort women, 12, 348, 350
  estimate of amount of claims for, 116–17
  Hsia Shu-chin's lawsuit for, 319–20
  Li Hsiu-ying's lawsuit for, 12–13, 50, 350
  role of citizen-led movements in efforts for, 6, 347–50, 352
conscription, 99–100, 101, 102, 112
conservative revisionists
  attempts to trivialize or deny the Nanking Atrocity, 47, 51–53, 116, 294, 330–36, 360
  delimitation of the Nanking Atrocity, 59, 295
  on the murder of defeated stragglers, 46
  on the murder of POWs, 40, 73, 78
  See also deniers; revisionists
Coville, Cabot, 202, 216
Cowdrey, Albert E., 288
Craigie, Robert, 156–57
Crop Investigation in the Nanking Area and Sundry Economic Data (Bates), 255
CST (Chungshant'ang), 67, 105, 377, 379, 380–82, 383
culpability, 116, 121–30, 142, 144, 145

D
defeated stragglers
  Japanese imprisonment of, 188
  justification of the murder of, 249
  loss of will after T'ang's desertion, 37, 41, 43–44, 231
  massacre of, by Japanese troops, 44–46, 65, 96, 103, 370–72, 374
  in the NSZ, 92, 231–32, 238, 322–23, 373
deniers
  academics and nonacademics as, 311, 327, 365

campaigns for textbook reforms, 304–5, 306
estimates of the Nanking death toll, 248–49, 374, 382, 383
on the execution of POWs, 249, 323–25, 358, 359, 372
on KMT units as responsible for atrocities, 7, 322–23, 356
on the lack of documented proof from the wartime era, 248–49, 262, 369
on neutrality violations of other countries, 18
protests against museum displays on the Nanking Atrocity, 308–9
rejection of Chinese sources, 6–7, 376
See also conservative revisionists; Fujioka Nobukatsu; Higashinakano Osamichi; revisionists
Documents of the Nanking Safety Zone (Hsü)
account of the attack on the Hsias, 320, 321
estimate of Nanking's population, 88–89, 91
as a primary source, 152, 361, 374
Dönitz, Karl, 368, 369
Dower, John, 365
Drea, Edward, 300
Dresden, 368
Durdin, F. Tillman, 88, 91, 103, 230–31, 236, 257

E
Eckstein, Gustav, 258–59
Eguchi Keiichi, 32, 343–44, 362
Eisenhower and the German POWs (Bischof & Ambrose), 288, 290, 291
Eisenhower, Dwight D., 286–87, 288
Endô Takaaki, 76, 78
epithets, 394–98
Espy, James, 91, 105
Etô Takami, 15
Eykholt, Mark, 220, 285, 295–96, 297, 298

F
fabrication thesis, 333–34
Falkenhausen, Alexander von, 18
Farrar, L. L., 360
Fauvet, Jacques, 287
Ferguson, Niall, 386
Finn, Richard B., 290
Fitch, George
criticism of the Japanese, 239, 256

departure for Shanghai, 243
estimates of Nanking's population, 89, 91
on the IC, 88, 232, 234, 235
on the inauguration of the SSA, 199, 200
on the SGC, 205, 241
smuggling of film negatives, 240–41
Fogel, Joshua A., 22, 285, 291, 292, 293, 298
Forster, Ernest, 103, 236
France, 286, 292
Frazer, Angus, 276
Fujioka Nobukatsu
criticism of *The Rape of Nanking,* 306, 307
crusade for textbook reform, 304–5, 340, 341
view of the Nanking Atrocity, 248–49, 307–9, 316, 328n12, 342, 365
Fujiwara Akira
on derogatory terms, 396
on Iris Chang, 360
on the Nanking Atrocity, 16, 19, 59, 73, 295, 343
Fukuda Tokuyasu, 209, 241

G
genocide, 276–81. *See also* Holocaust
Germany, 9–10, 17–18, 49, 315, 358–59. *See also* Holocaust
Gluck, Carol, 290, 293
Goette, John, 259
Goldhagen, Daniel, 22
Gollanz, Victor, 287
good citizen certificates, 93–94, 95, 96, 214–15
Great Britain, 249, 292, 358–59
Greater East Asia War thesis, 331–32, 335–36
Greenbie, Sydney, 259
Green, Roland, 287–88
Gries, Peter Hays, 274, 394
Grobman, Alex, 386
Gypsies, The (Frazer), 276

H
Haffner, Sebastian, 367
Hague Convention Concerning Laws and Customs of War, 323–25
Hanaoka Incident, 347
Hara Takeshi, 378, 380–82
Hata Ikuhiko
apology for the Nanking Atrocity, 388–89

categorization of Japanese factions in the
Nanking controversy, 331
estimate of Nanking's population, 91
on Japanese soldiers' lack of control, 96
on the Nanking death toll, 274, 362, 378
negative encounters with Chinese and
Chinese-Americans, 389, 393n106
on weapons in the NSZ, 18
Hata Kenuske, 73, 74
Hayden Act, 12, 365
Heilbrunn, Jacob, 299
Higashinakano Osamichi
background of, 311, 312
on defeated stragglers, 249, 322–23, 358
denial of the Nanking Atrocity, 248,
307–9, 316–19, 328n12, 342
flawed critique of primary sources, 22–23,
325–27
Kokka hasan, 312, 314–15
lawsuit against, 319–20
on the Nanking death toll, 106–7, 379–80
"Nanking gyakusatsu" no tettei kenshô,
316–19
on *The Rape of Nanking,* 306, 307, 308
use of pejorative terms, 313, 324, 396, 397
view of POW executions as legal, 249,
323–25
Hirohito, 30, 120, 124, 157–58, 359
Hiroshima, 292, 364
Hirota Kôki, 25n26, 30, 151, 156–57,
176n28, 384
History of the Second World War (Liddell-Hart),
296
"Hitler Myth," The (Kershaw), 360
Holocaust
comparisons of the Nanking Atrocity to
the, 6, 268, 275–81, 282, 363–67, 385
effect on the formation of Jewish identity,
271, 272–73
Germany's postwar atonement for the,
9–10
verbal impact of the, 299–300
Honda Katsuichi
collection of primary sources on the
Nanking Atrocity, 300
criticism of the Japanese Defense Agency,
296
examination of the East German
government system, 315

flawed memories of Chinese informants
used by, 128–29
on the geographic range of the Nanking
Atrocity, 34
interviewing techniques of, 142
on the massacre of POWs, 73
on the Nanking death toll, 16, 362
on a 100-man killing contest, 115, 121–26,
140, 141, 143, 333
publications on the Nanking Atrocity,
320–21, 330
rejected lawsuit against, 135, 145
Hoo Chai-tsai, 253
Hora Tomio
as co-founder of a Society to Study the
Nanking Incident, 116
essay on the Nanking Incident, 115, 119,
330
exposure of Tanaka's altering of Matsui's
diary, 334
on the massacre of POWs, 73
on a 100-man killing contest, 117, 118–19,
136–39, 141, 143, 333
Howard, Michael, 291
Hsiakwan, 65, 215–16, 235
Hsia Shu-chin, 319–21
Hsü Ch'uan-yin, 160, 204, 206, 210, 221, 240
Hsü Shuhsi, 88–89, 91, 320, 326–27
Huang Kuanghan, 18
Huang Yueh-hsuan, 205, 219
Hu Chin-T'ao, 9
Huttenbach, Henry R., 277, 280

I

IC. *See* International Committee (IC)
identification papers, 93–94, 95, 96, 214–15
Ienaga Saburô, 43, 48, 119, 126
Iinuma Mamoru, 32, 63
illusion thesis, 333, 334, 360
Imai Akio. *See* Suzuki Akira
Imperial Headquarters, 32, 33, 34, 57, 62
IMTFE. *See* International Military Tribunal for
the Far East (IMTFE)
Indian National Army (INA), 167
Inoie Mataichi, 44, 45
Inoue Hisashi, 250, 296, 382
In Peace Japan Breeds War (Eckstein), 258–59
International Committee (IC)
achievements of the, 238–39, 243

attempts to arrange a Sino-Japanese truce,
229–31
collection of missing people data, 104
complaints about Japanese soldiers'
conduct, 96–97, 153
conflicts with the SSA, 208–10, 212,
214–15, 241
cooperation with and resistance to the
Japanese, 239–41, 242
delegation of city government functions to
the, 90, 92, 228, 229
estimate of people remaining outside the
NSZ, 91
estimate of rapes by Japanese soldiers, 58
estimate of the Nanking death toll, 103,
109, 110, 112
formation of the, 227–28
funding of the, 229
handling of medical services, 236
inability to remove Chinese soldiers from
the NSZ, 231, 232–33, 238, 240
international appeals for financial aid,
254–56
Japanese objections to the, 200
ordering of Nanking's populace into the
NSZ, 90, 238
role in shaping the IMTFE's perception of
Japanese conduct, 152
struggles in obtaining and distributing
food, 210, 212, 213, 233–35, 242
subgroups of the, 229
See also Nanking International Relief
Committee; Nanking Safety Zone
(NSZ)
International Military Tribunal for the Far East
(IMTFE)
adoption of Nuremberg precedent, 363–64
as the basis for Japanese awareness of the
Nanking Atrocity, 50–51, 261, 338
counts in the indictment, 151–52, 164,
175n9
decision not to prosecute Mukai and Noda,
131
estimate of massacred POWs, 73
estimate of the Nanking death toll, 20,
204, 249, 268, 298, 377
execution of Japanese war criminals, 8,
25n26
Japanese reactions to the, 127, 149–50

lack of chemical warfare charges against
Japan, 387
Matsui's defense strategy during the,
152–56, 163, 175n20, 175n22
Pal's dissent to the verdicts at the, 150,
158–62, 176n39
reliability of evidence at the, 294, 295–96,
382
revisionist criticisms of the, 10–11
testimonies of Chinese victims and foreign
witnesses, 47
timeframe established for the Nanking
Atrocity, 87
verdict on Hirota, 156–57, 176n28
verdict on Matsui, 156, 175n27, 269,
293–94
See also Nanking War Crimes Trials; Pal,
Radhabinod
International Relief Committee. *See*
International Committee (IC)
Irokawa Daikichi, 140
Isa Kazuo, 44–45
Ishida Yûji, 345
Ishihara Shintarô, 143, 309, 349, 350
Ishikawa Mizuho, 316
Ishikawa Tatsuzô, 374
Ishiwara Kanji, 30
Itakura Yoshiaki, 52, 75–76, 97, 334–35
Itô Takashi, 135, 340

J
Jacquinot de Besange, Father, 227, 228, 229,
384
Japan
American prejudice against, 257–59,
261–62, 291–92, 297, 299
Anti-Comintern Pact with Germany, 17, 49
apologies for war crimes, 14–15, 120, 310
censorship of accounts of the Nanking
Atrocity, 50, 260–61, 262, 268, 374
citizen-led movements in, 345–52
comparisons of, to Nazi Germany, 22,
363–67
conflicts with China prior to Nanking,
29–33
development of identity in, 282
financial aid to the PRC, 11, 12
lawsuits against, for war crimes, 347–49,
350, 352

military documents on the Nanking
Atrocity, 369–74
mourning practices in, 13–14
peace treaty with the KMT on Taiwan, 8
peace treaty with the PRC, 8, 12, 120
separation from the League of Nations,
253–54
signing of the San Francisco Peace Treaty,
119
strategic blunders in the attack on
Nanking, 34–36
textbooks in
censored descriptions of the Nanking
Atrocity in, 9, 14–15, 51, 332, 349,
352
objections to negative depictions of
Japan in, 304–5, 306, 340, 341
use of chemical weapons, 138, 252–53,
254, 261, 386–87, 388
veterans and bereaved families in, 337–40,
344
Japan Fights for Asia (Goette), 259
Japan (Timperley), 257–58
Jaranilla, Delfin, 166
Jen Chi-yü, 319
Jenin, 357, 358, 366, 385
Jenkins, Russell, 292
Jen Yuan-tao, 218

K
Kaikô, 51–52
Kaikôsha, 51–52, 74–75, 334
Kaji Wataru, 261
Kalb, Marvin, 300
Kan'in Kotohito, 47, 386
Kanno Yoshio, 76, 77, 78, 79, 82
Kaochun county, 63, 65, 66
Kao Kuan-wu, 218, 219
Kasahara Tokushi
on burials in rural areas, 382
on the defense of Nanking, 34
delimitation of the Nanking Atrocity, 362
on derogatory terms, 395, 396, 398
estimate of Nanking's initial population, 20
on flaws in Higashinakano's work, 22–23
on flaws in Smythe's sampling method, 375
on fleeing Chinese troops, 373
on Japanese occupation policy, 387
on Li Hsiu-ying, 385

on the massacre of Chinese civilians, 343–44
on the massacre of Chinese soldiers, 73,
343–44, 370–72
on the Nanking death toll, 19, 295, 360,
384
Nankin jiken, 342–43
PRC's censorship of, 25n24
on T'ang Sheng-chih, 12
Katogawa Kôtarô, 52, 334
Katô Norihiro, 144–45
Katô Yôko, 395
Kellogg-Briand Pact, 162
Kennedy, David M., 290
Kershaw, Ian, 360
Kiang Tse-min, 307
killing contest. *See* 100-man killing contest
Kimura Takuji, 23, 51, 52, 304
Kirby, William C., 363
Kissinger, Henry, 119
Kitamura Minoru, 92, 98, 358, 374
KMT. *See* Kuomintang (KMT)
Kobayashi Yoshinori, 316, 328n24, 340, 396,
397
Koizumi Jun'ichirô, 14, 26nn30–31
Kokka hasan (Higashinakano), 312, 314–15
Komori Yoshihisa, ix, 11, 394, 398
Komuro Naoki, 324, 396
Kondô Eishirô, 77
Konoe Fumimaro, 29, 30
Kônô Yôhei, 311
Koo Wei-jun, 251–53
Korea, 15, 50, 51, 300, 347–48, 357
Koyama Kazunobu, 307–8, 328n12
Kozuka Kinshichi, 120
Krakowski, Shmuel, 385
Krauthammer, Charles, 357, 358
Krishna Menon, V. K., 165
Kröger, Christian, 103, 243
Kumazawa Kyôjirô, 136, 139
Kuomintang (KMT)
denouncement of Japanese war crimes,
249, 250, 251–53, 254
effect of the Sian Incident on the, 35
estimate of the Nanking death toll, 269
fleeing of troops into the NSZ, 322–23
funding of Smythe's surveys, 92, 98, 374
indictment of Chinese collaborators, 3
on the Japanese government's use of
pejoratives, 395

peace treaty with Japan, 8
postwar trials held by the, 11, 269
PRC's denouncement of the, 4
role in Chinese deaths, 13
scorched earth tactics, 381
training by German military advisers,
    17–18
view of a 100-man killing contest, 140
wartime view on the Nanking Atrocity,
    254, 261
Kuper, Leo, 276
Kurosu Tadanobu, 77
Kuyung county, 61–62, 65
Kyoto Exhibition on War for the Sake of Peace,
    346

L
League of Nations, 249, 251–52, 253–54, 261
Lebanese civil war, 277
Lemkin, Raphael, 276–77
Levi, Primo, 385
Liang Hung-chih, 57
Liddell-Hart, Basil H., 296
Lieber Rules, 373
Li Hsiu-ying, 12–13, 50, 350, 385
Lishui county, 61, 65, 66
Li Tsung-jen, 230
Liu, F. F., 296
Liu, James T. C., 149–50
Lotus Lake murders, 221
Lou Hsiao-hsi, 203
Loyal Subject certificates, 93–94, 95, 96,
    214–15
Lu Su, 295–96, 377, 378, 382, 383
Lynn, John A., 386

M
MacArthur, Douglass, 269
Ma Ch'ao-chün, 228, 229
MacInnis, Donald, 292
Magee, John, 103, 109, 160, 215, 237, 320
Ma Lieh-ch'eng, 14
Manchurian Incident, 30
Manchurian Myth, The (Mitter), 360
Mao Tse-tung, 130, 269
Marco Polo Bridge Incident, 8, 29, 35, 71,
    260, 394
Margalit, Avishai, 283
Marianas Turkey Shoot, 359

Marquand, Robert, 361
Marrus, Michael R., 277
Maruyama Susumu, 205, 382
Masahiro Yamamoto. *See* Yamamoto, Masahiro
Masuda Rokusuke, 45–46
Matsui Iwane
    advice to T'ang to surrender, 36–37, 260
    criticism of Japanese soldiers, 278
    defense of, at the IMTFE, 152–56, 163,
        175n20, 175n22
    enshrinement in the Yasukuni Shrine, 9
    execution of, 11, 25n26, 51
    IMTFE charges against, 151–52
    IMTFE verdict, 156, 175n27, 269, 293–94
    military positions held by, 31, 333
    opinion of the SGC, 242
    orders to troops, 32, 45, 201
    on rapes and looting, 48
Matsumura Toshio, 12–13, 16, 319–20, 350
Matsuoka Isao, 201, 215
McCallum, James, 91, 103, 109, 238
McDougall, Stuart, 165, 177n61
media
    coverage of atrocities in Nanking, 249–251,
        257–259, 260–261, 262, 268
    coverage of a 100-man killing contest,
        128–30, 142, 145, 280
    effect on the Japanese view of culpability,
        127–28
Meguro Fukuji, 82–83
Mei Ju-ao, 159–60
Menken, Arthur, 87, 233, 236
Miki Takeo, 13
Military History of Modern China, A (Liu), 296
Mills, W. Plumer, 221, 227, 228, 230
minimalist thesis, 334–35
Mishima Yukio, 120
Mitter, Rana, 360
Miyamoto Shôgo, 79
Miyazawa Kiichi, 51
Mizutani Sô, 44, 45
Moriô Migaku, 312, 318, 328n29
mourning practices, 13–14
Mufushan massacre, 20, 39–40, 42, 70–85,
    359, 378
Mukai Toshiaki, 25n26, 117–18, 125–26,
    128–35, 137–42
Murayama Tomiichi, 304, 337
My Lai, 357, 358, 366, 385

N
Nagasaki, 292
Nakajima Kesago, 38, 334
Nakamura Akira, 307–8, 328n12
Nakasone Yasuhiro, 13, 14, 346
Namikawa Eita, 340, 341
Nandy, Ashis, 166–67
Nanking
    estimates of civilian casualties in, 96–107,
        109–11, 112, 255
    estimates of the population in
        after the attack, 92–96
        before the attack, 20, 87–90, 96, 111,
            295, 376
    reopening of foreign embassies in, 242–43
    See also Nanking Safety Zone (NSZ);
        Nanking Special Administrative District
        (NSAD)
Nanking 1937, 309
Nanking Atrocity
    approaches to studying the, 297–99,
        342–45, 385–89
    comparisons to the Holocaust, 6, 268,
        275–81, 282, 299–300, 363–67, 385
    death toll from the
        difficulties in achieving an accurate
            count, 58–59
        early postwar Chinese sources on,
            376–82
        importance of, 298–99, 363, 366
        Japanese military documents on,
            369–74, 384
        later postwar Chinese sources on,
            383–84
        variations in, 3–4, 5, 8, 16, 20, 362–63
        wartime documents by Westerners on,
            374–76
    deniers of the. *See* deniers
    effect on Chinese diaspora communities,
        174n6, 267, 270–73
    geographic and temporal delimitations of
        the, 34, 57, 59, 86–87, 295, 361–63,
        384
    memorial for the, 8, 269, 274
    revisionists' view of the. *See* conservative
        revisionists; revisionists
    social ramifications from research and
        citizen-led movements on the, 345–52
    terminology for the, 16–17, 23, 57, 359–61

underlying causes of the, 36
U.S. debates about the, 285–86, 293
See also Nanking Special Administrative
    District (NSAD)
"Nanking gyakusatsu" no tettei kenshô
    (Higashinakano), 316–19
Nanking International Relief Committee, 104,
    217, 243, 254–56, 379. *See also*
    International Committee (IC)
*Nanking Massacre in History and Historiography,
    The* (Fogel), 285, 291, 293
Nanking Military Tribunal (NMT). *See*
    Nanking War Crimes Trials
Nanking Population, The (Bates), 255–56
Nanking Safety Zone (NSZ)
    civilians killed in the, 47
    creation of the, 37, 227–29, 256
    defeated stragglers in the, 92, 231–32, 238,
        322–23, 373
    execution of suspected Chinese soldiers
        within the, 44–46, 103, 105, 209,
        231–32
    food distribution in the, 233–35, 238
    geographic size of the, 60
    housing in the, 238
    media coverage of the, 250
    medical services in the, 236–38
    ordering of Nanking's populace into the,
        90, 91, 92, 238
    policing of the, 231–33, 238
    population of the, 68, 87, 89–93, 235,
        238, 243, 256
    rapes in the, 49
    SSA's closing of the, 214–15
    See also International Committee (IC)
Nanking Self-Government Committee
    (SGC)
    conflict with the IC, 208–10, 241
    creation of the, 197, 199, 205, 241
    dissolution of the, 217–18, 220
    distribution of food, 211–13, 242
    funding of the, 207–80, 216
    goals of the, 200, 208
    members of the, 202, 203, 204–6, 218–19,
        241–42
    recruitment for brothels, 203–4
    relocation of refugees back to their homes,
        214–15, 243
    SSA's control over the, 207, 209

Nanking Special Administrative District
(NSAD)
  atrocities within the, 58, 60–64, 65, 68
  counties within the, 57, 60–63
  estimate of the death toll in the, 59, 66–68,
    343, 374
  population of the, 60, 68
Nanking Special Service Agency (SSA)
  attempt to blame war crimes on Chinese
    soldiers, 322
  conflicts with the IC, 208–10, 212,
    214–15, 241
  control over the SGC, 207, 209
  creation of the, 201
  estimate of Nanking's population, 94
  inauguration of the, 198–200, 217
  issuing of Loyal Subject certificates, 214–15
  links with the RSS, 202–4, 378
  murder of defeated Chinese troops, 202
  use of Chinese labor, 211
Nanking War Crimes Trials
  estimate of the Nanking death toll, 20,
    377, 382
  execution of Mukai and Noda, 8, 25n26,
    117, 118, 131, 360
  Mukai's defense at the, 132, 133
  records on a 100-man killing contest, 136
  revisionist criticisms of the, 10–11
  temporal delimitation of the Nanking
    Atrocity, 87
  See also International Military Tribunal for
    the Far East (IMTFE)
Nankin jiken (Kasahara), 342–43
Nankin senshi, 40, 48, 52, 74, 75
Naruse Kanji, 135, 136
New Sun, The (Yashima), 259
New York Times, 250, 251, 257
Nihon seinen kyôgikai, 306–7
Nishio Kanji, 305, 340, 365–67, 377–78, 396,
  397
Nixon, Richard, 119
NMT. *See* Nanking War Crimes Trials
Noda Tsuyoshi
  arguments on the guilt of, 117–18,
    125–26, 137–39, 140, 141–42
  arguments on the innocence of, 128–30,
    132, 133–35, 140, 141–42
  execution of, 25n26, 117, 118
Noguchi Takehiko, 368

No Gun Ri, 357, 358, 366, 385
Nonaka Hiromu, 332, 349
Novick, Peter, 385
NSAD. *See* Nanking Special Administrative
  District (NSAD)
NSZ. *See* Nanking Safety Zone (NSZ)

O
Okaka International Peace Center, 310, 311
Okamura Yasuji, 48
Okinawa, 359
Okumiya Masatake, 362–63
Ômori Minoru, 117
100-man killing contest
  early portrayals of the, 117–19
  as fabricated, 20, 128–35, 141–42, 360
  as factual, 136–39, 140, 141–42, 360
  link between culpability and debates about
    a, 121–27, 144, 145
  media coverage of a, 251, 260, 280
  significance of debates over a, 115–16, 142,
    143, 333
  sociopolitical background of debates about
    a, 119–21
Onoda Hirô, 120
Ono Kenji
  criticism of Lu Su's testimony, 383
  on the murder of Chinese POWs, 73
  research on murdered Chinese POWs,
    39–40, 345, 359, 367, 378, 382
  on war crimes outside of Nanking, 19–20
Operation Burn All, Kill All, Plunder All,
  343–44, 388
Ôta Hisao, 385
Ôta Kôzô, 311
Other Losses (Bacque), 22, 286–91, 292, 294,
  298, 299
Our Enemy (Young), 258
Overmans, Ruediger, 288, 289, 298

P
Pact of Paris, 162
Pal, Radhabinod
  complaints about the political ends of the
    IMTFE, 165–66, 364
  contradictions in arguments of, 170–71
  desire for a widened scope of inquiry, 171–72
  dissenting verdict of, at the IMTFE, 21,
    150, 158–65, 176n39, 281

political beliefs of, 167–70, 173
portrayal of, in *Puraido,* 9
Peacekeeping Law, 19, 28n86
pejoratives, 394–98
People's Republic of China (PRC)
　censorship in the, 8, 25n24, 269, 270
　criticism of wartime losses reported by, 12–13
　denouncement of the KMT, 4
　entry into the United Nations, 119
　financial aid from Japan, 11, 12
　fourth generation's political views, 273–74
　intolerance of different views of the
　　Nanking Atrocity, 385–89
　linking of the Nanking Atrocity to the
　　Holocaust, 6, 364
　mourning practices in the, 13
　objections to the Peace Osaka conference,
　　310
　officially sanctioned view of the Nanking
　　Atrocity, 5, 7–8, 86, 274
　peace treaty with Japan, 8, 12, 120
　protests against Japanese textbooks, 51
　rift with Taiwan, 271
　use of the Nanking Atrocity to shame
　　potential trading partners, 269–70
Pernikoff, Alexander, 258, 259
poison gas
　Japan's use of, 138, 252–53, 254, 261,
　　386–87, 388
　Nazi Germany's use of, 277–78
Pradervand, Jean-Pierre, 287
PRC. *See* People's Republic of China (PRC)
Prideaux-Brunce, H. I., 243
prisoners of war (POWs)
　estimates of the murder of, by Japanese
　　troops, 359, 370–72, 374
　justifications for the execution of, 41–42,
　　48, 249, 323–24, 367, 372–73
　lack of food or water for, 187, 188, 373
　massacre of, near Mufushan, 20, 39–40,
　　42, 70–85, 359
　systematic mass executions of, by Japanese
　　troops, 38–40, 42–43, 65, 334
　U.S. treatment of, 286–89, 358
Puraido, 9

R
Rabe, John
　attempts to arrange a truce, 230–31
　on Chinese soldiers in the NSZ, 18, 231,
　　232–33, 240
　departure from Nanking, 243
　documentation of the attack on the Hsias,
　　221, 320
　efforts to obtain food for refugees, 89–90,
　　233–34, 235
　estimate of Nanking's population, 87,
　　89–90, 91, 92, 376
　estimate of the Nanking death toll, 12, 59,
　　102–3, 104, 109–11, 290, 376
　Iris Chang's use of the diary of, 289, 290,
　　300, 301n27
　PRC's depiction of, 4
　on rapes by Japanese soldiers, 49–50, 97
　role of, in the NSZ, 21, 199, 228
　on the SSA, 200, 210
　superficial cooperation with the Japanese,
　　239, 240, 242
　on the training of KMT troops, 17–18
　on treatment for the wounded, 236–37
Rape of Nanking, The (Chang)
　attempts to publish a Japanese translation
　　of, 307, 328n11, 360
　comparison of the Nanking Atrocity to the
　　Holocaust, 6, 268, 275, 276, 299
　critical reviews of, 289–90, 291, 292,
　　306–7, 308
　errors in, 22, 307
　manipulation of statistics in, 293–94
　popularity of, in America, 285–86
　reactions of professional historians and
　　general readers to, 292–93, 297
　use of Rabe's diary in, 289, 290, 300, 301n27
rapes
　estimates of the number of, by Japanese
　　soldiers, 8, 58, 97, 298
　high incidence of, by Japanese soldiers,
　　47–50, 58, 64, 96
　Japanese army's attempts to reduce the
　　incidence of, 50, 222
　during the Lebanese civil war, 277
　murder of rural women to conceal, 64
　in the NSAD, 61, 63, 64, 65, 66
　of refugees as they returned home, 215
　during the SSA inauguration holiday, 200
　trauma from, 58, 61
Red Swastika Society (RSS)
　burials at Hsiakwan, 103

founding of the Nanking branches of the, 202, 378
groups buried by the, 101, 106
links with the SSA, 202–4, 378
petition to the SGC for assistance, 214
problems with the burial records of, 104, 109, 111, 378–79, 380, 383
records on the number of burials by the, 67, 98, 105, 108, 377–78, 381–82
soup kitchens operated by the, 222n2
registration cards, 93–94, 95, 96, 214–15
Republic of China
    creation of the, 395
    development of identity in the, 282
    Reformed Government of the, 217, 218, 219, 362, 376
    wartime media reports in the, on Japanese war crimes, 249–51
revisionism, 19
revisionists, 10–11, 293–96, 344, 361. *See also* conservative revisionists; deniers
Riggs, Charles, 196, 199, 210, 214
Ritchie, Donald, 366
Röling, B. V. A., 159, 167, 176n28
Rosen, Georg, 49, 221–22, 320, 321, 322, 379
RSS. *See* Red Swastika Society (RSS)
Rummel, R. J., 276
Rumsfeld, Donald, 358, 359

S
Saigô Takamori, 313–14
Saitô Jirô, 76
Sakamoto Takao, 340, 365, 396–97
Sakata Shigeki, 201, 202
Sakhalin, 347, 348
San Francisco Peace Treaty, 8, 9, 10, 51, 119, 382
Sankei shinbun, 305, 306, 340–41
Sasaki Motokatsu, 374
Sasaki Tôichi, 25n26, 38, 65
Satô Eisaku, 119
Satô Shinju, 132, 138
Sawada Masahisa, 42
Scharffenberg, Paul, 90, 92, 197, 235
Schell, Orville, 291
scorched earth tactics, 91, 92, 93, 108, 381
SEA. *See* Shanghai Expeditionary Army (SEA)
SEF. *See* Shanghai Expeditionary Army (SEA)
Sejima Ryûzô, 311
Senjinkun (Tôjô), 120

Senô Kappa, 128
Senshi sôsho, 40
SGC. *See* Nanking Self-Government Committee (SGC)
Shanghai, 31, 71, 185, 278, 279, 386–87
Shanghai Evening Post, 250
Shanghai Expeditionary Army (SEA)
    actions en route to Nanking, 33–34, 37
    creation of a, 35
    massacre of defeated stragglers, 44, 45
    orders to kill all POWs, 74
    reorganization of, 31–32
    use of chemical weapons, 386–87
    See also Central China Area Army (CCAA)
Sheng Cheng, 377, 378
Shermer, Michael, 386
Shiga Naoya, 339
Shih Mei-yu, 132
Shijime Akira, 139–40
Shônen (Senô), 128
Short-War Illusion, The (Farrar), 360
Shôwa emperor, 30, 120, 124, 157–58, 359
Sixty-fifth Regiment, 39, 70–82, 84–85, 187, 188, 345. *See also* Amano Saburô
Smedley, Agnes, 107, 358
Smith, Arthur L., Jr., 288
Smith, Bradford, 258
Smythe, Lewis S. C.
    description of surveys of, 51, 59, 66–67
    estimate of forced labor, 99–100
    estimate of Nanking's population, 89, 90, 93
    estimate of the Nanking death toll, 98, 102, 103, 107, 112, 255
    flaws in the surveys of, 60, 67, 95, 375
    on the IC, 234, 235, 240, 242
    KMT funding of surveys by, 92, 98, 374
    on Nanking residents' fear of Japanese soldiers, 376, 377
    on NSZ police taken by the Japanese, 231
    on the punishment of collaborators, 232
    role in the creation of the NSZ, 227
    on T'ao Hsi-san, 205
    on Wang Cheng-tien, 196, 197, 222
    War Damage in the Nanking Area, 66, 92–96, 98, 100–101, 255, 374–76
Snow, Edgar, 107, 358
Society for a Liberated View of History, 304, 308, 309, 340

Society to Create a New Japanese History Textbook, 305, 308, 341
Society to Honor Our War Heroes, 332, 335, 336–39, 349
Society to Study the Nanking Incident
formation of the, 51, 344
members of the, 73, 116
research on the murder of POWs, 78
role in scholarship on the Nanking Atrocity, 116, 330, 332–33, 334
Society to Survey and Study the Nanking Incident, 342–44
Sperling, Eduard, 221, 230, 240
SSA. *See* Nanking Special Service Agency (SSA)
Steiner, Jesse, 258, 259
Steward, Albert, 215–16, 217
Sun Shu-jung, 205, 206, 209, 213, 218, 219
Suzuki Akira
criticism of *The Rape of Nanking*, 307
death of, 144
denial of the Nanking Atrocity, 5, 135–36, 145, 333, 360
interviewing techniques developed by, 142
on a 100-man killing contest, 115, 128–32, 135, 140, 141, 333
on the murder of POWs, 74
problematic sources used by, 137–38, 333
refusal to correct errors, 143–44
Suzuki Jirô, 125–26, 132, 136, 138

T
Tadokoro Chieko, 141, 142–43
Taiwan, 5, 8, 11–12, 269, 271
Takashi Yoshida. *See* Yoshida, Takashi
Takemoto Genji, 262
Takigawa Masajirô, 363–64
Tanabe Mastake, 387
Tanaka Kakuei, 119–20
Tanaka Masaaki
alteration of primary sources, 145, 334, 389
blaming of the Chinese for atrocities, 322
denial of the Nanking Atrocity, 248, 296, 333–34, 358, 364
lawsuit against the Japanese government, 15
on the murder of POWs, 323
on the Nanking death toll, 5, 20, 249
Tanaka Ryûkichi, 50
Tanaka Saburô, 80, 81

Tanaka Toshiyuki, 345
T'ang Chia-hsüan, 310
T'ang Sheng-chih
agreement to demilitarize the NSZ, 18
decree for noncombatants to move to the NSZ, 91, 92
desertion of Nanking, 4, 37, 41, 43, 231
desire for a 3-day truce, 230–31
on disorder in the NSZ, 228–29
ordering of units to shoot fleeing Chinese soldiers, 12
refusal to surrender, 36–37, 260, 366
Tanizawa Eiichi, 396, 398
T'ao Chueh-san, 206, 219
T'ao Hsi-san
imprisonment of, 219
participation in the SSA's inauguration, 199, 200, 208
as part of the Reformed Government, 218–19
role in the SGC, 203, 205, 206, 213, 224n35, 241
Ta-t'u-sha, 3, 359, 385
Tawantzu, 70, 84
Taylor, Frederick, 368
Tenth Army, 31–32, 34, 36, 37, 47, 386. *See also* Central China Area Army (CCAA)
Thayer, Nathaniel, 365
Three 'Alls' Operations, 343–44, 388
T'ien-an-men Square, 361, 368
Timperley, Harold J.
accounts of a 100-man killing contest, 117–18, 138, 140
deniers' criticism of, 358
Japan, 257–58
problems with the findings of, 97, 379
publication of works by, 240
What War Means. See What War Means (Timperley)
Tôjô Hideki, 9, 120, 127
Tokyo War Crimes Trials. *See* International Military Tribunal for the Far East (IMTFE)
Torpedo Encampment, 70, 77, 84
Toyama Takeo, 132
Trevor-Roper, Hugh, 368, 369, 385
Tuan Yuep'ing, 295
Tungchou, 260
Turkey, 267, 275, 276, 279

U
United Nations, 119, 149, 277, 395
United States
    accounts of the Nanking Atrocity, 249,
        257–59, 261–62, 292–93, 297
    air raids on Japanese targets in Chinese
        cities, 13
    atomic warfare used by the, 365
    attempt to block the PRC from the United
        Nations, 119
    debates about the Nanking Atrocity,
        285–86, 293
Uno Shintarô, 136, 139

V
Vautrin, Minnie, 7, 104, 204, 206, 227, 379
Vietnam War, 119, 122
Villa, Brian Loring, 288, 299
Vincent, John, 367

W
Wade-Giles system, xi
Wakabayashi, Bob Tadashi, x–xi, 20, 23, 333,
    339
Wang Cheng-tien
    distribution and transportation of food,
        210, 211–12, 214, 242
    participation in the SSA's inauguration, 199
    roles in the IC and SGC, 21, 196–97, 199,
        206, 210, 220–22
Wang Ch'un-sheng, 205, 206, 219
Wang, Jimmy. *See* Wang Cheng-tien
Wang Kopang, 90, 96
war crimes trials. *See* International Military
    Tribunal for the Far East (IMTFE);
    Nanking War Crimes Trials
War Damage in the Nanking Area (Smythe), 66,
    92–96, 98, 100–101, 255, 374–76
Watada Susumu, 73, 144, 333
Watanabe Shôichi, 145, 249, 262, 324, 395,
    396
Webb, William, 159, 281
Weizsacker, Richard von, 364, 365
Wen Chia-pao, 9
What War Means (Timperley)
    on atrocities at Nanking, 256, 257
    criticism of, 325, 326, 379–80
    estimate of Nanking's population, 88–89,
        91

estimate of the Nanking death toll, 97–98,
    106–7, 379–80
    translation into Japanese, 261
Will, George F., 291, 292
Wilson, Robert
    documentation of the attack on the Hsias,
        321
    estimate of Nanking's population, 91
    estimate of the Nanking death toll, 104–5
    on Japanese brutality in Nanking, 256
    on the Japanese decree requiring citizens to
        register, 94
    on the lack of artillery attacks on the NSZ,
        233
    on medical staff in Nanking, 237
    role of, after the attack on Nanking, 236
    on the SGC's ties to the RSS, 199, 203,
        204
Wu Chang-te, 121

Y
Yamada Detachment, 71, 77, 78–83, 84–85,
    345. *See also* Sixty-fifth Regiment
Yamakawa Saki, 396
Yamamoto Isoroku, 17, 343
Yamamoto, Masahiro, x, xi, 19, 22, 97, 384
Yamamoto Shichihei
    attempts to prove Mukai and Noda
        innocent, 128, 132–35, 141
    debates on a 100-man killing contest, 115,
        122–26, 142, 145, 333
    denial of the Nanking Atrocity, 5, 145, 333
    estimate of Chinese military casualties, 135,
        143
    public support for, 339
    suspicion of B-class war crimes committed
        by, 122–23, 127
Yamashita Tomoyuki, 176n37
Yamazaki Tomoko, 396
Yanagawa Heisuke, 31, 33, 386
Yang Daqing, 286, 294, 298, 300, 331,
    344–45
Yashima, Taro, 259
Yasukuni Shrine, 9, 13–14, 23, 336, 337, 339
Yokoi Shôichi, 120
Yoshida, Takashi, ix, xi, 22–23, 47, 294, 298
Yoshida Yutaka, 34, 73, 325, 335, 343, 351
Young, James, 258
Yüleiying, 70, 77, 84